SANDRA GUSTAFSON'S

GREAT SLEEPS PARIS

TENTH EDITION

CHRONICLE BOOKS

SAN FRANCISCO

TENTH EDITION
ISBN: 0-8118-4037-9
ISSN: 1074-505X

Manufactured in the United States of America.

Cover design: Julie Vermeer
Book design: Words & Deeds
Typesetting: Jack Lanning
Series editor: Jeff Campbell
Author photograph: Marv Summers

Distributed in Canada by
Raincoast Books
9050 Shaughnessy Street
Vancouver, British Columbia V6P 6E5

10 9 8 7 6 5 4 3 2 1

Chronicle Books LLC
85 Second Street
San Francisco, California 94105

www.chroniclebooks.com
www.greateatsandsleeps.com

For Jacob, Geneviève, Diana, and Alessandra,
with love

Contents

To the Reader **7**

Tips for Great Sleeps in Paris **10**

How to Use *Great Sleeps Paris* **13**

    Big Splurges and Cheap Sleeps **13**

    Stars **13**

    Reservations **14**

    Deposits **17**

    Checking In/Checking Out **17**

    Rates: Paying the Bill **18**

    Complaints **19**

    Breakfast **19**

    English Spoken **20**

    Smoking/Nonsmoking Rooms **20**

    Facilities and Services **20**

    Nearest Tourist Attractions **21**

    Transportation **21**

    Maps **21**

General Information **22**

    When to Go **22**

    Holidays and Events **22**

    What to Bring **23**

    Tourist Offices and American Embassy **26**

    Disabled Travelers **26**

    Tours **28**

    Classes **32**

    Services **33**

    Money Matters **34**

    Insurance **39**

    Discounts **40**

    Health Matters **42**

    Emergency Numbers **44**

    Safety and Security **45**

Staying in Touch   47

Transportation   51

Time   56

Standards of Measure   57

Voltage   57

Arrondissement Map   58

Hotel Listings by Arrondissement   59

First Arrondissement   61

Second Arrondissement   79

Third Arrondissement   83

Fourth Arrondissement   90

Fifth Arrondissement   107

Sixth Arrondissement   138

Seventh Arrondissement   174

Eighth Arrondissement   201

Ninth Arrondissement   216

Eleventh Arrondissement   221

Twelfth Arrondissement   232

Thirteenth Arrondissement   234

Fourteenth Arrondissement   238

Fifteenth Arrondissement   248

Sixteenth Arrondissement   255

Seventeenth Arrondissement   271

Eighteenth Arrondissement   286

Other Options   295

Apartment Rental Agencies   296

Bed and Breakfast in a Private Home   308

Boat on the Seine   309

Camping Out   310

Hostels   311

Residence Hotels   317

Student Accommodations   323

Shopping: Great Chic   **327**

    Tips for Great Shopping   **328**

    Shopping Hours   **330**

    Size Conversion Charts   **330**

    Tax Refund: *Détaxe*   **331**

    Customs   **332**

    Consignment Shops: *Dépôts-Ventes*   **332**

    Department Stores   **333**

    Designer Discount Boutiques   **333**

    Sales: *Soldes*   **334**

    Getting It All Home   **335**

    Shopping Areas   **336**

    Discount Shopping Streets   **338**

    Passages   **340**

    Shopping Malls   **341**

    Store Listings by Arrondissement   **344**

    Flea Markets: *Les Marchés aux Puces*   **392**

    Food Shopping Streets and Outdoor Roving Markets   **393**

    A Shopper's Glossary   **397**

    Shops by Type   **399**

Glossary of French Words and Phrases   **403**

Index of Accommodations   **409**

Index of Shops   **413**

Readers' Comments   **415**

To the Reader

You, who have ever been to Paris know;
And you who have not been to Paris, go.
　　　　　　　—*John Ruskin*,
　　　　　　　　A Tour through France (1835)

The crowds in the streets, the lights in the shops, the elegance, variety, and beauty of their decorations, the brilliant cafés with their vivacious groups at little tables on the pavement soon convince me that this is no dream: that I am in Paris . . .
　　　　　　　—*Charles Dickens*

La Belle France continues to beckon visitors to her shores. Indeed, it should not be surprising that Paris is one of the most popular travel destinations in the world, playing host to more than 26 million visitors yearly, or nearly ten times the city's population. This number translates into 130,000 tourism-related jobs and adds nearly 8 billion euros to the economy. The American passion for Paris has not ebbed despite wars, riots, occupations, differing politics, and the rise and fall of hemlines and the dollar. Whether seen for the first time or the tenth, Paris never leaves you, and it becomes a never-ending love affair for most of us. Walk a block, turn a corner, in Paris there is always something interesting, something beautiful and new, something that has been there forever but that you never noticed until now. No matter what time of year you visit, you will find it impossible to keep from losing your heart to the city, with its grand boulevards, beautiful men and women, breathtaking monuments and museums, glorious food, famous art, and sweeping views—from place de la Concorde up the Champs-Élysées, from the steps of the Sacré Coeur over the entire city, and standing at Trocadéro looking across the fountains to the Eiffel Tower.

The first priority for visitors is to get a roof over their heads. Despite Paris's reputation for high prices, there are fifteen hundred hotels in all price ranges, so travelers can enjoy a pleasant stay in the city, no matter what their budget may be. However, the French have learned to make do with cramped quarters, sitting elbow-to-elbow in bistros, standing nose to-nose on a crowded métro, or inching their way through narrow, traffic-clogged streets. This intimacy is part of the city's charm, and it translates even to the size of hotel rooms, which by American standards are very small.

The essence of any Parisian hotel is its individuality, and no two are alike. You can, of course, find here the most luxurious pleasure palaces in the world, and it is always possible to check into the Hilton or any other big-name chain hotel. But only in Paris can you sleep in a romantic hideaway in Montmartre and be served breakfast in bed while looking out the window and seeing all of Paris below, rent an eighteenth-century apartment with views of the place des Vosges (the oldest square in Paris), or check into a suite in a renovated hotel a block from the Ritz but light-years away in price.

It is certainly true that a trip to Paris will cost more today than it did a few years ago, but what doesn't? Europe—or Paris—on $20 or $30 a day is ancient history and rarely exists for any traveler. Most of those romantically threadbare hotels of our youth are thankfully gone for good. More and more smaller hotels are being renovated, adding bathrooms, fluffy towels, Internet hookups, and buffet breakfasts served in sixteenth-century stone-walled *caves* (or cellars). This, of course, adds up to higher prices. Yet there are still many ways to save money and maximize the buying strength of the dollar without feeling *nouveau pauvre* in the process, and *Great Sleeps Paris* shows you how.

Great Sleeps Paris is a highly selective guide to the accommodations that I have discovered to be the best value in their category, be it a no-star with the shower and toilet down the hall; an antique-filled, three-star Left Bank hotel with a Jacuzzi in the marble bathroom, or an antique-filled apartment on l'Île St-Louis with a magnificent view of Notre Dame and the Seine. The purpose of this book is to offer fail-safe advice for first-time visitors, as well as for Paris veterans, on the best-priced accommodations for a range of tastes and needs. The selections include hotels—from the center of Paris to the fringes—for lovers and honeymooners, nostalgia buffs, backpackers, and families. Other options include camping, renting an apartment, or living in a hostel, and for students, a wealth of inexpensive beds awaits.

Each hotel listing has been included because I feel it has something special to offer. Some represent a particular style or era; others have been beautifully restored; and some are in nontourist neighborhoods where people like you and me live and work, send their children to school, get their cars repaired, eat lunch, shop, and go to the dentist. Some accommodations are basic, many are charming, and a few are starkly modern. Most are moderately priced, some are inexpensive Cheap Sleeps, and some fall into the Big Splurge category for those with more flexible budgets and demanding tastes. All have one vital feature in common: the potential for providing a memorable stay that will make you feel you have discovered your own part of Paris, one that you will savor and want to return to as often as possible.

It is important for readers to know that no hotel can purchase a listing or ask to be included in this book. I pay my own way, and I do all the research and writing for the book myself; the buck stops right here. In reviewing the hotels, I pull no punches and call the shots as I see them, good, bad, and otherwise, including giving the specifics about the best and worst rooms, so that you will know exactly what to expect when you check into your room during your Parisian holiday.

What are the guidelines I use for selecting a hotel? The two primary concerns are value for money and cleanliness, followed by location, pleasant surroundings in the room, and management attitude and service. On my visits to the hotels, which are always unannounced, I wipe my fingers across the door tops, check closets, turn on the showers, look for mold, flush toilets, spot thin towels and waxed or sandy toilet paper, open and close windows, bounce on the beds, look under them for dust, and visit the dining room where breakfast is served. I have stumbled along dimly lit corridors, climbed endless flights of stairs, and been squeezed into minuscule cage elevators that seem to have been in operation since the fall of the Bastille, all so that I can warn you about avoiding the same.

In addition to giving the value-conscious traveler the inside track to the best hotel prices in Paris, *Great Sleeps Paris* offers insider information on shopping. If you are like I am and believe the eighth deadly sin is paying full retail price for anything, then you will love the "Great Chic" shopping section (see page 327). This section leads you to everything from designer discount shops and big-name cosmetics to the latest models of shoes—all sold for less than their regular retail price.

On my most recent trip for the tenth edition of this guide, I inspected every hotel and shop that's listed, along with scores of others that did not make the final cut for one reason or another. In so doing, I walked hundreds of miles, wearing out my walking shoes in the process, and was asked for directions 75 times. And yet, no matter what the weather, how long the day, or the personalities and moods of the people I met along the way, it never seemed like work. I loved every minute of it, and can't wait to pack my bags and return to Paris to do it all again. I hope that *Great Sleeps Paris* shows you how to cut corners with style, so that whatever your budget, you need not give up the good life by lowering your standards. If I can help you select that special hotel that makes your stay in Paris truly memorable and sets the stage for many return visits, I will have done my job well. I wish you *bonne chance* and *bon voyage.*

Tips for Great Sleeps in Paris

Paris is planted in my heart.
> —*Endre Ady, Hungarian lyric poet*

1. Unless you enjoy standing in long lines in French government tourist offices or rail stations, or wandering the streets looking for a hotel, never arrive in Paris without confirmed hotel reservations.

2. Before you make a hotel reservation, log onto www.pagesjaunes.fr. Type in the hotel's address (or that of almost any Paris business or residence) and you can see one or more photos of the building. Click again, and there is a map of the surrounding area, which is very helpful in gaining a sense of the views you will encounter each day. Click on Rues Commerçantes, and you will go on a virtual tour of every business in the block.

3. Dealing directly with the hotel almost always insures the best rate. When calling the hotel, always ask for the best rates being offered for weekends, families, the off-season, and so on. When negotiating price, remember the higher the rack rate for the hotel, the more negotiating room there will usually be, especially in slow periods. If a hotel has an Internet site, *always* check it to find out about specials. If the hotel has a toll-free 800 number, the rates quoted are usually regular or premium rates. However, special rates are sometimes available, so it doesn't hurt to ask. No matter how you reserve your room, bring paper copies of your confirmations to present upon check-in.

4. Luxury does not necessarily have to be beyond your budget if you go when everyone else does not. The weather may not always cooperate in the off-season months, but there will be far fewer tourists, and hotels will be cutting deals. The two fashion weeks in mid-January, from Easter through June, September, October, and ten days around Christmas and New Year's are considered high season and the hardest times to find a hotel room in Paris. During the height of winter and summer, hotel rates are at their lowest.

5. You pay for the room, not for the number of people occupying it. Back rooms often face blank walls or dreary courtyards and are usually smaller, but they cost less and are quieter. Twin beds cost more than a double, and any room with a private shower and toilet will generally be less than one with a bathtub. If you ask for a double room, you must specify whether you want a double bed or twin beds. During major trade shows, international exhibitions, and the designer fashion shows in the fall and early spring, many hotels add a supplement.

6. Don't be surprised if your shower, either stall or over the bathtub, has no curtain. In smaller hotels, towels are usually changed every two or three days.

7. Many hotels do not allow outside guests to visit you in your room. This is an iron-clad rule in hostels, student digs, and almost every no-star and one-star hotel in Paris.

8. If you pay a deposit, always ask about the hotel's refund policy. Some smaller hotels have draconian ideas about refunds, which may leave you out of luck if you have to cancel at the last minute or leave earlier than planned.

9. If you have booked an apartment and paid a chunk of money in advance or have a nonrefundable and nonchangeable airline ticket, seriously consider purchasing trip insurance. If you have to change dates, interrupt travel, or cancel altogether, you will be grateful for it. For further details, see Insurance, page 39.

10. Always check out the room before you check in. Confirm the rate and discuss the cost of any extras (such as telephone calls, both local and long distance, and logging onto the Internet) ahead of time, not when paying the bill. All hotels must clearly post their rates by the reception desk, but they are not required to list "hidden" charges they may add on later.

11. Avoid eating breakfast at your hotel if you want to save money. Instead, join the Parisians standing at the bar at the corner café. Only a few hotels now include breakfast in their prices, and even if you do not take it, many hotels will not deduct it, saying, "It is offered." Still, it doesn't hurt to ask to have the "offer" deducted. However, if you partake of your hotel's buffet breakfast, please do not take advantage and load your pockets and bags with enough extra food to sustain you and your family for lunch and/or snacks during the day. Hoteliers take a very dim view of this cheap trick.

12. Wash loads of clothes at the local laundromat and take your cleaning to the neighborhood dry cleaner yourself. Laundry and dry cleaning sent from the hotel can blow a budget. If you do wash out a few things, be sure they do not drip over carpeting or fabric. And please, do not hang things in the windows!

13. Notify the hotel if you expect to arrive after 6 P.M. Even if you paid the room deposit, the hotel can technically resell your room to someone else if they do not know your arrival time.

14. Change money at a bank, never at a hotel.

15. For security's sake, avoid rooms on the *rez-de-chaussée,* or ground floor. In France, the ground floor is what Americans call the first floor; the French first floor *(premier étage)* is our second floor.

16. Paris is a very noisy city both day and night, making it heaven for night owls and a nightmare for insomniacs. Traffic, sirens, motor scooters, and voices magnify on the narrow streets, echoing throughout the night. Street-cleaning crews and trash trucks start their rounds at zero-dark-hundred, jarring awake many a sleeper. If noise is a problem, ask for a room away from the street, in the back of the hotel, or facing an inner courtyard. For added insurance, buy or bring earplugs (*boules de quièss*).

17. In the winter, hotels often schedule remodeling and/or repainting. This can involve anything from adding a coat of paint or remodeling a few bathrooms to months of time-consuming cleaning and exterior repairs that require scaffolding and sheets of plastic covering the windows. Work crews at these sites arrive at dawn and leave at dusk, and at no time are they or their machines quiet or conducive to peace. Before making final reservations, ask the hotel if it, or any of the buildings immediately around it, will be undergoing repairs or renovations during your stay. If it will be, consider carefully whether you want to put up with the noise and new paint smells.

18. It is important to realize that a *hôtel* is not always a hotel. The word *hôtel* has more than one meaning in French. Of course, it means a place offering lodging, but it also means a mansion or town house, like the Hôtel Lambert, or a large private home (a *hôtel particulière*). The city hall is the *Hôtel de Ville;* auctions are held at the *Hôtel des Ventes; Hôtel des Postes* refers to the general post office; and the *Hôtel des Invalides,* once a home for disabled war veterans, is now the most famous military museum in the world and the final resting place of Napoléon Bonaparte. Finally, if you are in the hospital, you are in a *Hôtel-Dieu.*

19. Traveler: Know thyself. It has often been said that all a person needs for adventure is the desire to have one. Your trip to Paris (or to any other destination) should be an adventure filled with treasured memories that last a lifetime. During any adventure, there will always be surprises. If you aren't willing to risk some unexpected turns in your plans, but insist on absolute predictability, especially in your accommodations, then I recommend you do one of two things: reserve a room at the Hôtel Ritz (Tel 01-43-16-30-30, www.ritzparis.com), or invest your travel money elsewhere and stay home.

How to Use
Great Sleeps Paris

Big Splurges and Cheap Sleeps

Most of the hotels in this guide are in the midrange price category. However, a few are higher priced and designated as "Big Splurges" and a few are true budget accommodations and designated as "Cheap Sleeps." Big Splurge hotels have amenities, ambiance, services, and an overall appeal that will suit those celebrating special occasions or those with more flexible budgets and demanding tastes. Even though their rates are higher, they still offer the same good value for money as the other accommodations in this guide. All Big Splurge hotels are marked with a dollar sign ($). The index includes a separate list of these special hotels.

Conversely, those looking to maximize their travel dollar without sacrificing cleanliness and a good night's sleep should look for the Cheap Sleep hotels, which are denoted with a cent symbol (¢) and are also listed separately in the index. These budget-priced hotels are in safe and sometimes pleasant locations and maintain excellent quality for their price category. Those on a budget could also consider hostels or, if you qualify, student accommodations, which are listed under "Other Options," page 323.

Stars

Hotels throughout France are controlled by a government rating system that ranks them from no stars to four-star deluxe. Every hotel must display prominently the number of stars it has.

Because the number of stars has to do with the size of the room, the distance from the bed to the light switch, and whether or not there is an elevator, and absolutely nothing to do with the level of cleanliness, decor, attitude of management or personnel, location, or value for money, you cannot always judge the quality or even the price of a hotel by its stars. In older hotels, many of the rooms are not standardized, and they can range in size and price from a dark little cavelike cell in the back to a sumptuous suite facing a leafy garden.

However, the star ratings do act as a general guide. A no-star hotel is usually mighty basic, with few, if any, private bathrooms, no elevator, and someone behind the desk who speaks limited English. Many of them, however, are spotlessly clean, well located, and excellent budget values. A one-star hotel has minimum facilities, but again, it may be well located and very clean. Two stars means a comfortable hotel with direct-dial phones in all rooms and an elevator in buildings of four or more stories.

Three stars indicates a very comfortable hotel where all rooms have direct-dial phones, a majority have private plumbing, and there is an elevator. A four-star hotel is first class all the way, usually with a restaurant, and a four-star deluxe is a virtual palace, with every service you could dream of. This book covers no-star to three-star hotels, with the exception of a handful of four-stars that were too good to leave out.

Reservations

People always ask me, "Do I need advance hotel reservations in Paris?" The answer is yes, positively! In order to be assured of a room, you must reserve as far in advance as possible. Paris experiences some of the worst hotel bottlenecks in Europe, and a confirmed reservation, even on the slowest day in the low season, will save you frantic hours spent searching for a room after your arrival. It will also save you money, since without advance reservations you will probably be forced to take something beyond your budget, perhaps in a part of the city you do not like. Do not reserve for more nights than you think you will need. If you decide to leave before you intended, or if you want to switch hotels, you may not get back any money you have paid ahead, or you could be charged on your credit card for the nights you do not stay. The easiest way to reserve is to let your travel agent do all the work. However, it is not hard to do it yourself, and frankly, with the ease and speed of the telephone, faxes, email, and the Internet, it is not only easy but better because you will be able to ask questions, inquire about exact rates, and arrange just what you want without going through an intermediary. In addition, the hotel may pass along to you their savings of the travel agent's commission, have special prices for reserving on their Website, or negotiate a better rate. After reserving by one of these methods, you will be asked to guarantee your booking by fax with a major credit card, or in a few cases, a money order in euros.

The one way *not* to reserve is by letter. Transatlantic mail can take more than two weeks each way—and if there is a strike, who knows how long mail will take to reach its destination? Now with the speed and ease of email, a letter makes no sense; in fact, in today's world, writing for reservations is about as *au courant* as the bustle. In other words, don't do it.

When reserving, discuss the following points:

1. Dates of stay, time of arrival, and number of persons in the party.
2. Size and type of room (double or twin beds, extra beds, adjoining rooms, suite, and so on).
3. Facilities needed: private toilet, shower and/or bathtub, or hall facilities if acceptable.
4. Location of room: view, on the street, on the courtyard, or in the back of the hotel.

5. Rates. Determine what the nightly rate will be, including the per-person City of Paris tourist tax, called the *taxe de séjour* (see "Rates: Paying the Bill," page 18, for details). Be sure to state whether or not you will be eating breakfast at the hotel (and remember you will save money if you do not).

6. Deposit required and form of payment.

7. Refund policy if you should have to cancel, and penalty if you check out earlier than planned. Request a confirmation by fax or email (print it out), and take it with you to the registration desk.

Email and the Internet

The attraction and convenience of email and the Internet has swept the French hotel industry to the degree it has in the States. Even some of the smallest hotels have realized that an email address and/or a Website can increase business significantly. Whenever applicable, each hotel's email and/or Internet address have been given. In some cases, hotels subscribe to a general service rather than have their own. Because the digital revolution is still growing so rapidly in France, please be understanding and patient and expect some snafus.

Fax

All but the smallest budget hotels in Paris have joined the electronic age and have, at the very least, a fax machine. Faxing is the best way to secure a confirmed booking because it ensures that all parties get the details correct. Insist on a confirmation fax from the hotel, acknowledging your reservation and all pertinent details. To fax a hotel in Paris, dial 011+33, and then the fax number in Paris, remembering to drop the first zero. For instance, if the fax is 01-42-12-34-56, compose 011+33+1-42-12-34-56.

Telephone

Always call Paris during regular, local weekday business hours to avoid talking to a hotel night clerk who has no authority to negotiate prices. The best times to get anything done in Paris is between 10 A.M. and noon, and between 3 and 6 P.M. Before calling, write down all your requests and questions. The hotel will ask you to send a fax with your credit card number as a guarantee for your reservation. In this fax to the hotel, cite the details of the conversation, the name of the person with whom you spoke, and the date and time of the call. It is vital to ask the hotel to fax you a confirmation of your reservation in return, and then take it with you in case there are any problems at check-in. To dial direct to Paris from the United States, dial 011+33, and then the number of the hotel, dropping the first 0 of the ten-digit phone number. For instance, if the hotel phone number is 01-42-11-22-33, you dial 011+33+1-42-11-22-33.

Making Your Reservation in French

If the hotel in question has no English-speaking staff, or you just want to try your luck with French, here are a few simple phrases for making your reservation (see also the glossary, page 403).

Bonjour/Bonsoir madame/monsieur.
Hello/Good evening, madam/sir.

Parlez-vous anglais?
Do you speak English?

Je voudrais réserver ____ chambre(s) (tranquille) pour une/deux/trois personne(s) qui donne sur (le jardin/la rue/la cour) à deux lits (avec un grant lit/ à un lit) avec salle de bains et WC (avec douche ou bain et WC/sans douche ou bain et WC) pour ____ nuit(s) à partir du ____ au ____.
I would like to reserve ____ (quiet) room(s) for one/two/three person(s) that is/are on (the garden/the street/the courtyard) with two beds (one big bed/one regular-size bed) with bath and toilet (with shower or bath and toilet/without shower or bath and toilet) for ____ night(s) beginning on ____ to ____.

Je voudrais prendre la (les) chambre(s) avec (sans) le petit dejéuner.
I would like to have the room(s) include (without) breakfast.

Quel est le tarif?
What is the price?

Quel est votre tarif meilleur? Avez-vous des prix basse-saison?
What is your best price? Do you have a low-season rate?

Voici mon numero de carte de credit.
Here is my credit card number.

Mon numéro de fax/email est_____.
My fax/email number is_____.

Veuillez-vous confirmer ma reservation des que possible?
Would you please confirm this reservation as soon as possible?

Merci beaucoup, madame/monsieur.
Thank you very much, sir/madame.

If you are sending a confirmation fax, you will want to add:

Vous trouvez ci-joint____ (mon carte de credit) à titre d'arrhes.
You will find attached ____ (my credit card number and expiration date) as a first-night deposit.

Auriez-vous le bonté de bien vouloir me confirmer cette réservation dès que possible? Je vous remercie de votre obligeance, et je vous prie de croire, monsieur/ madame, à l'assurance de mes sentiments distingués.
Would you please be kind enough to confirm this reservation as soon as possible? Thank you for your assistance.
Yours sincerely,

Deposits

After making a reservation, most hotels will require at least a one-night deposit, even if you have been a guest there before. This is smart insurance for both sides. The easiest way to handle a deposit is with a credit card. If the hotel does not take credit cards, there are other options. You can sometimes send your own personal check, which the hotel will only cash if you are a no-show. They will return the uncashed check to you upon arrival. The next best option from your standpoint is to send the hotel an international money order in U.S. dollars. This can be converted into euros by the hotel, and it saves you from having to secure a deposit in euros on this side of the Atlantic. While this option is more convenient for you, it is added work for the hotel, costs them money to exchange, and some, especially in the lower price ranges, simply refuse. If your hotel insists on a deposit in euros, you will have to purchase them in the form of a money order or a wire transfer through your bank.

Checking In/Checking Out

The lobby is usually one of the most attractive parts of a hotel, both because first impressions are important and because it is where the owner and manager spend their day. When you arrive at your hotel, ask to see your room. This is a normal and expected practice in all hotels in France. If you are dissatisfied, ask to see another room. Keep going until you are satisfied. After approving the room, reconfirm the rate and whether or not you will be eating breakfast at the hotel. This advance work prevents any unpleasant surprises at checkout time.

In most hotels, you pay for the room, not for the number of persons occupying it. Thus, if you are alone and occupy a triple, you will pay the triple price, unless negotiated otherwise. Watch out! Most rooms are set up for two, and the few singles tend to be tiny and located on a top floor without much view or along the back facing a blank wall. Single travelers may be more comfortable in a small double. Most hotels have two kinds of double rooms: those with a double bed *(un grand lit)* and those with twin beds *(deux lits)*. If you ask for a double, you will get a room with a double bed, so when reserving, be sure to be specific about exactly what type of bed arrangement suits you.

In Paris, the hotel day begins and ends at noon. If you overstay, you can be charged the price of an extra day. If you are arriving before noon after a long international flight, the room will probably not be ready if the hotel is fully booked. If you must have your room at 8 or 9 A.M., you will have to book (and pay) for it the night before. If you think you might arrive after 6 P.M., be sure to notify the hotel; otherwise, your room can legally be given away, even if you have a deposit.

Rates: Paying the Bill

Just like French restaurant menus, hotel rates and the number of stars must be posted.

The city of Paris levies a visitor's tax on persons not liable for the resident tax (a tax raised on habitual residents of the City of Paris). This visitor's tax, called the *taxe de séjour,* applies to all forms of paying accommodations: hotels and tourist residences, furnished flats, holiday campsites, and RV parking. The tax is charged per person, per night. The amount ranges from 0.15€ for guests staying at no-star hotels and campgrounds to 1.07€ for those patronizing four-star hotels. Some hotels charge it over and above the quoted rate, which is technically illegal, but no one seems to be looking; others include it in the total hotel rate. All *Great Sleeps Paris* listings note the specific amount for each hotel and whether or not this tax is included or extra in the daily rate. However, policies on this tax change, so to avoid confusion, be sure to inquire at the time of booking whether or not the *taxe de séjour* is included or extra. The proceeds of the *taxe de séjour* are allocated for the development and promotion of tourism in Paris.

The French government no longer tightly controls hotel prices, but they do give special authorization for hotels to increase prices by a certain percentage every year. Many hotels do this around April; others have held steady for two and three years at a time. It usually depends on the economy. Most hotels offer different rates at different times of the year, getting what they can when they can, based on the law of supply and demand. This is especially true during the fashion and trade shows, when hotels in premium Paris locations have been know to double prices—and have people fight to pay them. All rates listed in *Great Sleeps Paris* are for full price and do not reflect any special deals. If a hotel does offer discounted rates at certain times of the year, that fact is noted, but not the amount of the discount because that can change, and in your favor. The rates tell whether or not breakfast is extra or included and, if included, whether or not the hotel will allow you to deduct it if not taken. While I have made every effort to be accurate on the rates, I cannot control changes or fluctuations of the dollar against the euro, inflation, yearly percentage rate hikes, owner whims, or grand renovations that result in higher prices. So, be prepared for the prices to vary (unfortunately, usually upward).

All listings state which credit cards are accepted. The favored cards are Visa and MasterCard. American Express is third, and Diners Club a very distant fourth, thanks to their vendor charges and slow payments. In most hotels, payment is required one night in advance. Some low-priced hotels, youth hostels, and student accommodations do not accept credit cards. It is cash up front in euros only. I have yet to see one of these hotels bend on this important point, so be prepared.

The following abbreviations are used to denote which credit cards a hotel will accept:

American Express	AE
Diners Club	DC
MasterCard	MC
Visa	V

Hotel exchange rates are terrible. If you plan to pay your bill in cash, convert your money at a bank before checkout time (see "Currency Exchange and Traveler's Checks," page 36). Before leaving the hotel, go over your bill carefully, question anything you do not understand, and get a receipt marked *paid.*

Complaints

If you have a serious complaint about some aspect of your hotel stay (and this does not mean noise or mismatched colors in your room), complain directly to the manager, not to the desk clerk, who has no authority and will rarely pass on your comments to the boss for fear of losing his or her job. If the problem cannot be resolved at this level, then put your concerns in writing and send them to the Direction du Tourisme, 2, rue Linois, 75015, Paris; Métro: Charles-Michels. I encourage you to also let me know about any major problems you encounter. While I cannot intercede on your behalf, it is important for me to know if a hotel is no longer measuring up so that I can take up the matter with the hotel on my next visit (see "Readers' Comments," page 415, for an address).

Breakfast

Hotel breakfasts are almost always a bad buy. Hotels stand to make as much as a 200 percent profit on this meal, so they naturally encourage their guests to eat it at the hotel. It is much cheaper, and twice as interesting, to join the locals at the corner café for a *café crème* and a croissant, or to stop by a neighborhood *pâtisserie* or *boulangerie* that has a few tables and chairs and indulge in freshly baked treats. Almost every Parisian hotel charges extra for their Continental breakfast, which consists of coffee, tea, hot chocolate, bread, croissants or other rolls, butter, and jam. Some throw in a glass of juice or a piece of cheese. If you want anything beyond this (for example, an egg or fruit), it will cost dearly and is usually not worth the extra expenditure.

Many hotels are now offering a buffet downstairs for the same price as a Continental, which they will serve in your room. An all-you-can-eat buffet—with cereals, yogurt, hard-boiled eggs, cheese, cold meat, and fruit added to the standard Continental fare—can sometimes be worth the price, especially if you plan to skip lunch. But please! Do not treat the buffet as a free feed for the rest of the day by loading up a bag with the fixings for lunch and a predinner snack. This is extremely bad form, and hoteliers will be furious if they catch you doing it. Be aware of the "breakfast is offered" ruse. No, it isn't . . . you are paying for it in the room rate; it just has not been separately charged, and it will be virtually impossible to have anything deducted, even if you do not eat it. Of course, if a hotel charges for breakfast separately, it should not be on your bill unless you ate it.

Unless otherwise noted, none of the hotels listed serve meals other than breakfast.

English Spoken

All the hotel listings in this book state whether or not English is spoken. If you do not speak any French and want to avoid the stress of trying to communicate without it, it is important to know whether someone at the hotel speaks English. If you can dust off a few French phrases, smile, and display good will, you will find that the hotel staff will prove to be friendly and go out of their way to help you. While it is fun to practice your high-school French, it is not fun to try to deal with a problem while struggling to speak it.

Smoking/Nonsmoking Rooms

Bon chance on this one! Statistics show that 50 percent of Parisian men are smokers and 30 percent of Parisian women light up. I think these figures are very low, considering that three tons of cigarette butts are cleaned off the streets of Paris every day! Statistics are even higher for other countries whose residents vacation in Paris and smoke in their hotel rooms. Many hotels will say they have nonsmoking rooms "on request." What that really means is that, if you ask when reserving, the maid will open the window and spray air freshener on the day you arrive. Or, as one hotel owner seriously said to me when questioned about nonsmoking rooms, "Yes, we do have nonsmoking rooms. We always remove the ashtrays in rooms of our nonsmoking guests." If the hotel provides exclusive nonsmoking rooms, it is definitely noted under the Facilities and Services category. Fortunately, most of the hotel breakfast dining rooms are nonsmoking. The index has a list of hotels that have rooms exclusively set aside for nonsmoking guests (see page 412).

Facilities and Services

A brief summary at the end of each hotel listing states which facilities and services are offered by the hotel. They may include: air-conditioning (if in some rooms only, this is noted), bar, conference room, direct-dial telephone, hair dryer, elevator, Internet in lobby (if there is a public terminal available for the use of all guests; in-room data ports for personal laptop computers are not noted), laundry service, minibar, parking, room service, television with either French or international reception, pay-per-view television or videos, safe in office or in the room (and whether there is a charge), and exclusive nonsmoking rooms. Of course, the better the hotel, the more offerings there will be.

Nearest Tourist Attractions

Each hotel listing tells you if the hotel is on the Right or Left Bank and gives you the nearest tourist attractions within a reasonable walking distance.

Transportation

The closest métro and RER stops are given with each hotel listing. That is not to say that taking the bus might not be a better way for you to get where you want to go. It is beyond the scope of *Great Sleeps Paris* to give the bus routes, but there are free métro and bus maps available in métro stations and at your hotel. When in doubt, just ask at the hotel desk. You can bet that person rides either the métro or the bus to work. (See "Transportation," page 51, for information on public transportation in Paris.)

Maps

"There is never any ending to Paris and the memory."
—*Ernest Hemingway*

The maps in *Great Sleeps Paris* are meant to help locate all the hotels and shops; they are not meant to replace detailed street maps to guide you as you walk about the city. On this book's maps, hotels are marked with bullets, shops with triangles, and key tourist sites and métro and rail stations are noted.

The free maps you will pick up at your hotel are worth what you paid for them: nothing. If you plan to be in Paris for more than a day, a necessary investment, and one that will last forever, is a copy of the *Plan de Paris par Arrondissement*. This Parisian "bible" offers a detailed map of each arrondissement, with a completely keyed street index, métro and bus routes, tourist sites, churches, and other valuable information. It is available at major newsstands and bookstores and costs between 8€ and 13€. All Parisians have a copy, and so should you.

General Information

When to Go

Whoever does not visit Paris regularly will never be elegant.
—Balzac, 1815

If you don't travel when you can, your heirs probably will.
—Anonymous

How wonderful it would be to drop everything and fly to Paris whenever the spirit moved us! If such romantic impulses do not quite fit into your schedule or budget, then the high and low seasons must be taken into consideration. These times of year affect not only the availability of hotel rooms and the rates but also airline fares. High season in Paris is considered to be the two fashion weeks in mid-January for *haute couture,* again in March for *pret-a-porter* (the spring and fall trade shows), Easter through June, September, October, and ten days around Christmas and New Year's. It is very important for Paris visitors to note that when fashion and large trade shows fill the city to the bursting point, many hotels add on surcharges of up to 50 percent. Dates vary slightly from year to year, so the best bet is to check with the French Government Tourist Office in New York or Los Angeles for the latest information. This leaves July, August, November, the first three weeks of December, and parts of January to Easter, as the best times to go to Paris. The drawback in July and August is that you will be sharing your Parisian holiday with many other tourists and very few French. Despite government pleadings and tourist demands, August is still the traditional vacation month for most Parisians, and many restaurants and shops are closed for at least a week or two, if not the entire month. The good news is that hotels are always open—and many offer lower rates—and everything is easier to come by, including métro seats, café tables, and good-natured waiters.

Holidays and Events

Holidays *(les jours fériés)* are vital dates to bear in mind when planning any trip to Paris. Banks, post offices, and most retail stores are all closed, and museums that are open may run on different time schedules. In addition, banks may be closed a half day before each holiday as well as the day after in some instances. The traffic is horrendous, especially if the holiday falls on a Tuesday or Thursday, since many French take off Monday or Friday to make it a long weekend. Restaurant holiday policies vary with the rise and fall of the economy. Always call ahead to make sure—even if they say they are open, they may change their mind and be closed. Skeleton or third-string crews often man the hotel desks, and there is a laid-back attitude during a holiday period, resulting in quick excuses for things not working. It can all add up to some very frustrating times for a traveler.

January 1	New Year's Day	*Jour de l'An*
Easter Sunday		*Pâques*
and Monday		*et Lundi de Pâques*
Ascension Day	*Ascension*	(40 days after Easter)
Whit Monday	Lundi de Pentacôte	(second Monday after Ascension)
May 1	Labor Day	*Fête du Travail*
May 8	VE Day	Armistice 1945
July 14	Bastille Day	*Quatorze Juillet/Fête Nationale*
August 15	Assumption Day	*Assomption*
November 1	All Saints' Day	*Toussaint*
November 11	Armistice Day	Armistice 1918
December 25	Christmas Day	*Noël*

For motorists, the time to avoid is the last weekend in August, when Parisians return from their vacations en masse via the autoroutes. This grand *rentrée* creates traffic snarls of world-class proportions.

Events

The two best sources for events in Paris are the weekly magazines *Pariscope: Une Semaine de Paris* and *l'Officiel des Spectacles*. They come out on Wednesday, cost 4€, and are sold at every kiosk in the city. In these magazines you will find listings for the opera, theater, films, concerts, art exhibitions, special events, naughty nightlife, weekly TV programs, swimming-pool hours, and interesting guided tours. Although the magazines are printed in French (with the exception of a small English-language section in *Pariscope* devoted to weekly highlights), a non–French speaker can quickly decipher the information.

What to Bring

I think every wife has a right to insist upon seeing Paris.
—*Sydney Smith, British author (1771– 1845), from letter to Countess Grey, September 11, 1835*

Why buy good luggage? You only use it when you travel . . .
—*Casey Stengel*

If you follow only one piece of advice in *Great Sleeps Paris,* let it be this: Travel light. Porters are no longer roaming airports or train stations, and bellboys are almost relics of the past for most hotels. Therefore, you are going to have to carry your own luggage, and believe me, after the first ten minutes, even when pulling luggage on wheels, less is definitely best.

My travel rule of thumb is this: Take twice as much money as you think you will need and half as much clothing. Keep it simple, color coordinate your outfits, and remember, this is Paris, not Mars, so you can go out and buy something wonderful if you need to fill a gap in your travel wardrobe. For travel products and travel clothing, I think one of the best sources is Magellan's Travel Catalog (Tel: 800-962-4943, www.magellans.com).

One of the favorite pastimes of Parisians and their expatriate friends is to sit in a café along a busy boulevard and pick out the tourists. You can spot them a mile away, in their summer tank tops and shorts, a bottle of water dangling from a hook on their belts—and in winter, bundled up in parkas as if the ski slopes were just around the corner. Of course, they all wear jogging shoes and the men have baseball caps . . . often turned backward.

Parisians are some of the most stylish people on earth. They are also some of the most conservative in their dress. Yes, you will see some off-the-wall outfits on bionic, buffed bodies, but you will never see short shorts and skimpy tops on any well-groomed Parisian man or woman. Big-city clothes are the call of the day, no matter what the weather may bring.

Naturally, you will leave your heavy wool coat and long johns at home when you visit Paris in August. But what kind of coat makes sense in May or June? Knowing the monthly average temperatures will help:

January	45.5°F	(7.5°C)
February	44.8°F	(7.1°C)
March	50°F	(10.2°C)
April	60.3°F	(15.7°C)
May	61–62°F	(16.6°C)
June	75°F	(23°C)
July	77°F	(25.1°C)
August	78°F	(25.6°C)
September	69–70°F	(20.9°C)
October	61.7°F	(16.5°C)
November	53°F	(11.7°C)
December	46°F	(7.8°C)

If you are going during the warm months, wear light cottons and comfortable shoes. Synthetics don't breathe and add to the heat discomfort. For winter visits, layering makes sense, and so do a lined raincoat, a set of silk long underwear, and a hat (since 70 percent of body heat goes out through your head). Jeans are universal and certainly acceptable for sight-seeing and casual dining. However, they are not considered in vogue at more expensive restaurants or if you are invited to someone's home. Men will feel comfortable wearing slacks and a nice shirt or turtleneck, along with a jacket if it is cool. Women will feel best in simple, well-tailored outfits. Gauzy, lime-green jumpsuits with sequined

Eiffel Tower T-shirts, along with jogging shoes for every occasion, spell tourist and can lead to such problems as poor service or being a target of pickpockets.

When packing your bags, use every bit of space to its fullest: stuff your shoes, roll your sweaters and underwear, use plastic garment bags between layers to prevent wrinkling and pack so things will not slip and slide to one end. Pack your toiletries and cosmetics in a sealable, waterproof bag. You only need one experience with the mess caused by airline pressure blowing off the top of your shampoo or nail polish remover to know what I am talking about.

Aside from the obvious documents, money, airline tickets, medicines, emergency telephone numbers, and clothing, the following is a list of useful items. It is by no means exhaustive, nor do I suggest you take every item on it, but it is a list of things you might consider bringing.

- Your favorite shampoo and soap
- As many moist towelettes as you can fit in, and a bottle of antiseptic hand wash
- Packaged wipes for shoe cleaning, make-up removal, nail polish removal
- Sunscreen lotion and sunglasses
- French dictionary and/or phrasebook
- Portable radio with earphones
- Pedometer to keep track of the number of miles you walk, so you can impress your friends when you return
- First-aid kit
- Sewing kit, with a pair of decent scissors
- Travel tool kit with Swiss army knife, screwdriver, tape, stapler, packing tape, Scotch tape, string
- A few hangers you can toss out at the end of the trip. You may be surprised at the condition and scarcity of hotel hangers.
- Rubber doorstop as a security measure
- For drip-dry laundry: blow-up hangers, clothesline with clothespins, or clothespins you can hang up; and a small container of spot remover to use on tough stains before you wash your clothes in your room sink or bathtub. (However, don't pack laundry soap; it's cheap and readily available in all Paris supermarkets.)
- Adapter plug and a transformer for electrical appliances (see "Voltage," page 57), and a grounded surge protector for your computer
- A sturdy suction hook for the back of the bathroom or bedroom door

- Suction-cup magnifying mirror
- Alarm clock with lighted face
- Mosquito repellent (summer)
- Flashlight
- Reading material
- Umbrella
- Camera
- Extra batteries (including a camera battery)
- Calculator
- Lint remover roller, clothes brush
- Extra fold-up bag for shopping purchases and a few sheets of bubble wrap for wrapping breakables you might buy

Tourist Offices and American Embassy

The main office of the Office de Tourisme de Paris is at 127, avenue des Champs-Élysées, 75008; Métro: Charles-de-Gaulle-Étoile; Tel: 08 92-68-31-12 (0.33€ per minute); Internet: www.paris-touristoffice.com; Open: in summer daily 9 A.M.–8 P.M., in winter Mon–Sat 9 A.M.–8 P.M., Sun and holidays 11 A.M.–6 P.M. It is a one-stop shop for information on Paris, has a nice boutique, can make hotel reservations, changes money, sells phone cards and museum cards, and makes reservations for concerts and shows, For information on Paris and Île de France, contact Espace du Tourisme d'Île de France at Carrousel du Louvre, 99, rue de Rivoli, 1st; Métro: Palais Royal–Musée du Louvre; Internet: www.pidf.com; Open: Mon, Wed–Sun 10 A.M.–7 P.M.

In the United States, the French government tourist offices are located at 444 Madison Avenue, New York, NY 10020; Tel: 212-838-7800; and 9454 Wilshire Boulevard, Beverly Hills, CA 90212; Tel: 310-271-6665. They are open Monday to Friday 10 A.M. to 4 P.M. You can send them an email at fgto@gte.net or surf their Website at www.francetourism.com.

In Paris, the American Embassy is at 2, avenue Gabriel, 75008; Métro: Concorde; Tel: 01-43-12-22-22; Internet: www.amb-usa.fr. Consulate/visas/passport services: 2, rue St-Florentin, 75001; Métro: Concorde. Passports: Mon–Fri 9 A.M.–12:30 P.M., 1–3 P.M. Visas: telephone for appointment between 2 and 5 P.M.

Disabled Travelers

Paris is improving for wheelchair-bound travelers, but it still has a long way to go. Many hotels in *Great Sleeps Paris* do have rooms that have been somewhat refitted for handicapped guests, but the facilities may consist only of a wide door, a grab-bar by the tub, or just the fact that the room is on the *rez-de-chaussée* (ground floor). An English language guide, *Access in Paris* by Gordon Couch and Ben Roberts (Quiller Press), is available for around £7 (British pounds). Contact them at RADAR, Unit 12, City Forum, 250 City Road, London EC1V 8AS; Tel: 44 (0) 207-250-3222.

There are several agencies you can contact. L'Office de Tourisme de Paris has some information for disabled travelers at www.parisbienvenu.com. The main office in Paris is at 127, avenue des Champs-Élysées, 75008; Métro: Charles-de-Gaulle-Étoile. Tel: 08-92-68-31-12 (0.49€ per minute), www.paris-touristoffice.com. Another Website to check is www.jaccede.com, which also has information for disabled visitors. A toll-free number offers advice in French for disabled persons living or visiting Paris (08-00-03-37-48). The Association des Paralysés de France publishes a magazine, *Faire Face,* which covers issues pertinent to the disabled in France. They also publish *Guide Musées, Cinémas, Théâtres À Paris; Loisirs des Parisiens* (dealing with libraries, parks, and gardens in Paris); *Vie Pratique* (general living in Paris); and *Tourisme à Paris* (hotels and transportation). Their office is at 22, rue du Père-Guérain, 75013; Métro: Place d'Italie, Tel: 01-44-16-83-83; Fax: 01-44-16-83-80; Email: info@apf.asso.fr; Internet: www.apf.asso; Open: Mon–Fri 9 A.M.–12:30 P.M., 1:30–6 P.M.

Very few of the métros and buses are suitable for wheelchair use. The métro line 14 and the RER Lines A and B are accessible and so are some SNCF trains. For information in English and a list of the most accessible métro and RER stations, call RATP, place de la Madeleine, 75008; Tel: 08-92-68-41-41; Open: daily 6 A.M.–9 P.M. The telephone number for SNCF is 08-92-35-35-35. Theoretically, taxis are obliged to pick up passengers in wheelchairs, but don't count on it. It is better to reserve with one of the following companies who specialize in service for the handicapped. They like a forty-eight–hour notice.

Airhop (to and from airports), 01-41-29-01-29. Open: Mon–Fri 9 A.M.–noon, 1:30–6:30 P.M.

Amhap, 01 56-61-91-00

GiHp, 01-41-83-15 15. Open: Mon–Fri 7.30 A.M.–8 P.M.

Neuf Orthopedio sells wheelchairs, canes, and other accessories for the handicapped. They are at 9, rue Léopold Bellan, 75002; Tel: 01-42-33-83-46; Métro: Sentier; Open: Mon–Fri 9 A.M. –6 P.M.

Other information for disabled travelers can be obtained from the following organizations in the United States:

Directions Unlimited
720 N. Bedford Road
Bedford Hills, NY 10507
Telephone: 800-533-5343
A travel agency with an agent who specializes in accessible travel for the disabled.

Moss Rehabilitation Hospital
Telephone: 215-456-5882
Internet: www.mossresourcenet.org
Open: Mon–Fri 9 A.M.–5 P.M.
Can refer disabled travelers to travel agents who specialize in travelers with disabilities.

Society for the Advancement of Travel for the Handicapped, Inc.
347 Fifth Avenue
New York, NY 10016
Telephone: 212-447-7284
Internet: www.sath.org

Tours

The people whom I focus on below provide tours in Paris and environs as well as other unique services. In addition to being multilingual, talented, and very well qualified, these professionals are passionate about what they do and possess an intimate, detailed knowledge of Paris, a city they have come to love and call their own through years of living and working here. Indeed, any of these tours are wonderful ways to enhance your trip and learn more about the fascinating City of Light.

Mike's Bike Tours

24, rue Edgar Faure, 75015
Métro: Dupleix (office), Bir-Hakeim (bike tour start)
For the young in spirit, not to mention in body, Mike's day and night bike tours are great ways to experience Paris. All you have to do is show up, pay your money, and enjoy the three- to four-hour ride; tours meet at the south leg (Pilier Sud) of the Eiffel Tower on the Champ-du-Mars. You will be provided with a helmet, five-speed bike, rain gear if necessary, an English-speaking guide, and a day or night of unequalled fun. All ages are welcome (as long as you can ride a bike), bikes are sized to fit everyone from a child to his or her grandparents, and there's a twenty-five biker per tour maximum. Once you have spun through Paris, move on to one of Mike's tours of Versailles or Monet's Giverny. Reservations are required for both of these day trips. At their office, you will find a multitude of help: a DSL Internet line and a computer with an English keyboard, Starbucks coffee, free (and clean) bathrooms, phone cards, free daily storage of backpacks, and loads of information about other destinations in France and Europe. If your travels take you to Amsterdam, Barcelona, or Munich, Mike has bike tours of these cities.
Telephone & Fax: 01-56-58-10-54
Internet: www.MikesBikeToursParis.com
Credit Cards: None, only euros, US dollars, or traveler's checks
Hours: Day tours commence at 11 A.M., night tours at 7 P.M.
Prices: Day tour, student 22€, adult 24€; night tour, student 26€, adult 28€; everybody Versailles 50€, Giverny 65€

Paris Garden Walks

Discover the world famous gardens of Paris. The guides are professional artists, landscape designers, or art and architectural historians. Each guide views a garden from a different perspective, so every walk is different, even if you see the same garden several times. All the walks are conducted in English, last at least one hour, and require a minimum of three people. Reservations are mandatory, and payment is in cash before the start of the walk, or in advance by euro check. Call or email for the current schedule.

Telephone & Fax: 01-47-41-21-59
Email: parisgarden@free.fr
Credit Cards: None, euro cash or check
Prices: 10€ per person

Paris Muse

Ellen McBreen, a graduate of New York University with a doctorate in art history, can now be your private guide to the museums of Paris. As this university lecturer says, "My time with you is less expensive than a university class and a lot more fun." Besides, you are in Paris, the masterpieces are in front of you, and Ellen is at your side to make them come alive for you in fascinating ways. Her tours, for no more than four people, are tailored to your schedule and your interests, and are absolutely private to you and your friends or family. She also specializes in art tours for children. Of course, the price includes admission not only to the museums but to the special shows, and there is no waiting on line at any time. What better way to appreciate and understand the magnificent art treasures in Paris than with this delightful muse.

Telephone: 06-73-77-33-52
Internet: www.parismuse.com
Credit Cards: None. Pay online through PayPal, with a U.S. check, or in euros in Paris.
Price: per person, 60€ (90-minute tour), 110€ (2½-hour tour)

Paris Personalized

Antoinette Azzurro is from Australia, but her love of her adopted city of Paris is infectious. After being with her for only a short while on one of her private walking itineraries, you will quickly become caught up in the beauty, history, and magic of the city, and catch Antoinette's enthusiasm in the bargain. Her walking itineraries are designed for the discerning traveler wanting more than the average run-of-the-mill group tour. Her list of wonderful Paris experiences is endless. Antoinette leads you to places that few tourists see, focusing on history with interesting anecdotes, footnotes, and fascinating stories that provide new insights to the city, whether you are a first-time visitor or a Paris veteran. All her walks are private, last either a half or whole day, and can be tailored to the participants' special interests. She also can organize trips with a car and

English-speaking driver and licensed guide to take you to Vaux-le-Vicomte, the Châteaux of the Loire, the Normandy beaches, Giverny, and the Burgundy and Champagne regions. For something really memorable, ask her to organize a private hot-air balloon ride, a private wine tasting with local Parisians, private cooking lessons in Normandy in a converted fifteenth-century convent home, or a crack-of-dawn tour of Rungis, the largest wholesale food market in Europe. This last is a must for any foodie. To record your day, a private photographer can be arranged who will create a photo book of your adventure. For a never-to-be-forgotten gift for the special lady in your life, ask Antoinette to arrange a "Day of Beauty," which includes massage, steam bath, facial, manicure and pedicure, hair styling, and even a complete makeover.

Antoinette is available year-round, with the exception of January, when she leaves Paris for her own travel adventure. It is important to note that all tours are private to you and your own group, whether it be just one person, a couple, or a family, and that Antoinette meets her guests at their hotel. For further details, check her Website, then telephone or email to reserve one of the best days you will ever spend in Paris.

Telephone: 01-48-00-82-38, (cell) 06-63-24-59-40

Email: aazzurro@hotmail.com

Internet: www.parispersonalized.com

Credit Cards: None, cash only

Prices: Half-day private walking tour, per group: $300 half day, $500 full day

Paris Walks

10, rue Samson, St Denis, 93200

If you are fluent in French, finding an interesting walking tour in Paris is easy. Just look in the most recent issue of *Pariscope* and you will find several possibilities every day of the week. For those whose French is limited, an English-language walking tour with British expatriates Oriel and Peter Caine is the solution. The Caines are licensed "blue badge" guides in France. They and a small group of assistants have put together a series of well-researched group walking tours through parts of Paris that the casual visitor is likely to miss. Their comments are both educational and entertaining, filled with little-known tidbits that humanize the particular area covered. The tours are given year-round and last approximately two hours; all you have to do is to show up at the appointed time and place wearing comfortable shoes and be ready to learn and enjoy. With advance notice, customized private tours (for five to six people) and family tours geared toward making Paris fun for children are available.

Telephone: 01-48-09-21-40

Fax: 01-42-43-75-51

Internet: www.paris-walks.com

Credit Cards: For general walking tours, cash only; for customized tours, V

Price: General walking tour, 10€ adult, 7€ student, 5€ child; customized tours: half-day, 195€; full day, 320€

Promenades Gourmandes

187, rue du Temple, 75003

Not only did I learn a lot about cooking, but I had the opportunity to meet a wonderful person!

—*George Brooks, attorney-at-law*

It doesn't matter who you are—everyone from gourmet chefs to fledging novices will learn something from the dynamic Parisian chef Paule Caillat, whose love of cooking and culinary heritage transform everything she touches. Paule, who was born and raised in Paris and college-educated in the States, gives private and group cooking lessons, but I can assure you they are a quantum leap from the ordinary, stilted classes I have often attended. Menus are selected according to the season, student preferences, and a careful eye for product availability in your home country. Cooking with Paule means getting hands-on, from shopping at the market right through enjoying what you have prepared. On the trip to the outdoor market, you will learn how to recognize the best ingredients, discern the different types of bread and cheese, distinguish a French apricot from one imported from Israel and know which one to buy, select the perfect meats and fish, and avoid anything that is not absolutely fresh. Through her knowledge of food, you will also be able to place the products you buy into their historical and geographical context in France. After lunch (if you have signed up for a full-day session), Paule will take you on a Promenade Gourmande (gourmet walking tour) to visit famous bakeries, kitchens of well-known restaurants, the bistros of rising young chefs, landmark kitchen equipment emporiums, saffron producers, and much more. If you are not a serious chef but appreciate gourmet foods, join one of her three-hour gourmet walking tours in Paris, which are as much fun as they are interesting and informative.

Cooking lessons and gourmet tours in Paris are not the half of Paule and her enthusiasm about food. She also leads small groups on excursions to areas in France that are specifically known for their exceptional food products. The trips include train travel, all meals and accommodations, and visits to points of interest.

Paule is a delightful, dynamic, knowledgeable woman. If you love food and cooking, please treat yourself to one of her cooking lessons, gourmet walks, or trips. You won't regret it for a minute. As one very happy participant said, "This was the best day I have ever spent in Paris, and the highlight of my entire trip!" I agree, and so does everyone lucky enough to spend time with Paule.

NOTE: Sometimes Paule takes a short vacation in August.

Telephone & Fax: 01-48-04-56-84, (cell) 01-16-72-79-00

Email: paule.caillat@wanadoo.fr

Internet: www.promenadesgourmandes.com
Credit Cards: None, cash only
Prices: Half day, $200; two half days, $360; full day, $290; two full days, $560; gourmet walking tour without cooking class, $90

Classes

L'École des Fleurs au Crillon

10, place de la Concorde, 75008
Métro: Concorde

Four types of French floral arranging classes are held at one of the most prestigious hotels in the world, the Hôtel de Crillon. Christian Tortu, one of the premier names in French floral designs, has created these exceptional classes given by the finest Parisian florists who have been personally chosen for their innovative talent and their artistic expertise.

Start with a Discovery class, which offers an introduction to bouquet arranging and an initial approach to floral decoration. These classes last ninety minutes and accommodate a maximum of fifteen students. At the end of the class, you keep your bouquet, its vase, and the instructions and know-how to re-create it when you get home.

Master classes last two hours and have up to ten participants. In addition to hands-on floral arranging, students receive a multitude of ideas and insider's hints about the latest trends in French floral style. At the end of the class, you take home what you have created and an École des Fleurs apron.

Flower Day covers everything from basic techniques to complex creations. At the end of the class, you take your creation with you and receive an École des Fleurs diploma. If you plan to be in town for a while, consider the Five-Class Bouquet Package, which is a cycle of five weekly classes in which students experience floral art in all its forms: the round bouquet, the foliage bouquet, the green and white centerpiece, and table decorations with flowers, fruits, and vegetables. Throughout the five-week course, your work will be critiqued by the teachers and, at the end, you will receive an École des Fleurs diploma.

During the year, special classes are held on various themes: Valentine's Day, tulips, weddings, springtime, and more. If you love flowers and flower arranging, you will be in floral heaven . . . not to mention in the magnificent Hôtel de Crillon. Classes are held in French or English, and must be reserved and paid for in advance. There are no walk-ins allowed, and no classes are held in August.

Telephone: 01-55-90-59-60
Fax: 01-47-04-50-21
Internet: www.ecoledesfleurs.com
Credit Cards: None, euro cash only
Prices: Discovery Class, 100€; Master Class, 250–300€; Flower Day (includes brunch), 350€, Five-Class Bouquet, 400€

Services

Computer Consultant

Karl Leino is a computer consultant specializing in Macintosh systems. Let's face it, the last thing you want is a problem with your computer, especially if you need it as a business tool. In addition to helping clients troubleshoot anything concerning a Mac, he will set up an Internet account in Paris for you, so you will be ready to log on immediately the moment you arrive. If you have questions before you leave home or when you get here, Karl is the Mac computer expert to call. Even if you don't have a Mac and run into problems, he will be able to refer you to a colleague who can help. He also has Mac contacts in other major cities when you are on the move and run into a problem. Karl is Swedish and speaks fluent English, comes to wherever you are in Paris, is extremely patient, and follows up on every consultation to make sure all is going well for you. Karl's rates are very fair, when you consider he makes house calls.

Telephone: 06-63-82-42-88

Email: oniel@mac.com

Credit Cards: None, euro cash only

Prices: Depends on the complexity of the consultation

Hairdresser—Franck Fann Coiffeur

5, rue d'Ormesson, 75004 (see map page 84)

Métro: St-Paul

Where to get your hair cut, a manicure, massage, or facial? It is always a problem in a strange city, especially if you cannot communicate very well. Relax—now you have Franck and his congenial staff ready to see to all your beauty needs. Franck is wonderful at cutting, coloring, and styling both men's and women's hair, and he speaks English. In fact, he has given me the best haircuts I have ever had. I only wish I could convince him to move to the States so I could go to him on a regular basis. He likes Miami, Florida . . . so there is hope! The other operators are all competent and professional, especially Florence, who gives manicures, and Flora, who does therapeutic massages and facials in the *hammam* (spa).

In French salons, all services are individually priced and tipped, from the shampoo to the blow dry. At Franck's the prices are very reasonable; it should run around 40 to 45€ for a haircut, from 45€ up for massages and facials, and from 24€ for manicures, all plus tips. Except for massages and facials, appointments are not necessary. However, it doesn't hurt to call ahead to let them know you are coming, especially if you want Franck. He is only here on Wednesday, Friday, and Saturday, when you will see his snazzy sports car parked illegally in front of the shop. Whenever you go, please say hello to everyone for me . . . and encourage Franck to open a second salon in the States very soon.

Telephone: 01-48-04-50-62

Credit Cards: MC, V (minimum 50€)

Open: Mon–Sat 10 A.M.–7 P.M.

Money Matters

There are few certainties when you travel. One of them is that the moment you arrive in a foreign country, the American dollar will fall like a stone.

—Erma Bombeck

If you charge big items on your credit card, carry some traveler's checks, convert as you go, and use ATMs, you will do fine. Also, remember to carry a few of your own personal checks. If you suddenly run out of money, you can use them to get cash advances, provided the credit card you have allows this. Try to have a few euros on hand when you arrive. This gets you out of the airport faster and keeps you from having to wait in line to get enough money to get into Paris. True, you may pay more for this convenience, but if you change $200 or so before you leave home, you will never miss the few cents extra it may cost. If you cannot get euros locally, you can order them by telephone or online, and they will arrive by Federal Express within two business days. Please contact Travelex/Thomas Cook, 630 Fifth Avenue, New York, NY 10101; Tel: 800-287-7362; Internet: www.travelex.com; Open: Mon–Fri 8:30 A.M.–7 P.M., EST.

The Euro

The euro became the official currency of the fifteen countries of the European Union, of which France is a member, on January 1, 2000, and it is now the sole legal tender for these countries. The euro consists of one hundred cents and comes in the following denominations: coins—one cent, two cents, five cents, ten cents, twenty cents, fifty cents, one euro, and two euros; and notes—5, 10, 20, 50, 100, 200, and 500 euros. At press time $1.09 bought one euro. The official Website is: www.euro.gouv.fr.

Automatic Teller Machines

Automatic teller machines (ATMs) are all over Paris. You can use your bank ATM card, American Express, or a Visa or MasterCard. There will be fees involved, but you will be getting a wholesale conversion rate that is better than you would get at a bank or currency exchange office. Naturally, you are limited to the amount you can withdraw by the type of account you have and your cash advance balance and limit. Please—and I cannot stress this enough—do not assume your ATM card or credit card PIN (personal identification number) will automatically work in Paris. They might, but you may have to obtain a special PIN or enroll in a special program. Contact the card issuer for the steps you need to take, and allow plenty of time. Setting up an account can take several weeks but costs the cardholder nothing. For the Paris Cirrus locations and the details that you will need to use your card there, call 800-4-CIRRUS (424-7787); Internet: www.mastercard.com. For foreign Plus locations and information, call 800-THE-PLUS (843-7587); Internet: www.visa.com. To enroll in the

American Express foreign ATM program, call 800-CASH-NOW (227-4669); Internet: www.americanexpress.com. Check the following Websites for worldwide ATM locations: Visa, www.visa.com/pd/atm, and MasterCard, www.mastercard.com/atm.

Credit Cards

For the most part, I recommend using a credit card whenever possible. The benefits are many. It is the safest way to purchase things because it eliminates the need for carrying large sums of cash, which you must obtain by standing in line at a bank or at another money-changing facility. The credit-card company gives the rate of exchange on the day the receipt from the expenditure is submitted, and this can work to your advantage if the dollar is rising. It also provides you with a written record of your purchases, and best of all, you often get delayed billing of up to four to six weeks after you have returned home. Emergency personal check cashing and access to ATM machines are benefits of many cards, as is free travel insurance. Check with your issuing bank to determine the benefits you have . . . you may be pleasantly surprised. Be careful, however, because many credit card companies have slapped on a foreign-use surcharge of 1 to 5 percent per transaction. The cards tied to airline miles are some of the worst offenders, making the accumulation of frequent flyer miles not very attractive when you consider you are paying more to get it, and when you want to cash in those miles, not being able to do it because of a myriad of exceptions and exclusions. Again, check with the issuing bank of the credit cards you plan to use on your trip, and allow enough time to make necessary changes to another card.

Take a copy of all of your credit card numbers with you, and treat it with the same importance you do your passport. Lock it up in the hotel safe—don't keep it in your wallet or purse. Save your receipts to check against the statement when it arrives. Errors are frequent. American Express card members have a host of back-up services, including their American Express Global Assist program, which can be reached twenty-four hours a day, seven days a week, at 800-333-2639, or collect from abroad at 715-343-7977. This is a service for any American Express cardholder who needs emergency medical, legal, or financial assistance while traveling. Operators at this number will accept collect calls and give information on currency rates, weather, visa and passport requirements, customs, and embassy and consular telephone numbers and addresses. They also will help with urgent message relays, lost luggage location, prescription assistance, emergency hotel check-in if you have lost your credit card, and translations. It is worth having an American Express card just for this service.

Finally, remember, in Europe a MasterCard is Eurocard, and Visa is Carte Bleu. Every listing in *Great Sleeps Paris* tells you whether or not plastic money is accepted and what kind. Thankfully, most hotels accept at least one credit card.

If, heaven forbid, your cards are lost or stolen, call one of these twenty-four–hour hotlines in Paris, or call collect in the United States to report the loss as soon as possible.

In Paris:

American Express	01-47-77-72-00, 01-47-14-50-00
Diners Club	08-00-22-20-73
MasterCard (Eurocard)	01-45-67-84-84
Visa (Carte Bleu)	08-36-69-08-80

From Paris, you can call the following U.S. numbers or visit the Websites to report a theft or loss of your cards:

American Express	Toll-free 800-233-5432; collect 336-393-1111; www.americanexpress.com
Diners Club	Toll-free 800-234-6377; collect 702-797-5532; www.dinersclubnorthamerica.com
MasterCard	Toll-free 800-307-7309; collect 636-722-7111; www.mastercard.com
Visa	Toll-free 800-336-8472; collect 410-581-9994, or toll-free within France 0800-901-179; www.visa.com

Cash Advances

If you are stuck for cash, don't panic. You can use your American Express, Diners Club, MasterCard, or Visa to get cash, either by writing a personal check and presenting your card, or going to a bank that gives cash advances for whatever card you are carrying (see also "Wiring Money to Paris," page 37).

American Express: Cardholders can get fast money by writing personal checks. For more information, contact American Express Global Assist at 800-333-2639 in the U.S.

Diners Club: For any Diners Club cardholder, a cash advance of $500 a day, or $1,000 a week, is easy. Just present the card and a picture ID at any Eurochange bank.

MasterCard or *Visa:* Available through banks displaying these card signs.

Currency Exchange and Traveler's Checks

Every time you exchange currency, someone is making a profit, and I assure you, it is not you. The worst exchange rates are at the airport and rail stations. The second-worst rates are at hotels, restaurants, shops, and most change offices that litter the tourist trails. These places should be avoided at all cost when it comes to money changing. Your best currency exchange rate will usually be at a bank. Banking hours are Monday through Friday, 9:30 A.M. to 5 P.M. All banks close at noon the day before a public holiday, and all remain closed on public holidays and the day after Christmas, Easter, and Pentecost.

The use of traveler's checks has been almost totally replaced by ATMs, making currency exchange much less important than it once was. However, for some, traveler's checks may be preferable because if they are lost or stolen, there is recourse and they will be replaced, especially if you have American Express Traveler's Checks (Tel: 08-00-90-86-00). Estimate your needs carefully when changing money. If you overbuy, you will lose twice, buying and then selling.

You will not always get a better rate for traveler's checks than for cash, but the real cost lies in what you spent to get the traveler's checks in the first place and the commission cost to convert them. If your bank, credit union, or automobile club offers American Express traveler's checks for no commission, by all means try to get them in euros. This eliminates your exchange problems, including reading one word further in this section about currency exchange. If you are unable to get your traveler's checks in euros, you can cash American Express traveler's checks commission-free at the American Express office in Paris. The drawbacks here are that the exchange rates are not always the best, and the lines can be slow and oh, so long. The office is at 11, rue Scribe, 75009; Métro: Opéra (exit rue Scribe). Exchange office: Tel: 01-47-77-79-50; Open: Mon–Fri 9 A.M.–6 P.M. Sat until 5 P.M. For other services at American Express: Tel: 01-47-77-51-20; Open: Mon–Fri 9 A.M.–4 P.M.

Another bank with a multitude of services is Citibank, which has regular banking services plus currency exchange, traveler's checks, and cash advance with Visa cards. They accept Cirrus and most other ATM cards, and have English-speaking representatives. They're at 125, avenue Champs-Élysées, 75008; Métro: Charles-de-Gaulle-Étoile; Tel: 01-53-23-33-60; Open: Mon–Sat 10 A.M.–6 P.M., change office closes at 5 P.M.

You can also change money at Comptoir de Change Opera at 9, rue Scribe, 75009; Métro: Opéra; Tel: 01-47-42-20-96; Open: Mon–Fri 9 A.M.–5:15 P.M., Sat 9:45 A.M.–4:15 P.M. Another popular *bureau de change* with the Parisian locals is MULTIChange. There are several locations, but the most central, and the one that gives the same rate for dollars and traveler's checks, is at 7, rue de Castiglione, 75001; Métro: Tuileries; Tel: 01-40-15-61-16; Internet: www.multi-change.com; Open: Mon–Sat 9:30 A.M.–6:30 P.M. Call this branch for the location nearest you.

Wiring Money to Paris

When your money is history in Paris before you are, and you have exhausted (or preferred not to use) any of the above discussed ways to increase your cash flow, there is one recourse left: Call home for money. The fastest way to refill your wallet is to have the money wired from someone in the States using a moneygram. The transfer is accomplished in minutes and the sender pays the fees, which are based on the amount sent. Here is what to do:

Contact the sender in the United States, who in turn will send the money to you in either of two ways: by going to a Western Union office located in his or her city or via a credit card given over the telephone. If the money is sent by credit card, there is a $500 limit. To send the money in person, the sender must call 800-926-9400 (twenty-four hours a day, 365 days a year). This is an information line that will provide the sender with the location of the agents nearest his or her home and any other particulars for sending the money. To send money by credit card, call 800-325-6000, Monday to Friday 6 A.M. to 4:30 P.M., MST. The Website is www.westernunion.com. No matter which way the money is sent, the cash-strapped person in Paris will be notified of the transaction and given a ten-digit confirmation number and an address to go to in Paris to pick up the money (using a photo ID). Money transfers take less than thirty minutes. CCF is the agent that handles Western Union transactions in Paris. The main office is at 4, rue du Cloître–Notre-Dame, 75005; Métro: Cité; Tel: 01-40-51-28-46; Open: daily 9 A.M.–5 P.M. As you face Notre Dame Cathedral, rue du Cloître–Notre-Dame is the first street on the left.

Post offices now provide Western Union money transfer services (08-25-00-98-98).

Tipping

How much is too much, and what is enough? Here are a few guidelines for appropriate tipping in Paris.

By law in France, a service charge of 15 percent is added to all hotel and restaurant bills. This service charge *is* the tip, so that when you receive your final bill at a restaurant, you don't need to tip anything more. While this eliminates the need for tips in general, there are certain times when an additional tip is appropriate.

Bars, cafés, restaurants	Leave a few extra euro cents in a bar or café, and up to 10 percent if the waiter in a restaurant has gone to extra lengths for you.
Hair salons	10 to 15 percent to anyone who has worked on you, including the shampoo girl
Hotels	Bellboys 1€ per bag; housekeepers about 3€ for a three-day stay; room service 1€
Taxis	10 to 15 percent on the metered fare, not for the supplements added for extra baggage

The bottom line on tipping in Paris is the same as anywhere else in the world: It is a matter of personal choice. If you liked the service, reward it; if not, do not feel guilty about not leaving an additional cent.

NOTE: Beware of the tipping scam. There is an increasingly common practice in restaurants of putting the entire amount of the bill, to which a 15 percent service has already been added, in the top box of the charge slip, leaving the boxes marked "tip" and "total" empty. Do not be intimidated.

Draw a line from the top figure to the total at the bottom and then write in the total figure yourself. If you are choosing to tip on top of this total (and remember you do not have to), leave it in cash. Often tips left on credit cards are not properly distributed.

Insurance

No one plans on a medical crisis during a trip, wants to cut the trip short, or abandon it altogether due to some emergency or sudden change of plans. Travel insurance is seldom a great bargain, but it does buy you protection and, just as importantly, peace of mind should unfortunate circumstances occur.

Hotel cancellations less than forty-eight hours prior to arrival can result in charges unless the room can be used by another customer. This is small potatoes and frankly, not worth covering with an insurance policy. However, if you have prepaid a large portion of your trip, especially if you have rented a flat and paid a big chunk in advance, you would be crazy not to buy cancellation insurance. French serviced apartments, individual apartment owners, and the agencies representing them are often merciless when it comes to refunds. Their policy is very simple: no refunds. Period.

Before your departure, check with your health-care plan to see what, if any, medical coverage you will have when you travel, and seriously consider taking out a supplemental policy to fill in the gaps. The amount you spend in supplemental insurance will be nothing compared to a foreign medical emergency for which you have to pick up the tab. If you do need medical care, many medical facilities will require that you pay for your treatment in full at the time of service. Don't assume that they will file claims for you or participate in any medical plan you may belong to. It will generally be up to you to get your claim processed and be reimbursed.

Read through your renter's or homeowner's policy to check whether it covers you in any way when you are traveling, and if it is lacking, again consider adding a floater policy for the duration of your trip, especially if you are traveling with a laptop or other expensive equipment.

Finally, if you are an American Express Card member, call 800-297-2900 to find out about their coverage for members traveling 150 miles from home within a thirty-one day period. American Express Global Assist is another service for American Express cardholders who need emergency medical, legal, or financial assistance while traveling (see "Credit Cards," page 35). Below is a list of travel insurers with policies to suit many needs:

Access America, Inc.: 800-284-8300, www.accessamerica.com

Insure.com (comparison quotes from multiple companies): www.insure.com (click on Travel)

Medex Insurance Services: 800-732-5309, www.medexassist.com

Medjet Assistance (worldwide medical transports): 800-963-3538, www.medjetassistance.com

Safeware (will insure laptops for an annual premium): www.safeware.com

Wallach & Co.: 800-237-6615, www.wallach.com

Discounts

Hotels

When booking a hotel room, it's always worth asking if any discounts are being offered, even in the middle of high season—you might get lucky. It makes good sense to check hotel Websites or to call toll-free numbers to see about special package deals or lower rates. Savvy travelers check with airlines or their travel agents for package deals that include airfare coupled with a hotel at a fraction of the cost if paid for separately. Often included are airport transfers and/or car rentals. In July and August, many hotels offer a published 10 percent discount, and for others, you have to ask. Some hotels will give an automatic 5 to 10 percent discount to *Great Sleeps Paris* readers, and I have noted these in the listings.

The Internet is full of sites offering discount airfares. It is beyond the scope of *Great Sleeps Paris* to go into detail about them, other than to advise readers to definitely check into them. The savings are often significant enough to enable some to upgrade on a hotel or stay longer.

Museums

For avid museum-goers in Paris, there are now one-, three-, and five-day French passes that provide direct access to more than sixty museums and monuments, including the Louvre, Musée d'Orsay, Musée Picasso, and Versailles. Called the *Paris Carte Musées—Monuments,* or Paris Museum Pass, it covers your admission for each museum (but you must pay extra to see the special exhibitions or take guided tours); it also allows you to go to the head of any line, or through a special entrance, without waiting. You can also revisit your favorites as many times as you want at no extra charge.

In most museums, entry is free for anyone under eighteen, and reduced prices are available for those between eighteen and twenty-five. Museums are generally closed on Monday or Tuesday. Depending on the time of year and the museum, entrance on the first Sunday of the month is free to anyone, but the crowds can be frightening. If you have the museum pass, you will at least avoid standing in lines to get in, and that is worth the price of the pass, especially when it is freezing cold, pouring rain, or scorching hot. The passes are on sale in the participating museums, main métro and RER stations, branches of FNAC, and tourism offices in Paris, including the one at 127, Champs-Élysées. In Paris, the pass costs 15€ for one day, 30€ for three days, and 45€ for five days. For further information, contact interMusées at 4, rue Brantôme, 75003; Tel: 01-44-61-96-60; Internet: www.intermusees.com. The passes can also be purchased before leaving the United States through Challenges International, Inc., 10 East 21st Street, Suite 600, New York, NY 10010; Tel:

212-529-9069; Fax: 212-529-4838; Internet: www.ticketsto.com; Open: Mon–Fri 8:30 A.M.–5:30 P.M.

If you do not have a museum pass, here are some tips to avoid standing forever on line at the Pyramide entrance to the Louvre. If traveling on the métro, get off at the Palais Royal–Musée du Louvre stop and use the entrance directly from the métro platform. Another way is to use the Porte des Lions entrance to the Denton wing. To do this, stand with your back toward the Tuileries Garden. On each side of the Louvre are stairs (next to angels) that lead to the underground entrance. Another less populous entry is from the Galeries du Carrousel, the shopping mall under the museum.

If your travels will be taking you beyond Paris, consider purchasing the National Museum Pass, which is valid for one year and allows unlimited free entrance (without having to stand on line) to more than one hundred national museums and monuments in France, sixteen of which are in and around Paris. The pass is on sale at participating museums and monuments, and costs around 50€. For further information, see www.monum.fr.

Seniors

If you have reached your sixtieth birthday, in France you are a member of the *troisième age* (third age) and are eligible for a Carte Vermeil (CV). This card entitles you to a number of significant discounts, including reductions on air and rail travel as well as on the bus and métro in Paris. If you are going to be in Paris (or France) for a short time, it may not be worthwhile to get the Carte Vermeil. However, you would be surprised at the senior discounts available, especially for concerts, theater performances, and cinemas. Always ask. The answer will often be yes.

The French domestic airline, Air Inter, honors "third agers" by giving 25 to 50 percent reductions on regular nonexcursion ticket prices. On French trains, you can save between 25 and 50 percent of the cost of a first- or second-class compartment and 10 percent of an excursion ticket. These air and rail reductions are not available during all times of the year, and restrictions do apply. However, if you can cash in on the savings, they can be significant. Other benefits include reduced entrance rates for theaters, museums, and cinemas.

The Carte Vermeil is valid for one year from June 1 to May 31 of the following year. The card cannot be purchased in the United States, but it is available at any major railway station in France. Do not expect clerks to speak English, but you won't need much French to communicate your wishes, as most of them are used to dealing with foreigners who are privy to this super deal. When you go to purchase your card, you will have to show your passport as proof of age. For more information, contact Rail Europe; Tel: 800-438-7245; Internet: www.raileurope.com; or the French Government Tourist Office, 444 Madison Ave., New York, NY 10020; Tel: 212-838-7806. However, be prepared for frustrating waits that could speed your aging process.

Members of the AARP (American Association of Retired Persons) are entitled to discounts on air tickets, rooms in selected major chain hotels, and some train and car rentals. Always inquire when booking a reservation. Elderhostel, another organization for seniors, operates programs throughout Europe, and many are in France. Contact them at 75 Federal Street, Boston, MA 02110-1941; Tel: 877-426-8056; Internet: www.elderhostel.org.

Students and Teachers

The best discounts for students and teachers are available with the International Student Identity Card (ISIC) and the International Teacher Identity Card (ITIC). Both are available in the United States through STA (Tel: 800-226-8624; Internet: www.statravel.com), require a one-inch–size passport photo, and cost around $25. The card can also be issued in Paris through student travel agencies and at the CROUS office at 39, avenue Georges-Bernanos, 5th; Métro: Port-Royal; Tel: 01-40-51-36-00; Open: Mon–Fri 9 A.M.–4:30 P.M. To learn about additional benefits of these superb travel discount cards, see Student Accommodations in "Other Options," page 323. Anyone age twenty-six or younger, whether a student or not, can buy the Carte 12/25, which allows a 50 percent reduction on certain SNCF train travel.

Theater and Concerts

You can buy half-price tickets for selected concerts, theaters, ballets, and other shows on the day of the performance only at the Kiosque Théâtre in the eighth arrondissement (for complete details, see the "Shopping" chapter, page 378).

Health Matters

It is not difficult to stay healthy in Paris. The main complaints seem to be hangovers and/or exhaustion from too much late-night partying, and the usual stomach upsets caused from too much rich food. The water is safe to drink, but I always advise buying bottled water if only because it tastes better. Water from decorative fountains is not safe. Of course, it is always prudent to pack an extra set of glasses, an adequate supply of whatever medications you need, and a copy of prescriptions, perhaps translated into French. If you need medical attention, contact one of the following:

The American Hospital	63, boulevard Victor Hugo, Neuilly; Métro: Porte Maillot, or bus No. 82; Tel: 01-46-41-25-25
The Franco-British Hospital (Hôpital Franco-Britannique)	3, rue Barbès, Levallois-Perret (a suburb of Paris); Métro: Anatole-France; Tel: 01-46-39-22-22

AIDS: Hotline in English Tel: 01-44-93-16-32; Open: Mon–Fri 11 A.M.–3 P.M.

SIDA Information Service Tel: 08-00-84-08-00; Open: Mon, Wed, Fri 2–7 P.M.

Burns: Hôpital de St-Antoine 184, rue du Faubourg-St-Antoine, 75012; Métro: Faidherve-Chaligny; Tel: 01-49-28-26-09; Open: 24 hours.

Poisons: Hôpital Fernand Widal
 200, rue du Faubourg-St-Denis, 75010; Métro: Gare du Nord; Tel: 01-40-05-48-48

Children: Hôpital Necker 149, rue de Sèvres, 75015; Métro: Duroc; Tel: 01-44-49-40-00

Children, Burns: Hôpital Armand-Trousseau
 26, avenue du Dr. Arnold-Netter, 75012; Metro: Bel Air; Tel: 01-44-73-62-54

Association Française d'Acuponcture
 3, rue de l'Arrivée, 75015; Métro: Montparnasse; Tel: 01-43-20-26-26; Open: Mon–Thur 8:30 A.M.–12:30 P.M., 1:30–5:30 P.M., Fri 8:30 A.M.–4:30 P.M. Lists professional acupuncturists.

Homeopathic Doctors: Academie d'Homeopathie
et des Medecines Douces 2, rue d'Isly, 75008; Metro: St-Lazare; Tel: 01-43-87-60-33; Open: Mon–Fri 10 A.M.–6 P.M. Must have an appointment. Many pharmacies also sell homeopathic medicines.

SOS Cardiac Tel: 01-47-07-50-50, Open: 24 hours.

SOS Dentist Tel: 01-43-37-51-00; Open: 8 A.M.–8 P.M.

SOS Doctor (SOS Médecins) Tel: 01-43-37-77-77, 01-47-07-77-77; Open: 24 hours.

SOS Help Tel: 01-46-21-46-46. Open: 3–11 P.M. Bilingual crisis hotline.

SOS Nurse Tel: 01-40-24-22-23, 06-08-34-08-92. Will make house calls.

Airparif	Tel: 01-44-59-47-64; Open: Mon–Fri 1 A.M.–5:30 P.M. Information about pollution levels and air quality in Paris.
Alcoholics Anonymous	Tel: 01-46-34-59-65

Pharmacies

Pharmacies are marked with a green neon cross. They are serious places where health-care advice is given out, and quality skin- and hair-care products are sold by knowledgeable personnel. The pharmacist can help with many minor medical complaints, in addition to dispensing a prescription if you need one. A system of on-duty pharmacies ensures that at least one pharmacy in each arrondissement is always open. A closed pharmacy will have a sign giving the address of the nearest open pharmacy.

Pharmacie Dhèry	84, avenue des Champs-Élysées, 75008; Métro: George V; Tel: 01-45-62-02-41; Open: 24 hours a day, 365 days a year.
American Pharmacy	Pharmacie Anglo-Américaine, 6, rue Castiglione, 75001; Metro: Tuileries; Tel: 01-42-60-72-96; Open: Mon–Sat 10 A.M.–7:30 P.M.
Pharmacie des Halles	10, boulevard de Sebastopol, 75004; Métro: Châtelet; Tel: 01-42-72-03-23; Open: Mon–Sat 9 A.M.–midnight, Sun 9 A.M.–10 P.M.
Pharma Presto-Night	Tel: 01-42-42-42-50; Open: daily 24 hours. This is a pharmacy delivery service.
To find nearest all-night pharmacy	Tel: 01-45-62-02-41

Emergency Numbers

In an emergency, dial these numbers. They are free from any phone, including pay phones, and are staffed twenty-four hours a day.

Emergency from a mobile phone	112
Police	17
Fire	18
Ambulance	15 or 01-45-67-50-50
Medical Emergency	15
Poison	01-40-05-48-48

Safety and Security

In comparison to other cities, Paris is not a dangerous place. It is still important, however, to take the same sensible precautions you would in any major metropolitan city in the world. Foreigners are easily spotted by their language, clothes, guidebooks, maps, and cameras. Pickpockets usually work in pairs or larger groups. The victim seldom knows what has happened until it's too late. A woman's handbag with a zipper or clasp is no problem for a pickpocket if it is dangling out of the owner's sight, or lying on the floor in a restaurant or shop. A man's wallet in an outside pocket makes for very easy pickings. Be vigilant at ATMs. Don't let anyone come near you or ask you a question when you are withdrawing money. Never leave anything of importance locked in a car, and that includes the trunk.

If you are robbed or attacked, report the incident immediately at the police station in the arrondissement where the incident happened. Call 01-43-12-23-47 for the closest *commissariat*. Someone speaks English Monday to Friday 9 A.M. to 5 P.M.; on the weekends there is a duty officer to help. If you are going to file a claim with your own insurance company, you will need this police report. In general, keep the following advice in mind as you tour Paris:

1. Be aware of your surroundings and do not go down dark streets at night, especially alone.

2. Wear a money belt or a neck pouch *inside* your clothing and carry only what you need with you: passport (not mandatory for Americans in Paris), some money, and so on. Carry your purse with the strap around your neck and the clasp against your body, away from the street side. Fanny packs are magnets for thieves . . . they can cut and grab one in no time. If you do wear one, don't wear it on your fanny; wear it in front of you, string the strap through your belt loops, and keep only a small amount of money in it. Do not carry any valuables in your wallet, purse, or bag. These all belong in the hotel safe. Thread a safety pin through the toggle on your backpack's zipper to pin it closed.

3. Try to blend in and keep a low profile: don't wear flashy jewelry, wild colors, or prints, or speak in a booming voice.

4. Keep a close eye on your possessions, and do not leave packages or suitcases unattended on the métro or when making a phone call or hailing a taxi. Be careful of your camera.

5. Trust your instincts: If a situation seems suspect, it probably is, so beat a hasty retreat. Beware of pickpockets, especially on the métro Line 1 between Châtelet and Charles-de-Gaulle and on Line 4 between Châtelet and Porte de Clignancourt, and in tourist areas along boulevard Haussmann, rue de Rivoli, Les Halles, the Arc de Triomphe, the Eiffel Tower, St. Michel, and Montmartre. Watch out for the bands of gypsy children who will surround you and

distract your attention by fluttering papers in your face, and then strip you of your valuables before you can think to say, "Stop thief!" Another popular ruse for men is the "coin toss." Someone drops a few coins in front of you, and you instinctively lean over to help pick them up, while another hand is reaching into your back pocket and grabbing your wallet. It's so fast, you will never know what happened, and may not even trace the loss of your wallet to this trick.

6. Thieves in métro stations lurk around the turnstiles and try to grab your bag as you go through, or they reach for it as the train door closes. Always avoid métro stations late at night, especially Stalingrad, Châtelet–Les Halles, Barbès-Rochechouart, Pigalle, and Anvers.

7. If you are alone, don't say so to a wide audience. Also, make sure someone at home knows your itinerary, and arrange times to call to check in, just to let them know all is well.

8. Before leaving home, make two photocopies of every document that is crucial to the successful completion of your trip—such as your passport, airline tickets, hotel vouchers, credit card numbers (or the number of your credit card registry), and necessary prescriptions (including the one for contact lenses). Leave one copy at home with someone you can always contact, and take the other copy with you and treat it with the same importance you do your money and passport. In the horrible event that your documents are lost or stolen, you have a record of your various numbers, and the process of replacing everything will be easier.

9. *Always* lock up important papers, airline tickets, traveler's checks, extra money, and so on in the hotel safe. Even if there is a charge for this, it is well worth it when you consider the cost, inconvenience, and hassle of a theft. *Never* leave anything of value in your hotel room, even in a locked suitcase.

The U.S. Department of State publishes a pamphlet called *A Safe Trip Abroad.* For a copy, write the Superintendent of Documents, U.S. Government Printing Office, Washington, DC 20402.

Hotel Security

Security in your hotel mostly pertains to theft. Note that hotel liability tends to be limited and often provides slim protection for the traveler. If an item is stolen from your room, you may have little recourse unless you can prove negligence. Here are some points to consider:

1. Avoid rooms on the ground floor and those near fire escapes.

2. Do not leave any valuables exposed in your room, even when you are sleeping.

3. When you leave your room, close and lock the windows and do not leave (or hide) any valuables. Lock them up in the hotel safe. There isn't a hiding place a thief doesn't know about.

4. Valuables include more than money and jewelry. Consider camcorders, cameras, computers, personal and travel documents, cell phones, and so on.

5. If you leave luggage at the hotel after you check out, be sure the storage area is secure, and do not leave any bag containing valuables.

6. If you are a victim of a theft, insist on filing a complete report with the local police immediately. The more documentation you have, the better your chances are for compensation from your own insurance company.

Most important: If you don't absolutely need it in Paris, don't take it with you.

Lost and Found

If you have lost something in a public space or on public transport, contact the Bureau des Objets Trouvés. You must go in person with an ID to fill out a form detailing the date, time, and place where you lost the item. Very little English is spoken. Claims can take weeks. If you are leaving Paris before the claim can be processed and your lost item is (hopefully) found, you must appoint a proxy to retrieve your item. If you lost an object in a street opening, a sewer worker will try to rescue that key or diamond earring that fell through the sewer grate. You will need to know the street and cross street where you lost your valuables.

Bureau des Objets Trouvés (Lost and Found)
36, rue des Morillons, 75015
Métro: Convention
Telephone: 08-21-00-25-25
Open: Mon, Wed, Fri 8:30 A.M.–7 P.M., Tues, Thur (not in July or August) 8:30 A.M.–8 P.M.

Staying in Touch

The need to stay in touch is right up there with a safe flight, a good meal, and a comfortable bed.
—Ann Dimon, travel writer for the
Toronto Sun

Email and the Internet

The worldwide love affair with the Internet and email is rapidly becoming a part of everyday life in France. More and more hotels are installing Internet terminals in the lobby and providing modems in the rooms. Almost every telephone has a second plug. However, logging on from your hotel room can be far from hassle-free and very expensive by U.S. standards. To avoid paying an arm and a leg to surf the Internet or to send email, go to a cyber café. Here are a few good ones:

easyEverything

31–37 boulevard de Sébastopol, 75001 (see map page 62)
Métro: Châtelet
You won't have to wait to check your emails or surf the net in this hyper-cyber café, which has 375 terminals operating twenty-four hours a day, seven days a week. Prices are reasonable, especially in the middle of the night.
Telephone: 01-40-41-09-10
Open: 24 hours, 365 days a year

Web Bar

32, rue de Picardie, 75003 (see map page 84)
Métro: Filles du Calvaire
This is one of the best all-around cyber cafés in Paris. Not only is it a place to handle your email and Internet business, but it's a place to eat, listen to music, partake in a poetry reading, see a short film, and generally hang out.
Telephone: 01-42-72-66-55
Internet: www.webbar.fr
Open: Mon–Fri 8:30 A.M.–2 A.M, Sat & Sun 11 A.M–2 A.M.

Zeidnet

18, rue de la Bucherie, 75005 (see map page 108)
Métro: Maubert-Mutualité, St-Michel
Zeidnet offers every Web service currently out there. Their computers have either English or French keyboards, which is a real bonus. After struggling with a French keyboard elsewhere, you will happily come here, which is a two-minute walk from Notre Dame. If you buy a block of minutes, whatever you have left does not expire. You can also fax, photocopy, and order hot and cold drinks. The patient and helpful staff speaks English, but unfortunately, they do not accept credit cards.
Telephone & Fax: 01-44-07-20-15
Internet: www.zeidnet.com
Open: Mon–Sat 10 A.M.–11 P.M., Sun noon–8 P.M.

If you are going to be in Paris for more than a few days and know you will be doing a lot of communicating via the Internet, buy a subscription card that is good for either a couple of hours or up to 250. For a worldwide list of cyber cafés, consult www.cybercafes.com.

If you do wish to bring a laptop, before you leave home, check with your local Internet provider for a French local-access telephone number to use when emailing and going online. You will then be charged in local

French telephone units and avoid the cost of dialing a U.S. provider number when you are sending email or going online. You can set up a free email account through Yahoo! Mail (www.mail.yahoo.com) or Hotmail (www.hotmail.com). In Paris you will need your user name or ID number and your account password. To avoid all of this extra work, let a Parisian computer expert set up your foreign account (see "Services," page 33).

Post

How quaint! I cannot imagine too many travelers in Paris are spending much of their time writing letters. For postcards, you can buy stamps at any tobacconist shop. This eliminates standing in line at the post office, and the price is exactly the same.

Every *quartier* has a post office; they are open Monday to Friday 8 A.M. to 7 P.M., Saturday until noon. I have never found one yet that did not have a long line. The main post office (52, rue du Louvre: Métro: Louvre-Rivoli; Tel: 01-40-28-76-00) is open twenty-four hours daily for *Poste Restante,* telephones, telegrams, stamps, and faxes, and for sending boxes not exceeding two kilos. Larger boxes have to be sent during regular post office hours. All post offices sell boxes in various sizes; the price includes the shipping, and there is no weight limit.

If you do not have an address in Paris, you can use *Poste Restante.* Mail addressed to you must have your name in block capitals, followed by the words *Poste Restante,* then the main Paris post office address: 52, rue du Louvre, 75001, Paris. To get your mail, you must show your passport and pay a small fee for each letter you receive. If you have an American Express account, you can also receive mail c/o American Express, 11, rue Scribe, 75009; Métro: Opéra; Tel: 01-47-14-50-00 (main office); Open: Mon–Fri 9 A.M.–6 P.M., Sat 9 A.M.–5 P.M.

If speed is a factor in sending parcels, then Federal Express is probably the answer. Warning: It is not cheap! For further information on shipping and Fedex, see "Getting It All Home," page 335.

Telephone

French telephone numbers have ten digits. Paris numbers begin with 01, and the rest of France is divided into four regional zones with prefixes 02, 03, 04, and 05. Free telephone numbers begin with 08; cell phone numbers begin with 06. If you are calling France from abroad, leave off the 0 at the beginning of the ten-digit number; dial 0+country code+area or city code+number. For instance, if you are in the United States, and the Paris number is 01-42-22-33-44, dial 011-33-1-42-22-33-44.

Making a call from a public telephone is not as simple as dropping a coin into the pay telephone, dialing 0, and requesting connection. Most public phones in Paris now require a prepaid phone card *(télecarte),* which you buy in increments or units *(unités).* To make a call, pick up the phone, insert the card into a slot on the phone, wait for the dial tone, and then start dialing the number. The amount of your call is automatically deducted from the remaining value. These cards offer several advantages: you do not need a pocketful of change; calling from a public phone eliminates the surcharges in hotels; and the card has no expiration date, so you can use what is left on your card on your next trip. Where to buy the *télecarte?* Post offices, *tabacs,* airports, and train and métro stations all sell them. Telephone books are in all post offices and hotels. Check the French Telecom Website (www.wanadoo.fr) to find any listed residential or business phone number; click on *annuaires* in either English or French.

Every time you pick up a phone in Paris, it will cost you money, even if you are calling next door. If you call between a cell phone and a land line, the rates will be staggering. Always try to dial cell to cell or land line to land line to avoid this excessive rate. If you are calling abroad, the rates can be downright frightening. Avoid going through your hotel switchboard when calling home. Even if you reverse the charges or use a telephone service such as AT&T, you will likely be hit with a surcharge, sometimes up to 100 percent of the cost of the call. Check with the hotel operator about your hotel's policy, as they all differ. To avoid the surcharge, use an international calling card that you purchase in Paris from the same places that sell the domestic *télecartes* discussed above. It is important to remember that the domestic card won't work on international calls, and vice-versa. However, you *can* buy a *télecart* that is good for both domestic and international calls (France et International-Delta Multimedia). Or, before leaving home, purchase a phone card from a warehouse club (for example, Costco or Sam's Club). Some cost about $20 for four hours of talk time. These cards are simple, painless, and definitely the least expensive way to stay in touch.

For further savings, call when the rates are low. Within France and Europe, the cheaper hours are Monday to Friday 7 P.M. to 8 A.M., Saturday noon to 8 A.M. Monday. The cheaper rates to the United States and Canada are Monday to Friday 7 P.M. to 1 P.M., Saturday to Sunday all day. Remember, when calling the United States, Paris is six hours ahead of Eastern Standard Time and nine hours ahead of Pacific Standard Time.

Here are some helpful numbers for domestic or international calls:

To call Paris from the United States	011+33+number
To call the United States from Paris	00+1+area code+number
To reach an English-speaking operator	
AT&T	0800-99-00-11
MCI	0800-99-00-19
Sprint	0800-99-00-87
Directory information	12
Operator	10
International information	32-12+country code (1 for United States)
Time	3699

Traffic	08-26-02-20-22
Weather	
Paris	08-92-68-02-75
For France and abroad	08-99-70-12-34

Fax

To send a fax to Paris from the United States, dial 011+33+the number. Remember to eliminate the 0 at the beginning of the ten-digit number; for instance, if the fax number is 01-47-12-34-56, dial 011-33-1-47-12-34-56. To fax the U.S. from Paris, dial 00+1+area code+number.

Transportation

Public transportation in and around Paris is some of the best in Europe. Because it is so efficient, why would any foreign traveler willingly subject him- or herself to driving in this city? Isn't this supposed to be a vacation? Parking is impossible, traffic is from hell, gasoline is expensive, and the one-way streets will drive you crazy. Did you know that of Paris's 988 miles of streets, 435 miles are one way?! Behind the wheel, Parisian drivers are kamikaze pilots taking no prisoners. They think nothing of driving and parking on the sidewalk, blocking traffic on narrow streets, cutting in and out with inches to spare, and flashing their lights to indicate displeasure (honking the horn is forbidden until the moment of impact). Then there is the *priorité à droite* to get used to: this gives the right of way to the car approaching from the right, regardless of the size of the street, the traffic on it, or the safety hazard of the moment. Add to this frightening horror show the insane motorcyclists who drive on the sidewalk when the traffic is too thick for them to squeeze through it. The best reason to drive a car in Paris is to get out of town and head for the provinces.

Save yourself a great deal of aggravation by using the métro, the buses, the RER suburban railway, and your own feet to get around the city. Paris is a city that invites walking, and exploring the narrow streets or strolling along the grand boulevards is the best way to discover it. However, even as a pedestrian, you must keep up your guard. In Paris, anyone behind the wheel of a car, or traveling by any kind of wheeled conveyance—inline skates, bicycle, scooter, or motorcycle—considers the pedestrian a monumental nuisance in the effort to get from A to B in the least amount of time possible. Even when the pedestrian has a green light, don't assume that drivers will concede the right of way. By law, drivers are only required to come to a full stop at a red light. When there is a crosswalk, whether or not it has a flashing amber light or a sign saying *priorité aux pietons* (priority to pedestrians), drivers will ignore this and step on the gas.

Getting to and from the Airports

Roissy–Charles-de-Gaulle Airport

For general information in English, twenty-four hours daily, call 01-48-62-12-12.

A taxi is the easiest and most comfortable way to get from Roissy to Paris, but it is expensive. The ride into central Paris takes about fifty minutes on a good day; during rush hour, add at least thirty minutes. Taxis will take no more than three people and add at least a 1€ surcharge for every piece of luggage. Fares range between 35€ and 50€ during the day and are higher from 8 P.M. to 7 A.M. A 15 percent tip is expected.

A more economical way is to take the direct RER B train to Paris. There is direct access from Terminal 2. A free shuttle bus (look for the word *navette*) runs from Terminal 1 and takes passengers to Terminal 2 and the Roissy train station, where you board the Roissy Rail into the city, with stops at Gare du Nord, Châtelet–Les Halles, St-Michel, Luxembourg, Port Royal, and Denfert-Rochereau. The train leaves every twenty-five minutes between 5 A.M. and 11 P.M. and costs around 9€. The train trip takes around forty-five minutes, and the shuttle to the airport station about fifteen.

Air France buses (you do not have to be a passenger on one of their flights to use them) leave from both terminals every twelve minutes from 5:45 A.M. to 11:30 P.M.; they take about forty to fifty minutes to reach Paris and cost around 10€. The buses stop at place de la Porte Maillot/Palais des Congrès, Arc de Triomphe/Charles-de-Gaulle-Étoile at avenue Carnot, Gare Montparnasse at 113, boulevard Vaugirard, and Gare de Lyon. For information, call 01-48-64-45-01.

The RATP-operated Roissybus runs every fifteen to twenty minutes from 5:45 A.M. to 11 P.M. between the airport and rue Scribe, near place de l'Opéra, and beside the American Express office; it takes about an hour and costs around 9€, and that includes all of your luggage. At Roissy–Charles-de-Gaulle airport, the bus departs for Paris from air terminals 2B and 2D, gate 11, and air terminals 2A and 2C, gate 10. Tickets are sold on the bus. Call the main RATP number (08-92-68-41-14) for information in English; or the Roissybus direct line (01-49-25-61-87, Mon–Fri 8:30 A.M.–5:30 P.M., except bank holidays).

There are also various shuttle services between both Roissy–Charles-de-Gaulle and Orly Airports. These take passengers door-to-door from the airport to their hotel. Advance reservations are necessary. Airport Connection (01-44-18-36-02) operates mini-bus services from the main airports to and from your hotel. The price is 24€ per person, with a discount for two or more persons. Another such company is Airport Shuttle (08-21-80-08-01), which costs 23€ for one person, with better rates for two or more.

Orly Airport
For information in English, daily 6 A.M. to 11:30 P.M., call 01-49-75-15-15.

A taxi to and from Orly to Paris takes twenty to forty minutes and costs between 18 and 28€, plus 1€ for each piece of luggage.

The high-speed Orlyval shuttle train runs daily every seven minutes from 6 A.M. to 10 P.M. to RER B station Antony. It costs 9€ and takes thirty minutes; to La Défense, 11€, fifty minutes; and to Châtelet–Les

Halles, 9€, thirty-five minutes. In Paris: take the RER Line B toward St-Rémy-les-Chevreuse as far as Antony and change to the Val line to Orly Ouest or Orly Sud. For more information, call RATP information (08-92-68-41-14).

There is the Orlybus that links Orly airport to the RER Line B at place Denfert-Rochereau. Buses de part from Orly-Sud (gate H, platform 4) every fifteen to twenty minutes from 6 A.M. to 11:30 P.M.; it costs 6€ and takes thirty minutes. In Paris, the bus leaves from Denfert-Rochereau RER or métro station. Tickets can be purchased on the Orlybus. For more information, call customer service (01-40-02-32-94, Mon–Fri 8:30 A.M.–5:30 P.M.).

Air France buses leave both terminals every twelve minutes between 6 A.M. and 11 P.M. to the Air France air terminal at Les Invalides or Montparnasse. The fare is around 8€ and the trip takes between thirty and forty-five minutes, depending on traffic.

Métro and Regional Express Railway (RER)

With 370 stations, the Paris métro system is one of the most efficient in the world. The system has fourteen lines, each identifiable by its number and destination. Paris and the suburbs are divided into five zones, but most visitors only go to zones 1 and 2, which cover the city center and all métro lines. Métro and RER trains run from 5:30 A.M. until 12.30 A.M.

The RER (Regional Express Railway) has five lines in Paris—A, B, C, D, and E—and is joined to the city métro network and some of the SNCF trains (France's national train system). Using a combination of the métro and the RER, you can get within walking distance of almost everything you would want to see and do in the city.

If you will be in Paris only a short time and plan on seeing a lot, the *Paris Visite* ticket is worth considering. This go-as-you-please ticket is good for one, two, three, or five days, and it is valid for the bus, metro, RER, and the SNCF trains to Disneyland Paris, Versailles, Fontainebleau, and Roissy–Charles-de-Gaulle and Orly airports. Another benefit is that it offers reductions on a few museums and tourist sites in Paris. It is available at main métro stations, any RER or SNCF station, and from the Paris Tourist Information Office. Rates depend on how many days you need and zones you travel to. Prices range from 5€ to 46€. Children under twelve pay half price.

Another short-range option is a one-day *Mobilis* pass, which ranges from 5€ to 17.95€, depending on how many zones you will be traveling in. It does not include the airports or reduced rates for tourist sites, nor does it cover trips to Versailles or Disneyland.

You can buy individual tickets (1.30€), but a *carnet* of ten (9.60€) is much more practical and cheaper. Either of these can be purchased at métro stations, tourist offices, or *tabacs*. If you are staying in Paris more than a few days, buy the weekly *Carte Hebdomadaire* (13.75€) valid

Monday through Sunday, or the monthly *Carte d' Orange Coupon Mensuel* (46.50€), valid from the first day of the month. Both allow unlimited travel in zones 1 and 2 on the métro and buses. Always hold on to your ticket. If you are caught without it, you will be fined. To buy either type of métro pass, you must have a passport-size photo (there are photo booths in some larger métro stations). To make your purchase, go to the cashier window in almost any major métro station, or head to the RATP offices: place de la Madeleine, 75008; Métro: Madeleine; Open: May–Sept only, Mon–Fri 8:30 A.M.–noon, 1–4:30 P.M., Sat 8:30 A.M.–noon, 2–4:30 P.M. The other RATP office is at 53 bis, quai des Grands Augustins, 75006; Métro: St-Michel; Open: year-round Mon–Sat, same hours. For general information in English, call 08-92-68-41-14. The unofficial Website for the Paris métro is perso.wanadoo.fr/ratpinfo/dossiers.htm, but it's in French only. For the most detailed Paris maps showing all streets with metro stops, consult the *Plan de Paris par Arrondissement* (see page 21).

Important warning: Buy your métro or bus tickets and passes from official cashiers inside métro stations or from one of the RATP offices listed above. Do not, under any circumstances whatsoever, buy from independent shysters who work the train stations claiming to be authorized RATP employees, which they are not. They are cheats out to steal your money through their scam.

Bus

Because the métro is so fast and efficient, visitors often overlook the buses in Paris. The routes of each bus line are generally posted at each stop. They are also listed in the back of the *Plan de Paris par Arrondissement* (see page 21), or you can pick up a free bus map, *Autobus Paris-Plan de Reseau,* at tourist offices in major métro stations, or probably at your hotel. If you have a métro ticket, or a weekly or monthly métro pass, these will all work on the bus; just show your pass to the driver.

Warning: Do not punch your weekly ticket when you board the bus; just show it. Punching it will render it unusable. You can punch your *individual* ticket, which, if you don't already have one, you can purchase from the bus driver. Always hold on to your ticket until you get off the bus. If caught without it, you will be fined.

All buses run Monday to Saturday from 6:30 A.M. to 8:30 P.M. Some continue until 12:30 A.M., and some run on Sunday. The Noctambus runs all night, but the routes are fewer. *Paris Bus, Métro, RER Routes,* a pamphlet printed by the RATP, lists several scenic bus routes and gives directions to major museums and monuments. For RATP information in English, call 08-92-68-41-14, or visit the Website at www.ratp.fr.

The Paris Montmartrobus is an inexpensive, fun way to see Montmartre with the least amount of walking involved. The electric bus starts at the Jules Joffrin métro stop, goes up to Sacré Coeur, and then down to place Pigalle. En route, you will pass the pretty streets and corners of

Montmartre that make it so famous. If you have a Carte d'Orange, you can get on and off the bus as many times as you wish without paying extra fare. Bring your camera.

Taxi

The challenge of finding a taxi in Paris often rivals that of New York City on a busy Friday afternoon. Add rain to that and you are better off riding public transportation or walking. Hailing a cab on a corner is difficult. It is smarter to go to a taxi stand; they are located on most major thoroughfares and at all the railroad stations. Taxis are required by law to stop for you if the large white light on top is on unless it is the driver's last half hour on duty, the passenger is less than fifty meters from a taxi stand, there are three or more in your group, or you are drunk. A glowing orange light means the taxi is not available. Taxi drivers will take you anywhere you want to go in Paris or to either airport, follow a route of your choosing, accept all handicapped passengers, and give you a receipt. They are not required to take animals (even though they may have their own dog riding with them in the front seat), take more than three persons, or accept an unreasonable amount of luggage. They might do any of these things, but the driver will probably add a supplemental charge. There is a minimum fee of 1€ for every piece of luggage, more if it is heavy or unwieldy.

Normal taxi fares are based on area and time of day. Beneath the taxi light are three little lights—A, B, and C. One of these will light up according to what tariff applies. The tariff is also shown on the meter display inside the taxi. A 15 percent tip is customary. If you want an early-morning taxi to take you to the airport, book it the night before. If you need a taxi at a specific time and don't want to chance not finding one, call ahead. If you do call a taxi, the fare starts when the driver gets the call, not when you get in. Here is a list of some of the bigger taxi companies; all take credit cards (minimums vary).

Alpha	01-45-85-85 85
Artaxi	01-42-03-50-50
01Taxi	01-49-17-01-01 (24 hours a day)
Taxi G7	01-47-39-47-39, 01-41-27-66-99
Taxis Bleu	08-25-16-10-10

Paris taxi drivers are quite honest and above-board, and they provide receipts upon request. Ask for *un reçu, s'il vous plait.*

Train

The SNCF is the acronym for the French national train system. There are six train stations in Paris:

Gare d'Austerlitz	Trains to/from the southwest of France and Spain
Gare de l'Est	Trains to/from Alsace and southern Germany

Gare de Lyon	Trains to/from the southeast of France, the Alps, Provence, and Italy
Gare du Nord	Trains to/from Brussels, London via the Chunnel, and other destinations to the north
Gare Montparnasse	Trains to/from the west, Brittany, and Bordeaux
Gare St-Lazare	Trains to/from the northwest and Normandy

At each station is a métro stop with the same name.

You can buy tickets at the station or call ahead to reserve your seat, but you must pick it up within forty-eight hours. Your ticket will have your departure station printed on it. If you are under twenty-six years old, you can save up to 50 percent on TGV fares with the Carte12/25, but even without the card, you still get a 25 percent reduction. People over sixty also get good deals with a Carte Vermeil (see "Seniors," page 41). You can also save considerable money by booking at least fifteen days in advance of your travel date. Before boarding the train you must remember to validate your ticket in an orange *composteur;* these are located at the beginning of the platforms, and when the conductor checks your ticket, he could fine you for not having done it. For information, go to the ticket offices in any one of the above listed stations, or call 08-92-35-35-35.

Private Car and Driver or Chauffeured Limousine

For the ultimate comfort and convenience in Paris transportation, hire a private car and driver to take you where you want to go, whether it be to ride to and from the airports, to arrive unruffled for a Big Splurge dinner, or to admire Paris at night when the City of Light is at her most beguiling. I have found the following to be reliable, on time, and very polite; both speak English and are especially recommended for airport transfers: Jean Poittier, Tel & Fax: 01-47-91-49-95, (cell) 06-60-50-96-80, and Henri Rouah, Tel: 06-60-44-64-65. Prices depend on the services required.

More expensive will be a chauffeured limousine with a bilingual driver from Paris Major Limousines: Tel: 01-44-52-50-00; Fax: 01-44-52-50-05; email: pml@easynet.fr; Internet: www.lst-limousine-services.com. It's a minimum of four hours, except for city or airport transfers. Prices start at 99€ for city transfer, 134€ for airport transfer, and 247€ for three passengers and four-hour use of the car. They accept AE, DC, MC, and V.

Time

France is one hour ahead of Greenwich Mean Time (GMT). Time is based on the twenty-four-hour clock. To check the time and set your clock, dial 36-99. Paris is six hours ahead of Eastern Standard Time and nine hours ahead of Pacific Standard Time. Daylight saving time is observed from April 1 to October 31.

Standards of Measure

France uses the metric system. Here are the conversions:

1 inch = 2.54 centimeters	1 centimeter = 0.4 inch
1 mile = 1.61 kilometers	1 kilometer = 0.62 mile
1 ounce = 28 grams	1 gram = 0.04 ounces
1 pound = 0.45 kilograms	1 kilogram = 2.2 pounds
1 quart = 0.95 liter	1 liter = 1.06 quarts
1 gallon = 3.8 liters	

How much is that in miles, feet, pounds, or degrees? Here is how to do the conversions:

Kilometers/miles: To change kilometers to miles, multiply the kilometers by .621. To change miles to kilometers, multiply the miles by 1.61.

Meters/feet: To change meters to feet, multiply the meters by 3.28. To change feet to meters, multiply the feet by .305.

Kilograms/pounds: To change kilograms to pounds, multiply the kilograms by 2.20. To change pounds to kilograms, multiply the pounds by .453.

Celsius/Fahrenheit: To change Celsius to Fahrenheit, double the Celsius figure and add 30. If the Celsius figure is below zero, double the sub-zero number and subtract it from 32.

Voltage

French electrical circuits are wired at 220 volts. You will need a transformer and an adapter plug for appliances you bring that operate on 110 volts. Things such as hair dryers and hair curling irons may have switches that convert the appliance from one voltage to another. This only eliminates the need for a transformer, not for the adapter plug. If you are planning on using a computer, be sure you have a surge protector and the adapter plug; otherwise, you could end up damaging your machine. Don't worry if you find yourself without the proper adapters or transformers. Go to the basement of the BHV department store (see page 358) and take the appliance with you. If they don't have what you need, chances are it doesn't exist.

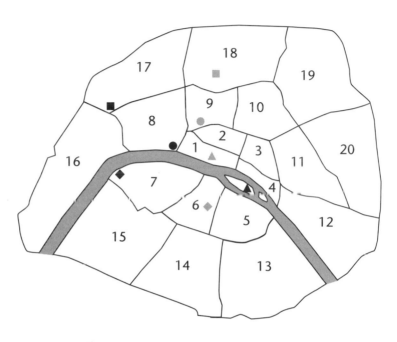

- ● Place de la Concorde
- ■ Arc de Triomphe
- ▲ Notre Dame
- ◆ Tour Eiffel

- ● Opéra
- ■ Sacré Cœur
- ▲ Louvre
- ◆ Jardin du Luxembourg

HOTEL LISTINGS BY ARRONDISSEMENT

Paris has more than nine million inhabitants occupying 432 square miles. Despite these numbers, it is a very compact city, bound by a ring road known as the *périphérique* and divided into twenty districts called *arrondissements.* Anything outside the *périphérique* is the *banlieu* and is considered the suburbs. The River Seine divides Paris into the Right Bank *(Rive Droite)* and the Left Bank *(Rive Gauche).* In the late nineteenth century, Paris was reorganized and modernized by Baron Haussmann, the far-sighted planner who gave the city its wide boulevards, beautiful parks, and system of arrondissements that make up the city today. Each arrondissement has a character all its own, as well as its own mayor, city hall, police station, and central post office.

Knowing which arrondissement is which is the key to understanding Paris and quickly finding your way around. Starting with the first arrondissement, which is the district around the Louvre, the numbering of districts goes clockwise in a rough spiral. From a visitor's standpoint, the arrondissements of greatest interest are the first through the eighth, although there are interesting things to see and do in all of them. For instance, Montmartre occupies most of the eighteenth, and to attend a performance at the Opéra Bastille, you must journey to the eleventh. For mailing purposes, the Paris postal code prefix is 750, which is followed by a two-digit number indicating the arrondissement: 75001 is the code for the first, 75002 for the second, and so on. For every address in *Great Sleeps Paris,* the postal code is given.

In addition to each arrondissement being numbered, it also has a name (and in some cases, two) by which its residents often refer to it. The first arrondissement is commonly referred to as Louvre, the second as Bourse, and so on (see below). For example, Parisians might say, "I live in the sixth, Luxembourg." Some arrondissements have two sections, and each section has its own name. In this case, a resident would specify which: "I live in the eleventh, République."

First	Louvre
Second	Bourse
Third	Marais
Fourth	Hôtel de Ville
Fifth	Panthéon
Sixth	Luxembourg
Seventh	Invalides

Eighth	Élysée
Ninth	Opéra
Tenth	Magenta
Eleventh	République (northern section), Voltaire (southern section)
Twelfth	Bercy (eastern section), Reuilly (western section)
Thirteenth	Bibliothèque Nationale de France (eastern section), Italie (western section)
Fourteenth	Observatoire (eastern section), Montparnasse (western section)
Fifteenth	Vaugirard (eastern section), Grenelle (western section)
Sixteenth	Passy
Seventeenth	Ternes (western section), Batignoles (eastern section)
Eighteenth	Butte Montmartre (western section), La Chapelle (eastern section)
Nineteenth	La Villette (northern section), Buttes Chaumont (southern section)
Twentieth	Ménilmontant (northern section), Père Lachaise (southern section)

First Arrondissement

Paris began on Île de la Cité, and Parisians still regard it as the center not only of their city but of all France. Anchored in the middle of the Seine, Île de la Cité has some of the oldest and most treasured monuments of Paris. La Conciergerie is the Gothic prison where thousands, including Robespierre and Marie-Antoinette, were incarcerated during the French Revolution. Le Palais de Justice, a royal palace, became the seat of the judicial system after the French Revolution. Ste-Chapelle, located within Le Palais de Justice, has seven-hundred-year-old, breathtakingly beautiful red-and-blue stained-glass windows. The Tuileries Gardens, Musée de l'Orangerie, and Louvre Museum form the cornerstone of this regal *quartier*. In the first arrondissement you will find Les Halles, with Forum des Halles housing two hundred or more boutiques along with movie theaters, fast-food joints, and the largest métro station in the world (which has the reputation of being unsafe after dark). Two famous churches are here: St-Germain-l'Auxerrois, the Gothic church parish of French kings, and St-Eustache, the largest Gothic Renaissance church in Paris. For many, place Dauphine, with its white brick buildings, is one of the most peaceful and harmonious in the city. The palaces surrounding the moneyed place Vendôme include the famed Cartier jewelry store, the Ministry of Justice, and the world-renowned Ritz Hôtel, where room prices are within the budget of any average emir or Texas oil mogul.

RIGHT BANK
Conciergerie
Île de la Cité
Les Halles & Forum des Halles
Louvre
Musée de l'Orangerie
Musée des Arts Décoratifs
Palais de Justice
Palais Royal
place Dauphine
place Vendôme
Pont Neuf
Ste-Chapelle
St-Eustache
St-Germain-l'Auxerrois
Tuileries Gardens

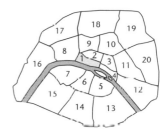

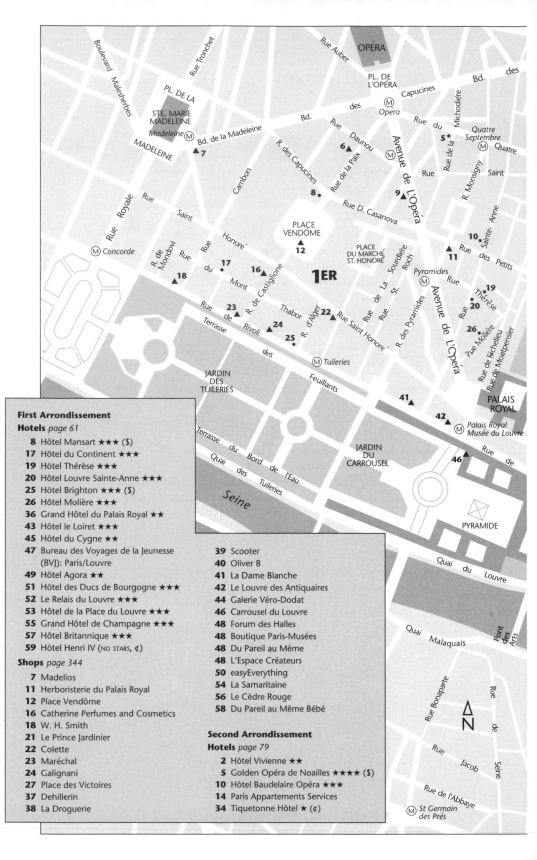

OPÉRA

PL. DE L'OPÉRA

PL. DE LA STE. MARIE MADELEINE

MADELEINE

PLACE VENDÔME

PLACE DU MARCHÉ ST. HONORÉ

1ER

PALAIS ROYAL

Palais Royal Musée du Louvre

JARDIN DES TUILERIES

JARDIN DU CARROUSEL

Seine

PYRAMIDE

First Arrondissement

Hotels *page 61*

- **8** Hôtel Mansart ★★★ ($)
- **17** Hôtel du Continent ★★★
- **19** Hôtel Thérèse ★★★
- **20** Hôtel Louvre Sainte-Anne ★★★
- **25** Hôtel Brighton ★★★ ($)
- **26** Hôtel Molière ★★★
- **36** Grand Hôtel du Palais Royal ★★
- **43** Hôtel le Loiret ★★★
- **45** Hôtel du Cygne ★★
- **47** Bureau des Voyages de la Jeunesse (BVJ): Paris/Louvre
- **49** Hôtel Agora ★★
- **51** Hôtel des Ducs de Bourgogne ★★★
- **52** Le Relais du Louvre ★★★
- **53** Hôtel de la Place du Louvre ★★★
- **55** Grand Hôtel de Champagne ★★★
- **57** Hôtel Britannique ★★★
- **59** Hôtel Henri IV (NO STARS, ¢)

Shops *page 344*

- **7** Madelios
- **11** Herboristerie du Palais Royal
- **12** Place Vendôme
- **16** Catherine Perfumes and Cosmetics
- **18** W. H. Smith
- **21** Le Prince Jardinier
- **22** Colette
- **23** Maréchal
- **24** Galignani
- **27** Place des Victoires
- **37** Dehillerin
- **38** La Droguerie
- **39** Scooter
- **40** Oliver B
- **41** La Dame Blanche
- **42** Le Louvre des Antiquaires
- **44** Galerie Véro-Dodat
- **46** Carrousel du Louvre
- **48** Forum des Halles
- **48** Boutique Paris-Musées
- **48** Du Pareil au Même
- **48** L'Espace Créateurs
- **50** easyEverything
- **54** La Samaritaine
- **56** Le Cèdre Rouge
- **58** Du Pareil au Même Bébé

Second Arrondissement

Hotels *page 79*

- **2** Hôtel Vivienne ★★
- **5** Golden Opéra de Noailles ★★★★ ($)
- **10** Hôtel Baudelaire Opéra ★★★
- **14** Paris Appartements Services
- **34** Tiquetonne Hôtel ★ (¢)

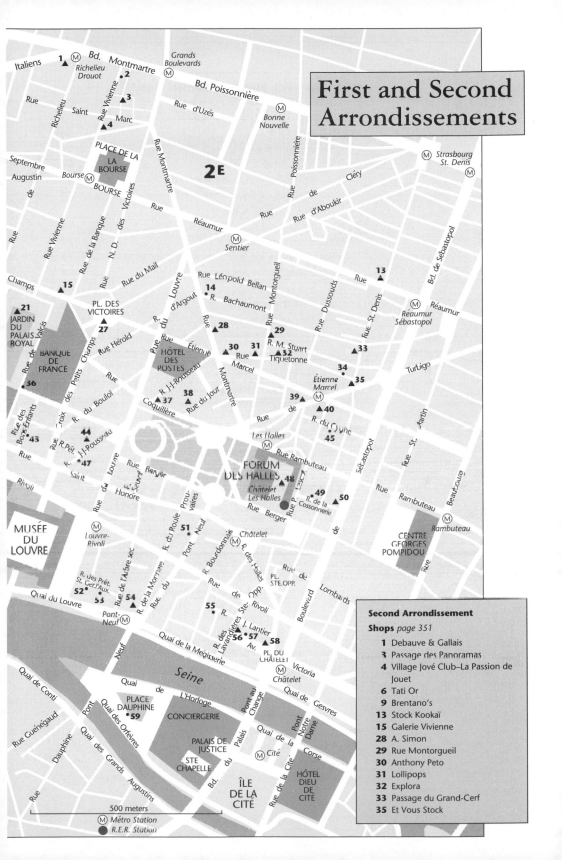

First and Second
Arrondissements

2E

Italiens
Bd. Montmartre
Grands Boulevards
Richelieu Drouot
Bd. Poissonnière
Rue d'Uzès
Bonne Nouvelle
Rue Vivienne
Saint Marc
Rue
Septembre
Augustin
de
Bourse
PLACE DE LA
LA BOURSE
BOURSE
Rue Montmartre
Rue d'Aboukir
Strasbourg
St. Denis
Cléry
de
Rue
Réaumur
N. D. des Victoires
Rue de la Banque
Rue Vivienne
Champs
15
Réaumur
Sentier
Bd. de Sébastopol
Rue du Mail
Rue Léopold Bellan
14
R. Bachaumont
PL. DES VICTOIRES
27
21
JARDIN DU PALAIS ROYAL
Rue Hérold
HÔTEL DES POSTES
28
Rue Montorgueil
29
R. M. Stuart
30   31
Rue Tiquetonne
32
33
Réaumur
Sébastopol
Rue St. Denis
Rue Dussouds
13
Rue
34
Étienne Marcel
35
Turbigo
BANQUE DE FRANCE
36
des Petits Champs
R. du Bouloi
R. J-J. Rousseau
37   38
Coquillière
Rue du Jour
Rue Étienne
Rue Marcel
39
de
R. du Cygne
40
45
Rue
Sébastopol
Rue St. Martin
Rue des Bons Enfants
43
R. Pél.
44
R. J-J. Rousseau
47
Rivoli
Rue
Saint
Rue du Louvre
Rue Berger
Les Halles
Rue Rambuteau
FORUM DES HALLES
48
Châtelet Les Halles
49   50
Rue de la Cossonnerie
Rue
Rambuteau
de
Rambuteau
CENTRE GEORGES POMPIDOU
MUSÉE DU LOUVRE
Louvre-Rivoli
R. du Roule
51
Pont Neuf
Châtelet
R. Bourdonnais
Rue de la Ferronnerie Ste. Opp.
PL. STE.OPP.
Rue de Rivoli
Rue du Pont Neuf
Prouvaires
R. St. Germ.l'Aux.
R. des Prêt.
52   53
R. de l'Arbre sec
R. de la Monnaie
Rue du
54
55
R.
J. Lantier
56 57
58
Av.
PL. DU CHÂTELET
Rue des Lavandières
Rue
de
Opp.
Rue du
Boulevard
Lombards
Victoria
Châtelet
Quai du Louvre
Pont-Neuf
Quai
de
L'Horloge
Seine
PLACE DAUPHINE
59
CONCIERGERIE
Quai de la Mégisserie
Quai des Orfèvres
Quai des Grands Augustins
Rue Guénégaud
Pont Neuf
Quai de Conti
Dauphine
PALAIS DE JUSTICE
STE CHAPELLE
PALAIS
Bd. du
Pont au Change
Pont Notre Dame
Quai de Gesvres
Quai de la Corse
Cité
Corse
ÎLE DE LA CITÉ
Rue de la Cité
HÔTEL DIEU DE CITÉ

500 meters

Ⓜ Métro Station
● R.E.R. Station

Second Arrondissement

Shops *page 351*

  1 Debauve & Gallais
  3 Passage des Panoramas
  4 Village Joué Club–La Passion de Jouet
  6 Tati Or
  9 Brentano's
 13 Stock Kookaï
 15 Galerie Vivienne
 28 A. Simon
 29 Rue Montorgueil
 30 Anthony Peto
 31 Lollipops
 32 Explora
 33 Passage du Grand-Cerf
 35 Et Vous Stock

HOTELS IN THE FIRST ARRONDISSEMENT

Grand Hôtel de Champagne ★★★	64
Grand Hôtel du Palais Royal ★★	65
Hôtel Agora ★★	66
Hôtel Brighton ★★★ ($)	67
Hôtel Britannique ★★★	68
Hôtel de la Place du Louvre ★★★	69
Hôtel des Ducs de Bourgogne ★★★	70
Hôtel du Continent ★★★	71
Hôtel du Cygne ★★	71
Hôtel Henri IV (NO STARS, ¢)	72
Hôtel le Loiret ★★★	73
Hôtel Louvre Sainte-Anne ★★★	74
Hôtel Mansart ★★★ ($)	74
Hôtel Molière ★★★	76
Hôtel Thérèse ★★★	77
Le Relais du Louvre ★★★	77

OTHER OPTIONS
Student Accommodations
Bureau des Voyages de la Jeunesse (BVJ): Paris/Louvre	324

($) indicates a Big Splurge; (¢) indicates a Cheap Sleep

GRAND HÔTEL DE CHAMPAGNE ★★★ (55)
17, rue Jean-Lantier, at 13, rue des Orfèvres, 75001
Métro: Châtelet (exit rue de Rivoli, *nos impairs*, or
Bertin Poirée); RER Châtelet–Les Halles
43 rooms, all with shower or bath and toilet

Hidden on a small corner near the River Seine and the Châtelet métro stop, the family-owned Grand Hôtel de Champagne appeals to travelers looking for an A+ location for exploring the Louvre, the islands, St-Michel, and St-Germain-des-Prés.

If you look carefully in the sitting area off the reception, you will see 1562 carved in one of the original wooden pillars; this is the date that the building was constructed, making it the oldest structure on rue Jean-Lantier. Before its present charmed transformation, it served as a residence for members of the tailor and shoemaker guilds, an inn during the Empire period, and until 1854, a Christian girls' school.

Different themes are carried out in each of the forty-three rooms and suites, with the colorful interiors running

TELEPHONE
01-42-36-60-00; toll-free from U.S. 800-44-UTELL

FAX
01-45-08-43-33

INTERNET
www.hotelchampaigneparis.com

CREDIT CARDS
AE, DC, MC, V

RATES
Single 150€, double 165–200€, suites 240–320€; *taxe de séjour* 0.91€ per person, per day

BREAKFAST
Buffet downstairs or Continental in room, 12€ per person

ENGLISH SPOKEN
Yes

the gamut from masculine modern to frankly feminine. Many have hand-painted murals done by artists over the years (perhaps in lieu of a final payment?). All rooms on the first floor are nonsmoking. Room 304 has a fanciful scene of Venice on the bathroom wall. No. 105, a room with twin beds, is done in a red-and-white English print; the nice corner bath makes up in part for the lack of sitting and luggage space. No. 301 is a deluxe suite daringly done in shades of lavender and turquoise. It has the advantage of a separate toilet and sink off the sitting area in addition to a fantasy bathroom with double sinks and a sunken tub. I also like the walk-in closet. Rooms 502, 504, and 505 have terraces. Frankly, the only thing going for No. 502 is the balcony. I don't like the low cross beams, the open rack that subs for a closet, or the lack of tub in the bathroom. A better choice is suite 504, done in Victorian red, with neighborhood views from its two balconies.

Management is justifiably proud of its buffet breakfast served downstairs. Designed to appeal to lumberjack appetites, it includes fresh fruit, juices, a variety of breads and rolls, several selections of meat and cheese, pâté, eggs, and cereals. After this meal, you won't need to eat until dinnertime.

FACILITIES AND SERVICES: Air-conditioning, direct dial phone, elevator (to most floors), hair dryer, laundry service, minibar in suites, TV with international reception, office safe (no charge), 1st floor exclusively nonsmoking

NEAREST TOURIST ATTRACTIONS (RIGHT BANK): Les Halles and Forum des Halles, Centre Georges Pompidou (Beaubourg), Louvre, Île de la Cité, Île-St-Louis, St-Michel, St-Germain-des-Prés

GRAND HÔTEL DU PALAIS ROYAL ★★ (36)
4, rue de Valois, 75001
Métro: Palais Royal–Musée du Louvre
85 rooms, all with shower or bath and toilet

The minimalistic lobby and reception areas are softened by posed orchid and lily floral arrangements that look almost real in this modern choice midway between the Bourse (stock exchange) and the Louvre. All the eighty-five blue-and-yellow rooms are the same. They face outward, display exceptionally high housekeeping standards, and have bare hardwood floors, simple blue-and-white bedspreads and curtains, and functional

TELEPHONE
01-42-96-15-35
FAX
01-40-15-97-81
EMAIL
h-palais-royal@wanadoo.fr
CREDIT CARDS
MC, V
RATES
Single 110€, double 120€; extra bed 25€; *taxe de séjour* included

BREAKFAST
Buffet 10€ per person

ENGLISH SPOKEN
Yes

bathrooms with stall showers or tub/shower combinations and sink space. Toiletries are limited to a sliver of soap. You'll find no cable TV, no safe, no minibars, and no unpleasant surprises. Instead you can count on a decent, clean hotel room that is modestly priced for the area.

FACILITIES AND SERVICES: Direct-dial phone, elevator, hair dryer, French TV, 2 handicapped rooms

NEAREST TOURIST ATTRACTIONS (RIGHT BANK): Palais Royal, Louvre, Tuileries Gardens, Seine

HÔTEL AGORA ★★ (49)
7, rue de la Cossonnerie, off rue Pierre Lescot, 75001
Métro: Etienne-Marcel; RER Châtelet–Les Halles
29 rooms, all with shower or bath and toilet

TELEPHONE
01-42-33-46-02

FAX
01-42-33-80-99

EMAIL
hotel.agora.f@wanadoo.fr

INTERNET
www.123france.com/hotel-agora

CREDIT CARDS
AE, MC, V

RATES
Single 65–100€, double 91–120€, triple 135€; *taxe de séjour* 0.76€ per person, per day

BREAKFAST
Continental 8€ per person

ENGLISH SPOKEN
Yes

The decor at the Hôtel Agora is an eclectic pastiche of flea-market nostalgia that gives new meaning to the phrases frou-frou and hand-me-downs. The rooms are not large nor are the bathrooms, but if you want something different in an active, animated section of Paris, read on.

The location, in the midst of a Les Halles block of touristy shops on a pedestrian street, is hardly inspiring. A short flight of stairs leads to a reception room with living plants draped all over the windows and a birdcage with a stuffed monkey eating a banana. A mirrored breakfast room has two covered tables and a sitting area to one side with several antique pieces and a photo of an Italian film star, who stayed here in leaner times.

The hallways are painted a gloomy battleship gray, but the rooms are whimsically individual, mixing the old with the new in a way that comes together. Number 26 is a nice double in green with two large windows. No. 31, with twin beds, features an armchair covered in a leopard print, a fireplace, and a gold-framed headboard with hand-painted flowers. In No. 64, you will have a rooftop view of St-Eustache Church, sleep in a double bed, and use a small bathroom with a mini corner shower and wash basin. Room 66, on the top floor, is a sweet single with a slat park chair and a white bedspread with appliquéd floral hearts. Room 61 is the biggest and will hold three, but I think it is better for two. It is dominated by a nineteenth-century painting of a woman and a mixture of similar-era art scattered on the walls. A Tunisian wood sculpture looms over the twin beds. The warm mustard-colored No. 51 is one of my favorites. Besides its tiny terrace, I like the entryway with its large oval mirror, the marble fireplace, and the gold scrolled piece of wood that forms a backdrop for the bed.

FACILITIES AND SERVICES: Direct-dial phone, elevator (starts 1st floor), hair dryer, TV with international reception, office safe (no charge)

NEAREST TOURIST ATTRACTIONS (RIGHT BANK): Heart of Les Halles, Forum des Halles, Centre Georges Pompidou (Beaubourg), Louvre, Île de la Cité, Île St-Louis

HÔTEL BRIGHTON ★★★ ($, 25)
218, rue de Rivoli, 75001
Métro: Tuileries

60 rooms, all with shower or bath and toilet

The Hôtel Brighton dates from the end of the nineteenth century and takes its name from the friendship that developed between Great Britain and France during the reign of Queen Victoria. Overlooking the Tuileries Gardens and many of the most beautiful Parisian monuments, it is also only a short walk from the Louvre, place Vendôme, wonderful shopping, the Opéra, and the Seine.

The hotel has undergone a complete redecoration and the results are impressive, indeed. Naturally those with the million-dollar views of Paris are the most expensive; however, all are nice and have the advantage of space . . . which is very hard to come by in most Parisian hotels. Number 401 is a large, quiet twin on the back with a rooftop view. The room includes a desk, luggage space, and a bathroom large enough to hold a table and small stool in addition to the regular bathroom fixtures. Another choice on the back is No. 403, with a double brass bed and a leather armchair. The long, narrow marble bathroom is light and has a shower over the tub. Also on the back is No. 305, with a working-size desk, big bathroom, and a small balcony with a peek at the Tuileries. These rooms are nice if you are willing to sacrifice a view and accept a certain minimum amount of noise. Frankly, when staying here, I want a room with a view, because they are nothing short of spectacular, encompassing almost all of Paris from the Arc de Triomphe and La Defense to the Eiffel Tower, Invalides, Notre Dame, and more. Yes, there is some noise, but double windows and air-conditioning buffer most of it. Take No. 309, for example, a large room with vintage furniture, leather armchair, mirrored dresser with a tulip light, good desk, and a huge bathroom with a separate tub, stall shower, and enclosed toilet.

TELEPHONE
01-47-03-61-61

FAX
01-42-60-41-78

EMAIL
hotel.brighton@wanadoo.fr

INTERNET
www.esprit-de-france.com

CREDIT CARDS
AE, DC, MC, V

RATES
Single or double 120–240€, triple 170–260€; *taxe de séjour* included

BREAKFAST
Continental 10€ per person

ENGLISH SPOKEN
Yes

Also under the same ownership are the Hôtels de la Place du Louvre, Mansart, Parc Saint-Séverin, and d'Orsay (see pages 69, 74, 129, and 184).

FACILITIES AND SERVICES: Air-conditioning (planned), direct-dial phone, elevator, hair dryer, laundry service, minibar, TV with international reception, room safe (no charge)

NEAREST TOURIST ATTRACTIONS (RIGHT BANK): Tuileries Gardens, place de la Concorde, Louvre, Musée d'Orsay, place de la Madeleine, place Vendôme, shopping, Seine

HÔTEL BRITANNIQUE ★★★ (57)
20, avenue Victoria, 75001
Métro: Châtelet; RER Châtelet–Les Halles
40 rooms, all with shower or bath and toilet

TELEPHONE
01-42-33-74-59
FAX
01-42-33-82-65
INTERNET
www.hotel-britannique.fr
CREDIT CARDS
AE, DC, MC, V
RATES
Single 140€, double 165–190€, suite 295€; lower rates depend on season and availability; *taxe de séjour* included
BREAKFAST
Buffet or Continental in room 14€ per person
ENGLISH SPOKEN
Yes

The history of this hotel goes way back. In 1870–71, it was run by a Quaker mission to aid war victims. During World War I, it was where war casualties recuperated. Today it is a gracefully restored, sound choice between Châtelet and Hôtel de Ville. In the refashioning of the hotel several years ago, the owners wisely kept many original parts. The winding stairway with polished banister and the carved reception counter are two examples of how the old can blend beautifully with the new. Granite hallways lined with red print carpet lead guests to their rooms, which are behind eggplant-purple doors. Best choices are on the top three floors, just high enough to escape the brunt of the street noise; they have more light and avoid blank-wall views on the back. For a street-side balcony, ask for something on the fifth floor. The rooms, though small, are professionally decorated in soft colors with tone-on-tone wallpaper, faux marble accents, and print fabrics. For more space, reserve the suite (No. 12), done in yellow and burgundy. In addition to the bedroom, the sitting area has a comfortable sofa bed with a pretty tapestry of grapes hanging over it. Three windows let in lots of light and the double-mirrored closet provides ample unpacking room.

Classical music soothes early morning diners in the pretty breakfast room. A buffet is laid out here, or you can have a Continental breakfast sent to your room for the same price. The sunken, mirrored lounge, with eye-level windows on the street, is accented with some lovely old heirlooms. Be sure to notice the birdcage, the early record player, and the intricately detailed model of an old sailing vessel.

FACILITIES AND SERVICES: Bar, direct-dial phone, elevator, hair dryer, minibar, terrycloth robes in all rooms, TV with international reception, room safe (no charge)

NEAREST TOURIST ATTRACTIONS (RIGHT BANK): Louvre, Tuileries Gardens, Centre Georges Pompidou (Beaubourg), Les Halles & Forum des Halles, Seine, Île de la Cité, Île St-Louis, St-Michel

HÔTEL DE LA PLACE DU LOUVRE ★★★ (53)
21, rue des Prêtres St-Germain-l'Auxerrois, 75001
Métro: Pont-Neuf, Louvre-Rivoli

20 rooms, all with shower or bath and toilet

The name of the hotel gives you a hint. From the front door the Louvre is only a five-minute stroll, the quais along the Seine a block away, and all the Left Bank has to offer is just a few minutes across the Pont Neuf to St-Michel. The hotel is imaginatively done from start to finish. Portions of the original stone walls are artistically exposed to the dramatically modern entry. Murals on curving walls lead to a tented sitting area with a purple chamois wall covering highlighted by black and tangerine leather and chrome furniture. A multicolored curtain hangs above the front window, which faces the St-Germain-l'Auxerrois Church across the street.

All of the rooms are named for famous artists whose work hangs in the Louvre. The brilliant pink, third-floor Picasso room has a view of the church, marble-top bedside tables, a corner desk, mirrored wardrobes, and a wonderful upstairs bathroom with a skylight. If you check into the green-and-white Kandinsky double, you will have good luggage space and a salmon-colored tile bath with gray monogrammed towels and plenty of shelf space. The Robert Delaunay room on the second floor has a good view of the church and the side of the Louvre.

There are two rooms I would avoid. The Francis Picaba is a two-room suite that has a sleeping loft and a bathroom ceiling so low over the tub-shower combination that anyone over five feet could not stand upright. Same for the Jackson Pollack—the shower is comfortable for short people only.

Breakfast is served in the original fourteenth-century stone-walled *cave* in the basement.

This hotel is under the same management and ownership as the Hôtels Brighton, Mansart, Parc Saint-Séverin, and d'Orsay (see pages 67, 74, 129, and 184).

FACILITIES AND SERVICES: Air-conditioning in most rooms, bar, direct-dial phone, elevator, hair dryer,

TELEPHONE
01-42-33-78-68

FAX
01-42-33-09-95

EMAIL
hotel.place.louvre@wanadoo.fr

INTERNET
www.esprit-de-france.com

CREDIT CARDS
V

RATES
Single 95–125€, double 125–150€, triple 160€; *taxe de séjour* included

BREAKFAST
Continental 10€ per person

ENGLISH SPOKEN
Yes

minibar, TV with international reception, room safe (no charge)

NEAREST TOURIST ATTRACTIONS (RIGHT BANK): Louvre, Tuileries Gardens, Seine, Les Halles & Forum des Halles, Centre Georges Pompidou (Beaubourg), Île de la Cité, Île St-Louis, St-Michel, St-Gremain-des-Prés

HÔTEL DES DUCS DE BOURGOGNE ★★★ (51)
19, rue du Pont Neuf
Métro: Pont-Neuf; RER Châtelet–Les Halles
50 rooms, all with shower or bath and toilet

TELEPHONE
01-42-33-95-64; toll-free in the U.S. and Canada 800-528-1234 (Best Western)

FAX
01-40-39-01-25

INTERNET
www.hotel-paris-bourgogne.com, www.bestwestern.fr

CREDIT CARDS
AE, DC, MC, V

RATES
Single 98–150€, double 150–180€, triple (w/ folding bed) 180€, triple/quad 245€; children under 12 free; *taxe de séjour* included

BREAKFAST
Buffet 12€ per person

ENGLISH SPOKEN
Yes

When you walk in the door, you can't miss the English hat rack with its collection of vintage hats. The owner originally had it in the lobby as a place for guests to hang their coats, but it was too fragile for this purpose. Rather than dispose of it, he went to the flea market and bought a collection of fanciful *chapeaux*. Now the hat rack, with the hats, has become the symbol of the hotel, and no one would think of hanging a coat on it. Another interesting feature along the wall leading to the downstairs breakfast room is the rogues' photo gallery of French and American astronauts, which is a tribute to the many clients who come here to attend meetings at the *Centre Nationale Spatial Français* (at the end of the street).

Besides the hat rack and photos, there are many appealing things about the hotel, which is affiliated with Best Western. First, the A+ location puts guests in the heart of Paris. Next, children under twelve are free, and discounts are often available on the Internet. The traditional, air-conditioned rooms are very clean, 20 percent are exclusively nonsmoking, all have double windows, and bathrooms have good mirror and sink space. Finally, the staff, headed by friendly Nathalie Dupont, the manager, is always ready to help. Always ask her about special off-season and promotional rates.

FACILITIES AND SERVICES: Air-conditioning, conference room, direct-dial phone, elevator, hair dryer, laundry service, minibar, public parking across the street, tea and coffee maker, TV with international reception, office safe (no charge), 20 percent of rooms nonsmoking

NEAREST TOURIST ATTRACTIONS (RIGHT BANK): Louvre, Les Halles & Forum des Halles, Centre Georges Pompidou (Beaubourg), Seine, Île de la Cité

HÔTEL DU CONTINENT ★★★ (17)
30, rue du Mont-Thabor, 75001
Métro: Tuileries, Concorde
26 rooms, all with shower or bath and toilet

A fresh renovation with Art Deco overtones has brought this well-located choice back up to speed. Primary colors are used in many of the bedrooms to create a space that is clean-cut and comfortable. A mirrored elevator takes guests to the rooms that have yellow leather armless chairs, red bedside tables, and new baths with Formica-style wood-pattern countertops. Good shelf and closet space add appeal, and a painting of Paris in each room reminds you of where you are lucky enough to be. I like the rooms that face the street, which though in the heart of Paris, is small and relatively quiet. Rooms on the back can be dark, especially No. 10, a depressing single with poor security.

FACILITIES AND SERVICES: Air-conditioning, bar, direct-dial phone, elevator (to most floors), hair dryer, laundry service, minibar, TV with international reception, office safe (no charge)

NEAREST TOURIST ATTRACTIONS (RIGHT BANK): Tuileries Gardens, Louvre, place Vendôme, place de la Concorde, place de la Madeleine, Seine

TELEPHONE
01-42-60-75-32
FAX
01-42-61-52-22
EMAIL
continen@cybercable.fr
INTERNET
www.hotelducontinent.com
CREDIT CARDS
AE, DC, MC, V
RATES
Single 130–170€, double 170–190€, suite 190€ (for 2), 240€ (for 3); *taxe de séjour* 0.91€ per person, per day
BREAKFAST
Continental 10€ per person
ENGLISH SPOKEN
Yes

HÔTEL DU CYGNE ★★ (45)
3, rue du Cygne, 75001
Métro: Étienne-Marcel; RER Châtelet–Les Halles
20 rooms, 18 with shower or bath and toilet

Reliable two-star hotels in this corner of Les Halles are very scarce, so I was happy to find the Hôtel du Cygne, located in a seventeenth-century building on a short, pedestrian-only street leading off the busy boulevard de Sebastopol. The owners, Mme. Elaine Gouge and her daughter Isabelle, have taken this old hotel and made it livable and appealing on almost every count. The pretty tiled entryway leads to a homey sitting room with a yellow leather armchair and comfortable sofa. The charming, partially skylighted breakfast area has cushioned chairs, a collection of old Paris photos, potted palm, and a swan *(cygne) jardinière*—the symbol of the hotel.

While the hallways could use a facelift, the rooms, which subscribe to the Laura Ashley style of decorating, are excellent value for the price. In fact, some three-star hotel rooms can't begin to compare with the twenty here, almost all of which have a desk and chair, luggage

TELEPHONE
01-42-60-14-16
FAX
01-42-21-37-02
EMAIL
hotel.cygne@wanadoo.fr
INTERNET
www.hotelducygne.fr
CREDIT CARDS
MC, V
RATES
Single 75–85€, double 98–120€, triple 140€; *taxe de séjour* included
BREAKFAST
Continental 6€ per person
ENGLISH SPOKEN
Yes

rack, bedside tables with good lights, and decent towels in the bathrooms. Mme. Gouge told me she couldn't find curtains or bed skirts to go with the pretty bed quilts so she bought the material and made them herself. The twin-bed nests have bathtubs; the single- and double-bed rooms come with showers. For best results, request a room that has a new bathroom. Room 35, with a bright Provençal theme and original beams, is the biggest. The divided room has the beds on a platform mezzanine, and below, a sitting area with a sofa bed, table, and chairs. If you are willing to walk up one flight of stairs (from the third to the fourth floor), you can enjoy the quiet, quaint, and romantic No. 41, which is under the eaves, with windows along the mansard roof; it has a shower and a marble desk. Single travelers should book Room 11, which faces out and has a wicker armchair, but avoid Room 38, which has no closet or drawer space, and No. 18 unless you are willing to walk up a flight of stairs to the shower and toilet.

FACILITIES AND SERVICES: Direct-dial phone, no elevator (4 floors), hair dryer in most bathrooms, TV with international reception, room safe (no charge)

NEAREST TOURIST ATTRACTIONS (RIGHT BANK): Les Halles and Forum des Halles, Centre Georges Pompidou (Beaubourg)

HÔTEL HENRI IV (NO STARS, ¢, 59)
25, place Dauphine, 75001
Métro: Pont-Neuf

20 rooms, 2 with shower and toilet, 2 with shower only, 16 with no shower or toilet

TELEPHONE
01-43-54-44-53
CREDIT CARDS
None, cash only
RATES
Single 26€, double 36–72€, triple 52€, shower 3€; *taxe de séjour* 0.30€ per person, per day
BREAKFAST
Included (hot beverage, bread and butter)
ENGLISH SPOKEN
Yes

Four hundred years ago, King Henri IV's printing presses occupied this narrow townhouse on Île de la Cité's pretty place Dauphine. Today, it is a twenty-room hotel that has been touted in every budget guide to Paris, becoming a mecca for the seriously thrifty and anyone else eager for a romantically threadbare hotel adventure in Paris. Despite improvements, such as hall linoleum, new wallpaper in a few rooms, and showers installed in four rooms, all guests must continue to be philosophical about both the accommodations and the plumbing. Remember, you cannot pour a quart into a pint . . . which here means that short of gutting the building and starting over, not much can be done to modernize or even upgrade. The rooms, which passed their prime decades ago, could be a shock to some: the furniture looks like leftovers from a garage sale, the lighting is dim, the mattresses are spongy, most of the bedspreads have seen better days, and the exposed pipes gurgle and sputter all day and all night. On the other hand, it is so cheap, so perfectly located, and so quiet, and the owners (M. and Mme. Balitrand and their son, François, who now runs it) are so friendly, that thousands of young-at-heart guests continue to flock here from around the world and reserve many months in advance.

FACILITIES AND SERVICES: None. No elevator (4 floors); office open for reservations 8 A.M.–7 P.M.

NEAREST TOURIST ATTRACTIONS (ON ÎLE DE LA CITÉ): place Dauphine, Île de la Cité, Île St-Louis, St-Michel, St-Germain-des-Prés, Louvre, Seine

HÔTEL LE LOIRET ★★★ (43)
5, rue des Bons Enfants, 75001
Métro: Palais Royal–Musée du Louvre
31 rooms, all with shower or bath and toilet

The rooms at the three-star Hôtel le Loiret are up to one-third less than those just around the corner in a nationally known two-star chain hotel. Alain and Madeleine Diguet have owned the hotel for twenty-five years. Even though their rooms and bathtubs are small, the good location, lots of perks, and friendly tabs keep guests returning regularly. Each of the compact rooms has been customized with built-ins to take advantage of every inch of space, and eleven new baths have been added. In addition to the standard amenities, each guest is given a private fax and telephone number with voice mail. The fax, phone number, and computer connection can be allocated when reserving or upon check-in. You also can order a meal to be sent in by a catering service.

NOTE: The Ministry of Culture is engaged in an enormous multilevel construction project across the street. The building, which will eventually hold nine hundred employees, was scheduled for completion before press time. However, if you are considering this hotel, be sure to confirm that the building is finished. Otherwise, you will be contending with nonstop dirt, dust, and noise.

FACILITIES AND SERVICES: Direct-dial phone and fax with private number and message, elevator (to most floors), hair dryer, Internet in lobby, laundry service, minibar, parking 20€ per day, room service by outside caterer, TV with international reception, room safe (no charge)

NEAREST TOURIST ATTRACTIONS (RIGHT BANK): Louvre, Tuileries Gardens, Palais Royal, Seine

TELEPHONE
01-42-61-47-31

FAX
01-42-61-36-85

INTERNET
www.hotelleloiret.com

CREDIT CARDS
MC, V

RATES
Single 87–95€, double 101–110€; *taxe de séjour* included

BREAKFAST
Continental 8€ per person

ENGLISH SPOKEN
Yes

HÔTEL LOUVRE SAINTE-ANNE ★★★ (20)
32, rue Ste-Anne, 75001
Métro: Palais Royal–Musée du Louvre, Pyramides
20 rooms, all with bath or shower and toilet

TELEPHONE
01-40-20-02-35
FAX
01-40-15-91-13
INTERNET
www.louvre-ste-anne.fr
CREDIT CARDS
AE, DC, MC, V
RATES
Single 124–140€, double 140–155€, superior 155–190€; *taxe de séjour* included
BREAKFAST
Buffet 10€ per person
ENGLISH SPOKEN
Yes

This hotel was completely renovated in 1997. The owners, M. and Mme. Bernie, said the work took one year to complete to their stringent specifications, and believe me, they did a great job. Each air-conditioned room is color-coordinated in soft peach with blue or green accents, and the marble bathrooms have towel warmers and stretch tubs. All the spotless rooms can be recommended, but if it is a view of Sacré Coeur you are after or a balcony, those rooms are on the fifth floor. On the ground level there is a handicapped room with a proper shower and seat, plus plenty of maneuvering room for a wheelchair. In the morning, a hot buffet breakfast, including bacon and eggs with potatoes, is served in a stone room brightened by a bouquet of sunflowers atop yellow-and-blue tablecloths. The reception staff, headed by Mounira and Nadege, complements the excellent quality of the hotel in every way.

FACILITIES AND SERVICES: Air-conditioning, direct-dial phone, elevator (to most floors), hair dryer, 1 handicapped-accessible room, laundry service, minibar, TV with international reception, room safe (no charge)

NEAREST TOURIST ATTRACTIONS (RIGHT BANK): Opéra, Louvre, Tuileries Gardens, Palais Royal, shopping

HÔTEL MANSART ★★★ ($, 8)
5, rue des Capucines, at place Vendôme, 75001
Métro: Opéra, Madeleine
57 rooms, all with shower or bath and toilet

TELEPHONE
01-42-61-50-28
FAX
01-49-27-97-44
EMAIL
hotelmansart@wanadoo.fr
INTERNET
www.esprit-de-france.com
CREDIT CARDS
AE, DC, MC, V
RATES
1–2 persons 110–185€, deluxe 235–298€; extra bed 18€; lower rates depending on season and availability; *taxe de séjour* included
BREAKFAST
Buffet or Continental in room 11€ per person
ENGLISH SPOKEN
Yes

If staying at the Ritz appeals except for the price (upwards of $750 per night for a double, breakfast extra), consider staying at Hôtel Mansart, named after the architect of Louis XIV, who designed the place Vendôme, Versailles, and the dome on Les Invalides. The hotel used to be the Hôtel Calais, a rambling wreck totally devoid of style, with labyrinth halls, creaking floors, and turn-of-the-century plumbing. Not anymore! What a stunning transformation the owners have achieved.

By not making any structural changes other than adding spectacular new bathrooms, the owners kept the spirit of the building intact. You will still find long hallways, high ceilings, marble fireplaces, stained-glass windows, well-loved period furnishings, and in some cases, slightly sloping floors. No two rooms are alike, but all reflect the same high level of style and good taste. Some favorites include No. 603, a top-floor choice done in blue and gray with a mirrored armoire, marble bedside tables, and a tile bathroom with double sinks. Room 400 is a large, twin-bedded room with good work space, plenty of light, and a bathroom large enough to accommodate a long tub and a marble-top table. Number 505, a sunny, rear room with twin beds, has a separate stall shower in addition to a stretch-out bathtub that is perfect for luxurious bubble baths. Rooms 506, 507, and 508 have their own terraces. Number 502, facing the street, is enormous, with a fireplace, built-in armoire, large round table with chairs, and a writing desk. A showcase room is No. 204, overlooking place Vendôme. This room is done in royal blue with gold carpeting, and its high ceilings, collectable furniture, and lovely oil painting over the marble dresser are reminiscent of hotels on the Grand Tour of Europe that our grandmothers stayed in decades ago. A similar room is No. 204, with a corner view to the place Vendôme. It has a half-canopied king-size bed, a round table that could easily seat six, and a large leather-top desk. You must go up a few steps to the bathroom and dressing area, but the bathroom, lighted by three windows, has a separate stall shower and a long tub.

The stark simplicity of the lobby is created by an interesting mixture of geometric wall designs based on the gardens at Versailles. Antique chairs and love seats and tiny glowing ceiling lights complete the room by elegantly mixing a touch of contemporary with the past. A Continental breakfast is served in a formal room with arched stained-glass windows and suede-cloth-covered chairs placed around tables draped with damask cloths. Everything works together throughout this impressive hotel and adds up to a smart address in a fine location.

Four other hotels are under the same ownership: Hôtels Brighton, de la Place du Louvre, Parc Saint-Séverin, and d'Orsay (see pages 67, 69, 129, and 184).

FACILITIES AND SERVICES: Air-conditioning in some rooms, bar, direct-dial phone, elevator (to most floors), hair dryer, Internet in lobby, minibar, TV with international reception, room safe (no charge)

NEAREST TOURIST ATTRACTIONS (RIGHT BANK): Opéra, place Vendôme, place de la Madeleine, place de la Concorde, Tuileries Gardens, Louvre, shopping

HÔTEL MOLIÈRE ★★★ (26)
21, rue Molière, 75001
Métro: Palais Royal–Musée du Louvre, Pyramides
32 rooms, all with shower or bath and toilet

TELEPHONE
01-42-96-22-01
FAX
01-42-60-48-68
EMAIL
molière@gaif.fr
INTERNET
www.hotel-moliere.fr
CREDIT CARDS
AE, DC, MC, V
RATES
Single 125€, double 145–175€,
triple 175€, apartment 275€;
extra bed 16€; lower rates in off-
season on request; *taxe de séjour*
included
BREAKFAST
Buffet 12€ per person
ENGLISH SPOKEN
Yes

The Molière is a sedate, midcity choice. The faux-finished, pillared lobby has azure blue velvet armchairs and an Art Nouveau beaded lamp on the reception desk. Toward the back is another sitting area with a red sofa and an assortment of magazines and daily newspapers, and just beyond is the breakfast room with glass-top tables and metal chairs, overlooking a small interior garden. The mirrored elevator has a bust of Molière and a trompe l'oeil painting of his books.

The rooms, which are above average in size and layout, are tastefully done in a rather formal French style. The amount of living space is exceptional; the views, even along the back, are pleasant; and the location puts guests within walking distance of many of the tourist "musts" of Paris. If you are looking for space, book No. 56, a three-room suite with two bedrooms and a sitting room done in soft mauve. The sitting room offers a comfortable sofa, two armchairs, and a desk. The double bedroom has a wonderful brass bed with matching dressing table, marble bedside tables, a walk-in closet with wide shelves and double hanging space, and a tango-size bathroom. Finally, there is a small single bedroom that would be perfect for a child. Similar in size and layout is No. 67, on the top floor with views of surrounding rooftops. Less grand, but no less comfortable, is No. 41, a double with a new bathroom that has a magnifying mirror, large tub, and sink space. The bedroom, with a brass bed and a mirrored armoire, has good living space. Room 42, also with a new bathroom, is another good choice if you want twin beds. Number 43 is a pleasant single with a large working desk and a stall shower.

FACILITIES AND SERVICES: Air-conditioning, bar, direct-dial phone, elevator (to most floors), hair dryer, Internet in lobby, laundry service, minibar, TV with international reception, room safe (no charge)

NEAREST TOURIST ATTRACTIONS (RIGHT BANK): Louvre, Tuileries Gardens, Palais Royal, shopping, Opéra

HÔTEL THÉRÈSE ★★★ (19)
5–7, rue Thérèse, 75001
Métro: Palais Royal–Musée du Louvre
43 rooms, all with shower or bath and toilet

Hôtel Thérèse occupies a perfect location in the heart of the elegant Right Bank, close to the Louvre, Palais Royal, and shopping along rue St. Honoré. When Sylvie de Lattre (who also owns Hôtel Verneuil, see page 199) purchased it, she spent months renovating it from top to bottom in her unique and graceful style. Now gleaming from her remarkable effort, it is a success by all accounts and provides a sleek, contemporary address for the discerning traveler. The small downstairs bar and library is furnished in brown leather, dark burgundy accented with a flourish of eggplant, indirect lighting, and potted orchids. The sitting room, imaginatively painted in deep mustard, is furnished with comfortable armchairs and displays pieces from her interesting art collection. The stairway to the sixth floor is used as exhibition space for her collection of 1890 photographs of Roman statues. The breakfast room serves as the focal point for her collection of Chinese tea caddies. Seating is on brown wicker chairs with white cushions secured with a big bow in back. All of the rooms are exceptional and again demonstrate her remarkable use of colors: plum with yellow, soft green with vanilla and chocolate. The deluxe and superior rooms are naturally the most popular because they offer more living space, either twins or king-size beds, spacious marble bathrooms with separate stall showers, and often a window. Lower rates in August and frequent promotions on the Website keep the demand for Hôtel Thérèse high.

FACILITIES AND SERVICES: Air-conditioning, bar, conference room, direct-dial phone, elevator (to most floors), hair dryer, Internet in lobby, laundry service, robes in deluxe rooms, TV with international reception, room safe (no charge)

NEAREST TOURIST ATTRACTIONS (RIGHT BANK): Palais Royal, Louvre, Tuileries Gardens, Opéra, shopping

LE RELAIS DU LOUVRE ★★★ (52)
19, rue des Prêtres St-Germain-l'Auxerrois, 75001
Métro: Louvre-Rivoli, Pont-Neuf
20 rooms, all with shower or bath and toilet

Just down the street from the Hôtel de la Place du Louvre (see page 69) is Le Relais du Louvre, another top three-star pick hard by the Musée du Louvre. The small

TELEPHONE
01-42-96-10-01

FAX
01-42-96-15-22

EMAIL
hoteltherese@wanadoo.fr

INTERNET
www.hoteltherese.com

CREDIT CARDS
AE, DC, MC, V

RATES
Single or double standard 130€, double superior 170€, double deluxe 200€, junior suite 275€; extra bed 28€; *taxe de séjour* included

BREAKFAST
Buffet 15€

ENGLISH SPOKEN
Yes

TELEPHONE
01-40-41-96-42

FAX
01-40-41-96-44

INTERNET
www.relaisdulouvre.com

CREDIT CARDS
AE, DC, MC, V

RATES
Single 105€, double 138–
158€, superior double 195€,
junior suite 212–265€,
apartment 395€; extra bed
25€; parking 15€ per day; *taxe
de séjour* included

BREAKFAST
Continental in room only 10€
per person

ENGLISH SPOKEN
Yes

lobby, draped in coral-colored linen, offers comfortable seating. A massive fresh floral spray sitting atop an antique bureau adds color. The rooms live up to the elegant promise of the lobby. All are attractively furnished with designer fabrics and have good closet space, full-length mirrors, and marble bathrooms with fluffy towels. Number 35, a standard twin-bedded room, offers an armchair covered in a quilted pink hydrangea pattern and a writing desk overlooking the church across the street. Appealing prints of Victorian ladies hang on the walls. If you need a little more space, consider the junior suites: Nos. 51 and 52. Number 51 is an L-shaped room on the back with a walnut chest of drawers, sofa, armchair, and a large bathroom with a skylight. Number 52 has a direct view of the gargoyles on the St-Germain-l'Auxerrois Church. If there are four in your group, request rooms 24 and 25, which connect and can be joined to form a nice family suite. Even larger is the apartment occupying the entire sixth floor. Aside from a beautiful, fully equipped kitchen complete with dishwasher, microwave, refrigerator, and separate freezer, the apartment has two television sets, a tape player, a comfortable living area with two sofas, and a wall of windows that let in light all day long. The singles are small and on the back, but the interior view is not depressing. An added bonus are Brigitte and Marie, the friendly, English-speaking staff.

FACILITIES AND SERVICES: Air-conditioning, direct-dial phone, hair dryer, elevator, laundry service, minibar, TV with international reception, room safe (no charge)

NEAREST TOURIST ATTRACTIONS (RIGHT BANK): Louvre, Tuileries Gardens, Seine, Île de la Cité, St-Michel

Second Arrondissement

The second arrondissement is known as the area of finance (around the stock exchange, or Bourse), the press, and the rag trade (around place du Caire). It makes up for its small size with the beautiful Victorian shopping passages and the boutiques around place des Victoires. The second is within walking distance to the Marais, Centre Georges Pompidou (Beaubourg), the Palais Royal, and the Louvre Museum. The southern half around rue Montorgueil has some of the best food markets and shops in Paris. The seedy northern section around rue d'Aboukir should definitely be avoided, and so should rue St-Denis, home of Paris hookers and other assorted netherworld characters.

RIGHT BANK
Bourse
passages
place des Victoires
rue Montorgueil shopping
  street

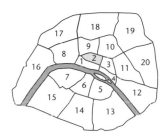

HOTELS IN THE SECOND ARRONDISSEMENT
(see map page 62)

Golden Opéra de Noailles ★★★★ ($)	79
Hôtel Baudelaire Opéra ★★★	80
Hôtel Vivienne ★★	81
Tiquetonne Hôtel ★ (¢)	82

OTHER OPTIONS
Apartment Rental Agencies

Paris Appartements Services	304

($) indicates a Big Splurge; (¢) indicates a Cheap Sleep

GOLDEN OPÉRA DE NOAILLES ★★★★ ($, 5)
9, rue de la Michodière, 75002
Métro: Opéra, Quatre-Septembre
61 rooms, all with shower or bath and toilet

If you are allergic to gilt and cherubs, you will appreciate this postmodern hotel, which owner Martine Falck has turned into a smart, zen-inspired site with different bold color schemes of gray, black, chocolate brown, and midnight blue distinguishing each floor. To make sure that all aspects of the hotel were in their proper alignment in the universe, three different artists and mediums were consulted, along with a Feng Shui expert. The pleasing results are evident to anyone. The street entrance leads into a wide-spaced reception room with designer chairs

TELEPHONE
01-47-42-92-90; toll-free in the U.S. 800-344-1212 (Golden Tulip Hotels)

FAX
01-49-24-92-71

EMAIL
goldentulip.denoailles@ wanadoo.fr

INTERNET
www.hoteldenoailles.com

CREDIT CARDS
AE, DC, MC, V

RATES
Single 190€, double 200€, superior room 225€, suites 260€; ask about promotional rates; *taxe de séjour* included

BREAKFAST
Buffet 15€ per person

ENGLISH SPOKEN
Yes

and tables overlooking a full bar and an atrium garden. To one side, a massive marble table with a dramatic floral display is flanked by two wrought-iron sculptures that represent good luck for Feng Shui followers.

All sixty-one rooms and suites can be recommended, from the twelve rooms that open onto their own garden to the smart suites to the smallest room. Rooms have all the twenty-first-century perks: halogen lighting, built-ins, separate Internet phone jacks, adequate desk space, smart bathrooms, room service, and a Shiatsu masseuse on call. Room 305, with a wooden backdrop behind the bed and a state-of-the-art bathroom, is let as a standard double. It has an inside view but is light and very pleasant. For more space, reserve No. 210, a superior double. It doesn't have as much seating space as some others, but it has a large bathroom with double sinks and a separate enclosed toilet. The fifth and sixth floors are newly revamped with brown leather–lined walls. The rooms are large on these floors and have a distinctly masculine feel. Most have light and feature all new bathrooms with Japanese-style opaque sliding doors dividing the bathroom and bedroom. Added bonuses for many are the free sauna and workout gym, the exclusive nonsmoking rooms in three garden rooms and the entire fifth and sixth floors, and the attractive promotional rates on the weekend and in low season.

FACILITIES AND SERVICES: Air-conditioning, bar, conference room, direct-dial phone, elevator, gym and sauna, hair dryer, laundry service, minibar, Shiatsu masseuse on call, TV with international reception, room service, room safe (no charge), some nonsmoking rooms

NEAREST TOURIST ATTRACTIONS (RIGHT BANK): Opéra, shopping at Galeries Lafayette and Au Printemps, Palais Royal, Louvre

HÔTEL BAUDELAIRE OPÉRA ★★★ (10)
61, rue Ste-Anne, 75002
Metro: Quatre-Septembre, Pyramides
29 rooms, all with shower or bath and toilet

TELEPHONE
01-42-97-50-62

FAX
01-42-86-85-85

EMAIL
hotel@noos.fr

INTERNET
www.paris-hotel.net

CREDIT CARDS
AE, DC, MC, V

The area around this hotel has an interesting history. When Cardinal Richelieu bought the Palais Royal, he developed the area around it, including the rue Ste-Anne. The Hôtel Baudelaire Opéra began as a shop, then became a *hôtel particuliere* (private town home). It is named after Baudelaire, the writer, who lived here in 1854 and wrote letters to his mother pleading, "Do not refuse me both your money and your company at the same time." The hotel now welcomes your visit and asks a fair price for it. It is owned by a friendly couple that bought it a few years ago and has spent considerable time and money on improvements, which on the whole have been very successful. However, despite several rooms with balcony views of the old Bibliothèque Nationale, attractive color-coordinated fabrics, and new beds and carpets, the tightly fitted rooms will never be anything but small. Yet they are a good three-star value if you are traveling light and plan to spend little time in your hotel room.

FACILITIES AND SERVICES: Direct-dial phone, elevator, hair dryer, minibar, TV with international reception, some trouser presses, room safe (no charge)

NEAREST TOURIST ATTRACTIONS (RIGHT BANK): Opéra, Palais Royal, place des Victoires, shopping

RATES
Single 120€, double 140–150€, duplex for 2–3 people 180€; *taxe de séjour* 0.86€ per person, per day

BREAKFAST
Continental 7.50€ per person

ENGLISH SPOKEN
Yes

HÔTEL VIVIENNE ★★ (2)
40, rue Vivienne, 75002
Métro: Richelieu-Drouot, Grands Boulevards
45 rooms, 30 with toilet, all with shower or bath

The picture on the reception desk was taken at the hotel in 1917. The little girl in the photo was born in this hotel, which her parents owned along with a restaurant next door. The present owner, Claudine Haycraft, bought the hotel from the family twenty-eight years ago. Since then, she has slowly redone it, making it a popular budget destination in this part of Paris. She recently bought the noisy bar next door and was able to expand the reception and sitting areas. The rooms are kept spotlessly clean by a team of career housekeepers. Room decor falls into the typical two-star category: mix-and-match furniture, some chenille here and there, and industrial-strength carpeting. Ten rooms have balconies. New beds throughout and remodeled bathrooms in most rooms have improved things immeasurably. Best rooms in the house? I think No. 14, which faces the street and is large enough to feel at home in for more than overnight; No. 6, a double on the street with two windows opening onto a balcony; and No. 3, in bright orange, yellow, blue, and aqua, also with a balcony, new tiled bathroom, and sleeping space for four.

FACILITIES AND SERVICES: Direct-dial phone, elevator (to most floors), hair dryer, TV with international reception, office safe (no charge)

NEAREST TOURIST ATTRACTIONS (RIGHT BANK): Bourse, Palais Royal, Opéra

TELEPHONE
01-42-33-13-26

FAX
01-40-41-98-19

EMAIL
paris@hotel-vivienne.com

CREDIT CARDS
MC, V

RATES
Single 55–65€, double 70–90€; extra bed is 30 percent of room rate; children under 10 are free; *taxe de séjour* 0.65€ per person, per day

BREAKFAST
Continental 6€ per person

ENGLISH SPOKEN
Yes

TIQUETONNE HÔTEL ★ (¢, 34)
6, rue Tiquetonne, 75002
Métro: Étienne-Marcel; RER Châtelet–Les Halles
46 rooms, 30 with shower and toilet, no bathtubs

TELEPHONE
01-42-36-94-58
FAX
01-42-36-02-94
CREDIT CARDS
MC, V
RATES
Single 30–42€, double 50€
(double beds only); shower
4.57€; hall shower 5€; *taxe de
séjour* included
BREAKFAST
Continental 7€ per person (no
croissants)
ENGLISH SPOKEN
Yes

Anyone looking for an old-fashioned, budget-minded family hotel that offers basic, clean rooms in central Paris will hit pay dirt here. The vintage hotel has been run for more than half a century by Mme. Sirvain, who is accompanied by her niece Marie-Jo, and the hotel dog, Ganish, a strapping German shepherd who surveys the scene from a command post in the lobby.

All the doubles have showers, but only some singles do, and with limited success. For example, in No. 34, you enter the pink-papered room through the bathroom, red curtains hang at the windows, and furniture consists of a bed and a hard chair . . . but it is clean and sunny. There is nothing wrong with No. 20, provided you can live in a room with an orange chenille bedspread, red curtains, and floral wallpaper in peach, pink, and green. Furnishings include a small table with a laminated top displaying sailing ships and two hard chairs. The bathroom has a shelf over the sink and a curtain shielding the enclosed tile shower. Number 30, an inside double with a shower and toilet, demonstrates an attempt to color coordinate the aqua-blue chenille spread with the blue trim on the curtains.

Rock-bottom prices insure popularity in a part of Paris that is animated, active, and very much alive almost around the clock. So book early, but don't plan on a room in August or during the week between Christmas and New Year's, when the family shuts the hotel and goes on their own vacation.

FACILITIES AND SERVICES: Elevator, reception open 7:30 A.M.–midnight

NEAREST TOURIST ATTRACTIONS (RIGHT BANK): Les Halles & Forum des Halles, Centre Georges Pompidou (Beaubourg), rue Montorgueil (one of the most popular shopping streets in Paris)

Third Arrondissement

This area includes the northern parts of the revitalized Marais, a thirteenth-century swampland that later became the residential suburb of the French nobility. Later still it fell from favor, and until it was rescued by Minister of Culture André Malraux in the 1960s, it was the worst slum in Paris. The magnificent seventeenth-century *hôtels particulieres* (private mansions) have been turned into museums, the most famous of which is the Musée National Picasso. The Musée des Arts et Métiers, occupying the medieval abbey of St-Martin-des-Champs, has a fascinating collection of industrial and scientific objects displayed on the abbey's altars, apses, and choir stalls. The Musée Cognacq-Jay showcases the mostly French Rococo collection of Ernest Cognacq, founder of La Samaritaine department store, and his wife, Louise Jay.

RIGHT BANK
French National Archives
Marais
Musée Carnavalet (City of Paris Museum)
Musée Cognacq-Jay
Musée des Arts et Métiers
Musée National Picasso (Hôtel Salé)

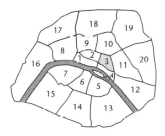

HOTELS IN THE THIRD ARRONDISSEMENT

Austin's Arts et Métiers Hôtel ★★★	**86**
Hôtel des Chevaliers ★★★	**86**
Hôtel du Séjour (NO STARS, ¢)	**87**
Paris-France Hôtel ★★	**88**
Tulip Inn Little Place ★★★	**88**

OTHER OPTIONS
Apartment Rental Agencies
Kudeta Home	**302**

(¢) indicates a Cheap Sleep

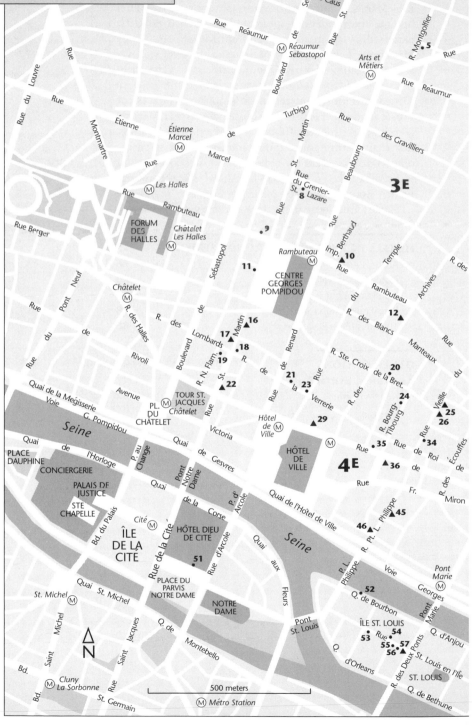

Third and Fourth Arrondissements

3E

4E

Strasbourg St. Denis Ⓜ

Boulevard

Rue

1

R. Sal. de Caus

Martin

Sebastopol

de

St.

Rue

R. Montgolfier

5

Rue

Rue

Réaumur

de

Réaumur Sebastopol Ⓜ

Rue

Rue Réaumur

Boulevard

Arts et Métiers Ⓜ

Rue

des Gravilliers

Rue du Louvre

Rue

Rue

Montmartre

Étienne

Étienne Marcel

de

Turbigo

Rue

Beaubourg

R. des

Marcel

Rue

Marcel Ⓜ

Martin

St.

Les Halles Ⓜ

Rambuteau

Rue du Grenier-St. Lazare

8

Rue

Temple

Rue Berger

FORUM DES HALLES

Châtelet Les Halles Ⓜ

9

Imp. Berthaud

10

Rue

du

Archives

R. des

11

Rambuteau Ⓜ

Rambuteau

Pont Neuf

Châtelet

Sebastopol

CENTRE GEORGES POMPIDOU

R. des Blancs

12

Manteaux

Rue

du

Rue

Châtelet Ⓜ

R. des Halles

R. des

de

16

Martin

20

Rue

de

Lombards

17

18

Renard

R. Ste. Croix de la Bret.

Rivoli

Avenue

Boulevard

R. N. Flam.

19

R.

de

24

Rue

Quai de la Mégisserie

Voie

G. Pompidou

PL. DU CHÂTELET

TOUR ST. JACQUES Châtelet

St.

22

21

23

la

Verrerie

R. Bourg-Tibourg

25

26

Vieille

Rue

des Écouffes

de

Seine

Quai

de

l'Horloge

P. au Change

Victoria

Hôtel de Ville Ⓜ

29

35

34

Rue

PLACE DAUPHINE

CONCIERGERIE

Quai de Gesvres

HÔTEL DE VILLE

Rue

de Roi

R. des

PALAIS DE JUSTICE

Pont Notre Dame

HÔTEL DE VILLE

36

de

Fr.

R. des

Miron

STE CHAPELLE

Bd. du Palais

Cité Ⓜ

de la Corse

P. d' Arcole

Quai de l'Hôtel de Ville

Rue

ÎLE DE LA CITÉ

HÔTEL DIEU DE CITÉ

Rue de la Cité

Rue d'Arcole

Quai

aux

Seine

R. Pt. L. Philippe

45

46

Quai St. Michel

St. Michel

51

PLACE DU PARVIS NOTRE DAME

Fleurs

P. L. Philippe

Pont Marie

Voie

Pont Marie

St. Michel

Q. de

NOTRE DAME

Pont St. Louis

52

Q. de Bourbon

Q. d'Anjou

△ N

Saint Jacques

Q. de Montebello

Pont St. Louis

Q.

ÎLE ST. LOUIS

54

53

Rue

55

57

56

St. Louis en l'île

Cluny La Sorbonne Ⓜ

Rue

Saint Jacques

St. Germain

d'Orleans

R. des Deux Ponts

ST. LOUIS

Q. de Bethune

Bd.

Saint

500 meters

Ⓜ Métro Station

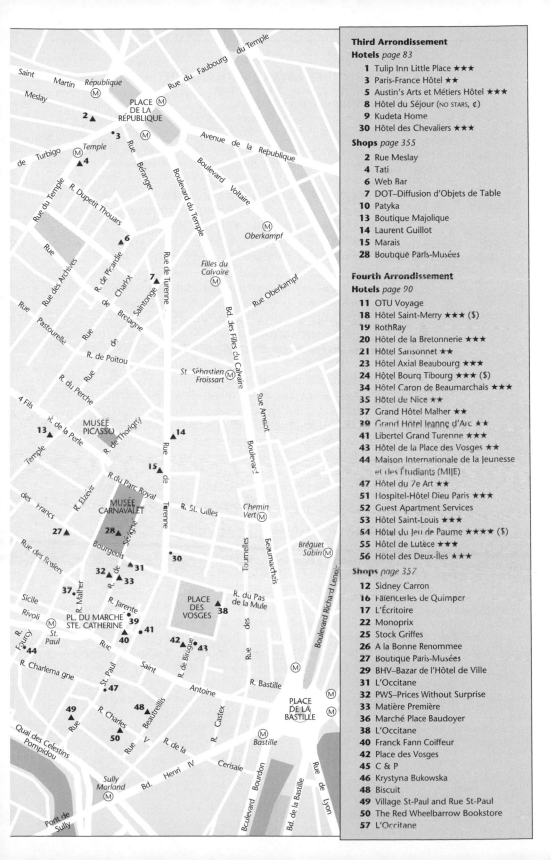

Third Arrondissement

Hotels *page 83*

1 Tulip Inn Little Place ★★★
3 Paris-France Hôtel ★★
5 Austin's Arts et Métiers Hôtel ★★★
8 Hôtel du Séjour (NO STARS, ¢)
9 Kudeta Home
30 Hôtel des Chevaliers ★★★

Shops *page 355*

2 Rue Meslay
4 Tati
6 Web Bar
7 DOT–Diffusion d'Objets de Table
10 Patyka
13 Boutique Majolique
14 Laurent Guillot
15 Marais
28 Boutique Paris-Musées

Fourth Arrondissement

Hotels *page 90*

11 OTU Voyage
18 Hôtel Saint-Merry ★★★ ($)
19 RothRay
20 Hôtel de la Bretonnerie ★★★
21 Hôtel Sansonnet ★★
23 Hôtel Axial Beaubourg ★★★
24 Hôtel Bourg Tibourg ★★★ ($)
34 Hôtel Caron de Beaumarchais ★★★
35 Hôtel de Nice ★★
37 Grand Hôtel Malher ★★
39 Grand Hôtel Jeanne d'Arc ★★
41 Libertel Grand Turenne ★★★
43 Hôtel de la Place des Vosges ★★
44 Maison Internationale de la Jeunesse et des Étudiants (MIJE)
47 Hôtel du 7e Art ★★
51 Hospitel-Hôtel Dieu Paris ★★★
52 Guest Apartment Services
53 Hôtel Saint-Louis ★★★
54 Hôtel du Jeu de Paume ★★★★ ($)
55 Hôtel de Lutèce ★★★
56 Hôtel des Deux-Îles ★★★

Shops *page 357*

12 Sidney Carron
16 Faïenceries de Quimper
17 L'Écritoire
22 Monoprix
25 Stock Griffes
26 A la Bonne Renommee
27 Boutique Paris-Musées
29 BHV–Bazar de l'Hôtel de Ville
31 L'Occitane
32 PWS–Prices Without Surprise
33 Matière Première
36 Marché Place Baudoyer
38 L'Occitane
40 Franck Fann Coiffeur
42 Place des Vosges
45 C & P
46 Krystyna Bukowska
48 Biscuit
49 Village St-Paul and Rue St-Paul
50 The Red Wheelbarrow Bookstore
57 L'Occitane

AUSTIN'S ARTS ET MÉTIERS HÔTEL ★★★ (5)
6, rue Montgolfier, 75003
Métro: Arts et Métiers

29 rooms, all with shower or bath and toilet

TELEPHONE
01-42-77-17-61
FAX
01-42-77-55-43
EMAIL
austins.amhotel@wanadoo.fr
CREDIT CARDS
AE, DC, MC, V
RATES
Single 92€, double 120€; *taxe de séjour* included
BREAKFAST
Buffet downstairs or Continental in room 7€ per person
ENGLISH SPOKEN
Yes

For a three-star family-owned hotel with more than its share of charm and facilities, this place is great. If it were in a more centrally located, touristy area, it would cost half again as much. However, this area is rapidly becoming gentrified and is considered very "in" with many Parisians. A spacious living room done in warm gold and deep brown is a welcoming beginning. The twenty-nine soundproofed rooms have every comfort. Faux finishing and fabric-covered walls in the bedrooms form the backdrop for the cream-colored furnishings, with either red or yellow and blue coordinated spreads and curtains. Bathrooms are nice, especially those with a glass-enclosed shower stall. The best rooms face front; those along the back might be a bit calmer, but the tradeoff is a view of peeling buildings and metal grates.

Also under the same ownership is Austin's Saint-Lazare, a three-star hotel on rue d'Amsterdam, across from Gare St-Lazare. While the hotel is nice, the neighborhood is not recommended, unless you want to be in the shadow of one of Paris's largest rail stations.

FACILITIES AND SERVICES: Direct-dial phone, elevator, hair dryer, TV with international reception, office safe (no charge)

NEAREST TOURIST ATTRACTIONS (RIGHT BANK): Musée des Arts et Métiers, Centre Georges Pompidou (Beaubourg)

HÔTEL DES CHEVALIERS ★★★ (30)
30, rue de Turenne, 75003
Métro: Chemin-Vert

24 rooms, all with shower or bath and toilet

TELEPHONE
01-42-72-73-47
FAX
01-42-72-54-10
EMAIL
info@hoteldeschevaliers.com
INTERNET
www.parishotels.com
CREDIT CARDS
MC, V
RATES
1–2 persons 135–140€, triple 165€; *taxe de séjour* included
BREAKFAST
Continental 9€ per person
ENGLISH SPOKEN
Yes

The location near the Picasso Museum and on the edge of the vibrant Marais puts the Hôtel des Chevaliers on the list of desirable, good-value sleeps in Paris. A yellow fabric-lined sitting room has a small bar, where you can read an assortment of international newspapers, and a piano, which guests are invited to play. The smartly done rooms are not large, but they are soundproofed by double-paned windows and brightened by attractive fabrics and fresh flowers. Attention to detail is evident throughout, from welcome chocolates and complimentary umbrellas to a basket of nice toiletries in each bath. I think the rooms on the third and fourth floors are preferable. Those on the fifth floor require climbing one flight of stairs, and the rooms, while still appealing for many, are even tighter, given the configuration of the sloping roof lines. The five facing the inner courtyard are the least pleasant. The only other drawback I found was the location of the room safes—on the floor in either the closet or the bathroom, forcing one into a prone position to gain access. Sixteenth-century exposed supports line the stairway leading to the downstairs breakfast room, fashioned from an old *cave* (cellar), with the original water well still in one corner. Nicely upholstered chairs are placed around well-lit tables, where breakfast is served on individual trays. Management, headed by owner Mme. Truffaut, is very outgoing and friendly, and repeat guests are many.

FACILITIES AND SERVICES: Bar, direct-dial phone, hair dryer, elevator (to most floors), laundry service, minibar, TV with international reception, room safe (no charge)

NEAREST TOURIST ATTRACTIONS (RIGHT BANK): Marais, place des Vosges, Musée National Picasso, Bastille, Opéra Bastille

HÔTEL DU SÉJOUR (NO STARS, ¢, 8)
36, rue du Grenier-St-Lazare, 75003
Métro: Rambuteau, Étienne-Marcel

20 rooms, 8 with shower and toilet, 4 with shower only

If the bottom line is saving money, then visitors who do not mind a theatrically run-down, five-story walk-up will definitely be interested in this clean Cheap Sleep for their Paris sojourn. The building has been a hotel for three hundred years and is, and probably always will be, a quantum leap from modern. You enter from the street and walk up steps with a black rubber strip anchoring the laminated woodlike covering. Jean and Maria, the owners for over eight years, have been making improvements on a cautious basis, starting with new mattresses, hall toilets, and some paint. In the past year or so, they added several showers and double windows. Singles or pairs can snooze in No. 20, a top-floor perch with a sink. The floor is uneven, but there is plenty of light. Duos can go for Nos. 12 or 13; No. 12 has a bare floor. Room 10 is a sunny double facing out with a pink chenille–draped bed. If there are two of you, and you each plan on bathing, definitely go for a room like No. 10 or 15, each of which has its own shower, toilet, and sink. Though showerless rooms are cheaper at first glance, once you

TELEPHONE & FAX
01-48-87-40-36

CREDIT CARDS
None, cash only

RATES
Single 30€, double 42–55€; shower 4€; *taxe de séjour* included

BREAKFAST
Not served

ENGLISH SPOKEN
Limited

add in the extra cost for the shared hall showers, you will end up spending more.

FACILITIES AND SERVICES: None

NEAREST TOURIST ATTRACTIONS (RIGHT BANK): Centre Georges Pompidou (Beaubourg), Musée des Arts et Métiers

PARIS-FRANCE HÔTEL ★★ (3)
72, rue de Turbigo, 75003
Métro: Temple, République
46 rooms, all with shower or bath and toilet

<!-- sidebar -->
TELEPHONE
01-42-78-00-04
FAX
01-42-71-99-43
INTERNET
www.paris-france-hotel.com
CREDIT CARDS
MC, V
RATES
Single 70€, double 75–86€, triple 109€; *taxe de séjour* included
BREAKFAST
Continental 5€ per person
ENGLISH SPOKEN
Yes

This hotel opened its doors in 1910, marking the end of the Belle Epoque in Paris. All that remains today of its gilded past are the original tiles on the main ground floor. As anyone on a budget knows, trying to find a decent two-star hotel in Paris is no easy task, and now more than ever, it requires leaving tourist central to find something. While hardly in the thick of things, this neighborhood does have some appeal. Thrifty shoppers will be happy to know there is a Monoprix and a small branch of Tati just up the street. Also within walking distance are the Musée des Arts et Métiers, two métro stops, and two excellent bus lines (Nos. 80 and 84) for further excursions. The rooms have that decor-by-Kmart look, televisions are pitched on the ceiling, the chairs are hard, and management has not invested in shower curtains. However, the rooms are clean, have enough space for you and some luggage, and won't jar your senses with wild, mismatched colors and patterns. Some rooms on the sixth through eighth floors have views of the Church of Ste-Elisabeth across the street, but no matter your room, you will hear her chimes. A Continental breakfast is served cafeteria-style downstairs or in your room for the same price.

FACILITIES AND SERVICES: Direct-dial phone, elevator (to most floors), hair dryer, Internet in lobby, TV with international reception, room safe (no charge)

NEAREST TOURIST ATTRACTIONS (RIGHT BANK): Musée des Arts et Métiers

TULIP INN LITTLE PLACE ★★★ (1)
4, rue Salomon de Caus, 75003
Métro: Réaumur-Sébastopol, Strasbourg–St-Denis
57 rooms, all with shower or bath and toilet

<!-- sidebar -->
TELEPHONE
01-42-72-08-15; toll-free in U.S. 800-344-1212 (Golden Tulip Hotels)
FAX
01-42-72-45-81

Overlooking the green Arts et Métiers Square, this hotel has an impressive facade with carved stones, scrolled balconies, and marble columns that is reminiscent of the roaring twenties. Inside, fabric-covered walls and drapes frame the entrance to the restaurant, where guests admire the lovely original stained-glass windows and floral-patterned ceiling. The comfortable sitting room is furnished with back-to-back sofas and barrel armchairs, and to one side, a mosaic-tile bar overlooks a well-tended garden. The fifty-seven rooms have built-ins that allow for more space, and they are decorated in blends of orange, warm mustard, and green. They have all the three-star necessities, including modems and bathrooms with toiletries and a lighted magnifying mirror, but nothing about them says Paris. Best bets are those on the top floor with a balcony, with the exception of No. 62 with its dizzying mix of swirled and striped wallpaper. The hotel restaurant serves lunch from Monday to Friday, and dinner Monday to Thursday, but consider eating here only if you are desperate.

FACILITIES AND SERVICES: Air-conditioning, bar, direct-dial phone, elevator, hair dryer, laundry service, minibar, TV with international reception and pay-for-view movies, office safe (no charge)

NEAREST TOURIST ATTRACTIONS (RIGHT BANK): Centre Georges Pompidou (Beaubourg), Musée des Arts et Métiers

EMAIL
LittlePlaceHotel@compuserve.com

INTERNET
www.hotelbook.com/
goldentulip

CREDIT CARDS
AE, DC, MC, V

RATES
Single 140€, double 160€, triple 180€; *taxe de séjour* included

BREAKFAST
Buffet 12€ per person

ENGLISH SPOKEN
Yes

Fourth Arrondissement

RIGHT BANK
Centre Georges Pompidou
(Beaubourg)
continuation of the Marais
Hôtel-de-Ville (City Hall)
Île St-Louis
Maison de Victor Hugo
Notre Dame Cathedral on Île
de la Cité
place des Vosges
rue des Rosiers (Jewish Quarter)
Village St-Paul antiques dealers

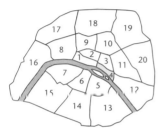

The fourth arrondissement stretches from the Marais through the ancient Jewish Quarter on the rue des Rosiers to the Île St-Louis in the middle of the Seine. It is an area perfectly suited to exploring on foot, lending itself to discovery at almost every turn. Its immense charm arises from a wonderful mixture of past and present. Notre Dame Cathedral, the geographical and spiritual heart of France, sits majestically on the Île de la Cité. In front of the cathedral is a bronze plaque (Kilometer Zéro) from which all distances in France are measured. Legend has it that if you stand on the plaque, make a wish, and twirl on your heel, your wish will come true.

Place des Vosges, with its historic pink-brick town houses set above wide arcade walkways, is the oldest square in Paris and one of the most beautiful. Victor Hugo resided here at No. 6. Not too far away is the architecturally controversial modern art museum, the Centre Georges Pompidou (also known as the Beaubourg), which logs more visitors each year than the Eiffel Tower.

L'Île St-Louis is one of the most desirable, and admittedly expensive, places to reside in Paris. The island is a capsule of all that is Parisian, with interesting shops, art galleries, boutiques, Baroque mansions, lines for the famous Berthillon ice cream, and lovely views along the romantic quais. To capture the enchantment of Paris, stay on Île St-Louis. But be forewarned: you may never want to leave! Many people like being on the island because they are only steps away from Notre Dame Cathedral, Ste-Chapelle, and the Conciergerie; within walking distance of the Latin Quarter, St-Germain-des-Prés, the Marais; and close to all the excitement and nightlife around the Bastille Opéra. Only a few feel isolated and frustrated by its narrow streets, weekend crowds, and lack of easy parking. Personally, I love it, but I am biased because this is where I lived the first year I spent in Paris.

HOTELS IN THE FOURTH ARRONDISSEMENT
(see map page 84)

Grand Hôtel Jeanne d'Arc ★★	**92**
Grand Hôtel Malher ★★	**92**
Hospitel-Hôtel Dieu Paris ★★★	**93**
Hôtel Axial Beaubourg ★★★	**94**
Hôtel Bourg Tibourg ★★★ ($)	**95**
Hôtel Caron de Beaumarchais ★★★	**96**
Hôtel de la Bretonnerie ★★★	**97**
Hôtel de la Place des Vosges ★★	**98**
Hôtel de Lutèce ★★★	**99**
Hôtel de Nice ★★	**99**
Hôtel des Deux-Îles ★★★	**100**
Hôtel du Jeu de Paume ★★★★ ($)	**101**
Hôtel du 7e Art ★★	**102**
Hôtel Saint-Louis ★★★	**103**
Hôtel Saint-Merry ★★★ ($)	**104**
Hôtel Sansonnet ★★	**105**
Libertel Grand Turenne ★★★	**106**

OTHER OPTIONS
Apartment Rental Agencies

Guest Apartment Services	**300**
RothRay	**306**

Student Accommodations

Maison Internationale de la Jeunesse et des Étudiants (MIJE)	**325**
OTU Voyage	**326**

($) indicates a Big Splurge

GRAND HÔTEL JEANNE D'ARC ★★ (39)
3, rue de Jarente, 75004
Métro: St-Paul, Bastille

TELEPHONE
01-48-87-62-11
FAX
01-48-87-37-31
EMAIL
information@hoteljeannedarc.com
INTERNET
www.parishotels.com
CREDIT CARDS
MC, V
RATES
Single 60–70€, double 75–80€, triple 110€, quad 130€; *taxe de séjour* included
BREAKFAST
Continental 6€ per person
ENGLISH SPOKEN
Yes

36 rooms, all with shower or bath and toilet

The Grand Hôtel Jeanne d'Arc sits on a quiet street leading into the Marais. Discovered long ago by astute, wallet-conscious travelers, the hotel offers spotless rooms with a minimum of snags and tears. Sometimes it is hard to account for different types of decorating tastes, and I admit to being baffled about a few of the choices in the public areas of this hotel. My prize for the most bizarre mirror on the Continent goes to the one done by a local artist that hangs near the reception and defies rational description. The strange taste in art carries to the bright primary-colored fish painted on the first- and second-floor stairways. Fortunately, the rooms do not keep pace with the unusual decoration elsewhere, and they are actually quite plain by comparison.

Rooms 11 or 12 are good bets if there are two of you. Number 60, with its sloping eaves and rooftop views, is a good choice for parties of three, and Nos. 53 and 63 for parties of four. If you are alone, avoid No. 31, with its dorm-style furniture and an old pink tiled shower. Instead, request No. 51, a small top-floor room with a desk, open closet, sunny view, and a compact bathroom with a stall shower. Recent improvements include new stairway carpeting and halls repapered in faux orange vinyl. Repeat customers comprise the bulk of the clientele, so book early if this one appeals to you.

FACILITIES AND SERVICES: Direct-dial phone, elevator, TV with international reception, office safe (no charge)

NEAREST TOURIST ATTRACTIONS (RIGHT BANK): Marais, place des Vosges, Musée National Picasso, Bastille Opéra, rue des Rosiers (Jewish Quarter), Seine, Île St-Louis, Île de la Cité

GRAND HÔTEL MALHER ★★ (37)
5, rue Malher, 75004
Métro: St-Paul

TELEPHONE
01-42-72-60-92
FAX
01-42-72-25-37
EMAIL
ghmalher@yahoo.fr
INTERNET
www.grandhotelmalher.com
CREDIT CARDS
AE, DC, MC, V

31 rooms, all with shower or bath and toilet

When the good-value awards are presented, the Grand Hôtel Malher is always a winning two-star, thanks to its many three-star features and excellent family-run management. The lobby is dominated by a lovely gold mirror and two square black leather chairs and matching sofa attractively arranged against a backdrop of centuries-old stone walls. Fresh flowers soften the setting. Breakfast is served in a seventeenth-century vaulted wine cellar. Rooms with twin beds face the street; those facing the interior court have double beds. Rooms 30, 32, and 62 are standard doubles on the back with space and good light in the bathroom. Other good choices are on the sunny top floors in rooms with balconies. Room 34, a pine furnished twin with a little balcony, faces front and has a big bathroom with two windows. Number 64, a suite, is ideal for a couple with one child; it has a double and twin bed and an extra-large sink area in the gray tiled bathroom. Pamela and Didier Fossiez are your gracious hosts, and your stay with them should be delightful.

FACILITIES AND SERVICES: Conference room, direct-dial phone, elevator, hair dryer, minibar, TV with international reception, office safe (no charge)

NEAREST TOURIST ATTRACTIONS (RIGHT BANK): Marais, place des Vosges, Bastille Opéra, Musée National Picasso, rue des Rosiers (Jewish Quarter), Seine, Île de la Cité, Île St-Louis, St-Germain-des-Prés

RATES
Single 110–117€, double 125–135€, junior suite 180€; very good lower rates in off season; *taxe de séjour* included

BREAKFAST
Continental 8€ per person

ENGLISH SPOKEN
Yes

HOSPITEL-HÔTEL DIEU PARIS ★★★ (51)
1, place du Parvis Notre-Dame de Paris, 75004
Galerie B-2, 6ème étage
Métro: Cité

14 rooms, all with shower or bath and toilet

Wanted: A quiet, comfortable hotel room on the doorstep of Notre Dame Cathedral, only seconds away from all the fun and frolic going on around place St-Michel and the Left Bank. Impossible? *Mais non!* Not if you check into the Hospitel-Hôtel Dieu Paris, located within the walls of Paris's oldest and most prominent hospital: L'Hôpital Hôtel Dieu Paris. Originally opened to serve relatives of patients, the fourteen rooms in this historical monument are now open to anyone. Frankly, I had my doubts when I first heard about it—I could just imagine the depressing rooms with linoleum floors and institutional furnishings, all smelling like Lysol. How wrong I was. Actually, the hotel has a great deal going for it. In addition to the dynamite location, its contemporary rooms, done with Art Deco overtones and in vibrant primary colors, are blissfully quiet and several are exclusively nonsmoking. The tiled baths are above average; it is, of course, absolutely spotless; and above all, the low prices are amazing for this expensive, touristy section of Paris. Reception is open from 7 A.M. to 10 P.M. daily, and room service for hot meals is available daily

TELEPHONE
01-44-32-01-00

FAX
01-44-32-01-16

EMAIL
hospitelhoteldieu@wanadoo.fr

INTERNET
www.hotel-hospitel.com

CREDIT CARDS
MC, V

RATES
Single 90€, double 100€; *taxe de séjour* included

BREAKFAST
Continental 7.50€ per person

ENGLISH SPOKEN
Yes

between 11 A.M. and 9 P.M. The only downside is that the hotel is situated on the sixth floor under a mansard roof, so there are no real windows, only skylights—but they are ample and let in plenty of light and sunshine, and from the even-numbered rooms, you can see the tower of Notre Dame. The closet and drawer spaces are not geared to long stays, and you might see a few hospital patients in bathrobes en route to your elevator. If you can live with this, it is a real value.

NOTE: To locate the hotel within the hospital, enter directly through the door just beside the main door. The entrance is marked. The hotel is located on the sixth floor of Building 2 (look for Galerie B-2, *6ème étage*).

FACILITIES AND SERVICES: Direct-dial phone, elevator, hair dryer, 2 handicapped-accessible rooms, TV with international reception, room service, room safe (no charge), several nonsmoking rooms

NEAREST TOURIST ATTRACTIONS (ISLAND IN THE SEINE): Île de la Cité, Île St-Louis, Seine, St-Michel, St-Germain-des-Prés

HÔTEL AXIAL BEAUBOURG ★★★ (23)
11, rue du Temple, 75004
Métro: Hôtel-de-Ville

39 rooms, all with shower or bath and toilet

Dark woods, liberal use of eggplant, plum, deep brown and honey colors, and stylized floral arrangements set the minimalistic tone in Véronique Turmel's stylish hotel. The breakfast room is an interesting blend of classic and modern, mixing fifteenth-century stone walls with lavender linen stretch covers on armless chairs. Black doors with buffed silver handles lead to the subdued rooms. Number 62 on the top floor is one of the biggest standard rooms, with a large bed but only stools for seating. It has a street view and a compact sandy-gray marble and tile bath with a heated towel rack. Room 64 is a smaller version of No. 62, but it has a more interesting view of the top of the Hôtel de Ville and the BHV department store. If you can live with some street noise, No. 17, in eggplant tones, has more space, a bit of character thanks to its beams, and a writing desk and two chairs. Even the television has a bigger screen.

FACILITIES AND SERVICES: Air-conditioning, direct-dial phone, elevator, hair dryer, Internet in lobby, laundry service, minibar, TV with international reception, room safe (no charge)

TELEPHONE
01-42-72-72-22
FAX
01-42-72-03-53
INTERNET
www.axialbeaubourg.com
CREDIT CARDS
AE, DC, MC, V
RATES
Single 105–120€, double 140–175€; *taxe de séjour* included
BREAKFAST
Buffet 10€ per person
ENGLISH SPOKEN
Yes

NEAREST TOURIST ATTRACTIONS (RIGHT BANK): Centre Georges Pompidou (Beaubourg), BHV department store, Seine, Île de la Cité, Île St-Louis, Marais, Les Halles

HÔTEL BOURG TIBOURG ★★★ ($, 24)
19, rue du Bourg-Tibourg, 75004
Métro: Hôtel-de-Ville

30 rooms, all with shower, bath, and toilet

The Hôtel Bourg Tibourg is a testament to over-the-top opulence befitting a château, not a hotel with some rooms so small that tables and chairs are not viable options, and crawling over the bed to get from one side of the room to the other may comprise a large part of your daily aerobic workout. Despite its lack of space, the hotel has a visually rich quality about it and certainly does not stint on rich fabrics, fringes, and frills. This is especially evident in the ground-floor sitting area, which incorporates a heavy tapestry-covered high-back settee, dark cocoa armchairs, and a massive wrought iron chandelier hanging over thick hemp carpeting. An enviable framed collection of prints of early French fashions and tradespeople lines one wall. Tucked around the corner by the atrium garden is a fringed chaise lounge and floor lamp. The elevator hides behind a brass studded suede-covered door. The rooms are all very small, and if you like the Ali Baba school of decorating, quite well done, especially No. 54, which is enveloped in velvet hanging behind and over the bed and on the closet doors. Double windows opening onto a tiny balcony provide a slight sense of expanse. The bathroom includes a tub and the latest in free-standing sinks. No. 51, a mini-single, also has drapes that match the backdrop behind the bed and the covering of the narrow closet. There is no work space or chair, but you can relax in the stretch bathtub framed in mosaic tiles. No. 21 is a slightly larger single on the back facing a wall. It is a quiet, corner choice, with a small table and an extra chair. Breakfast is served on round tables in a small seventeenth-century stone cellar downstairs; work space is limited or nonexistent in the rooms, so guests are invited to work here during the day. In addition to the visual bang that the hotel gives, it has a central Marais address and is popular with artists and fashionistas eager to experience the luster of luxe.

FACILITIES AND SERVICES: Air-conditioning, direct-dial phone, elevator, hair dryer, laundry service, minibar, TV with international reception, room safe (no charge)

TELEPHONE
01-42-78-47-39

FAX
01-40-29-07-00

EMAIL
hotel.du.bourg.tibourg@
wanadoo.fr

INTERNET
www.hoteldubourgtibourg.com

CREDIT CARDS
AE, DC, MC, V

RATES
Single 158€, double 210€, deluxe 265€, suite 370€; *taxe de séjour* included

BREAKFAST
Continental 14€ per person

ENGLISH SPOKEN
Yes

NEAREST TOURIST ATTRACTIONS (RIGHT BANK): Marais, Seine, Île St-Louis, Île de la Cité, rue des Rosiers (Jewish Quarter), place des Vosges

HÔTEL CARON DE BEAUMARCHAIS ★★★ (34)
12, rue Vieille-du-Temple, 75004
Métro: Hôtel-de-Ville, St-Paul
19 rooms, all with shower or bath and toilet

TELEPHONE
01-42-72-34-12
FAX
01-42-72-34-63
INTERNET
www.carondebeaumarchais.com
CREDIT CARDS
AE, MC, V
RATES
1–2 persons 147–165€; extra bed 16€; *taxe de séjour* included
BREAKFAST
Continental 11€ per person
ENGLISH SPOKEN
Yes

Named after the boisterous author of *The Marriage of Figaro* and *The Barber of Seville,* the Caron de Beaumarchais is close to place des Vosges, interesting shopping in the Marais, the Jewish Quarter, and the Bastille Opéra. The beautifully restored hotel, opened for business in June 1993, is run by father and son owners Étienne and Alain Bigeard. Between them they have all the credentials necessary to run a fine, small hotel. Service and attention to guests' needs are dwindling commodities in today's hotel market, but not here. Every time I have been in the hotel, guests could not say enough about the care and consideration extended to them during their stay, and this is backed up by the many glowing letters I have received from contented readers who have stayed here.

The downstairs lobby features a Louis XVI fireplace, a rare piano *forte,* copies of eighteenth-century murals, an antique game table laid out with authentic old playing cards, and a tiny atrium garden off to one side. Breakfast with freshly squeezed orange juice, assorted pastries, fresh fruit, and yogurt is served in a comfortable room that lends itself to lingering while thumbing through the collection of guidebooks left here for everyone's use. If guests prefer, a Continental breakfast will be brought on a tray to their rooms. A café au lait and the *Herald-Tribune* can also be brought to your room for a small charge.

The nineteen bedrooms are small, but effective design and elegant eighteenth-century decor overcome this. No detail has been overlooked in providing a coordinated look. The Gustavian III–style furniture was made specially for the hotel. Original pages from *The Marriage of Figaro* are framed and hang in each room. Hand-painted and signed ceramic tiles highlight the bathrooms, where even the color of the soap in the soap dish has been taken into consideration. All rooms are air-conditioned and soundproofed, and six have balconies with tables and chairs. In operating the hotel, the family strives to re-create a typically French atmosphere where guests feel at home and want to return. They achieve their goal with great success.

FACILITIES AND SERVICES: Air-conditioned, direct-dial phone, elevator, hair dryer, magnifying mirrors, minibar, robes, TV with international reception, office safe (no charge)

NEAREST TOURIST ATTRACTIONS (RIGHT BANK): Place des Vosges, Marais, rue des Rosiers (Jewish Quarter), Centre Georges Pompidou (Beaubourg), Seine, Île St-Louis, Île de la Cité, Musée National Picasso, Bastille Opéra

HÔTEL DE LA BRETONNERIE ★★★ (20)
22, rue Ste-Croix-de-la-Bretonnerie, 75004
Métro: Hôtel-de-Ville

29 rooms, all with shower or bath and toilet

A stay in this captivating hotel will make you feel like an inhabitant of old-world Paris. Set in a restored seventeenth-century town house in the heart of the picturesque Marais, it is just minutes from the Beaubourg, place des Vosges, the Musée National Picasso, the banks of the Seine, and Notre Dame. High praise goes to longtime owner Valérie Sagot for providing a warm welcome to her many returning guests, who rightfully consider this to be one of the best small hotels in Paris.

Quality and taste are evident from the minute you enter the comfortable cross-beamed lobby and vibrant red sitting room, with a large tapestry on one wall and tapestry-covered armchairs. The twenty-two rooms and seven suites are individually decorated, and all are recommended. For a special treat, reserve No. 25 with modern British colonial wicker and a four-poster metal bed. Bathroom touches include fabric wall coverings, a deep tub, and an inset sink with plenty of space for all the cosmetics one could possibly need. The suites are not only stunning, but great value, especially No. 5, which has two rooms and two bathrooms done in soft rose and green. Number 28 is another beautiful two-room suite with a double bathroom to die for . . . just wait until you sink into the massive oval tub. Room 35 is also wonderful; magnificently done in pale yellow and green with enviable antiques, it consists of a bedroom, a separate sitting room, and one of the most beautiful three-star marble baths in Paris. For something smaller but just as appealing, try Room 14 or 29, both with a four-poster canopy bed. Breakfast is served in the arched, stone-walled *cave* (cellar), with colorful dried floral arrangements complementing the rich French red decor.

TELEPHONE
01-48-87-77-63

FAX
01-42-77-26-78

INTERNET
www.bretonnerie.com

CREDIT CARDS
MC, V

RATES
1–2 persons, classic 110€, charming 145€, junior suite 180€; *taxe de séjour* 0.86€ per person, per day

BREAKFAST
Continental 9.50€ per person

ENGLISH SPOKEN
Yes

FACILITIES AND SERVICES: Direct-dial phone, elevator, hair dryer, laundry service, minibar, TV with international reception, room safe (no charge)

NEAREST TOURIST ATTRACTIONS (RIGHT BANK): Centre Georges Pompidou (Beaubourg), rue des Rosiers (Jewish Quarter), Marais, place des Vosges, Bastille Opéra, Musée National Picasso, Seine, Île de la Cité, Île St-Louis

HÔTEL DE LA PLACE DES VOSGES ★★ (43)
12, rue de Birague, 75004
Métro: Bastille
16 rooms, all with shower or bath and toilet

TELEPHONE
01-42-72-60-46
FAX
01-42-72-02-64
EMAIL
hotel.place.des.vosges@gofornet.com
INTERNET
www.hotelplacedesvosges.com
CREDIT CARDS
AE, DC, MC, V
RATES
1–2 persons, older rooms 120€, top floor room with bath 140€, 5 new rooms 202€; *taxe de séjour* included
BREAKFAST
Continental 6€ per person
ENGLISH SPOKEN
Yes

Renovating a hotel in Paris can be a trying experience thanks to mountains of red tape, building constraints, and historical conservation demands, not to mention expense. The determined owners of this prime Marais hotel are forging ahead and slowly redoing it. Their philosophy ("Buy the best and cry only once") is evident in the quality materials used in the five new rooms, which also prove the adage small is beautiful. Masterful attention to detail is apparent from the nonallergic quilts on top-of-the-line beds to the lighted alcoves beside the bed that replace the need for side tables. Two telephone lines in every room let you access email and talk on the phone at the same time. It is the Marais, so naturally the five new rooms have heavy beams, exposed stone walls, and hardwood floors. You don't have to travel light to stay in one of these rooms: the beds were especially designed to be high enough to slide a regulation suitcase under, and an armoire provides shelf and hanging space. The five-star marble bathrooms have state-of-the-art shower heads and six wall massage jets. The rack rate on the new rooms is somewhat deceiving: though quoted at 202€ per night, if guests ask for "the discovery rate," the price drops to 140€ per night, which is much more like it.

What about the other eleven rooms? They, too, are small with little or no seating but are well-maintained so that guests do not feel second class by staying in one. If a bathtub is important, the only one in the hotel is in the largest (nonrenovated) room on the top floor.

FACILITIES AND SERVICES: Bar, direct-dial phone, elevator (starts 1st floor), fans, hair dryer, laundry service, TV with international reception, room safe (no charge)

NEAREST TOURIST ATTRACTIONS (RIGHT BANK): Place des Vosges, Marais, Musée National Picasso, Opéra Bastille, Seine, Île St-Louis, Île de la Cité

HÔTEL DE LUTÈCE ★★★ (55)
65, rue St-Louis-en-l'Île, 75004
Métro: Pont Marie

23 rooms, all with shower or bath and toilet

Île St-Louis is a small island, a mere six blocks long and two blocks wide, in the middle of the Seine. Every day and night, and especially on the weekends, crowds of tourists and Parisians surge down the main street, browsing through the boutiques and art galleries or stopping for ice cream at the famed Berthillon. Lovers of this unique part of Paris check into either the Lutèce or the Deux-Îles, both owned by husband-and-wife team Roland and Elisabeth Buffat. Stepping inside the Hôtel de Lutèce from the island's main street, you are welcomed by bouquets of fresh flowers and a large stone fireplace surrounded by soft couches and armchairs. The rooms at the Lutèce are not large by any standard, but they are nicely decorated and have the requisite exposed beams, Provençal prints, and pretty rooftop views (that is, if you are lucky enough to secure a top-floor room). For a slight increase in space, reserve the double bedded duplex, up ten steps off the landing between the third and fourth floors; it faces the court, so it will be very quiet. Because the hotel exudes charm from top to bottom, it is booked months ahead, so you should reserve as far in advance as possible.

The following hotels are under the same ownership: Hôtel des Deux-Îles (page 100), the Hôtel Henri IV in the 5th (page 125), and Galileo Hôtel in the 8th (page 204).

FACILITIES AND SERVICES: Air-conditioning, direct-dial phone, elevator (to most floors), hair dryer, laundry service, TV with international reception, room safe (no charge)

NEAREST TOURIST ATTRACTIONS (ISLAND IN THE SEINE): Île St-Louis, Île de la Cité, St-Germain-des-Prés, Latin Quarter, St-Michel, Bastille Opéra, place des Vosges, Marais

TELEPHONE
01-43-26-23-52
FAX
01-43-29-60-25
INTERNET
www.hotel-ile-saintlouis.com
CREDIT CARDS
AE, MC, V
RATES
Single 132€, double 155€, triple 170€; *taxe de séjour* 0.91€ per person, per day
BREAKFAST
Continental 12€ per person
ENGLISH SPOKEN
Yes

HÔTEL DE NICE ★★ (35)
42bis, rue de Rivoli, 75004
Métro: Hôtel-de-Ville

23 rooms, all with shower or bath and toilet

When I first walked into the Hôtel de Nice, I was blinded by the use of turquoise everywhere: on the stairs leading to the reception, on the doors to the rooms, even on the wood trim and around the light switches in the hall. But after awhile, I was so busy looking at the

TELEPHONE
01-42-78-55-29
FAX
01-42-78-36-07
CREDIT CARDS
MC, V

RATES
Single 65€, double 100€,
triple 120€, quad 145€; *taxe de
séjour* included
BREAKFAST
Continental 6€ per person
ENGLISH SPOKEN
Yes

pleasantly cluttered hotel, I forgot all about this blast of color. The main sitting room, which also serves as the reception and breakfast room, has a certain *grand-mère's* parlor look, complete with oriental rugs on the floors, paisley prints tossed over tables and chairs, and a portrait of Lady Diana Cooper mixed in with the eclectic collection of artwork and a variety of green plants.

The rooms are as generously flossy as the public areas. Noise can be a nuisance, especially if your room faces the rue de Rivoli, a major thoroughfare in this part of Paris. Floral bedspreads, tartan cushions, Indian elephant fabric curtains, mismatched antique chairs, and old prints pasted onto the bathroom door sum up the look in No. 11. The bathroom has a tub and shower combination, good towels, and some sink space. Number 5, a tight double, is a study in mustard yellow with limited negotiating room around the foot of the bed. It is saved by a balcony overlooking the leafy square below. No, it isn't the Paris hotel for the masses, but if you like a hopscotch of colors in quirky surroundings, book now.

FACILITIES AND SERVICES: Direct-dial phone, hair dryer, elevator (starts 1st floor), French TV, office safe (no charge)

NEAREST TOURIST ATTRACTIONS (RIGHT BANK): Centre Georges Pompidou (Beaubourg), Marais, place des Vosges, rue des Rosiers (Jewish Quarter), Seine, Île de la Cité, Île St-Louis

HÔTEL DES DEUX-ÎLES ★★★ (56)
59, rue St-Louis-en-l'Île, 75004
Métro: Pont Marie
17 rooms, all with shower or bath and toilet

TELEPHONE
01-43-26-13-35
FAX
01-43-29-60-25
EMAIL
hotel.2iles@free.fr
INTERNET
www.hotel-ile-saintlouis.com
CREDIT CARDS
AE, MC, V
RATES
Single 133€, double 150€;
taxe de séjour 0.91€ per person,
per day
BREAKFAST
Continental 12€ per person
ENGLISH SPOKEN
Yes

The Hôtel des Deux-Îles is a beautiful seventeenth-century mansion owned by decorator Roland Buffat and his wife, Elisabeth. This hotel displays their touches at every turn, from the lobby with its atrium garden and antique birdcage to the Louis XIV tiled bathrooms. The snug breakfast area downstairs has a big fireplace and several secluded nooks with soft overstuffed sofas, making it a perfect place to start your Paris day. The rooms are very small, but they are well done with provincial prints, fabric wall coverings, bamboo furniture, and tiled baths. The very essence of Paris can be viewed from the top-floor windows.

The owners also run Hôtel de Lutèce (page 99), Hôtel Henri IV (page 125), and Galileo Hôtel (page 204).

FACILITIES AND SERVICES: Air-conditioning, direct-dial phone, elevator, hair dryer, Internet in lobby, laundry service, TV with international reception, room safe (no charge)

NEAREST TOURIST ATTRACTIONS (ISLAND IN THE SEINE): Île St-Louis, Île de la Cité, Latin Quarter, St-Michel, St-Germain-des-Prés, Marais, place des Vosges, Bastille Opéra

HÔTEL DU JEU DE PAUME ★★★★ ($, 54)
54, rue Saint-Louis-en-l'Île, 75004
Métro: Pont Marie
30 rooms, all with bathtub, shower, and toilet

At the beginning of the seventeenth century, Louis XIII decided to build a royal tennis court patterned after those in England. The result was the Jeu de Paume, which existed on this site for more than one hundred years. After several other owners and years of neglect, it was completely refashioned in 1988 and now is a stunning, secluded hotel of impressive caliber. Many original features remain including the dramatically high-pitched, open cross-beamed roof that once accommodated the gallery spectators. This open area is the focal point of the hotel and lends itself well to deep-seated chairs and sofas nicely placed throughout. An artful glass elevator whisks guests to the beautifully executed rooms, which are not lavish, but all boast themed decorating and comfortable furnishings.

Room 6 is a blue and yellow ground-floor single opening onto the garden. In addition to a marble bath with gold and silver fixtures, the room itself has plenty of work and living space. Number 205 is a large twin with two windows also overlooking the garden. Number 12 is a junior suite on two levels. In the downstairs sitting room, the mirrored wall reflecting the stone floors gives a sense of space. Here you will find a sofabed, television, table and chairs, and a small bathroom with a shower. Upstairs, you have double windows with a view of the garden, twin beds, a large walk-in closet, and an Italian tile bathroom with a marble sink set into a wooden console. The location in the heart of Paris on l'Île St-Louis is ideal in every respect. In fact, it simply does not get anymore romantic, or Parisian, than this.

FACILITIES AND SERVICES: Bar, billiard room, conference room, direct-dial phone, elevator, hair dryer, Internet in lobby, laundry service, minibar, room service for light

TELEPHONE
01-43-26-14-18
FAX
01-40-46-02-76
INTERNET
www.jeudepaumehotel.com
CREDIT CARDS
AE, DC, MC, V
RATES
Single 162€, double 225–290€, junior suite 475€; dog 10€; *taxe de séjour* 1.15€ per person, per day
BREAKFAST
Continental 15€ per person
ENGLISH SPOKEN
Yes

snacks, sauna, TV with international reception, room safe (no charge)

NEAREST TOURIST ATTRACTIONS (ISLAND IN THE SEINE): Île St-Louis, Île de la Cité, Latin Quarter, St-Michel, St-Germain-des-Prés, place des Vosges, Marais, Bastille Opéra

HÔTEL DU 7E ART ★★ (47)
20, rue St-Paul, 75004
Métro: St-Paul, Bastille

TELEPHONE
01-44-54-85-00
FAX
01-42-77-69-10
CREDIT CARDS
AE, DC, MC, V
RATES
1–2 persons 75–130€; extra bed 25€; *taxe de séjour* 0.65€ per person, per day
BREAKFAST
Continental 7.62€ per person
ENGLISH SPOKEN
Yes

22 rooms, all with shower or bath and toilet

The theme of this hotel is "yesterday's and today's movies." If you are a movie buff, especially if you love old films, you must at least drop by to admire the hotel's fabulous collection of film posters. For instance, the sitting room displays an irreverent takeoff on the Last Supper with Marilyn Monroe as the central figure and twelve male film stars, ranging from Laurel and Hardy to Elvis and Frankenstein, sitting and gesturing along the laden table.

The rooms are not posh, nor are they large, but they do have funky character . . . and at least one or two framed film posters. Room 27, a back double with a miniature bathroom squeezed into a closet, sports a *L'Est d'Eden* with James Dean, *Les Trafiquants de la Nuite* (The Long Haul) starring Victor Mature and Diana Dors, and *Ne Me Quitter Jamais* (Never Let Me Go) with Clark Gable and Gene Tierney. Room 21, with beige grass-cloth walls and brown paisley quilted spreads on twins, can fit three, but I think it's better for two. Posters here include *The Swan* with Grace Kelly and *Niagara* with Marilyn Monroe, Joseph Cotten, and Jean Peters. From a nostalgic standpoint, my favorite in this room is *Scandle en Floride,* featuring Ronald Reagan and Shirley Temple. Number 18 is a real hoot, with *How to Marry a Millionaire,* starring Marilyn Monroe, hanging over the bed, and on the adjacent walls, Maureen O'Hara and Charles Laughton in *Quasimoto* and Charlie Chaplin in *The Kid.* In the bathroom, posters are imposed on some tiles and the shower curtain continues the film theme. If you can't live without your own bit of film memorabilia or collectable kitsch, check out the small boutique, and the front window display—almost everything is for sale.

FACILITIES AND SERVICES: Bar, direct-dial phone, no elevator (4 floors), hair dryer available, laundry room for guests, TV with international reception, room safe (no charge)

NEAREST TOURIST ATTRACTIONS (RIGHT BANK): Antiques and boutiques along rue St-Paul, Marais, place des Vosges, Musée National Picasso, Bastille Opéra, Seine, Île de la Cité, Île St-Louis, Latin Quarter

HÔTEL SAINT-LOUIS ★★★ (53)
75, rue St-Louis-en-l'Île, 75004
Métro: Pont Marie

19 rooms, all with shower or bath and toilet

Real estate prices for even the tiniest studio on Île St-Louis are mind-boggling, so you can imagine there are no hotel bargains here. This former swamp was transformed into an elegant residential area in the seventeenth century, and it is still the favorite of artists, actresses, heiresses, and members of the Rothschild family. The tree-lined quays, magnificent town houses with spectacular views, and narrow main street make it so intimate and romantic that it is one of the most enchanting and picturesque places to stay in Paris. The Hôtel Saint-Louis boasts those quintessentially charming Parisian hotel status symbols: exposed wood beams, arched stone basement breakfast room, tapestry-rich fabrics, a few well-positioned antiques, and big bouquets of fresh flowers. The rooms, which all face out, are small, even by Paris standards, but if you get one on the fourth or fifth floor with a balcony, this helps. Numbers 51 and 52, hidden under the eaves, are the largest rooms, both with original beams and two balconies, including one off the bathroom with a peek at the Seine. Number 41, either a twin- or king-bedded room, has two windows overlooking its balcony. In No. 42, the balcony is on the corner. The bathroom is narrow, but it does have good light and some shelf space.

FACILITIES AND SERVICES: Air-conditioning, direct-dial phone, elevator to half floors (some stairs required), hair dryer, laundry service, French TV , room safe (no charge)

NEAREST TOURIST ATTRACTIONS (ISLAND IN THE SEINE): Île St-Louis, Île de la Cité, Notre Dame, Latin Quarter, St-Germain-des-Prés, place des Vosges, Marais, Bastille Opéra

TELEPHONE
01-46-34-04-80

FAX
01-46-34-02-13

EMAIL
slouis@cybercable.fr

INTERNET
www.hotelsaintlouis.com

CREDIT CARDS
MC, V

RATES
Single 140€, double 155–220€; extra bed 62€; *taxe de séjour* 0.91€ per person, per day

BREAKFAST
Continental 9.50€ per person

ENGLISH SPOKEN
Yes

HÔTEL SAINT-MERRY ★★★ ($, 18)
78, rue de la Verrerie, 75004
Métro: Châtelet, Hôtel-de-Ville; RER Châtelet–Les Halles

11 rooms, 1 suite, all with shower or bath and toilet

TELEPHONE
01-42-78-14-15
FAX
01-40-29-06-82
EMAIL
hotelstmerry@wanadoo.fr
INTERNET
www.hotelmarais.com
CREDIT CARDS
MC, V
RATES
1–2 persons 160–230€, suite 335€ for 2, 375€ for 3, 405€ for 4; *taxe de séjour* included
BREAKFAST
Continental in rooms only, 11€ per person
ENGLISH SPOKEN
Yes

The former presbytery of the seventeenth-century Gothic church of St-Merry is now the most unusual hotel in Paris, and it qualifies as its own tourist attraction! It is the labor of love of former owner M. Crabbe, who for more than forty years worked to create a true Gothic masterpiece. His immense pride in his achievement is well deserved, and the results are spectacular.

The hotel is located on a pedestrian walkway, and the entrance is through a short hallway with exposed beams and stone steps leading up to the lobby and reception area. Each room in the hotel is different and showcases a wonderful collection of authentic Gothic church and castle memorabilia mixed with custom-made pieces. All the back rooms share a common wall with the church, and wherever possible this stone wall has been kept visible. Room 9 contains a carved stone flying buttress, which flows from the floor to the ceiling over the bed. Others have rough red tiles from the Château de l'Angeres in the Loire Valley, hand-carved mahogany pews, converted confessionals serving as headboards, and impressive eight-lamp chandeliers. All of the windows in the hotel are stained glass, and the balcony rails still bear the St-Merry Church crest. Since each room is unique, room rates vary accordingly, depending on the plumbing and the level of Gothic detailing.

For years M. Crabbe worked on Room 20, the Gothic Suite, and it is finally completed. It isn't just a hotel suite—it is an experience! The approach is through an entry hall and up seventeen steps into a huge, pitched-roof room with cross beams, a baronial dining table seating six, skylights, a ten-foot clock, a fireplace, a wall of carved wooden shelves, and a large sofabed where you can view the big-screen television. The bedroom is equally dramatic, with a view of the church. Even the bathroom is fabulous, with an ornately carved door depicting the three wise men, Mary, Joseph, and baby Jesus.

While you are here, please don't miss visiting the St-Merry Church adjoining the hotel. It has a beautiful choir and the oldest church bell in Paris, cast in 1331.

A cautionary note: In 2002, M. Crabbe sold the hotel, and I am not the only longtime loyalist who hoped this day would never come. The new owner has another hotel in the neighborhood that is not covered in *Great Sleeps Paris* because I think it offers absolutely no value and is not well maintained. Those of us who admire M. Crabbe and his marvelous achievement at the Hôtel St-Merry sincerely hope the new proprietor will properly care for this unique, historic hotel and not let it fall by the wayside.

FACILITIES AND SERVICES: Direct-dial phone, no elevator (4 floors), hair dryer, laundry service, TV in suite, room safe (no charge)

NEAREST TOURIST ATTRACTIONS (RIGHT BANK): Centre Georges Pompidou (Beaubourg), BHV department store, Marais, place des Vosges, Seine, Île de la Cité, Île St-Louis

HÔTEL SANSONNET ★★ (21)
48, rue de la Verrerie, 75004
Métro: Hôtel-de-Ville

26 rooms, 22 with shower or bath and toilet

The Sansonnet offers far better two-star values than most of its competitors in the neighborhood. The hotel is clean and reasonably modern. A colorful aquarium sits at the lobby entrance, which is up an easy flight of stairs from the street. Several of the singles without facilities are minuscule, but if you have only a small suitcase and plan to use your room only for sleep, these are buys. The doubles are good-sized, with uniform color schemes and blended fabrics. The closets have shelves and most of the showers have doors. Rooms facing the street are subject to noise, and those on the back all have a shower. Everything is kept spic and span by Liliane, who has been the housekeeper here for more than twenty-five years. The address couldn't be better located for exploring the area around the Beaubourg and the Forum des Halles. For sightseeing and shopping farther afield, it is a ten-minute walk to the islands, St-Michel, the big department stores on rue de Rivoli, and a number of recommended restaurants (see *Great Eats Paris*).

FACILITIES AND SERVICES: Direct-dial phone, no elevator (4 floors), hair dryer, TV with international reception, office safe (no charge)

NEAREST TOURIST ATTRACTIONS (RIGHT BANK): Centre Georges Pompidou (Beaubourg), BHV department store, Marais, place des Vosges, Seine, Île de la Cité, Île St-Louis

TELEPHONE
01-48-87-96-14

FAX
01-48-87-30-46

EMAIL
hotelsansonnet@wanadoo.fr

INTERNET
www.hotel-sansonnet.com

CREDIT CARDS
MC, V

RATES
Single 45–70€, double 74–80€; showers free; *taxe de séjour* included

BREAKFAST
Continental 5.34€ per person

ENGLISH SPOKEN
Yes

LIBERTEL GRAND TURENNE ★★★ (41)
6, rue de Turenne, 75004
Métro: St-Paul, Bastille
41 rooms, all with shower or bath and toilet

TELEPHONE
01-42-78-43-25
FAX
01-42-74-10-72
EMAIL
H2760@accor-hotels.com
INTERNET
www.libertel-hotels.com
CREDIT CARDS
AE, DC, MC, V
RATES
Single 155€, double 170–190€, suite 245€; lower rates depend on season and availability; *taxe de séjour* included
BREAKFAST
Buffet 14€ per person
ENGLISH SPOKEN
Yes

The Libertel hotel group has many smart lodgings in various price categories scattered throughout Paris. All are done from top to bottom with coordinated colors and furnishings. Libertel Grand Turenne offers forty-one charming rooms done in blues, greens, or soft reds with attractive accent pieces and pretty prints on the walls. The first and second floors are devoted entirely to non-smokers. There are several categories of rooms, and despite their slight increase in price, I recommend the Superior rooms because they offer more space, especially for a double. There is one exception, however, and that is No. 603, a top-floor Superior double. The big bathroom with windows and a tub is nicely appointed, but the slanted wall makes it awkward for a tall person. Junior suites are popular with some, but I don't think they offer enough value to justify the higher price tags. The hotel location, only a five-minute walk from place des Vosges, offers visitors a convenient base for exploring one of the most interesting *quartiers* in Paris. From here it is a pleasant stroll to the Musée National Picasso, Île de la Cité, Île St-Louis, the Bastille Opéra, and all the wild and woolly nighttime fun in the eleventh arrondissement. In addition, many restaurants listed in *Great Eats Paris* are close by.

FACILITIES AND SERVICES: Direct-dial phone, elevator, hair dryer, laundry service, minibar, some tea and coffee makers, TV with international reception, office safe (no charge)

NEAREST TOURIST ATTRACTIONS (RIGHT BANK): Place des Vosges, Musée National Picasso, Bastille Opéra, Seine, Île St-Louis, Île de la Cité

Fifth Arrondissement

The fifth is named the Latin Quarter for the students who came during the Middle Ages to study at the Sorbonne, which was founded in 1253 and remains a center of student life to this day, though not much Latin is spoken here anymore. The arrondissement stretches from the colorful street *marché* on rue Mouffetard to the dome of the Panthéon, and beyond to the Seine and through the botanical wonders of the Jardin des Plantes (opened by Louis XIV's doctor for the king's health). This ancient, interesting, and exhilarating part of Paris is crisscrossed with networks of narrow, curved streets lined on both sides with bookshops, restaurants, and cafés that surge with action twenty-four hours a day. It is youthful, cosmopolitan, bohemian, and fun. Even though St-Michel has lost its penniless chic, it is still the soul of the Latin Quarter. Crowds of all ages and types gather daily around the St-Michel fountain to flirt, eat, drink, argue, pose, and watch the sidewalk entertainment. The area around place de la Contrescarpe is where Hemingway lived when he was a starving writer new to Paris. You can see two of his addresses: 39, rue Descartes, a studio; and 74, rue de Cardinal-Lemoine, where he lived with his wife, Hadley. Also of interest in the fifth is the Musée Rodin, the twelfth-century Église St-Julien-le Pauvre, the Manufacture des Gobelins (tapestry workshops), and the Cluny baths, which form part of the Musée du Moyen Age (known as the Musée de Cluny) and are regarded as the most important Roman ruins in Paris.

LEFT BANK
Musée de Cluny
Jardin des Plantes
Latin Quarter
rue Mouffetard
Panthéon
Sorbonne

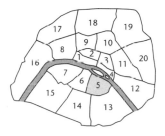

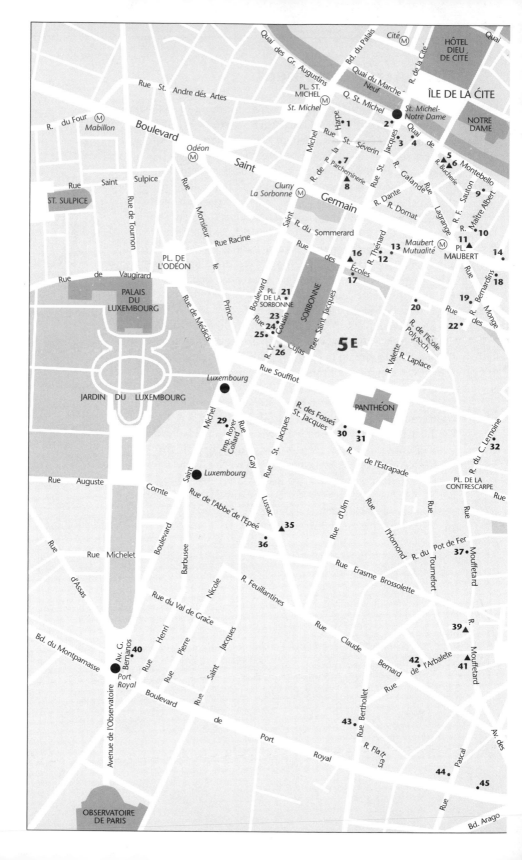

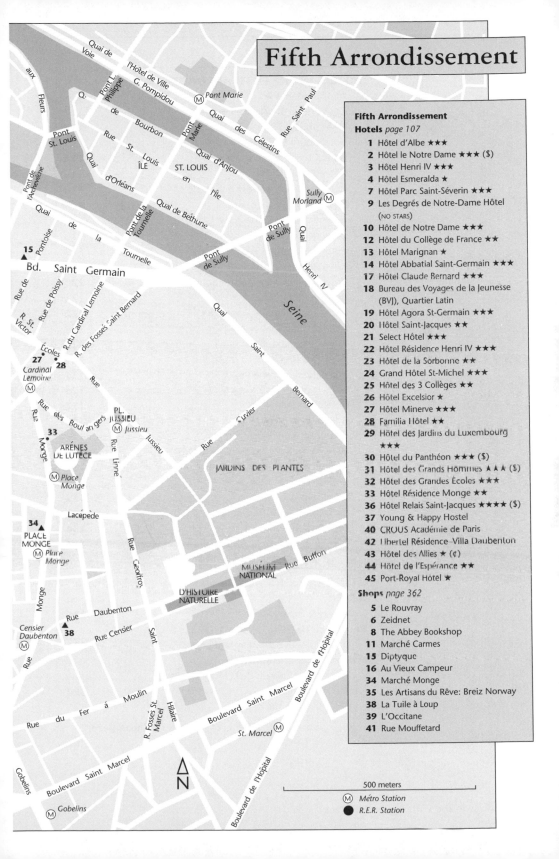

Fifth Arrondissement

Fifth Arrondissement

Hotels *page 107*

1 Hôtel d'Albe ★★★
2 Hôtel le Notre Dame ★★★ ($)
3 Hôtel Henri IV ★★★
4 Hôtel Esmeralda ★
7 Hôtel Parc Saint-Séverin ★★★
9 Les Degrés de Notre-Dame Hôtel (NO STARS)
10 Hôtel de Notre Dame ★★★
12 Hôtel du Collège de France ★★
13 Hôtel Marignan ★
14 Hôtel Abbatial Saint-Germain ★★★
17 Hôtel Claude Bernard ★★★
18 Bureau des Voyages de la Jeunesse (BVJ), Quartier Latin
19 Hôtel Agora St-Germain ★★★
20 Hôtel Saint-Jacques ★★
21 Select Hôtel ★★★
22 Hôtel Résidence Henri IV ★★★
23 Hôtel de la Sorbonne ★★
24 Grand Hôtel St-Michel ★★★
25 Hôtel des 3 Collèges ★★
26 Hôtel Excelsior ★
27 Hôtel Minerve ★★★
28 Familia Hôtel ★★
29 Hôtel des Jardins du Luxembourg ★★★
30 Hôtel du Panthéon ★★★ ($)
31 Hôtel des Grands Hommes ★★★ ($)
32 Hôtel des Grandes Écoles ★★★
33 Hôtel Résidence Monge ★★★
36 Hôtel Relais Saint-Jacques ★★★★ ($)
37 Young & Happy Hostel
40 CROUS Académie de Paris
42 Libertel Résidence-Villa Daubenton
43 Hôtel des Allies ★ (¢)
44 Hôtel de l'Espérance ★★
45 Port-Royal Hôtel ★

Shops *page 362*

5 Le Rouvray
6 Zeidnet
8 The Abbey Bookshop
11 Marché Carmes
15 Diptyque
16 Au Vieux Campeur
34 Marché Monge
35 Les Artisans du Rêve: Breiz Norway
38 La Tuile à Loup
39 L'Occitane
41 Rue Mouffetard

500 meters

Ⓜ *Métro Station*
● *R.E.R. Station*

HOTELS IN THE FIFTH ARRONDISSEMENT

Familia Hôtel ★★	111
Grand Hôtel St-Michel ★★★	112
Hôtel Abbatial Saint-Germain ★★★	113
Hôtel Agora St-Germain ★★★	113
Hôtel Claude Bernard ★★★	114
Hôtel d'Albe ★★★	115
Hôtel de la Sorbonne ★★	116
Hôtel de l'Espérance ★★	116
Hôtel de Notre Dame ★★★	117
Hôtel des Allies ★ (¢)	118
Hôtel des Grandes Écoles ★★★	119
Hôtel des Grands Hommes ★★★ ($)	119
Hôtel des Jardins du Luxembourg ★★★	120
Hôtel des 3 Collèges ★★	121
Hôtel du Collège de France ★★	122
Hôtel du Panthéon ★★★ ($)	122
Hôtel Esmeralda ★	123
Hôtel Excelsior ★	124
Hôtel Henri IV ★★★	125
Hôtel le Notre Dame ★★★ ($)	126
Hôtel Marignan ★	127
Hôtel Minerve ★★★	128
Hôtel Parc Saint-Séverin ★★★	129
Hôtel Relais Saint-Jacques ★★★★ ($)	130
Hôtel Résidence Henri IV ★★★	131
Hôtel Résidence Monge ★★	132
Hôtel Saint-Jacques ★★	132
Les Degrés de Notre-Dame Hôtel (NO STARS)	133
Port-Royal Hôtel ★	134
Select Hôtel ★★★	136

OTHER OPTIONS

Hostels
Young & Happy Hostel	316
Residence Hotels
Libertel Résidence–Villa Daubenton	321
Student Accommodations
Bureau des Voyages de la Jeunesse (BVJ), Quartier Latin	324
CROUS Académie de Paris	325

($) indicates a Big Splurge; (¢) indicates a Cheap Sleep

FAMILIA HÔTEL ★★ (28)
11, rue des Écoles, 75005
Métro: Cardinal Lemoine, Maubert-Mutualité

30 rooms, all with shower or bath and toilet

Many hotels on rue des Écoles are run by foreign managers for absentee owners residing in other countries. As a result, service, cleanliness, and upkeep are often drastically reduced because no one at the hotel has any stake in it or really cares. You will find none of this at the Familia Hôtel. M. and Mme. Gaucheron, who have owned the hotel for a decade, have now turned the operating duties over to their son, Eric, whose hands-on management and high-energy enthusiasm keep him on top of things every minute. Speaking rapid-fire French, Spanish, or English, he never stops doing whatever is necessary to ensure that all guests are looked after properly. His wife, Sylvie, helps in the afternoon or whenever she is not looking after their toddler, Charles, who is the apple of his grandfather's eye and adored by all the staff at the hotel.

The family is constantly on the lookout for ways to improve the hotel. One very successful project involved chipping away years of plaster and paint from the walls to expose the original stone from 1850, which now serves as a perfect backdrop for Eric's collection of original tapestries. Many rooms also have exposed walls; others have frescoes of famous Parisian landmarks. Room 62 has the Canal St-Martin painted over the twin beds, No. 43 has the famed Pont Neuf in sepia tones, and No. 25 highlights the place des Vosges. I like No. 52, with the Pont Alexandre III and the Eiffel Tower gracing one wall and its little outdoor terrace with a view of Notre Dame. The same artist painted the mural of old Paris along the front entry.

The bedrooms are all very well done and are on a rotating schedule for maintenance and improvements, which guarantees nothing ever extends beyond its due date. Some rooms will have new mattresses one year, others a new marble bathroom, while still others will be repainted and recarpeted. Double-glazed windows and many expensive touches such as special Canadian cherry-wood closet doors, and antique reproduction furnishings designed specifically for the hotel are standard issue. If you want a bird's-eye view of Notre Dame Cathedral, ask for a front room on the fifth or sixth floor. For a room with a balcony, you want something on the second or fifth floors, facing the street. Staying at the Familia puts

TELEPHONE
01-43-54-55-27

FAX
01-43-29-61-77

EMAIL
familia.hotel@libertysurf.fr

INTERNET
www.hotel-paris-familia.com

CREDIT CARDS
MC, V

RATES
Single 71–116€, double 81–116€, triple 131€, quad 145€; *taxe de séjour* 0.65€ per person, per day

BREAKFAST
Continental 6€ per person

ENGLISH SPOKEN
Yes

guests only a few minutes from St-Germain-des-Prés, the islands, and all the famous cafés in the Latin Quarter. Métro connections are good, and so is bus transportation.

If the Familia is booked, don't worry. The family now owns the Hôtel Minerve next door (see page 128), which they completely renovated into a very smart three-star.

FACILITIES AND SERVICES: Direct-dial phone, hair dryer, elevator, minibar, TV with international reception, office safe (no charge)

NEAREST TOURIST ATTRACTIONS (LEFT BANK): Seine, Île St-Louis, Île de la Cité, Jardin des Plantes

GRAND HÔTEL ST-MICHEL ★★★ (24)
19, rue Cujas, 75005
Métro: Cluny–La Sorbonne; RER Luxembourg
45 rooms, all with shower or bath and toilet

The Grand Hôtel St-Michel is an upscale pick between the boulevard St-Michel and the Panthéon. It has an elegant look, which starts in the formal lobby and sitting rooms and continues along the tone-on-tone soft yellow hallways. Rooms, which are color coordinated in orange, yellow, and blue, are large enough to actually live in and are equipped with modems, individual air-conditioning controls, and nice bathrooms. Those on the top floors have Panthéon views: in No. 503, a suite, you can see the dome from both balconies, including one off the bathroom. Number 602 is a large, light double done in soft blue. Room 604 has a view from both windows and one of the best bathrooms in the house. Singles will appreciate No. 303, a corner room with a street view, which is bigger than some deluxe doubles in other hotels. It is nicely outfitted with a large armoire hiding an eye-level safe, pretty hand-painted furniture with red and salmon accents, and a nice bath with chrome and brass fittings. Transportation connections are unbeatable: the RER Line B, which goes to either Orly or Roissy–Charles-de-Gaulle airports, eight bus lines, and the métro are all within an easy walk.

FACILITIES AND SERVICES: Air-conditioning, bar, conference room, direct-dial phones, elevator, hair dryer, laundry service, TV with international reception, room safe (no charge)

NEAREST TOURIST ATTRACTIONS (LEFT BANK): Panthéon, Sorbonne, Jardin du Luxembourg, Musée de Cluny, St-Michel

TELEPHONE
01-46-33-33-02

FAX
01-40-46-96-33

EMAIL
grand.hotel.st.michel@wanadoo.fr

INTERNET
www.grand-hotel-st-michel.com

CREDIT CARDS
AE, DC, MC, V

RATES
Single 135€, double 180€, suite 265€; *taxe de séjour* included

BREAKFAST
Buffet or Continental 12€ per person

ENGLISH SPOKEN
Yes

HÔTEL ABBATIAL SAINT-GERMAIN ★★★ (14)
46, boulevard St-Germain, 75005
Métro: Maubert-Mutualité

43 rooms, all with shower or bath and toilet

The Abbatial Saint-Germain offers comfort, convenience, and location. True, the rooms are generally small by American standards, but they are the norm in this popular section of Paris, and they are carefully cleaned by a team of housekeepers headed by Maria, who has spent over a quarter century working here. The spirit of the nineteenth-century building is evident from the original cross beams along the halls, tapestry-covered furniture, and white antiqued furniture. The plaster plaques of nymphs and cherubs that grace almost every room, and the rooms decorated in fiery orange seem a little too much, but to each his own. The fifth- and sixth-floor rooms have balconies with views of Notre Dame and the Panthéon, and the sunny street-side rooms are soundproofed with double-glazed windows. Also under the same ownership is the Hôtel Agora St-Germain (see below).

FACILITIES AND SERVICES: Air-conditioning, direct-dial phone, elevator, hair dryer, laundry service, minibar, public parking across the street, TV with international reception, room safe (no charge)

NEAREST TOURIST ATTRACTIONS (LEFT BANK): St-Michel, Musée de Cluny, Seine, Île de le Cité, Île St-Louis

TELEPHONE
01-46-34-02-12
FAX
01-43-25-47-73
EMAIL
Abbitial@club-Internet.fr
INTERNET
www.abbatial.com
CREDIT CARDS
AE, DC, MC, V
RATES
Single 107€, double 135–160€, triple 191€; free baby cot; *taxe de séjour* included
BREAKFAST
Buffet or Continental 9€ per person
ENGLISH SPOKEN
Yes

HÔTEL AGORA ST-GERMAIN ★★★ (19)
42, rue des Bernardins, 75005
Métro: Maubert-Mutualité

39 rooms, all with shower or bath and toilet

The Agora St-Germain continues to represent a success story for both owners and guests. The customized rooms with pretty silk wall coverings, ample space, and marble-tile bathrooms are beautifully maintained. Several have balcony views of St-Nicholas de Chardonnet, which is the only church in Paris that still conducts services in Latin. An interior garden gives the sitting area and lobby more dimension, and makes it a pleasant place to linger and read the daily newspapers. A Continental breakfast is served in a stone-walled dining room with baskets of flowers and linen napkins on each table. The friendly owners, Pascale and Michèle Sahuc, and their staff see to the wishes of every guest. Firmly recommended by all who have stayed here, this haven for weary travelers is less than five minutes away from good restaurants (see *Great*

TELEPHONE
01-46-34-13-00
FAX
01-46-34-75-05
EMAIL
agorastg@club-Internet.fr
INTERNET
www.AgoraSaintGermain.com
CREDIT CARDS
AE, DC, MC, V
RATES
Single 116€, double 140–155€, triple 169€; *taxe de séjour* included
BREAKFAST
Continental 9€ per person
ENGLISH SPOKEN
Yes

Eats Paris) and close to all the charm and excitement of this part of the Left Bank. Also under the same ownership is the Abbatial St-Germain on boulevard St-Germain (see above).

FACILITIES AND SERVICES: Air-conditioning, direct-dial phone, elevator, hair dryer, laundry service, minibar, TV with international reception, room safe (no charge)

NEAREST TOURIST ATTRACTIONS (LEFT BANK): Musée de Cluny, Panthéon, St-Michel, Seine, Île de la Cité, Île St-Louis

HÔTEL CLAUDE BERNARD ★★★ (17)
43, rue des Écoles, 75005
Métro: Maubert-Mutualité, Cluny–La Sorbonne
35 rooms, all with shower or bath and toilet

TELEPHONE
01-43-26-32-52
FAX
01-43-26-80-56
EMAIL
claudebernardhotel@minitel.net
INTERNET
www.hotelclaudebernard.com
CREDIT CARDS
AE, DC, MC, V
RATES
Single 130€, double 150€, suite 297€; extra bed 40€; taxe *de séjour* 1€ per person, per day
BREAKFAST
Continental 10€ per person
ENGLISH SPOKEN
Yes

The Claude Bernard continues to be a Latin Quarter favorite with many fans, thanks to its key location as a base for exploring St-Michel, St-Germain-des-Prés, and the islands in the Seine—but for this edition, I cannot recommend it. Over the years, the hotel has had its ups and downs. Things picked up considerably a few years ago thanks to a new owner with fresh ideas, but on last visit, the dear old Claude Bernard was on a downward slide and looked very tired and worn out. When I arrived to re-inspect the hotel, the desk clerk did not acknowledge my presence (I had an appointment), but instead spent ten minutes on a personal phone call, all the while aware that I was standing in front of him. As I glanced around, the lobby reminded me of an airport lounge with curved, tufted banquette seating. Ashtrays were piled high and a week's worth of newspapers lay scattered about. As I went through the hotel, I found the hall carpeting dirty. The rooms, which admittedly have size in their favor, still had the same shabby pine furniture that has needed a strong dose of TLC for years. The provincial fabrics were faded, the paint chipped, the bathrooms dated, and the toiletries not only skimpy, but cheap. The tremendous triple and quad rooms are still geared for families, in that there is nothing rambunctious children could do to damage them. As always the rooms facing the street should be considered off-limits for all but comatose sleepers who wear heavy-duty earplugs.

Sorry Claude, but I have to be honest and report the facts as I find them. Hopefully the next time around, you will have someone in charge who cares, because your loyal customers are saddened by your present state.

FACILITIES AND SERVICES: Air-conditioning, bar, direct-dial phone, elevator (to most floors), hair dryer, Internet in lobby, minibar, TV with international reception, office safe (warning: 25€ per stay!)

NEAREST TOURIST ATTRACTIONS (LEFT BANK): Musée de Cluny, St-Michel, Luxembourg Gardens, St-Germain-des-Prés, Seine, Île de la Cité, Île St-Louis

HÔTEL D'ALBE ★★★ (1)
1, rue de la Harpe, 75005
Métro: St-Michel; RER St-Michel–Notre-Dame
45 rooms, all with shower or bath and toilet

This is the perfect site for Latin Quarter night owls and other urbanites who consider 11 P.M. the shank of the evening and the crack of dawn bedtime. Rue de la Harpe is just off place St-Michel, the twenty-four-hour, nonstop, pulsating hub of this *quartier*. The street itself is lined with restaurants and cafés geared to tourists out for a good time. So, I must warn you, while this hotel has a good location, good value, and is the best on the street, it is going to be very noisy unless you use earplugs, sleep with the double glazed windows tightly shut, and keep the air-conditioning on in a room on the top two floors. Above-average closet space and new bathrooms complement well-maintained, spotless rooms that have coordinated colors, striped walls, and quilted bedspreads. Best choices are the corner rooms with three windows, but remember that they will be noisy. If there are four of you, look elsewhere; there aren't any quads. The bright modern breakfast room faces the street and plays relaxing classical music while you enjoy a morning croissant and café au lait.

FACILITIES AND SERVICES: Air-conditioning, direct-dial phone, hair dryer, elevator (to most floors), Internet in lobby, laundry service, minibar, TV with international reception, room safe (no charge), 5th and 6th floors exclusively nonsmoking

NEAREST TOURIST ATTRACTIONS (LEFT BANK): St-Michel, Musée de Cluny, Seine, Île de la Cité, Île St-Louis, St-Germain-des-Prés

TELEPHONE
01-46-34-09-70
FAX
01-40-46-85-70
EMAIL
albehotel@wanadoo.fr
INTERNET
www.hotelalbe.fr
CREDIT CARDS
AE, DC, MC, V
RATES
Single 110–120€, double 130–156€, triple 166€; *taxe de séjour* included
BREAKFAST
Buffet 10€ per person
ENGLISH SPOKEN
Yes

HOTEL DE LA SORBONNE ★★ (23)
6, rue Victor Cousin, 75005
Métro: Cluny–La-Sorbonne; RER Luxembourg
37 rooms, all with shower or bath and toilet

TELEPHONE
01-43-54-58-08
FAX
01-40-51-05-18
INTERNET
www.hotelsorbonne.com
CREDIT CARDS
AE, MC, V
RATES
Single or double 85–115€; *taxe de séjour* included
BREAKFAST
Continental 6€ per person
ENGLISH SPOKEN
Yes

A new proprietor, a quick cosmetic facelift, and a friendly crew headed by Frédéric Lopez have turned this once dumpy dowager into a popular two-star. It is owned by a husband-and-wife team who have several other wonderful three-star hotels on the Left Bank (see below), and when I heard this was their latest acquisition, I knew it would be a winner. The hotel is located in a small courtyard off the street. There is no lobby, but a pretty breakfast room with a bulldog guarding a gas-log fireplace is a welcome place to sit during the day. Upstairs the rooms have all been repainted and updated with simple prints and fabrics, faux woods, and wrought-iron light fixtures. The only choices I do not recommend are the eight rooms similar to No. 31, which have bathrooms so small that you cannot shut the door once you are inside. Despite the sixteen-stair climb to reach Nos. 61 and 62, these rooms are the most popular, thanks to their Panthéon views and new bathrooms; the mansard roof lines could be a problem, however, if you are tall.

Also under the same ownership in the fifth arrondissement: Hôtel des Grands Hommes (page 119), Hôtel du Panthéon (page 122), and Hôtel Résidence Henri IV (page 131).

FACILITIES AND SERVICES: Direct-dial phones, elevator (to most floors), hair dryer, TV with international reception, office safe (no charge)

NEAREST TOURIST ATTRACTIONS (LEFT BANK): Sorbonne, Panthéon, Jardin de Luxembourg, Musée de Cluny, St-Michel, St-Germain-des-Prés

HÔTEL DE L'ESPÉRANCE ★★ (44)
15, rue Pascal, 75005
Métro: Censier-Daubenton, Gobelins
38 rooms, all with shower or bath and toilet

TELEPHONE
01-47-07-10-99
FAX
01-43-37-56-19
EMAIL
hotel.esperance@wanadoo.fr
CREDIT CARDS
AE, DC, MC, V
RATES
Single 70–80€, double 80–90€, triple 105€; *taxe de séjour* included

Baubles, bangles, and beads—and then some—describes the effusive frilly decor and the effervescent owner, Mme. Ellen Aymard, awaiting you at this hotel. Fortunately, you are not sleeping in her downstairs lobby, which is loaded with bowers of oversized fake flowers, Yugoslavian colored crystal, a doll collection, and an extensive array of hand-crocheted pillow covers, doilies, and lamp throws. Add to this a gurgling fountain and reproduction eighteenth-century furniture, and some might need blinders to get to their rooms, which are all quite nice and tame by comparison. The color scheme revolves around coordinated yellow and soft-rose florals. Cleanliness is always stressed. The bathrooms are all nice, and most have heated towel racks. At night you will always find a mint on your pillow. Room 11 is a double with a private garden and a large bathroom suitable for the handicapped. If you want quiet, book No. 21, a double on the back with its own balcony. I think No. 35 is too crowded for three, and the ugly sofabed looked uncomfortable. The location is an interesting one, close to rue Mouffetard and within easy transportation access to most Left Bank and Latin Quarter points of interest.

FACILITIES AND SERVICES: Bar, direct-dial phone, elevator, hair dryer, minibar, TV with international reception, office safe (no charge)

NEAREST TOURIST ATTRACTIONS (LEFT BANK): Rue Mouffetard, Jardin des Plantes, Manufacture des Gobelins (tapestry workshop)

BREAKFAST
Continental 7€ per person
ENGLISH SPOKEN
Yes

HÔTEL DE NOTRE DAME ★★★ (10)
19, rue Maître Albert, 75005
Métro: Maubert-Mutualié; RER St-Michel–Notre-Dame
34 rooms, all with shower or bath and toilet

Walk along the Seine, turn onto a winding, cobblestone street lined with century-old buildings, and suddenly you will come to this quintessential Parisian hotel. The traditional Pierre Deux–designed fabrics go hand in hand with the Asian mirrored screen that reflects the antique furnishings, polished beams, and collection of French porcelain in the reception and sitting areas. The garden breakfast room filled with an attractive mixture of blooming flowers and green plants is one of the nicest places in Paris to start your day. Framed prints of teacups, teapots, and flower bouquets on the marble-top tables add more color. Oriental-style rugs and red-and-green-checked tissue-covered walls lead to the pleasing, well-planned rooms, which reflect the same standards of high quality and elegant coziness. This is an ancient building, so small is the operative word when it comes to room size. However, comfort is never compromised, and you can expect lovely coordinated quarters, marble bathrooms, and all the beams and stone walls this part of Paris is known for.

TELEPHONE
01-43-26-79-00
FAX
01-46-33 50 11
EMAIL
hotel.denotredame@libertysurf.fr
INTERNET
www.hotel-paris-notredame.com
CREDIT CARDS
MC, V
RATES
1–2 persons 145–160€; *taxe de séjour* 0.86€ per person, per day
BREAKFAST
Continental 8€ per person
ENGLISH SPOKEN
Yes

FACILITIES AND SERVICES: Air-conditioning in some rooms, direct-dial phone, elevator, hair dryer, TV with international reception, room safe (no charge)

NEAREST TOURIST ATTRACTIONS (LEFT BANK): Seine, Île de la Cité, l'Île St-Louis, Musée de Cluny, St-Michel, St-Germain-des-Prés

HÔTEL DES ALLIES ★ (¢, 43)
20, rue Berthollet, 75005
Métro: Censier-Daubenton

38 rooms, 21 with shower or bath and toilet

TELEPHONE
01-43-31-47-52
FAX
01-45-35-13-92
CREDIT CARDS
MC, V
RATES
Single 34–57€, double 42–57€, triple 58–75€, quad 93€; hall shower 2.50€; *taxe de séjour* included
BREAKFAST
Continental 5€ per person
ENGLISH SPOKEN
Yes

Three generations of contented clientele continue to reserve rooms in this serviceable, frugal pick at the bottom of the fifth arrondissement. The location is not central by any means, but it is within walking distance to all the action and color around rue Mouffetard. The desk is open from 7 A.M. to 10:30 P.M., but keys are given to guests.

Aside from a talking glass elevator, it is obvious that money has not been spent on fancy decorating touches, but all the rooms are clean, with a minimum of rips, tears, or dents in sight. The best part is that the rooms come with price tags no serious bargain hunter can ignore. The plain-Jane Room 22 is a steal, with a huge bathroom, twin beds, and nice wallpaper. It is, however, next to the hall shower. Number 2 is also across from a hall shower, and like most of the other rooms, is hose-down simple in every respect. It does have its own bathroom with orange sorbet–colored fixtures and a window. Unfortunately, No. 49 reminds me that chenille bedspreads are still available; however, the enormous robin's-egg-blue bath with a glass shower is better than many three star hotels can offer. If you are solo, avoid No. 51; even though it has a view of the dome of l'Église du Val de Grace on the grounds of a nearby military hospital, the bed is too soft and lumpy. A better nest for singles is sunny No. 52, with tiny flowered wallpaper and a stall shower in the bathroom. Room 5, on the street, has space to spare, a double bed, wallpaper, and a bathroom with a stall shower.

FACILITIES AND SERVICES: Elevator, office safe (no charge)

NEAREST TOURIST ATTRACTIONS (LEFT BANK): Rue Mouffetard

HÔTEL DES GRANDES ÉCOLES ★★★ (32)
75, rue du Cardinal-Lemoine, 75005
Métro: Cardinal-Lemoine, Place Monge
51 rooms, all with shower or bath and toilet

It is unanimous—everyone *adores* this hotel.

Once found, this hotel address is one that its loyal followers whisper only to a select few. Nestled in a beautiful garden and hidden from the world by towering wooden doors opening off the street, it is definitely one of the most romantic havens of peace and quiet in Paris. The grandmotherly owner, Leonore LeFloch, and her receptionist, Marie, treat their guests like family members. As you can imagine, reservations for this very special hotel are essential months in advance.

Two facing houses make up the hotel. In both, the rooms are decorated with a feminine touch, sparing no ruffle or pretty flowered fabric from the Laura Ashley school of decorating. Almost all of the rooms in both buildings look out onto the large tree-shaded garden with trellised roses, singing birds, spring daffodils, and summer wildflowers. Tables and chairs are placed here, making it a lovely spot for reading and sipping a cool drink. When you look out of your window between April and October, you will imagine you are in a French country village, not in the middle of Paris.

The hotel is an uphill climb from the métro, but once there you are close to place de la Contrescarpe, which played such an important part in Hemingway's Paris. You can also walk to rue Mouffetard, famous for its colorful, daily street *marché,* some good places to eat (see *Great Eats Paris*), and inexpensive clothing stores geared to cute young things.

FACILITIES AND SERVICES: Direct-dial phone, elevator (to most floors), hair dryer, no TV, office safe (no charge)

NEAREST TOURIST ATTRACTIONS (LEFT BANK): Rue Mouffetard, place de la Contrescarpe, Panthéon, Jardin des Plantes

TELEPHONE
01-43-26-79-23

FAX
01-43-25-28-15

EMAIL
Hotel.Grandes.Ecoles@wanadoo.fr

INTERNET
www.hotel-grandes-ecoles.com

CREDIT CARDS
MC, V

RATES
1–2 persons 100–125€; extra bed 20€; parking 30€; *taxe de séjour* included

BREAKFAST
Continental 8€ per person

ENGLISH SPOKEN
Yes

HÔTEL DES GRANDS HOMMES ★★★ ($, 31)
17, place du Panthéon, 75005
Métro: Maubert-Mutualité; RER Luxembourg
32 rooms, all with shower or bath and toilet

The Hôtel des Grands Hommes is a popular three-star choice, thanks to the personal management of the owner, Corinne Brethous-Moncelli. The hotel faces the Panthéon—the final resting place of many of France's great, including Voltaire, Rousseau, Victor Hugo,

TELEPHONE
01-46-34-19-60

FAX
01-43-26-67-32

INTERNET
www.hoteldesgrandshommes.com

CREDIT CARDS
AE, DC, MC, V

RATES
Single 210€, double 225€,
triple 255€, suite 285–292€;
extra bed 15.24€; excellent
rates in low season; *taxe de séjour*
included

BREAKFAST
Buffet 10€ per person

ENGLISH SPOKEN
Yes

Alexandre Dumas, and Pierre and Marie Curie. In addition to its knockout location, it has historical significance: it is where André Breton invented automatic writing in 1919. The rooms have benefited from a recent redecoration using Greek and Roman classical themes and bold color schemes that mix eggplant with brown, and azure blue with verdant green. The gracious formal lobby is decorated in peach colors with faux marble finishes and outfitted with plenty of soft seating, a small corner bar, and an atrium garden filled with blooming plants. While all the rooms are very nice, I would request one of the spacious front rooms with a balcony on the fifth and sixth floors, where you can have breakfast and gaze onto the Panthéon across the street and see Sacré Coeur gleaming in the distance. Not only do the rooms on the back have no view, but some are so tightly fitted that you can hardly get around the bed.

Also under the same ownership is the Hôtel du Panthéon next door (page 122), the Hôtel Résidence Henri IV (page 131), and Hôtel de la Sorbonne (see page 116).

FACILITIES AND SERVICES: Air-conditioning, bar, direct-dial phone, elevator, hair dryer, minibar, TV with international reception, room safe (no charge)

NEAREST TOURIST ATTRACTIONS (LEFT BANK): Panthéon, Sorbonne, Musée de Cluny, Jardin du Luxembourg, St-Michel

HÔTEL DES JARDINS DU LUXEMBOURG ★★★ (29)
5, Impasse Royer-Collard, 75005
Métro: Cluny–La Sorbonne; RER Luxembourg
26 rooms, all with shower or bath and toilet

TELEPHONE
01-40-46-08-88

FAX
01-40-46-02-28

EMAIL
jardinslux@wanadoo.fr

CREDIT CARDS
AE, DC, MC, V

RATES
Single or double 140–150€,
suite 155€; *taxe de séjour*
included

BREAKFAST
Buffet or Continental in room
10€ per person

ENGLISH SPOKEN
Yes

On his first trip to Paris in 1885, Sigmund Freud lived at this address, which was then the Hôtel de la Paix. When he noticed that the curtains around his bed were green, he applied chemical tests to make sure they did not contain arsenic.

Freud is long gone, as are the green curtains. In their place is this charming boutique hotel with casually elegant guest quarters, the best of which overlook the quiet street. The lobby is filled with personal touches that set the tone for the rest of the hotel. In one corner, a park bench is lined with colorful pillows; in another is a mirrored hat and coat rack. A cloisonné table holds a selection of magazines, and kilim rugs scattered on hardwood floors add color. The intimate breakfast room has marble-top bistro tables, each with its own brass reading light. Some of the rooms are a bit tight, so if you require space, book a superior or the sixth floor minisuite, which has a tip-of-the-Eiffel-Tower view. Two other good bets are No. 24, a twin with rooftop and sky views, and nicely turned out with brown fabric walls that blend with the blue and green fabric colors, and No. 25, a double with a nice bathroom and a peek at the Eiffel Tower. Next to the hotel, there are also two ground floor superior rooms with separate entrances. They do have space, but absolutely no privacy from the street-facing windows unless you keep the curtains permanently drawn. For security, the windows do not open, which means the only fresh air comes from the transom over the door. Another minus is the lack of closets; instead, there is only a movable clothes rack.

FACILITIES AND SERVICES: Air-conditioning, direct-dial phone, hair dryer, elevator, laundry service, minibar, sauna (free), TV with international reception, room safe (no charge)

NEAREST TOURIST ATTRACTIONS (LEFT BANK): Jardin du Luxembourg, Panthéon, Sorbonne, Musée de Cluny, St-Michel, St-Germain-des-Prés

HÔTEL DES 3 COLLÈGES ★★ (25)
16, rue Cujas, 75005
Métro: Maubert-Mutualité; RER Luxembourg
44 rooms, all with shower or bath and toilet

This hotel takes its name from the three colleges on the Montagne–St-Geneviève: La Sorbonne, founded in the thirteenth century; the fifteenth-century Collège St-Barbe, the oldest private school in France; and the prestigious Collège de France. It is in a good Left Bank neighborhood between the Sorbonne and the Panthéon, and within easy walking distance to a multitude of restaurants and shops. The small, off-white lobby has a California look, with modern chairs, large green plants, and bleached wooden floors. The pocket-size rooms have all the necessities: luggage racks, desks and chairs, full-length mirrors, wall-mounted television sets, and fitted bathrooms. What they are missing is extra space. The best from a size standpoint are No. 62 with a Sorbonne view, No. 63 with sloping roof, and No. 64. Number 46 is a nice selection for the single traveler. The glass-roofed lounge off the lobby showcases a large, central tree that's surrounded by rattan chairs.

TELEPHONE
01-43-54-67-30

FAX
01-46-34-02-99

INTERNET
www.3colleges.com

CREDIT CARDS
AE, DC, MC, V

RATES
Single 67€, 1–2 persons 86–94€, large 6th floor rooms for 1–2 people 120€, triple 140€; *taxe de séjour* included

BREAKFAST
Continental 8€ per person

ENGLISH SPOKEN
Yes

FACILITIES AND SERVICES: Direct-dial phone, elevator, hair dryer, laundry service, TV with international reception, room safe (no charge)

NEAREST TOURIST ATTRACTIONS (LEFT BANK): Panthéon, Sorbonne, Jardin du Luxembourg, St-Michel, Musée de Cluny

HÔTEL DU COLLÈGE DE FRANCE ★★ (12)
7, rue Thénard, 75005
Métro: Maubert-Mutualité, Cluny–La Sorbonne
29 rooms, all with shower or bath and toilet

TELEPHONE
01-43-26-78-36
FAX
01-46-34-58-29
EMAIL
hotel.du.college.de.france@wanadoo.fr
INTERNET
www.hotel-collegedefrance.com
CREDIT CARDS
AE, MC, V
RATES
Single 81€, double 90–100€, triple 107–117€; free for children under 14; *taxe de séjour* included
BREAKFAST
Continental 7€ per person
ENGLISH SPOKEN
Yes

Well placed in the heart of the Latin Quarter and across the street from the Collège de France, this is an outstanding value for a two-star hotel. The immaculate rooms are uniformly done. The best ones are on the top floors; they have wooden beams and paneling, glimpses of Notre Dame Cathedral, and in summer are equipped with portable fans. One room on the second floor and some on the fifth have a balcony. If you want connecting rooms, they will be on the first or second floors. Room 62 is the largest and most requested, probably due to the two floor-to-ceiling windows opening onto a small balcony, where you can see the Collège de France. The bathrooms are modern, with hair dryers, large towels, and space for more than just a toothbrush. The lobby and breakfast room feature rust red fabrics, which goes well with the collection of healthy green plants, and a statue of Joan of Arc guards the entryway. Jean Marc, the very personable owner, and his excellent staff have proven their motto: "If you are a client once, you will always be one." The popularity of this little hotel is reflected in its guest register, which is almost filled months ahead, so plan accordingly.

FACILITIES AND SERVICES: Direct-dial phone, fans, elevator (to most floors), hair dryer, TV with international reception, office or room safe (no charge)

NEAREST TOURIST ATTRACTIONS (LEFT BANK): Musée de Cluny, St-Michel, St-Germain-des-Prés, Sorbonne, Panthéon, Luxembourg Gardens, Seine, Île de la Cité, Île St-Louis

HÔTEL DU PANTHÉON ★★★ ($, 30)
19, place du Panthéon, 75005
Métro: Maubert-Mutualité; RER Luxembourg
36 rooms, all with shower, bath, and toilet

TELEPHONE
01-43-54-32-95
FAX
01-43-26-64-65
EMAIL
hotel.pantheon@wanadoo.fr

The Hôtel du Panthéon is an elegantly converted eighteenth-century town house that faces the imposing place du Panthéon in the fifth arrondissement. The métro is about five blocks away, but if you love this part of Paris, you know that almost everything is within walking distance. From the ground up, the hotel benefits from the impeccable taste and preservationist sensibilities of the gracious owner, Corinne Brethous-Moncelli, who also owns Hôtel des Grands Hommes next door (see page 119), the Hôtel Résidence Henri IV (see page 131), and Hôtel de la Sorbonne (see page 116).

The large entry leads to the attractive lounge that has a small atrium garden to one side and a panoramic view of the Panthéon. The Continental breakfast is served under the stone arches in the house's original cellar or in the privacy of your room. Guests will feel at home immediately in any one of the thirty-six rooms, harmoniously decorated with antique furniture, perfectly coordinated fabrics, textile-covered walls, nicely framed artwork, and floor-length curtains from fourteen-foot ceilings. Several with canopy beds are romantic choices for honeymooners. The twenty-three front rooms facing the Panthéon are naturally in demand, especially the five with balconies on the fifth floor. However, if you need absolute silence and calm, the viewless back rooms will guarantee this. The bathrooms are spacious, many with free-standing sinks, separate stall showers, and enclosed toilets.

FACILITIES AND SERVICES: Air-conditioning, conference room, direct-dial phone, elevator, hair dryer, laundry service, magnifying mirrors, minibar, porter, TV with international reception, room safe (no charge)

NEAREST TOURIST ATTRACTIONS (LEFT BANK): Panthéon, Sorbonne, Luxembourg Gardens, Musée de Cluny, St-Michel

INTERNET
www.hoteldupantheon.com

CREDIT CARDS
AE, DC, MC, V

RATES
Single 190€, double 220€, triple 260€; *taxe de séjour* included

BREAKFAST
Buffet or Continental 11€ per person

ENGLISH SPOKEN
Yes

HÔTEL ESMERALDA ★ (4)
4, ruc St Julien-le-Pauvre, at quai de Montebello, 75005
Métro: St-Michel; RER St-Michel–Notre-Dame
19 rooms, 16 with shower or bath and toilet

Warning: This hotel is not for perfectionists!

The Esmeralda is an unconventional hideaway directly across the Seine from Notre Dame Cathedral. It has been owned for years by Madame Bruel, a sculptor and writer who lived in England and studied at Oxford. She and her former husband owned the first Bateaux Mouches that now take tourists up and down the Seine. After a bitter divorce, she bought the Esmeralda because she could see her beloved Seine from many of the windows. She told me most of the rooms at the time were occupied

TELEPHONE
01-43 54 19-20

FAX
01-40-51-00-68

CREDIT CARDS
None, cash only

RATES
Very small single 30€, 1–2 persons 60€, triple 95€, quad 105€; *taxe de séjour* included

BREAKFAST
Continental 6€ per person

ENGLISH SPOKEN
Yes

by "permanent residents," all of whom shared one bathroom! She has made some improvements since then . . . notice I said some. This is a hotel people either love or absolutely hate. For some, its faded charm with a definite past holds great appeal, especially when sitting by one of the large windows and looking across the Seine to Notre Dame bathed in moonlight.

Maybe it does not have the most modern accommodations in town, but it does have one of the best Left Bank locations and some of the most interesting guests. The lack of embellishments, which might disappoint some, is the lure that brings others back again and again. This is a hotel with character for people with character.

No two rooms are alike, and they definitely are light years away from modern. Just like the unique owner, they flout convention and are eccentric to the core. Some are the size of a walk-in closet; others have chandeliers, marble fireplaces, and picture-perfect postcard views of Notre Dame Cathedral over the gardens of St-Julien-le-Pauvre, Paris's oldest church. All the rooms are reached by passing through a stone-walled lobby and climbing up a circular flight of ancient stairs. Some of the floors slant, a few areas need more than just a coat of paint, and others have only a nodding acquaintance with the housekeeper. It is also noisy. But its many cult followers do not care because just being at the Esmeralda spells Paris for them. Be sure to bring earplugs and reserve way in advance.

FACILITIES AND SERVICES: Direct-dial phone, no elevator (4 floors), office safe (no charge)

NEAREST TOURIST ATTRACTIONS (LEFT BANK): Seine, St-Michel, Île de la Cité, Île St-Louis, St-Germain-des-Prés, Musée de Cluny

HÔTEL EXCELSIOR ★ (26)
20, rue Cujas, 75005
Métro: Cluny–La Sorbonne; RER Luxembourg
66 rooms, all with shower or bath and toilet

TELEPHONE
01-46-34-79-50

FAX
01-43-54-87-10

EMAIL
htexcel5@club-Internetpoint.fr

INTERNET
www.excelsiorlatin.com

CREDIT CARDS
AE, MC, V

Acceptable one-star hotels are becoming an endangered species in this part of Paris. Either they have been totally renovated into three- or four-star addresses, or are so run-down and filthy that, for me, considering them is absolutely out of the question. Enter the Excelsior, which is still a one-star and still acceptable . . . as long as you can live without air-conditioning or a direct-dial telephone in your room, don't need an elevator for the first two floors, and don't mind open closets, hard chairs, and some wear and tear around the edges. The rooms are clean, colors match, and the location is excellent. If you don't like noise, you will have to put up with some blank wall views in the second building. Room 204, a double, is one of these, but it does have newer carpeting, matching drapes and spreads, and a better closet, though the bathroom has a half tub. Number 34 is a safe twin selection. It faces front and has a bathroom with a shower over the tub. Forget No. 33—the toilet, sink, and shower are in an open area with no door, and in No. 21, you enter the room through the bathroom! All rooms are payable in advance and only registered guests are allowed past reception.

FACILITIES AND SERVICES: Elevator (starts 2nd floor), hair dryer available, TV with international reception, office safe (no charge)

NEAREST TOURIST ATTRACTIONS (LEFT BANK): Panthéon, Sorbonne, Jardin du Luxembourg, Musée de Cluny, St-Michel, St-Germain-des-Prés

RATES
Single 70€, double 75€, triple 92€, quad 95€; lower rates in off-season on Internet; *taxe de séjour* included
BREAKFAST
Continental 6€ per person
ENGLISH SPOKEN
Yes

HÔTEL HENRI IV ★★★ (3)
9–11, rue Saint-Jacques, 75005
Métro: Cluny–La Sorbonne, Maubert-Mutualité; RER St-Michel–Notre-Dame
23 rooms, all with shower or bath and toilet

The wonderful Hôtel Henri IV, the latest jewel in the crown of owners Roland and Elisabeth Buffat, proves that style does not have to come with high price tags. The sophisticated design and great value of their other hotels are both clearly evident in their newest venture. The brick-floor lobby is done in soft sea green, accented by an antique Portuguese-tile wall and comfortable dark brown–leather armchairs. The halls are done in the same soft green, with linen-textured walls adding interest above the wainscoting. The tasteful rooms all repeat the same putty and white colors, on the stucco walls and wicker furnishings. All have luggage and closet space, a comfortable chair, desk space with modem lines, and attractive bathrooms with tub-and-shower combinations and heated towel racks. I like the rooms on the higher floors, not only because they are light and airy, but because some have views of the top of Notre Dame Cathedral. Some of the rooms facing the interior hotel courtyard have small balconies.

Also under the same ownership are Hôtel de Lutèce and Hôtel des Deux-Îles, both on Île St-Louis (see pages 99 and 100), and Galileo Hôtel (see page 204).

TELEPHONE
01-46-33-20-20
FAX
01-46-33-90-90
EMAIL
hotel-henri-IV@wanadoo.fr
INTERNET
www.hotel-henri4.com
CREDIT CARDS
AE, MC, V
RATES
Single135€, double 155€, triple 175€; *taxe de séjour* 0.90€ per person, per day
BREAKFAST
Continental 11€ per person
ENGLISH SPOKEN
Yes

FACILITIES AND SERVICES: Air-conditioning, direct-dial phone, elevator, hair dryer, Internet in lobby, laundry service, minibar, TV with international reception, room safe (no charge)

NEAREST TOURIST ATTRACTIONS (LEFT BANK): Seine, St-Michel, Île de la Cité, l'Île St-Louis, Musée de Cluny, Jardin du Luxembourg

HÔTEL LE NOTRE DAME ★★★ ($, 2)
1, quai St-Michel, 75005
Métro: St-Michel; RER St-Michel–Notre-Dame
26 rooms, all with shower or bath and toilet

TELEPHONE
01-43-54-20-43
FAX
01-43-26-61-75
EMAIL
hotel.lenotredame@libertysurf.fr
INTERNET
www.lenotredame.com
CREDIT CARDS
AE, DC, MC, V
RATES
1–2 persons 150€ (no view), 200€ (view), duplex for 3–4 250€; *taxe de séjour* 0.86€ per person, per day
BREAKFAST
Continental 7€ per person
ENGLISH SPOKEN
Yes

Hôtel le Notre Dame offers twenty-six beautiful rooms, all with the latest bathrooms and bold color plans. Reserve one of the eighteen rooms with a view, and you will look out across the *bouquinistes* (second-hand booksellers) lining the quays along the Seine and to the great western facade of the famed cathedral. Unless the windows are tightly shut and you are using earplugs, you will go to sleep and wake with the sounds of Paris, but for many of us, the majestic view will be worth it.

Entrance to the hotel is through a mirrored ground-floor hall and up a short flight of steps. The beautiful sitting room and breakfast area off the reception area have picture windows facing Notre Dame Cathedral and river. Warm dark woods show off the gold tartan-covered walls and form a backdrop for the comfortable seating that invites you to linger for hours and watch *tout* Paris surge by.

The rooms are decorated with an attractive mix of antiques and reproductions. If space is a prime concern, opt for No. 61, two-story duplex. When you walk in, *voila!* The river and Notre Dame are in full view. Upstairs there is a glass partition and a rooftop window with more views. In No. 63, it's more of the same. However, in No. 62, under a pitched roof, the windows are high, and unless you are right in front of them, you won't have the view. I love the contemporary bathroom in No. 52, and the three windows in the room that allow you to lie in bed and gaze at the cathedral. In No. 53, you can still see the church but not from bed; the new marble bathroom has a heated towel rack and good light. You definitely do not want to stay in Room 25 or 55, both of which face a back airshaft and noisy fan.

FACILITIES AND SERVICES: Air-conditioning, direct-dial phone, elevator (starts 1st floor; 1 flight of stairs to reception), hair dryer, minibar, TV with international reception, room safe (no charge)

NEAREST TOURIST ATTRACTIONS (LEFT BANK): Seine, St-Michel, Île de la Cité, Île St-Louis, St-Michel, Musée de Cluny, St-Germain-des-Prés

HÔTEL MARIGNAN ★ (13)
13, rue de Sommerard, 75005
Métro: Maubert-Mutualité, Cluny–La Sorbonne
30 rooms, 8 with shower or bath and toilet, 7 with toilet and sink, 15 with sink only

The Marignan lives up to the three Cs of all lower-priced accommodations: it is clean, convenient, and cheap, especially from October through February (but not between Christmas and New Year's) when rooms booked for three nights or more are 25 percent less than the published prices. The hotel is usually jammed year-round with a frugal crowd of students, backpackers, and professors. A spirit of camaraderie prevails in this busy spot, making it impossible to feel lonely for long. The linoleum-lined rooms are above average for a one-star. Mattresses are good, a third of the rooms have full facilities, and space is a reality, but don't look for views from the back singles or much in the way of reading lights. Breakfast, which is generous by one-star standards (cheese, fruit salad, and orange juice along with bread and jam, but no croissant) is included in the rate and cannot be deducted. Guests are allowed to bring in food, store it in the kitchen refrigerator, warm it in the microwave, and eat it in the dining room, but no eating is allowed in the rooms. Guests can also use the washer/dryer to wash travel-weary clothing and iron out the wrinkles with the hotel iron.

To his credit, long-term owner Paul Keniger has provided guests with a wealth of information on Paris, including a large detailed map of the *quartier* showing the métro stops, banks, pharmacies, money-changing offices, bakeries, and tourist sites. The management also clearly states the rules of the hotel, and guests are expected to abide by them or move out. They are listed in plain sight at the check-in desk, so no one can claim "I didn't know" not to put suitcases on the bed or to slam doors; not to eat or leave empty bottles or cans in the room; not to take a shower before 7 A.M. or after 10:45 P.M.; and never to go barefoot in public areas or on the stairs. And by all means, turn off the light when leaving.

TELEPHONE
01-43-54-63-81
FAX
01-43-54-63-81
EMAIL
reserv-marignan@wanadoo.fr
INTERNET
www.hotel-marignan.com
CREDIT CARDS
MC, V
RATES
Single 47–70€, double 60–85€, triple 90–110€, quad 100–125€, 5 people 125–155€; showers free; *taxe de séjour* included
BREAKFAST
Included, cannot be deducted
ENGLISH SPOKEN
Yes, and German

Between March and September, reservations are taken for a minimum of two nights.

All reservations can be guaranteed by a credit card. To pay by credit card, tabs must exceed a minimum of 120€ in off-season and 250€ in high season. Full refunds are granted if cancellation is more than seven days before arrival; otherwise, they charge the price of the room for one night.

FACILITIES AND SERVICES: Dining area, direct-dial phones, no elevator (6 floors), basement laundry and ironing area (no room laundering allowed), French TV on request, hair dryer in some rooms and also on request, office safe (no charge)

NEAREST TOURIST ATTRACTIONS (LEFT BANK): Musée de Cluny, St-Michel, St-Germain-des-Prés, Seine, Île de la Cité, Île St-Louis

HÔTEL MINERVE ★★★ (27)
13, rue des Écoles, 75005
Métro: Cardinal Lemoine, Maubert-Mutualité
54 rooms, all with shower or bath and toilet

TELEPHONE
01-43-26-26-04
01-43-26-81-89

FAX
01-44-07-01-96

EMAIL
minerve@hotellerie.net

INTERNET
www.hotel-paris-minerve.com

CREDIT CARDS
MC, V

RATES
Single 79–130€, 93–140€,
triple 145€; *taxe de séjour*
included

BREAKFAST
Continental 8€ per person

ENGLISH SPOKEN
Yes, and Spanish

Eric Gaucheron had two important life-changing events in 1999: his wife, Sylvie, bore him a son, and he bought the fifty-four-room Hôtel Minerve, next door to the Familia Hôtel, which he and his family have owned for many years (see page 111). Despite the fact that the Minerve occupies an 1850 noble building, before Eric renovated it completely, the hotel was, in a word, terrible. No more! Thank goodness energy, imagination, and enthusiasm are three attributes Eric has in spades. Twenty-four workmen toiled relentlessly for months to meet his exacting standards, and a phoenix rose from the ashes.

Everything is new: the mattresses; the attractive, custom-made antique-style furnishings; the coordinated fabrics; and of course, the marble-tile bathrooms with monogrammed towels. In addition to all the usual comforts, such as international television reception and triple-glazed windows to buffer the noise, all rooms have modems, four have cathedral ceilings, five have hand-painted ceilings, two have interior patios, ten have balconies, and many have hand-painted frescoes of French monuments. It is hard to pick a favorite, but I do like No. 607. The wall behind the bed was an old chimney, and from the balcony you have a view of Notre Dame and a twelfth-century abbey. Another favorite is No. 403, with a fresco of Monet's gardens at Giverney. Room 507 has two windows looking onto a balcony and a large bathroom with a tub. If you need absolute quiet, No. 608, with hand-painted scenes from the Greek Parthenon, double closets, and good lighting, is on the back and can sleep three. Both of the two inside patio rooms (Nos. 102 and 103) are also quiet.

A mural montage of Paris greets guests as they enter the hotel. Original 150-year-old tapestries hang on the exposed stone walls in the lobby and in the downstairs breakfast room. The appealing lobby has burnt orange and gold armchairs and settees arranged in groups for twos and threes. Toward the back is a glass-enclosed atrium with a fountain and bamboo trees. Along one wall is an antique bookcase holding some of Eric's antique book collection and a lovely old clock. Recent additions include two conference rooms, which seat thirty but can hold fifty for small weddings or private receptions. It all adds up to an impressive three-star hotel.

FACILITIES AND SERVICES: Conference rooms (2), direct-dial phone, elevator, hair dryer, minibar, TV with international reception, room safe (no charge)

NEAREST TOURIST ATTRACTIONS (LEFT BANK): Jardin des Plantes, Seine, Île-St Louis, Île de la Cité

HÔTEL PARC SAINT-SÉVERIN ★★★ (7)
22, rue de la Parcheminerie, 75005
Métro: Cluny–La Sorbonne, St-Michel;
RER St-Michel–Notre Dame
27 rooms, all with shower or bath and toilet

Dyed-in-the-wool aficionados of life around St-Michel, who also like elegantly understated surroundings, will love this hotel. The owners are to be applauded for creating an alluring, modern establishment that is serene, serious, and pleasing to the eye. For someone very, very special, reserve No. 70, the private penthouse suite with its own elevator entrance. The wraparound terrace provides unequaled views of Notre Dame, St-Séverin Church (one of the most popular in Paris for weddings), the Panthéon, Collège de France, Tour Montparnasse, and in the distance, the Eiffel Tower and the Sacré Coeur on Montmartre. The interior of this dream suite glows with a blend of antiques and contemporary furnishings. The other rooms in the hotel display the same standards of excellence, and many have impressive views. The management and staff are exceptional in their attention and service for all of their guests. For those who want up-to-the-minute convenience and luxury in the heart of old Paris, the Parc

TELEPHONE
01-43-54-32-17

FAX
01-43-54-70-71

EMAIL
hotel.parc.severin@wanadoo.fr

INTERNET
espirit-de-france.com

CREDIT CARDS
AE, DC, MC, V

RATES
Single 105€, double 125–140€, suites 195–295€; children under 12 free; *taxe de séjour* included

BREAKFAST
Buffet downstairs or Continental in room 10€ per person

ENGLISH SPOKEN
Yes

Saint-Séverin is a favorite choice of many discriminating *Great Sleeps Paris* readers.

For other hotels under the same ownership, see Hôtel Brighton (page 67), Hôtel de la Place du Louvre (page 69), Hôtel Mansart (page 74), and Hôtel d'Orsay (page 184).

FACILITIES AND SERVICES: Air-conditioning, bar, direct-dial phone, elevator, hair dryer, Internet in lobby, laundry service, minibar, TV with international reception, room safe (no charge)

NEAREST TOURIST ATTRACTIONS (LEFT BANK): Musée de Cluny, St-Michel, St-Germain-des-Prés, Seine, Île de la Cité, Île St-Louis

HÔTEL RELAIS SAINT-JACQUES ★★★★ ($, 36)
3, rue de l'abbé de l'Épée, 75005
Métro: RER Luxembourg
23 rooms, all with shower, bath, and toilet

TELEPHONE
01-53-73-26-00; toll-free in the U.S. 800-44-UTELL

FAX
01-43-26-17-81

EMAIL
nevers.luxembourg@wanadoo.fr

INTERNET
www.relais-saint-jacques.com

CREDIT CARDS
AE, DC, MC, V

RATES
1–2 persons 200–325€; lower off-season rates; *taxe de séjour* 1€ per person, per night

BREAKFAST
Buffet 14€ per person

ENGLISH SPOKEN
Yes

A beautiful Louis XV furnished salon with Aubusson tapestries and a marble fireplace flanked by bookcases set the regal tone at this lovely boutique hotel, which is on the road that pilgrims once took on their way to Santiago de Compostela in Spain. The theme of the hotel celebrates the grace and beauty of the castles of the Loire Valley and reflects the meticulous care that the Bonneau family has put into making sure that their guests are pampered with a combination of the traditions of the past and the luxurious amenities of the present. The stunning collection of photographs of the Loire hanging in the common areas and the glass-roofed breakfast room are the work of the family patriarch, who was named the best French photographer of the year in 1961. In keeping with the theme, each room is named after a château in the Loire and furnished in one of four traditional styles: Louis XV, Louis XVI, Empire, and Portuguese Manuelian. Room 402, named after the Château Usse, is done in the latter, with handmade twisted dark mahogany wood offsetting the lace linens. The stunning desk was originally a type of office trunk used for traveling from castle to castle. Number 203, Château Beaugency, decorated in soft aqua, is Louis XVI. The customized gold-trimmed furnishings include a console cabinet containing a television, safe, and minibar. Château Blois, and two others like it, are Empire. The bathrooms in all are beautifully done in marble with plenty of mirrors, excellent light, and all the towels and toiletries you would expect. Most of the bedrooms face out, but the few that do not look out onto walls that have been painted to resemble country garden themes.

FACILITIES AND SERVICES: Air-conditioning, bar, business center, conference room, direct-dial phone, elevator, hair dryer, handicapped room, Internet in business center, laundry service, minibar, trouser press, TV with international reception, 24-hour room service, room safe (no charge), some nonsmoking rooms

NEAREST TOURIST ATTRACTIONS (LEFT BANK): Jardin du Luxembourg, Panthéon, Sorbonne, Musée de Cluny, St-Michel

HÔTEL RÉSIDENCE HENRI IV ★★★ (22)
50, rue des Bernardins, next to Square Paul Langevin, 75005
Métro: Maubert-Mutualité, Cardinal Lemoine
14 rooms, all with shower or bath and toilet and fully fitted kitchenette

Over twenty years ago, when I began writing my Paris hotel guide, this hotel had another name and an image of faded respectability. Several years ago it was taken over by Corinne Brethous-Moncelli, who owns other recommended hotels in the fifth arrondissement. I have found that whatever Mme. Moncelli touches is transformed with style and distinction, and this property is no exception. Quietly situated opposite the leafy Square Paul Langevin, at the end of rue des Bernardins, the hotel offers fourteen spacious rooms, each with the added plus of fully fitted kitchenettes, as well as all the hotel services and facilities that a guest could want. I think the best buys are the beautiful two room suites because they offer separate sitting areas, marble fireplaces, and just enough extra space to make a long stay very comfortable. Number 22 has a magnificent gold-framed mirror over its fireplace. Hand-painted moldings and the original ceiling are carried through to the bedroom, which has a large armoire and a corner fireplace to add to its charm. Rooms 50 and 52 can be joined to accommodate a family. Number 1 on the ground floor is done in soft gray and cream and has a skylight in the bathroom. It faces the street and has no fireplace, but it is large enough for three. The hotel is peaceful and calm, yet it is minutes away from almost everything on a visitor's A-list of things to see and do around the *quartier* of St-Michel.

Also under the same ownership are Hôtel des Grands Hommes (page 119), Hôtel du Panthéon (page 122), and Hôtel de la Sorbonne (page 116).

TELEPHONE
01-44-41-31-81

FAX
01-46-33-93-22

INTERNET
www.residencehenri4.com

CREDIT CARDS
AE, DC, MC, V

RATES
1–2 persons 133€ (no kitchenette)–163€, triple 193€, quad 223€; *taxe de séjour* included

BREAKFAST
Continental 9€ per person

ENGLISH SPOKEN
Yes

FACILITIES AND SERVICES: Two air-conditioned rooms, direct-dial phone, elevator (does not go to lower ground floor breakfast room), hair dryer, fitted kitchenettes, TV with international reception, room safe (no charge)

NEAREST TOURIST ATTRACTIONS (LEFT BANK): Panthéon, Sorbonne, Jardin du Luxembourg, Musée de Cluny, St-Michel

HÔTEL RÉSIDENCE MONGE ★★ (33)
55, rue Monge, 75005
Métro: Place Monge, Cardinal Lemoine
36 rooms, all with bath or shower and toilet

TELEPHONE
01-43-26-87-90
FAX
01-43-54-47-25
EMAIL
hotel-monge@wanadoo.fr
INTERNET
www.hotelmonge.com
CREDIT CARDS
MC, V
RATES
Single 62–75€, double 78–120€; extra bed 16€; *taxe de séjour* 0.91€ per person, per day
BREAKFAST
Continental 7€ per person
ENGLISH SPOKEN
Yes

It isn't posh by any means, just a modest family hotel run by a delightful owner, Mme. Chatillon. The exceptionally clean, well-priced rooms are done in rose, blue, peach, pale green, or yellow. All are absolutely spotless and in perfect order, thanks to the three housekeepers who have worked here for twenty years. Number 31 is one of the best in the house. This quiet room is done in hues of salmon and blue with two windows overlooking a playground (which was once a Roman amphitheater) and a bathroom with both a tub and shower. Number 32 is also a nice double with good leg room and a large, light bathroom. Three can fit comfortably in No. 22, which has the bonus of a balcony. I can't say much for No. 23, a single on the front where it is a tight squeeze to sit at the desk, which is almost covered by the TV, and the closet door will never open all the way. You can expect some noise in Rooms 1 and 15 because they face the street. Imitation flowers and plants abound, especially in the breakfast room, which is overflowing with many bright varieties sitting in floral trimmed pots.

FACILITIES AND SERVICES: Air-conditioning, direct-dial phone, elevator, hair dryer, minibar, TV with international reception, office safe (no charge)

NEAREST TOURIST ATTRACTIONS (LEFT BANK): Rue Mouffetard, Jardin des Plantes

HÔTEL SAINT-JACQUES ★★ (20)
35, rue des Écoles, 75005
Métro: Maubert-Mutualite, Cluny–La Sorbonne; RER St-Michel–Notre-Dame
35 rooms, 31 with shower or bath and toilet

TELEPHONE
01-44-07-45-45
FAX
01-43-25-65-50
EMAIL
hotelsaintjacques@wanadoo.fr
INTERNET
www.hotel-saintjacques.com

Rooms with half as much appeal often cost twice as much as those at this outstanding two-star choice near the Sorbonne. From the doorstep you can easily walk to Notre Dame, the Panthéon, the Louvre, the islands, and all the interesting streets that make up this part of the Latin Quarter. Concern for artistic details, first-rate services, and loads of amenities underscore the fact that affordable does not need to mean lacking in style or substance. The pretty frescoes in the sitting room of a Victorian trio along the Seine and in the street-side breakfast room of Notre Dame were done by a painter who left his job as an English teacher to follow his passion for art. The thirty-five reasonably priced rooms are a mixture of modern comforts that flow easily with sculptured moldings, coordinated decor, and views of Notre Dame and the Panthéon. Everyone likes the tissue-lined No. 5, which has an original 1870 ceiling and two windows draped in fabrics that match the bed. The bathroom has a large tub and a shower guard. From the corner balcony in No. 8, you have a view of Notre Dame on the right and the Panthéon on the left. The new bathroom has an enclosed stall shower and painted tile detailing around the mirror. In No. 28, guests who don't mind climbing a few stairs are rewarded with another balcony and a new bathroom. Also on the sixth floor is No. 31, a roomy single done in the bright colors of Provence. Guests staying longer than a week can request their own private fax and phone lines.

FACILITIES AND SERVICES: Direct dial phone, elevator (to most floors), fans on request, hair dryer, Internet in lobby, magnifying mirrors in largest rooms, TV with international reception, room safe (no charge)

NEAREST TOURIST ATTRACTIONS (LEFT BANK): Sorbonne, Pantheon, Musée de Cluny, St-Michel, Jardin du Luxembourg, St-Germain-des-Prés

CREDIT CARDS
AE, DC, MC, V

RATES
Single 50–76€, double 86–115€, triple 135€; free hall showers; *taxe de séjour* included

BREAKFAST
Continental 8.50€ per person

ENGLISH SPOKEN
Yes

LES DEGRÉS DE NOTRE-DAME HÔTEL (NO STARS, 9)
10, rue des Grands Degrés, 75005
Métro: Maubert-Mutualité; RER St-Michel–Notre-Dame
10 rooms and 2 studio apartments, all with shower or bath and toilet

It takes a youthful mind-set and an agile body to stay at this hotel, which blatantly ignores trends and creates its own individual style. For starters, the ten rooms are located on four floors reached by a steep winding staircase hardly one person wide. Once you have schlepped your luggage to your room, you won't have to worry about where to put it all—the rooms are large and there is plenty of closet and drawer space. The colors are coordinated and the furnishings have that certain flea market, collectable flair. Number 36 (a three-flight

TELEPHONE
01 55 42 88 88

FAX
01-40-46-95-34

CREDIT CARDS
MC, V

RATES
Hotel 1–2 persons 100–160€; studio apartments 160€; *taxe de séjour* included

BREAKFAST
Continental with fresh orange juice included

ENGLISH SPOKEN
Yes

workout) has a wood floor, dark furnishings, and a long bathroom with a huge tub, freestanding sink, and toilet behind a pocket door. In No. 24, a huge double up two flights, you can enjoy the neighborhood view from the three double windows or admire the nude painting over the bed. The bathroom is a study in kelly green, and until the peeling ceiling is repaired, or better yet, a new bathroom installed, don't book this room. For my money, the best accommodations are the two studio apartments next to the hotel; you don't have to climb stairs to reach them, and they are absolute knockouts in terms of space, good looks, and amenities. Number 8 has polished inlaid hardwood floors in a sitting room with a double bed, large desk with five drawers, bookshelves framing a nice window, two large closets, a bathroom with a power shower, washing machine, and a fully fitted kitchen with a four-burner cooking top, microwave, and double sink—and all for about half the price of most hotel suites in this part of Paris.

FACILITIES AND SERVICES: Bar, direct-dial phone with private number, elevator (for studio/suites only; 4 floors), hair dryer, restaurant, French TV, room safe (no charge)

NEAREST TOURIST ATTRACTIONS (LEFT BANK): Seine, Île de la Cité, Île St-Louis, St-Michel, Musée de Cluny

PORT-ROYAL HÔTEL ★ (45)
8, boulevard de Port Royal, 75005
Métro: Gobelins

48 rooms, 20 with shower or bath and toilet

If you are looking for maximum value without sacrificing quality in either surroundings or service, you will find the Port-Royal Hôtel impossible to beat. In fact, it is so far ahead of most other one-star hotels in Paris (and many two- and three-star hotels for that matter) that there simply is no contest. I will admit that I had my doubts at first, as I trudged on and on down the long boulevard de Port Royal in a driving rainstorm looking for the hotel. Once inside, however, I found it nothing short of amazing. It is obvious that Claudine and Thierry Giraud are paying close attention to every detail and carrying on the traditions set by their father, who owned the hotel for over seventy years. On top of being an absolute steal for the money, it is spotless and, thanks to Claudine, exceptionally well decorated. The usual one-star dime-store taste—dusty plastic floral arrangements, mismatched colors, and exhausted, sagging furniture—

TELEPHONE
01-43-31-70-06

FAX
01-43-31-33-67

INTERNET
www.portroyalhotel.fr.st

CREDIT CARDS
None, cash only

RATES
Single (sink only) 39–53€, double (sink only) 50–53€, 1–2 persons (shower & toilet) 76€, deluxe 85–90€; showers in hall 2.50€; *taxe de séjour* included

BREAKFAST
Continental 5€ per person

ENGLISH SPOKEN
Yes

is nowhere in sight. Instead, everything is in perfect order, from her magnificent collection of orchids and other blooms in the downstairs areas to the blue carpeted hallways with security and fire doors, to the well-coordinated rooms, all with attractive fabrics, touches of faux finishing, wicker and wrought-iron furnishings, and ceiling fans. Those on the front have double-paned windows that allow for peaceful sleep. Many have beautiful new bathrooms, especially No. 2, a double on the back, and No. 11, with floral inserts on the tile walls wrapping around the deep tub. Even the showers have doors, a rare find in Paris and almost a curiosity in one-star hotels. Those selecting the smallest rooms need not feel deprived; these have many of the nice touches of their more expensive neighbors, including a piece of candy on the pillow at night.

The facade has been repainted, enhancing the Art Deco glass gracefully curving over the front door. The inviting street-side sitting room, with its comfortable chairs and beautiful live green and flowering plants, belies the hotel's budget category. So does the breakfast room, overlooking a neatly manicured interior garden. Real flowers on the tables, caned chairs with upholstered seats, and an interesting collection of the family's antique woodworking tools add to the appeal.

The hotel is easily accessible to St-Michel, the Musée d'Orsay, the Louvre, and the Champs-Élysées by bus. It connects to Orly by direct bus from the métro stop. Close by is a huge shopping complex with 150 boutiques and a branch of Au Printemps department store. Also near are cinemas—including the Grand Ecran, which boasts the largest screen in Europe— and a selection of restaurants and cafés (see *Great Eats Paris*). Free street parking is available Monday to Friday 7 P.M. to 9 A.M. and all day Saturday, Sunday, holidays, and in August; otherwise, underground parking is three minutes away on foot and costs around 20€ per day. All in all, it adds up to one of the best hotels for the money in Paris.

NOTE: Reservations are accepted by phone 7 A.M. to 7 P.M. only.

FACILITIES AND SERVICES: Direct-dial phone, elevator, hair dryer and iron available, nearby parking, French TV (in sitting room), office safe (no charge)

NEAREST TOURIST ATTRACTIONS (LEFT BANK): Gobelins Museum, rue Mouffetard

SELECT HÔTEL ★★★ (21)
1, place de la Sorbonne, 75005
Métro: Cluny–La Sorbonne; RER Luxembourg

68 rooms, all with shower or bath and toilet

TELEPHONE
01-46-34-14-80
FAX
01-46-34-51-79
INTERNET
www.selecthotel.fr
CREDIT CARDS
AE, DC, MC, V
RATES
1–2 persons standard 145€,
superior 165€, triple 180€,
duplex 225€; extra bed 30
percent of room rate; *taxe de
séjour* 0.86€ per person, per day
BREAKFAST
Complimentary buffet or
Continental
ENGLISH SPOKEN
Yes

In 1937, Eric Sevareid paid 50¢ a night at the Select. Things have changed . . . considerably.

The Select has one of the most spectacular interior garden courts in Paris, complete with blooming tropical plants and a fountain. The lobby and reception area are studies in ultramodern design, with chrome and black leather furniture offset by posters of Paris. This sleek approach is carried into the intimate bar, breakfast room, and seating alcoves tucked around the skylighted garden. Hallways showcase the work of Hyppolite Romain, who was commissioned specially to do all of the paintings you see.

Most of the rooms have as much modernistic appeal as the public areas, especially the renovated sites overlooking the garden court, the place de la Sorbonne in front, or the facade of the Sorbonne. Some of those on the backside and in the annex have all the perks but are dark, viewless, and done in some hideous wallpapers and colors. An exception, well, maybe for some, is No. 32. It has an interior view, but the area is filled with green plants to soften the outlook. The room itself feels like an exhibit space at the Centre Pompidou. Curved metal doors halfway shield the room from the bathtub and stainless steel sink with a long, narrow mirror. The toilet is enclosed, but there is no privacy for bathing or brushing your teeth. Other than the bed and a metal chair with a leather seat cushion, everything is built-in. The only color comes from the light gray bedspread with a pear, eggplant, and squash pattern. *Chaque à son gout!* Avoid No. 41, a duplex, due to the treacherous spiral staircase descending to the cavelike downstairs bedroom. Two of the nicest are Nos. 33 and 53, which display the original stone wall of the hotel and centuries-old oak beams. Two large floor-to-ceiling windows open onto the place de la Sorbonne below. Comfortable armchairs, good reading lights, a large working desk, hidden storage space, and a split bathroom make these favorites for longer stays. Number 29 is a roomy triple with beams and recessed lighting. It features a double closet in the entry, a stone wall behind the bed, a comfortable chair, double sinks in a marble bathroom, and a side view of the Sorbonne. Rooms 23 and 25 facing the place de la Sorbonne also have the modern look; I like the work and luggage space these rooms offer. An ideal Latin Quarter location, lower off-season rates, three-star creature comforts, and the friendly reception staff (headed by Jeanine for more than twenty years and by Isabelle for seven) make the Select Hôtel a front-runner in the *quartier*. Unfortunately, it no longer costs only 50¢ a night.

FACILITIES AND SERVICES: Air-conditioning, bar, direct-dial phone, elevator, hair dryer, TV with international reception, office safe (no charge)

NEAREST TOURIST ATTRACTIONS (LEFT BANK): Sorbonne, Jardin du Luxembourg, Pantheon, St-Michel, Musée de Cluny, Seine

Sixth Arrondissement

LEFT BANK
École des Beaux-Arts
excellent shopping
Jardin du Luxembourg
Odéon National Theater
St-Germain-des-Prés Church
St-Sulpice Church

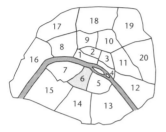

Literary and artistic Paris is the heart of the sixth, which is a continuation of the Latin Quarter and one of the most stimulating parts of the city. Intellectual, elegant, and very appealing, it has tiny side streets, old buildings, antique shops, designer boutiques, a thriving café life, and more atmosphere block for block than anyone could ever soak up. The square by the Église St-Germain-des-Prés, the oldest Roman abbey church in Paris, is the main focus of the district. Les Deux Magots and Café de Flore, the two most celebrated cafés in Paris, were the hangouts of Hemingway, Sartre, Simone de Beauvoir, and James Joyce. Today they are jammed with Parisians and tourists alike engaged in some of the best people-watching in the universe. Most of the major fashion designers have opened boutiques here, making the area a luxury shopping destination for world-class fashionistas. The École Nationale Supérieure des Beaux-Arts, the city's most famous fine-arts school, is in a former convent that is open to the public for exhibitions. The Jardin du Luxembourg, one of Paris's most loved parks, draws more than three million joggers and walkers per year. The city employs seventy-two gardeners and spends eleven million euros per year to maintain it. At one end of the gardens is the Italianate Palais du Luxembourg, which was built for Marie de Médici and is now occupied by the French Senate.

HOTELS IN THE SIXTH ARRONDISSEMENT

Artus Hotel ★★★ ($) **142**
Atlantis Saint-Germain-des-Prés ★★★ **143**
Au Manoir Saint-Germain-des-Prés ★★★★ ($) **144**
Dhely's Hôtel ★ **145**
Grand Hôtel de l'Univers ★★★ ($) **145**
Grand Hôtel des Balcons ★★ **146**
Hôtel Aviatic ★★★ ($) **147**
Hôtel Danemark ★★★ **148**
Hôtel Danube ★★★ **149**
Hôtel Dauphine Saint-Germain-des-Prés ★★★ ($) **150**
Hôtel de Chevreuse ★ **151**
Hôtel de Fleurie ★★★ **151**
Hôtel de l'Abbaye ★★★ ($) **152**
Hôtel de l'Odéon ★★★ **154**
Hôtel des Académies ★ (¢) **154**
Hôtel du Dragon (NO STARS) **155**
Hôtel du Lys ★★ **156**
Hôtel Ferrandi ★★★ **157**
Hôtel Jardin Le Bréa ★★★ **158**
Hôtel Left Bank Saint-Germain ★★★ ($) **158**
Hôtel le Régent ★★★ ($) **159**
Hôtel Le Relais Médicis ★★★ ($) **161**
Hôtel le Sainte-Beuve ★★★ **162**
Hôtel le Saint-Grégoire ★★★★ ($) **163**
Hôtel Novanox ★★★ **164**
Hôtel Relais Saint-Sulpice ★★★ ($) **165**
Hôtel Saint-André-des-Arts ★ **165**
Hôtel Saint-Germain-des-Prés ★★★ ($) **166**
Hôtel Saint-Paul ★★★ **167**
Le Madison Hôtel ★★★ ($) **168**
Le Relais Hôtel du Vieux Paris ★★★★ ($) **170**
Millésime Hôtel ★★★ ($) **171**
Pension les Marronniers (NO STARS, ¢) **172**
Welcome Hôtel ★★ **173**

OTHER OPTIONS
Residence Hotels

Hôtel Résidence des Arts ($) **320**

($) indicates a Big Splurge; (¢) indicates a Cheap Sleep

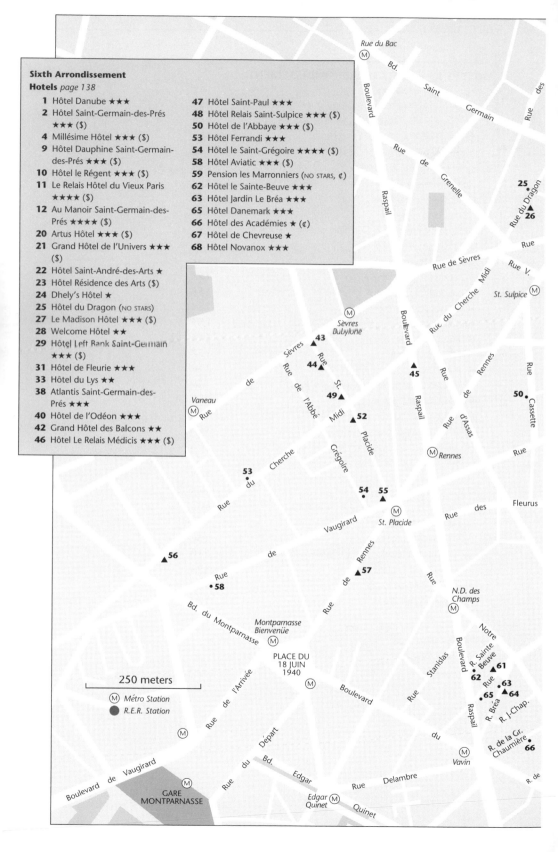

Sixth Arrondissement

Hotels *page 138*

1 Hôtel Danube ★★★
2 Hôtel Saint-Germain-des-Prés ★★★ ($)
4 Millésime Hôtel ★★★ ($)
9 Hôtel Dauphine Saint-Germain-des-Prés ★★★ ($)
10 Hôtel le Régent ★★★ ($)
11 Le Relais Hôtel du Vieux Paris ★★★★ ($)
12 Au Manoir Saint-Germain-des-Prés ★★★★ ($)
20 Artus Hôtel ★★★ ($)
21 Grand Hôtel de l'Univers ★★★ ($)
22 Hôtel Saint-André-des-Arts ★
23 Hôtel Résidence des Arts ($)
24 Dhely's Hôtel ★
25 Hôtel du Dragon (NO STARS)
27 Le Madison Hôtel ★★★ ($)
28 Welcome Hôtel ★★
29 Hôtel Left Bank Saint-Germain ★★★ ($)
31 Hôtel de Fleurie ★★★
33 Hôtel du Lys ★★
38 Atlantis Saint-Germain-des-Prés ★★★
40 Hôtel de l'Odéon ★★★
42 Grand Hôtel des Balcons ★★
46 Hôtel Le Relais Médicis ★★★ ($)

47 Hôtel Saint-Paul ★★★
48 Hôtel Relais Saint-Sulpice ★★★ ($)
50 Hôtel de l'Abbaye ★★★ ($)
53 Hôtel Ferrandi ★★★
54 Hôtel le Saint-Grégoire ★★★★ ($)
58 Hôtel Aviatic ★★★ ($)
59 Pension les Marronniers (NO STARS, ¢)
62 Hôtel le Sainte-Beuve ★★★
63 Hôtel Jardin Le Bréa ★★★
65 Hôtel Danemark ★★★
66 Hôtel des Académies ★ (¢)
67 Hôtel de Chevreuse ★
68 Hôtel Novanox ★★★

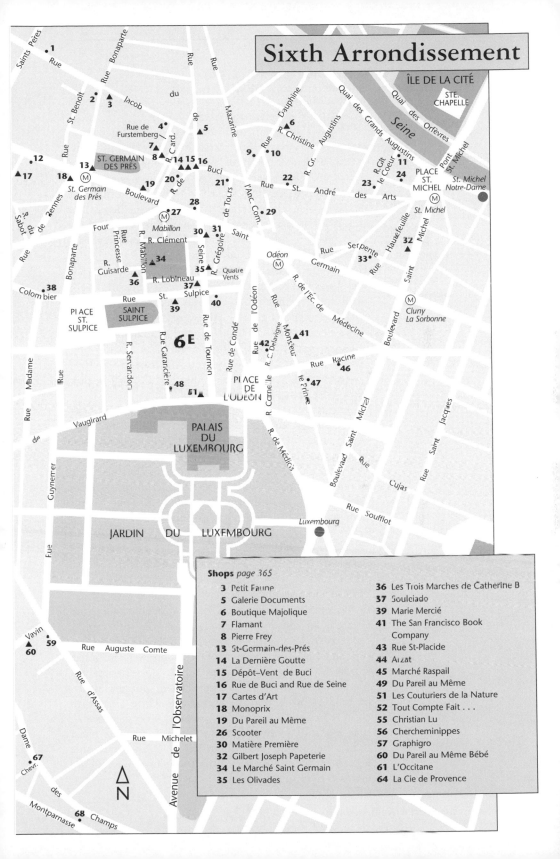

Sixth Arrondissement

ÎLE DE LA CITÉ

STE. CHAPELLE

Seine

PLACE ST. MICHEL

St. Michel Notre-Dame

ST. GERMAIN DES PRÉS

St. Germain des Prés

PLACE ST. SULPICE

SAINT SULPICE

6E

PLACE DE L'ODÉON

PALAIS DU LUXEMBOURG

JARDIN DU LUXEMBOURG

Luxembourg

Shops *page 365*

3 Petit Faune
5 Galerie Documents
6 Boutique Majolique
7 Flamant
8 Pierre Frey
13 St-Germain-des-Prés
14 La Dernière Goutte
15 Dépôt–Vent de Buci
16 Rue de Buci and Rue de Seine
17 Cartes d'Art
18 Monoprix
19 Du Pareil au Même
26 Scooter
30 Matière Première
32 Gilbert Joseph Papeterie
34 Le Marché Saint Germain
35 Les Olivades

36 Les Trois Marches de Catherine B
37 Soulciado
39 Marie Mercié
41 The San Francisco Book Company
43 Rue St-Placide
44 Arzat
45 Marché Raspail
49 Du Pareil au Même
51 Les Couturiers de la Nature
52 Tout Compte Fait . . .
55 Christian Lu
56 Chercheminippes
57 Graphigro
60 Du Pareil au Même Bébé
61 L'Occitane
64 La Cie de Provence

ARTUS HÔTEL ★★★ ($, 20)
34, rue de Buci, 75006
Métro: Mabillon
27 rooms, all with shower or bath and toilet

TELEPHONE
01-43-29-07-20
FAX
01-43-29-67-44
INTERNET
www.artushotel.com
CREDIT CARDS
AE, DC, MC, V
RATES
1–2 persons 190–235€, duplex 300€, junior suite 320€; *taxe de séjour* included
BREAKFAST
Continental in room or breakfast room included; cannot be deducted
ENGLISH SPOKEN
Yes

Down the street from the picturesque Buci street *marché* is the Artus Hôtel. To say this hotel is "different" is the understatement of the year. The owners have mixed an aggressively imaginative interior with an old period French building, and the results are nothing short of spectacular. The entrance announces immediately that this is a hotel where creativity and pure whimsy have been raised to new levels. A wood-plank walkway leads guests to the reception desk, where three clocks display time around the world. To one side, zebra-patterned armchairs and comfortable sofas suggest lingering over a drink from the honor bar, which is an old stone fountain with a face spouting water. All twenty-seven guest-room doors were crafted and hand-painted by nine local artists and defy description; photos of them hang in the lobby. And if you take the elevator, you will miss the graffiti-covered stairway, authentically done by a knowledgeable New York artist.

The rooms are simple yet extremely well planned. Burnt sienna–colored walls offset crisp white duvet covers on leather-trimmed beds with built-in headboards hiding closets. Long, blond wall desks with halogen lights and a fabric-draped chair complement open-slat wooden armoires. Instead of the usual, mundane Do Not Disturb sign, an amusing plank of wood hangs on the door to announce either "Go Ahead Make My Bed" or "Shhh—I'm Asleep or Busy." Which rooms are best? I can recommend them all, but No. 162, a top-floor junior suite with an electric bed, circular Jacuzzi bath for two, and a balcony with a pair of chaise lounges, wins by a nose. A close second is No. 140, a duplex with a huge upstairs bathroom that has skylight views of St-Germain Church; an old-fashioned, claw-foot bathtub (and a modern stall shower for diehards); a beautiful antique sink; an easy chair; and an adobe-tile floor with an Indian rug under a marvelous wicker *coiffeuse* (dressing table). Number 123 has double windows facing out and, in the bathroom, black marble lining the white sink with chrome fittings. Clothes hang in two clever closets: one that looks like the gates to a fortress, and the other hidden behind the bed. Room 121 is a standard double with a built-in curved desk and windows overlooking bamboo trees in the courtyard.

The downstairs breakfast room is no less unusual, with modern chairs covered in rose, green, pumpkin, and purple leather. A steamer trunk that doubles as a buffet holds daily newspapers, a mirror made from beer caps set in cement, a collection of Jim Beam ceramic whiskey bottles, and a little roadster round out the experience. In the back part, you can check your emails or access the Internet in the hotel's cyber space while sitting in a red-leather dentist's chair.

FACILITIES AND SERVICES: Air-conditioning, bar, direct-dial phone, elevator, hair dryer, 2 handicapped rooms, Internet in cyber café, laundry service, minibar, robes for suites & duplex, room service, TV with international reception, office safe (no charge)

NEAREST TOURIST ATTRACTIONS (LEFT BANK): St-Germain-des-Prés, Seine, Île de la Cité, St-Michel, Musée de Cluny, excellent shopping

ATLANTIS SAINT-GERMAIN-DES-PRÉS ★★★ (38)
4, rue Vieux Colombier, 75006
Métro: St-Sulpice, St-Germain-des-Prés

27 rooms, all with shower or bath and toilet

Located opposite St-Sulpice Church, this hotel is in the thick of things in this corner of the St-Germain-des-Prés *quartier*. Within an easy five-to-ten-minute walk, you can be sipping a café at either Les Deux Magots or Café de Flore on the boulevard St-Germain, shopping at Bon Marché department store, browsing along the narrow streets lined with designer boutiques, or jogging off that last pastry in the Jardin du Luxembourg. The clean and efficient air-conditioned rooms are maintained by a staff of housekeepers who take their job seriously. Reaching them, however, means getting into an unbelievably small elevator, even for one. Furnishings are an interesting fusion of Art Deco and traditional French with brass beds, comfortable armchairs, good wardrobe space, and nicely coordinated fabrics. Those ending in the number one or on the back are the largest, and a few have balconies. The tiled bathrooms are modern and functional. The downstairs sitting room with assorted artwork adds another pleasant dimension to the hotel, as does the skylighted breakfast room with a grandfather clock in one corner. The desk staff is always helpful.

FACILITIES AND SERVICES: Air-conditioning, direct-dial phone, elevator, hair dryer, laundry service, minibars, TV with international reception, room safe (no charge)

TELEPHONE
01-45-48-31-81
FAX
01-45-48-35-16
INTERNET
www.hotelatlantis.com
CREDIT CARDS
AE, DC, MC, V
RATES
1–2 persons 123–183€, triple 206€; ask about promotional rates; *taxe de séjour* included
BREAKFAST
Continental 10€ per person
ENGLISH SPOKEN
Yes

NEAREST TOURIST ATTRACTIONS (LEFT BANK): St-Sulpice, St-Germain-des-Prés, excellent shopping

AU MANOIR SAINT-GERMAIN-DES-PRÉS ★★★★ ($, 12)
153, boulevard St-Germain 75006
Métro: St-Germain-des-Prés
32 rooms, all with shower or bath and toilet

TELEPHONE
01-42-22-21-65; toll-free in U.S. and Canada 800-528-1234 (Best Western)
FAX
01-45-48-22-25
INTERNET
www.paris-hotels-charm.com
CREDIT CARDS
AE, DC, MC, V
RATES
Single 178€, double 178–250€; extra bed 25€; lower off-season rates; *taxe de séjour* 1€ per person, per day
BREAKFAST
Complimentary buffet or Continental, served in room
ENGLISH SPOKEN
Yes

For a dynamic St-Germain-des-Prés address in the very heart of the famous *quartier,* reserve a room in this gracious hotel. Over the years, it has retained its dignified demeanor, displaying all the trappings of a grand hotel, yet none of the stuffiness. The downstairs boasts one of the prettiest series of garden-themed sitting and dining areas of any Left Bank hotel. In the breakfast room, the garden motif is carried out on green faux-finished wood and matching hobnail upholstery on the chairs and banquettes. Eight garden frescoes, a basket of dried fruits and leaves on each table, and a flowered carpet complete the attractive scene. The bar has groupings of cushioned wicker chairs and an old-fashioned sedan chair in one corner. Next to it on the left, a trompe l'oeil painting of a cat snoozing on a chair could convince you to try to touch its fur. In the sky-lighted conservatory, a trio of Majolica plates hang over the sofa, and an old tapestry trunk with a collection of men's hats reminds us of turn-of-the-century clothing formalities. Jardinieres hold green and blooming plants, and two glass cases display a beautiful collection of antique floral plates

The coordinated rooms are generously proportioned; have twin, queen-, or king-size beds; and are well furnished with all the comforts you would expect, including a Jacuzzi in every bathroom. Windows are double-glazed and the rooms are air-conditioned. If you need guaranteed quiet, request a room on the courtyard, but be aware that the view will not be interesting.

Also under the same ownership is the Hôtel Left Bank Saint-Germain (see page 158).

FACILITIES AND SERVICES: Air-conditioning, bar, direct-dial phone, elevator, hair dryer, Internet in lobby, Jacuzzis, laundry service, TV with international reception, room safe (no charge)

NEAREST TOURIST ATTRACTIONS (LEFT BANK): St-Germain-des-Prés, excellent shopping, Seine, St-Michel, Musée de Cluny, Île de la Cité

DHELY'S HÔTEL ★ (24)
22, rue de l'Hirondelle off place St-Michel, 75006
Métro: St-Michel; RER St-Michel–Notre Dame
21 rooms, none with toilet or bathtub, 10 with shower

If you would rather splurge on dinner or a new outfit rather than on a night's sleep, this top-drawer budget hotel, steps from the Seine and place St-Michel, is the place. Many cut-rate choices in this Left Bank neighborhood are severely lacking in housekeeping, but not this one. Everything is shipshape, from the hall toilets and ground-floor showers to the rooms, most of which have pretty floral wallpaper and window boxes with real flowers. The larger rooms have carpeting; the smaller ones have linoleum floors. Of course, the higher you climb, the lower the price and the better the view. While the hotel is basic, it does have some redeeming architectural details, such as the original sixteenth-century tiled entryway and classified historical stairway, open beams, and exposed stone walls. In its most infamous moment, it was the home of Anne de Pisseleu, the favorite mistress of François Premier, king of France from 1515 to 1547. For the last twenty-four years, the hotel has been owned by Mme. Kenniche.

FACILITIES AND SERVICES: Direct-dial phone, no elevator (5 floors), TV with international reception, office safe (no charge)

NEAREST TOURIST ATTRACTIONS (LEFT BANK): St-Michel, St-Germain-des-Prés, St-Michel, Musée de Cluny, Seine, Île de la Cité, Île St-Louis

TELEPHONE
01-43-26-58-25
FAX
01-43-26-51-06
EMAIL
delhys@wanadoo.fr
CREDIT CARDS
AE, DC, MC, V
RATES
Single 50–70€, double 55–70€, triple 75–100€; shower 4€; *taxe de séjour* 0.46€ per person, per day
BREAKFAST
Continental 5.50€ per person
ENGLISH SPOKEN
Yes

GRAND HÔTEL DE L'UNIVERS ★★★ ($, 21)
6, rue Grégoire-de-Tours, 75006
Métro: Odéon, Mabillon
34 rooms, all with shower or bath and toilet

If you like tapestries, brocades, oriental rugs, thick beams, stone walls, and rich, heavy fabrics offset by bowers of real blooming plants, check into this quiet hotel on a pedestrian street just off the boulevard St-Germain-des-Prés. The hotel is owned by the same family who runs Hôtel Saint-Germain-des-Prés, a longtime favorite with *Great Sleeps Paris* readers (see page 166). It also has the same style of decorating, including masses of fabulous blooming plants and flowers. When I asked how they were maintained in both hotels, I was told the manager goes weekly to Rungis, the famous wholesale food and flower market outside of Paris. No wonder these floral displays are always at their peak of perfection.

TELEPHONE
01-43-29-37-00; toll-free in the US 800-528-1234 (Best Western)
FAX
01-40-51-06-45
EMAIL
grandhotelunivers@wanadoo.fr
INTERNET
www.hotel-paris-univers.com
CREDIT CARDS
AE, DC, MC, V
RATES
Single 180€, double 195€, deluxe 210–225€; extra bed 15€; *taxe de séjour* included

BREAKFAST
Complimentary American
buffet
ENGLISH SPOKEN
Yes

Each floor has a different color theme, and the doors to all the bedrooms have been hand-painted by an artist from the École des Beaux Arts. No two rooms are exactly alike, but all are well done in terms of colors and design. The marble bathrooms have nice sink space and good lighting. Three rooms on the sixth floor have views of the top of Notre Dame. Room 65, a double superior in rose with two windows, has a mezzanine area with a desk and a comfortable chair. Room 62 brings spring to life any time of year with its cheerful tulip print fabrics. Number 36 is a double with good closet and luggage space, but the bathroom is smaller and the three windows face a wall. The fourth floor is reserved exclusively for nonsmoking guests.

FACILITIES AND SERVICES: Air-conditioning, bar, direct-dial phone, elevator, hair dryer, Internet in lobby, laundry service, minibar, robes in superior rooms, trouser press in some rooms, TV with international reception, room safe (no charge), 4th floor nonsmoking

NEAREST TOURIST ATTRACTIONS (LEFT BANK): St-Germain-des-Prés, Jardin du Luxembourg, Seine, Île de la Cité, St-Michel, Musée de Cluny

GRAND HÔTEL DES BALCONS ★★ (42)
3, rue Casimir-Delavigne, 75006
Métro: Odéon, Cluny–La Sorbonne
50 rooms, all with shower or bath and toilet

TELEPHONE
01-46-34-78-50
FAX
01-46-34-06-27
INTERNET
www.balcons.com
CREDIT CARDS
AE, DC, MC, V
RATES
Single 85–125€, double 105–155€, triple 185€; *taxe de séjour* included
BREAKFAST
Buffet or Continental 10€ per person
ENGLISH SPOKEN
Yes

The Grand Hôtel des Balcons is one of the most dignified, inexpensive hotel choices in this part of the Left Bank, and it's a perennial favorite with older, cost-conscious budgeteers who have found that it is a much better value than the other three-star hotels on the same block.

The impressive lobby is a masterpiece of Art Nouveau design, with glorious stained-glass windows and masterfully turned wood. There are always beautiful fresh-flower displays, arranged by the owner's wife, who is a recognized international ikebana expert. On the reception desk is a tin of cookies, which you are invited to enjoy along with afternoon tea. Uniformed maids are relentless in keeping everything dust free. To management's credit, rooms have been redecorated with nice wallpaper and new bedspreads. Each has a desk, at least one chair, and good reading lights. Many have double windows. Those ending in the number one are on the corner and have balconies. Almost all have that one hard-to-find luxury in Paris . . . space. For these, request one of the eight that are similar to No. 204. Vintage baths tend to be small but are spotless. The location is tops, close to lots of budget restaurants (see *Great Eats Paris*) and near place de l'Odéon, boulevard St-Michel, St-Germain-des-Prés, and one of the city's most popular parks, the Jardin du Luxembourg.

FACILITIES AND SERVICES: Direct-dial phone, elevator, hair dryer, TV with international reception, office safe (no charge)

NEAREST TOURIST ATTRACTIONS (LEFT BANK): Jardin du Luxembourg, St-Sulpice, excellent shopping, St-Michel, Musée de Cluny

HÔTEL AVIATIC ★★★ ($, 58)
105, rue de Vaugirard, 75006
Métro: Falguière, St-Placide, Montparnasse-Bienvenüe

43 rooms, all with shower or bath and toilet

Part of the hotel dates from the seventeenth century when the Marquise de Maintenon lived here and raised the children of Madame de Montespan and Louis XIV. The hotel is named after the World War I French aviators based at the Issy-les-Moulineaux airfield who came to live here to be closer to their hangars, and when not on duty, the Parisian life. Today, Art Deco glass and a black wrought-iron awning over the door—flanked by matching lamps—set the welcoming stage for this business-like hotel. The lobby has faux-marble columns and small groupings of velvet chairs and antique marble chests topped with bouquets of fresh flowers. To one side is the breakfast room, papered with vintage Parisian art posters.

A wide, winding stairway with overhead skylights leads guests up to forest-green carpeted hallways and the forty-three rooms in two buildings. There is more than just a touch of class in these well-thought-out chambers, which all have built-in luggage racks, good space to spread out and work, armchair seating, ample closets, soundproofing, and telephones in the bathrooms. The rooms in the front building are bright and airy, with pretty views of the surrounding Montparnasse neighborhood. Those in the back are sunny, but they don't have much of a view. The millennium suite is perfect for the person who needs a mini-office when traveling. Here you can sit at the leather-topped desk, send and receive faxes or emails, and log online for the cost of a local phone call. A change of ownership led to redecoration

TELEPHONE
01-53-63-25-50

FAX
01-53-63-25-55

INTERNET
www.aviatic.fr

CREDIT CARDS
AE, DC, MC, V

RATES
1–2 persons: traditional 170€, superior 199€, millennium 210€, suites 297€; extra bed 25€; free baby bed or for child under 12; excellent lower rates in off-season; parking 22€

BREAKFAST
Buffet 12€ per person

ENGLISH SPOKEN
Yes

and improvements in most of the rooms, which now carry higher price tags. However, they have low-season discounts and deals throughout the year, so it's possible to avoid the sometimes Big Splurge rates.

FACILITIES AND SERVICES: Air-conditioning, bar, direct-dial phone, elevator, hair dryer, laundry service, minibar, robes in some rooms, parking, TV with international reception, room safe (no charge)

NEAREST TOURIST ATTRACTIONS (LEFT BANK): Montparnasse

HÔTEL DANEMARK ★★★ (65)
21, rue Vavin, 75006
Métro: Vavin, Notre-Dame-des-Champs
15 rooms, all with shower, bath, and toilet

TELEPHONE
01-43-26-93-78
FAX
01-46-34-66-06
INTERNET
www.hoteldanemark.com
CREDIT CARDS
AE, DC, MC, V
RATES
Single 115–130€, double 130–150€; *taxe de séjour* 0.86€ per person, per day
BREAKFAST
Continental 9€ per person
ENGLISH SPOKEN
Yes

For the Nurit family, nothing seems to be too much trouble when it comes to pleasing their guests. They have a special fondness for Americans, many of whom have been repeat guests for years, even before the hotel was what it is today. The Nurits are proud of their fifteen-room hotel in Montparnasse, and they should be. It is an imaginative lesson in how to take an old student-style hotel and turn it into an eye-catching spot.

Cool blues and grays dominate the downstairs color scheme, with artist-inspired furnishings that look like exhibits from New York's Museum of Modern Art. The walls are dotted with a collection of dramatic posters of Parisian landmarks and famous race cars, along with bold paintings done by an architect friend of the family. Each floor has just three rooms, which are done in soft yellows, green, lavender, or cocoa brown. While compact, they contain everything necessary for a comfortable stay. All rooms have their own Italian marble bathroom with heated towel racks, good make-up lighting, and in a few, a Jacuzzi. The rooms from the third floor up have no interior views. Those on the front face a pretty, white-brick apartment building with terrace gardens, and those on the top floor are under sloping, beamed ceilings with skylights.

FACILITIES AND SERVICES: Direct-dial phone, hair dryer, elevator, some Jacuzzis, minibar, TV with international reception, office safe (no charge)

NEAREST TOURIST ATTRACTIONS (LEFT BANK): Montparnasse, Jardin du Luxembourg

HÔTEL DANUBE ★★★ (1)
58, rue Jacob, 75006
Métro: St-Germain-des-Prés
40 rooms, all with shower or bath and toilet

This building has had an interesting vantage on history. The American Treaty of Independence from Britain was signed next door on September 3, 1783. David Hartley represented the King of England and Benjamin Franklin, John Jay, and John Adams were the American representatives. During World War II, from September 1939 to June 1940, it was the home of General Sikorsky, head of the Polish government in exile. Today it is the Hôtel Danube, a St-Germain charmer with forty rooms offering good value for the price. The hotel is very well managed by Séverin Ferrand, and the desk staff are the friendliest and most accommodating in the neighborhood. It is also one of the few hotels that offers complimentary Internet access for guests to send and receive emails.

A red floral wallpapered entry has a multicolored tile floor. To one side is an inviting sitting room with a fireplace flanked by two cane wing-back chairs. Just beyond an interior courtyard is a breakfast room with a collection of blue-and-white Asian porcelain on display.

The large bedrooms are individually decorated with a mixture of styles that range from colonial Chinese and Indian to mid-Victorian and tropical. Most bathrooms are in marble. Double windows in Room 15 open onto the street. Two cane chairs are positioned around a glass-top table. Other appointments include a marble-top chest of drawers, lighted closet, and gray monogrammed towels in the bathroom. Room 10 is the same size, and it has a beautiful double brass bed and Pierre Frey matching fabrics, but the bathroom has an older style of tile. In No. 35, guests can spread out in a two-room suite and look out onto a pink-and-white wall that has wisps of tree branches cleverly painted on it. For what Room 40 (on the courtyard) may lack in view, it more than makes up for in space. Number 41, a two-room apartment in pink and blue, is another large choice. It has an antique double bed in one room and two regular doubles in the second. The new marble-tile bathroom has a tub with a handheld shower over it and sink space for toiletries. Number 54 is a new room that's too elfin for two, but it probably would suit one person with light luggage. There are five rooms similar to No. 6, which has a table

TELEPHONE
01-42-60-94-07 (reservations),
01-42-60-34-70

FAX
01-42-60-81-18

INTERNET
www.hoteldanube.fr

CREDIT CARDS
AE, DC, MC, V

RATES
1–2 persons 110–160€,
apartment (2–4 persons) 225€;
extra bed 40€; *taxe de séjour*
0.91€ per person, per day

BREAKFAST
Continental 10€ per person

ENGLISH SPOKEN
Yes

flanked by two armchairs, a marble-top dresser, lighted closets, an older style bath, and a good working desk.

FACILITIES AND SERVICES: Direct-dial phones, elevator (to most floors), hair dryer, complimentary Internet in lobby, laundry service, TV with international reception, office safe (no charge)

NEAREST TOURIST ATTRACTIONS (LEFT BANK): Excellent shopping, St-Germain-des-Prés, Seine, St-Michel, Musée de Cluny, Île de la Cité, Île St-Louis

HÔTEL DAUPHINE SAINT-GERMAIN-DES-PRÉS
★★★ ($, 9)
36, rue Dauphine, 75006
Métro: Odéon
30 rooms, all with shower or bath and toilet

In the early days, the first and second floors of Parisian town homes were for the nobility, the higher floors for the servants. This explains the larger rooms and higher ceilings you will encounter in this seventeenth-century building. Unfortunately, the rooms on the back (except on the top floor) and those ending in the number 4 face a boring back view, but they are quiet and certainly have the same high decorating standards and amenities found in the rest of the hotel. Otherwise, there is plenty to choose from, including Nos. 55, 56, 65, and 66, which are exclusively reserved for nonsmoking guests. Number 61 is a blue-and-white sloped-roof suite that can accommodate up to four. The mansard windows let in plenty of light and have a view of Notre Dame Cathedral and the dome of Panthéon. Room 68 is frankly feminine, with its pink and white candy-striped walls blending perfectly with florals and checks. It has good light, a rooftop view, and the same excellent granite and marble bathroom features found in the rest of the hotel, plus heated towel racks, monogrammed towels, a drying line, large mirror, and a basket of quality toiletries.

A special feature of your morning routine here is the large breakfast buffet, which includes pastries and croissants baked in the hotel kitchen, fresh fruit, and cereals, as well as such extras as yogurt, ham, sausage, pâté, cheese, and mushrooms.

FACILITIES AND SERVICES: Air-conditioning, bar (24-hour service), direct-dial phone with fax, Internet in lobby, elevator, hair dryer, laundry service, minibar, TV with international reception, room service for light snacks, room safe (no charge), several nonsmoking rooms

TELEPHONE
01-43-26-74-34; toll-free from the U.S. 800-44-UTELL

FAX
01-43-26-49-09

INTERNET
www.dauphine-st-germain.com

CREDIT CARDS
AE, DC, MC, V

RATES
1–2 persons 194–208€; suite 1–2 persons, 260€; 3–4 persons 316€; extra bed 56€; lower rates in off-season; *taxe de séjour* included

BREAKFAST
Buffet 16€ per person

ENGLISH SPOKEN
Yes

NEAREST TOURIST ATTRACTIONS (LEFT BANK): St-Germain-des-Prés, St-Michel, Musée de Cluny, Seine, Île de la Cité, Île St-Louis, excellent shopping

HÔTEL DE CHEVREUSE ★ (67)
3, rue de Chevreuse at rue Notre-Dame-des-Champs, 75006
Métro: Vavin
23 rooms, 15 with shower or bath and toilet

Nothing resembles a one-star at the Chevreuse but the prices. A hotel of some sort has been here for fifty years, but it took a new owner with some imagination to turn it into an eye-catching spot where no one need feel they are scrimping in order to stay within budget. It is all well done, from the minute you walk into the reception and lobby, which shows off the owner's penchant for collecting. The room is divided by a bookcase holding vintage flower vases and a photo of the hotel as it was. Nearby is a 1930s clock, a trombone made into a floor lamp, and an old hat and umbrella rack next to a church pew. The sofa and chairs are covered in contemporary combinations of blue, white, and yellow. A small breakfast room with four tables and light metal and wood chairs is to one side.

Rooms are simple compositions with open closets, metal chairs, and built-ins. Since in-room showers resemble phone booths, and the shared hall showers are clean, acceptable, and free, you are actually better off and money ahead booking a showerless room. If you are on the fifth floor, you can keep fit because there is no elevator in the building.

FACILITIES AND SERVICES: Direct-dial phone, French TV, no elevator (5 floors), office safe (no charge)

NEAREST TOURIST ATTRACTIONS (LEFT BANK): Montparnasse, Jardin du Luxembourg

TELEPHONE
01-43-20-93-16
FAX
01-43-21-43-72
CREDIT CARDS
MC, V
RATES
Single 40€, 1–2 persons 65–70€, 1–3 persons (largest room) 90€; free hall showers; *taxe de séjour* 0.50€ per person, per day
BREAKFAST
Continental 7€ per person
ENGLISH SPOKEN
Yes

HÔTEL DE FLEURIE ★★★ (31)
32–34, rue Grégoire-de-Tours, 75006
Métro: Mabillon, Odéon
29 rooms, all with shower or bath and toilet

If you enjoy the colorful, round-the-clock atmosphere of St-Germain-des-Prés, then the dynamic Hôtel de Fleurie is for you. This exceptional hotel is owned and managed by the Marolleau family, who for two generations owned Brasserie Balzar (see *Great Eats Paris*). When they sold the brasserie, they bought this down-and-out hotel, and with a year of hard work, they completely

TELEPHONE
01-53-73-70-10 (reservations),
01-53-73-70-00
FAX
01-53-73-70-20
INTERNET
www.hotel-de-fleurie.fr
CREDIT CARDS
AE, DC, MC, V

RATES
Single 130–150€, double 165–185€, deluxe room 240–325€, family rooms (up to 4 persons) 290–320€; extra bed (only in deluxe rooms) 25€; children under 12 free; lower rates in off-season; *taxe de séjour* included
BREAKFAST
Buffet downstairs or Continental in room 10€ per person, 5€ for children under 12
ENGLISH SPOKEN
Yes

transformed it into a delightful three-star that has become a hands-down favorite with readers of *Great Sleeps Paris*.

The facade of the hotel has been restored to its former glory and is embellished with statues that are lighted at night. The lobby and sitting rooms are models of gracious comfort and charm. A spiral staircase leads from the reception desk down to a stone-walled *cave*, where a full buffet is served at tables covered with Provençal prints. Continental breakfasts, which include fresh orange juice, pound cake, and cheese in addition to the usual croissants and fresh bread, are served only in the rooms.

Almost all of the rooms have modern marble bathrooms and a good layout. Several connect to make nice family options. Room 60, on the top floor with no elevator access, overlooks a beautiful mosaic-tiled building across the street. Other deluxe choices include Nos. 11, 14, 24, and 34 Nos. 14 and 24 have new bathrooms and *toile de Jouy* wall covering in red and white. Closet and living space is excellent, and there's plenty of light from the two windows. Room 54, a standard double, has a writing table, white cane headboard, lighted mirrored closet in the entry, and heated towel racks in the bathroom. Number 50, with a double bed, has a small window with a view and a pink marble bathroom; it would be nice for a single visitor. For reservations of more than seven nights, the hotel offers a three-day museum pass that enables visitors to bypass the lines at almost every museum and monument in Paris and at Versailles.

FACILITIES AND SERVICES: Air-conditioning, bar, direct-dial phone, elevator (to most floors), hair dryer, Internet in lobby, laundry service, magnifying mirrors, minibar, TV with international reception, robes, slippers, tea and coffee makers in deluxe rooms, room safe (no charge)

NEAREST TOURIST ATTRACTIONS (LEFT BANK): St-Germain-des-Prés, Seine, Île de la Cité, excellent shopping, St-Michel, Musée de Cluny

HÔTEL DE L'ABBAYE ★★★ ($, 50)
10, rue Cassette, 75006
Métro: St-Sulpice
44 rooms, all with shower or bath and toilet

In the sixteenth and seventeenth centuries, the Abbaye Saint-Germain was a Catholic convent. Today it is a very special hotel for those who love its quiet

TELEPHONE
01-45-44-38-11
FAX
01-45-48-07-86
EMAIL
hotel.abbaye@wanadoo.fr

location near St-Sulpice, its discreet staff, and its commendable service. The entrance is off the street through fifteen-foot-high green doors that open onto a cobblestone courtyard, where the nuns once gathered before going to chapel for daily prayers. The central reception room is handsomely furnished with magnificent antiques and comfortable sofas centered around a marble fireplace. Behind this are an exquisite salon with intimate seating, a wood-burning fireplace, a profusion of flowers, and a nice bar with big wicker armchairs. The addition of a glassed-in winter and summer garden where breakfast can be served has enhanced the hotel's charm and desirability even more.

Returnees vie for the top-floor terrace suites, with their arched ceilings, fireplaces, and rooftop views, or the two ground-floor rooms with private gardens. Number 303 is a two-level oriental suite with a downstairs sitting room that boasts a fireplace, sofa, two chairs, lots of closets, and two big windows. Also on this level is a huge marble bathroom with six feet of sink space, a separate toilet, an enclosed glass shower, and a deep tub. Upstairs, the twin or king bedroom opens onto its own terrace. In addition, there are more lighted closets and a small half bathroom. One favorite is No. 34, a large twin done in florals. I like the granite bathroom with six shelves, a separate shower, and deep tub. Another is No. 32, a nicely appointed, light room with a view over the trees and a sunken bathtub that is just right for one. For those who shun traditional and embrace cutting edge minimalism, the three suite-salons might be appealing. These new rooms combine masculine, monochromatic colors of linens and leathers, lots of glass and chrome, and stunning bathrooms behind glass doors.

Because l'Abbaye is such a unique and outstanding choice, it is higher in price, and it is included for those with flexible budgets who are looking for a memorably romantic Parisian address.

FACILITIES AND SERVICES: Air-conditioning, bar, direct-dial phone, elevator, hair dryer, Internet in lobby, porter, trouser press in suites, TV with international reception, room service for light snacks, room safe (no charge)

NEAREST TOURIST ATTRACTIONS (LEFT BANK): Jardin du Luxembourg, St-Sulpice, St-Germain-des-Prés, excellent shopping

INTERNET
www.hotel-abbaye.com

CREDIT CARDS
AE, MC, V

RATES
1–2 persons: standard 205€, *grande* 305€, suite-salon 385€, suite-duplex 440€; *taxe de séjour* included

BREAKFAST
Continental included, cannot be deducted

ENGLISH SPOKEN
Yes

HÔTEL DE L'ODÉON ★★★ (40)
13, rue St-Sulpice, 75006
Métro: Odéon

TELEPHONE
01-43-25-70-11
FAX
01-43-29-97-34
EMAIL
hotelodeon@wanadoo.fr
INTERNET
www.paris-hotel-odeon.com
CREDIT CARDS
AE, DC, MC, V
RATES
Single 125–190€, double 160–237€, family room 252–270€; lower off-season and promotional rates; *taxe de séjour* included
BREAKFAST
Continental 11€ per person
ENGLISH SPOKEN
Yes

29 rooms, all with shower or bath and toilet

Hôtel de l'Odéon has become a popular Paris destination for travelers who want luxury and impeccable service in a distinguished hotel that is still small enough to maintain a personal touch. The staff is exceptional; the prices are excellent, especially in low season; and the location is top drawer.

The interior is in the style of a seventeenth-century inn, beautifully blending antique charm and atmosphere with all the modern conveniences one expects in a top three-star hotel. In the charm department, the Odéon has it all: high beamed ceilings, original stone walls, stunning furniture, massive tapestries, intricately scrolled brass-and-metal beds with hand-crocheted coverlets, blooming flower boxes under the windows, lovely oil and watercolor paintings hanging throughout, and a manicured atrium garden off to one side of the skylighted breakfast area. On the convenience side, the baths are large and the bedside lighting is good. Double-paned windows keep street noise to a minimum, air-conditioning allows warm-weather comfort, and the closets are large enough for more than the contents of an overnight bag.

FACILITIES AND SERVICES: Air-conditioning, direct-dial phone, elevator (to most floors), hair dryer, Internet in lobby, laundry service, TV with international reception, room safe (no charge)

NEAREST TOURIST ATTRACTIONS (LEFT BANK): St-Sulpice, Jardin du Luxembourg, St-Germain-des-Prés, excellent shopping

HÔTEL DES ACADÉMIES ★ (¢, 66)
15, rue de la Grande Chaumière, 75006
Métro: Vavin

TELEPHONE
01-43-26-66-44
FAX
01-43-26-03-72
CREDIT CARDS
MC, V
RATES
Single 41€, double 56–68€; free shower; dogs free, no cats; *taxe de séjour* included
BREAKFAST
Continental (only bread and jam) in room, 7€ per person
ENGLISH SPOKEN
None

21 rooms, 17 with shower or bath and toilet

When planning your trip to Paris, you may begin to wonder where all the nonmillionaires sleep. Many of them have been sleeping at Hôtel des Académies for years because they do not have to dig too deeply into their pockets to pay the final bill. The owner, Mme. Charles, who was born in the hotel more than eighty years ago and still lives there, runs it with a firm hand, not standing for a soupçon of hanky-panky. Assisting her with the welcoming formalities is her dog, Diavoletto, which she describes as "a street dog, a little bit Labrador." She is a devoted dog lover and welcomes guests who arrive with their own well-behaved canines.

Her plain, little, upstairs Montparnasse location delivers small but spotless rooms at unheard-of rates to a band of devoted regulars, who keep in touch by sending her postcards and souvenirs that she once proudly displayed in her tiny reception room. On my last visit I noticed that the postcard collection had been replaced by a new telephone system, but most of the knickknacks are still there, along with a cage of songbirds. There are no extras here, and the rooms mix 1950s chrome and plastic with varying color and pattern schemes. But with these breathtakingly low prices, especially for those who are willing to hike a few floors up to save even more money, who cares? Certainly not the generations of families who return year after year making it their home base in Paris.

FACILITIES AND SERVICES: Direct-dial phones, elevator (to most floors), TV with international reception, office safe (no charge)

NEAREST TOURIST ATTRACTIONS (LEFT BANK): Montparnasse, Jardin du Luxembourg

HÔTEL DU DRAGON (NO STARS, 25)
36, rue du Dragon, 75006
Métro: St-Sulpice, St-Germain-des-Prés, Sèvres-Babylone
28 rooms, all with shower and toilet

Talk about a Great Sleep in Paris!

Despite its no-star status, the Hôtel du Dragon is one of the last outposts for decent budget anchorage in the heart of the Left Bank. Sprinkled throughout the public rooms and in some of the guest rooms are furnishings that belonged to the owner's grandparents when they started the hotel almost a century ago. The spotless rooms are bedecked in flowered or striped wallpaper and coordinating fabrics that look more up to date than some three-star hotels I could name. They have space, beams, decent closets, adequate lights, and new bathrooms. Of course, there is no elevator, and for air-conditioning you must open the window. However, you do get orange juice with your morning baguette and jam; a television tuned to French, German, or CNBC in your room; and a warm welcome from the Rabier-Roy family, who have owned the hotel since the 1920s.

The bottom line for prudent sleepers in Paris: You get a great sleep for your money, and today, that is not always easy to find.

TELEPHONE
01-45-48-51-05

FAX
01-42-22-51-62

EMAIL
hotel.du.dragon@wanadoo.fr

INTERNET
www.hoteldudragon.com

CREDIT CARDS
AE, MC, V

RATES
Single 75€, double 95€, triple 108€; extra bed 30% of room rate; *taxe de séjour* included

BREAKFAST
Continental 8€ downstairs, 9€ in room, per person

ENGLISH SPOKEN
Yes

FACILITIES AND SERVICES: Direct-dial phone, no elevator (4 floors), hair dryer, TV, office safe (no charge)

NEAREST TOURIST ATTRACTIONS (LEFT BANK): Heart of St-Germain-des-Prés, wonderful shopping and browsing

HÔTEL DU LYS ★★ (33)
23, rue Serpente, 75006
Métro: Odéon, Cluny–La Sorbonne

22 rooms, all with shower or bath and toilet

<table>
<tr><td align="right">TELEPHONE</td></tr>
<tr><td align="right">01-43-26-97-57</td></tr>
</table>

The location is dynamite, the prices are still in line, and if you hit the right room, your stay should be very nice. The hotel is owned by Marie-Hélène Decharne, who took it over when her father retired after fifty years. She has since made some welcome improvements, and the result is a small hotel with more charm and romantic appeal than many in the area charging twice as much.

TELEPHONE
01-43-26-97-57

FAX
01-44-07-34-90

EMAIL
hoteldulys@wanadoo.fr

INTERNET
www.hoteldulys.com

CREDIT CARDS
MC, V

RATES
1–2 persons: small room 95€, large room 110€, triple 125€; *taxe de séjour* included

BREAKFAST
Continental included, cannot be deducted

ENGLISH SPOKEN
Generally, yes

The rooms are done in a cozy French style with beams, a stone wall here and there, and matching bedspreads and curtains. If you are reserving by telephone, please bear in mind that Mme. Decharne is usually at the hotel only on weekday mornings from 9 A.M. to noon. When reserving, I would request No. 11, one of the better twin-bed rooms with a high beamed ceiling and stone wall. Two windows opening onto flower boxes let in plenty of light, and the room has two chairs, a large armoire, and a blue-tiled bath with a nice tub. No. 16, in blue and white, has a new tiled bath with an enclosed shower. I would not request No. 14 because of its strange WC perched on a platform; No. 10, whose only window is in the bathroom; or No. 9, which has a new bathroom and an old door used as a headboard, but is rather dark, and the TV is pitched from the ceiling above the closet. If climbing to the fourth floor doesn't give you the vapors, No. 19, a twin done in blue and white, has a balcony and a Napoleon III chest of drawers that has been in the hotel forever. Also here is No. 20, a nice triple with pretty pink walls and a new bathroom.

NOTE: Mme. Decharne's husband, Pascal Bennett, is a noted Paris photographer who gives lessons in either French or English. The classes naturally deal in the best way to photograph Paris; thus, your classroom is the city. The classes are for one to four persons, last for two hours, and cost around 40€. If you are interested, sign up for a space when you book your room.

156 Hotels in the Sixth Arrondissement

FACILITIES AND SERVICES: Direct-dial phone, no elevator (4 floors), hair dryer, TV with international reception, office safe (no charge)

NEAREST TOURIST ATTRACTIONS (LEFT BANK): St-Michel, St-Germain-des-Prés, St-Michel, Musée de Cluny, Seine, Île de la Cité, Île St-Louis

HÔTEL FERRANDI ★★★ (53)
92, rue du Cherche-Midi, 75006
Métro: Vaneau, Falguière
42 rooms, all with shower or bath and toilet

Thoroughly dignified in every way, the hotel is unusually successful in combining the best in old-world style with modern comforts and expectations. The attractive owner, Mme. La Fond, and her exceptional staff are on top of the details that make a difference in a guest's stay. The downstairs sitting area is defined by an ornate marble fireplace and a crystal chandelier. Loads of comfortable chairs, fresh flowers, attractive art, and daily newspapers in French and English create a pleasing place to relax. Stained-glass windows add color to the front hall. The interior hallways, lined with ocher fabric to keep noise to a minimum, are gracefully joined by a winding staircase painted in a mustard toned, faux-marble finish.

The rooms, all of which face the front, are furnished with period antiques and are color coordinated in soft shades of blues, browns, and pinks. Most have extra closet and luggage space and are just the ticket for those of us who do not travel lightly. For longer stays, I like Room 50, a ground-floor, two-room apartment with a roomy pink marble bathroom, or No. 43, with a four-poster bed, ornamental ceiling, plenty of drawer and closet space, good light, and inviting armchairs. Other favorites are No. 23, with a blue-and-white half-canopy bed, marble fireplace, and massive armoire; and No. 46, a deluxe twin or king in blue with a pink marble bathroom. Number 27, with a brass bed, double closet, and single chair, is the least expensive room; it's perfect for one. Some of the bathrooms, especially in the smaller rooms, tend to be cramped, but most are equipped with heated towel racks. Motorists will appreciate the hotel garage, and shoppers will love the many discount shopping stores within easy reach.

FACILITIES AND SERVICES: Air-conditioning, bar, direct-dial phone, elevator, hair dryer, laundry service, some minibars, private parking (must reserve ahead), TV with

TELEPHONE
01-42-22-97-40

FAX
01-45-44-89-97

EMAIL
hotel.ferrandi@wanadoo.fr

INTERNET
www.123france.com

CREDIT CARDS
AE, DC, MC, V

RATES
1–2 persons 105–130€, deluxe room 170–220€, suite for 2 persons 260€; private parking 22€ per day; *taxe de séjour* 0.85€ per person, per day

BREAKFAST
Continental 10€ per person

ENGLISH SPOKEN
Yes

international reception and pay-for-view channels, office safe (no charge)

NEAREST TOURIST ATTRACTIONS (LEFT BANK): Montparnasse, Le Bon Marché department store, good shopping

HÔTEL JARDIN LE BRÉA ★★★ (63)
14, rue Bréa, 75006
Métro: Vavin, Notre-Dame-des-Champs
23 rooms, all with shower or bath and toilet

TELEPHONE
01-43-25-44-41
FAX
01-44-07-19-25
EMAIL
brea.hotel@wanadoo.fr
INTERNET
www.jardinlebrea-paris-hotel.com
CREDIT CARDS
AE, DC, MC, V
RATES
Standard single 125€, double 140€, triple 165€; superior single/double 160€, triple 165€; extra bed 17€; *taxe de séjour* 0.91€ per person, per day
BREAKFAST
Buffet 11€ per person, Continental in room 10€ per person
ENGLISH SPOKEN
Yes

The floral theme of this attractive Montparnasse hotel starts the minute you enter the street-side orange-and-yellow sitting room, which has a framed art collage of rose petals and a big bouquet of silk red poppies in the window. Further charm is added by a marble-framed black-metal fireplace and a terracotta-tiled bar facing a winter garden. The small, compact rooms have all been redone in yellow and Provençal red, and reflect good taste and three star comforts. Two rooms (Nos. 7 and 8) open onto the garden. Number 7 is a small yellow double with a stall shower; No. 8, a king, has slightly more space, but for some the twelve steps down a narrow spiral stairway to reach the bathroom would not be appealing. Room 11, a twin on the courtyard, has a large bathroom with good lighting; No. 14, a double on the street, has the advantage of a bathtub and more luggage space; and so does No. 4, a superior with a king bed, two windows, and a large white tiled bathroom. A buffet breakfast is laid out in a stone-walled room with wicker chairs and yellow clad tables.

NOTE: The elevator does not go to the top two floors where the superior rooms are located.

FACILITIES AND SERVICES: Air-conditioning, bar, direct-dial phone, elevator to first floor only, hair dryer, Internet in lobby, laundry service, TV with international reception, room safe (no charge)

NEAREST TOURIST ATTRACTIONS (LEFT BANK): Montparnasse, Jardin du Luxembourg

HÔTEL LEFT BANK SAINT-GERMAIN ★★★ ($, 29)
9, rue de l'Ancienne Comédie, 75006
Métro: Odéon
31 rooms, all with shower or bath and toilet

TELEPHONE
01-43-54-01-70; toll-free in the U.S. and Canada 800-528-1234 (Best Western)
FAX
01-43-26-17-14

It is hard to imagine a small hotel in Paris more appealing than this one, which is, quite frankly, just the sort of hotel that makes you fall in love with Paris in the first place. Located in the ever-popular St-Germain *quartier* and convenient to everything, it is run by Claude Teil and his family, who also operate Au Manoir Saint-Germain-des-Prés a few blocks away (see page 144). So it is no surprise to find the Hôtel Left Bank Saint-Germain just as beautiful, from the entrance where guests all admire an adorable antique baby carriage filled with authentically dressed vintage dolls to the large top-floor suite with dormer window views onto Notre Dame, Ste-Chapelle, and Centre Georges Pompidou (Beaubourg). To add to the overall allure, there are fresh flowers everywhere, museum-quality Aubusson tapestries, polished antiques mixed with special handmade furnishings from Perigord, excellent eighteenth-century reproductions, open oak beams, stone walls, and a very helpful, English-speaking staff.

The standard-size rooms are done in rich paisley prints with built-in minibars and room safes. The bathrooms are excellent and the courtyard views pleasant. The connecting rooms that house up to four are comfortable choices because they have desk space, larger baths, and out-of-sight storage space. In Suite 604, one window on the pitched roof has a tip-toe view of the Eiffel Tower, and at the other end of the room, the view is of Notre Dame, Centre Georges Pompidou, and Ste-Chapelle. The huge room that sleeps up to five has a red-velvet settee, two desks, a dressing table, and a nice bathroom, but I was disappointed to see the worn upholstery on the chairs.

FACILITIES AND SERVICES: Air-conditioning, direct-dial phone, elevator, hair dryer, Internet in lobby, laundry service, minibar, TV with international reception, room safe (8€ per stay), several nonsmoking rooms

NEAREST TOURIST ATTRACTIONS (LEFT BANK): St-Germain-des-Prés, St-Michel, Musée de Cluny, Seine, Île de la Cité, Île St-Louis, wonderful shopping

INTERNET
www.paris-hotels-charm.com

CREDIT CARDS
AE, DC, MC, V

RATES
Single 200€, double 216€, triple 240€, quad 264€, suite 320€; *taxe de séjour* 0.86€ per person, per day

BREAKFAST
Complimentary buffet or Continental

ENGLISH SPOKEN
Yes

HÔTEL LE RÉGENT ★★★ ($, 10)
61, rue Dauphine, 75006
Métro: Odéon
25 rooms, all with shower or bath and toilet

For Parisian atmosphere in a setting of nonstop activity, it is hard to top the Régent, which offers guests traditional charm in a renovated eighteenth-century building. Fresh flowers and green plants add soft touches

TELEPHONE
01-46-34-59-80

FAX
01-40-51-05-07

EMAIL
hotel.leregent@wanadoo.fr

INTERNET
www.france-hotel-guide.com/
h75006leregent.htm
CREDIT CARDS
AE, DC, MC, V
RATES
1–2 persons 140€, deluxe 200–
215€; lower rates in off-season;
taxe de séjour included
BREAKFAST
Continental 12€ per person
ENGLISH SPOKEN
Yes

to the stone entry and reception areas, which are decorated with antiques and tapestry-covered chairs. A selection of Les Deux Magots teas, jams, champagne, and dishes is for sale in a display case . . . and why not? Both the famous café and this hotel are under the same ownership. The airless stone-walled breakfast room with a copy machine under the winding staircase needs a makeover; until that happens, enjoy breakfast in your room, or be more Parisian and go to the corner café. If mobility is an issue, note that the elevator does not descend to the dining room on the lower ground floor.

All the rooms are well maintained and have the creature comforts most deem necessary, with the added bonus of terry robes (which are available upon request) and trouser presses. The bathrooms are modern, but the real showstoppers are in the rooms on the highest floors. For one of the prettiest pink-tiled bathrooms in Paris, request Room 52. Number 41, a large twin with three windows, also has an outstanding spacious bathroom with monogrammed towels, a lighted magnifying mirror, and a deep glass-enclosed tub and shower. Just like it is Room 11 on the first floor, which is in shades and patterns of orange; however, because it faces front, guests should expect some street noise. Room 53 is a wood-paneled twin with a view to the top of Notre Dame. If I had to pick a favorite room, I would select No. 62, nestled under the eaves on the sixth floor. From the room, you can see Notre Dame Cathedral. Sitting on the balcony, you look over the rooftops to La Tour Montparnasse.

The staff is very pleasant. It should be noted, however, that they are unable to promise specific rooms, but will note special requests and do their best to accommodate them.

FACILITIES AND SERVICES: Air-conditioning, direct-dial phone, elevator (starts 1st floor), hair dryer, Internet in lobby, laundry service, minibar, robes upon request, trouser press and magnifying mirrors in some rooms, TV with international reception, room safe (no charge)

NEAREST TOURIST ATTRACTIONS (LEFT BANK): St-Germain-des-Prés, Seine, Île de la Cité, Île St-Louis, excellent shopping

HÔTEL LE RELAIS MÉDICIS ★★★ ($, 46)
23, rue Racine, 75006
Métro: Odéon, Cluny–La Sorbonne
16 rooms, all with shower or bath and toilet

The jury is still out on whether heaven is as divine as a stay at Le Relais Médicis. I will admit it was love at first sight the minute I walked into this picture-perfect dream hotel, where something artistic and imaginative catches your eye at every turn—it might be a humorous bench with black bears carved on each end, or the antique metal toys and Majolica spice jars displayed behind the desk. The total look of the hotel is characteristically French, with the mix of patterns, shapes, sizes, and colors all adding up to a stunning visual effect. In the lush salon, lovely oil paintings are set off by vibrant fuchsia fabric-covered walls and antique birdcages, which add a light touch. Garden paintings define the spring-time feel of the breakfast room, where even the lights reflect the floral theme. Vintage black-and-white photos displayed throughout the halls of the hotel add notes of interest.

Two lifts take guests to the sixteen floral-themed bedrooms, all of which I could live in happily for a long Parisian stay. For instance, in No. 22 you are surrounded by soft greens and corals, with floral dust ruffles complementing the cotton bedspreads. An enviable display of turn-of-the-century colored prints of young women and children are offset by a solo modern painting. The marble bath has reproduction antique chrome fittings and the mirrored wardrobe is large enough to hold everything you brought with you. In Room 36, a deluxe double with twin beds, there is a sofa and a comfortable chair, windows overlooking both the garden and street, and an interesting painting of a bridge scene, divided into four panels. A huge double bookcase occupies one wall, and a four-drawer marble dresser another. If you occupy the quiet and secluded double-bedded No. 39, the color scheme is a soft orange sorbet, and the view is of the buildings across the way. Frankly feminine No. 26, which is similar to No. 36, is a cheerful, large, beamed room with twin beds, three windows, and an adorable old desk. Colors and fabrics are coordinated in blue and yellow; decorative accents include a gold clock and an assortment of old tins. Room 24 is a smaller double with a marble-top dresser. The mirrored wall gives the illusion of more space in this room, which is still big enough to

TELEPHONE
01-43-26-00-60

FAX
01-40-46-83-39

EMAIL
relais-medicis@wanadoo.fr

INTERNET
www.relaismedicis.com

CREDIT CARDS
AE, DC, MC, V

RATES
Single 188€, double 208€, deluxe 239–258€; excellent lower rates in off-season; *taxe de séjour* included

BREAKFAST
Complimentary Continental

ENGLISH SPOKEN
Yes

accommodate a round table and two chairs, the perfect place to enjoy a Continental breakfast.

FACILITIES AND SERVICES: Air-conditioning, bar, direct-dial phone, elevator, hair dryer, Internet access (planned), laundry service, magnifying mirrors in most rooms, minibar, *peignoirs* (bathrobes) in all rooms, porter, TV with international reception, room safe (no charge)

NEAREST TOURIST ATTRACTIONS (LEFT BANK): St-Michel, Musée de Cluny, Jardin du Luxembourg, St-Germain-des-Prés, shopping

HÔTEL LE SAINTE-BEUVE ★★★ (62)
9, rue Sainte-Beuve, 75006
Métro: Vavin, Notre-Dame-des-Champs
22 rooms, all with shower, bath, and toilet

Nicely positioned between the Jardin du Luxembourg and the boulevard Montparnasse, the Hôtel Sainte-Beuve makes my short list of top upmarket hotel choices in this corner of Paris. The hotel and the street were named for Charles Sainte-Beuve, a poet and contemporary of Victor Hugo. As the story goes, he went to a dinner party and left with Victor Hugo's wife.

The hotel was artfully designed by decorator David Hicks, who boldly combines fabric patterns and furnishings in a harmony of colors. The result is an atmosphere that is rich in a contemporary French way, with many touches that give it a feeling of easy-going elegance. In the comfortable lounge are two over-size sofas and armchairs grouped around a lovely wood-burning fireplace. Gray tweed hallways lined with antique Parisian prints lead to the bedrooms, all of which display a sense of style and grace. In No. 18, the modern poppy-red and beige colors set off the antique mirrored vanity dressing table and marble-top bedside chests. The easy-to-live-in room has good closet space and a bathroom with two windows. Number 12, a standard room on the back with a city view, can connect with No. 11 to form a family suite. For the largest room, reserve La Chambre "Sainte-Beuve," a huge two-room suite with sisal floor covering topped with a tiger rug. Two oversized twin beds covered in white linens blend with the soft beige tones, leather-top writing desk, and an interesting collection of oriental pots displayed along one wall. The closet and storage space never ends; in addition to a six-drawer walnut dresser, you have shelves in the bathroom and more in the room itself. Breads and pastries from the famous Gérard Mulot Pâtisserie are served for breakfast.

TELEPHONE
01-45-48-20-07

FAX
01-45-48-67-52

EMAIL
saintebeuve@wanadoo.fr

INTERNET
www.paris-hotel-charme.com

CREDIT CARDS
AE, DC, MC, V

RATES
1–2 persons standard 135€, classic 178€, superior 195€, deluxe 235€, La Chambre "Sainte-Beuve" 275€, connecting rooms 325€; lower rates in August; *taxe de séjour* 0.86€ per person, per day

BREAKFAST
Continental 14.50€ per day

ENGLISH SPOKEN
Yes

FACILITIES AND SERVICES: Air-conditioning, bar, direct-dial phone, elevator, hair dryer, Internet in lobby, laundry service, minibar, bathrobes and slippers, room service, TV with international reception, video on request, room safe (no charge)

NEAREST TOURIST ATTRACTIONS (LEFT BANK): Montparnasse, Jardin du Luxembourg

HÔTEL LE SAINT-GRÉGOIRE ★★★★ ($, 54)
43, rue de l'Abbé Grégoire, 75006
Métro: St-Placide

20 rooms, all with shower or bath and toilet

Everyone raves about it because on all counts the Hôtel le Saint-Grégoire is a stunning hotel. I will warn you: After one or two nights at this hotel, you will face a dilemma—you will wish you never had to leave Paris. It is, admittedly, on the high side in peak season, but I can assure you it is one of the most popular Big Splurges in the book because so many readers believe it is worth the extra money, not only for the comfort and surroundings, but for the welcome and assistance extended by the staff, skillfully headed by M. François de Béné.

The color scheme is purple, yellow, orange, red, and beige . . . and it works. Decorator David Hicks has created an elegantly intimate atmosphere in this twenty-room hotel by mixing period antiques with handsome modern pieces and sprinkling interesting fabrics, patterned throw rugs, and rich silks throughout a garden setting. As a result, the hotel conveys a feeling of well-being, from the fireplace in the rose-filled lobby to the linen-covered tables in the *cave* dining room, where freshly squeezed orange juice and yogurt are served with the Continental breakfast.

Please forward all mail to me care of Room 100, a bright yellow, ground-floor double opening onto a small garden. It has a marble-top coffee table, a bureau large enough to hold the contents of my suitcase, and two comfortable chairs for lazy late-night reading. The bath has heated towel racks and enough towels to last (almost) forever. If this room is not available, I would be supremely happy in either No. 102, a junior suite, also on a garden—which has its own entryway leading to a large room with a sofa, two easy chairs, and a table at one end—or No. 16, a large room with a terrace on the back of the hotel. Room 14 is a pink double, also with its own terrace, and just perfect if you are alone. Families can request that Rooms 24 and 26 be combined. Number 24

TELEPHONE
01-45-48-23-23

FAX
01-45-48-33-95

INTERNET
www.hotelsaintgregoire.com

CREDIT CARDS
AE, DC, MC, V

RATES
1–2 persons 175€, superior 215€, suite and rooms with private terrace 215–248€; dog 12€; lower rates in off-season; *taxe de séjour* included

BREAKFAST
Continental 12€ per person

ENGLISH SPOKEN
Yes

is a small, peach-colored room with a wall hat rack; No. 26 is a larger double with a nice writing table, armoire, and black marble-top dresser, and it has a light bath with a separate enclosed toilet.

Also under the same ownership is the Hôtel le Tourville in the seventh and their newest, Hôtel Le Lavoisier, in the eighth (see pages 193 and 210).

FACILITIES AND SERVICES: Air-conditioning, bar, direct-dial phone, elevator, hair dryer, laundry service, TV with international reception, office safe (no charge)

NEAREST TOURIST ATTRACTIONS (LEFT BANK): Montparnasse, Le Bon Marché department store, excellent shopping

HÔTEL NOVANOX ★★★ (68)
155, boulevard du Montparnasse, 75006
Métro: Vavin, Raspail; RER Port Royal
27 rooms, all with shower or bath and toilet

From the outside it doesn't inspire. But inside, the future beckons at the Novanox, an impressive example of what a sense of style and imagination—with a little money thrown in—can do. Hats off to owner Bertrand Plasmans, who, several years ago, gambled everything and took an old hotel and fashioned a modern re-creation with the latest designs and contemporary craftsmanship. The yellow-and-blue lobby, with dangling mobile lights, reminds me of a playful fairyland—everywhere you look the faces of Greek gods and goddesses are softly painted on the walls and depicted on the upholstered chairs and couches. At one end of the lobby is a breakfast area overlooking an enclosed, plant-rimmed sidewalk terrace. Dainty croissants and buttery brioches fill the breakfast baskets and are accompanied by an assortment of jams and a pot of sweet butter. A portion of cheese and fresh fruit round out the meal.

The rooms along the front have a chocolate-brown color scheme, with contemporary furniture specially built to fit the design of each room, and sparkling white-tile baths. The quiet rooms on the back are larger, and though not yet refurbished, still very nice. The toiletries are from Roger and Gallet, the fresh flowers from the owner's mother's garden, the carpet imported from Belgium, and the ideas all from M. Plasmans. The result? Still *magnifique!*

M. Plasmans' latest hotel acquisition is the Hôtel Saint-Thomas-d'Aquin, a two-star in the seventh arrondissement (see page 197).

TELEPHONE
01-46-33-63-60
FAX
01-43-26-61-72
EMAIL
hotel-novanox@wanadoo.fr
INTERNET
www.hotel-novanox.com
CREDIT CARDS
AE, DC, MC, V
RATES
1–2 persons 112–124€; extra bed 28€; look for special promotions on Website; *taxe de séjour* included
BREAKFAST
Continental 9€ per person
ENGLISH SPOKEN
Yes

FACILITIES AND SERVICES: Bar, direct-dial phone, elevator, hair dryer, laundry service, minibar, TV with international reception, room safe (no charge)

NEAREST TOURIST ATTRACTIONS (LEFT BANK): Montparnasse, Jardin du Luxembourg

HÔTEL RELAIS SAINT-SULPICE ★★★ ($, 48)
3, rue Garancière, 75006
Métro: Mabillon, Odéon
26 rooms, all with shower, bath, and toilet

An inspired use of pattern and colonial African design characterizes the public areas of this attractive choice that is close to designer boutique shopping and promenades through the Jardin du Luxembourg. The intimate sitting room, housing a small honor bar, is enhanced by an unusual collection of colorful beetles mounted under glass and a dhurrie rug tossed onto the plank floor. The large skylighted breakfast room has a contemporary tapestry of the Jardin du Luxembourg and hand-painted floor tiles from Provence set into an oak floor. In keeping with the theme of the hotel are tables and chairs crafted from twisted bamboo and wood, and a pretty garden bench covered with African prints. To one side is the entrance to the complimentary guest sauna. The twenty-six livable rooms are done in shades of cream, biscuit, and toffee, or soft green with wrought-iron bed frames and cushioned cane chairs complemented by a table from the 1930s or a vintage chest. Most face the street and have a view of St. Sulpice Church; a few others overlook a quiet central courtyard. All the bathrooms have a bathtub and shower combination, and are brightened by a colorful lizard design set into the tiles.

FACILITIES AND SERVICES: Air-conditioning, bar, conference room, direct-dial phone, elevator, hair dryer, laundry service, minibar, sauna, TV with international reception

NEAREST TOURIST ATTRACTIONS (LEFT BANK): St. Sulpice Church, Jardin du Luxembourg, St-Germain-des-Prés, excellent shopping

TELEPHONE
01-46-33-99-00
FAX
01-46-33-00-10
EMAIL
relaissstsulpice@wanadoo.fr
CREDIT CARDS
AE, DC, MC, V
RATES
1–2 persons 160–195€, triple 235€; *taxe de séjour* included
BREAKFAST
Buffet 12€ per person
ENGLISH SPOKEN
Yes

HÔTEL SAINT-ANDRÉ-DES-ARTS ★ (22)
66, rue St-André-des-Arts, 75006
Métro: Odéon, St-Michel
32 rooms, all with shower or toilet

The Saint-André-des-Arts continues to improve—well, sort of. Some of the airless, trainlike bathrooms with hot-red toilet seats are still in use, but some more enjoyable stretch tubs have been included in a few of the

TELEPHONE
01-43-26-96-16
FAX
01-43-29-73-34
EMAIL
hsaintand@wanadoo.fr

INTERNET
www.123france.com
CREDIT CARDS
MC, V
RATES
Single 67€, double 84–87€,
triple 104€, quad 114€; *taxe de
séjour* included
BREAKFAST
Complimentary Continental
ENGLISH SPOKEN
Yes

new bathrooms. Various rooms have also had quickie facelifts (that is, a coat of paint has been slapped on). Much also stays the same. The carved misericord, which priests used to sit on and lean against during long masses, continues to grace the entry, along with a row of raffia stools under the window, an exhausted black leather sofa, and two folding tables—one of which holds a TV with a stack of CDs on top and another holds the CD player. Most importantly, the friendly manager still stands behind his ruling philosophy, "We are a hotel without extras, including the charges." For instance, a Continental breakfast is complimentary, but "if you want it served in your room, you take it there," says the manager.

The location is strategic, the prices low, and the unconventional crowd of fashion groupies, hip musicians, budding actors, and starving backpackers is party-loving and carefree. For some people, the rooms are so small that cabin fever sets in immediately. Others may object to the unpleasant symphony of noises drifting through the walls at all hours or to the low-watt lights dangling from the ceilings. Nonsmokers won't appreciate that housekeepers are allowed to smoke on the job. But none of that matters to the devoted regulars, for whom this wrinkled hotel still has a tattered charm they love to romanticize and an attitude by the management they eagerly applaud.

FACILITIES AND SERVICES: Direct-dial phone, no elevator (4 floors), hair dryer, TV and video at reception, office safe (no charge)

NEAREST TOURIST ATTRACTIONS (LEFT BANK): St-Germain-des-Prés, St-Michel, Musée de Cluny, Seine, Île de la Cité, Île St-Louis

HÔTEL SAINT-GERMAIN-DES-PRÉS ★★★ ($, 2)
36, rue Bonaparte, 75006
Métro: St-Germain-des-Prés

30 rooms, all with shower or bath and toilet

TELEPHONE
01-43-26-00-19
FAX
01-40-46-83-63
EMAIL
hotel-saint-germain-des-
pres@wanadoo.fr
INTERNET
www.hotel-st-ger.com
CREDIT CARDS
AE, MC, V

The hotel brochure states: "At the end of your visit, you are already longing to come back to this magical place." How true it is—the Saint-Germain-des-Prés is just the kind of small hotel everyone hopes to find, and return to, in Paris. Superbly located in the very *coeur* of St-Germain, only a few minutes from two of the city's most famous cafés—Les Deux Magots and Café Flore—it has a long history of famous guests. It began in 1778 as a Masonic lodge to which Voltaire, Benjamin Franklin, and U.S. Navy captain John Paul Jones belonged. After it became a hotel, it housed philosopher Auguste Comte, American playwright Elmer Rice, and authors Henry Miller and Janet Flanner. Ms. Flanner lived here for years and wrote her Letters from Paris column for the *New Yorker* from her top-floor suite.

The hotel is known for its lovely displays of fresh flowers, which are massed everywhere, from the entryway with its Venetian glass chandelier and hand-painted celestial ceiling to the antique- and tapestry-filled salon overlooking a walled garden filled with blooming hydrangeas and azaleas. The well-lit individualized rooms have hand-painted doors and brass or canopy beds, and they are done in dark woods and fabric-covered walls. The quiet suites face the courtyard. With their separate sitting rooms, they are captivating, especially No. 26, which has oriental rugs tossed on polished inlaid wooden floors, a canopy bed, leaded-glass windows, flower boxes, and a marble bath with Art Nouveau lights and fixtures. Space is well used in No. 25, a double on the back where built-in closets frame the bed; a small desk, chair, and luggage bench offer comfort. Air-conditioning in all the rooms is an added bonus on hot days in this noisy part of Paris.

The hotel's deserved popularity today is due in no small measure to the thoughtfulness of its staff members, who go to great lengths to cater to the needs of their guests. Everyone who stays here agrees that it is definitely worth the Big Splurge.

The Grand Hôtel de l'Univers, also in the sixth arrondissement, is under the same ownership (see page 145).

FACILITIES AND SERVICES: Air-conditioning, bar, direct-dial phone, elevator, hair dryer, Internet in lobby, laundry service, minibar, robes and slippers in suites and deluxe rooms, room service for light meals, TV with international reception, room safe (no charge)

NEAREST TOURIST ATTRACTIONS (LEFT BANK): St-Germain-des-Prés, wonderful shopping, Seine

RATES
1–2 persons 160–195€, superior 255€, suite 310€; *taxe de séjour* included

BREAKFAST
Complimentary Continental

ENGLISH SPOKEN
Yes

HÔTEL SAINT-PAUL ★★★ (47)
43, rue Monsieur-le-Prince, 75006
Métro: Odéon, Cluny–La Sorbonne
31 rooms, all with shower or bath and toilet

In the seventeenth century, this building served as a hostel for Franciscan monks. During World War II, the breakfast room served as a shelter during the air raids. In the early 1960s, the hotel was full of American students studying at the Sorbonne. For the past forty years, it has

TELEPHONE
01-43-26-98-64

FAX
01-46-34-58-60

EMAIL
hotel.saint.paul@wanadoo.fr

INTERNET
www.hotelsaintpaulparis.com

CREDIT CARDS
AE, DC, MC, V
RATES
Single 112–128€, double 128–
158€, suite 174–190€, duplex
204€; see Website or ask about
special promotions; *taxe de séjour*
included
BREAKFAST
Continental 10€, American
(eggs and ham) 13€, per person
ENGLISH SPOKEN
Yes

been a hotel owned by the Hawkins family and is now competently run by their daughter, Marianne, and her husband, Daniel, who are ably assisted by an accommodating staff and the black-and-white house cat, Spoutnick. The family's collection of antiques, oriental rugs, and watercolor paintings has been used in the hotel with elegant results. The seasonal fresh flower bouquets that grace the public areas are grown and arranged by one of the housekeepers, who has been with the hotel for over two decades.

Custom-made curtains, fabric-covered walls, and interesting brass and four-poster beds combine with modern baths to create the pleasing rooms. There are four rooms similar to No. 31, a single overlooking the garden and done in beige grass cloth with a white brass bed. Room 14 has a high ceiling that accommodates a four-poster bed with a tapestry-covered headboard and matching canopy. Twin sleigh beds and plenty of sunshine add to the enjoyment of Room 13, located on the front of the hotel. In No. 35, the fresco of bookshelves holds a painting of Spoutnick; the room is on the street and has a very nice bathroom. One of my favorites is No. 51, with terracotta linen walls. Situated under the eaves, it has a cozy bedroom with a small sitting room and a bird's-eye view of École de Médecine. For those wanting more space, No. 2, a duplex with twin beds downstairs and a circular stairway leading to a second bedroom with a double bed and bath, is a good choice.

FACILITIES AND SERVICES: Air-conditioning, direct-dial phone, elevator, hair dryer, laundry service, minibar, TV with international reception, room safe (no charge)

NEAREST TOURIST ATTRACTIONS (LEFT BANK): Jardin du Luxembourg, St-Germain-des-Prés, St-Michel, Musée de Cluny

LE MADISON HÔTEL ★★★ ($, 27)
143, boulevard St-Germain 75006
Métro: Mabillon, St-Germain-des-Prés
54 rooms, all with shower, bath, and toilet

TELEPHONE
01-40-51-60-00
FAX
01-40-51-60-01
INTERNET
www.hotel-madison.com
CREDIT CARDS
AE, DC, MC, V

Le Madison Hôtel evokes the charm of a bygone era, when families packed trunks, set sail across the Atlantic, and spent months doing *Le Grand Tour* of Europe. Built in 1924, the hotel has played host to some famous guests. Nobel Prize winner Albert Camus wrote *l'Étranger* while living here; Hemingway was a regular at the bar, as was Juliette Greco, who was known as "the queen of St-Germain" in the fifties. André Malraux had his mistress ensconced here, and today, singer Carol King calls it her Paris home.

The beautiful reception and sitting areas are done in classic French style with tapestries, rich velvet upholstery, oriental rugs, dramatic window treatments, and graceful antiques. Personal touches make guests feel at home: a picture of the owner's mother hanging over the wood-burning fireplace, bouquets of fresh flowers scattered about, books and magazines to thumb through, a bowl of candies.

The rooms blend modern amenities and comforts with conventional fabrics and furnishings, accented by some unusual touches. For instance, each floor has a different painting on the door to the elevator. The bathroom in No. 27 is done entirely in lipstick red, right down to the tiles and towel racks. Color was also not lost on No. 28, which positively glows in shades of fiery orange. Aside from needing dark glasses to stay in this room, it has a dismal back view, as do all rooms ending in 2, 7 or 8. No one could fault No. 71, a charming single in green and turquoise with a view of St. Sulpice. In addition to excellent luggage space, a decent desk and a mirrored closet, it has a pink-tile bathroom with a good shower and marble sink. Room 23, which can sleep two or three, has an amusing collection of antique golf prints. From No. 74, a yellow and green double, you have a sweeping view encompassing Montmartre, St-Germain-des-Prés Church, and the tip of La Samaritane department store. The bed is king-size, the bathroom marble, and the space excellent. Room 86, lavishly done in lavender and tawny gold, has the same view.

In No. 87, a two-room suite, you have only a peek at St-Germain-des-Prés Church but enough space to swing three cats and entertain two dozen of your closest friends. The sitting room is pleasingly decorated in blue and green with coordinating tartan curtains pulled back to let in plenty of light. It is furnished with a green leather sofa, two comfortable armchairs, and a desk large enough to plug in your laptop and actually get some work done. The twin bedroom has more closet and luggage space than you will ever need and a well-lit bathroom with a separate stall shower and double sinks.

Two other hotels are under the same family ownership: Hôtel Bourgogne & Montana, and Terrass Hôtel (see pages 179 and 293).

RATES
Single 150–190€, double 200–250€, executive 300€, suite/apt 400€; extra bed 65€; off-season rates Jan–Feb, Aug; animal 14€; *taxe de séjour* included

BREAKFAST
Complimentary buffet in breakfast room or Continental in room

ENGLISH SPOKEN
Yes

FACILITIES AND SERVICES: Air-conditioning, bar, direct-dial phone, hair dryer, elevator, Internet in lobby, laundry service, magnifying mirrors, TV with international reception, robes in deluxe rooms and suites, room safe (no charge)

NEAREST TOURIST ATTRACTIONS (LEFT BANK): St-Germain-des-Prés, shopping, Seine, Musée de Cluny, St. Michel

LE RELAIS HÔTEL DU VIEUX PARIS ★★★★ ($, 11)
9, rue Gît-le-Coeur, 75006
Métro: Odéon; RER St-Michel–Notre-Dame
19 rooms, all with shower, bath, and toilet

TELEPHONE
01-44-32-15-90
FAX
01-43-26-00-15
INTERNET
www.vieuxparis.com
CREDIT CARDS
AE, DC, MC, V
RATES
Single 220€, double 280€, suite 380€; *taxe de séjour* included
BREAKFAST
Continental 13€ per person
ENGLISH SPOKEN
Yes

Romance and nostalgia in a picture-perfect setting sum up Le Relais Hôtel du Vieux Paris. The building dates from the late 1400s, as do most of the others on this narrow lane just off the Seine. As King Henri IV passed by the street, he said, *"Gist mon coeur"* (Here lies my heart), because this was where his favorite mistress lived—thus, the name of the street and the spirit that still pervades it.

In its heyday in the 1950s and early 1960s, the hotel had no proper name, just a street number. It was the haunt of the movers and shakers of the beat generation: Allen Ginsberg, Harold Norse, William S. Burroughs, Harold Chapman, Thelma Shumsky, and many others. Guests painted, wrote, talked, and planned, and the inflexible Mme. Rachou presided over it all while standing on a box behind the little zinc bar. There were no carpets, no telephones, and the nineteenth-century electrical system was hit-or-miss. Toilet facilities consisted of a hole in the floor on each stair landing. In the mid-1960s, Mme. Rachou suddenly sold the hotel. The new owners named it, carpeted and painted the rooms, added phones, and, of all things, even installed private bathrooms in some rooms. Canvases, manuscripts, and sketches that may have been worth millions of dollars were burned in the battle to disinfect the hotel.

Currently under its third owner, Mme. Claude Odillard, the hotel has been completely redone and today bears no resemblance to its previous life. The guests are chic and well traveled, and few are aware of the hotel's history—all that remains are photos of some of its earlier guests. Placed throughout the public areas of the hotel are pieces from Mme. Odillard's own collection of antiques. The thirteen individually decorated rooms and seven suites, which are coordinated in Pierre Frey fabrics and top-of-the-line furnishings, all have something special to offer. In No. 28, a blue floral double or twin, there is a massage shower; in No. 27, an executive double overlooking the street, there is a small sitting area. Number 25, a two-room suite in blue and white with its original beamed ceiling, also has a separate sitting area, as well as a Jacuzzi and a quiet vantage point. It is not surprising that the top-floor suite is always in demand: in addition to the king-size bedroom, sitting area, and marble bathroom on the first level, there is a mezzanine bedroom with a skylight that children adore.

Of further interest to many guests, the entire hotel is nonsmoking. A private limousine is available for airport pickup and departures, or day trips outside of Paris. Guests are urged to buy their tickets for the Louvre and Musée d'Orsay at the hotel reception, which means you do not have to waste time standing in those long lines. Honeymooners are toasted with a bottle of chilled champagne, and everyone is personally welcomed and made to feel at home in this very lovely hotel with an amazing history.

FACILITIES AND SERVICES: Air-conditioning, direct-dial phone, elevator, hair dryer, laundry service, TV with international reception, bathrobes and Jacuzzis in suites, room safe (no charge), wholly nonsmoking

NEAREST TOURIST ATTRACTIONS (LEFT BANK): St-Germain-des-Prés, St-Michel, Musée de Cluny, Seine, Île de la Cité, Île St-Louis

MILLÉSIME HÔTEL ★★★ ($, 4)
15, rue Jacob, 75006
Métro: St-Germain-des-Prés
22 rooms, all with shower, bath, and toilet

If art is one of the cornerstones of your Parisian trip, the Millésime is a perfect launching pad for walks to the Louvre, Musée d'Orsay, or the Cluny. Also within easy strolling distance are dozens of private art galleries and dealers in the neighborhood. For trips farther afield, a quick métro or bus ride takes you to the Rodin, Centre Georges Pompidou, or Picasso. This top-drawer location is also a heavenly address for dedicated shop hounds and those that want to adopt the café life.

The hotel is built around a pretty Provençal-style courtyard with trailing greenery and summer flowers. The interior is done in the warm countryside colors of this popular region: sunny yellow, earthy adobe, azure blue. Most of the rooms have pleasing neighborhood views. They are simply fitted with creature comforts and

TELEPHONE
01-44-07-97-97

FAX
01-46-34-55-97

INTERNET
www.millesimehotel.com

CREDIT CARDS
AE, DC, MC, V

RATES
1–2 persons 175–190€, Millésime room 215€; extra bed 45€; ask about special promotional offers; *taxe de séjour* included

BREAKFAST
Buffet 15€, Continental 12€, both per person

ENGLISH SPOKEN
Yes

white-tile bathrooms, which admittedly are nothing other than small in the standard rooms. The largest room is the Millésime suite with a sloping ceiling and cross support beams framing the window. Room 50, a one-flight walk up, is the only single on the fifth floor. It is designed to combine with No. 51, which has a larger bathroom, more sitting and work space, and a romantic view of the St-Germain-des-Prés Church. Breakfast is served in an arched stone cellar, where bright orange chairs are placed around white linen–covered tables. The fourth floor is exclusively nonsmoking.

FACILITIES AND SERVICES: Air-conditioning, direct-dial phone, elevator (to most floors), hair dryer, Internet in lobby, laundry service, room service for light snacks, TV with international reception, room safe (no charge), 4th floor nonsmoking

NEAREST TOURIST ATTRACTIONS (LEFT BANK): St-Germain-des-Prés, Seine, excellent shopping

PENSION LES MARRONNIERS (NO STARS, ¢, 59)
78, rue d'Assas (first floor on left, stairway A), 75006
Métro: Vavin, Notre-Dame-des-Champs
12 rooms, 2 with shower and toilet

TELEPHONE
01-43-26-37-71
FAX
01-43-26-07-72
EMAIL
o_marro@club-Internet.fr
INTERNET
www.pension-marronniers.com
CREDIT CARDS
None, cash only
RATES
Single 27–61€, double 54–82€; special rates for long stays; one month or longer, 20% discount; *taxe de séjour* 0.15€ per person, per day
BREAKFAST
Included Mon–Sat; dinner included from Mon–Fri; Sat lunch only
ENGLISH SPOKEN
Yes

The days of family-run pensions in France, and especially in Paris, are numbered, according to a documentary on the subject filmed here. This *incroyable* Cheap Sleep, across the street from one of the entrances to the Jardin du Luxembourg, is presided over by Marie Poirier, whose family members have been here since the turn of the century. At the Pension les Marronniers, the philanthropically low prices include not only a Continental breakfast but a three-course dinner with cheese. With advance notice, special dietary needs can be catered to. Students, Frenchmen from the provinces doing a work-study program, and smart budgeteers fill this third-floor walkup, which has the Laura Ashley decorating seal of approval in the dining and living rooms. Mel, a black sheepdog, is in charge of providing a friendly welcome. The bedrooms might seem primitive to many, but all are cleaned on a regular basis, and the linens changed weekly. Reservations are absolutely essential months in advance, and guests who stay for a long time are preferred. Meals are part of the program and cannot be deducted for any reason.

FACILITIES AND SERVICES: Direct-dial phones, no elevator (2 floors), minibar, TV and video in lounge, office safe (no charge)

NEAREST TOURIST ATTRACTIONS (LEFT BANK): Montparnasse, Jardin du Luxembourg

WELCOME HÔTEL ★★ (28)
66, rue de Seine, at boulevard St-Germain, 75006
Métro: Odéon, Mabillion, St-Germain-des-Prés
30 rooms, all with shower or bath and toilet

Unpretentious, clean rooms with well-worn furniture in a fun-filled location are combined with moderate prices to make a stay here more than welcome. Composed of thirty rooms on six floors, this spot on the corner of rue de Seine and boulevard St-Germain is directly across from the picturesque rue de Buci street *marché*. Because many of the rooms are on the small side, as are the closets, it is an especially suitable stopover for singles. Those wanting more spacious accommodations should ask for a corner room with a view (Nos. 21, 51, or 53). The best is No. 53, done up in pink. The plus here is the large bath (for this hotel) with a tub and shower nozzle above. Other popular picks are No. 54, the best single because it has a writing table and a view, and No. 62, an attic nest with beams and a peaked ceiling. The worst is No. 64, with an open closet, a bathroom with no shelf space, and windows too high to see out. Despite double windows, quiet is not the rule here. For the least noisy bunks, request rooms that face rue de Seine (Nos. 21 or 51), not boulevard St-Germain. Top-floor rooms can get hot and stuffy in warm weather, but they are very desirable otherwise.

FACILITIES AND SERVICES: Direct-dial phone, elevator, French TV, office safe (no charge for access from 8 A.M — 6 P.M.)

NEAREST TOURIST ATTRACTIONS (LEFT BANK): St-Germain-des-Prés, Seine, shopping

TELEPHONE
01-46-34-24-80

FAX
01-40-46-81-59

CREDIT CARDS
MC, V

RATES
Single 75–95€, double 95–110€, triple 125€; *taxe de séjour* included

BREAKFAST
Continental 9€ per person

ENGLISH SPOKEN
Yes

Seventh Arrondissement

LEFT BANK
Assemblée Nationale
Champ-de-Mars
École Militaire
Les Egouts de Paris
Eiffel Tower
Les Invalides
Musée d'Orsay
Musée Rodin
UNESCO

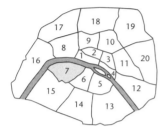

Known affectionately as "Seventh Heaven," this quiet, luxurious residential area is full of stately mansions built before the Revolution and now occupied by diplomats, government workers, well-to-do Parisians, and expatriates. The Champ-de-Mars served as the parade ground for the École Militaire and is the backyard of the Eiffel Tower. Also on the Champ-de-Mars is one of Paris's newest and most moving monuments: the Mur Pour la Paix (The Wall of Peace) based on the Wailing Wall in Jerusalem. It was built in 2000 to honor the hopes of peace in the new millennium. One part holds computer banks where people can write their own messages for peace here or on the Website (www.murpourlapaix.com).

Built as a military hospital and still used for this purpose, Les Invalides is the home of four world-famous military museums and is the final resting place of Napoléon Bonaparte. To the west of Les Invalides is the École Militaire, a military academy built by Louis XV; Napoléon trained there. If you are interested in experiencing the sewers of Paris *(les egouts de Paris),* which date from the Second Empire and were designed by Baron Haussmann, the museum at 93, quai d'Orsay runs guided tours. Tours of the Assemblée Nationale (the lower house of French parliament) are held on Saturdays when the chamber is not in session. Not to be missed are two museums: the Musée d'Orsay, originally a train station and now a repository of masterpieces of the Impressionists, and the lovely statues in the Musée Rodin. For premier antique shopping, stroll along the quai Voltaire and rue du Bac. Finally, there is the Eiffel Tower, which is best viewed across the river from Trocadéro. The 1,070-foot tower hosts six million visitors per year.

HOTELS IN THE SEVENTH ARRONDISSEMENT

Grand Hôtel Lévêque ★★ 178
Hôtel Bersoly's Saint-Germain ★★★ 178
Hôtel Bourgogne & Montana ★★★★ ($) 179
Hôtel de la Paix ★★ 180
Hôtel de la Tulipe ★★★ 181
Hôtel de Londres Eiffel ★★★ 181
Hôtel de l'Université ★★★ 182
Hôtel de Varenne ★★★ 183
Hôtel d'Orsay ★★★ 184
Hôtel Duc de Saint-Simon ★★★ ($) 185
Hôtel du Champ de Mars ★★ 186
Hôtel du Palais Bourbon ★★ 187
Hôtel Eber Mars ★★ 188
Hôtel Kensington ★★ 189
Hôtel Latour-Maubourg ★★★ 190
Hôtel Lenox Saint-Germain ★★★ 191
Hôtel les Jardins d'Fiffel ★★★ 192
Hôtel le Tourville ★★★★ ($) 193
Hôtel Muguet ★★ 194
Hôtel Relais Bosquet ★★★ 195
Hôtel Saint-Dominique ★★ 196
Hotel Saint Thomas-d'Aquin ★★ 197
Hôtel Valadon ★★ 198
Hôtel Verneuil ★★★ 199
Splendid Hôtel ★★★ 200

OTHER OPTIONS
Boat on the Seine

Bateau Sympatico 309

($) indicates a Big Splurge

Seventh Arrondissement

Seine

Pont des Invalides

Quai   d'Orsay

Branly

PL. DE LA RESISTANCE

Quai

l'Université

Rue Jean

Rue

Rue Maubourg

Avenue de la Bourdonnais

Rue   de

Avenue Rapp

Avenue

Rue Malar

Nicot

•1

Surcouf

Tour

Pont d'Iéna

R. Monttessuy

Av. Sacy

Saint

Dominique

•4

la

▲5

Branly

TOUR EIFFEL

Av. G. Eiffel

Av. Anatole

R. Sédillot

R. Amélie

6• •7

de

•9

Av. Pierre

Rue

Bosquet

Rue

Grenelle

La Tour Maubourg Ⓜ

Port de Suffren

Quai

Champ de Mars Tour Eiffel

Rue   •8

R. l'Exposition

Rue

de

•15

Av. Ch.

12•

R. Augereau

13•

14.

Cler

Av. G. Gréard

Av. Rey

de

Bouvard

Avenue de la Bourdonnais

R. du Champs de Mars

•22

•11

Avenue

PARC DU CHAMP DE

France

23•

24•▲

Rue   Jean

de

Suffren

Av. J.

MARS

Loti

31•

Chevert

•25

Rue

de

la

Fédération

Floquet

Av. C. Risler

École Militaire Ⓜ

•32

Avenue de Tourville

Rue

Desaix

Av. de la Motte Picquet

Rue

de

33•

Boulevard

de

Grenelle

Rue   Duplex

PLACE JOFFRE

ÉCOLE MILITAIRE

Avenue

Duquesne

PLACE DUPLEIX

Lowendal

Rue

d'Estrées

Dupleix Ⓜ

Grenelle

Av. de la Motte Picquet

Avenue

PLACE DE FONTENOY

Av.

Ségur

Breteuil

Rue   Fondary

La Motte Picquet Grenelle Ⓜ

Bd. de Grenelle

Avenue

de

de

Saxe

•36

Avenue   de

Av. Émile Zola

Ⓜ

Avenue Émile Zola

Rue   Frémicourt

PLACE CAMBRONNE

Ⓜ

Cambronne

Boulevard

Suffren

Ségur Ⓜ

PLACE DE BRETEUIL

Rue de la Croix   Nivert

Garibaldi

Sèvres Lecourbe

Ⓜ

500 meters

Ⓜ Métro Station

● R.E.R. Station

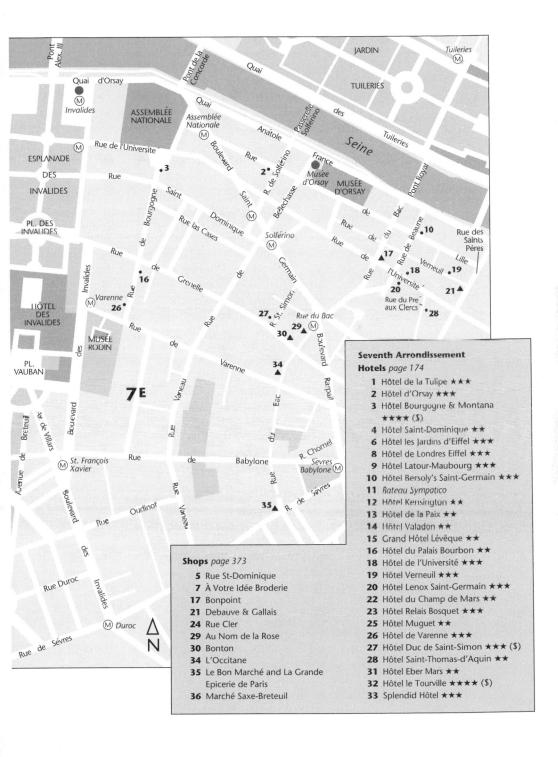

GRAND HÔTEL LÉVÊQUE ★★ (15)
29, rue Cler, 75007
Métro: École Militaire, Latour-Maubourg

TELEPHONE
01-47-05-49-15
FAX
01-45-50-49-36
INTERNET
www.hotel-leveque.com
CREDIT CARDS
AE, MC, V
RATES
Single 60€, double 90–99€,
triple 120€; free showers; *taxe
de séjour* 0.76€ per person,
per day
BREAKFAST
Continental 8€ per person
ENGLISH SPOKEN
Yes

50 rooms, 45 with shower and toilet, 5 singles with sink only

Committed cheap sleepers who like the seventh arrondissement love the Lévêque. Among the colorful food shops that line the rue Cler, it is close to all the things that one often forgets are so important on a trip: banks, a post office, good transportation, do-it-yourself laundries, cleaners, well-priced shops, cafés for a midmorning cup of hot chocolate, a street *marché,* and several exceptional cheese shops and *charcuteries* that inspire picnickers.

The hotel has benefited from yearly improvements and now boasts a glass elevator and spiffy, no-nonsense rooms. Closets and shelves are spacious enough, but drawer space is limited. The best rooms face the front. Three on the fifth floor have balconies where you can observe the wonderful street scene below. In Nos. 51 and 52, you can lie in bed and see the Eiffel Tower. The hotel is always busy, and I predict it will be even more in demand thanks to the many improvements. If you are interested in staying here, book ahead at least one month and more during peak periods.

FACILITIES AND SERVICES: Air-conditioning, direct-dial phone with private number, elevator, fans, hair dryer in most rooms, Internet in lobby, TV with international reception, room safe (5€ per stay)

NEAREST TOURIST ATTRACTIONS (LEFT BANK): Champ-de-Mars Park, Eiffel Tower, lively street *marché* on rue Cler

HÔTEL BERSOLY'S SAINT-GERMAIN ★★★ (10)
28, rue de Lille, 75007
Métro: Rue du Bac, St-Germain-des-Prés

TELEPHONE
01-42-60-73-79
FAX
01-49-27-05-55
EMAIL
hotelbersolys@wanadoo.fr
INTERNET
www.bersolyshotel.com
CREDIT CARDS
AE, DC, MC, V
RATES
1–2 persons 115–125€; pet
10€ per day; private parking
30€ per day; *taxe de séjour*
included

16 rooms, all with shower or bath and toilet

Bersoly's Saint-Germain continues to be a very good value three-star, which has been owned since the mid-1980s by Mme. Carbonnaux. The old stone walls and floors in the lobby are clean and polished, and the flowery downstairs breakfast room is set with Villeroy and Boch china. Then there is the location: only minutes away from the Musée d'Orsay, the Louvre, serious shopping, and equally serious restaurants (see *Great Eats Paris*).

Every air-conditioned bedroom has been named for a famous French artist. In each case, a reproduction of one of that artist's paintings hangs in the room, and the mood and color scheme of the room are taken from the painting. If you like bold reds and black, request the ground-floor Picasso room, with its entrance off the atrium. This is also the room you will get if you bring your pet to the hotel. If you prefer pastels, the Seurat or Sisley rooms are the ones to ask for. The twin- or king-bed Gauguin room can be joined with the Turner to form a family suite. The room to avoid is No. 10, the Van Gogh—not only is it dark, but guests must crawl over a brown fringed chair to reach the mini-bathroom.

FACILITIES AND SERVICES: Air-conditioning, bar, direct-dial phone, electric tea kettle, fans, elevator (to most floors), hair dryer, Internet in lobby, laundry service, private parking, room service, TV with international reception, room safe (no charge)

NEAREST TOURIST ATTRACTIONS (LEFT BANK): Musée d'Orsay, Louvre, Tuileries Gardens, interesting art galleries, shopping

HÔTEL BOURGOGNE & MONTANA ★★★★ ($, 3)
3, rue de Bourgogne, 75007
Métro: Assemblée-Nationale; RER Invalides
32 rooms, all with shower or bath and toilet

The formal Bourgogne & Montana, facing the Palais Bourbon, is located in a posh diplomatic neighborhood between Les Invalides and St-Germain. Famous neighbors include Lionel Jospin and fashion designer Karl Lagerfeld. Across the street is one of the best *pâtisseries* in the *quartier,* and next door, the Loulou de la Falaise boutique sells her fantasy collection of clothing, jewelry, and purses at equally fanciful prices. Combining a taste for tradition with a dignified clientele, the hotel is both regal and efficient, with large reception rooms and a historically classified 1924 elevator with lovely old iron-work and an open front that enables you to see the floors as you ascend.

No two rooms are the same, and many are in odd shapes, which not only adds interest but extra space. If cost is not too much of a factor, book a room on the fifth or sixth floor. I always hope for No. 67, a junior suite with wonderful views of place de la Concorde, the Madeleine Church, the Assemblée Nationale, and the roof of the Grand Palais. When the buildings are illuminated at night, it is pure fairyland. Done in blue and yellow, this twin-bed room has antiques, a comfortable sofa, large television, built-in closet, luggage space, and a divided bathroom with two sinks. If this is not available, ask for No. 61 with a mansard roofline and a round bathtub.

BREAKFAST
Continental 10€ per person

ENGLISH SPOKEN
Yes

TELEPHONE
01-45-51-20-22; toll-free from U.S. 800-44-UTELL

FAX
01-45-56-11-98

INTERNET
www.bourgogne-montana.com

CREDIT CARDS
AE, DC, MC, V

RATES
Single 150–180€, double 170–240€, suite 300–350€; extra bed 60€; animal 14€; lower off-season rates; *taxe de séjour* included

BREAKFAST
Complimentary buffet

ENGLISH SPOKEN
Yes

Room 54 has a courtyard view and a gleaming tile bathroom with excellent fittings. Room 42 is a standard choice in simple hotel decor, but it does offer space. Special rates during the off-season make this excellent choice even more affordable for many.

Also under the same ownership are Le Madison Hôtel in the sixth (see page 168) and Terrass Hôtel in Montmartre (see page 293).

FACILITIES AND SERVICES: Air-conditioning, bar, direct-dial phone, elevator, hair dryer, laundry service, minibar, free parking on the square (if you are lucky), *peignoirs* (bathrobes) in deluxe rooms and suites, TV with international reception and pay-for-view channels, office safe (no charge)

NEAREST TOURIST ATTRACTIONS (LEFT BANK): Musée d'Orsay, Musée Rodin, Invalides, Seine, Tuileries Gardens, Louvre

HÔTEL DE LA PAIX ★★ (13)
19, rue du Gros Caillou off rue de Grenelle, 75007
Métro: École Militaire

23 rooms, all with shower or bath and toilet

TELEPHONE
01-45-51-86-17
FAX
01-45-55-93-28
EMAIL
hotel.de.la.paix@wanadoo.fr
CREDIT CARDS
MC, V
RATES
Single 61€, double 91–100€, triple 111€; lower rates in Feb and Aug (but not for single rooms); *taxe de séjour* 0.80€ per day, per person
BREAKFAST
Continental in breakfast room 7€, in room 9€, per person
ENGLISH SPOKEN
Yes

The Hôtel de la Paix proves the point that style need not come at a hefty price. Everything is new, from the lobby and sitting room to the ground-floor handicapped room to the glass elevator. The modern rooms are quiet and comfortable, done in attractive coordinated colors and simple, contemporary dark wood. An interesting print or poster adds warmth. While only two rooms on the top floor have a tip-of-the-Eiffel-Tower view, none of the others offer grim overlooks. Another selling point is the tiled baths, especially the one in No. 9 with the ooh-la-la oval tub that you might find in a four-star deluxe. The owner is on site every day to make sure that her guests' needs are being met, that housekeeping is up to snuff, and that everything is running smoothly. She works very hard, and the result is this Great Sleep in the seventh.

FACILITIES AND SERVICES: Air-conditioning in 2 rooms, direct-dial phone, elevator (starts 1st floor), hair dryer, handicapped room, TV with international reception, room safe large enough for a laptop (no charge)

NEAREST TOURIST ATTRACTIONS (LEFT BANK): Eiffel Tower, Champ-de-Mars, UNESCO, Invalides

HÔTEL DE LA TULIPE ★★★ (1)
33, rue Malar, 75007
Métro: Latour-Maubourg

22 rooms, all with shower or bath and toilet

For years this former convent was a tired and tattered penny-pincher's choice *sans charme*. Thanks to the efforts of Jean-Louis Fortuit, a French film actor turned hotelier, and his charming wife, Caroline, it is finally a very sweet and romantic choice. The twenty-two rooms are tightly snuggled around a tree-shaded garden patio. Bright prints in Provençal colors, grass cloth–covered walls, wrought-iron and wicker furniture, beams galore, ancient stone walls, and peaceful garden views work nicely together, creating the illusion that the small rooms are in a country cottage miles away from Paris. If romance is on your itinerary, book No. 24, which once served as the chapel and still has two of the original stone walls and three windows opening onto the patio. If it's space you need, reserve the two-room, two-bath suite that can sleep five. From the hotel, you are in close range for bargain shopping along rue St-Dominique, soaking up the market atmosphere along rue Cler, and trying many of the favored restaurants in *Great Eats Paris*. For tourist endeavors, the Eiffel Tower is within walking distance for most and so is Les Invalides, the Seine, and the Musée d'Orsay.

FACILITIES AND SERVICES: Direct-dial phone, no elevator (2 floors), fans on request, hair dryer, minibar, parking (must be reserved), TV with international reception, room safe (no charge)

NEAREST TOURIST ATTRACTIONS (LEFT BANK): Eiffel Tower, Champ-de-Mars, Invalides

TELEPHONE
01-45-51-67-21

FAX
01-47-53-96-37

INTERNET
www.hoteldelatulipe.com

CREDIT CARDS
AE, DC, MC, V

RATES
Single 100€, double 130€, triple 165€, suite 250€; extra bed 22.87€; lower rates in Aug; parking 20€ per day; *taxe de séjour* included

BREAKFAST
Continental 9€ per person

ENGLISH SPOKEN
Yes

HÔTEL DE LONDRES EIFFEL ★★★ (8)
1, rue Augereau, 75007
Métro: École Militaire

30 rooms, all with shower or bath and toilet

Realistic prices, a very quiet location in the tony seventh arrondissement, easy walking distance to the Eiffel Tower and Champ-de-Mars, shopping, and a good métro connection add up to this fine hotel selection. Making it even more attractive is the hardworking owner, Isabelle Prigent, who told me, "I put my heart in this hotel. I want it to be just like my house." Isabelle has indeed succeeded at creating a very welcoming hotel where her guests can relax and feel quite at home.

The well-thought-out bedrooms are named after Isabelle's favorite French poets, and they all display her

TELEPHONE
01-45-51-63-02

FAX
01-47-05-28-96

INTERNET
www.londres-eiffel.com

CREDIT CARDS
AE, DC, MC, V

RATES
Single 99€, double 130–140€, triple 165€; extra bed 17€; lower off-season rates; *taxe de séjour* included

BREAKFAST
Continental 7€ per person

innate good taste: everything matches and is color coordinated, right down to the bows on the lamp shades. I like her collection of whimsical prints of old-fashioned makeup cases and beauty supplies, which hangs throughout. Rooms 52, 54, 62, and 64 have Eiffel Tower views. Rooms 101 (for two) and 103 (a triple) are quiet ground-floor choices overlooking the garden. The six larger rooms in the back building are also quiet, but there is no elevator. Off the reception area is an airy, yellow faux-finished breakfast room with chairs draped in orange fabric anchored by a wheat-colored bow. Isabelle is at the hotel every day, along with her friendly fox terrier, Ketty, to tend to her guests and extend her warm hospitality.

FACILITIES AND SERVICES: Air-conditioning, direct-dial phone, elevator (to most floors), hair dryer, Internet in lobby (no charge), minibar, TV with international reception

NEAREST TOURIST ATTRACTIONS (LEFT BANK): Eiffel Tower, Champ de Mars, UNESCO, Invalides

HÔTEL DE L'UNIVERSITÉ ★★★ (18)
22, rue de l'Université, 75007
Métro: Rue du Bac
27 rooms, 25 with shower or bath and toilet

There is a certain vintage charm about this old dowager that is reassuring to her many devoted returnees. Even the hotel brochure plays up the fact this is an *old-fashioned* hotel. What it does not say is that the owner has been here for at least fifty years and change does not come easily to her. This is clearly not a hotel for anyone in the fast track. It is, however, well loved by those who feel most comfortable in older homes where the same chair and sofa have been in place for years . . . and covered in the same fabric, too. All twenty-seven rooms are different, but each is furnished in an antique style with big armchairs, thick beamed ceilings, flocked wallpaper, heavy drapes hanging from brass poles, and fireplaces in many. Bedspreads may or may not fit, and colors in most rooms are as dated as the bathrooms. On the bright side, the location is tops and the rooms have space, a commodity in very short supply in most Parisian hotels. Many overlook the Ministry of Finance and a pretty garden. In No. 32, I like the sunny window that lets in the sounds of children playing nearby. The huge antique armoire and mirrored dresser will hold everything you brought to Paris, and all that you buy here as well. In No. 35, nothing really matches, but somehow it all goes together. Two windows

TELEPHONE
01-42-61-09-39
FAX
01-42-60-40-84
EMAIL
hoteluniversite@wanadoo.fr
INTERNET
www.hoteluniversite.com
CREDIT CARDS
AE, MC, V
RATES
Single (shower, no toilet) 80–125€, double 150–160€, terrace room 190–200€, triple 200–240€; *taxe de séjour* included
BREAKFAST
Continental 9€ per person
ENGLISH SPOKEN
Yes

overlook the ministry, and the semi-antique furnishings create a certain worn-slipper comfort. From the sunny top-floor Room 52, you can see the tip of the Eiffel Tower. You sleep in a brass bed, shower in a pink marble bathroom, and sit on your own terrace. Two armchairs, a round table, and six-tiered bookshelf lend more homey touches. You also get to climb one flight of stairs because the elevator does not go to this floor. Until it has been completely redone, I would not sleep in No. 23, a single facing front. Not only is there no closet (a curtain hides a clothes rack), no table, and no chair, but the wallpaper is hideous, the carpet worse . . . and never mind those worn-out velvet drapes.

Under the hotel is an amazing seventeenth-century crypt that was built with stones dating back to Gallo-Roman times in the first century. The chapel belonged to the Knights of the Temple of Solomon, who fought Pope Clément the Fifth. It is now used as a conference room, but it still looks like a massive hall in a feudal castle where the knights of the round table presided.

FACILITIES AND SERVICES: Air-conditioning, direct-dial phone, elevator (to most floors), hair dryer, laundry service, some minibars, TV with international reception, room service for light meals, room safe (no charge)

NEAREST TOURIST ATTRACTIONS (LEFT BANK): Musée d'Orsay, Musée Rodin, Seine, Tuileries Gardens, Louvre, shopping

HÔTEL DE VARENNE ★★★ (26)
44, rue de Bourgogne, 75007
Métro: Assemblée-Nationale, Varenne; RER Musée d'Orsay
24 rooms, all with shower or bath and toilet

Over the years, I never gave up hope that someone would pull this establishment out of the decorating doldrums and create a charming hotel. *Enfin!* It has been revived and is now a delightful garden hotel in the heart of the cosmopolitan seventh. The revival is apparent in the attitude of the staff, who stand firmly behind the hotel motto "Guest service is our top priority—nothing will be spared to make your stay as pleasant as possible." The rooms, which have enough space for a luggage rack and comfortable armchair, have been refitted with Napoléonic-style furniture, and they have gold tissue–covered walls and blue or red upholstery and drapery fabrics. The bathrooms are done in beige and tan tile with granite sinks. On the fourth floor, the rooms have

TELEPHONE
01-45-51-45-55
FAX
01-45-51-86-63
INTERNET
www.hoteldevarenne.com
CREDIT CARDS
AE, MC, V
RATES
1–2 persons 115–135€; extra bed 25€; *taxe de séjour* included
BREAKFAST
Continental 9€ per person
ENGLISH SPOKEN
Yes

mansard rooflines. One of the nicest features of the hotel is the newly landscaped private garden. Tables and chairs are here for guest enjoyment, whether it be for a relaxing afternoon drink or an early breakfast on a warm morning. Now boasting a brand new look and all the required amenities, this small hotel offers good value for those seeking a moderate hotel room in a very desirable area.

FACILITIES AND SERVICES: Air-conditioning, direct-dial phone, elevator, hair dryer, laptop on loan for a modest hourly fee, minibar, TV with international reception, room safe (no charge)

NEAREST TOURIST ATTRACTIONS (LEFT BANK): Musée d'Orsay, Musée Rodin, Invalides, Seine, Tuileries Gardens, Louvre

HÔTEL D'ORSAY ★★★ (2)
93, rue de Lille, 75007
Métro: Assemblée-Nationale, Solférino; RER Musée d'Orsay
41 rooms, all with shower or bath and toilet

TELEPHONE
01-47-05-85-54

FAX
01-45-55-51-16

EMAIL
hotel.orsay@wanadoo.fr

INTERNET
www.esprit-de-france.com

CREDIT CARDS
AE, DC, MC, V

RATES
Single 135€, double 165€, suite 280€; *taxe de séjour* included

BREAKFAST
Continental 9€ per person

ENGLISH SPOKEN
Yes

In its past life, the Hôtel d'Orsay was two hotels. Now the renovated, side-by-side eighteenth-century buildings are an exercise in understated elegance and good taste. The sedate location is ideal for walking either to the Louvre via the new Solferino footbridge over the Seine or to the Musée d'Orsay just a few blocks away.

The warmly decorated rooms are rich with comforts. Several that overlook a quiet garden are light and cheerful. Room 10 is one of these. It is a plain room with fabric-covered headboards and matching curtains, and because it is smaller, it would suit one guest very well. The largest rooms have twin beds and a bathtub in the bathroom. I like No. 12 because it has extra room and a stylish color scheme in peach, blue, and white. Two windows allow plenty of daylight and the glass-top work desk is ample. In No. 60 the maroon-and-blue checkered bedspreads coordinate with the floral draperies in the pitched roof suite to add a contemporary note, while the double sink in the mirrored bathroom adds convenience. Two comfortable chairs, twins or a king-size bed, plus a sunny balcony make this choice even more desirable. Until the peeling wallpaper has been repaired in No. 15 and No. 17, I would avoid these choices, despite their large bathrooms. An American-style breakfast buffet is served beneath an opaque glass ceiling in a stark setting highlighted by three framed splashes of color on the walls.

Hotels under the same ownership and management include Hôtel Brighton (page 67), Hôtel Mansart (page 74), Hôtel de la Place du Louvre (page 69), and the Hôtel Parc Saint-Séverin (page 129).

FACILITIES AND SERVICES: Direct-dial phone, elevator (to most floors), hair dryer, Internet in lobby, laundry service, TV with international reception, room safe (no charge)

NEAREST TOURIST ATTRACTIONS (LEFT BANK): Musée d'Orsay, Musée Rodin, Seine, Louvre, Tuileries Gardens

HÔTEL DUC DE SAINT-SIMON ★★★ ($, 27)
14, rue de St-Simon, 75007
Métro: Rue du Bac
29 rooms and 5 suites, all with shower or bath and toilet

Everyone has his or her first hotel in Paris, and this was mine. Of course, in those days it bore about as much resemblance to what it is today as a simple one-star does to the Hôtel Ritz. Over the years, and through many changes, my enthusiasm for the hotel has not dimmed, and it still tops my short list of ideal small Parisian hotels.

I am drawn to the Duc de Saint-Simon for many reasons, especially its intimate romantic feeling, wonderful sense of privacy, overall beauty, and high degree of personalized service. Built around a courtyard garden, many of the individually decorated rooms, with exclusive fabrics designed especially for the hotel, open onto this green view, while several larger rooms and suites open onto their own private terraces. Everything is beautifully coordinated: the monograms on the sheets and towels match the room color, as do the drinks tray and limoges china used for room service. When I first walked into No. 19, a large suite on the first floor, I thought, This is it—I am never leaving! The antique-filled sitting room has comfortable seating, a lovely writing desk, and good lighting. The quiet bedroom has its own television and a double bed where, in the morning, you are awakened by the birds singing outside your garden window. The older-style bathroom has all the nice extras: heated towel racks, a magnifying mirror, a tub with a water shield, and a telephone. I like all the other rooms in this very special hotel, but a favorite has always been No. 11, which is decorated in rich fabrics with a corner sitting area and windows that open onto the gardens, seemingly bringing them inside. Another beautiful room is No. 37. It is a soft, feminine room with a floral theme carried

TELEPHONE
01-42-22-07-52 (reservations),
01-44-39-20 20

FAX
01-45-48-68-25

EMAIL
duc.de.saint.simon@wanadoo.fr

CREDIT CARDS
AE, MC, V

RATES
1–2 persons 235–297€, suite 370–395€; extra bed 30% of room rate, *taxe de séjour* included

BREAKFAST
Continental 15€ per person

ENGLISH SPOKEN
Yes

out on the wallpaper, curtains, spread, and lamp shades. I also like the two-drawer antique dresser, framed embroideries, and the roomy bathroom with its inset sink, shelf space, and separate stall shower. Room 34 has a double bed framed by lighted closets and a view overlooking the terraces below. It is elegantly decorated with warm yellow and rose floral colors and furnished with a comfortable armchair, four-drawer marble dresser, and crystal chandelier.

The owners of the hotel, M. and Mme. Lindqvist, have been antiques collectors of note for many years and have used their handsome collection throughout the hotel, from the beautiful grandfather clock in the lobby to the graceful marble-top dressers in the bedrooms. The downstairs seventeenth-century cellar bar has pillowed niches and quiet corners just big enough for two to sip drinks and talk about life and love.

The prices for a stay here are high, no doubt about it. But for those seeking a quietly elegant, discreet stay in Paris, this should be the hotel of choice.

FACILITIES AND SERVICES: Air-conditioning in some rooms, bar, direct-dial phone, elevator, hair dryer, laundry service, magnifying mirrors, TV with international reception in suites (otherwise on request), robes, room service for light snacks, room safe (no charge)

NEAREST TOURIST ATTRACTIONS (LEFT BANK): Musée d'Orsay, Musée Rodin, Seine, Tuileries Gardens, Louvre, St-Germain-des-Prés, excellent shopping

HÔTEL DU CHAMP DE MARS ★★ (22)
7, rue du Champ de Mars, 75007
Métro: École Militaire

25 rooms, all with shower or bath and toilet

Under the competent ownership of Françoise and Stéphane Gourdal, the Hôtel du Champ de Mars is a stylish choice for guests who want to watch their budget but not feel deprived in the process.

The hotel's look reflects the time, talent, enthusiasm, and downright hard work of this delightful couple, who transformed it from stem to stern. The French way with color is often daring. Others might have stopped short of the mix of brightly hued fabrics, but Françoise had both the courage and good taste to pull it off. Her love of flowers is the underlying theme throughout. In the downstairs breakfast room, round tables draped in orange-and-yellow plaid hold bouquets of dried flowers. An old chest with a bowl of potpourri, framed fruit

TELEPHONE
01-45-51-52-30

FAX
01-45-51-64-36

EMAIL
stg@club-Internet.fr

INTERNET
www.hotel-du-champ-de-mars.com

CREDIT CARDS
MC, V

RATES
Single 75–80€, double 80–84€, triple 100€; *taxe de séjour* included

BREAKFAST
Continental 7€ per person

ENGLISH SPOKEN
Yes

prints hanging on the stone walls, and soft background music create a relaxing place for morning coffee and croissants. The series of golf prints hanging by the elevator are a nod to her husband's enthusiasm for the game.

White doors with big brass doorknobs lead to the yellow-and-blue rooms, all of which are named after French flowers. Tournesol (No. 25) is a pretty yellow-and-blue double with three floral prints over the bed and two windows that let in light from the front of the hotel. Myosotis (No. 55), on the front, is a single with great allure thanks to its small entry, light blue interior, and glimpse of the Eiffel Tower. Mimosa (No. 54) is another pleasant single with a nice view onto the court and rooftops beyond. If it is twin beds you want, ask for Muguet (No. 24). You enter Lilas (No. 4) through a little garden; the striped wallpaper, curtains, bedspreads, and rug are color coordinated in yellow, blue, and white to create a very sweet setting.

Last, but certainly not least, guests will find excellent discount shopping, several banks, a main post office, the métro, a street *marché* on rue Cler, and lots of favorite *Great Eats Paris* restaurants all close at hand.

FACILITIES AND SERVICES: Direct-dial phone, elevator, hair dryer, TV with international reception, room safe (no charge)

NEAREST TOURIST ATTRACTIONS (LEFT BANK): Eiffel Tower, Champ-de-Mars, Invalides, École Militaire, UNESCO

HÔTEL DU PALAIS BOURBON ★★ (16)
49, rue de Bourgogne, 75007
Métro: Varenne

32 rooms, 29 with shower, bath, and toilet

The Palais Bourbon has long been a reliable staple for readers of *Great Sleeps Paris* looking for a respectable budget hotel suitable for the entire family. The hotel is in a quiet residential area of Paris that is only a half block from the Musée Rodin, five minutes from Invalides, about ten minutes from the Musée d'Orsay, and just across the Seine from the Tuileries Gardens. The Claudon family has owned, managed, and lived in the hotel for more than fifty years, and they keep a steely eye out for anything, or anyone, out of line. Madame Claudon, who is a grandmother with more energy than most people half her age, told me, "I work all the time. I am of another time." It must agree with her, since she has a spring in her step and a twinkle in her eye that could not possibly go unnoticed.

TELEPHONE
01-44-11-30-70

FAX
01-45-55-20-21

EMAIL
HTLBOURBON@aol.com

INTERNET
www.hotel-palais-bourbon.com

CREDIT CARDS
MC, V

RATES
Single 50–101€, double 125€, triple 145€, quad 165€; extra bed 9.15€; *taxe de séjour* included

BREAKFAST
Continental included, cannot be deducted

ENGLISH SPOKEN
Yes

The hotel may not be the snazziest place to sleep in the *quartier,* but it is one of the best budget values, not only in the seventh, but in the entire city. The rooms are very large by Parisian standards and extremely clean, thanks to vigilant housekeeping and an ongoing maintenance program. The lobby has been redone and the breakfast room expanded to the centuries old *cave* in the basement. Continuing improvements include air-conditioning in all rooms, the addition of more tiled bathrooms (many with bidets), hardwood floors throughout, and new beds. Popular rooms are No. 3, which can connect with the room next door if larger quarters are needed; No. 4, a quiet double; and No. 1, a twin, also on the back. Number 8 is a large, light twin room facing the street, and No. 24, a back double on the top floor, has a queen-size bed and beamed ceiling.

Because the hotel is so popular, reservations are essential as far in advance as possible. When booking, please be sure to inquire about the cancellation and change in departure date policies, which are stricter than most.

FACILITIES AND SERVICES: Air-conditioning in all rooms with bathrooms, direct-dial phone (on request, private numbers given at no charge), elevator (to most floors), hair dryer, some magnifying mirrors, some minibars, TV with international reception, room safe (no charge)

NEAREST TOURIST ATTRACTIONS (LEFT BANK): Musée Rodin, Musée d'Orsay, Invalides, Tuileries Gardens

HÔTEL EBER MARS ★★ (31)
117, avenue de la Bourdonnais, 75007
Métro: École Militaire

24 rooms, all with shower or bath and toilet

For years this hotel was unfortunately owned and run by a sour-faced fellow and his equally dour wife who ruled their hotel like potentates granting rooms only to a chosen few. Despite their unwavering rudeness, I was intrigued by their amazing collection of Art Deco furnishings. However, after years of snarling responses that left me literally standing on the street, I finally gave up on them and their property.

On a recent visit to Paris, I happened to walk by the hotel and saw a crew of plaster-covered workmen tearing apart the front of the building. Eureka! I was happy to learn the hotel had been sold, and I was especially delighted to know that it had been purchased by Jean-Marc Eber, who owns Hôtel Eber Monceau, one of the nicest small boutique hotels in the seventeenth

TELEPHONE
01-47-05-42-30

FAX
01-47-05-45-91

EMAIL
hotelebermars@wanadoo.fr

INTERNET
www.hotelseber.com

CREDIT CARDS
AE, MC, V

RATES
1–2 persons 75–110€; triple 135€; extra bed 25€; *taxe de séjour* included

BREAKFAST
Continental 10€ per person, served all day

ENGLISH SPOKEN
Yes

arrondissement (see page 280). M. Eber was not completely finished with his renovations for this edition, but I am going to trust that he will finish the hotel in the same fashion that he has started it. He assured me that by the time you are reading this, the transformation should be done.

He has certainly had his work cut out for him. This hotel required far more than a quick coat of paint, new carpeting, and a big vase of flowers on the receptionist's desk. Everything—from the front door handle to the stairs, electrical system, and, of course, beds—has had to be either thrown out or redone. Amazingly enough, the bathrooms were not bad; though somewhat dated in terms of tile colors, they were in remarkably good condition and have the advantage of being spacious, so they remain. The rooms also have that hard-to-find-Paris commodity: space. All have been repapered, recarpeted, and refitted in a linear 1930s look using neutral colors. At press time, the downstairs reception, sitting, and breakfast rooms, as well as the facade, were under piles of construction rubble and clouds of dust. No doubt, M. Eber's hard work will make these sparkle. I wish him great success.

FACILITIES AND SERVICES: Direct-dial phone, elevator, hair dryer, French TV, office safe (no charge)

NEAREST TOURIST ATTRACTIONS (LEFT BANK): Eiffel Tower, Champ-de-Mars, Invalides, École Militaire, UNESCO

HÔTEL KENSINGTON ★★ (12)
79, avenue de la Bourdonnais, 75007
Métro: École Militaire; RER Pont de l'Alma
25 rooms, all with shower or bath and toilet

The location could not be better. It is five minutes to the métro, ten to the nearest RER stop. Only two blocks away is the Champ-de-Mars, with La Tour Eiffel at one end and the impressive École Militaire at the other. This grand Parisian park is the perfect place for an early morning walk or jog, a midday picnic, or great people-watching anytime. In addition, you will be staying in one of the most expensive pockets of Parisian real estate.

The use of wicker and bright orange and yellow fabrics creates a stylish statement in the lobby and reception area, which also has a fireplace with a mirrored backdrop. The cork-covered walls and the odd hall carpeting don't do a thing for me, but they are serviceable and in good shape. The rooms don't quite qualify as monastic cells, but you will hardly be "livin' large" in

TELEPHONE
01-47-05-74-00

FAX
01-47-05-25-81

INTERNET
www.hotel-kensington.com

CREDIT CARDS
AE, DC, MC, V

RATES
Single 56€, double 71–86€; extra bed 16€; *taxe de séjour* 0.76€ per person, per day

BREAKFAST
Continental 7€ per person

ENGLISH SPOKEN
Yes

any of them. They are plain but pleasant, done in basic beige fabrics and blond furnishings. Those on the fourth, fifth, and sixth floors offer some sort of vantage on the Eiffel Tower. Bathrooms are as *petite* as the rooms. One of the nicest choices is No. 34, a double on the street. One of the least desirable is No. 23, also on the street, and a few inches larger, but with a bathroom that needs work. The good news about this budget pick is that you won't be tempted to spend time lounging in your room, and most importantly, your final tab will not cause sticker shock, leaving you with more time and money to spend enjoying Paris to the fullest.

FACILITIES AND SERVICES: Direct-dial phone, elevator, French TV, room safe (no charge)

NEAREST TOURIST ATTRACTIONS (LEFT BANK): Eiffel Tower, Champ-de-Mars, École Militaire, UNESCO, Invalides

HÔTEL LATOUR-MAUBOURG ★★★ (9)
150, rue de Grenelle, 75007
Métro: Latour-Maubourg
10 rooms, all with shower or bath and toilet

TELEPHONE
01-47-05-16-16
FAX
01-47-05-16-14
INTERNET
www.latourmaubourg.com
CREDIT CARDS
MC, V
RATES
Single 125–145€, double 160–185€, suite 245–305€ (sleeps 2 adults and 2 children); lower rates in Aug; *taxe de séjour* included
BREAKFAST
Complimentary Continental
ENGLISH SPOKEN
Yes, and German

The Hôtel Latour-Maubourg is a hotel of character with an exceptional, welcoming spirit of friendliness that has impressed many readers who now consider it their home in Paris. Facing Invalides across a small park, this town house was in the Klein family for more than 150 years and was their home until they opened it to paying guests. For many years they ran it as an elegant pension-hotel that guests never wanted to leave. In fact, one guest arrived when it first opened and was one of the last to leave when it closed in 1993. Now the Klein family is gone, replaced by Victor and Maria Orsenne, their three children, and their dogs, Faust and Othello. Dog lovers will be interested to know that Faust is 60 percent beagle and a foundling that the Orsennes rescued and brought home the day they knew they would have this hotel. Othello, also a foundling, is the latest canine member of the Orsenne entourage.

When the Orsennes took over, they closed the hotel to totally redo it. They reopened in the spring of 1994, with exceedingly graceful results. They wisely kept the best pieces of furniture, recovering them to give a more up-to-date look. The beautiful wooden staircase was shined and polished, and the gorgeous high ceilings were cleaned and repainted. All of the landscape and Anonymous Ancestor paintings were dusted and rehung, and a glass case holding Maria's family collection of dolls dating from 1858 was added. The former dining room, with a large fireplace, now doubles as a sitting room and breakfast area. American guests will especially appreciate the fresh orange juice and daily *Herald Tribune* that come with the generous Continental breakfast.

The rooms display uniformity and a warm sense of color. The furniture reflects the 1930s and 1940s and was custom crafted for the hotel. Rooms have soundproof doors, a two-line phone with alarm clock, and an outside line for laptops. Some of the bathrooms are new. I wondered about those that seemed to be older. In talking with a guest, she told me that the 1930s style tubs are long and deep, so you can stretch out and have the bubbles come right up to your chin. The marble fireplaces are still in place and so are the tall, double French windows that open onto the tiny park across the street, where you can watch pensioners in berets feeding the pigeons or discussing the latest political scandal. Beds are covered with either pillowy duvets or blankets . . . it is your choice (be sure to state your preference). The first-floor suite and two other rooms facing south are air-conditioned. If you are a non-smoker, Room 21 is exclusively reserved for nonsmoking guests. Another bonus is this room's nighttime view of the gilded dome of the Invalides.

Victor and Maria Orsenne are a busy couple. Their newest endeavor is the Hôtel Valadon, a smart two-star a few blocks away (see page 198).

FACILITIES AND SERVICES: Air-conditioning in suite and 2 deluxe rooms, direct-dial phone, electric fans, no elevator (2 floors), fax in rooms (extra charge), Internet in lobby, hair dryer, laundry service, minibar, TV with international reception, office safe (no charge), 1 nonsmoking room

NEAREST TOURIST ATTRACTIONS (LEFT BANK): Invalides, Champ-de-Mars, Eiffel Tower, Musée Rodin

HÔTEL LENOX SAINT-GERMAIN ★★★ (20)
9, rue de l'Université, 75007
Métro: Rue du Bac; RER Musée d'Orsay
34 rooms, all with shower or bath and toilet

Featuring a beautiful Art Deco–style lobby and adjoining jazz bar, the Lenox appeals to a design-conscious crowd who appreciate the trendy boutiques and interesting art galleries in the *quartier*. The Lenox Club Bar pays homage to the jazz greats of the twentieth century with its life-size, wood marquetry inlays, collection of musical

TELEPHONE
01-42-96-10-95

FAX
01-42-61-52-83

INTERNET
www.lenoxsaintgermain.com

CREDIT CARDS
AE, DC, MC, V

RATES
1–2 persons 120–150€, attic room 200€, duplex 270€; *taxe de séjour* 0.86€ per person, per day

BREAKFAST
Buffet 12.50€, Continental in room 10€, per person

ENGLISH SPOKEN
Yes

instruments, and large framed black-and-white photos and posters. Indian rosewood and leather armchairs may tempt you into a long stay, and that's possible, since the bar is open to the public and hotel guests from 4:30 P.M. to 1:30 A.M.

The lobby is well done in polished marble and wood with leather seating arrangements. Two large animal statues—an elephant and a panther—guard the room. An Egyptian fresco sets the tone for the downstairs breakfast room as well as the glass elevator. In a design departure from the rest of the hotel, the rooms are classically done in coordinating colors and fabrics. Those on the fourth and fifth floors have small balconies. Bathrooms have good lighting and space. Number 51, the attic room, is a two-level affair with yellow faux-finished furniture and a mezzanine bathroom with a skylight. In the *au courant* non-colors of beige-on-beige, No. 54 is another two-level suite with the bedroom on one level and a sitting room and bath on the other.

FACILITIES AND SERVICES: Air-conditioning, bar, direct-dial phone, elevator, hair dryer, Internet in lobby, laundry service, magnifying mirrors, bathrobes in deluxe rooms, TV with international reception, room safe (no charge)

NEAREST TOURIST ATTRACTIONS (LEFT BANK): Musée d'Orsay, Musée Rodin, Seine, Tuileries Gardens, Louvre

HÔTEL LES JARDINS D'EIFFEL ★★★ (6)
8, rue Amélie, 75007
Métro: Latour-Maubourg, École Militaire
80 rooms, all with shower or bath and toilet

TELEPHONE
01-47-05-46-21; toll-free in the U.S. 800-44-UTELL

FAX
01-45-55-28-08

INTERNET
www.hoteljardinseiffel.com

CREDIT CARDS
AE, DC, MC, V

RATES
Single 120–135€, double 140–165€; extra bed 33€; ask about promotional and lower off-season rates; parking 20€ (must reserve ahead); *taxe de séjour* included

BREAKFAST
Buffet 12€, Continental in room 15€, per person

ENGLISH SPOKEN
Yes

Les Jardins d'Eiffel has built a solid reputation as a hotel offering many services. The quiet rooms and suites are simply coordinated and well appointed with wooden built-ins and the latest in modern bathrooms, including lighted magnifying mirrors and telephones. Rooms on the third through the fifth floors have views of the Eiffel Tower. In addition, family communicating rooms have private corridor entrances; nonsmokers can reserve anything on the fourth or fifth floor of the front building and all rooms in the new wing; and motorists can park in the private hotel garage (by prior reservation). Should you need a doctor, one is on call twenty-four hours a day. A new nonsmoking wing provides garden and executive rooms done in bright primary colors and bold print fabrics. The hotel will book reservations, organize sightseeing trips, rent a car for you—with or without driver—and confirm airline tickets.

FACILITIES AND SERVICES: Air-conditioning, babysitting, bar, concierge, direct-dial phone, doctor on 24-hour call, dogs allowed, hair dryer, handicapped-accessible rooms, elevator, Internet in lobby, laundry and cleaning services, minibar, parking (16.77€ per 24-hour period), trouser press, TV with international reception, room safe (no charge), some nonsmoking rooms

NEAREST TOURIST ATTRACTIONS (LEFT BANK): Invalides, Eiffel Tower, Champ-de-Mars, École Militaire

HÔTEL LE TOURVILLE ★★★★ ($, 32)
16, avenue de Tourville, 75007
Métro: École Militaire

30 rooms, all with shower, bath, and toilet

If the Hôtel le Saint Grégoire appeals to you, you will also adore the Tourville. It has been created by the same owners and design team and has infused a breath of fresh air into this part of the conservatively staid seventh arrondissement, known best for its diplomatic missions and upper-bourgeois lifestyle, not for anything *avant-garde*. The creative interiors knowingly mix antiques, beautiful fabrics, original prints, and a collection of Northern African tribal rugs, blending them around twenty-first-century comforts. Beautiful fresh flowers are the hallmark of the hotel and they are everywhere, from miniature rosebuds floating in a bowl on the reception desk to a fragrant bouquet welcoming guests to one of the suites. The lobby, in pumpkin and yellow, has seating on a large button-tufted couch and four azure blue linen chairs placed around a circular table. A collection of books and an oil painting behind the couch give the room an old-world feel. Room 104, a junior suite, leads off the back of this area but is separated from it by a clever little private sitting space that has two wicker chairs and a mahogany chest with the top drawer filled with pinecones.

The other rooms are exceptional in every detail. The three junior suites have Jacuzzis, and all rooms have some antiques and nicely framed prints in a background of sand, rose, or golden yellow. The standards face avenue de Tourville, but the windows have double glazing, which helps to buffer noise. Room 100 is one of these; it's nicely done with an antique chest in the entryway and a dhurrie rug beside the bed. The bathroom is distinguished by marble insets around the sink and bathtub. It is perfect for one, but for two, it could be a

TELEPHONE
01-47-05-62-62
FAX
01-47-05-43-90
EMAIL
hotel@tourville.com
INTERNET
www.hoteltourville.com
CREDIT CARDS
AE, DC, MC, V
RATES
1–2 persons standard 145€, superior 215€, room with private terrace 240€, junior suite 310€; extra bed 17€; occasional lower rates in off-season; *taxe de séjour* included
BREAKFAST
Continental 12€ per person
ENGLISH SPOKEN
Yes

tight squeeze. Room 16, a superior that comfortably sleeps three or four, has two doors opening onto a large terrace and a large marble bathroom. Occupying the entire top floor are two junior suites: No. 60 in white wicker and No. 62 with dormer windows and an old-fashioned washstand.

The staff is friendly, yet professionally efficient. A stay here in any room will certainly encourage you to settle right in, open a bottle of champagne, and rejoice in what Paris is all about.

The following hotels are under the same ownership and direction: Hôtel le Saint-Grégoire in the sixth (see page 163) and Hôtel Le Lavoisier in the eighth (see page 210).

FACILITIES AND SERVICES: Air-conditioning, bar, direct-dial phone, elevator, hair dryer, Jacuzzis in junior suites, laundry service, pets allowed (no charge), TV with international reception, office safe (no charge)

NEAREST TOURIST ATTRACTIONS (LEFT BANK): Invalides, Eiffel Tower, Champ-de-Mars, École Militaire, UNESCO

HÔTEL MUGUET ★★ (25)
11, rue Chevert, 75007
Métro: Latour-Maubourg, École Militaire
48 rooms, all with shower or bath and toilet

The Hôtel Muguet continues to be one of the smartest, most stylish two-star values in Paris. Savvy readers obviously agree and are on to this one; they come here in droves, making it necessary to reserve the view rooms or suite at least six months in advance. Staying here will make anyone feel like a privileged budget traveler, especially in the suite, with its lovely tiled bathroom. The rooms are air-conditioned, which is a rare extra in a two-star, let me assure you. All are outfitted in country-style furniture with color schemes in either pink, yellow, or blue, and those on the first and second floors are exclusively nonsmoking. Everything is well coordinated; mirrored wardrobes are generous; and from Nos. 61 and 62, on the sixth floor, you can see the Eiffel Tower. From No. 63, your vista is over Invalides. On the fifth floor, ask for No. 51, with a balcony and good Eiffel Tower view. Another room I like is No. 41, a triple with three twin beds. The advantage here is the small sitting room and the large bath with yellow and gray accents. Three new doubles opening onto a garden terrace have been added, two with stall showers and the third with a

TELEPHONE
01-47-05-05-93

FAX
01-45-50-25-37

EMAIL
muguet@wanadoo.fr

INTERNET
www.hotelmuguet.com

CREDIT CARDS
AE, MC, V

RATES
Single 87€, double 97–105€, triple 135€; *taxe de séjour* included

BREAKFAST
Buffet 8€ per person

ENGLISH SPOKEN
Yes

bathtub. Also new this time is a glass-roofed winter garden that allows Mme. Pelettier to show off her talent with plants.

Thankfully, the parts of the hotel that give it character also remain. The black and gray-green marble facade is intact, and so is the lovely grandfather clock next to the reception desk. No one has replaced the colorful flowers and lush green plants in the garden with plastic versions, and more important, the attractive owners, the Pelettier family and their two poodles, Framboise and Mandarine, still live at the hotel and are always ready with their friendly smiles to make their guests feel very special and at home. In this effort, they are ably assisted by their outstanding receptionist, Jacqueline Bonnet. I think Mme. Pelettier's comment to me perfectly sums up the philosophy of the hotel: "Everything is done with the comfort of the client in mind."

The immediate neighborhood could hardly be dubbed "the miracle mile," but it is quiet both day and night. After a nice ten-minute stroll, you can be at Invalides viewing Napoléon's tomb or on a park bench at the Champ-de-Mars, admiring the Eiffel Tower while eating a gourmet picnic put together from the food shops that line rue St Dominique and rue Cler. Good restaurants are within very easy walking distance (see *Great Eats Paris*), and so is discount shopping (see "Shopping," page 338).

FACILITIES AND SERVICES: Air-conditioning, direct-dial phone, elevator (to most floors), hair dryer, Internet in lobby, magnifying mirrors, TV with international reception, room safe (no charge), 2 nonsmoking floors

NEAREST TOURIST ATTRACTIONS (LEFT BANK): Invalides, Champ-de-Mars, Eiffel Tower, École Militaire, UNESCO, Musée Rodin

HÔTEL RELAIS BOSQUET ★★★ (23)
19, rue du Champ de Mars, 75007
Métro: École Militaire

40 rooms, all with shower or bath and toilet

The Relais Bosquet offers guests exceptional comfort, space, and peacefulness in a renovated forty-room hotel built around a courtyard. Each room has all the three-star perks as well as an iron and ironing board, electrically controlled shutters, tea- and coffee-making facilities, Internet access, and an assortment of current periodicals. Two rooms are exclusively nonsmoking. If you are traveling with an infant, the hotel will provide a

TELEPHONE
01-47-05-25-45

FAX
01-45-55-08-24

INTERNET
www.relaisbosquet.com

CREDIT CARDS
AE, DC, MC, V

RATES
Single 130–150€, double 145–165€; extra bed 30€; parking 14€ per day; special rates Nov 15–March 30 (except week between Christmas and New Year's), July 15–Aug 30; *taxe de séjour* included
BREAKFAST
Large Continental 10.50€; coffee, juice, roll 5.50€, per person
ENGLISH SPOKEN
Yes

free baby bath, chair, food warmer, and bed. Secure private parking is available at a very modest rate. Decor is attractively uniform hotel-issue in all the rooms, with creamy wall coverings and nice-quality furnishings. Brass poles, artistically hung with soft pillows covered in the same material as the curtains, are mounted as headboards behind the beds. Baths have three-tiered rolling carts and nice towels. Top room choices are No. 52, a large twin superior on the back with excellent space in both the room and the bathroom, which includes a stretch-out tub and separate enclosed shower; No. 54, which can serve as a small double or generous single; and No. 32, a big room for two with double sinks in the well-lit bathroom. The street is quiet, so consider No. 53 with two windows facing front as a good option. The hardworking owner, Philippe Hervois, is on site daily and pays careful attention to the needs of his guests. The upscale residential area of the seventh arrondissement is close to the Champ-de-Mars, Eiffel Tower, and Invalides, offers some great dining choices, and has easy access by métro or bus to the rest of Paris.

FACILITIES AND SERVICES: Air conditioning, free baby equipment, direct-dial phone, dogs accepted (no charge), electric fans, elevator, hair dryer, iron and ironing board, Internet in lobby (planned), minibar, parking, tea and coffee maker, TV with international reception, room safe (no charge), 2 nonsmoking rooms

NEAREST TOURIST ATTRACTIONS: Champ-de-Mars, Eiffel Tower, École Militaire, UNESCO, Invalides, Musée Rodin

HÔTEL SAINT-DOMINIQUE ★★ (4)
62, rue St-Dominique, 75007
Métro: Latour-Maubourg
34 rooms, all with shower or bath and toilet

TELEPHONE
01-47-05-51-44
FAX
01-47-05-81-28
EMAIL
saint-dominique.reservations@wannadoo.fr
INTERNET
www.hotelstdominique.com
CREDIT CARDS
AE, DC, MC, V
RATES
Single 97€, double 114–131€; always ask about lower rates; *taxe de séjour* included

In the 1700s, this building housed Dominican nuns who prayed in a downstairs chapel. Today, it is a quaint hotel on a busy shopping street, and the chapel is the breakfast room. An English country theme begins in the beamed lobby and continues through the tight rooms, which are furnished in pine and wicker and have soft, billowing curtains dressing the windows. Matching spreads, coordinated wall coverings, and a pretty Provençal-style breakfast room are other positive points. My favorite rooms are the two that open onto the terrace, where breakfast is served on warm spring and summer mornings. I also like No. 8, a twin on the back: although the floors slant a bit, the roomy bedroom and bathroom, with a rolling cart for toiletries, save the day. The rooms do not boast exciting views, not all have a chair (only a backless stool), the furniture needs a big shot of TLC, and the elevator does not service the back building nor the breakfast room. While these may be deterrents for some, many guests overlook them in favor of a tranquil stay in a hotel with reasonable rates.

FACILITIES AND SERVICES: Direct-dial phone, elevator to most rooms, minibar, TV with international reception

NEAREST TOURIST ATTRACTIONS (LEFT BANK): Invalides, Eiffel Tower, Champ-de-Mars, École Militaire

BREAKFAST
Continental 8€ per person

ENGLISH SPOKEN
Yes

HÔTEL SAINT-THOMAS-D'AQUIN ★★ (28)
3, rue Pré-aux-Clercs, 75007
Métro: St-Germain-des-Prés
21 rooms, all with shower or bath and toilet

Talented hotelier Bertrand Plasmans, who owns the Hôtel Novanox (see page 164), has magnificently transformed this once dull two-star into a smartly designed example of urban chic in the heart of the Rive Gauche. The hotel's high standards appeal to those seeking a modern escape for less per night than the cost of a coin purse at many of the top designer boutiques in the neighborhood. The soft cream walls form the perfect backdrop for the interesting palette of chocolate and cocoa colors on the furnishings and fabrics. Not all is monochromatic . . . every so often there is an unexpected dash of muted color; perhaps a lavender easy chair in No. 518, the top-floor room with a mansard roof; Provençal red and gold offsetting the stylized black bed and tables in No. 102; or a green checked bedspread in No. 103. The best rooms face the quiet street. A few on the back overlook a nearby hotel's glass elevator, and you probably don't want one of these. Bathrooms are fitted with excellent toiletries and monogrammed towels. The very moderate rates for the top-drawer neighborhood have made the much-sought-after rooms hard to come by, unless you book as far in advance as possible. Bravo, M. Plasmans, on another great success!

FACILITIES AND SERVICES: Bar, direct-dial phones, elevator (to most floors), fans, hair dryer, French TV, room safe (no charge)

NEAREST TOURIST ATTRACTIONS (LEFT BANK): St-Germain-des-Prés, Musée d'Orsay, Seine

TELEPHONE
01-42-61-01-22

FAX
01-42-61-41-43

EMAIL
hotelsaintthomasdaquin@
wanadoo.fr

INTERNET
www.hotel-st-thomas-
daquin.com

CREDIT CARDS
AE, DC, MC, V

RATES
1–2 persons 110€; *taxe de séjour* included

BREAKFAST
Continental 9€ per person

ENGLISH SPOKEN
Yes

HÔTEL VALADON ★★ (14)
16, rue Valadon, off rue de Grenelle, 75007
Métro: École Militaire
12 rooms, all with shower (1 with bathtub) and toilet

TELEPHONE
01-47-53-89-85
FAX
01-44-18-90-56
INTERNET
www.hotelvaladon.com
CREDIT CARDS
MC, V
RATES
Single 85€, 110€ in family
room, double 99–110€, 125€
in family room; triple 125€,
140€ in family room; *taxe de
séjour* included
BREAKFAST
Complimentary Continental
ENGLISH SPOKEN
Yes

Victor and Maria Orsenne spent one year and serious money transforming this dumpy one-star hotel with an uncertain pedigree into a perky budget choice with a neo-industrial look and feel. Inspired by the black, white, and gray colors of a favorite piece of fabric, the couple added carpets and furnishings, and to avoid an overdose of somber black and white, they infused splashes of red throughout. Each room is designed to comfortably sleep three under duvets placed on a twin and a queen-size bed. The floors are hardwood, the closets and shelves open, and the prints and photos on the wall remind guests they are in Paris. Six smoke-free rooms guarantee guests can breathe easily. A red strip here, a red line there, add a bit of life to the gray-tile bathrooms. One of the nicest rooms is No. 2 on the back, provided going down stairs to the large, well-lighted bathroom would not be a problem. The subterranean Nos. 1 and 2 might not appeal to claustrophobics. The only light is from a sky-light and a tiny six-by-twelve-inch window over a built-in desk. To create more space, the rooms combine, but the bathroom connects them. Breakfast is served in a two-tone room with gray and red cushioned chairs around bare black tables. In keeping with the family atmosphere of the hotel, guests are invited to use a shared refrigerator in the breakfast room, borrow the hotel's dishes and cutlery, and enjoy light snacks here (but please, never in the rooms). The desk is covered from 7:30 A.M. to 8:30 P.M., and guests are given keys and codes for access otherwise.

The Orsennes also own the Hôtel Latour-Maubourg (see page 190).

FACILITIES AND SERVICES: Bar, direct-dial phone, elevator (to most rooms), hair dryer, Internet in lobby, TV with international reception, room safe (no charge), 6 non-smoking rooms

NEAREST TOURIST ATTRACTIONS (LEFT BANK): Eiffel Tower, Champ-de-Mars, Invalides, École Militaire, UNESCO

HÔTEL VERNEUIL ★★★ (19)
8, rue de Verneuil, 75007
Métro: Rue du Bac; RER Line C Musée d'Orsay
26 rooms, all with shower or bath and toilet

For museumgoers, the Hôtel Verneuil is ideally located within walking distance to the Musée d'Orsay, the Louvre, and the Musée Rodin. Antique lovers are in heaven, and so are browsers and shoppers—the tantalizing shops and boutiques that line this area could keep them busy for a week. The owner, Sylvie de Latte, is continually full of ideas and plans for her small and charming hotel. In a seventeenth-century building that retains its original cross beams and rough stone walls, it is a haven of peace and comfort where I always feel as though I am a guest in a lovely French home. Mme. de Latte is an art collector, and she has skillfully hung many of her favorite pieces throughout the hotel. The black-and-white photos are by her son, who lived in India. The vaulted stone-cellar breakfast room is down a winding spiral staircase with no elevator access.

The rooms are all personalized with rich fabrics, solid furnishings, interesting photos, and prints. Some have canopy beds, most have wood-beam ceilings and ornate doors, and those ending in number 2 or 4 have wall murals of Parisian landmarks. Comfortable seating and adequate closet space are not an issue. The room and marble bathroom sizes vary; the biggest is No. 302, a romantic favorite, and the smallest No. 308. However, the charm and feeling of well-being in this wonderful hotel never wavers.

For Mme. de Latte's other hotel, see Hôtel Thérèse (page 77).

FACILITIES AND SERVICES: Air-conditioning in some rooms, bar, direct-dial phone, elevator (starts 1st floor), hair dryer, Internet in lobby, laundry service, minibar, robes in deluxe rooms, TV with international reception, room safe (no charge)

NEAREST TOURIST ATTRACTIONS (LEFT BANK): Musée d'Orsay, Seine, Tuileries Gardens, Louvre

TELEPHONE
01-42-60-82-14

FAX
01-42-61-40-38

EMAIL
hotelverneuil@wanadoo.fr

INTERNET
www.hotelverneuil.com

CREDIT CARDS
MC, V

RATES
Single 125€, double 150€, deluxe suite 195€; extra bed 24€; *taxe de séjour* included

BREAKFAST
Continental 12€ per person

ENGLISH SPOKEN
Yes

SPLENDID HÔTEL ★★★ (33)
29, avenue de Tourville, at 1, avenue Duquesne, 75007
Métro: École Militaire

TELEPHONE
01-45-51-29-29;
01-45-54-24-77

FAX
01-44-18-94-60

INTERNET
www.splendidhotel.biz

CREDIT CARDS
AE, DC, MC, V

RATES
Single 125€, double 148€, suite 220€; extra bed 20€; lower rates in off-season; parking 12€ per day; *taxe de séjour* included

BREAKFAST
Continental 9€ per person

ENGLISH SPOKEN
Yes

48 rooms, all with shower or bath and toilet

Before 1992, the Splendid was anything but—now it lives up to its name on almost every count. Done in an Art Deco theme with soft blond wood and pastel wall colorings, the modernized rooms and serviceable baths offer all the comforts three-star sleepers demand. All rooms face out and have some type of street or city view. Balconies on the fifth and sixth floors offer views of the École Militaire. While sitting by the window in one of the junior suites (No. 507 or 607), you can see the Eiffel Tower. If you would rather work, there is a fax and a computer plug. Windows are double-glazed to shield against the nonstop traffic at this busy intersection, but on hot nights, you better have those earplugs handy or be prepared to swelter behind shut windows, because there is no air-conditioning.

A large downstairs corner bar is a good place to go for a relaxing drink. Another pleasant spot is the breakfast room: if the strong coffee doesn't wake you up, surely the green armchairs in the bright orange room trimmed with light pink will. The hotel is minutes from rue Cler, a pedestrian market street where well-dressed, basket-toting locals shop for their vegetables, flowers, meats, cheeses, and fresh morning croissants; several excellent restaurants (see *Great Eats Paris*) are within a five-minute walk, and the métro is a two-minute walk. Hotel guests are given 20 percent reduction on the services of the J. Bogatti Coiffure and Beauté salon next to the hotel.

FACILITIES AND SERVICES: Bar, direct-dial phone, elevator, fax in suites, hair dryer, Internet in lobby, laundry service, minibar, parking by reservation only, robes in suites, TV with international reception, room safe (2.50€ per day)

NEAREST TOURIST ATTRACTIONS: UNESCO, Eiffel Tower, Champ-de-Mars, École Militaire, Invalides

Eighth Arrondissement

The ten-lane Champs-Élysées, sweeping dramatically from the Arc de Triomphe to the place de la Concorde, is the most famous avenue and parade ground in the world, and it is definitely worth a serious look and stroll. But save the shopping, partying, and eating for less touristy and unspoiled areas. This is the traditional watering hole for show-biz celebrities, glamour girls on the way up or down, tourists in baseball caps, heavy-set men and their young companions, and anyone else who wants to hide behind dark glasses twenty-four hours a day. The flame on the tomb of the unknown soldier burns under the Arc de Triomphe, and the view from the top is inspiring. Twelve avenues radiate from the Arc de Triomphe, forming the world-famous, death-defying traffic circle known as l'Étoile.

The place de la Concorde is the largest square in Paris. Two of its most famous occupants are the luxurious Hôtel de Crillon and the American Embassy. It is thrilling to stand on this strikingly beautiful square and be surrounded by some of the greatest landmarks in the world: the Tuileries Gardens, the Louvre, and the view up the Champs-Élysées to the Arc de Triomphe, across the Seine to the Palais Bourbon, and up the rue Royale to the Madeleine Church, built as a replica of a Greco-Roman temple by Napoléon I. In the evening, when it is all illuminated and the fountains are playing, it becomes a sight you will never forget.

Famous names in *haute couturière* are displayed in boutiques lining rue Faubourg St-Honoré and avenue Montaigne. World-class gourmet shopping surrounds the place de la Madeleine.

RIGHT BANK
American Embassy
Arc de Triomphe
Champs-Élysées
elegant shopping on rue St-Honoré and rue du Faubourg St-Honoré
Étoile
Grand Palais
Madeleine Church
Petit Palais
place de la Concorde
shopping at Au Printemps and Galeries Lafayette
Tuileries Gardens

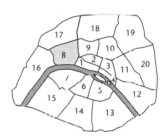

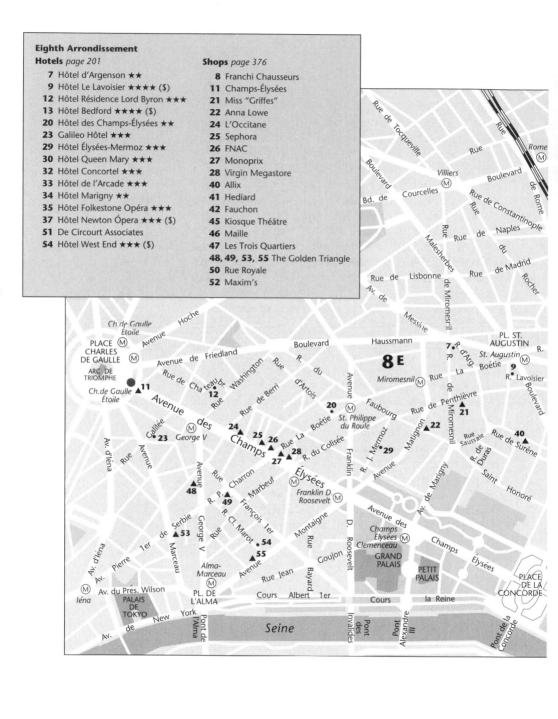

Eighth Arrondissement

Hotels *page 201*

- **7** Hôtel d'Argenson ★★
- **9** Hôtel Le Lavoisier ★★★★ ($)
- **12** Hôtel Résidence Lord Byron ★★★
- **13** Hôtel Bedford ★★★★ ($)
- **20** Hôtel des Champs-Élysées ★★
- **23** Galileo Hôtel ★★★
- **29** Hôtel Élysées-Mermoz ★★★
- **30** Hôtel Queen Mary ★★★
- **32** Hôtel Concortel ★★★
- **33** Hôtel de l'Arcade ★★★
- **34** Hôtel Marigny ★★
- **35** Hôtel Folkestone Opéra ★★★
- **37** Hôtel Newton Ópera ★★★ ($)
- **51** De Circourt Associates
- **54** Hôtel West End ★★★ ($)

Shops *page 376*

- **8** Franchi Chausseurs
- **11** Champs-Élysées
- **21** Miss "Griffes"
- **22** Anna Lowe
- **24** L'Occitane
- **25** Sephora
- **26** FNAC
- **27** Monoprix
- **28** Virgin Megastore
- **40** Allix
- **41** Hediard
- **42** Fauchon
- **45** Kiosque Théâtre
- **46** Maille
- **47** Les Trois Quartiers
- **48, 49, 53, 55** The Golden Triangle
- **50** Rue Royale
- **52** Maxim's

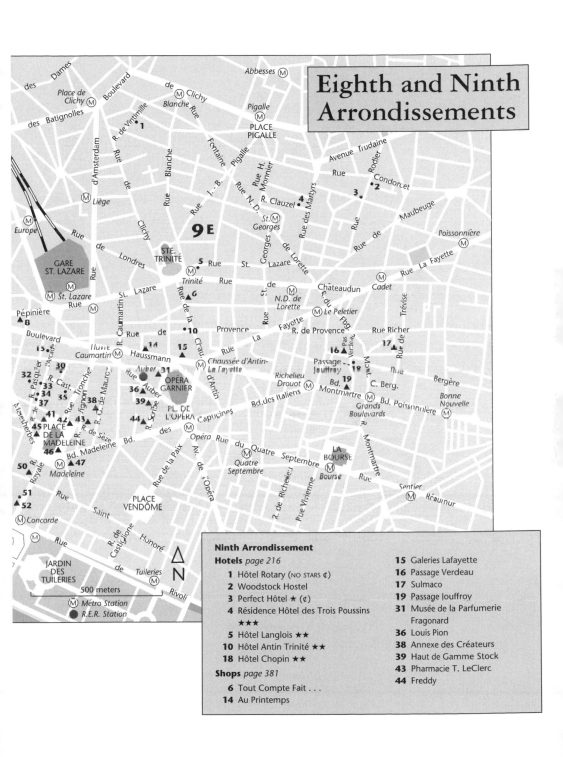

Eighth and Ninth Arrondissements

9E

Ninth Arrondissement

Hotels *page 216*

1 Hôtel Rotary (NO STARS ¢)
2 Woodstock Hostel
3 Perfect Hôtel ★ (¢)
4 Résidence Hôtel des Trois Poussins ★★★
5 Hôtel Langlois ★★
10 Hôtel Antin Trinité ★★
18 Hôtel Chopin ★★

Shops *page 381*

6 Tout Compte Fait . . .
14 Au Printemps

15 Galeries Lafayette
16 Passage Verdeau
17 Sulmaco
19 Passage Jouffroy
31 Musée de la Parfumerie Fragonard
36 Louis Pion
38 Annexe des Créateurs
39 Haut de Gamme Stock
43 Pharmacie T. LeClerc
44 Freddy

500 meters

Ⓜ Métro Station
● R.E.R. Station

HOTELS IN THE EIGHTH ARRONDISSEMENT

Galileo Hôtel ★★★   204
Hôtel Bedford ★★★★ ($)   205
Hôtel Concortel ★★★   206
Hôtel d'Argenson ★★   206
Hôtel de l'Arcade ★★★   207
Hôtel des Champs-Élysées ★★   208
Hôtel Élysées-Mermoz ★★★   209
Hôtel Folkestone Opéra ★★★   209
Hôtel Le Lavoisier ★★★★ ($)   210
Hôtel Marigny ★★   211
Hôtel Newton Opéra ★★★ ($)   212
Hôtel Queen Mary ★★★   213
Hôtel Résidence Lord Byron ★★★   214
Hôtel West End ★★★ ($)   215

OTHER OPTIONS
Apartment Rental Agencies

De Circourt Associates   299

($) indicates a Big Splurge

GALILEO HÔTEL ★★★ (23)
54, rue Galilée, 75008
Métro: George-V, Charles-de-Gaulle-Étoile; RER Charles-de-Gaulle-Étoile
27 rooms, all with shower or bath and toilet

TELEPHONE
01-47-20-66-06
FAX
01-47-20-67-17
EMAIL
hotelgalileo@wanadoo.fr
INTERNET
www.galileohotel.com
CREDIT CARDS
AE, DC, MC, V
RATES
Single 131€, double 153€;
taxe de séjour 0.91€ per person,
per day
BREAKFAST
Continental 10€ per person
ENGLISH SPOKEN
Yes

Contented guests with sophisticated, artistic temperaments continue to fill Roland and Elisabeth Buffat's popular hotels on the Île St-Louis: Hôtel de Lutèce and Hôtel des Deux-Îles (see pages 99 and 100), and their newest, the Hôtel Henri IV on rue St-Jacques (see page 72). The fourth option to tempt them is the Galileo, a Right Bank hotel that re-creates an elegant French town home in an oasis of calm, only a few steps from the Champs-Élysées.

Like the flowers in the boutique lobby and garden, guests are beautifully arranged in the elegantly pristine rooms, all fashioned alike in comforting colors of beige, brown, and cocoa. No. 403, a double with two armchairs, a desk, and gray marble bath, has a *Rear Window*–type view onto the life within the nearby apartment building. Room 200, facing a walled garden, is the largest twin. On the ground floor, it has a small sitting area and a huge marble bathroom. I also like No. 203, with an entryway that leads to a quiet queen-bed room with a small purple chair in a sitting corner and a long workspace overlooking the garden. The room size jackpot is shared by two on the fifth floor (Nos. 501 and 502). In addition to being the biggest, their allure comes from their delightful glass-covered, screened verandas with wicker seating that invite year-round usage. Butcher block tables adorn the below-ground, mirrored dining room, and green plants and posters of familiar Paris landmarks and buildings add interest.

FACILITIES AND SERVICES: Air-conditioning, direct-dial phone, elevator, hair dryer, Internet in lobby, minibar, TV with international reception, room safe (no charge)

NEAREST TOURIST ATTRACTIONS (RIGHT BANK): Champs-Élysées, Arc de Triomphe

HÔTEL BEDFORD ★★★★ ($, 13)
17, rue de l'Arcade, 75008
Métro: Madeleine, Havre-Caumartin
145 rooms, all with shower, bath, and toilet

Generally, the eighth arrondissement provides a stay on the dull side in terms of active day-to-day Parisian living. It is predominantly a business district that is busy Monday to Friday during the day, but in the evening and on weekends, the sidewalks are rolled up and you have the streets to yourself. However, all is not lost when staying at the Bedford. Shop hounds will be happy bagging buys at Galeries Lafayette and Au Printemps, the two famous Parisian department stores less than a ten-minute walk away, and foodies will have a field day with all the nearby gourmet food emporiums surrounding place de la Madeleine. Guests are also within easy strolling distance to the Champs-Élysées, Tuileries Gardens, and the Seine.

The hotel provides unobtrusive and efficient service in a low-key, discreet atmosphere reminiscent of the 1940s. Rooms won't dazzle, but they will impress with their size and layout. Most come equipped with a desk, two comfortable chairs, luggage space, and large closets with shelves and enough hanging space. Bathrooms follow suit in size with plenty of monogrammed towels and deep tubs with either a shower overhead or separate. A bonus for many is the beautiful nineteenth-century dining room with its original painted-glass domed ceiling. A formal lunch is served here, and in the evening, guests eat in a smaller grill room. Lower December and August rates are drawing cards for many.

TELEPHONE
01-44-94-77-77

FAX
01-44-94-77-97

INTERNET
www.hotel-bedford.com

CREDIT CARDS
AE, MC, V

RATES
Single 160€, double 176–228€, triple 228€, suite 320€; lower rates in Aug and Dec; *taxe de séjour* included

BREAKFAST
Buffet or Continental 12€ per person

ENGLISH SPOKEN
Yes

FACILITIES AND SERVICES: Air-conditioning, bar, direct-dial phone, elevator, hair dryer, laundry service, minibar, restaurant, room service, TV with international reception, room safe (no charge)

NEAREST TOURIST ATTRACTIONS (RIGHT BANK): Madeleine Church, place de la Concorde, Opéra, Champs-Élysées, Tuileries Garden, shopping (rue du Faubourg St-Honoré or at Au Printemps and Galeries Lafayette department stores)

HÔTEL CONCORTEL ★★★ (32)
19–21, rue Pasquier, 75008
Métro: Madeleine
46 rooms, all with shower or bath and toilet

TELEPHONE
01-42-65-45-44
FAX
01-42-65-18-33
EMAIL
concortel@wanadoo.fr
INTERNET
www.hotelconcortel.com
CREDIT CARDS
AE, DC, MC, V
RATES
Single 115–142€, double 130–165€, triple 189€; ask about special off-season and business rates; private parking 20.6€ per day; *taxe de séjour* included
BREAKFAST
Continental 7€ per person
ENGLISH SPOKEN
Yes

For many years, the conveniences and comforts of the Concortel have appealed to many seeking a midcity location to combine sight-seeing with business. The hotel consists of two blocks of rooms joined by a courtyard that is filled in the spring and summer with bright blooming plants. The color-coordinated bed chambers are well arranged and offer the space and perks that travelers desire. High-speed Internet access will soon be in the rooms—a distinct advantage to those who must stay constantly in touch. The desk staff is exceptional, especially Pierre—who has been here more than twenty-seven years, speaks wonderful English, and is always ready to help—and Remy, the porter, who has been here a decade and also speaks English. Lower rates in August make this hotel even more attractive.

FACILITIES AND SERVICES: Air-conditioning, bar, conference room, direct-dial phone, elevator (to most floors), hair dryer, laundry service, minibar, porter, private parking, radio, TV with international reception and pay-for-view, room safe (no charge)

NEAREST TOURIST ATTRACTIONS (RIGHT BANK): Champs-Élysées, Madeleine Church, place de la Concorde, Opéra, shopping (rue du Faubourg St-Honoré or at Galeries Lafayette and Au Printemps department stores)

HÔTEL D'ARGENSON ★★ (7)
15, rue d'Argenson, at 111 boulevard Haussmann, 75008
Métro: Miromesnil
28 rooms, 26 with shower or bath and toilet

TELEPHONE
01-42-65-16-87
FAX
01-47-42-02-06
CREDIT CARDS
MC, V

Veteran Paris visitors know that the business-centered eighth arrondissement is normally Big Splurge territory. Coming to the rescue is this twenty-eight-room, second-floor walkup, perched above Rene Saint-Ouen, one of the most famous bakeries in Paris. How famous? It was selected to provide all the baguettes to the Élysée Palace, and that is quite an honor. Those who are familiar with this part of Paris know that noise is part of the deal, and it won't escape you at this hotel. However, if cost is your guiding light, give this one consideration.

You first enter the small wood-paneled salon, which has two chairs. Martine, the owner's daughter, is usually behind the desk, along with her black-and-brown cocker spaniel, Flash. The fifties-style rooms that once varied from frankly fussy to downright tacky have been toned down to some extent. In most rooms, at least the curtains and bedspreads match somewhat, and the wild wallpaper has been removed from the ceilings. I have trouble with the mustard yellow– and beer brown– colored tiles in the bathrooms, which definitely don't go with the plaid towels. Rooms on the second and fifth floors have balconies. There are no twin-bed rooms, but an extra bed can be added at no additional cost if there are only two of you and you want to sleep separately. The hotel is notable because it is cheap and clean, and the rooms are big enough to satisfy almost anyone. Martine's husband stays on top of maintenance.

FACILITIES AND SERVICES: Direct-dial phone, elevator (to most floors), fans, hair dryer at desk, French TV, room safe (no charge)

NEAREST TOURIST ATTRACTIONS (RIGHT BANK): Champs-Élysées, shopping at Au Printemps and Galeries Lafayette department stores

RATES
Single 62–78€, double 74–85€, triple 97€; *taxe de séjour* included

BREAKFAST
Continental in room included, cannot be deducted

ENGLISH SPOKEN
Yes

HÔTEL DE L'ARCADE ★★★ (33)
9, rue de l'Arcade, 75008
Métro: Madeleine
41 rooms, all with shower, bath, and toilet

Good taste is everywhere evident at the Hôtel de l'Arcade, and no wonder when you learn it was decorated by Gerard Gallet, who also did the Orient Express. Everything about the hotel is exceptional, and something complimentary can be said about all the sound-proofed rooms. The divided lobby, done in celery green and beige, is softened further with fresh flowers and green plants. Wingback chairs, sofas, and a writing desk are complemented by a decorative stone fireplace. The crowning touch is a beautiful green wrought-iron chandelier with twelve candle lights entwined with white metal flowers. A banquette, the owner's collection of

TELEPHONE
01-53-30-60-00

FAX
01-40-07-03-07

EMAIL
contact@hotel-arcade.com

INTERNET
www.hotel-arcade.fr

CREDIT CARDS
AE, MC, V

RATES
Single 140–169€, double 185€, triple 225€, duplex 225€; free baby cot; special promotion rates Dec and Aug; *taxe de séjour* included

BREAKFAST
Buffet downstairs or
Continental in room 10€ per
person
ENGLISH SPOKEN
Yes

black-and-white etchings, and windows shaded by white linen café curtains set the stage for the street-side breakfast room.

All the soundproofed bedrooms have beige walls with wood built-ins, good closets, and appealing bathrooms. They all face front, so there will be no depressing wall views, and the standard rooms connect. Two floors are exclusively nonsmoking. Room 602 is a good choice for two. The corner location with three large windows, two closets, armchair seating, and a lovely, light bathroom make it an inviting choice for a longer stay. Number 605 is one of four duplexes. It is a two-story suite with double televisions, three telephones (including one in the bathroom), and an upstairs bedroom with a small balcony and a skylight. When guests return from an evening out, they find the evening housekeeper has changed the towels and turned down the beds. Lower summer and winter rates make this smart hotel an even more exceptional value.

FACILITIES AND SERVICES: Air-conditioning, conference rooms, direct-dial phone, elevator, hair dryer, magnifying mirrors, minibar, TV with international reception, room safe (no charge), 2 floors exclusively nonsmoking

NEAREST TOURIST ATTRACTIONS (RIGHT BANK): Madeleine Church, place de la Concorde, Opéra, Champs-Élysées, shopping (rue du Faubourg St-Honoré or at Au Printemps and Galeries Lafayette department stores)

HÔTEL DES CHAMPS-ÉLYSÉES ★★ (20)
2, rue d'Artois, 75008
Métro: St-Philippe-du-Roule

36 rooms, all with shower or bath and toilet

TELEPHONE
01-43-59-11-42
FAX
01-45-61-00-61
CREDIT CARDS
AE, DC, MC, V
RATES
Single 88–100€, double 95–103€, triple 120€; *taxe de séjour* included
BREAKFAST
Continental 8€ per person
ENGLISH SPOKEN
Yes

During World War II, this hotel housed Dutch and American soldiers. It now houses mostly business travelers who want a moderate, reliable nest near the Champs-Élysées and the Arc de Triomphe.

The thirty-six attractive rooms and modern baths have coordinated colors and good space usage, and most importantly, they provide many three-star amenities for two-star prices. Bathrooms are nice, and many have enclosed stall showers. Adding to the hotel's popularity is the Art Deco sitting room with a multicolored mural and Erté-style lamp. Behind the inlaid wooden bar is a glass-roofed atrium with a small pool framed by Grecian columns and a wraparound mural of the Parc Monceau. In the breakfast room, be sure to notice the nostalgic black-and-white photos of the owner of the hotel as a little girl, being held by her parents and grandparents.

FACILITIES AND SERVICES: Air-conditioning, bar, direct-dial phone, elevator, hair dryer, laundry service, some magnifying mirrors, minibar, TV with international reception, room safe (no charge)

NEAREST TOURIST ATTRACTIONS (RIGHT BANK): Champs-Élysées, Arc de Triomphe

HÔTEL ÉLYSÉES-MERMOZ ★★★ (29)
30, rue Jean-Mermoz, 75008
Métro: St-Philippe-du-Roule, Miromesnil
27 rooms, all with shower or bath and toilet

What sets the Élysées-Mermoz apart from dozens of other three-star hotels in the area, which is only a short walk from the Champs-Élysées, place de la Concorde, and the Tuileries Gardens? Friendly, personalized service for one thing, competitive rates for another, and rooms and suites done in Pierre Frey fabrics and quality furnishings. The largest rooms face the street, which is quiet; smaller quarters and the suites overlook an interior courtyard. The mirrored bathrooms in all are modern, with heated towel racks, good sink space, and separate glass-enclosed showers (in the suites). The breakfast room has an Italian flair to it, thanks to its burnt umber colors and tile floor. The inviting sitting room is casually outfitted with wicker and bamboo seating under a skylight roof. You could hear a pin drop in the evening and on the weekends when workers in this nine-to-five business area lock their office and shop doors and go home.

FACILITIES AND SERVICES: Air-conditioning, conference room, direct-dial phone, elevator, hair dryer, laundry service, magnifying mirrors, minibar, TV with international reception, room safe (no charge)

NEAREST TOURIST ATTRACTIONS (RIGHT BANK): Champs-Élysées, Madeleine Church, place de la Concorde, Tuileries Gardens, shopping on rue Faubourg St-Honoré

TELEPHONE
01-42-25-75-30
FAX
01-45-62 87-10
EMAIL
elymermoz@worldnet.fr
INTERNET
www.hotel-elyseesmermoz.com
CREDIT CARDS
AE, DC, MC, V
RATES
Single 138–150€, double 150–170€, suite 222€; lower rates in Aug; *taxe de séjour* included
BREAKFAST
Continental 10.20€ per person
ENGLISH SPOKEN
Yes

HÔTEL FOLKESTONE OPÉRA ★★★ (35)
9, rue de Castellane, 75008
Métro: Madeleine, Havre-Caumartin
50 rooms, all with shower or bath and toilet

The Folkestone is part of the Best Western chain in Paris, and it's definitely one of the better choices in an area where prices are usually over the top. A stay here puts you in the middle of the business, high fashion, and entertainment precinct of the city.

TELEPHONE
01-42-65-73-09; toll-free from the U.S. and Canada 800-528-1234 (Best Western)
FAX
01-42-65-64-09
INTERNET
www.bwfolkestoneopera.com

CREDIT CARDS
AE, DC, MC, V

RATES
Single 145€, double 165€,
suite: 1 person 215€, 2 people
245€; lower rates in off-season;
taxe de séjour 0.91€ per person,
per day

BREAKFAST
Buffet 9€ per person

ENGLISH SPOKEN
Yes

An interesting collection of framed French country homes line the hallways leading to the contemporary bedrooms, which are decorated in peach, pale gray, and cream, with polished cotton fabrics on the beds and covering the windows. Five of the seven floors in the hotel are exclusively designated for nonsmokers. With the exception of the suites, most of the rooms do not have space as a virtue. The smallest doubles, at the back, have miniature bathrooms and no view. The bright rooms on the street offer more space and have double windowpanes to buffer noise. An exception on the front is No. 303, with so little extra space that you cannot open a suitcase unless it's on the bed, and once you do, there is only a tiny armoire to hold its contents. Room 203 is much better. Here you have a sofa and comfortable chair, working desk, luggage and closet space, and a large bath with a recessed tub. Another option for more space is to reserve one of the connecting rooms. From the hotel door, it is less than a fifteen-minute walk to shopping along rue du Faubourg St-Honoré or at Galeries Lafayette and Au Printemps, place de la Madeleine, place de la Concorde, the Tuileries Gardens, and the Champs-Élysées.

FACILITIES AND SERVICES: Air-conditioning, bar, direct-dial phone, elevator, hair dryer, Internet in lobby, laundry service, minibar, TV with international reception, room safe (no charge), 5 exclusive nonsmoking floors

NEAREST TOURIST ATTRACTIONS (RIGHT BANK): Madeleine Church, place de la Concorde, Tuileries Gardens, Opéra, shopping

HÔTEL LE LAVOISIER ★★★★ ($, 9)
21, rue Lavoisier, 75008
Métro: St-Augustin

30 rooms all with shower, bath, and toilet

TELEPHONE
01-53-30-06-06

FAX
01-53-30-23-00

INTERNET
www.hotellavoisier.com

CREDIT CARDS
AE, DC, MC, V

RATES
1–2 persons: superior 199–
320€, terrace room 245–261€,
junior suite 289–304€,
executive suite 385–401€;
extra bed 16€; *taxe de séjour*
included

BREAKFAST
Continental 12€ per person

Michel Bouvier's latest hotel venture was a hit before it opened. Paris insiders have continuously booked his other two hotels on the Left Bank: Le Saint-Grégoire in the sixth (see page 163), and Le Tourville near the Eiffel Tower in the seventh (see page 193). When word got out about Le Lavoisier, the trendsetters lost no time in filling the rooms. The nineteenth-century town-house hotel creation was placed confidently in the skillful hands of Jean-Philippe Nuel, who uses bold color combinations mixed with a sprinkling of antiques for character and interest in a thoroughly contemporary setting. The Georgian lobby and adjoining library bar are done in blackened pearwood furnishings surrounded by clay-colored walls with rose and white accents. A painting of two girls with their doll and teddy bear adds a warm touch to the room. The daring use of flamenco orange and adobe brown adds spice to the bare wood tables and wicker chairs in the breakfast room. Each table has its own light, so guests can scan the local papers while enjoying their breakfast. The rainbow of colors continues in the cerise-pink linen-lined halls that are richly carpeted in deep eggplant and lighted by stylized oak leaf sconces. While the rooms do not have the same dramatic colors as the public areas of the hotel, they are beautifully done in uniform good taste using quality fabrics and furnishings. Soft gray wood accents compliment the yellow and rose fabrics, polished black wood furnishings, and crisp white bed linens. Wooden shutters are used instead of curtains to control the light. Some rooms have private terraces, the suites have Jacuzzis, and all rooms have a separate computer line. The youthful staff is enthusiastic and helpful.

FACILITIES AND SERVICES: Air-conditioning, bar, direct-dial phone, hair dryer, elevator, Jacuzzi in suites, laundry service, room service, TV with international reception, office safe (no charge)

NEAREST TOURIST ATTRACTIONS (RIGHT BANK): Shopping at Au Printemps and Galeries Lafayette, Opéra, Madeleine Church

ENGLISH SPOKEN
Yes

HÔTEL MARIGNY ★★ (34)
11, rue de l'Arcade, 75008
Métro: Madeleine, Havre-Caumartin
32 rooms, 26 with shower or bath and toilet

Only a few hundred yards from the Madeleine Church and a bracing ten minutes from Gare St-Lazare and place de la Concorde is this reliable roost owned and aptly run for thirty years by the Maugars family. The neighborhood is dull as dishwater after 7 P.M. and on weekends, but the prices are right and the métro is close. The spotless rooms are reached by the same antique birdcage elevator that Marcel Proust used when he lived and wrote in the hotel. Most of the rooms are sunny, several connect, and those on the sixth floor, which have double beds only, have balconies where you can step outside and enjoy the view. The rooms that have been redone are preferable, especially No. 61, a double with a shower. The room is simply decorated in white textured wallpaper, with matching floral fabrics on both the bed and curtains. Another new room is No. 10, a cozy nest with blond wood furniture and a red leatherette accent wall. It has a shower and sink, but the

TELEPHONE
01-42-66-42-71
FAX
01-47-42-06-76
EMAIL
hotel-marigny@wanadoo.fr
INTERNET
www.hotelmarigny.com
CREDIT CARDS
MC, V
RATES
Single 80€, double 85–90€; extra bed 30€; supplement for air-conditioning (8€ older room, 10€ new room); *taxe de séjour* included
BREAKFAST
Continental 6€ per person
ENGLISH SPOKEN
Yes

toilet is outside in the hall. Number 112 is beamed twin on the front with a built-in closet and 1950s leather and chrome chairs, and a smart new black mosaic–tile bathroom. When I asked about the framed artwork over the bed (which resembles a crumpled painting by a frustrated ten year old), M. Maugar sighed, "It was the interior designer's idea, and so are those in the new salon." If you need more room and want everyone to be together, this room connects with the one next door, which has a double bed. Back rooms are equal in amenities and will be quiet, but you may find yourself in a room, such as No. 54, with a frosted window that affords absolutely no view.

FACILITIES AND SERVICES: Air-conditioning (for a surcharge), direct-dial phone, elevator, hair dryer in new rooms (otherwise available), minibar, French TV, office safe (no charge)

NEAREST TOURIST ATTRACTIONS (RIGHT BANK): Madeleine Church, Tuileries Gardens, place de la Concorde, shopping (rue du Faubourg St-Honoré, or at Au Printemps and Galeries Lafayette department stores)

HÔTEL NEWTON OPÉRA ★★★ ($, 37)
11, bis rue de l'Arcade, 75008
Métro: Madeleine
31 rooms, all with shower, bath, and toilet

Antiques are meshed with bold designer colors and patterns to create a hospitable and elegant atmosphere at the Newton Opéra. The thirty-one comfortable rooms are beautifully decorated with white faux-finished furniture trimmed in gold, fabric-covered walls, and plush carpets. They all have enough living space and creature comforts to ensure a pleasant stay. Beams are in some, and balconies with a table and chairs enhance others, notably No. 62 and No. 63, but always there are many small extras that add up to a memorable stay. Fresh flowers, a bowl of sweet potpourri, and a complimentary decanter of sherry are some of these welcoming touches. In the bathrooms, fluffy monogrammed towels and terrycloth robes are there for drying after relaxing under high pressure, pulsating showers with three jet streams. Double-glazed windows buffer the big-city street noise.

FACILITIES AND SERVICES: Air-conditioning, direct-dial phone, elevator, hair dryer, Internet in lobby, laundry service, magnifying mirror, minibar, trouser press, TV with international reception, room safe (no charge)

NEAREST TOURIST ATTRACTIONS (RIGHT BANK): Madeleine Church, place de la Concorde, Tuileries Gardens, Opéra,

TELEPHONE
01-42-65-32-13
FAX
01-42-65-30-90
EMAIL
newtonopera@easynet.fr
INTERNET
www.hotel-newton-opera.com
CREDIT CARDS
AE, DC, MC, V
RATES
1–2 persons 150–200€; *taxe de séjour* 1€ per person, per day
BREAKFAST
Buffet 13€ per person
ENGLISH SPOKEN
Yes

shopping (rue du Faubourg St-Honoré or at Au Printemps and Galeries Lafayette department stores)

HÔTEL QUEEN MARY ★★★ (30)
9, rue Greffulhe, 75008
Métro: Madeleine, Havre-Caumartin

36 rooms, all with shower or bath and toilet

Visitors to Paris who desire a distinguished hotel in the center of the city between the Opéra and the Madeleine Church will have a hard time doing better than the Queen Mary. The hotel's Scottish owner, David Byrne (who also owns Hôtel du Bois in the sixteenth; see page 261), has spared no effort to improve the creature comforts offered. As a result, every time I am here, I am impressed all over again.

Beautiful ceiling details and thick moldings soften the rooms, which are uniformly done with English carpeting, rich fabrics, and built-in mahogany furniture. Luxury accessories such as air-conditioning, double-glazed windows, twenty-channel TV plus pay-per-view channels, FM radio and alarm clock, two telephones, and beautiful bathrooms add to the appreciation of the rooms. Rooms on the second and fifth floors have balconies; superior rooms and suites face front. Those looking for extra-special accommodations will do well in the sunny, top-floor, beamed suite with its rooftop view, two televisions, private fax, and large gray-tile bathroom with its own window. Breakfast is served in a yellow-and-red basement dining room with murals of Tuscany. You have a choice of a regular Continental repast, one for slimmers, or a no-calories-barred American/English breakfast buffet that includes bacon, sausage, eggs, a daily selection of mushrooms, potatoes, or tomatoes, and corn flakes, along with your croissants, butter, and jam. Whatever breakfast you choose will be served on Limoges plates with English fruit designs.

Many thoughtful touches make the difference here: a decanter of sherry in each room, happy hour from 6 to 8 P.M. in the friendly blue-and-white bar off the entry, afternoon tea served in the salon, room service from nine international restaurants or light snacks prepared at the hotel, and drinks served in a tiny fountain garden when weather permits.

Shoppers take serious note: You are in ultra-chic Fashion Country here. The names Lanvin, Yves St-Laurent, Jean-Paul Gaultier, and many more grace boutiques no more than a ten- to fifteen-minute browse from the hotel door.

TELEPHONE
01-42-66-40-50

FAX
01-42-66-94-92

EMAIL
hotelqueenmary@wanadoo.fr

INTERNET
www.hotelqueenmary.com

CREDIT CARDS
AE, DC, MC, V

RATES
Single 129€, double 149–179€, suite for 2–4 persons 239€; extra bed 55€; special rates on request; *taxe de séjour* included

BREAKFAST
American/English buffet or Continental 15€ per person

ENGLISH SPOKEN
Yes

FACILITIES AND SERVICES: Air-conditioning, bar, direct-dial phone, elevator, private fax in suites, hair dryer, Internet in lobby, laundry service, minibar, radio, room service, electric tea kettle (in suite), trouser press, TV with international reception and pay-per-view channels, room safe (2€ per day)

NEAREST TOURIST ATTRACTIONS (RIGHT BANK): Madeleine Church, place de la Concorde, Tuileries Gardens, Opéra, shopping (rue du Faubourg St-Honoré or at Au Printemps and Galeries Lafayette department stores)

HÔTEL RÉSIDENCE LORD BYRON ★★★ (12)
5, rue Chateaubriand, 75008
Métro: Charles-de-Gaulle-Étoile, George-V; RER Charles-de-Gaulle-Étoile
31 rooms, all with shower or bath and toilet

TELEPHONE
01-43-59-89-98
FAX
01-42-89-46-04
EMAIL
lord.byron@escapade-paris.com
INTERNET
www.escapade-paris.com
CREDIT CARDS
AE, DC, MC, V
RATES
Single 124€, double 152–169€, triple 219€, suite (2–4 people) 243–299€; *taxe de séjour* included
ENGLISH SPOKEN
Yes

The Résidence Lord Byron provides lodgings for half the price of many other hotels in this prestigious, expensive *quartier*. On a quiet, winding street still close to the bright lights and excitement of the Champs-Élysées, it is so peaceful that it's listed in the *European Guide to Silent Hotels*. The larger-than-average deluxe rooms overlook a garden courtyard where morning coffee and afternoon tea are served in the summer. In the spring, the garden is resplendent with tulips, daffodils, and fragrant narcissus. The hotel, formerly a *hôtel particulière* (privately owned town home), is furnished with a wide range of lovingly worn and near antiques, making no pretenses at modernization. However, it has just been redecorated in pleasing colors and coordinated fabrics. Number 2, with sliding glass doors between the bedroom and sitting room, is a good example of the newer look of the rooms: it has a sofa and two armchairs covered in blue suede cloth that blends nicely with the blue carpeting and gold curtains. The bathroom has double sinks and a shower guard by the bathtub. Number 22 is a roomy twin in a floral motif with a stall shower. Room 17, in gold and blue, is a single on the back with a view of the Eiffel Tower from the bathroom. Room 28 is a tight twin, but when squeezed into a triple, it is so cramped that one bed blocks access to the chest of drawers. If you reside on the fifth floor (an easy walk up a single flight of stairs), your room will be cheaper.

FACILITIES AND SERVICES: Air-conditioning in front building only, direct-dial phone, elevator (to most floors), fans, hair dryer, Internet in lobby, minibar, room service for light snacks, TV with international reception, room safe (no charge)

NEAREST TOURIST ATTRACTIONS (RIGHT BANK): Arc de Triomphe, Champs-Élysées

HÔTEL WEST END ★★★ ($, 54)
7, rue Clément Marot, 75008
Métro: Alma-Marceau, Franklin-D-Roosevelt
49 rooms, all with shower, bath, and toilet

The glossy, eye-catching hotel brochure has not one word of text. It doesn't have to because the pictures speak for themselves. After one glance, you know immediately that this is an elegant hotel in a glamorous and luxurious part of Paris. What is so surprising is the price, which is vastly less than most all-stars in the neighborhood. The hotel is located just off the Champs-Élysées in the middle of couture heaven around fashionable avenue Montaigne. The intimate sitting area and bar are rich in the French way, furnished in a fine style that mixes patterns, stripes, and velvets that ultimately come together in a charming way. The rooms are comfortable and equally suited to a business stay or one decidedly romantic. Streamlined marble bathrooms are in various sizes. In No. 101, the green marble sink stretched the width of the ten-by-eight-foot bathroom, which is larger than many Parisian hotel rooms. Rooms on the second and fifth floor have balconies either facing the street or an interior courtyard. If sheer luxury is on your agenda, reserve a suite, perhaps No. 102. In addition to a sitting room with two leather chairs, and a king-size bedroom with adjustable bedside lights, there is a walk-in closet and a wonderful bathroom with double sinks and separate shower and toilet units. The standard rooms are not as lavish, but you have all the amenities: tissue-covered walls that form neutral backdrops for the lush fabrics of the curtains and beds, adequate closet and luggage space, and always a desk should work demand your attention. Services are everything you would expect, from the helpful porter carrying your bags to the housekeeping staff who check your room twice a day and always turn down your bed at night.

FACILITIES AND SERVICES: Air-conditioning, honesty bar, concierge, direct-dial phone, elevator, hair dryer, Internet in lobby, laundry service, luggage room, porter, room service for light meals, TV with international reception and video, room safe (no charge)

NEAREST TOURIST ATTRACTIONS (RIGHT BANK): Champs-Élysées, designer shopping and browsing, Seine

TELEPHONE
01-47-20-30-78

FAX
01-47-20-34-42

INTERNET
www.hotel-west-end.com

CREDIT CARDS
AE, DC, MC, V

RATES
1–2 persons 175–190€, suite 275€; extra bed 40€; child under 12 years free; *taxe de séjour* included

BREAKFAST
Hot American buffet or Continental in room 18€ per person

ENGLISH SPOKEN
Yes

Ninth Arrondissement

RIGHT BANK
department stores (Au
Printemps and Galeries
Lafayette)
Opéra
Pigalle

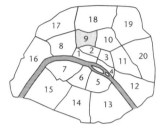

In the southern part of this arrondissement is the beautiful Second Empire Opéra National de Paris Garnier with its famous Chagall ceiling, along with many large banks and shopping at Galeries Lafayette and Au Printemps. At the northern end is the infamous Pigalle, a sleazy neighborhood lined with twenty-four-hour peep shows, bordellos, "ladies of the night"—anything, generally, that constitutes the seamier side of life. Avoid the métro stops Anvers, Pigalle, and Barbès-Rochechouart after dark.

HOTELS IN THE NINTH ARRONDISSEMENT
(see map page 202)

Hôtel Antin Trinité ★★	**216**
Hôtel Chopin ★★	**217**
Hôtel Langlois ★★	**218**
Hôtel Rotary (NO STARS, ¢)	**219**
Perfect Hôtel ★ (¢)	**220**

OTHER OPTIONS
Hostels
Woodstock Hostel	**315**
Residence Hotels
Résidence Hôtel des Trois Poussins ★★★	**322**

(¢) indicates a Cheap Sleep

HÔTEL ANTIN TRINITÉ ★★ (10)
74, rue de Provence, 75009
Métro: Chausée d'Antin–La Fayette; RER Auber
46 rooms, all with shower or bath and toilet

TELEPHONE
01-48-74-29-07
FAX
01-42-80-26-68
EMAIL
hotel@hotel-antin-trinite.fr
INTERNET
www.paris-hotel-antin.com
CREDIT CARDS
AE, DC, MC, V

Dedicated shop hounds can roll out of bed and into Galeries Lafayette, Au Printemps, and the myriad of other shops and department stores that line the streets of this part of Paris. If shopping is not your *raison d'etre,* you are minutes away from the magnificent Opéra, countless cafés and brasseries, and easy métro and bus connections to take you throughout Paris. The simple, surprise-free rooms are French, and that means small, but they are nicely done in coordinating colors of soft orange and yellow, blue, mocha, and rose. They each have a desk, chair, luggage rack, and enclosed stall showers, or tub and shower combinations. The reception staff is friendly and helpful. If you want to maintain your budget while staying in this part of Paris, this is a choice that won't disappoint.

FACILITIES AND SERVICES: Direct-dial phone, elevator (to most floors), hair dryer, TV with international reception, office safe (no charge)

NEAREST TOURIST ATTRACTIONS (RIGHT BANK): Shopping at Au Printemps, Galeries Lafayette, and all the shops surrounding them, Opéra

RATES
Single 100€, double 125€, triple 140€; *taxe de séjour* included

BREAKFAST
Buffet 10€ per person

ENGLISH SPOKEN
Yes

HÔTEL CHOPIN ★★ (18)
10, boulevard Montmartre (46, passage Jouffroy), 75009
Métro: Richelieu-Drouot, Grands Boulevards
36 rooms, all with shower or bath and toilet

Parisians were mall shoppers long before Americans. At the turn of the century, Paris had enclosed, skylighted shopping walkways called *passages*. Today, these lovely covered areas house a variety of restaurants and shops selling everything from art and antiques to dubious-quality clothing. The Hôtel Chopin is a listed historic monument occupying a unique location at the end of the passage Jouffroy. This *passage* has some interesting boutiques, including one specializing in dollhouses and toys, another in secondhand books, and the Musée Grevin, Paris's answer to a wax museum. The door to the hotel was opened the same year as the *passage* (1846), and it has never been locked. Given its longevity, please be prepared for some things that may not be totally *au courant*. Fortunately, the hotel has been redone, and now the rooms have bathrooms; the vibrant salmon pink and green hallways display some pretty painted chests, screens, and chairs; and the rooms, done up in hot pink and green, are all clean and quiet. The best rooms are on the top floors because they have skyline views and more natural light, but in No. 409, the tub is under a sloping eave, making upright showering a bit tricky for taller guests.

FACILITIES AND SERVICES: Direct-dial phone, elevator (to most floors; some stairs required), electric fans, hair dryer available, French TV, room safe (no charge)

NEAREST TOURIST ATTRACTIONS (RIGHT BANK): Shopping at Galeries Lafayette and Au Printemps, Opéra

TELEPHONE
01-47-70-58-10

FAX
01-42-47-00-70

CREDIT CARDS
AE, MC, V

RATES
Single 65–75€, double 75–85€, triple 100€; *taxe de séjour* included

BREAKFAST
Continental with fresh orange juice 9€ per person

ENGLISH SPOKEN
Yes

HÔTEL LANGLOIS ★★ (5)
63, rue Saint-Lazare, 75009
Métro: Trinité, St-Lazare

TELEPHONE
01-48-74-78-24
FAX
01-49-95-04-43
INTERNET
www.hotel-langlois.com
CREDIT CARDS
AE, MC, V
RATES
Single 79–80€, double 89–99€, suite 135€; extra bed 20€; *taxe de séjour* 0.78€ per person, per day
BREAKFAST
Continental 7.8€ per person
ENGLISH SPOKEN
Yes

27 rooms all with shower or bath and toilet

The history of the hotel states that the building was constructed in 1870 and used as a bank until 1896, when it became a hotel and was owned by the same family for over eighty years. A recent change in ownership resulted in a massive renovation, which combined the charm of the Belle Epoque and Art Nouveau styles inherent in the building. All the bathrooms have been redone, the windows sound-proofed, and satellite television and minibars installed. The furnishings have been restored or replaced with something from the era. All the paintings, sculptures, and other decorative objects are equally as authentic.

The rooms on the first and second floors are done in the style of the 1930s and 1940s; those on the top floors reflect the Belle Epoque style of the early 1900s. Five uniformed maids toil relentlessly to keep them in pristine order at all times. For a real *tour-de-force* in hotel rooms, reserve No. 11, with a massive bathroom and equally massive bedroom that has a wonderful blond laminated Art Deco wardrobe and its original ceramic-tile fireplace. Two wicker armchairs are positioned overlooking a small garden below. Room 15 has two fireplaces: one in the large bedroom and a marble one in the bathroom! Of course, neither one work, but they do add a certain panache. In No. 63, I like the arched sitting space with two soft armchairs padded in the same material as the headboard, the original tile fireplace, and the sky view over the back of the hotel. The only disappointment is No. 44, a suite with two lumpy futons, and no convenient place to plug in a laptop.

In 2001, the hotel was used in the filming of Universal Studio's remake of *Charade.* The hotel is a few minutes walk from the St-Lazare station and a taxi ride away from the Eurostar terminal at Gare du Nord. Also within walking distance is the Gustave Moreau Museum.

FACILITIES AND SERVICES: Direct-dial phone, elevator, hair dryer, TV with international reception, office safe (no charge)

NEAREST TOURIST ATTRACTIONS (RIGHT BANK): Opéra, shopping at Au Printemps and Galeries Lafayette department stores

HÔTEL ROTARY (NO STARS, ¢, 1)
4, rue Vintimille, 75009
Métro: Blanche, Liège

17 rooms with showers and sinks, none with toilet

The Hôtel Rotary appeals to those whose aesthetic mind-set matches that of the hotel's interior design guru, whose ample use of *junque* has created a glowing bouquet of gloriously tacky enclaves. For instance, take No. 5, "The Chinese Room." It has a green velvet–draped, inlaid mother-of-pearl bed fit for a king—or queen, as the case may be. Two old tapestries hang on the wall, oriental rugs are tossed on the floor, a bentwood hat rack subs for the closet, and the bathroom is in black and gold mosaic tiles. There isn't much light to read by, but is anyone really going to read here? I don't think so, because when you turn off all the lights, the ceiling sparkles like a star-studded midnight sky. The only window is opaque, but no matter—the interior will keep you plenty preoccupied. Room 8 is known as "The Grotto." Here you share the room with a statue of Aphrodite standing in a shallow bath backed by mirrors. A sea nymph motif encircles the room, which is dimly lit with glistening seashell lights. When you turn off the lights, Aphrodite continues to glow. Again the window in this room is opaque. Number 4 could be dubbed "The Red Room," thanks to its bright red ceiling and matching tiled bathroom with a hot-pink shower curtain. In the bedroom, the etching of a girl's face on the mirror was done by a friend of the hotel owner. If anyone staying here wants a "normal" room, perhaps No. 2 would qualify; its only claim to fame is the totally pink-bubble-gum-colored interior. By comparison, No. 3 is really boring, with its gun-metal gray floors and lavender walls. Amenities are few: no room phone, no elevator, and no cable television. The hotel is not close to much on a tourist map either, but perhaps the hotel itself is attraction enough.

FACILITIES AND SERVICES: No elevator (6 floors), hair dryer on request, French TV, office safe (no charge)

NEAREST TOURIST ATTRACTIONS (RIGHT BANK): Moulin Rouge

TELEPHONE
01-48-74-26-39

FAX
01-48-74-33-42

EMAIL
hotel.rotary@wanadoo.fr

CREDIT CARDS
None, cash only

RATES
Single 40€, double 45€, theme rooms 55–60€; *taxe de séjour* included

BREAKFAST
Continental in room only, no croissants, sometimes crêpes

ENGLISH SPOKEN
Yes

PERFECT HÔTEL ★ (¢, 3)
39, rue Rodier, 75009
Métro: Cadet, Anvers
42 rooms, 23 with shower and toilet

TELEPHONE
01-42-81-18-86
01-42-81-26-19

FAX
01-42-85-01-38

CREDIT CARDS
MC, V

RATES
Single 37–55€, double 43–55€, triple 58–70€; *taxe de séjour* included

BREAKFAST
Continental (no croissants) 4€ per person

ENGLISH SPOKEN
Yes

Finding budget accommodations in Paris is becoming more and more of an art. Sleeping cheap in the *centre ville* is nigh unto impossible, which forces the frugal into the fringes. The Perfect Hôtel is well named if your budget is on the ropes or you just want to cut corners. It's located in a tourist wilderness, so guests must be willing to master several routes of public transportation to get to action central. The rooms are neat and clean, scrape- and tear-free, and without the usual one-star garish color mismatches that are known to cause five-star nightmares. The best bets are top-floor rooms that have sky views and sunshine, or one with a balcony on the fifth floor. Since the public showers off the hall are free, you could opt for the cheapest rooms. The murals throughout the hotel and in some of the rooms were done by M. Mario, a friend of the owner. Breakfast is a breathtakingly low 4€ and is served in a plain room that has an interesting collection of old sailing ship models. Owners M. and Mme. Souer and their daughter are what the French call *sympa,* which means friendly and welcoming, and in any language, these attitudes are always appreciated.

FACILITIES AND SERVICES: Elevator, luggage storage, French TV in lounge, office safe (no charge)

NEAREST TOURIST ATTRACTIONS (RIGHT BANK): None, must use public transportation

Eleventh Arrondissement

The eleventh and twelfth arrondissements are known as *quartiers populaires* because they are traditional working-class neighborhoods where many foreigners settle. These are not hotbeds of tourist activity, but they do provide interesting glimpses of both the blue-collar Parisian way of life and the new-wave artists. Place de la Bastille joins the third, eleventh, and twelfth arrondissements and still serves as the rallying point for demonstrations, just as it did in the French Revolution. The column in the middle stands where the prison once was. The neighborhoods around the Bastille and the futuristic Opéra Bastille, which opened in 1989, are the city's new bohemia, full of art galleries, lofts, cafés, nightclubs, and boutiques featuring the apparel craze of the moment. Humming night and day, this area is definitely one of the "in" places for anyone who likes to walk on the wild side and stroll on the cutting edge. On the weekends after midnight, it is only recommended for the *very* hardcore night crawlers.

RIGHT BANK
Bastille
Opéra Bastille
place de la République

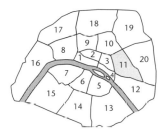

HOTELS IN THE ELEVENTH ARRONDISSEMENT

Daval Hôtel ★★	**224**
Garden Hôtel ★★	**224**
Hôtel Bastille de Launay ★★	**225**
Hôtel Beaumarchais ★★★	**225**
Hôtel de Nevers ★ (¢)	**226**
Hôtel Lyon-Mulhouse ★★	**227**
Hôtel Notre-Dame ★★	**227**
Hôtel Plessis ★★	**228**
Hôtel Résidence Alhambra ★★	**229**
Hôtel Rhetia ★ (¢)	**230**
Libertel Croix de Malte ★★	**230**

OTHER OPTIONS
Hostels

Auberge International des Jeunes	**312**
Auberge Jules Ferry	**313**

Residence Hotels

Home Plazza Résidence Hôtels: Bastille ★★★	
and Saint-Antoine ★★★	**319**

Student Accommodations

Maison Internationale des Jeunes (MIJCP)	**326**

(¢) indicates a Cheap Sleep

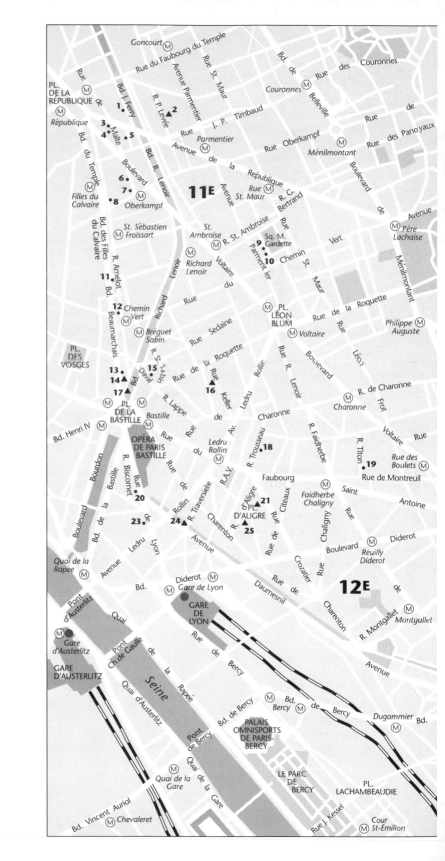

20ᴱ

CIMETIÈRE
DU
PÈRE LACHAISE

Eleventh Arrondissement

Hotels *page 221*

1 Auberge Jules Ferry
3 Hôtel de Nevers ★ (¢)
4 Hôtel Notre-Dame ★★
5 Hôtel Plessis ★★
6 Hôtel Résidence Alhambra ★★
7 Libertel Croix de Malte ★★
8 Hôtel Beaumarchais ★★★
9 Hôtel Rhetia ★ (¢)
10 Garden Hôtel ★★
11 Home Plazza Bastille ★★★
12 Hôtel Bastille de Launay ★★
13 Hôtel Lyon-Mulhouse ★★
15 Daval Hôtel ★★
18 Auberge International des Jeunes
19 Maison Internationale des Jeunes
   (MIJCP)
22 Home Plazza Saint-Antoine ★★★

Shops *page 384*

2 Porcelaine de Paris
14 Allicante
16 Anne Willi
17 Marché Richard-Lenoir

Twelfth Arrondissement

Hotels *page 232*

20 Hôtel le Pavillon Bastille ★★★
23 Centre Parisien de Zen

Shops *page 386*

21 Betty
24 Viaduc des Arts
25 Marché and Rue d'Aligre

N

500 meters

Ⓜ *Métro Station*
● *R.E.R. Station*

DAVAL HÔTEL ★★ (15)
21, rue Daval, 75011
Métro: Bastille, Bréguet Sabin
23 rooms, all with shower or bath and toilet

TELEPHONE
01-47-00-51-23
FAX
01-40-21-80-26
EMAIL
hoteldaval@wanadoo.fr
CREDIT CARDS
AE, DC, MC, V
RATES
Single 65€, double 69–80€,
triple 80€, quad 97€; *taxe de
séjour* included
BREAKFAST
Continental 8€ per person
ENGLISH SPOKEN
Yes

Monsieur Gonod and his German shepherd dog, Malko, run this Bastille budget hotel with good sense, good humor, and kindness. Valued mainly for its "in" location and conservative prices, the Daval Hôtel occupies a platinum position in the white-hot Bastille area, only a short promenade from the Opéra Bastille and all the cafés, boutiques, and galleries that characterize this popular *quartier,* as well as the Bastille hotspots that barflies gravitate to on the weekends. The blue rooms all have the same functional, easy-maintenance style: open closets, compact baths, built-in beds and side tables, quilted bed spreads, and industrial-strength carpeting. There are no twin beds, but all rooms are air-conditioned, which is an almost unheard-of luxury in this price range.

FACILITIES AND SERVICES: Air-conditioning, direct-dial phone, elevator, hair dryer, TV with international reception, room safe (no charge)

NEAREST TOURIST ATTRACTIONS (RIGHT BANK): Opéra Bastille, Bastille

GARDEN HÔTEL ★★ (10)
1, rue du Général-Blaise (facing Square M. Gardette), 75011
Métro: St-Ambroise, Rue St-Maur
42 rooms, all with shower or bath and toilet

TELEPHONE
01-47-00-57-93
FAX
01-47-00-45-29
CREDIT CARDS
AE, MC, V
RATES
Single 61€, breakfast included;
double 61€, breakfast extra;
triple 77€, breakfast extra;
extra bed 16€; *taxe de séjour*
0.75€ per person, per day
BREAKFAST
Continental 5.50€ per person
ENGLISH SPOKEN
Limited

Need a neat, clean, safe, and comfortable temporary abode in the eleventh arrondissement? If so, I cannot imagine topping one of Mme. Adams's spotless forty-two rooms, many of which have balconies facing the Square M. Gardette, a neighborhood gathering place that defines this corner of Paris. Her antiseptically clean hotel rooms, which are the pride and joy of the sweet housekeeper, Mme. Casablanca, are appointed with light pine built-ins, simple floral wallpaper, and lots of chenille. Color matches do not jar the senses, and the functional bathrooms have good towels. For breakfast, you can join other guests at a long communal table in a breakfast room accented with a poster of Dutch tulips. Real flowers and potted plants line the reception desk, where you can plot your excursions in Paris by consulting the framed map of the métro. The reception desk is staffed from 6 A.M. to 10 P.M.

FACILITIES AND SERVICES: Direct-dial phone, hair dryer available, elevator, French TV, office safe (no charge)
NEAREST TOURIST ATTRACTIONS (RIGHT BANK): Bastille

HÔTEL BASTILLE DE LAUNAY ★★ (12)
42, rue Amelot, 75011
Métro: Chemin Vert, Bastille
36 rooms, all with shower or bath and toilet

TELEPHONE
01-47-00-88-11
FAX
01-47-00-24-90
EMAIL
hotelbastilledelaunay@
wanadoo.fr
INTERNET
www.bastilledelaunay-paris-
hotel.com
CREDIT CARDS
AE, DC, MC, V
RATES
Single 65€, double 98–135€,
triple 161€; *taxe de séjour*
included
BREAKFAST
Buffet 10€ per person
ENGLISH SPOKEN
Yes

The Bastille de Launay is a moderate two-star near the Marais that won't set off firecrackers, but neither will its tariff burn a hole in your pocket. The pale, uncluttered rooms are all just about the same: small and uniformly furnished with a colorful blend of fabric prints and stripes, easy-care furniture, a framed print on the wall, and the TV pitched in a high corner. Basic baths have shower guards on the tubs, but could use a wattage increase in the lighting. The lobby has nice groupings of easy chairs, an attractive wall covering, and the usual green plant. Breakfast is served in a stone cellar. That's it for this tastefully done, affordable pit stop on the edge of a much more expensive area of the Marais.

FACILITIES AND SERVICES: Direct-dial phone, elevator, hair dryer, minibar, TV with international reception, office safe (no charge)

NEAREST TOURIST ATTRACTIONS (RIGHT BANK): Bastille, Opéra Bastille, Marais

HÔTEL BEAUMARCHAIS ★★★ (8)
3, rue Oberkampf, 75011
Métro: Filles-du-Calvaire, Oberkampf
31 rooms, all with shower or bath and toilet

TELEPHONE
01-53-36-86-86
FAX
01-43-38-32-86
INTERNET
www.hotelbeaumarchais.com
CREDIT CARDS
AE, MC, V
RATES
Single 70€, double 100€, suite
140€; *taxe de séjour* included
BREAKFAST
Continental 10€ per person
ENGLISH SPOKEN
Yes

The hotel is owned by four inveterate travelers (a banker, lawyer, architect, and travel agent) who decided to open the kind of hotel they always hope to find but seldom do. All I can say is that they have certainly succeeded in getting my vote of approval, and judging from their bookings, that of many others as well. The architect partner had his hand in the overall imaginative design, which merges high style with quality materials and classic lines. In the tiled lobby, an Afghan rug defines the seating space, which mixes orange, green, and yellow barrel chairs with clean-lined gray metal tables. A glass display case holds three shelves of various pyramids, including one that looks like a rocket launch. No one tried to camouflage the big metal heat exhaust pipe, which is in full view behind the reception desk. But never mind—it takes a page from the Centre

Georges Pompidou school of decorating and fits right in. Breakfast is served at marble bistro tables with opaque plastic-backed chairs that overlook an interior garden with a central magnolia tree.

The rooms are upbeat and cheerful, each with Italian-designed lighting and a sunburst and a framed modern art print on the walls. In No. 56, a single with a shower, the view is of the dome of the Cirque de l'Hiver (winter circus building). Room 55, a double on the front, has yellow walls, red fruit print bedspreads, and a brightly tiled bathroom. Number 2, a double on the first floor facing the hotel patio, is the largest room, with two wicker chairs and a Mark Rothko poster over the bed. The suites are good buys if more space is a priority but a bathtub is not . . . they only have showers. I like their sitting areas with cushioned armchairs, more work space, amusing cactus lights, and mirrored wardrobes.

FACILITIES AND SERVICES: Air-conditioning in most rooms, direct-dial phone, elevator (to most floors), hair dryer, TV with international reception, room safe (no charge)

NEAREST TOURIST ATTRACTIONS (RIGHT BANK): Bastille, Marais, five-minute walk to place de la République with five métro lines, buses, and taxi stand

HÔTEL DE NEVERS ★ (¢, 3)
53, rue de Malte, at avenue de la République, 75011
Métro: Oberkampf, République
32 rooms, 24 with shower or bath and toilet

For cash-strapped globetrotters beholden to the bottom line, Paris hotel prices usually lead to one of two catastrophes: either of budget or of well-being. Coming to the rescue is this clean little Cheap Sleep near place de la République. For fourteen years, Alain and Sophie Bourderau and their cats—Misty stretched out in reception and Lea, a Scottish feline with attitude—have been dispensing their one-star, bright-colored, mixed-pattern, plebeian-furnished time-warped roosts to scores of visitors who are happy with a bed and not much more. For bathless abodes, guests have one toilet per floor, and only one shower on the third, but all complaints are quieted when you get your bill and realize that these are some of the lowest prices in Paris.

FACILITIES AND SERVICES: Direct-dial phone, elevator (to most floors), email in lobby, hair dryer on request, no TV, office safe (no charge)

TELEPHONE
01-47-00-56-18
FAX
01-43-57-77-39
INTERNET
www.hoteldenevers.com
CREDIT CARDS
MC, V
RATES
1–2 persons 32–50€, triple 59€, quad 75€; showers 5€; *taxe de séjour* 0.35€ per person, per day
BREAKFAST
Continental in room 5€ per person
ENGLISH SPOKEN
Yes

NEAREST TOURIST ATTRACTIONS (RIGHT BANK): Five-minute walk to place de la République and good public transportation, Marais

HÔTEL LYON-MULHOUSE ★★ (13)
8, boulevard Beaumarchais, 75011
Métro: Bastille
40 rooms, all with shower or bath and toilet

The hotel is named for Lyon and Mulhouse, two stops that stagecoaches made when leaving Paris from the Bastille. This has been a hotel since 1920, and when looking at the early photos, you will see that from the outside nothing has changed, except that the saplings out front are now mature trees whose branches reach the top floor. There is absolutely nothing fancy or pretentious about the plain rooms, but they are very good value, not only for their more than ample size but for their spare, coordinated looks, Internet access, views, and bathrooms with elongated tubs. The only view rooms are singles, and they are Nos. 43, 44, and 46, three cozy top-floor nests under the eaves with vistas of the Eiffel Tower and Montparnasse, Invalides, and the Panthéon. I would avoid No. 45, which somehow got lost in sequential numbering and is on the ground floor. Yes, it has space, not only in the room, but in the bathroom; however, the down side is the continuous 6 A.M. to 1 A.M. métro rumble. Room 30, a quiet quad on the back, has a partial view of the Opéra Bastille, double sinks in the bathroom, and a separate toilet unit. Just once while you are here, take the stairs and notice the pair of pictures hanging in the hallways showing what Paris has lost—that is, the Bastille—and what it has won—the Opéra Bastille.

FACILITIES AND SERVICES: Direct-dial phone, elevator, hair dryer, TV with international reception, office safe (1.60€ per day)

NEAREST TOURIST ATTRACTIONS (RIGHT BANK): Bastille, Opéra Bastille, Marais, interesting shopping

TELEPHONE
01-47-00-91-50
FAX
01-47-00-06-31
EMAIL
hotelyonmulhouse@wanadoo.fr
INTERNET
www.1-hotel-paris.com
CREDIT CARDS
AE, DC, MC, V
RATES
Single 60€, double 70–90€, triple 95€, quad 110–125€; *taxe de séjour* included
BREAKFAST
Continental 6€ per person
ENGLISH SPOKEN
Yes

HÔTEL NOTRE-DAME ★★ (4)
51, rue de Malte, near avenue de la République, 75011
Métro: Oberkampf, République
48 rooms, 31 with shower or bath and toilet

For those who want to spend time exploring Paris and require only a comfortable bed in a decent hotel close to transportation, this hotel run by Joseph and Anne-Marie, a husband-and-wife team, should fill the

TELEPHONE
01-47-00-78-76
FAX
01-43-55-32-31
INTERNET
www.hotel-notredame.com
CREDIT CARDS
AE, MC, V

RATES
Single 40–62€, double 69–
73€, triple 86€, quad 91€;
free shower; *taxe de séjour*
included

BREAKFAST
Continental 7€ per person

ENGLISH SPOKEN
Yes

bill. The working-class neighborhood is made up of shops supplying life's necessities, but it holds little to capture most tourists' attention. However, the place de la République, with a métro station, taxi stand, and several bus routes crossing it, is only a five-minute walk from the hotel door.

A gray-blue and white interior extends from the reception on one side to the breakfast room, which doubles as a TV lounge and waiting room. It is simple and a bit sterile, but a clean beginning. All rooms have been renovated, and they are appealing as long as you don't mind open closets and limited drawer space. Those on the sixth floor have balconies and rooftop views of Paris, and these are much better than those along the back, which have no view at all. My top choices include No. 64, a pretty yellow room for one with a balcony and stall shower; No. 65, done in soft beige with a balcony, double bed, and a stall shower in the bathroom; and No. 27, a twin on the front with a bathtub, two chairs, and five shelves in addition to the exposed closet. For those in any of the five bathless roosts, there is a free shower on the first floor, and for those in one of the twelve shower-only rooms, there is a toilet on every floor.

FACILITIES AND SERVICES: Direct-dial phone, elevator, hair dryer available, French TV in most rooms, office safe (no charge)

NEAREST TOURIST ATTRACTIONS (RIGHT BANK): Not much; five-minute walk to place de la République for métro and bus connections

HÔTEL PLESSIS ★★ (5)
25, rue du Grand Prieuré, near avenue de la République, 75011
Métro: Oberkampf, République
50 rooms, 38 with shower or bath and toilet

TELEPHONE
01-47-00-13-38

FAX
01-43-57-97-87

EMAIL
hotel.plessis@club-Internet.fr

CREDIT CARDS
AE, DC, MC, V

RATES
Single 35–67€, double 40–
70€; free shower; *taxe de séjour*
included

BREAKFAST
Buffet 7€ per person

ENGLISH SPOKEN
Yes

The hotel was built in 1925, and since 1953, it has been run by members of the Montrazat family, who take pride in their well-priced, clean, friendly accommodations that pennywise travelers from around the globe call home when in Paris. The safe neighborhood is hardly a tourist command post; rather, it's a place where you will see a mix of old ladies in fuzzy slippers tossing baguettes to the pigeons, children playing, and men gathered in cafés.

The six overstuffed Naugahyde armchairs in the faux wood–paneled lobby that also fits in a cold drink machine, and mezzanine bar with an upright piano, tell you that no one has called in a decorating team for years, if ever. However, you are not sleeping here, but in one of the perfectly adequate, clean chambers where the colors go together, there is space for your luggage, a chair to sit on, and the shower has a curtain. Rooms on the fifth floor have balconies; those without toilets and showers definitely say budget. There are good restaurants nearby and nightlife around the Bastille. The Marais is only two métro stops away, and you are a heartbeat from place de la République, where buses, métros, or taxis can take you wherever you want to be in the city.

FACILITIES AND SERVICES: Bar, direct-dial phone, elevator, fans, hair dryer, Internet in lobby, TV with international reception in rooms with bathrooms, office safe (no charge), one sitting room for nonsmokers

NEAREST TOURIST ATTRACTIONS (RIGHT BANK): Not much; short walk to place de la République for bus and métro connections

HÔTEL RÉSIDENCE ALHAMBRA ★★ (6)
11 bis and 13, rue de Malte, near boulevard Voltaire, 75011
Métro: Oberkampf, Filles-du-Calvaire
56 rooms, all with shower or bath and toilet

Here is a textbook example of getting what you pay for. Out of the way? Yes, more than a New York minute to get to what's really happening. Close to the métro? Yes, five major lines serve place de la République. A good deal? Yes, a pleasant Parisian stopover that would cost much more in tonier parts of the city.

The hotel is better than the neighborhood suggests. Automatic doors lead from the street into the light wood–paneled lobby, which looks onto a country garden. Open closets, no drawers, a built-in desk, and one chair sum up the rooms. Plumbing is of recent vintage in the tiled bathrooms, which have either a stall shower or shower and tub combined. Thirty-three of the rooms overlook what has to be the prettiest hotel garden on the Right Bank—at least of all the out-of-the-way two-stars. If you are lucky and secure one of these prime spots, you will overlook rose bushes, seasonal flowers, and trees, all lovingly tended by the owner's sister. Tables and chairs are set outside in the summer, making it an especially nice place to have your morning croissant.

FACILITIES AND SERVICES: Direct-dial phone, elevator, Internet in lobby, TV with international reception, office safe (no charge)

TELEPHONE
01-47-00-35-52
FAX
01-43-57-98-75
INTERNET
www.hotelalhambra.fr
CREDIT CARDS
AE, MC, V
RATES
Single 60€, double 65–71€, triple 93–105€, quad 116€; *taxe de séjour* 0.76€ per person, per day
BREAKFAST
Continental 7€ per person
ENGLISH SPOKEN
Yes

NEAREST TOURIST ATTRACTIONS (RIGHT BANK): None; short walk to place de la République for métro and bus connections

HÔTEL RHETIA ★ (¢, 9)
3, rue du Général-Blaise, near avenue Parmentier, 75011
Métro: St-Ambroise

24 rooms, 16 with shower or bath and toilet

TELEPHONE
01-47-00-47-18
FAX
01-48-06-01-73
CREDIT CARDS
None, cash only
RATES
Single 32–39€, double 37–45€, triple 54€; extra bed 10€; shower 1.50€; *taxe de séjour* included
BREAKFAST
Continental 3€ per person
ENGLISH SPOKEN
Limited

Keep the prices cheap enough and people will come back again and again, and they do—from Sweden, Belgium, Singapore, Australia, England, the United States, and Canada. As one guest from Sydney, Australia, put it, "It is neat, clean, tidy, homey . . . all you need." I agree. Not all the rooms have private bathrooms, but they do come with a television. Most are minimally furnished in the usual one-star way, with a well-used collection of furniture and bedspreads that don't quite fit anymore. At only 3 euros per person, breakfast can be considered a gift—grab it! The red hall and stairway carpets are worn; the neighborhood is safe and quiet (for Paris); and fourteen rooms along the front face the Square Maurice Gardette, which serves as the neighborhood gathering place. You are within reasonable walking distance to all the nightlife the area is known for, and you are a métro ride to everything else that is interesting. Please note, if you are calling or faxing for reservations, the front desk is open for business from 7:15 A.M. to 10 P.M.

FACILITIES AND SERVICES: Direct-dial phone, no elevator (6 floors), French TV, laundromat on corner

NEAREST TOURIST ATTRACTIONS (RIGHT BANK): Marais, Bastille

LIBERTEL CROIX DE MALTE ★★ (7)
5, rue de Malte, 75011
Métro: République, Oberkampf

29 rooms, all with bath, shower, and toilet

TELEPHONE
01-48-05-09-36
FAX
01-43-57-02-54
EMAIL
H2752-GM@accor-hotels.com
INTERNET
www.accor-hotels.com
CREDIT CARDS
AE, DC, MC, V
RATES
Single 95€, double or duplex 105€; extra bed 30€; *taxe de séjour* included

A stay at this upgraded two-star near the Bastille can satisfy luxury-loving Right Bank natures as well as those with fun-loving Left Bank streaks. Admittedly it is a few degrees from Tourist Central, but transportation is quick and easy from place de la République.

Rooms are well done, baths are modern, and the professional staff congenial. The vivid color palette is taken from the reproduction paintings of Walasse Ting that hang throughout the hotel. An unusual collection of boxed and acrylic art is displayed in the lobby, which flows into a bright glassed-in dining area with gaily upholstered chair cushions. The hotel has two buildings that face a winter garden with trompe-l'oeil frescoes. The first building, which has an elevator, has the best rooms. For example, in No. 7, the Ting poster of four brightly colored birds sets the turquoise tone for everything in the room: beds, side tables, wardrobe, stool, lampshades, and chair. Numbers 1 and 4 have their own little terraces, but the rooms are so small that you can barely walk around the end of the bed. The other building has duplex two-story rooms with spiral staircases that would not be safe for anyone traveling with children. Otherwise, the only duplex to definitely avoid is No. 207, where guests will have to contend with a painting of a sprawled nude woman over the bed and take a dangerous, winding fire-escape-style staircase to get to the bathroom, where the low roof will force most people to shower on their knees.

FACILITIES AND SERVICES: Bar, direct-dial phone, elevator (to most floors), hair dryer, laundry service, TV with international reception, office safe (no charge), two floors exclusively nonsmoking

NEAREST TOURIST ATTRACTIONS (RIGHT BANK): None; near place de la République with métro and bus connections

BREAKFAST
Buffet 9€ per person

ENGLISH SPOKEN
Yes

Twelfth Arrondissement

RIGHT BANK
Bercy Village
Bois de Vincennes
Musée d'Afrique et d'Océanie
Opéra Bastille
Viaduc des Arts

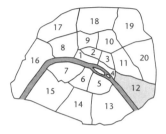

The twelfth leads away from the place de la Bastille and the Colonne de Juillet, a monument to the Parisians killed in the revolutions of 1830 and 1846. One of the district's nicest attractions is the Viaduc des Arts. Once a railway viaduct, it now showcases craft and new-wave design boutiques on the street level, and a pleasant green space—called the Promenade Plantée—runs along the top. Farther east is the vast Bois de Vincennes (with a lake, Buddhist temple, flower gardens, and a racetrack) and the Musée d'Afrique et d'Océanie, which has an outstanding collection of African tribal artifacts. The old brick wine warehouses at Bercy Village, across the river from the new Bibliothéque National, have been restored and developed into a pedestrian mall with shops, wine bars, cafés, and nightlife.

HOTELS IN THE TWELFTH ARRONDISSEMENT (see map page 222)

Hôtel le Pavillon Bastille ★★★   **233**

OTHER OPTIONS
Residence Hotels

Centre Parisien de Zen   **317**

HÔTEL LE PAVILLON BASTILLE ★★★ (20)
65, rue de Lyon, 75012
Métro: Bastille

25 rooms, all with shower, bath, and toilet

The only colors used in the hotel are shades of blue and yellow. This theme is carried out from the front terrace and the lobby through to the bedrooms and right down to the bowl of candies wrapped in yellow and blue foil. It sounds a bit over the top, but it works, and the boutique hotel is fused harmoniously into a contemporary whole. Close to the Marais and almost across the street from the Opéra Bastille, it is the perfect address if the opera is on your must-do list. If so, the hotel can book tickets, subject to availability. They should be requested when you reserve, with as much lead time as possible. Judicious use of mirrors in the bedrooms adds to the feeling of light and space, halogen lighting adds a modern touch, and cushioned window seats in some substitute for chairs. There is no air-conditioning, which means you have to open your window for air, making room position here important. The biggest choices are along the back, and these escape some of the traffic noise of front facing rooms. Seven rooms connect, and there is one suite with a small sitting room off the double bedroom. The breakfast room is brightly done in aqua—of course, with yellow and blue accents. A series of framed architectural prints hangs on the walls. The staff is young and enthusiastic.

FACILITIES AND SERVICES: Bar, direct-dial phone, elevator, hair dryer, Internet in lobby, laundry service, minibar, TV with international reception, room safe (no charge)

NEAREST TOURIST ATTRACTIONS (RIGHT BANK): Bastille, Opéra Bastille, Marais

TELEPHONE
01-43-43-65-65

FAX
01-43-43-96-52; U.S. toll-free
800-233-2552

EMAIL
hotel-pavillon@akaMail.com

INTERNET
www.pavillon-bastille.com

CREDIT CARDS
AE, DC, MC, V

RATES
1–2 persons 135€, suite or connection rooms 225€; *taxe de séjour* included

BREAKFAST
Buffet or Continental in room 12€ per person

ENGLISH SPOKEN
Yes

Thirteenth Arrondissement

LEFT BANK
Bibliothèque Nationale de
France–François Mitterand
Butte aux Cailles
Chinatown
Gobelins tapestry factory
(Manufacture des Gobelins)

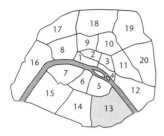

This large, working-class area is generally thought of as a tourist-free zone. It is the sort of place dedicated Parisian visitors see on their seventh or eighth trip, after they have done everything else they thought important. The area does hold some interesting surprises and should not be totally overlooked. There is the still-functioning Manufacture Nationale des Gobelins tapestry factory, which is open to the public. A stroll around the winding streets of the Butte aux Cailles district provides a delightful look at one of Paris's oldest yet least known and untouched parts, but one that is getting renewed attention from insiders who think the eleventh has become passé. The arrondissement also has a huge Asian population, which produces some of the best, and certainly the cheapest, Asian meals to be had on avenue de Choisy, the main street of Chinatown. The Bibliothèque Nationale de France–François Mitterand, designed to replace the Bibliothèque National, is a multimillion euro project, covering 288,000 square meters along the Seine across from the Ministry of Finance. This enormous new library, built to resemble four open books, has incited as much controversy as the Opéra Bastille did (and still does).

HOTELS IN THE THIRTEENTH ARRONDISSEMENT

Hôtel La Manufacture ★★★	**236**
Le Vert Gallant ★★★	**237**

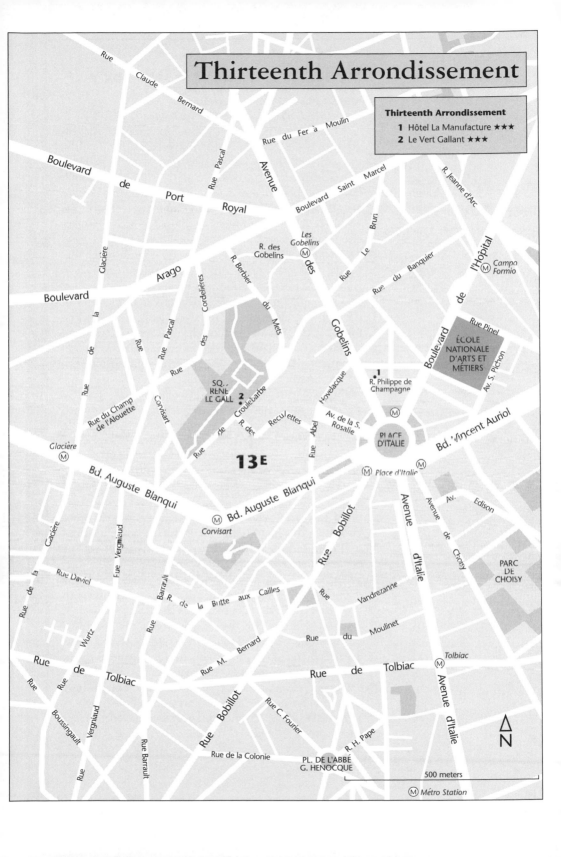

HÔTEL LA MANUFACTURE ★★★ (1)
8, rue Philippe de Champagne, 75013
Métro: Place d'Italie, Gobelins
57 rooms, all with shower or bath and toilet

TELEPHONE
01-45-35-45-25
FAX
01-45-35-45-40
EMAIL
lamanufacture.paris@wanadoo.fr
INTERNET
www.hotel-la-manufacture.com
CREDIT CARDS
AE, DC, MC, V
RATES
Single 125€, double 133–
239€; *taxe de séjour* included
BREAKFAST
Continental 7.5€ per person
ENGLISH SPOKEN
Yes

Your quest stops here if you are looking for a stylish yet starkly designed hotel room in an area that's on the upswing with locals but largely ignored by most tourists. The hotel is just off the busy place d'Italie, which has a huge shopping mall and cinema multiplex. You are about a ten-minute brisk walk from the colorful rue Mouffetard, fifteen to teeming Chinatown, and a mere two hundred meters from the Gobelins tapestry factory. The Butte aux Cailles, one of the city's oldest neighborhoods, still retains its village-like atmosphere and is another pleasant walk from the hotel.

The hot coral slipcovered sofas and stool modules in the lobby are eye-catching to say the least, and so are the high-backed red-and-white-checked banquettes and ocean-liner deck chairs in the dining room. Paolo Conté, a contemporary Left Bank painter, was commissioned to do the artwork, which is in direct contrast with the traditional fruit prints that line one wall. A stainless steel, mirrored elevator takes guests to their rooms, which are on the cutting edge of modern, with simple lines, customized furniture, and crisp white bed coverings offset by red striped carpets. Two floors have balconies, and several rooms connect, but there are no suites. Some favorite rooms are on the seventh floor, especially No. 74, offering a view of the rooftops of Paris and the Eiffel Tower. Depending on the circumstances, the other view from this room could be considered infamous since it is a direct look at the *quartier* police department. The bathroom is large enough for two pedestal sinks, a table, and a tub. In No. 72, you have a similar view of police doings in the neighborhood. All rooms on the seventh floor have tea- and coffee-making facilities, bathrobes, and scales. From No. 49, all you see is the courtyard from inside a very small room. In No. 63, the five framed damsels dictated the pink colors in this balconied room.

FACILITIES AND SERVICES: Air-conditioning, bar, direct-dial phone, elevator, hair dryer, Internet in cyber café next door, laundry service, TV with international reception

NEAREST TOURIST ATTRACTIONS (LEFT BANK): Gobelins tapestry factory, Chinatown, Butte aux Cailles

LE VERT GALLANT ★★★ (2)
41–43, rue Croulebarbe, 75013
Métro: Place d'Italie, Gobelins

15 rooms and studios, all with shower or bath and toilet

TELEPHONE
01-44-08-83-50

FAX
01-44-08-83-69

CREDIT CARDS
AE, MC, V

RATES
1–2 persons 87–90€; extra bed 15€; parking 10€ per day; *taxe de séjour* included

BREAKFAST
Continental 7€ per person

ENGLISH SPOKEN
Yes

Balzac said it well: "Paris is an ocean in itself. There is always some spot never seen before, some unknown cavern, flower, pearls, delight hitherto unknown."

A stay at the appealing Le Vert Gallant provides that wonderful feeling of discovery, of finding an unknown corner of Paris for your very own. Located in the Gobelins district, this discreet garden hotel is a charming oasis for those who know Paris well and are looking for something a bit beyond the usual hotel room—and who are willing to sacrifice a dead-center location to get it. Across the street from the hotel is the René Le Gall Square, a green park filled with the sound of children's voices, *mamans* pushing strollers, and elderly men and women out for a few minutes of gossip or a quiet moment to read the papers. For anything else, you will need the métro, which is a ten-minute walk. Next door to the hotel is its restaurant, l'Auberge Etchegorry, a Basque retreat that offers hotel guests fantastic prices on prix-fixe meals. For more on this special restaurant, see *Great Eats Paris.*

The hotel is made up of fifteen rooms, all of which have windows framing a garden courtyard, which has thirty-seven grapevines. Your morning wakeup call will be the songs of birds in the trees, not the usual rude Parisian awakening of grinding garbage trucks or furious horn-honking motorists. If you want to cook during your stay, reserve a studio on the ground floor. The rooms above also have kitchens, but because of fire regulations, no actual cooking is allowed on the higher floors. All rooms have an uncluttered, modern look. Colors are soft and pleasing, the accessories appropriate, and the fabrics well coordinated. Bathrooms are small but modern. Two affordable parking places must be reserved ahead. Maïté and Henri Laborde, your hosts here and at their restaurant, attend graciously to their guests, which further contributes to the overall feeling of well-being one has when staying at this special hotel. A warning is in order: Before arrival, have your affairs in order at home—you may never want to leave.

FACILITIES AND SERVICES: Direct-dial phone, no elevator (2 floors), hair dryer, some kitchenettes, minibar, parking, TV with international reception, room safe (no charge)

NEAREST TOURIST ATTRACTIONS (LEFT BANK): Nothing; must use public transportation

Fourteenth Arrondissement

LEFT BANK
Catacombs
Montparnasse
Parc Montsouris

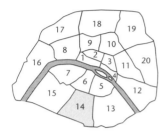

Montparnasse has become the victim of a tragically insensitive redevelopment policy exemplified by the Tour Montparnasse. During the 1920s and 1930s, the fourteenth was well known as the artistic headquarters of the modern art and literary worlds, where Picasso, Modigliani, Chagall, and Léger all had studios. Nostalgia buffs return today and head for the historic brasseries Le Dôme and La Coupole to rekindle memories of the famous patrons who ate and drank there, but they find the spirit is just not the same. Spirits of a different sort can be found at place Denfert-Rochereau, where the Catacombs are located. These underground cemeteries, created in 1785 as a hygienic alternative to the aboveground ones, hold the bones of six million Parisians, and during World War II, they were used as a headquarters by the French resistance. Another final resting place is the Cimetière du Montparnasse, where many famous writers and artists lie, including Paul Sartre and Simone de Beauvoir, Baudelaire, Maupassant, Samuel Beckett, and André Citroën. The Parc Montsouris, designed by Alphand during the time of Baron Haussmann, is one of the prettiest parks in Paris.

HOTELS IN THE FOURTEENTH ARRONDISSEMENT

Hôtel Daguerre ★★★	**239**
Hôtel de Blois ★ (¢)	**242**
Hôtel Delambre ★★★	**243**
Hôtel de l'Espérance (NO STARS, ¢)	**243**
Hôtel des Bains ★	**244**
Hôtel Istria ★★	**245**
Hôtel l'Aiglon ★★★	**246**
Hôtel Lenox Montparnasse ★★★	**247**

(¢) indicates a Cheap Sleep

HÔTEL DAGUERRE ★★★ (20)
94, rue Daguerre, near avenue du Maine, 75014
Métro: Denfert-Rochereau, Gaîté
30 rooms, all with shower or bath and toilet

For a reliable modern stay in this neck of the Paris woods, the Hôtel Daguerre is a top-notch choice. Even though it has recently been bumped up from two to three stars, nothing much has changed, including the prices. Paintings of the *bouquinistes* along the banks of the Seine and a mural of the Louvre accent the small sitting room and stone-walled breakfast area. The standard-issue rooms are comfortably furnished and have more than their share of perks, including heated towel racks. The even-numbered rooms face the street and have showers and more noise. The odd-numbered slots have tubs and are quiet. No room faces a blank wall. Two rooms are handicapped-accessible. The elevator does not go to the breakfast room and lands between the floors for the rooms, so there will always be a few steps to climb. The best feature of No. 501, a cheerful twin, is its glassed-in veranda looking toward Montmartre. If this room is booked, ask for No. 601, which has views of Sacré Coeur, or No. 301, with a pleasant view of the garden. If you want your own little terrace, try No. 1 or 2.

Also under the same ownership is the Hôtel La Régence Étoile in the seventeenth (see page 283).

FACILITIES AND SERVICES: Direct-dial phone, elevator (to half landings), hair dryer, Internet in lobby, minibar, TV with international reception, room safe (no charge)

NEAREST TOURIST ATTRACTIONS (LEFT BANK): Montparnasse, lively shopping street

TELEPHONE
01-43-22-43-54
01-56-80-25-80

FAX
01-43-20-66-84

EMAIL
hoteldaguerre@wanadoo.fr

CREDIT CARDS
AE, DC, MC, V

RATES
Single 72–85€, double 80€, suite 107–129€; extra bed 22€; *taxe de séjour* included

BREAKFAST
Buffet 10€ per person

ENGLISH SPOKEN
Yes

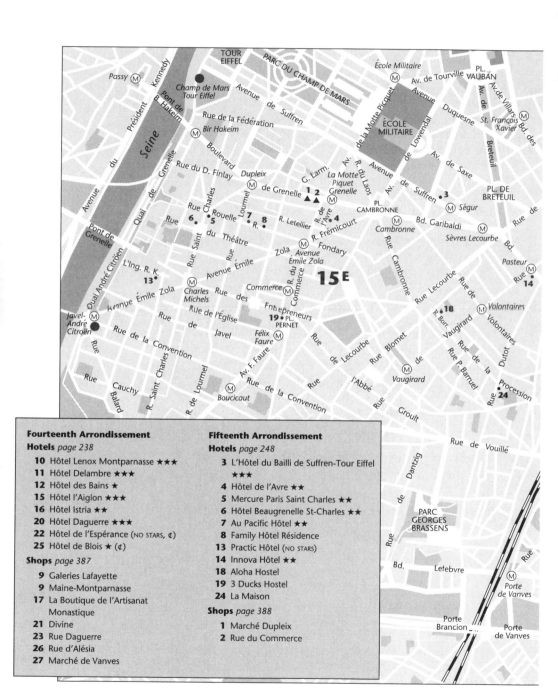

Fourteenth Arrondissement

Hotels *page 238*

- **10** Hôtel Lenox Montparnasse ★★★
- **11** Hôtel Delambre ★★★
- **12** Hôtel des Bains ★
- **15** Hôtel l'Aiglon ★★★
- **16** Hôtel Istria ★★
- **20** Hôtel Daguerre ★★★
- **22** Hôtel de l'Espérance (NO STARS, ¢)
- **25** Hôtel de Blois ★ (¢)

Shops *page 387*

- **9** Galeries Lafayette
- **9** Maine-Montparnasse
- **17** La Boutique de l'Artisanat Monastique
- **21** Divine
- **23** Rue Daguerre
- **26** Rue d'Alésia
- **27** Marché de Vanves

Fifteenth Arrondissement

Hotels *page 248*

- **3** L'Hôtel du Bailli de Suffren-Tour Eiffel ★★★
- **4** Hôtel de l'Avre ★★
- **5** Mercure Paris Saint Charles ★★
- **6** Hôtel Beaugrenelle St-Charles ★★
- **7** Au Pacific Hôtel ★★
- **8** Family Hôtel Résidence
- **13** Practic Hôtel (NO STARS)
- **14** Innova Hôtel ★★
- **18** Aloha Hostel
- **19** 3 Ducks Hostel
- **24** La Maison

Shops *page 388*

- **1** Marché Dupleix
- **2** Rue du Commerce

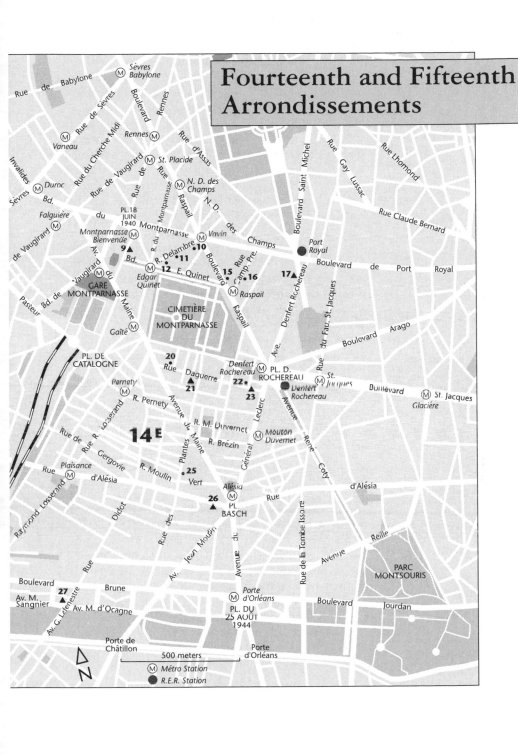

Fourteenth and Fifteenth Arrondissements

Rue de Babylone
Sèvres Babylone
Rue de Sèvres
Boulevard
Rennes
Rue d'Assas
Vaneau
Rue du Cherche Midi
Rennes
St. Placide
Invalides
Rue de Vaugirard
Rue d'Assas
Duroc
Bd.
Sèvres
Rue de Vaugirard
Rue
Rue
N. D. des Champs
Falguière
du
PL.18 JUIN 1940
Montparnasse
N. D.
des
Boulevard Saint Michel
Rue Gay Lussac
Rue Lhomond
de Vaugirard
Montparnasse Bienvenüe
9▲
Av.
R. du Montparnasse
Raspail
Vavin
Champs
Rue Claude Bernard
Bd.
R. Delambre
•10
•11
Port Royal
du
•12
E. Quinet
15
Rue Camp. Pre.
•16
17▲
Boulevard
de
Port
Royal
Vaugirard
Edgar Quinet
Boulevard
Denfert Rochereau
GARE MONTPARNASSE
Maine
Raspail
Rue du Fau. St. Jacques
Pasteur
Bd. de
Gaîté
CIMETIÈRE DU MONTPARNASSE
Raspail
Av.
Boulevard
Arago
PL. DE CATALOGNE
20
•
Rue
Daguerre
Denfert Rochereau
22▲
PL. D. ROCHEREAU
St. Jacques
Boulevard
St. Jacques
Pernety
21
23
Denfert Rochereau
Glacière
Avenue du Maine
Leclerc
R. Pernety
R. M. Duvernet
Mouton Duvernet
Avenue
Rue de R. Losserand
R. Brézin
René Coty
Rue de
Gergovie
R. Moulin
Plantes
Général
14E
Rue
Plaisance
d'Alésia
•25
Vert
d'Alésia
Alésia
Rue
d'Alésia
26▲
PL. BASCH
Rue de la Tombe Issoire
Didot
Rue des
Reille
PARC MONTSOURIS
Raymond Losserand
Rue
Av. Jean Moulin
Avenue
Avenue
Boulevard
27▲
Brune
Porte d'Orléans
Boulevard
Jourdan
Av. M. Sangnier
Av. M. d'Ocagne
Av. G. Lefebvre
PL. DU 25 AOÛT 1944
Porte de Châtillon
Porte d'Orléans
△
N
500 meters
Ⓜ Métro Station
● R.E.R. Station

HÔTEL DE BLOIS ★ (¢, 25)
5, rue des Plantes, 75014
Métro: Alésia, Mouton-Duvernet

25 rooms, 17 with shower or bath and toilet

TELEPHONE
01-45-40-99-48
FAX
01-45-40-45-62
CREDIT CARDS
AE, MC, V
RATES
Single 39–51€, double 41–
56€, triple 47–61€; free public
shower; *taxe de séjour* included
BREAKFAST
Continental 5€ per person
ENGLISH SPOKEN
Yes

When I first visited this hotel several years ago, it was my final hotel stop after a long, rainy day, and as I walked I thought, this place is about two blocks east of nowhere, and it better be very, very good. Luckily, Mme. Fontange's Hôtel de Blois turned out to be a winner in the one-star, budget hotel sweepstakes, and it still is. Cozy, clean, and homey are the words that spring to mind when I think of her cheery sitting room with windows overlooking the street. Breakfast is served here in the morning, and the room is always filled with fresh flowers, never dusty plastic ones.

Her overly feminine bedrooms are coordinated, thankfully displaying little of rainbow-palette color schemes and garage-sale Gothic furniture. Ask for Room 2, with a double bed, polished armoire, tiny-floral-print wall covering, and a big pink tile bathroom with new fittings and a shower curtain. Space is at more of a premium in No. 5, which is also rather dark and has a shower that needs attention, but it does have a table and dresser with a mirror and a TV pitched for easy viewing. Number 9, on the other hand, is a nice twin or triple with a good bathroom. Room 6 has a shower with doors, a double bed, and space to live in, but no view. I would not want to stay in No. 3, which has a poor layout due to how the shower and toilet were squeezed in. Oriental runners on white painted stairs and a different mural on each of the floors make climbing to your room a pleasant exercise. A self-service laundromat is right across the street, and if you need a workout, there is a public swimming pool a hundred meters behind the hotel.

Shopaholics take note: You are within a five-minute, bag-toting distance from one of the discount shopping meccas for savvy Parisians: rue d'Alésia (see page 339).

FACILITIES AND SERVICES: Direct-dial phone, no elevator (5 floors), hair dryer available, TV with international reception, office safe (no charge)

NEAREST TOURIST ATTRACTIONS (LEFT BANK): Discount shopping on rue d'Alésia; otherwise, must use public transportation

HÔTEL DELAMBRE ★★★ (11)
35, rue Delambre, 75014
Métro: Montparnasse-Bienvenüe, Vavin, Edgar-Quinet
30 rooms, all with shower or bath and toilet

I continue to be impressed. Patrick Kalmy's Hôtel Delambre still has my vote for the smartest rehab effort in the fourteenth arrondissement. A few years ago, he took a dog-eared one-star where surrealist André Breton once lived and transformed it from stem to stern into a snazzy three-star and—this is important—kept the prices within reason. In cleaning out the debris from the old hotel, M. Kalmy found some unlikely treasures he incorporated nicely in the lobby and breakfast room. In the street-side dining area, he cleverly displays an old metal garden gate, and two original regal columns stand by the elevators.

The rooms are well done in two dominant colors: red and blue or yellow and blue. Rooms 34 and 40, with white walls and enameled doors with wood detailing, are doubles with a built-in curved desk and an interesting view over a garden to a block of apartments beyond. Number 50, a two-room minisuite, combines the charm of sloping ceilings with smaller windows. The addition of a skylight, good closet space, and a large bathroom make this a popular choice. The hotel is within walking distance of the Luxembourg Gardens, and Montparnasse. Otherwise, public transportation is easy and close by.

FACILITIES AND SERVICES: Direct-dial phone, elevator (to most floors), electric fans, hair dryer, Internet in lobby, laundry service, TV with international reception, room safe (no charge)

NEAREST TOURIST ATTRACTIONS (LEFT BANK): Montparnasse, Jardin du Luxembourg

TELEPHONE
01-43-20-66-31
FAX
01-45-38-91-76
INTERNET
www.hoteldelambre.com
CREDIT CARDS
AE, MC, V
RATES
1–2 persons 85–95€, suite 150€; *taxe de séjour* included
BREAKFAST
Buffet 8€ per person
ENGLISH SPOKEN
Yes

HÔTEL DE L'ESPÉRANCE (NO STARS, ¢, 22)
1, rue de Grancey, 75014
Métro: Denfert-Rochereau
17 rooms, 6 with shower, none with toilet

Montparnasse is the neighborhood that made café-hopping famous, so there is no need to spend time in, or money on, your hotel room. You will be doing neither at Jackie Lacourarie's useful seventeen-room address that doesn't pretend to be stylish. It is situated right around the corner from rue Daguerre, a good place to observe the happenings on one of the more active shopping streets in the fourteenth arrondissement. Amenities are

TELEPHONE
01-43-21-41-04
FAX
01-43-22-06-02
EMAIL
hoteldelesperance@hotmail.com
CREDIT CARDS
MC, V
RATES
1–2 persons 35–60€, triple 61€; shower 3.50€; *taxe de séjour* 0.20€ per person, per day

BREAKFAST
Continental 5.5€ per person
ENGLISH SPOKEN
Yes

lean, but the rooms have double-glazed windows, are *très propre* (very clean), and free of cascading patterns and dizzying color schemes. Jackie bills herself as "the original French mother," which means she will take good care of you during her morning shift. Her son Laurent, who speaks English and is equally as hospitable, takes over in the afternoon. In digs like this, it is always budget-smart to book the cheaper, showerless rooms and use the hall facilities, which in this case are very good. It is also wise to book early, because there is seldom a vacancy.

FACILITIES AND SERVICES: No elevator (2 floors), hair dryer available, French TV, office safe (no charge)

NEAREST TOURIST ATTRACTIONS (LEFT BANK): Montparnasse

HÔTEL DES BAINS ★ (12)
33, rue Delambre, 75014
Métro: Edgar-Quinet

TELEPHONE
01-43-20-85-27
FAX
01-42-79-82-78
EMAIL
des.bains.hotel@wanadoo.fr
CREDIT CARDS
AE, MC, V
RATES
1–2 persons 75€, suite (1–4 persons) 100–137€; *taxe de séjour* included
BREAKFAST
Buffet 11€ per person
ENGLISH SPOKEN
Yes

41 rooms, all with shower or bath and toilet

Your surroundings are far from the usual lean one-star digs, especially the formal sitting room decorated with silk flowers in a graceful silver bowl, oriental rugs, and an oval dining table that would easily seat eight. For a one-star, the prices seem high, but for what you get, they are fair. Late risers will appreciate the set-back location from the street . . . all the rooms are quiet, at least for this part of Paris. The rooms aren't big on decorating frills, but they are a quantum leap from the Day-Glo colors and frayed-at-the-edges furnishings one usually contends with in one-star abodes. They come equipped with excellent bathrooms, TVs with international reception, hair dryer, room safe, and the possibility of private parking—an unheard-of extra in a one-star hotel.

Even though they lack much storage space, the best deals are the suites, all of which have a bedroom with one large bed and an adjoining room with twin beds. Oddly enough there are no towel racks in some, and when I asked about their absence, I was told the towels were changed daily. Another oddity for some might be the collection of paintings of reclining nude women that hang over the beds and adorn the walls, or in some cases are fashioned into side lights. Number 447 is a two-room selection facing the courtyard. It is open and simply done with hardwood floors, coordinated fabrics, and a corner glass shower in the bathroom. If you are at all claustrophobic, you won't want Suite 227, with only a tiny barred ceiling window in the second bedroom. On the other hand, Suite

772 would easily befit a three- or four-star property. Up a flight of stairs, this two-room suite is amazingly nice, with gray faux-finished beds and cane headboards. Ruby spreads and upholstered chairs match the tassels holding back the embroidered floor-to-ceiling floral print draperies. Each room comes equipped with its own TV, adequate seating, and open closet space. The large granite bathroom has a glass-enclosed stall shower, magnifying mirror, and extra hooks. Some of the doubles are really too small for two, unless you are staying only a night, have very limited luggage, or enjoy very cozy confines with your traveling companion. Better choices are No. 221, overlooking a garden, or No. 71, which can be a double or triple, and is sold as a suite. It is decorated in yellow and has a big bathroom with a glassed-in shower.

FACILITIES AND SERVICES: Direct-dial phone, elevator (to most floors), hair dryer, trouser press, TV with international reception, room safe (no charge)

NEAREST TOURIST ATTRACTIONS (LEFT BANK): Montparnasse, Jardin du Luxembourg

HÔTEL ISTRIA ★★ (16)
29, rue Campagne Première, 75014
Métro: Raspail
26 rooms, all with shower or bath and toilet

From this address you can wander the tree-lined boulevards and sit in the famous cafés that were the watering holes of Hemingway, Fitzgerald, and Henry Miller when they dominated the Montparnasse literary scene. In the 1920s and 1930s, when this was the *quartier* for artists and writers, the Istria was home to many of them, including Man Ray and his mistress Kiki de Montparnasse, Marcel Duchamp, Josephine Baker, and the Russian poet Vladimir Mayakovsky. Now, under the direction of Odile and Daniel Crétey, the hotel is a favorite for those seeking a convenient Montparnasse location. A pretty tiled entry with African art and pieces of country antiques, black-and-white photos of old Paris, and oriental rugs leads to a postage-stamp-size garden along the back of the hotel. Some of the rooms that overlook the garden are confining for two persons with any luggage. To avoid being cramped, request a third-floor nest. Remember, though, this building is old, and spacious rooms are not its strong suit; history, charm, and friendliness are.

FACILITIES AND SERVICES: Direct-dial phone, elevator (to most floors), hair dryer, laundry service, TV with international reception, room safe (no charge)

TELEPHONE
01-43-20-91-82
FAX
01-43-22-48-45
EMAIL
hotelistria@wanadoo.fr
CREDIT CARDS
AE, DC, MC, V
RATES
Single 96€, double 96–106€; extra bed 24€; *taxe de séjour* included
BREAKFAST
Continental 9€ per person
ENGLISH SPOKEN
Yes

HÔTEL L'AIGLON ★★★ (15)
232, boulevard Raspail, 75014
Métro: Raspail

47 rooms, all with shower or bath and toilet

The Hôtel l'Aiglon is a refined choice a quick walk from the Raspail métro stop. A formal tone pervades, from the faux book–lined bar to the beautifully redecorated rooms, all of which have been planned with discretion and good taste. Don't miss the original stained-glass windows over the stairway, which takes guests from the ground floor to a formal dining room with large sideboard and mahogany tables covered in starched white linen.

The rooms all face outward, and many have peaceful views over the Cimetière Montparnasse. They are color-coordinated, with textured fabrics, firm mattresses, good closet and luggage space, and bathrooms with windows. The eight suites are dreams come true, especially No. 55 with its soft blue colors. The sitting room is comfortably furnished with a desk, sofa bed, and easy chair, and it has a half bath to one side. Twin beds in the bedroom, with its own balcony, and a double-sink bathroom make up the rest. I also like Room 19, the only one with a kitchenette. It is handsomely done in kelly green and yellow with a pleasant sitting room, a large bedroom with a walk-in closet, and a beautiful bathroom. The advantage of Suite A is that both nicely appointed bedrooms have separate bathrooms, a real bonus for families. In No. 16, bright yellow and green are carried out on the quilted bedspread and curtains. The gray bathroom has gold and beige accents and a floral design in the shower. If you are *tout seul,* it is a perfect choice. Some people may not like the rooms on the top, or sixth, floor because the windows are higher than normal, but I find them quite charming. One of my favorite choices is No. 61. I like the room itself, with a three-drawer chest, a comfortable armchair, and print fabrics, but it is the bathroom that is the real star, with two windows and a view. I am also a fan of No. 67, with its sweeping view of the fourteenth arrondissement. And everyone enjoys the brand of service and hospitality provided by Jacques Rols and his excellent staff.

FACILITIES AND SERVICES: Air-conditioning, bar, direct-dial phone, elevator, hair dryer, kitchenette in one suite, laundry service, minibar, private parking (on request), TV with international reception, office safe (no charge)

TELEPHONE
01-43-20-82-42

FAX
01-43-20-98-72

EMAIL
hotelaiglon@wanadoo.fr

INTERNET
www.hotel-paris-aiglon.com

CREDIT CARDS
AE, DC, MC, V

RATES
1–2 persons 82–142€, suite (1–4 persons) 179–244€; extra bed 20€; parking 13.50€ per day; *taxe de séjour* 0.91€ per person, per day

BREAKFAST
Continental 6.50€ per person

ENGLISH SPOKEN
Yes

NEAREST TOURIST ATTRACTIONS (LEFT BANK): Montparnasse, Jardin du Luxembourg

HÔTEL LENOX MONTPARNASSE ★★★ (10)
15, rue Delambre, 75014
Métro: Vavin, Edgar-Quinet
52 rooms, all with shower or bath and toilet

The atmosphere is engaging and the clientele an international blend at the Lenox Montparnasse. The collection of furniture suggests Art Deco and the 1930s in both the lobby and large bar to one side. Green plants bring life to the area, beautiful sprays of fresh orchids give it wonderful color, and the ceiling painted like a beautiful cloud-filled Parisian day adds a light touch.

Rooms are nice, with just enough personality to set them apart from other mainstream Montparnasse hotels. If you want more leg room, reserve No. 69, a big twin with a corner sitting room, a tiny fireplace, and a rooftop view. It is softly decorated in blue and light gray. The bathroom has a rolling toiletry cart and blue and green inserts of flowers set against the white-tile walls. Rooms 10 and 14 are standard doubles, but I hope the guests are small people with only hand luggage. While the rooms are charming and have all the amenities, they are short on space. The bathroom in No. 10 is adequate, but in No. 14, *c'est trop petite.* That said, either would be just fine for a solo guest. Number 56 is a Club Room, which means it is slightly bigger than a standard room, and the bathroom has a tub. Number 60 is a good-value, twin-bedded suite beautifully done in blue and white with hand-painted window shutters and an old tile heater with a marble top. Seating is nicely arranged around a sofabed and two comfortable reading chairs. The top-floor, two-room suite, with its marble fireplace and clock, period furniture, and geometric upholstery, shows that an eclectic combination of styles and patterns can work if done correctly. Amusing etchings of French ladies of leisure with their dogs or coyly wrapped in fur—and not much else—grace the walls. The narrow bathroom has all the extras, including Roger and Gallet products.

FACILITIES AND SERVICES: Air-conditioning, bar, direct-dial phone, elevator, hair dryer, laundry service, parking, TV with international reception, office safe (no charge)

NEAREST TOURIST ATTRACTIONS (LEFT BANK): Montparnasse, Jardin du Luxembourg

TELEPHONE
01-43-35-34-50

FAX
01-43-20-46-64

EMAIL
hotel@lenoxmontparnasse.com

INTERNET
www.hotellenox.com

CREDIT CARDS
AE, DC, MC, V

RATES
1–2 persons: standard 120–130€, club 140–145€, suite for 2–3 persons 230–260€, parking 10€ per day; *taxe de séjour* included

BREAKFAST
Continental 11€ per person

ENGLISH SPOKEN
Yes

Fifteenth Arrondissement

LEFT BANK
Walking distance to:
Champ de Mars
Eiffel Tower
parts of Montparnasse
UNESCO

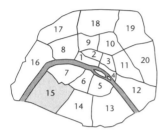

Home to a quarter of a million Parisians, the fifteenth is the biggest arrondissement, but it has few tourist attractions. If you enjoy seeing how the average Parisian lives, this is the perfect vantage point. La Ruche, which means beehive, was designed by Eiffel in 1900 as a wine pavilion. It is now used as artists' studios and occasionally is open to the public. The Parc André Citroën is a futuristic park built with computerized fountains, water jets, and even some green areas.

HOTELS IN THE FIFTEENTH ARRONDISSEMENT
(see map page 240)

Au Pacific Hôtel ★★	**248**
Hôtel Beaugrenelle St-Charles ★★	**249**
Hôtel de l'Avre ★★	**250**
Innova Hôtel ★★	**250**
L'Hôtel du Bailli de Suffren-Tour Eiffel ★★★	**251**
Mercure Paris Saint Charles ★★	**252**
Practic Hôtel (NO STARS)	**253**

OTHER OPTIONS
Hostels

Aloha Hostel	**311**
La Maison	**314**
3 Ducks Hostel	**315**

Residence Hotels

Family Hôtel Résidence	**318**

AU PACIFIC HÔTEL ★★ (7)
11, rue Fondary, 75015
Métro: Avenue Émile-Zola, Dupleix
57 rooms, all with shower or bath and toilet

TELEPHONE
01-45-75-20-49

FAX
01-45-77-70-73

EMAIL
pacifichotel@wanadoo.fr

INTERNET
www.au-pacific-hotel.com

CREDIT CARDS
MC, V

RATES
Single 50€, double 62€; *taxe de séjour* included

BREAKFAST
Buffet 6.50€ per person

This hotel and the Family Hôtel Résidence (a residence hotel, see page 318) are owned by Michèle Lepoutre, a gracious multilingual woman who took them over from her parents and grandmother. Both properties are on the same street in a blue-collar corner of Paris that is within a brisk fifteen-minute walk to the Eiffel Tower. At the Au Pacific, the rooms are sparse and spare with blond furniture and neutral colors. Eight in the back building have balconies, and now all have private facilities and television with French reception. Housekeeping is excellent; you won't see dirt or mold lurking in corners anywhere. The breakfast room is soberly yet very smartly furnished with the latest Italian designs in wood and chrome. Though amenities and prices are lean, the quality is never compromised. These are great budget sleeps, and euro-conscious, international guests stay here in droves.

FACILITIES AND SERVICES: Direct-dial phone, elevator (to most floors), hair dryer, French TV, office safe (no charge)

NEAREST TOURIST ATTRACTIONS (LEFT BANK): Champs de Mars, Eiffel Tower

HÔTEL BEAUGRENELLE ST-CHARLES ★★ (6)
82, rue St-Charles, at place St-Charles, 75015
Métro: Charles-Michels, Dupleix

51 rooms, all with shower or bath and toilet

This hotel is just as unassuming as its neighborhood, which offers a comfortable look at what everyday life is really all about in Paris, outside of the glittery and artsy *quartiers* that draw most visitors. You can spot the hotel from the place St-Charles . . . just look for the red awning and the boxwood bushes framing the entry. The lobby has Art Deco–style leather loveseats and armchairs. A modern breakfast room with black laminated tables and chairs is set apart by a bank of green plants. A glassed-in walkway joins the two buildings that make up the fifty-one-room hotel.

Several ground-floor rooms open onto the garden, and these are some of the best. Three rooms on the sixth floor have balconies and Eiffel Tower views, and one on the back, a single, also has a peek of the Eiffel Tower. All the rooms are small, especially the doubles with a shower, but decent closet space rescues them from feeling too cramped. Light, pastel-colored fabrics and blond furniture lend a modern touch. Peace and quiet prevails at night, as the neighborhood shuts down about 9 or 10 P.M.

NOTE: One of the best Monoprix stores in Paris is right around the corner. See page 360 for a description of this Parisian version of Wal-Mart, Target, and a huge supermarket all rolled into one.

FACILITIES AND SERVICES: Air-conditioning, direct-dial phone, elevator (to most floors), hair dryer, laundry service, minibar, small pets allowed (but not left alone in rooms), some trouser presses, TV with international reception, room safe (3.05€ per night!)

NEAREST TOURIST ATTRACTIONS (LEFT BANK): Eiffel Tower, Champ de Mars

TELEPHONE
01-45-78-61-63

FAX
01-45-79-04-38

EMAIL
beaugre@francenet.fr

INTERNET
www.hotelbeaugralize.com

CREDIT CARDS
AE, MC, V

RATES
Single 89–95€, double 90–96€; extra bed 30€; children under 12 free; lower rates in off-season; pets free, *taxe de séjour* 0.78€ per person, per day

BREAKFAST
Buffet 10€ per person

ENGLISH SPOKEN
Yes

HÔTEL DE L'AVRE ★★ (4)
21, rue de l'Avre, 75015
Métro: La Motte–Piquet-Grenelle, Avenue Émile-Zola
26 rooms, all with shower or bath and toilet

TELEPHONE
01-45-75-31-03
FAX
01-45-75-63-26
EMAIL
hotel.delavre@wanadoo.fr
INTERNET
www.hoteldelavre.com
CREDIT CARDS
AE, DC, MC, V
RATES
Single 61–72€, double 72–80€, triple 100€; extra bed for child under 8 years free; *taxe de séjour* included
BREAKFAST
Continental 7.50€ per person
ENGLISH SPOKEN
Yes

If you don't require much space and don't mind being somewhat in the boonies, then Bernard Vialette's twenty-six-room Hôtel de l'Avre is worth considering. The hotel is wrapped around a flowering spring and summer garden, where tables and umbrellas are set out for guests to enjoy breakfast or relaxing a moment from the rigors of sight-seeing. The garden-theme rooms are simple, yet a far cry from the standard-issue, charm-free two-star. Framed prints of herbs and flowers add interest to the rooms, and primary colors and striped fabrics keep them bright and cheerful. Closets are geared for short stays, and bathrooms for fast in-and-out use. Nine overlook the garden (which is at its best in warmer weather); another faces a day-care center. The largest rooms face the street, but this is a residential area, so quiet prevails after the sun sets. Good restaurants are nearby, and one of the biggest and most colorful roving street *marchés* sets up stalls only a block away on boulevard de Grenelle every Wednesday and Sunday morning.

FACILITIES AND SERVICES: Direct-dial phone, elevator, hair dryer, Internet in lobby, TV with international reception, office safe (no charge)

NEAREST TOURIST ATTRACTIONS (LEFT BANK): Eiffel Tower, Champ de Mars

INNOVA HÔTEL ★★ (14)
32, boulevard Pasteur, 75015
Métro: Pasteur
51 rooms, all with shower or bath and toilet

TELEPHONE
01-47-34-70-47
FAX
01-40-56-07-91
EMAIL
hotelinnova@wanadoo.fr
INTERNET
www.innova-paris-hotel.com
CREDIT CARDS
MC, V
RATES
1–2 persons 81–110€, triple 125€, quad 140€; air-conditioning supplement 12€ per day; *taxe de séjour* included
BREAKFAST
Continental 8€ per person

Laurent Cuypers's Innova Hôtel has fifty-one rooms. The street-side lobby is fashionably done in the color of the moment: sunny yellow. Breakfast is served in another large room facing the street; tables are covered in paisley prints and the ladder-back chairs have raffia seats. The curtains here and throughout the hotel were made by M. Cuypers's mother, and when you consider the sheer volume of work involved, congratulations are in order for a job beautifully done.

A new high-tech elevator beats climbing seven floors, and now all the television reception is via cable. All rooms have now been rehabbed, rewired, and redecorated, but fortunately not repriced. What can you expect? Nonthreatening accommodations, and many rooms with ornate ceiling details, luggage space, a hard chair or two, and yellow, blue, white, or red color schemes. Those fronting on the busy street will be noisy. Despite the noise, I do like No. 60, which gives occupants a glimpse of *quartier* life from its balcony. There will be less noise in No. 67, a twin on the back with not only space and a sky view, but a large bathroom with a heated towel rack. Families will sleep peacefully in No. 53, where there is not much of a gripping view, but it is quiet. Management under the direction of Jean-Pierre Fromont (who is on deck in the morning) is exceptional.

FACILITIES AND SERVICES: Air-conditioning, direct-dial phone, elevator, hair dryer, Internet in lobby, TV with international reception, office safe (no charge)

NEAREST TOURIST ATTRACTIONS (LEFT BANK): Montparnasse

ENGLISH SPOKEN
Yes

L'HÔTEL DU BAILLI DE SUFFREN-TOUR EIFFEL
★★★ (3)
149, avenue de Suffren, 75015
Métro: Ségur, Sèvres-Lecourbe

25 rooms, all with shower or bath and toilet

The hotel honors the memory of Admiral Pierre André de Suffren, who was appointed Bailli (chief magistrate) of the order of Malta and then proceeded on a trail of adventures that ranged from Saint Tropez to the Caribbean.

The royal blue carpet at the door suggests the type of first-class treatment you will receive at this dignified hotel owned by M. and Mme. Tardif, who spent two years in Lafayette, Louisiana. Madame Tardif told me they are fond of Americans, adding, "We try to make all of our guests feel at home." Given the bushel basket of amenities and services they offer, they meet, and exceed, their goal.

Tradition reigns supreme, from the downstairs living room outfitted with comfortable sofas and chairs and a baby grand piano to the mirrored garden-theme dining room and the fabric-lined elevator, which delivers guests to the twenty-five individually decorated rooms, a few of which are designated nonsmoking. Each one, warmly enhanced by indisputably good taste and harmony, displays a successful mix of reproduction furniture, quality fabrics, and thoroughly modern bathrooms, all of which have excellent towels, plentiful mirrors, clothes drying line, and three-tiered basket serving as extra space for toiletries. Room 304 has a ship theme, carried out in the regal colors of gold, blue, and red, and a framed collection

TELEPHONE
01-56-58-64-64

FAX
01-45-67-75-82

EMAIL
bailli.suffren.hotel@wanadoo.fr

INTERNET
www.baillitoureiffel.com

CREDIT CARDS
AE, DC, MC, V

RATES
Single 125–135€, double 137–148€, connecting rooms (2–4 people) 258–266€; extra bed 20€; ask about special rates and weekend packages; *taxe de séjour* included

BREAKFAST
Continental 11.50€, small Continental in room 8.50€, per person

ENGLISH SPOKEN
Yes

of nautical knots. The wood-paneled bathroom has a walk-in tiled shower complete with a porthole mirror and a bench for those who prefer to sit while showering. A vintage ship's sign warns: "On the order, abandon ship. Women and children first, follow me, Your Captain." For families, Nos. 403 and 404 can be combined into a two-room apartment. I would be happy in No. 503, a single on the front with a slightly oriental caste suggested by the grass-cloth-covered walls and the Thai carved woodwork on the closet doors and over the bed. After a long day, it is nice to join other guests in the living room and share a glass of the hotel's own wine, which comes from vineyards in Aix-en-Provence, or have a quiet meal in the hotel dining room.

FACILITIES AND SERVICES: Air-conditioning, bar, dining room, direct-dial phone, elevator, hair dryer, Internet in lobby, laundry service, some magnifying mirrors, minibar, *peignoirs* (bathrobes) and slippers for VIPs, room service for light meals, TV with international reception, some trouser presses, room safe (no charge), several non-smoking rooms

NEAREST TOURIST ATTRACTIONS (LEFT BANK): Champ de Mars, Eiffel Tower, Invalides, UNESCO

MERCURE PARIS SAINT CHARLES ★★ (5)
37, rue St-Charles, at 36, rue Rouelle, 75015
Métro: Dupleix, Charles-Michels
30 rooms, all with shower or bath and toilet

TELEPHONE
01-45-79-64-15
FAX
01-45-77-21-11
EMAIL
H1928@accor-hotels.com
INTERNET
www.mecure.com
CREDIT CARDS
AE, DC, MC, V
RATES
Single 86–105€, double 105–123€; extra bed 30€; children under 12 free; *taxe de séjour* included
BREAKFAST
Buffet 10€ per person
ENGLISH SPOKEN
Yes

This hotel now has a new name and hotel affiliation, which has resulted in a new facade, new decor, new mattresses, and some new bathrooms, but one thing has not changed: the warm hospitality that owner Claire Fournerie extends to all her guests. To some, the location might be considered a tourist backwater; for others, it represents a change of pace and is a safe bet for those insisting on peace in noisy Paris. I like it not only because it is well maintained and executed, but because it offers a vantage on a calmer day-to-day Parisian life. In the place St-Charles, old men sit quietly under the shade of the chestnut trees reading their newspapers and talking about old times. Pretty young girls with long ribbons and smocked dresses roller-skate along the sidewalks, and matrons walk their little dogs. Hurrying housewives carrying brimming shopping baskets go from shop to shop picking just the right ingredients for their evening meal. For trips away from the hotel, the métro stop is only a five-minute walk, and the RER Line C to Versailles is close to the Eiffel Tower, both of which are about a fifteen-minute walk if you window-shop along the way.

The hotel is done simply but with good taste and style. Each floor is coordinated in a different color: blue, pink, or yellow. The concise, spotless rooms have country-style, pine built-in furniture, and matching draperies and bedspreads. The book-theme lobby overlooks a small garden, which is especially inviting in the spring and summer. Be sure to examine the framed needlepoints hanging here. If you look carefully, you will see one done by every member of the family. One dating from 1907 was made by Mme. Fournerie's grandmother when she was a little girl. Another by the fireplace was done by her brother-in-law, and her son, Vincent, stitched the one hanging by the door when he was eight.

Mme. Fournerie always takes a personal interest in her guests and their well-being, and she would like to know when guests find her through *Great Sleeps Paris,* so please tell her you did.

NOTE: The café/bar/rotisserie/brasserie next door is also owned by Claire and her husband, Martial. Drop in Monday through Friday between noon and 2 P.M. for a typical working-class lunch and order the daily special. They are open for business from 7 A.M. to 8 P.M. weekdays only, and they serve drinks and cold sandwiches when lunch is not in progress.

FACILITIES AND SERVICES: Air-conditioning, bar (next door), direct-dial phone, elevator, hair dryer, laundry service, minibar, TV with international reception, no safe

NEAREST TOURIST ATTRACTIONS (LEFT BANK): Eiffel Tower, Champ de Mars

PRACTIC HÔTEL (NO STARS, 13)
20, rue de l'ingénieur Robert Keller, 75015
Métro: Charles-Michels; RER Javel–André Citroën
38 rooms, 27 with shower or bath and toilet

For a cheap bed in the fifteenth arrondissement, the Practic Hôtel, just behind the Centre Beaugrenelle shopping complex, attracts a loyal band of regulars who are looking to cut accommodation corners in order to enjoy other aspects of their stay in Paris. While it's definitely not a candidate for those who revel in Louis XV or Madame Pompadour surroundings, the hotel displays few of those depressing, exhausted, faded, and snagged interiors that plague many other budget addresses in Paris. You will be welcomed by one of the sweetest managers this side of heaven, Mme. Agnes Bihan, who

TELEPHONE
01-45-77-70-58

FAX
01-40-59-43-75

EMAIL
hotel.practic.hotel.15@wanadoo.fr

INTERNET
www.practichotel.fr

CREDIT CARDS
AE, MC, V

RATES
1–2 persons 47–81€, 3–4 persons 98€, suite 110€; extra bed 17€; free public showers; *taxe de séjour* included

BREAKFAST
Continental 8€ per person
ENGLISH SPOKEN
Yes

has been behind the desk since 1962. The owner of the hotel is Agnes Pouloux, who took over the reigns from her parents and grandparents who built the hotel. With help and encouragement from her husband, she is slowly improving the hotel by adding bathrooms and following a regular schedule of maintenance.

In dull brown with industrial-strength carpeting, the entry has a vase of flowers and old prints of Paris scattered around—the space definitely is past its due-date and needs a new look. But you don't live in the entry, so just keep going. I am a fan of No. 50, a double with soft gray-and-blue carpet, two desks, a view of the skyscraper apartments that line the Seine, and a beautiful bathroom with a stall shower. Double-glazed windows help to keep the noise levels down. Room 52 is just as nice and has plenty of space. Room 57, coordinated in yellow and blue with a stall shower, sleeps one. Number 59 is a two-room suite (don't forget we are in a no-star here) with blond furniture. One room has twin beds, the other just one twin. The bathroom comes with soap and shampoo and shower doors, all for around 100€. What a deal! Eight rooms have courtyard views, but they are not too bad. Breakfast is served in a blue-and-white first-floor dining room and includes cheese, fruit compote, juice, croissants, and bread and jam—an unheard-of spread for a no-star hotel.

NOTE: *Great Sleeps Paris* readers can get 10 percent off room rates. Shoppers will want to know that one of the best Monoprix stores in Paris is nearby (see "Shopping," page 360).

FACILITIES AND SERVICES: Direct-dial phone, elevator, hair dryer available, Internet in lobby, TV with international reception, office safe (no charge)

NEAREST TOURIST ATTRACTIONS (LEFT BANK): None; must use public transportation

Sixteenth Arrondissement

Known as a sedate, posh, and old-moneyed sector, the sixteenth is the home of the BCBG *(bon chic bon genre)* crowd, otherwise known as French yuppies. This is stylish territory, bordered by the Bois de Boulogne and the River Seine. Here you will see luxurious apartments along with prostitutes in BMWs on the avenue Foch and at night in the Bois de Boulogne luring customers. The Bois de Boulogne also has two thousand acres of lakes, gardens, two racetracks, and the Jardin d'Acclimatation, a children's amusement park. Fashionable shops line the unhurried and uncrowded rue de Passy and the avenue Victor-Hugo. The Trocadéro, directly across from the Seine and the Eiffel Tower, is the name for the gardens around the Palais de Chaillot, an imposing two-winged building that houses four museums. The spectacular view from the steps of the Trocadéro at night, across the Seine to the Eiffel Tower, with the illuminated pools, fountains, and statues between, is one you must not miss. Neither do you want to miss the Marmottan Museum, which houses a magnificent display of Claude Monet's water lily canvases; the Guimet, which has a collection of oriental and Asian art; or the Maison de Balzac, the home where Honoré de Balzac lived and worked.

RIGHT BANK
Avenue Foch
Bois de Boulogne
Jardin d'Acclimatation
Maison de Balzac
Marmottan Museum
Musée Guimet
Palais de Chaillot
Passy
Trocadéro

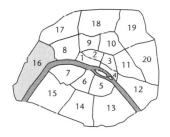

HOTELS IN THE SIXTEENTH ARRONDISSEMENT

Au Palais de Chaillot Hôtel ★★	258
Chambellan Morgane ★★★	259
Hôtel de Sévigné ★★★	259
Hôtel du Bois ★★★	261
Hôtel du Rond-Point de Longchamp ★★★	261
Hôtel Gavarni ★★★ ($)	262
Hôtel Keppler ★★	264
Hôtel Nicolo ★★	265
Hôtel Passy Eiffel ★★★	266
Hôtel Regina de Passy ★★★	266
Hôtel Résidence Foch ★★★	267
Hôtel Trocadéro La Tour ★★★	268
Hôtel Victor Hugo ★★★	268
Le Hameau de Passy ★★	269

OTHER OPTIONS
Camping Out

Les Campings du Bois de Boulogne	310

($) indicates a Big Splurge

Sixteenth Arrondissement

Bd. R. Wallace

Allée de Longchamp

Route de Suresnes

Allée de Longchamp

Boulevard Lannes

Av. Henri

Porte de la Muette

PL. DE COLOMBIE

BOIS

DE

BOULOGNE

Allée de la Reine Marguerite

Boulevard Suchet

Avenue Rachaël

Ch. Muette

La Muette Ⓜ

CARREFOUR DES CASCADES

Avenue de l'Hippodrome

Cloud

Av. de Ingres Beauséjour

Saint

Bd. Rue du

Rue de Ranelagh

Av. Mozart

Ranelagh Ⓜ

l'Assomption

Avenue

de

HIPPODROME D'AUTEUIL

Boulevard Suchet

Bd. de Montmorency

R. Jasmin

Mozart

Jasmin Ⓜ

Avenue

Rue La Fontaine

Théophile

Porte d'Auteuil

PL. DE LA PORTE DE D'AUTEUIL

Rue d'Auteuil Ⓜ

Michel Ange Auteuil Ⓜ

Av.

PL. DE BARCELONE Ⓜ

Avenue de la Porte d'Auteuil

Ⓜ Porte d'Auteuil

Église d'Auteuil Ⓜ

Boulevard

Porte Molitor

Murat

Ange

Michel Ange Molitor

Chardon Lagache

R. Mirabeau

Mirabeau

d'Auteuil

Rue Ⓜ Molitor

Avenue de

Rue du Château

Boulevard

Bd.

Michel

Lagache

Chardon

Versailles

Quai Louis Blériot

PARC ANDRÉ CITROËN

Avenue Robert Schuman

Exelmans Ⓜ Exelmans

Rue de

R. C. Farrère

PARC DES PRINCES

△ N

500 meters

Ⓜ Métro Station

● R.E.R. Station

Route de la Reine

Avenue

Pont de Garigliano

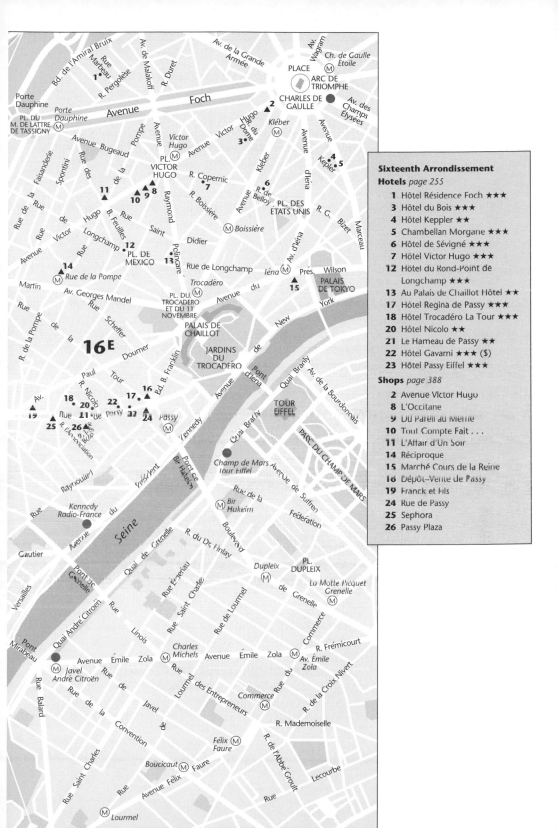

Sixteenth Arrondissement

Hotels *page 255*

1 Hôtel Résidence Foch ★★★
3 Hôtel du Bois ★★★
4 Hôtel Keppler ★★
5 Chambellan Morgane ★★★
6 Hôtel de Sévigné ★★★
7 Hôtel Victor Hugo ★★★
12 Hôtel du Rond-Point de
   Longchamp ★★★
13 Au Palais de Chaillot Hôtel ★★
17 Hôtel Regina de Passy ★★★
18 Hôtel Trocadéro La Tour ★★★
20 Hôtel Nicolo ★★
21 Le Hameau de Passy ★★
22 Hôtel Gavarni ★★★ ($)
23 Hôtel Passy Eiffel ★★★

Shops *page 388*

2 Avenue Victor Hugo
8 L'Occitane
9 Du Pareil au Même
10 Tout Compte Fait . . .
11 L'Affair d'Un Soir
14 Réciproque
15 Marché Cours de la Reine
16 Dépôt-Vente de Passy
19 Franck et Fils
24 Rue de Passy
25 Sephora
26 Passy Plaza

AU PALAIS DE CHAILLOT HÔTEL ★★ (13)
35, avenue Raymond Poincaré, 75116
Métro: Trocadéro, Victor-Hugo

28 rooms, all with shower or bath and toilet

TELEPHONE
01-53-70-09-09

FAX
01-53-70-09-08

EMAIL
hapc@wanadoo.fr

INTERNET
www.chaillotel.com

CREDIT CARDS
AE, DC, MC, V

RATES
Single 105€, double 120€, junior suite for 1–3 people 140€; extra bed 15€; free for child under 5 years; parking 16€ per day; discounts for readers of this guide; *taxe de séjour* 0.65€ per person, per day

BREAKFAST
Continental 9€ per person

ENGLISH SPOKEN
Yes

For up-to-the-minute appeal in an area not known for budget anything, look no further than this hotel. Two brothers, Cyrille and Thierry Pien, who received their master's in business administration in the United States, joined forces and completely gutted and revamped the twenty-eight-room hotel, which is nicely situated between the Trocadéro and the Champs-Élysées. The results are impressive, and so are the prices, especially for readers of *Great Sleeps Paris* who, upon mentioning this book, receive a 10 percent discount throughout the year on any Saturday or Sunday, and a whopping 15 percent anytime between July 15 and August 31. Reserve now, and don't forget to say who sent you!

From beginning to end, the hotel is a model of postmodern, casual French chic. Two potted trees frame the red awning entrance. To one side is a little summer terrace where breakfast can be served; otherwise, breakfast takes place in a yellow marbleized room with a half-mirrored wall reflecting five tables and armchairs. The bright bedrooms combine wicker with bold colors and have flashy bathrooms that include tubs and/or showers with corner shelves for shampoo and soap. All doubles face the street. There are five rooms similar in size to No. 34, a junior suite on the back. I like the walk-in closet, the small sitting area with red detailing around the ceiling, and the Dufy print over the bed. These rooms also have twin beds that can be adapted to a king. In addition to the usual amenities, the hotel offers room service for drinks, laundry service, and PC compatible plugs. For the area, it is impossible to imagine a better value.

FACILITIES AND SERVICES: Direct-dial phone, elevator (to half-landings; a few stairs required), hair dryer, laundry service, private parking by advance reservation, room service for drinks, TV with international reception, room safe (no charge)

NEAREST TOURIST ATTRACTIONS (RIGHT BANK): Trocadéro, shopping along avenue Victor-Hugo and in Passy, Arc de Triomphe, Champs-Élysées

CHAMBELLAN MORGANE ★★★ (5)
6, rue Kepler, 75116
Métro: George-V, Charles-de-Gaulle-Étoile

20 rooms, all with shower or bath and toilet

In 1984, when I began writing my Paris hotel guide, I fell in love with a little hotel in the sixteenth arrondissement called Résidence Morgane. It was run by a petite *grand-mère* who pampered her guests beyond the call of duty. She would make an omelet at midnight, keep your messages, forward your mail, and do your laundry and ironing if asked. When I returned a year later, Madame had left and the hotel had been taken over by a noncaring owner. Five years later, on a hunch, I decided to recheck the hotel, and I am so glad I did. Although Madame had not come back, new owners had masterminded a renovation that turned the hotel into the epitome of three-star elegance and classic luxury. Things have not changed since: the owner and her staff still do their utmost to please their international clientele.

The stage is set by the entrance and lobby, done in yellow and blue with white enamel woodwork and beautifully upholstered Louis XV–style antiques. The only holdover from the past is the old, copper Morgane nameplate by the front doorstep. Well-lighted halls lead to stylishly outfitted bedrooms with silk wall coverings, matching quilted spreads and curtains, a comfortable chair, and efficient mirrored and marbled bathrooms. Lower rates in July and August and on weekends, subject to availability, make this more attractive to a wider audience.

FACILITIES AND SERVICES: Air-conditioning, bar, conference room, direct-dial phone, elevator, hair dryer, laundry service, minibar, room service, TV with international reception, office safe (no charge), several nonsmoking rooms

NEAREST TOURIST ATTRACTIONS (RIGHT BANK): Champs-Élysées, Arc de Triomphe, Musée Guimet, Trocadéro

TELEPHONE
01-47-20-35-72

FAX
01-47-20-95-69

EMAIL
chambellan.morgane@wanadoo.fr

INTERNET
www.hotel-paris-morgane.com

CREDIT CARDS
AE, DC, MC, V

RATES
1–2 persons 145–160€; *taxe de séjour* included

BREAKFAST
Buffet 9.15€ per person

ENGLISH SPOKEN
Yes

HÔTEL DE SÉVIGNÉ ★★★ (6)
6, rue de Belloy, 75116
Métro: Bossière, Kléber

30 rooms, all with shower or bath and toilet

"My sole occupation is the immense joy of receiving you into my home." These words, written by the Marquise de Sévigné in a letter to her daughter on February 5, 1674, echo the welcome extended today by the owner of this hotel, Mme. Boileau, and her professionally trained staff.

TELEPHONE
01-47-20-88-90

FAX
01-40-70-98-73

EMAIL
hotel.de.sevigne@wanadoo.fr

INTERNET
www.hotel-paris-desevigne.com

CREDIT CARDS
AE, DC, MC, V

RATES
1–2 persons 145–170€; extra
bed 35€; see Website for
special promotions; parking
30€ per day; *taxe de séjour*
included
BREAKFAST
Continental 10€ per person
ENGLISH SPOKEN
Yes

Who was the Marquise de Sévigné? Marie de Rabutin-Chantal, Marquise de Sévigné (1626–1696), was a prolific letter writer who shed light on the political, social, and literary aristocratic life of high society and the nobility of the seventeenth century during the reign of Louis XIV. Orphaned at an early age, she was educated by her grandmother, who began a convent in Paris. The street, rue de Belloy, was on the edge of the convent's fields. Madame de Sévigné lived an elegant life in castles around France, but from 1677 to 1696, when she was in Paris, she held court in her town house, the Hôtel Carnavalet near the place des Vosges. The building is now a fascinating museum dedicated to the history of Paris from pre-Roman times to the present. Mme. Sévigné's desk and some of her letters are on display at the museum.

The hotel is an excellent three-star value and loaded with extras. The five floors of the hotel are named after people and places of significance in Madame Sévigné's life. The first floor is named after her husband's castle, Les Rochers; the second, Carnavalet, her home in Paris; third, Bourbilly, her grandmother's castle; fourth, Le Comte Roger Bussy-Rabutin, her cousin; and the fifth, Le Château de Grignan, her daughter's castle where Madame died. All thirty rooms are designed to cater to the comfort and well-being of their guests. In each you will find a large desk with both fax and computer connections, balconies on the second and fifth floors, plenty of closet and luggage space, and bathrooms with magnifying mirrors, space for toiletries, and good lighting. The rooms designated *chambres de charme* have all the above plus newer furnishings and a richer color scheme. The hotel is across from the place des États-Unis, a quiet green square only a few minutes from all the pomp and circumstance awaiting you along the Champs-Élysées.

FACILITIES AND SERVICES: Direct-dial phones in rooms and bathrooms, elevator, hair dryer, Internet in lobby, laundry service, minibar, parking by advance reservation only, TV with international reception and pay-for view channels, room service for light snacks, room safe (large enough to store a computer, no charge)

NEAREST TOURIST ATTRACTIONS (RIGHT BANK): Champs-Élysées, Arc de Triomphe, Musée Guimet, Trocadéro

HÔTEL DU BOIS ★★★ (3)
11, rue du Dome, at 29, avenue Victor-Hugo, 75116
Métro: Kléber, Charles-de-Gaulle-Étoile
41 rooms, all with shower or bath and toilet

For a stay on the exclusive avenue Victor-Hugo, just ten boutiques down from the Arc de Triomphe, and a direct RER line to Disneyland Paris from place d'Étoile, many consider the Hôtel du Bois to be a reasonable choice. The entrance to the hotel is in a passageway reached by steep steps from the avenue Victor Hugo level or on an upper level from rue Lauriston. You will recognize the hotel by the pretty planter boxes under each window. Owner David Byrne (see Hôtel Queen Mary, page 213) has done a commendable job in renovating the hotel. He has shined, polished, and redone all the rooms with coordinating Laura Ashley–style fabrics and mahogany furniture as well as a framed Hôtel du Bois poster and a watercolor painting. He also refitted the reception and breakfast areas, and gave the old bathrooms quickie facelifts, added enclosed showers, a shelf for toiletries, and a hook on the back of the door. Aside from reasonable rates for the high-rent area, the rooms are on two floors with no elevator. The best choices are the superiors with a bath and shower that face rue du Dome. The standard rooms with a shower are on the back side of both floors of the hotel, and look onto an ugly, depressing, blank gray wall; those on avenue Victor Hugo will experience some noise. The bottom line: This makes an affordable choice in an otherwise expensive neighborhood, but choose your room carefully.

FACILITIES AND SERVICES: Direct-dial phone, no elevator (2 floors), fans, hair dryer, Internet in lobby, minibar, TV with international reception and pay-per-view channels, room safe (no charge)

NEAREST TOURIST ATTRACTIONS (RIGHT BANK): Champs-Élysées, Arc de Triomphe, shopping along avenue Victor-Hugo

TELEPHONE
01-45-00-31-96
FAX
01-45-00-90-05
EMAIL
hoteldubois@wanadoo.fr
INTERNET
www.hoteldubois.com
CREDIT CARDS
AE, DC, MC, V
RATES
1–2 persons 105–167€; extra bed 48€; lower off-season Rates; *taxe de séjour* included
BREAKFAST
Buffet 12€, Continental 6€, per person
ENGLISH SPOKEN
Yes

HÔTEL DU ROND-POINT DE LONGCHAMP ★★★ (12)
86, rue de Longchamp, at place de Mexico, 75116
Métro: Trocadéro, Victor-Hugo
58 rooms, all with shower or bath and toilet

The area around the hotel dates back to the thirteenth century, when Longchamp was an austere abbey surrounded by fields and meadows belonging to a few farms. One of them was located right next to the hotel, and there is a plaque to commemorate Boileau and La

TELEPHONE
01-45-05-13-63
FAX
01-47-55-12-80
EMAIL
hotel.long@wanadoo.fr
INTERNET
www.rd-pt-longchamp.fr

CREDIT CARDS
AE, DC, MC, V
RATES
Single 98–194€, double 131–
200€, suite 335€; lower off-
season rates; *taxe de séjour*
included
BREAKFAST
Buffet or Continental in room
13€ per person
ENGLISH SPOKEN
Yes

Fontaine, two great French writers who came here to buy their fresh milk. Today the area is known as the "Golden Triangle," comprised of the Champs-Élysées, Trocadéro, and avenue Victor Hugo, and understandably one of the most prestigious residential areas in the capital.

The owner of this wonderful hotel, Gerard Dumontant, served as the president of the independent hoteliers in France, so you can imagine that his hotel reflects only the best . . . and let me assure you it does. The hotel appeals to traditionalists looking for exceptional value, classic service, and a multitude of facilities. The ground floor consists of a plant-filled lounge, a bar, and a billiards room with soft leather armchairs. Some of the rooms are decidedly Louis XIV, with four-poster beds and heavy curtains swooping from floor to ceiling. Others reflect more modern tastes. Views of the Eiffel Tower can be seen from rooms ending with the number 2. Several are superbly planned for businesspeople. These rooms double as an office and sitting room during the day and have a comfortable pull-down Murphy bed at night. All rooms have international television reception, air-conditioning, computer modems, and fabulous marble bathrooms.

FACILITIES AND SERVICES: Air-conditioning, bar, direct-dial phone, elevator, hair dryer, Internet in lobby, laundry services, minibar, room service, TV with international reception, room safe (no charge)

NEAREST TOURIST ATTRACTIONS (RIGHT BANK): Trocadéro, shopping on avenue Victor-Hugo

HÔTEL GAVARNI ★★★ ($, 22)
5, rue Gavarni, 75116
Métro: Passy
21 rooms and 4 suites, all with shower or bath and toilet

TELEPHONE
01-45-24-52-82
FAX
01-40-50-16-95
INTERNET
www.gavarni.com
CREDIT CARDS
AE, DC, MC, V
RATES
Single 99–150€, double 150–
200€, junior suite (1–2 people)
275–300€, suite (1–4 people)
450€; extra bed 20€; ask about
special promotional offers, and
always mention this guide
when reserving for possible
discounts; *taxe de séjour* included

The Hôtel Gavarni, glowing from a magnificent renovation, is a textbook example of what an owner with an unlimited budget can do if given the opportunity. The result of a year of hard work and an unimaginable amount of money is the boutique hotel of your dreams, offering discerning guests a sanctuary of privacy, discretion, and tranquillity in twenty-one rooms and four high-tech, sumptuous suites. The oohs-and-ahs begin in the wood-paneled ground floor lobby. On one side is a bar with a curved and tufted yellow and deep-rose banquette highlighted by four large, amusing paintings of ladies who lunch. Frosted-glass doors lead to the breakfast room that has five floral glass-top tables facing a mirrored buffet and a small garden and veranda beyond. This pretty *bijou* setting is accented by a large canvas of fruits and leaves painted in bold orange, yellow, and burgundy. The sitting area is lined with bookshelves filled with original editions of nineteenth-century French authors and framed copies of letters from Napoléon to Josephine. The hotel and street it is on are named after Gavarni, a nineteenth-century critic and lithographer. Hanging on each floor are one or two of his original signed and numbered lithographs.

The amenities in the suites rival, and in some cases exceed, what you would expect to find at a five-star deluxe property. Each suite has something special to offer, and is linked to its name by its hanging artwork, the logo etched on the shower doors, and the color-coordinated marble bathrooms. The Eiffel Suite has a stained-glass ceiling and crystal chandelier in the entryway, which leads to an enormous sitting room with a pair of closets flanking a working marble fireplace. The walls and ceiling are hand-detailed; the paintings and prints are of this famous landmark. Two inviting easy chairs and a large sofa provide luxurious comfort. The views of the Eiffel tower and the rooftops of Paris are through three windows or from chairs on the balcony. From the queen-size bed, you can stretch out and watch programming on the enormous plasma television set that has an LCD screen and DVD player. There is also DSL Internet access, a laptop available in case you did not bring your own, and a remote control panel with which guests can operate all the electrical components of the suite with a flick of a switch or turn of a dial. The marble bathroom has an artist-inspired ceiling filled with fluffy clouds over the Jacuzzi bathtub, separate shower with a shower head the size of a Frisbee, and double sinks. Guests in all suites have a special valet assigned to assist them from 7:30 A.M. to 10:30 P.M. in fulfilling any needs or requests they may have. Other suites include the Trocadéro and Vendôme, both junior suites with a courtyard view, and Versailles-Trianon, a full suite with a view of the Eiffel Tower. Not everyone is going to check into one of these suites, but the services and high-quality surroundings continue in the deluxe and standard rooms, which are personalized and customized right down to the soap and the matchboxes. Depending on size and location, many have marble fireplaces, granite bathroom sinks, draped beds, crystal lights, hand-painted ceilings, large television sets, and all the necessary technical hookups to stay connected.

BREAKFAST
Buffet 14€ per person
ENGLISH SPOKEN
Yes

Times change and so do places, and not always the way we want them to. Nowhere is this more evident than at the Hôtel Gavarni, which has gone from a modest family-owned two-star with soul to a high-stepping strutter with all the bells and whistles. Though the Hôtel Gavarni has gained a formal glow, it has lost that indefinable quality: soul.

FACILITIES AND SERVICES: Air-conditioning, bar, conference rooms, direct-dial phone with direct line in each room, fax in suites, elevator (to half-landings; a few stairs required), hair dryer, Internet in lobby, DSL in suites, laptops and printers available to rent, laundry service, minibar, room service, TV with satellite, room safe (no charge)

NEAREST TOURIST ATTRACTIONS (RIGHT BANK): Shopping in Passy, Trocadéro

HÔTEL KEPPLER ★★ (4)
12, rue Kepler, 75116
Métro: George-V, Kléber

49 rooms, all with shower or bath and toilet

For a two-star, family-run hotel, the Keppler offers much more than just a cheap sleep in a tony location. The lobby shows off a pretty fireplace and a small corner bar. The large dining room has upholstered mahogany chairs, blue walls, and Levelor blinds along the street-side windows. For the price, you cannot expect luxurious rooms with deep-pile carpeting and designer fabrics. They do, however, offer good value. The charmless surroundings have efficiently modern desks and chairs and ample closet and drawer space. Four rooms have balconies. On last inspection a few were showing signs of age, especially No. 6, which needed a new rug, the walls redone, and something else done with a big piece of cloth that tried to masquerade as a bedspread. Room 35 is acceptable, provided you don't mind the closet being in the blue bathroom. A team of uniformed housekeepers wearing beepers keeps everything shipshape, and management keeps an ear tuned to inappropriate noise. There are many repeat guests, and it is easy to understand their loyalty to this hidden Parisian value, where reservations (and a deposit) are required far, far in advance of your stay.

FACILITIES AND SERVICES: Bar, direct-dial phone, elevator, hair dryer available, luggage storage, TV with international reception, room safe (no charge)

NEAREST TOURIST ATTRACTIONS (RIGHT BANK): Arc de Triomphe, Champs-Élysées, Musée Guimet, Trocadéro

TELEPHONE
01-47-20-65-05
FAX
01-47-23-02-29
EMAIL
hotel.keppler@wanadoo.fr
INTERNET
www.hotelkeppler.com
CREDIT CARDS
AE, MC, V
RATES
1–2 persons 85€; extra bed 30% of room rate; baby cot 8€; *taxe de séjour* included
BREAKFAST
Continental 6€ per person
ENGLISH SPOKEN
Yes

HÔTEL NICOLO ★★ (20)
3, rue Nicolo, 75116
Métro: Passy, La Muette

28 rooms, all with shower or bath and toilet

Join diplomats visiting the nearby embassies, delegates to the European Organization for Economic Cooperation and Development, and other savvy travelers by staying at the discreetly hidden Hôtel Nicolo in the center of Passy. Because the hotel is set back off the street, your room will be blissfully free from the usual symphony of Parisian street noises. Now, it is even more alluring because the farsighted owner swept out the funky furnishings, flocked wallpaper, dated colors, and woebegone bathrooms. The results—and the prices—can be summed up in one word: Wow!

The mood suggests the Far East, particularly Indonesia. Check into No. 5, where the bed is backed by an antique Balinese screen and the wall is decorated by a colorful parrot print. Green and soft beige fabrics blend well with the overall oriental feeling in this room. In addition to a chest of drawers, a comfortable armchair, and excellent work space, you will have a fabulous new bathroom with double sinks and an Indonesian hand-painted floral frame around the mirror. The Art Deco suite, No. 21, sleeps four and is done in yellow with a collection of parrot prints decorating the walls. A sunken oval bathtub is the highlight of the lovely bathroom, which also has an Indonesian frame around the mirror. Another two-room suite, No. 32, has a sitting room with a blue leather sofa and armchair, and an antique Indonesian desk. The room overlooks the quiet courtyard, which is shaded in the spring and summer by a leafy green tree. Red-hot-red is the color of choice in the dramatic No. 11, which has a desk with brass pulls; black, red, and white prints of French villages; and a marvelous tub in the bathroom. Red is also the color of the ornate headboard in No. 24, which has a yellow bird print and a large framed poster portrait of Brad Pitt. Go figure!

FACILITIES AND SERVICES: Direct-dial phone, elevator (to most floors), ceiling fans, hair dryer, private parking (advance reservation only), TV with international reception, room safe (no charge)

NEAREST TOURIST ATTRACTIONS (RIGHT BANK): Passy, shopping, Trocadéro

TELEPHONE
01-42-88-83-40

FAX
01-42-24-45-41

EMAIL
hotel.nicolo@wanadoo.fr

INTERNET
www.123france.com

CREDIT CARDS
AE, DC, MC, V

RATES
1–2 persons 98–154€, triple 160€, suite or family room 174€; lower prices in Aug; parking 13€ per day; *taxe de séjour* 0.78€ per person, per day

BREAKFAST
Continental 6€ per person

ENGLISH SPOKEN
Usually

HÔTEL PASSY EIFFEL ★★★ (23)
10, rue de Passy, 75116
Métro: Passy, La Muette

TELEPHONE
01-45-25-55-66
FAX
01-42-88-89-88
EMAIL
passyeiffel@wanadoo.fr
INTERNET
www.passyeiffel.com
CREDIT CARDS
AE, DC, MC, V
RATES
Single 128€, double 130–
140€, triple 145€, suite 215€;
taxe de séjour included
BREAKFAST
Buffet 10€ per person
ENGLISH SPOKEN
Yes

50 rooms, all with shower or bath and toilet

The Hôtel Passy Eiffel, on the main street in Passy, provides a firsthand look at one of Paris's most exclusive neighborhoods, which has some of the best shopping you can find. The marble-lined foyer and lobby open onto a glassed-in winter garden with six rooms facing it. To one side is the sitting area with a comfortable sofa, an Internet terminal, and small bar. On the other is the breakfast room where a buffet is served every morning. Wood-beam ceilings add a sense of dimension to the variety of rooms, which are tasteful, clean, and very comfortable with pleasing views. Ten new bathrooms boast showers with massage jets. I think Nos. 1, 2, and 7 on the ground floor are very nice. They are viewless but are large enough that you won't feel closed in. Number 57 is a large twin on the back with a big bathroom and lots of space. If you are traveling solo, No. 61, also on the back, has good space, but for a view, balcony, bathtub, and more light, request No. 54. From the other top-floor rooms on the side street, guests can watch the elevator scale the Eiffel Tower as it takes tourists to the top. For breakfast, be sure to sample some of the honey bottled directly from the owner's beehives.

FACILITIES AND SERVICES: Air-conditioning, bar, direct-dial phone, elevator (to most floors), hair dryer, Internet in lobby, minibar, TV with international reception, office safe (no charge)

NEAREST TOURIST ATTRACTIONS (RIGHT BANK): Passy, shopping, Trocadéro

HÔTEL REGINA DE PASSY ★★★ (17)
6, rue de la Tour, 75116
Métro: Passy

TELEPHONE
01-55-74-75-75
FAX
01-40-50-70-62
01-45-25-23-78
EMAIL
regina@gofornet.com
INTERNET
www.hotel-paris-passy.com
CREDIT CARDS
AE, MC, V

64 rooms, all with shower or bath and toilet

Built in 1930 for the International Exhibition, this hotel is high on the Right Bank of the Seine across from the Eiffel Tower. The almost-grand lobby has a staircase framed by signed stained-glass windows. The hotel rooms have been restyled, and they are sophisticated and ultra-modern with geometric prints, chrome-and-leather furniture, and modern bathrooms. Closet and living space is ample. Fifteen rooms have small balconies where you can step out and look over the Passy neighborhood with the Eiffel Tower in the distance. One penthouse apartment and a junior suite, both with private rooftop terraces, boast impressive furnishings, marble bathrooms (one with a sunken tub), small bars, fully equipped kitchens, and enough wardrobe space for most of us to unpack and stay a year. Staff attitude has improved one hundred percent.

FACILITIES AND SERVICES: Air-conditioning, bar, direct-dial phone, elevator, hair dryer, laundry service, minibar, TV with international reception and pay-for-view channels, room safe (no charge)

NEAREST TOURIST ATTRACTIONS (RIGHT BANK): Passy, shopping, Trocadéro

RATES
1–2 persons 125–145€, junior suite 185€, penthouse apartment 277€; *taxe de séjour* included

BREAKFAST
Buffet 14€, Continental in room 10€, per person

ENGLISH SPOKEN
Yes

HÔTEL RÉSIDENCE FOCH ★★★ (1)
10, rue Marbeau, 75116
Métro: Porte Dauphine; RER Neuilly–Porte Maillot–Palais de Congrès
25 rooms, all with shower or bath and toilet

This hotel is on a quiet little street in one of Paris's most sought-after residential districts, not too far from Porte Maillot and the Palais de Congrès. It is run by the lovely Nelly Rolland, former owner of the Hôtel Gavarni (see page 262). Nelly is a graduate of the hotel management school in Lausanne, Switzerland, and she is young and full of life and new ideas. Her charm and innate sense of style are evident the minute you meet her, and it is clear they have carried over into her second hotel. The reception, lobby, and bar areas have an open plan layout looking onto a well-tended atrium garden. The rooms have character, thanks to decorative color combinations of golden orange, soft green, Williamsburg blue, and white. The traditional furnishings and matching fabric treatments are interspersed with contemporary conveniences such as built-in minibars, good drawer and closet space, and tiled baths with plenty of fluffy towels. Some, including the smallest doubles, have tip-of-the-Eiffel-Tower views. At press time, four suites were scheduled for complete renovation. Knowing Nelly, I'm sure they will be sensational, so be sure to inquire.

FACILITIES AND SERVICES: Air-conditioning in suites and superior rooms, bar, direct-dial phone, elevator (to each half-floor almost to top; some stairs required), hair dryer, Internet (DSL) in lobby, laundry service, minibar, room service, TV with international reception, room safe (no charge)

NEAREST TOURIST ATTRACTIONS (RIGHT BANK): Bois de Boulogne; otherwise, must use public transportation

TELEPHONE
01-45-00-46-50

FAX
01-45-01-98-68

INTERNET
www.residencefoch.com

CREDIT CARDS
AE, DC, MC, V

RATES
1–2 persons: standard room 127–150€, deluxe room 190–250€, family room (1–4 people) 150–250€, *taxe de séjour* included

BREAKFAST
Buffet 11€ per person

ENGLISH SPOKEN
Yes

HÔTEL TROCADÉRO LA TOUR ★★★ (18)
5 bis, rue Massenet, 75116
Métro: Passy, La Muette
41 rooms, all with shower or bath and toilet

TELEPHONE
01-45-24-43-03
FAX
01-45-24-41-39
EMAIL
trocadero-la-tour@magic.fr
INTERNET
www.hotels-la-tour.com
CREDIT CARDS
AE, DC, MC, V
RATES
Single 126€, double 142€,
triple 170€; extra bed 27€;
baby bed free; *taxe de séjour*
0.86€ per person, per day
BREAKFAST
Continental 9€ per person
ENGLISH SPOKEN
Yes

For a beautiful stay in Paris on a tranquil street in Passy, I like the formal Trocadéro La Tour, a family-owned hotel since the 1930s. The well-heeled French executive clientele appreciate the serene neighborhood close to the *bon ton* Passy shopping district; the professional services of the uniformed hotel staff—especially Thay, the courteous receptionist who has worked the desk for two decades—and, above all, the prices. These travelers know that if the hotel were in a more mainstream location, the prices would be nearly double.

Downstairs, the public rooms are paneled in rich walnut. Soft seating and a small library along one wall create an appealing English intimacy. Morning croissants are served in a little alcove overlooking a colorful patio. All the comfortable rooms are well furnished and impeccably maintained. Room 70, a corner double, has its own balcony looking out to the Eiffel Tower and La Tour Montparnasse, and a walk-in closet that is almost as large as some hotel rooms I have stayed in. If traveling alone, request No. 71, a top-floor single with an Eiffel Tower view terrace, or No. 51 with a small balcony, double closet with shelves, and a large bathroom. If quiet and space are top priorities, No. 25, a back sunny twin with two big windows, has a triple-drawer marble dresser, workable desk, three chairs, double luggage rack, and a bathroom with two sinks, a large tub, and oversize towels.

FACILITIES AND SERVICES: Air-conditioning, bar, direct-dial phone, elevator, hair dryer, Internet in lobby, laundry service, minibar, TV with international reception and pay-per-view movies, room safe (no charge), 10 nonsmoking rooms

NEAREST TOURIST ATTRACTIONS (RIGHT BANK): Passy, shopping, Trocadéro

HÔTEL VICTOR HUGO ★★★ (7)
19, rue Copernic, 75116
Métro: Victor-Hugo, Boissière
75 rooms, all with shower or bath and toilet

TELEPHONE
01-45-53-14-91 (for reservations), 01-45-53-76-01; toll-free in the U.S. and Canada
(Best Western) 800-528-1234
FAX
01-45-53-69-93
EMAIL
paris@victorhugohotel.com

This hotel has been a stalwart in the sixteenth arrondissement for years. For a long time, it seemed to be resting on its laurels and mired in the past. Not any more, thanks to the vim, vigor, and vitality of the second generation who have stepped up to the plate and now are in charge. Frankly, I hardly recognized the place: halls repainted and recarpeted, and hung with paintings and art posters. The still spotless and spacious rooms have shed their matronly appearance, especially the fifteen on the sixth and seventh floors, which overlook the vast reservoir behind the hotel. Rooms 75 and 77 are good examples. Both are large doubles with a balcony and reservoir views, and big new bathrooms. Harmonious, pastel colors in cream and rose with lavender accents add to their peaceful ambience. For views of the Eiffel Tower, ask for No. 73, which has four windows and a granite bathroom. Still firmly in place is the very pretty garden breakfast room, with its flagstone floor and fruit and vegetable vendor cart that is used for the buffet. Adding to the outdoor theme are the green lattice walls, Villeroy and Boch fruit-basket china, and Parisian poster–wrapped pillars that look just like those you see on all the city streets. An English club–style bar is lined with books by Victor Hugo and other great French writers. When I inquired about the fabulous kitsch carved Eiffel Tower light on the bar, I was told that *everyone* asks about it . . . and wants one, too. Sorry, this is a one-of-a-kind treasure the owner found in a flea market. Also still very much in evidence is the excellent staff, most of whom have been loyal employees for decades.

FACILITIES AND SERVICES: Air-conditioning, bar, direct-dial phone, elevator, hair dryer, Internet in lobby, Jacuzzis in some superior rooms, laundry service, mini-bar, tea- and coffee-making facilities, TV with international reception and pay-per-view movies, room safe (no charge), nonsmoking rooms on the 3rd and 7th floors and No. 82

NEAREST TOURIST ATTRACTIONS (RIGHT BANK): Champs-Élysées, Arc de Triomphe, shopping on avenue Victor-Hugo, Trocadéro

LE HAMEAU DE PASSY ★★ (21)
48, rue de Passy, 75116
Métro: Passy, La Muette
32 rooms, all with shower or bath and toilet

Hidden in a garden walkway off the busy rue de Passy, Le Hameau de Passy is a snappy two-star in this posh pocket of Paris. All the rooms face the garden and are done in the same style, with stark white walls, open closets, soft sheer curtains at the windows, and harmonizing fabrics and carpets. Ground-floor rooms in the three-story buildings have metal security shutters, but I still suggest asking for something on a higher floor. If you are

INTERNET
www.victor-hugo-hotel.com

CREDIT CARDS
AE, DC, MC, V

RATES
Single 140€, double 157–178€, triple 180–189€, deluxe 222€, suite 300€; always ask about special promotional and off-season rates; *taxe de séjour* included

BREAKFAST
Buffet 12€, Continental in room 10€, per person

ENGLISH SPOKEN
Yes

TELEPHONE
01-42-88-47-55

FAX
01-42-30-83-72

EMAIL
hameau.passy@wanadoo.fr

INTERNET
www.hameaudepassy.fr

CREDIT CARDS
AE, DC, MC, V

RATES
Single 98€, double 107–112€,
triple 126€, quad 142€; *taxe de
séjour* included

BREAKFAST
Complimentary Continental

ENGLISH SPOKEN
Yes

lucky and land in Building 4, the elevator takes the strain out of climbing up several flights to your room. Otherwise, in Buildings 1, 2, and 3, you will pay the same price and still have to hike up a winding outdoor metal stairway to get to your room. If this sort of exercise does not bother you, and you want to be only a whisper away from all the great shopping in Passy—including the designer discount and consignment clothing stores along rue de la Tour and rue de la Pompe—then consider this hotel. For details about this special shopping niche in Paris, see page 338.

FACILITIES AND SERVICES: Direct-dial phone, elevator (in one building only), hair dryer, TV with international reception, room safe (10€ for length of stay)

NEAREST TOURIST ATTRACTIONS (RIGHT BANK): Passy, shopping, Trocadéro

Seventeenth Arrondissement

The better half of the seventeenth arrondissement extends west from boulevard Malesherbes to the Arc de Triomphe. To the east and toward Gare St-Lazare, it is full of questionable characters dealing in the shadier side of life and residentially challenged local slummers and *clochards* (transients, bums) relaxing in doorways, guzzling beer or cheap wine. This is an area to avoid. The main attractions are the proximity to the Champs-Élysées and the Palais des Congrès, a convention center with restaurants, movie theaters, and the pickup and drop-off point for passengers going to and from Roissy–Charles-de-Gaulle Airport. There are many fine hotels in the better section of the arrondissement and the areas around them are safe. From many of them there is easy access to two RER lines: the A-line that goes to Disneyland-Paris and the C-line to Versailles, as well as excellent bus and métro connections to more tourist-inspired parts of Paris.

RIGHT BANK
Arc de Triomphe
Champs-Élysées
Palais des Congrès
Parc de Monceau

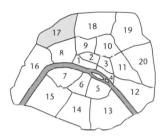

Hotels in the Seventeenth Arrondissement

Centre Ville Étoile ★★★	**274**
Hôtel Astrid ★★★	**274**
Hôtel Balmoral ★★★	**275**
Hôtel Bélidor ★ (¢)	**276**
Hôtel de Banville ★★★ ($)	**277**
Hôtel des Deux Acacias ★★	**279**
Hôtel Eber Monceau ★★★	**280**
Hôtel Étoile Péreire ★★★	**281**
Hôtel Flaubert ★★	**282**
Hôtel Jardin de Villiers ★★★	**283**
Hôtel La Régence Étoile ★★★	**283**
Hôtel Regent's Garden ★★★ ($)	**284**
Hôtel Villa des Ternes ★★★	**285**

Other Options
Apartment Rental Agencies
Irving Hutton Ltd	**302**

($) indicates a Big Splurge; (¢) indicates a Cheap Sleep

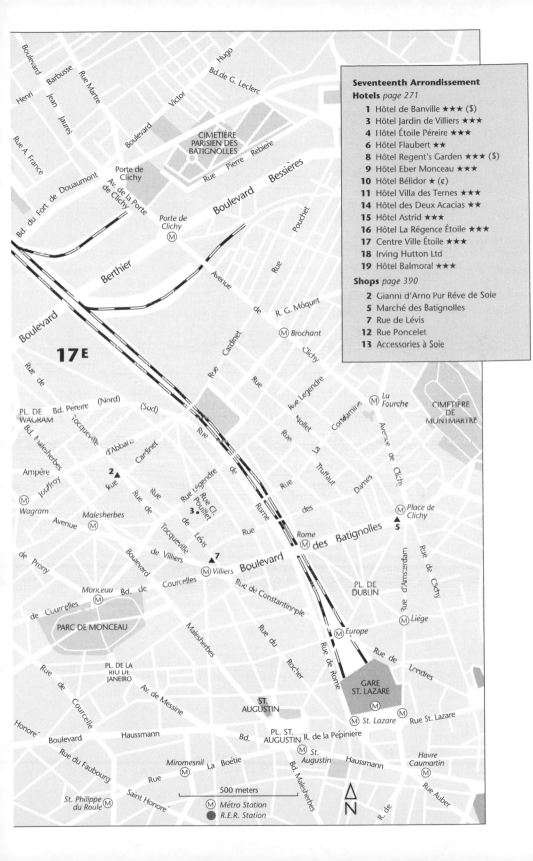

Boulevard Barbusse
Henri Jean Jaurès
Rue Martre
Victor
Hugo
Bd. de G. Leclerc
Rue A. France
Boulevard
CIMETIÈRE PARISIEN DES BATIGNOLLES
Rue Pierre Rebière
Bd. du Fort de Douaumont
Porte de Clichy
Av. de la Porte de Clichy
Porte de Clichy Ⓜ
Boulevard Bessières
Rue Pouchet
Berthier
Boulevard
Avenue
de
Rue
R. G. Môquet
Rue Cardinet
Ⓜ Brochant
Rue
Clichy
17ᴱ
Boulevard
Rue de
Rue
Rue Legendre
Rue Lemercier
Ⓜ Lu Fourche
CIMETIÈRE DE MONTMARTRE
PL. DE WAGRAM
Bd. Pereire (Nord)   (Sud)
Tocqueville
d'Abbans
Cardinet
Nollet
Contamine
Avenue de Clichy
Bd. Malesherbes
Rue
de
La
Truffaut
Dames
Ampère
Jouffroy
Rue
2 ▲
Rue Legendre
Rue Cl. Pouillet
3 ●
Rome
Ⓜ Place de Clichy
Ⓜ Wagram
Avenue
Malesherbes Ⓜ
Rue de Tocqueville
de Lévis
Rue
Rome
des
5 ▲
de Prony
Boulevard
de Villiers
▲ 7
Rome Ⓜ des Batignolles
Rue d'Amsterdam
Rue de Clichy
de Courcelles
Monceau Ⓜ
Bd. de
Courcelles
Ⓜ Villiers
Boulevard
Rue de Constantinople
PL. DE DUBLIN
Ⓜ Liège
PARC DE MONCEAU
Malesherbes
Rue du Rocher
Europe
Rue de Londres
PL. DE LA RIO DE JANEIRO
Rue de Courcelle
Av. de Messine
Rue de Rome
GARE ST. LAZARE
ST. AUGUSTIN
Honoré
Boulevard
Haussmann
Bd.
PL. ST. AUGUSTIN
R. de la Pépinière
Ⓜ St. Lazare
Ⓜ St. Augustin
Rue St. Lazare
Havre Caumartin
Rue du Faubourg
Miromesnil
La Boétie
Ⓜ
St. Augustin
Haussmann
Rue Auber
St. Philippe du Roule Ⓜ
Saint Honoré
500 meters
△ N
Ⓜ Métro Station
● R.E.R. Station
R. de

Seventeenth Arrondissement

Hotels *page 271*

1 Hôtel de Banville ★★★ ($)
3 Hôtel Jardin de Villiers ★★★
4 Hôtel Étoile Péreire ★★★
6 Hôtel Flaubert ★★
8 Hôtel Regent's Garden ★★★ ($)
9 Hôtel Eber Monceau ★★★
10 Hôtel Bélidor ★ (¢)
11 Hôtel Villa des Ternes ★★★
14 Hôtel des Deux Acacias ★★
15 Hôtel Astrid ★★★
16 Hôtel La Régence Étoile ★★★
17 Centre Ville Étoile ★★★
18 Irving Hutton Ltd
19 Hôtel Balmoral ★★★

Shops *page 390*

2 Gianni d'Arno Pur Rêve de Soie
5 Marché des Batignolles
7 Rue de Lévis
12 Rue Poncelet
13 Accessories à Soie

CENTRE VILLE ÉTOILE ★★★ (17)
6, rue des Acacias, 75017
Métro: Argentine, Charles-de-Gaulle-Étoile; RER Neuilly–Port Maillot–Palais des Congrès
16 rooms, all with shower or bath and toilet

TELEPHONE
01-58-05-10-00
FAX
01-47-54-93-43
EMAIL
hcv@centrevillehotels.com
INTERNET
www. paris-hotel-centre.com
CREDIT CARDS
AE, DC, MC, V
RATES
Single 125€, double 140–160€; extra bed 20€; lower off-season rates; *taxe de séjour* 0.92€ per person, per day
BREAKFAST
Continental 10€ per person
ENGLISH SPOKEN
Yes

Original, smart, and stylish are three words that well describe this Art Deco–inspired hotel close to the Arc de Triomphe and the Champs-Élysées. A three-story glass atrium joins the two buildings, which house only sixteen sleeping slots. An interesting collection of American cartoon prints enlivens the lobby and hallways. I also like the four Alsatian ceramic heaters that help keep the reception warm. The small masculine rooms, which haven't a ruffle in sight, display a judicious use of space and employ hard-edge colors of red, black, blue, and white along with black lacquered furnishings. Tiled and mirrored bathrooms are modern, with adequate shelf space and rolling carts for toiletries and stretch tubs for leisurely bathing. The personable staff goes beyond the call of duty in welcoming guests and pampering them in the evening by closing the curtains, turning down the beds, and putting a chocolate on the pillow. Nonsmokers will be happy to know there are five rooms exclusively reserved for them.

FACILITIES AND SERVICES: Air-conditioning, direct-dial phone, elevator, hair dryer, laundry service, minibar, *peignoirs* (bathrobes), TV with international reception, room safe (no charge), 5 nonsmoking rooms

NEAREST TOURIST ATTRACTIONS (RIGHT BANK): Arc de Triomphe, Champs-Élysées, Palais des Congrès

HÔTEL ASTRID ★★★ (15)
27, avenue Carnot, 75017
Métro: Charles-de-Gaulle-Étoile, Argentine
41 rooms, all with shower or bath and toilet

TELEPHONE
01-44-09-26-00
FAX
01-44-09-26-01
INTERNET
www.hotel-astrid.com
CREDIT CARDS
AE, DC, MC, V
RATES
Single 108€, double 122–123€, triple 150€, quad 157€; lower off-season rates; *taxe de séjour* included
BREAKFAST
Buffet 8€ per person
ENGLISH SPOKEN
Yes

Florence Guillet heads one of the best family-run hotels in Paris. Started by her grandfather in 1937, the Hôtel Astrid provides comfortable, moderately priced accommodations in this top-drawer part of the city. The colors throughout the hotel are cheerfully appropriate and blend well with the furnishings. Each floor has a theme. Starting from the top you have modern painters, then nature and birds, Paris bridges, Impressionists, and old Paris. Two of the nicest bedrooms have small balconies for viewing the Arc de Triomphe. The rooms are upgraded continually, and each one has its own individual ambience. Room 21, pictured on the hotel's brochure, is a nice choice because it is bigger. It has two armchairs, a marble fireplace, twin brass beds, good closets, and a new bathroom. I also like No. 25, which is done in pastels and has desk and luggage space, two chairs, and a double bed. The spotless bathroom has a stall shower, hooks, and a shelf for toiletries. Room 42, done in florals, and Room 36, a large, two-bedroom triple, also come with a large tile-and-granite bathroom.

Finally, the hotel is only about a five-minute walk from the Air France bus stop for Roissy–Charles-de-Gaulle Airport, so if you're traveling light, you can save money on cab fare. The RER stations are within a five-to-ten-minute walk.

FACILITIES AND SERVICES: Conference room (seats 6–8), direct-dial phone, elevator, hair dryer, laundry service, TV with international reception, room safe (no charge)

NEAREST TOURIST ATTRACTIONS (RIGHT BANK): Arc de Triomphe, Champs-Élysées, Palais des Congrès

HÔTEL BALMORAL ★★★ (19)
6, rue du Général Lanrezac, off avenue Carnot, 75017
Métro: Charles-de-Gaulle Étoile, Argentine
57 rooms, all with shower, bath, and toilet

The Hôtel Balmoral is well located, well run, and well priced.

First, the location. It is a three-minute walk to the métro, the RER Line A, and the Air France bus stop for Roissy–Charles-de-Gaulle Airport. You are only minutes away from the Champs-Élysées, boutique shopping along Victor Hugo, or great discount shopping on rue de la Pompe.

Guests immediately feel at home in the traditionally decorated rooms with their gracious period furnishings, old-fashioned comforts, and all the required modern amenities, including several reserved for nonsmoking guests. Business guests will appreciate No. 29, a large double with adequate space to spread out papers, plug in a computer, and comfortably work. Standard twin and double rooms make good use of space and overlook an interior courtyard, but they have dated one-inch-square mustard-colored tiles in the bathrooms. Speaking of color, if you like hot orange surroundings, check into No. 25, a deluxe double with two closets, a quiet outlook, and a large double-sink bathroom. Downstairs is a paneled breakfast room with leather hobnail chairs and a red bar with small alcove seating that seems perfect for a quiet drink or a confidential conversation with someone special.

TELEPHONE
01-43-80-30-50
FAX
01-43-80-51-56
EMAIL
balmoral@wanadoo.fr
INTERNET
www.hotel-balmoral.com
CREDIT CARDS
AE, DC, MC, V
RATES
Single 113–123€, double 138–153€, triple 163–178€; *taxe de séjour* included
BREAKFAST
Continental 10€ per person
ENGLISH SPOKEN
Yes

Finally, the price. This is an area full of three-star hotels that cost twice as much and offer half as much comfort and certainly less value. The Balmoral wins on all three counts.

FACILITIES AND SERVICES: Air-conditioning, bar, direct-dial phone, elevator, hair dryer, laundry service, magnifying mirror, minibar, porter, trouser press, TV with international reception, room safe (no charge), several nonsmoking rooms

NEAREST TOURIST ATTRACTIONS (RIGHT BANK): Arc de Triomphe, Champs-Élysées, Palais des Congrès

HÔTEL BÉLIDOR ★ (¢, 10)
5, rue Bélidor, 75017
Métro; Porte Maillot; RER Line C Neuilly–Port Maillot–Palais des Congrès
47 rooms, 18 with shower or bath and toilet, 3 rooms with shower only

TELEPHONE
01-45-74-49-91
FAX
01-45-72-54-22
CREDIT CARDS
V
RATES
Single 38–57€, double 43–63€; *taxe de séjour* included
BREAKFAST
Continental 5€ per person
ENGLISH SPOKEN
Yes

No serious economy-minded traveler in Paris can afford to overlook the Bélidor. A stay here provides you with a clean bed in a decent area just around the corner from the Palais des Congrès. It is an old-fashioned sort of hotel that has been in the same family over half a century. Their furniture fills the first of two breakfast rooms; it is the prettiest and is nonsmoking. In the second, there is a marble-and-brick fireplace and an upright piano, and you can smoke, but the ambience just isn't there. The owner is just as sweet as ever, the room colors and patterns are just as mixed, and all the electrical switch boxes are openly displayed over the radiator by the reception desk. The rooms are neat as pins, and those with bathtubs are larger than many two- and three-star rooms costing twice as much. However, if you book a bathless room, plan on sponge bathing because there is no communal *douche* (shower) in this hotel. If you can live with this, then please don't let the orange chenille and nontouristy location further deter you. After only a ten- or fifteen-minute métro journey, you can be standing under the pyramid at the Louvre, floating down the Seine on a *bateau mouche,* or strolling through the most romantic streets in St-Germain-des-Prés. It is crucial to remember to plan ahead for this one because it is booked weeks in advance all during the year.

NOTE: The RER station at Porte Maillot is enormous, so look for these directions in French for the correct exit: *sorti côté Paris, bd. Gouvion-Saint-Cyr côté impairs.* (In other words, exit on the Paris side of the métro station, on the odd-numbered side of boulevard Gouvion St-Cyr.)

FACILITIES AND SERVICES: Direct-dial phone, no elevator (5 floors), no communal showers, no TV, office safe (no charge)

NEAREST TOURIST ATTRACTIONS (RIGHT BANK): Palais des Congrès exhibition and convention center; otherwise, must use public transportation

HÔTEL DE BANVILLE ★★★ ($, 1)
166, boulevard Berthier, 75017
Métro: Porte-de-Champerret
38 rooms, all with shower or bath and toilet

The classic Hôtel de Banville is my idea of a wonderful, personalized Parisian hotel. It was built in 1928 by architect Jerome Bellat, who designed many of the magnificent buildings for which the seventeenth arrondissement is famous. From the beautiful lobby to the rooms filled with family antiques and heirlooms, you can tell immediately that this is a hotel where the owners know and care very much about what they are doing. The hotel has developed a large following of appreciative international guests who applaud the efforts of owner Mme. Lambert, her daughter, Marianne Lambert-Moreau, and their right-hand man, Jean-Pierre, who is also the talented artist who did all the paintings that hang throughout the hotel. A portrait of their dog, Charlie, the hotel mascot, is displayed over the reception desk. Charlie is very popular; in fact, he even receives mail from guests who have grown to love him during their repeated visits. Mme. Lambert grew up in the hotel business, and all of her family is involved in the industry in some way. Her background and expertise, combined with her impeccable good taste, are evident everywhere you look. Mme. Lambert told me, "I want this hotel to be like a private house, and I think I have realized my wish." I agree without question.

Every time I visit the hotel, I think, this is it. What more can be done to improve on perfection? And each time I find wonderful new additions. On this visit, it was the newly done staircase and hallways leading to bright-red enameled doors with gold fittings and the room number illuminated on the floor. On another visit, it was the stunning new bathrooms and a series of superior rooms, each with its own name and something outstanding and unique to recommend it. If someone had told me before I saw these absolutely fabulous bathrooms that an

TELEPHONE
01-42-67-70-16
FAX
01-44-40-42-77
EMAIL
hotelbanville@wanadoo.fr
INTERNET
www.hotelbanville.fr
CREDIT CARDS
AE, DC, MC, V
RATES
Standard: single 140€, double 165€; 1–2 persons, superior rooms: La Chambre d'Amélie, La Chambre Théodore de Banville, Les Pastourelles, and Les Preludes 200€; (smallest superior) La Chambre de Julie 116€; suite: L'Appartement de Marie 260€; parking 18€ per day; *taxe de séjour* included
BREAKFAST
Buffet 13€ per person
ENGLISH SPOKEN
Yes

open bathroom (with separate, enclosed toilets, of course) subtly incorporated into the main room itself would work, I would have had my doubts. I can assure you that they work magnificently . . . and I predict once you see these, you will be devising ways to remodel your own.

L'appartement de Marie is a suite aptly subtitled, "an invitation to dream." It is true. I cannot imagine a dream more romantic or wonderful that this fabulous two-room suite, with a wrought-iron canopy bed surrounded in soft, white gauze netting. The large, sunny sitting room, done in contemporary brick and beige colors, has a sweeping view from the Arc de Triomphe to the Tour Montparnasse. If the view does not capture your attention, the imaginative open bathroom surely will. Located within the suite—not behind closed doors—it features a double antique marble sink and huge bathtub, with an enclosed toilet to one side. Honeymooners should reserve the captivating *La Chambre d'Amélie,* where glass doors open onto a terrace filled with sunshine all day long. Seated in a comfortable chair, your vista includes Montmartre, the Eiffel Tower, Arc de Triomphe, Montparnasse, and more. In the open marble bathroom, you can float in the huge footed tub and see the Eiffel Tower. The *Théodore de Banville* room incorporates wood found in country farms to separate the bedroom from its walk-through marble bathroom. Here you see the tip of the Eiffel Tower from your balcony and sleep in a bed covered with a snowy white quilt. *Les Pastourelles* are also a series of superior rooms. It is impossible to select a favorite, but No. 1, with its red bathtub on legs, is very appealing. I also like the antique lamps, good desk space, and the red painted-wood backdrop behind the bed. Room 73 has a floral theme. It nicely sleeps three in quilt-covered beds, and has a big blue and white bathroom with flower accents. Room 74, with an Eiffel Tower view, is a double with gold-trimmed white furnishings. The red-and-white-striped carpet and barely gray wall coverings keep it elegantly casual. For a modern approach to living, book No. 62, done in gray-and-blue stripes. The simple wood headboard matches the bedside tables and desk. The chrome-fitted bathroom has a floating sink, large glass-enclosed shower, and a mirrored black-and-white mosaic-tile bath. Even the smallest room in the hotel, *La Chambre de Julie,* is done with elegance and gentle charm. Each year five new rooms are created. Notice I did not say redone—because they are true works of art worthy of a feature article in *Architectural Digest*. Even if you do not stay in one of the superior rooms, it would be impossible to be disappointed in any of the rooms in this outstanding hotel.

Breakfast is also special at the Banville. You can order a basic Continental or something more interesting: the *Dietetique* (which features wheat bread and yogurt), or go all out and have the *Pleinform,* which means sausage, eggs, and fruit juice along with your croissants and coffee.

The hotel is located on a busy boulevard lined with plane trees. The métro is close, and you can take the RER to the Musée d'Orsay and St-Michel or to Versailles. For buses, the No. 92 puts you at Étoile and the No. 84 drops you at place de la Concorde.

FACILITIES AND SERVICES: Air-conditioning, bar, two direct-dial phones per room, elevator (to most floors), hair dryer, Internet in lobby, parking can be arranged, some *peignoirs* and magnifying mirrors, porter, 24-hour room service for light meals, TV with international reception, room safe (no charge)

NEAREST TOURIST ATTRACTIONS (RIGHT BANK): None; must use public transportation

HÔTEL DES DEUX ACACIAS ★★ (14)
28, rue de l'Arc-de-Triomphe, 75017
Métro: Charles-de-Gaulle-Étoile, Argentine
31 rooms, all with shower or bath and toilet

Never mind its rather plain atmosphere—this choice will please bean counters wanting to stay within a certain budget and still be conveniently close to the Champs-Élysées and two convenient RER lines. It is owned by members of the Roubache family, who have fluffed and dusted it since taking over a few years ago from Mme. Delmas who ran it for seventy years and resisted change with an iron-willed determination. In back of the reception desk you will notice a huge map of the Paris métro system that dates back to the time that Mme. Delmas's parents owned the hotel. Fortunately, the Roubaches kept it for posterity . . . if not for nostalgic reasons.

No one could ever call this modest place modern, but now one can certainly call it improved in almost all respects. Upstairs, new paint, carpets, bedspreads, and redone bathrooms have perked up most of the rooms. Room 12, a frankly feminine roost, is done in soft yellow with a white metal and brass-tipped bed. Room 14 is in

TELEPHONE
01-43-80-01-85

FAX
01-40-53-94-62

EMAIL
hotelacacias@voila.fr

CREDIT CARDS
AE, MC, V

RATES
1–2 persons 85 110€, triple 115€, quad 150€; *taxe de séjour* 1€ per person, per day

BREAKFAST
Continental 7€ per person

ENGLISH SPOKEN
Yes

desert sand and has lots of closet and shelf space for the price, but it has an older bathroom. Room 18 is a very tight quad, but better as a triple; it has a new bathroom. The prize for the best remake goes to No. 50, with blue and white *toile de jouy* patterned wall covering, white wicker furniture, and a marble sink in the bathroom. The least expensive rooms are Nos. 52, 54, 56, and 58. These top-floor perches are not only cheap, but sunny and cheerful. Bathrooms are elfin, but at these rates you are lucky to have a shower and toilet to call your own. Hopefully, the upholstery and curtains in the sitting area adjoining the lobby are scheduled for renewal. At the moment, nothing matches, and the sofa belongs on the curb. However, look on the bright side: you are not living here, but in a sensibly priced, renewed room upstairs.

NOTE: Enclosed public parking is available across the street.

FACILITIES AND SERVICES: Direct-dial phone, elevator, hair dryer available, TV with international reception, no safe

NEAREST TOURIST ATTRACTIONS (RIGHT BANK): Champs-Élysées, Arc de Triomphe

HÔTEL EBER MONCEAU ★★★ (9)
18, rue Léon-Jost, 75017
Métro: Courcelles

18 rooms, all with shower or bath and toilet

TELEPHONE
01-46-22-60-70

FAX
01-47-63-01-01

INTERNET
www.hotelseber.com

CREDIT CARDS
AE, DC, MC, V

RATES
1–2 persons 120–150€, suite 210–250€; extra bed 25€; *taxe de séjour* included

BREAKFAST
Continental served all day 12€ per person

ENGLISH SPOKEN
Yes

Travelers longing for peace and quiet have at their disposal a group of French hotels whose owners have taken a vow of silence. The Hôtel Eber Monceau is one of the 275 members of Relais du Silence, an association of individually owned hotels dedicated to providing a silent and calm atmosphere where guests can feel at home. The entrance is along a tiled walkway that opens onto a beamed salon centered around a Henri II carved wooden fireplace. To the left of the reception desk is an inviting bar and breakfast area with comfortable armchairs. In back is a green patio, where metal tables and chairs are set out on warm days for al fresco breakfasts. The rooms tend to be small and are decorated in light beiges with good-looking American art prints and posters on the walls. The family rooms feature not only two rooms, but two bathrooms. In Room 55, guests have a lovely terrace that's shaded by an awning in the summer. There is no view, but there is plenty of light . . . and of course, peace and quiet. Many of the hotel clientele are from the world of fashion or entertainment, not a group known for its introverted behavior. However, owner Jean-Marc Eber and his diligent manager, Martin Duprez, say that those who want nonstop excitement should stay in St-Germain-de-Prés.

You will need public transportation for most things on a tourist agenda, but it might be interesting to walk by 25, rue de Chazelles, about two blocks away, to see where the Statue of Liberty was originally built. A photo of it under construction hangs by the hotel elevator. Also on display around the hotel are photos of the statue in varying stages of development and the signatures of those who attended the completion ceremonies.

M. Eber now has a second hotel, the Hôtel Eber Mars, not far from the Eiffel Tower (see page 188).

FACILITIES AND SERVICES: Air conditioning, bar, direct-dial phone, elevator, hair dryer, laundry service, minibar, room service from area restaurants, TV with international reception, office safe (no charge)

NEAREST TOURIST ATTRACTIONS (RIGHT BANK): Parc de Monceau

HÔTEL ÉTOILE PÉREIRE ★★★ (4)
146, boulevard Péreire, 75017
Métro: Péreire

26 rooms, all with shower or bath and toilet

The Étoile Péreire is a sophisticated hotel offering modern luxury at affordable prices. Occupying a distinctive building that is hard to identify as a hotel, it has benefited from several remodeling projects, and now from a new, enthusiastic owner, Laury Duquesnoy. Unfortunately, this attitude is not always extended by the reception staff, who can be icy and aloof.

The rooms all overlook a courtyard and are individually decorated around a specific color or theme. The result is a mixture of modern touched with the fanciful. The largest selections are the two-story duplexes with air-conditioning, ceiling fans, and skylights. Otherwise, the rooms are very nice but naturally smaller. In No. 205, a double, the green walls and latticework create a gardenlike feeling, and in No. 206, six wild animal prints define the room. No matter where you land, your bathroom will be modern and well supplied with Roger and Gallet products. Breakfasts are served in a white-and-gray basement dining room that displays the art of Jean Marais. Booths designed for two line the walls, and down the center is a communal table with silver leather

TELEPHONE
01-42-67-60-00

FAX
01-42-67-02-90

INTERNET
www.etoilepereire.com

CREDIT CARDS
AE, DC, MC, V

RATES
Single 130€, double 150€, duplex 205€; lower off-season rates; *taxe de séjour* included

BREAKFAST
Buffet 11€ per person

ENGLISH SPOKEN
Yes

chairs. Diners have a choice of twenty of the best quality jams, jellies, or honeys to accompany their croissants and fresh orange or grapefruit juice. If you want more, ham or bacon and eggs are available.

While hardly in the tourist mainstream, the hotel is close to Porte Maillot and the Air France air terminal. A large city park with tennis courts and plenty of picnic benches is across the street, as are several dining favorites listed in *Great Eats Paris*.

FACILITIES AND SERVICES: Air-conditioning in four duplexes, bar, direct-dial phone, elevator, hair dryer, Internet in lobby, laundry service, minibar in all rooms except singles with showers, TV with international reception, room safe (no charge), 2nd floor, superior rooms, and most of the duplexes nonsmoking

NEAREST TOURIST ATTRACTIONS (RIGHT BANK): Palais des Congrès

HÔTEL FLAUBERT ★★ (6)
19, rue Rennequin, 75017
Métro: Ternes, Péreire

TELEPHONE
01-46-22-44-35

FAX
01-43-80-32-34

INTERNET
www.hotelflaubert.com

CREDIT CARDS
AE, DC, MC, V

RATES
Single 90€, double 105€, triple 130€; extra bed 19€; *taxe de séjour* included

BREAKFAST
Buffet 8€ per person

ENGLISH SPOKEN
Yes

41 rooms, all with shower or bath and toilet

One of the most attractive features of this hotel is its lush garden overflowing with cascading vines and colorful seasonal plants. Bamboo furniture in the dining room and rooms lends a light tropical air. Singles or couples with scanty luggage, or who don't mind close quarters, can reserve one of the sunny yellow and blue rooms opening onto the garden. For a degree more space and better lighting, I like the top-floor *chambres*. Congenial owners, Françoise and Patrick Schneider, have refurnished the lobby with a leather couch and chair, placed stylized floral bouquets in the dining room, and added four new rooms. They couldn't make the existing ones bigger, but they did improve bathrooms and have polished the general decor. And they kept the most important aspect of the hotel: moderate prices that are good for this part of Paris, which is not known for much in the budget range.

FACILITIES AND SERVICES: Direct-dial phone, elevator, hair dryer, minibar, French TV, office safe (no charge)

NEAREST TOURIST ATTRACTIONS (RIGHT BANK): Parc de Monceau

HÔTEL JARDIN DE VILLIERS ★★★ (3)
18, rue Claude Pouillet, 71017
Métro: Villiers, Malesherbes

26 rooms, all with shower or bath and toilet

After years of keeping my eye on this neglected property, someone has finally turned it into the lovely hotel I always imagined it could be. New owner Pierre Bachy has completely and tastefully overhauled it from top to bottom, creating an intimate and welcoming hotel overlooking a flowered patio. The twenty-six rooms are harmoniously decorated in ruby, gold, and blue, with excellent beds and large screen television sets that have cable and pay-for-view movies. Even though they are a bit dark, I like the red and blue rooms on the back overlooking the quiet garden and patio. Throughout the hotel, M. Bachy has hung his marvelous collection of prints, some whimsical, others with animal themes. The stone *cave* breakfast room serves as a gallery for his own photography, which he shot during trips to the country town of Bracov in Romania, and in the wine regions of France. There is no denying the hotel is not close to the usual Parisian tourist hubs. It is, however, a block or two away from one of the most authentic shopping streets in the *quartier,* rue de Lévis, and within easy jogging or walking distance to the lovely Parc de Monceau.

FACILITIES AND SERVICES: Air-conditioning, direct-dial phone, hair dryer, elevator, Internet in lobby, laundry service, minibar, large screen TV with international reception and pay-for-view, office safe (no charge)

NEAREST TOURIST ATTRACTIONS (RIGHT BANK): Parc de Monceau

TELEPHONE
01-42-67-15-60

FAX
01-42-67-32-11

EMAIL
hoteljdv@wanadoo.fr

INTERNET
www.hotel-paris-etoile.com

CREDIT CARDS
AE, DC, MC, V

RATES
Single 85€, double 99€; *taxe de séjour* included

BREAKFAST
Complimentary Continental

ENGLISH SPOKEN
Yes

HÔTEL LA RÉGENCE ÉTOILE ★★★ (16)
24, avenue Carnot, 75017
Métro: Charles-de-Gaulle-Étoile, Argentine

38 rooms, all with shower or bath and toilet

The hotel is on the jacaranda-lined avenue Carnot, one of the spokes of the famed Étoile that radiates from the Arc de Triomphe. Because the prices are reasonable for a three-star, it is a good choice if you are a budget-minded business traveler in Paris and your work takes you to La Defense or the Palais des Congrès convention center. In addition, it is dependably decorated, and only a stone's throw or two from the bright lights and crowds along the Champs-Élysées.

A lighted nymphette statue in pristine alabaster greets guests as they enter the Directoire-style sitting

TELEPHONE
01-58-05-42-42

FAX
01-47-66-78-86

EMAIL
hotelregenceetoile@wanadoo.fr

INTERNET
www.parisplanet.com

CREDIT CARDS
AE, DC, MC, V

RATES
Single 95–120€, double 135–150€, triple 167€; *taxe de séjour* included

BREAKFAST
Buffet or Continental in room
11€ per person

ENGLISH SPOKEN
Yes

area, where comfortable velvet-covered armchairs and sofas flank a marble fireplace. A sparkling mirrored elevator takes you to the predictably acceptable upmarket rooms, which are in yellow and blue. Everything you need is here: air-conditioning, television with CNN, two chairs, a desk, a mirrored armoire, and heated towel racks in a twenty-first-century bathroom. Rooms with balconies on the fifth floors have views of the Arc de Triomphe. Breakfast is served downstairs in a room that has Turner-like murals wrapping around three of the walls, and the glass-top metal tables and chairs have gold-painted bows and garlands.

Also under the same ownership is the Hôtel Daguerre in the fourteenth (see page 239).

FACILITIES AND SERVICES: Air-conditioning, bar, direct-dial phone, elevator, hair dryer, Internet in lobby, laundry service, minibar, TV with international reception, room safe (no charge)

NEAREST TOURIST ATTRACTIONS (RIGHT BANK): Arc de Triomphe, Champs-Élysées

HÔTEL REGENT'S GARDEN ★★★ ($, 8)
6, rue Pierre-Demours, 75017
Métro: Ternes, Charles-de-Gaulle-Étoile (exit rue Carnot)
39 rooms, all with shower or bath and toilet

Originally built by Napoléon III for his personal physician, this building is now a refined garden hotel. Hidden behind a high brick wall, it seems a little far from the center of activity, but in fact, rue Pierre-Demours is only a few minutes' walk from the Champs-Élysées and the Arc de Triomphe.

The rooms offer affordable elegance with an ambiance of bygone days in Paris. They have been redone to reflect their former Second Empire glory and offer combinations of high-ceilings, crystal chandeliers, decorative moldings, marble fireplaces, brass or mahogany bedsteads, floor-to-ceiling mirrors, and authentic period furnishings. Many rooms connect for convenient family use, and several have large walk-in closets with built-in shelves and shoe racks. The bathrooms are luxuriously fitted with fluffy terry robes, heated towel racks, scented bubble bath and soaps, and plenty of light and mirrors for applying makeup. Most rooms overlook the garden, which is landscaped with large trees, stone statues, flowering walkways, and a terrace with tables for summer breakfasts or afternoon teas. Thank goodness the sitting

TELEPHONE
01-45-74-07-30; toll-free in the U.S. and Canada 800-528-1234 (Best Western)

FAX
01-40-55-01-42

EMAIL
hotel.regents.garden@wanadoo.fr

INTERNET
www.hotel-paris-garden.com;
www.bw-paris-hotel.com

CREDIT CARDS
AE, DC, MC, V

RATES
1–2 persons 118–220€, triple 180–255€, quad 265€; special promotional rates; parking 10€ per day; *taxe de séjour* included

BREAKFAST
Buffet 11€ per person

ENGLISH SPOKEN
Yes

areas and hallways have been redecorated. The fresh flower displays are as beautiful as ever, and the staff as helpful and courteous. Everyone who has ever stayed here, including myself, loves it, and you will, too.

FACILITIES AND SERVICES: Air-conditioning, direct-dial phone, elevator, hair dryer, Internet in lobby, minibar, parking in front on a first-come basis, TV with international reception, room safe (no charge), 2nd floor exclusively nonsmoking

NEAREST TOURIST ATTRACTIONS (RIGHT BANK): Champs-Élysées, Arc de Triomphe, Palais des Congrès

HÔTEL VILLA DES TERNES ★★★ (11)
97, avenue des Ternes, 75017
Métro: Porte Maillot (exit boulevard Gouvion St-Cyr)
39 rooms, all with shower or bath and toilet

The Villa des Ternes offers a good choice if you need to be near the Palais des Congrès or want to be within a five-minute walk to the RER. The classically restrained rooms, which are divided into three categories (standard, deluxe, and large), have an artistic rendering of a Parisian landmark or monument, tiled baths with a basket of toiletries, and a candy on your pillow. They offer guests a good use of space that is suitable for either a business sojourn or one dedicated to simply enjoying Paris. Quite frankly, if you are traveling solo, or don't mind being up close and personal with your traveling companion, the standard rooms offer all the amenities and for considerably less money. Downstairs, two book-lined sitting rooms face the street, and a cozy wood paneled bar doubles as a breakfast room. This is the sister hotel to the Hôtel Lenox Montparnasse (see page 247).

FACILITIES AND SERVICES: Air-conditioning, bar, direct-dial phone, elevator, hair dryer, laundry service, minibar, some trouser presses, TV with international reception, office safe (no charge)

NEAREST TOURIST ATTRACTIONS (RIGHT BANK): Palais des Congrès

TELEPHONE
01-54-81-94-94
FAX
01-53-81-94-95
EMAIL
hotel@hotelternes.com
INTERNET
www.villadesternes.com
CREDIT CARDS
AE, DC, MC, V
RATES
1–2 persons: standard 130€, club 162€, deluxe 216€; *taxe de séjour* included
BREAKFAST
Buffet 12€ per person
ENGLISH SPOKEN
Yes

Eighteenth Arrondissement

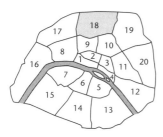

Montmartre is a rambling *quartier* full of contrasts, combining picture-postcard quaintness and razzle-dazzle. It was here that Toulouse-Lautrec drew the can-can girls dancing at the Moulin Rouge, and Picasso and Braque created Cubism at the Bateau-Lavoir on the place Émile Goudeau. The panoramic view from the steps of the Sacré Coeur at dawn or sunset, the many artists, and the intimate village atmosphere that prevails along the narrow streets—many of which are the same as when Utrillo painted them—continue to evoke the dynamic spirit and colorful past of this vibrant part of Paris, and it is a must-stop for any visitor. A walk down rue Lepic or rue des Abbesses, lined with bars and shops, leads to Pigalle, an area known for its bawdy nightlife. East of Montmartre is La Goutte d'Or, where many North Africans live, and to the north is the famed flea market at Porte de Clignancourt. Abbesses, one of the major métro stops, is one of two remaining métro stations that have their original Guimet-designed glass awning.

HOTELS IN THE EIGHTEENTH ARRONDISSEMENT

Ermitage Hôtel ★★	**287**
Hôtel Bonséjour (NO STARS, ¢)	**290**
Hôtel des Arts ★★	**290**
Hôtel le Bouquet de Montmartre ★★	**291**
Hôtel Prima-Lepic ★★	**292**
Hôtel Roma Sacré-Coeur ★★	**292**
Terrass Hôtel ★★★★ ($)	**293**
Timhôtel Montmartre ★★	**294**

OTHER OPTIONS

Apartment Rental Agencies
Paris Vacation Apartments	**304**

Bed and Breakfast in a Private Home
Alcôve & Agapes, Le Bed & Breakfast à Paris	**308**

Hostels
La Centrale de Réservations (FUAJ)	**313**
Le Village Hostel–Montmartre	**314**

Residence Hotels
Pierre & Vacances–Résidence Montmartre	**321**

($) indicates a Big Splurge; (¢) indicates a Cheap Sleep

ERMITAGE HÔTEL ★★ (5)
24, rue Lamarck, 75018
Métro: Lamarck-Caulaincourt, or bus No. 80 or No. 85

12 rooms, all with shower or bath and toilet

Close your eyes and imagine waking up in Paris in an antique-filled hotel high atop Montmartre with magical views over the entire city. Sound wonderful? It does, and it is all possible at the Ermitage, a poetic refuge run for many years by the engaging Maggie Canipel and her husband. Now they have retired, and their lovely daughter, Sophie, is in charge. However, Maggie still comes back now and then, and she fills in completely when Sophie and her family go on vacation. In the late 1970s, M. and Mme. Canipel sold everything they had and bought the Ermitage. They updated the plumbing, filled the old mansion with their collection of fine furniture, and began welcoming guests, continually outdoing themselves with their boundless energy and engaging smiles in order to make everyone feel at home. They succeeded beautifully and are now one of the favorite hotels for readers of *Great Sleeps Paris*. If this sounds appealing, book the Ermitage the minute you know the dates for your trip.

Any one of the twelve rooms could steal your heart, but my favorites are still Nos. 6 and 10—on the top floor, with tall French windows opening onto the morning sun and views of all Paris—and Nos. 11 and 12, which open onto their terrace garden. Number 2 is beautiful, with a magnificent set of nineteenth-century reproduction Louis XV bedroom furniture: a carved bed, two side tables, and a mirrored armoire. A crystal chandelier completes the picture.

True, you need strong legs and lungs to walk up the hill from the métro. However, once there, you will be richly rewarded not only by the warmth and hospitality of Sophie and her family, but by being in the center of one of the most picturesque parts of Paris. You can wander the streets once painted by Utrillo, peek into artists' ateliers, and have your portrait painted by one of the pseudo-artists lining the touristy place du Tertre. Decent restaurants in all price ranges are within easy walking distance (see *Great Eats Paris*).

FACILITIES AND SERVICES: Direct-dial phone, no elevator (3 floors), hair dryer, no TV, office safe (no charge)

NEAREST TOURIST ATTRACTIONS (RIGHT BANK): Montmartre, Sacré Coeur

TELEPHONE
01-42-64-79-22

FAX
01-42-64-10-33

CREDIT CARDS
None, cash only

RATES
Single 78€, double 88€, triple 115€, quad 130€; *taxe de séjour* included

BREAKFAST
Included, cannot be deducted

ENGLISH SPOKEN
Yes, also German and Italian

Eighteenth Arrondissement

Porte de St. Ouen

Porte de Clignancourt

1▲

Av. de la Porte de Clignancourt

Porte de St. Ouen Ⓜ

Boulevard Ney

Boulevard Ney

Porte de Clignancourt Ⓜ

Boulevard

PL. A. KAHN

Rue Ouen

Rue Leibniz

Rue Belliard

Rue Damrémont

Rue du

Rue Championnet

Rue Duhesme

Mont Cenis

R. Hermel

R.

Avenue de Saint

Rue Championnet

Rue Ordener

Vauvenargues

Poteau

du

Rue Ordener

Ⓜ Jules Joffrin

R. Guy Môquet

Ⓜ Guy Môquet

Rue

Rue

Marcadet

Duhesme

Rue

R. Hermel

Marcadet

Rue

Rue Lamarck

Rue Lamarck Caulaincourt

Rue

Rue Custine

Avenue de Saint Ouen

Joseph

de

Maistre

Rue Damrémont

Rue Caulaincourt

Ⓜ 2

Rue Caulaincourt

R. Lamarck

R. du Mont Cenis

R. Lamarck

Ramey

Ⓜ La Fourche

CIMETIÈRE DE MONTMARTRE

• 4

Av. Junot

Rue St. Vincent

• 5

Avenue de Clichy

Rue Caulaincourt

Rue

Rue

Rue

Lepic

Rue Tholozé

R.

R. Burq

Durantin

Lepic

Rue Ravignon

6 •

PL. DU TERTRE

SACRÉ CŒUR

Rue

R. Ch. Nodier

Muller

7 • 8 •

9 •

des

Abbesses

10 •

Rue des Trois Frères

R. Chappe

11 ▲

12 •

13 ▲

Rue

de

Ⓜ Blanche

R. Germain Pilon

PL. DES ABBESSES

Ⓜ Abbesses

R. des

14 •

Place de Clichy Ⓜ Ⓜ Bd.

PL. DE CLICHY

Rue

Clichy

15 ▲

d'Orsel

16 ▲

Rue

Avenue de Clichy

de

Douai

△ N

R. Houdon

Martyrs

Rue

17 •

Anvers Ⓜ

de

Rochechouart

Rue d'Amsterdam

Rue de Clichy

PL. PIGALLE

Ⓜ Pigalle

Boulevard

Rue

de

500 meters

Rue J. B. Pigalle

Avenue Trudaine

Ⓜ Métro Station

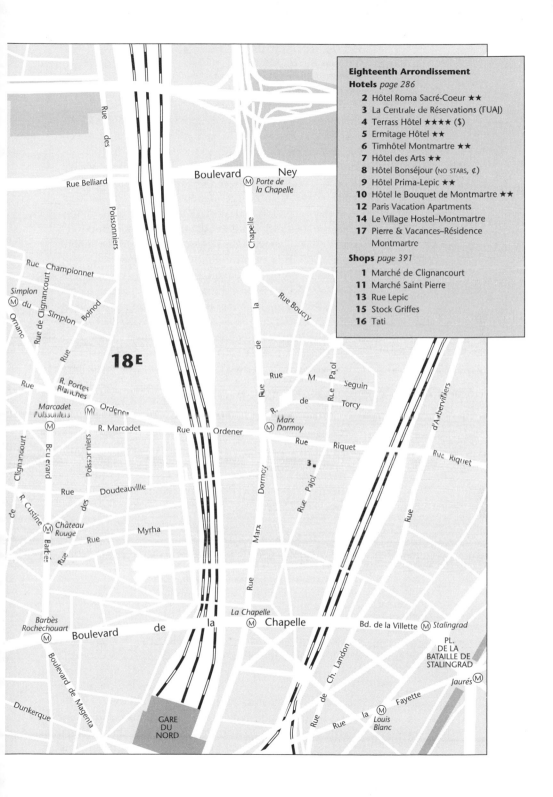

Rue des

Rue Belliard

Poissonniers

Boulevard Ney
Ⓜ Porte de
la Chapelle

Rue Championnet

Chapelle

Rue Boucry

Simplon
Ⓜ du
Simplon

Rue de Clignancourt

Boinod

la

de

18E

Ornano

Rue

R. Portes
Blanches

Rue
de
Seguin

Rue Pajol

M

Torcy

Rue

Marcadet
Poissonniers
Ⓜ

Ordener

R. Marcadet

Rue Ordener

Marx
Ⓜ Dormoy

Rue

Riquet

Rue Riquet

d'Aubervilliers

R.

Clignancourt

Bd Clignancourt

Poissonniers

Rue

des

Doudeauville

Dormoy

3.

Rue Pajol

Rue

R. Custine
Ⓜ Château
Rouge

Barbé

Rue

Myrha

Marx

Rue

de

La Chapelle

Barbès
Rochechouart
Ⓜ

Boulevard   de   la   Ⓜ Chapelle

Bd. de la Villette Ⓜ Stalingrad

PL.
DE LA
BATAILLE DE
STALINGRAD

Dunkerque

Boulevard de Magenta

GARE
DU
NORD

Rue de Ch. Landon

Rue

de

la

Ⓜ Louis
Blanc

Fayette

Jaurès Ⓜ

Eighteenth Arrondissement
Hotels *page 286*

   2 Hôtel Roma Sacré-Coeur ★★
   3 La Centrale de Réservations (FUAJ)
   4 Terrass Hôtel ★★★★ ($)
   5 Ermitage Hôtel ★★
   6 Timhôtel Montmartre ★★
   7 Hôtel des Arts ★★
   8 Hôtel Bonséjour (NO STARS, ¢)
   9 Hôtel Prima-Lepic ★★
  10 Hôtel le Bouquet de Montmartre ★★
  12 Paris Vacation Apartments
  14 Le Village Hostel–Montmartre
  17 Pierre & Vacances–Résidence
       Montmartre

Shops *page 391*

   1 Marché de Clignancourt
  11 Marché Saint Pierre
  13 Rue Lepic
  15 Stock Griffes
  16 Tati

HÔTEL BONSÉJOUR (NO STARS, ¢, 8)
11, rue Burq, 75018
Métro: Abbesses, Blanche
34 rooms, 5 with shower, none with bath or toilet

TELEPHONE
01-42-54-22-53
FAX
01-42-54-25-92
CREDIT CARDS
None, cash only
RATES
Single 25–38€, double 32–40€, triple 53€; extra bed 11€; shower 2€; *taxe de séjour* included
BREAKFAST
Continental 4€ per person
ENGLISH SPOKEN
Yes

Attention, tightwads! If money is your first concern, this old—but very clean—hotel should be one of your first picks. Occupying a hillside corner location, it is well protected from the low life and tourist mania that plagues Montmartre and its underbelly, Pigalle. It is run by Michel Bellart, who checks you in, and his hard-working wife, Amina, who is in charge of housekeeping and looking after their adorable little girl, Miriam. The clean rooms appeal to a young, intellectual, and sometimes impoverished crowd of international guests, who cheerfully ignore the mishmash of furniture and do not mind using hall facilities, or going to the first-floor communal shower and spending 2€ for a seven-minute wash. The cheapest rooms face walls and are bathless. If you can swing just a little more money, ask for one with a balcony (Nos. 23, 33, 43, or 53, the latter of which is the best because it has a nice Parisian view); No. 51, a triple with a tiny peek of the tip of the Sacré Coeur; or No. 55, a double with the same lofty view. The balcony rooms come with double beds. If you need twins, ask for No. 41 on the street, which also has more space and better bedspreads than some others. Breakfast can be part of the plan here if you are willing to spend 4€, but you can feel more Parisian by walking to one of the many cafés that line rue des Abbesses and rue Lepic.

FACILITIES AND SERVICES: None; no elevator (5 floors)

NEAREST TOURIST ATTRACTIONS (RIGHT BANK): Montmartre, Sacré Coeur

HÔTEL DES ARTS ★★ (7)
5 rue Tholozé, 75018
Métro: Abbesses, Blanche
50 rooms, all with shower or bath and toilet

TELEPHONE
01-46-06-30-52
FAX
01-46-06-10-83
EMAIL
hotel.arts@wanadoo.fr
INTERNET
www.arts-hotel-paris.com
CREDIT CARDS
AE, MC, V
RATES
Single 64€, double 78€; extra bed for child only 15€; *taxe de séjour* included
BREAKFAST
Buffet 7€ per person

The Lameyre family works as an honest, hard-working team, intent on providing good value for money. The attractively furnished lobby and breakfast rooms are especially appealing, with textured walls, fresh flowers, and a growing collection of local artwork depicting scenes and aspects of life in Paris and the village of Montmartre. Paintings of picturesque Montmartre are also in all the bedrooms. The rooms are redecorated on a revolving basis using bright colors, good quality furnishings, and nicely coordinated fabrics. Bathrooms are pristine. If you don't mind walking up a flight of stairs, the sixth-floor rooms have rooftop views of the white tip of Sacré Coeur, and in Nos. 60 and 62, you will see the tip of the Eiffel Tower and La Defense. If stairs don't appeal, request No. 55, a double with built-in closets. It is the smallest room in the hotel, but it has a western exposure with a view of the Eiffel Tower. The street is quiet, so at night you won't be awakened by wild, cruising party animals.

FACILITIES AND SERVICES: Direct-dial phone, elevator (to most floors), hair dryer, Internet in lobby, TV with international reception, office safes (private; no charge)

NEAREST TOURIST ATTRACTIONS (RIGHT BANK): Montmartre, Sacré Coeur

ENGLISH SPOKEN
Yes

HÔTEL LE BOUQUET DE MONTMARTRE ★★ (10)
1, rue Durantin, 75018
Métro: Abbesses

36 rooms, all with shower, 22 with bath and toilet

If you have a fondness for Montmartre, and you want to experience the fun and the village atmosphere of the area and still stay under budget, the Bouquet de Montmartre is a little honey of a hotel. Its second-floor lobby may be difficult to find, but the search is worth it.

The Gibergues family works hard to keep their Victorian hotel as nice as it is for the price. They are on duty from Monday to Saturday, 9 A.M. to 6 P.M., so when calling for reservations, bear this in mind. If you can wear blinders or dark glasses in your room, or do not mind living in a kaleidoscope of colors and patterns, then read on. Most of the bedrooms fall into the "cute and confusing" category; in Nos. 30 and 43, you have a view. In all the rooms, lacy curtains, velvet chairs with plastic covers, floral rugs, and busy wallpaper combinations march along with brightly tiled bathrooms in purple, lavender, royal blue, and aqua. All are positively spotless and tear-free. Breakfast is served in an ornate dining room with red velvet chairs, lacquered furniture, and globe lights— all of which serves to remind you that this is Montmartre.

From the hotel you can stroll in any direction and see something interesting. You can climb up to Sacré Coeur or crawl down the hill to Pigalle. For longer trips, jump on the Montmartobus, a minibus service that plies the winding streets snaking around the Butte; it is one of the most pleasurable rides you can take in Paris.

FACILITIES AND SERVICES: Direct-dial phone, no elevator (3 floors), no TV, office safe (no charge)

NEAREST TOURIST ATTRACTIONS (RIGHT BANK): Montmartre, Sacré Coeur

TELEPHONE
01-46-06-87-54

FAX
01-46-06-09-09

EMAIL
bouquet.montmartre@ club-Internet.fr

INTERNET
www.bouquet-de-montmartre.com

CREDIT CARDS
MC, V

RATES
Single 62€, double 65€, triple 81€, quad 85€; *taxe du séjour* included

BREAKFAST
Continental 5€ per person

ENGLISH SPOKEN
Limited

HÔTEL PRIMA-LEPIC ★★ (9)
29, rue Lepic, 75018
Métro: Abbesses, Blanche
38 rooms, all with shower or bath and toilet

TELEPHONE
01-46-06-44-64
FAX
01-46-06-66-11
EMAIL
reservations@hotel-prima-lepic.com
INTERNET
www.hotel-paris-lepic.com
CREDIT CARDS
AE, MC, V
RATES
Single 78€, double 93–123€, apartment/suite 2 people 150€, 3–4 people 170€; *taxe de séjour* included
BREAKFAST
Buffet 8€ per person
ENGLISH SPOKEN
Yes

Finally, it has been redone. Gone are the dusty ruffles and flourishes that hung in the dark halls, overpowering the worn-out, shabby bedrooms. Thanks to a new owner and an impressive infusion of euros, the hotel is now back among the Great Sleeps in Paris. Several features were not changed: the original mosaic-tile entryway with its heavily molded ceiling are still here, and so are the killer, white wrought-iron chairs and tables in the breakfast area. They are pretty to look at, but ten minutes into your café au lait and croissant, you know these chairs were not built for comfort. This is not the case for the vastly improved bedrooms. All are slightly different, but the colors are coordinated, even in the bathrooms, where the floor tiles blend with the colors used in the room. For a view onto the interesting market street, rue Lepic, ask for No. 24, Montmartre, done in blue and yellow with a white-dotted swill half-tester over the bed. Several rooms are similar to No. 15, among them Caulaincourt, which has a white bed with gauzy curtains on each side and a balcony large enough for a table and chairs. No. 12, Tholoze, done in lavender with floral lights, has a feminine flair to it. No. 27, Sacré Coeur, is a cozy double in yellow and green. There are three suites, but frankly nothing can be done to change the poor layout or the fact that you have to crawl up some steep steps to reach one of them. In the largest, one room has no window, the exposure is gloomy, and the floors slant. My best advice is to avoid the suites.

FACILITIES AND SERVICES: Direct-dial phone, dogs accepted, elevator (to most floors), hair dryer, luggage room, TV with international reception, room service, room safe (2€ per day)

NEAREST TOURIST ATTRACTIONS (RIGHT BANK): Montmartre, Sacré Coeur

HÔTEL ROMA SACRÉ-COEUR ★★ (2)
101, rue Caulaincourt, 75018
Métro: Lamarck-Caulaincourt
57 rooms all with shower or bath and toilet

TELEPHONE
01-42-62-02-02
FAX
01-42-54-34-92
EMAIL
hotel.roma@wanadoo.fr
CREDIT CARDS
AE, DC, MC, V

Quite honestly, this hotel is a bit of a gamble because its location is way out of the mainstream and does require some walking up and down hills. Still, it has cachet: Room 701 was where Georges Braque had his studio when Montmartre was in its artistic heyday in the 1920s.

It is easy today to picture the artist standing on the wraparound balcony, gazing at northern Paris on the horizon and painting. Other rooms of note are Nos. 506 and 507, with views to Sacré Coeur, and No. 704, with a balcony. Singles do not fare well: the rooms are meager and the outlooks discouraging, so if you are a lone voyager, pay a little more and get a small double. If a trio is traveling, book one of the connecting rooms rather than try to squeeze into a double with an extra (lumpy) bed that requires contortionist maneuvering to get around. The innocuous rooms are in nonclashing colors of soft peach, simple browns, and white. Management is agreeable, and the neighborhood is pretty in that it reflects a part of Paris untouched by the maddening tourist crowds.

FACILITIES AND SERVICES: Direct-dial phone, elevator (to most floors), hair dryer, minibar, TV with international reception, office safe (no charge)

NEAREST TOURIST ATTRACTIONS (RIGHT BANK): Montmartre (back side)

TERRASS HÔTEL ★★★★ ($, 4)
12, rue Joseph-de-Maistre, 75018
Métro: Lamarck-Caulaincourt
100 rooms, all with shower or bath and toilet

The Terrass Hôtel on the Butte Montmartre has some of the most spectacular views of Paris. In the summer months, the roof garden on the seventh floor with its panoramic view of the City of Light is the perfect place for a romantic lunch or dinner à deux. Otherwise, meals are served in a bright, corner dining room with windows onto the street. The hotel has been in the same family for four generations, and despite its size, has an easy atmosphere that recalls the peace of less turbulent times. The wood-paneled lobby and reception areas are formal but not pretentious. During most of the year, they are enlivened by changing art exhibitions of works by local artists.

The rooms are individually done in the best of traditional taste and fall into three categories: comfort, superior, and suite. All rooms benefit from a long list of amenities. Naturally, the view rooms are in great demand, but just because a room is viewless does not mean that it is inferior. Number 704, a superior, evokes romance and embodies the phrase "a room with a view." In addition, it has a large bathroom with a corner Jacuzzi. In No. 610, the view is not as spectacular, but it is there. The room benefits from a dramatic red fabric–covered wall in the sitting area and a small terrace. The rooms ending in the

RATES
Single 67–77€, double 88€, triple in connecting rooms 120€; extra bed 17€; lower rates subject to season and availability; *taxe de séjour* 0.76€ per person, per day

BREAKFAST
Continental 7€ per person

ENGLISH SPOKEN
Yes

TELEPHONE
01-46-06-72-85

FAX
01-42-52-29-11

INTERNET
www.terrass-hotel.com

CREDIT CARDS
AE, DC, MC, V

RATES
Single: comfort 194€, superior 220€, suite 311€; double: comfort 232€; superior 220€, suite 311€; triple: suite 360€

BREAKFAST
Complimentary buffet or Continental

ENGLISH SPOKEN
Yes

number eight are all the same: they have twin beds, large sitting areas, and handicapped bathrooms large enough to accommodate a wheelchair; those on the fifth and sixth floors are exclusively nonsmoking. Number 114, with gray velvet–covered walls, is a standard room with no view, but it has a terrace, excellent work space, and a draped bed.

Under the same ownership is Le Madison Hôtel (see page 168) and the Hôtel Bourgogne & Montana (see page 179).

FACILITIES AND SERVICES: Air-conditioning, bar, conference room, direct-dial phone, elevator, hair dryer, some Jacuzzis, laundry service, minibar, magnifying mirror, concierge and porter, two restaurants (both open to the public by reservation), room service, tea and coffee maker, TV with international reception and pay-for-view, nonsmoking rooms on 5th and 6th floors

NEAREST TOURIST ATTRACTIONS (RIGHT BANK): Montmartre, Le Cimetière de Montmartre

TIMHÔTEL MONTMARTRE ★★ (6)
11, rue Ravignan, 75018
Métro: Abbesses

60 rooms, all with shower or bath and toilet

TELEPHONE
01-42-55-74-79

FAX
01-42-55-71-01

INTERNET
www.timhotel.fr

CREDIT CARDS
AE, DC, MC, V

RATES
1–2 persons 120€, triple 165€; 15€ supplement for a view room; *taxe de séjour* included

BREAKFAST
Continental 9.50€ per person

ENGLISH SPOKEN
Yes

The rue Ravignan runs along the place Émile Goudeau. It was here that Picasso, Juan Gris, Modigliani, and others had studios in the Bateau-Lavoir. Picasso arrived at age 19 and painted the *Demoiselles d'Avignon* (which now hangs in the MOMA in New York). Cubism was also born here. In 1970, the famous landmark burned. This bit of art history trivia leads me to the Timhôtel, which is right on the place Émile Goudeau. Normally, I am not an advocate of any type of chain hotel. However, there are always exceptions, and this is a good one. In addition to its historic location, the hotel boasts views of Paris from ten rooms and of Sacré-Coeur in ten more. Each floor is painted yellow, has blue carpeting, and is named after a well-known Montmartre painter. The identical, dormitory-inspired rooms are hardly candidates for the style-obsessed, so if you don't get one with a view, why bother hiking the slopes of Montmartre to stay in a chain hotel?

FACILITIES AND SERVICES: Direct-dial phone, elevator, hair dryer, laundry service, TV with international reception, office safe (4€ per day), 15 nonsmoking rooms

NEAREST TOURIST ATTRACTIONS (RIGHT BANK): Montmartre, Sacré Coeur

Other Options

If hotel life is not for you, there are other reasonable and often quite inexpensive options that make sleeping sense in Paris. For the cheapest choice of all, consider a return to nature—that is, camping, which you can do just outside of Paris in the Bois de Boulogne. For a more total immersion in Parisian life, plan a stay with a French family in a B&B. For one of the most unusual sleeps in Paris, you can live luxuriously on your own private *péniche* (barge) docked on the Seine in the shadow of the Eiffel Tower. If you are a student or can go the hostel route, there are many excellent low-priced accommodations awaiting you. Other cost-saving possibilities are to stay in a residence hotel in a unit with a kitchenette, or to become truly Parisian and rent your own studio or apartment. The benefits of these last two choices are numerous, from having more space to spread out to the adventure of interacting with merchants while shopping for life's necessities in your own Parisian neighborhood.

OTHER OPTIONS
Apartment Rental Agencies	**296**
Bed and Breakfast in a Private Home	**308**
Boat on the Seine	**309**
Camping Out	**310**
Hostels	**311**
Residence Hotels	**317**
Student Accommodations	**323**

Apartment Rental Agencies

There is something about the rhythm of being in Paris and there is no city more beautiful. Period.
—*Holly Hunt, interior decorator*

If you want to live in Paris, not just be a visitor during your stay, then the best way to experience Paris *comme les Parisiens* is to rent a short-term apartment. Believe me, once you do it, you will not want to return to the confines of hotel living in the City of Light for any of your future visits. If you are going to be in Paris for more than a few days, extra space begins to matter. Not only does a stay in a Parisian apartment give you more elbow room than a hotel, and for less money in the long run, it makes you feel less frantic about seeing and doing absolutely everything. You are caught up instead with the fun and adventure of exploring and getting to know your own Paris *quartier,* which you will soon come to think of as your own, becoming a little Parisian in the process.

During the years I have researched Paris apartments, I have seen just about every nightmare possible—including total dumps that were not only filthy and unattractive but in terrible areas that have absolutely nothing to offer a tourist. Many are operated by huge firms, or are let by absentee owners who are on the scene to collect your money but then vanish, leaving you high and dry when maintenance problems arise, which they generally do. Just as with all of the hotels and shops listed in this book, I have personally visited every apartment agency listed and viewed a large sampling of what they offer before I considered recommending them to you.

Even though I mention it as the number-one tip in apartment renting, it bears repeating here: If you rent an apartment, be sure you clearly understand the payment, cancellation, and refund policies. It is beyond the scope of *Great Sleeps Paris* to detail the various policies you will encounter, but they are *never* in your favor. Therefore, it is absolutely essential that you purchase cancellation insurance, which is available through many state automobile associations, travel agents, and in some cases, through the apartment agency itself (see Insurance, page 39). This small investment will pay off tenfold if you have to change dates, cancel altogether, or must suddenly cut short your stay.

Tips on Renting a Paris Apartment

1. Most important: Know the deposit, payment, and cancellation policies, and buy cancellation insurance.

2. Lower rates are always negotiable for longer stays or during slow periods. *Always* ask. Once you determine a guaranteed rate, find out about extra charges such as linens, cleaning (whether weekly housekeeping service is included or extra, and what the final cleaning fee is), telephone, heating, electricity, and so on.

3. A picture is worth a thousand words. Most agencies now have Websites with pictures of their properties. This is fine for a start but does not cover all the bases. In addition to photos of the kitchen, bathroom, and storage space, always ask for pictures of the views taken from the windows of the apartments you are considering. You probably don't want to move into your apartment and find that you are facing dull, interior courtyards; ugly, blank walls, which the rental agency has billed as a "quiet, calm, or peaceful address"; or a main traffic street with nonstop noise.

4. Many Paris buildings are undergoing exterior cleaning, painting, and/or extensive renovation. Find out if your apartment is in one of these buildings, which will be covered in plastic sheeting and scaffolding, smelling like paint, and essentially crawling with workers who arrive early, make noise, create dust, and don't care that you can't open the windows, let alone see out of them, during what could be months of very disconcerting building repairs and work.

5. Be very specific when stating your needs: size of flat and number of occupants; whether you want a stall shower rather than a handheld shower nozzle in a half tub with no shower guard or curtain; and what sort of kitchen equipment you'd like—do you need only a microwave, do you want pots and pans for major cooking events, or are you just going to drink wine and eat baguettes and French cheese at the dining room table? Inquire about closet space and luggage storage. Don't forget to consider the beds. Will a sofabed do, or does your back demand something better than a folding bed, and if so, will you require a double bed or twin beds?

6. Is a television important for you—one that includes CNN, BBC, and Euro-Sport? Don't discount French TV, as it's a great way to improve your French comprehension. Is there a phone and how much are calls? Can you make both local and long-distance calls? Is there an answering machine, fax, and Internet hookup?

7. How far is the apartment from your center of interest? Where is the nearest market, laundry and dry cleaner, pharmacy, métro and bus stop, best café, and *pâtisserie?* Ask for a good local map with your address and the nearest métro stop pinpointed on it.

8. Is the apartment suitable for children? Is there a park or playground nearby?

9. Is there an elevator to your apartment? Many buildings in Paris do not have them. While that penthouse apartment with a dynamic view is romantically wonderful, consider carrying groceries, shopping purchases, and your luggage up and down. Think about this one carefully . . . stairs can get to be a problem, fast.

10. Upon arrival, will someone meet you at the apartment and show you the ropes, or do you have to go to an office in Paris to get the keys?

This is very important after a long international flight: dragging luggage and tired children through Paris in search of the keys to your Paris kingdom is not an attractive option.

11. What other services does the apartment rental company offer? Ask about drivers; itinerary planning throughout France and in other parts of Europe; ongoing reservations; and air travel arrangements and concierge services in Paris.

12. Check with your homeowner's or renter's insurance policy to see if it covers you for any damage that may occur while you are renting a foreign apartment. Many of these policies do cover you. If so, fax the information to the agency in question. Many times hefty deposits are taken, and unfortunately, you can be blamed for damages caused by another renter. To avoid this, upon arrival, go over the apartment very carefully and point out any damages or potential problems, no matter how small they may seem. When you leave, get a written statement that the apartment was in good condition when you left it.

APARTMENT RENTAL AGENCIES

Chez Vous	299
De Circourt Associates	299
France for Rent	300
Guest Apartment Services	300
Historic Rentals	301
Irving Hutton Ltd	302
Kudeta Home	302
Panache	303
Paris Appartements Services	304
Paris Vacation Apartments	304
Rendez-Vous À Paris Ltd	305
Rentvillas.com	306
RothRay	306

CHEZ VOUS
1001 Bridgeway, Suite 245
Sausalito, CA 94965

Chez Vous apartments offer you a Paris address in several of the best areas of the city, not in marginal, out-of-the-way *quartiers* that some apartment owners or agencies will try to convince you are interesting. The possibilities are in the first, fourth, fifth, sixth, and seventh arrondissements. None of the apartments are owner-occupied. All are on long-term lease to Chez Vous, who employs a staff in Paris to oversee maintenance, decorating, and guest services. The catalog listing the Paris properties is called Bonjour Paris!!!, and it not only gives you good information about their apartments but leaves nothing to chance in explaining the payment or cancellation policies. If you are venturing outside of Paris, and this type of stay appeals to you, ask about their other rental properties throughout France and in London.

TELEPHONE
415-331-2531

FAX
415-331-5296

INTERNET
www.chezvous.com

CREDIT CARDS
None, U.S. checks only

RATES
From $200 and up per night for 2–4 people (5-night minimum, starts any day of week); includes linens, final cleaning, and all utilities except telephone; housekeeping service extra

ENGLISH SPOKEN
Yes

DE CIRCOURT ASSOCIATES (51)
11, rue Royale, 75008
Métro: Concorde

De Circourt Associates was founded by Claire de Circourt to assist people moving to Paris, either for professional reasons or for a stay of at least two months. Claire de Circourt is a very savvy businesswoman who has lived and worked in New York City, so she knows the type of living accommodations most Americans want and the services they expect. Her customer service is superb because she always provides backup, or intermediary help, if any client ever has a problem. She has

TELEPHONE
01-43-12-98-00

FAX
01-43-12-98-08

INTERNET
www.homes-paris.com

CREDIT CARDS
AE, DC, MC, V

RATES
From 1,000–12,000€ per month, minimum-stay 2 months

active computerized listings of five thousand apartments and homes in Paris, and in the suburbs close to all the international schools, which are updated every fifteen days, plus a dynamic Website that is updated twice daily. It is also possible to reserve on her Website, and, of course, privacy and security are assured for clients who do this. Thanks to this sophisticated computerized search system, she or one of her exceptionally competent English-speaking staff will find you the place of your dreams at a price you can afford. Her office can also find an apartment in less than twenty-four hours. As she told me, "Clients can come in the morning, and by evening, have a contract in their pocket." The possibilities range from a romantic, beamed, one-bedroom walkup on Île de la Cité, to a zany artist's studio done in black and white with a bird-shaped chair, to the to-die-for apartment occupied by Robert Altman while he was on location in Paris filming *Prêt à Porter*. It is all up to you and your budget—whatever you want, chances are excellent De Circourt Associates will have it.

FRANCE FOR RENT
264 28th Street
San Francisco, CA 94131

TELEPHONE
Toll-free in the U. S.
866-437-2623

FAX
805-649-2689

INTERNET
www.FranceForRent.com

CREDIT CARDS
MC, V

RATES
Small studios for 3-month minimum 800€ per week; other studios and apartments from 1,000–5,000€ per week; lower rates for longer stays

ENGLISH SPOKEN
Yes

France for Rent has properties throughout France, but the emphasis is on Paris. Their Paris apartments are located in the most popular arrondissements and range in size from small studios and beamed Marais apartments to a fabulous town house on the Seine filled with magnificent art and all the latest high-tech gadgetry. All are positively nonsmoking, have cable television, CD stereo systems, and modern, well-equipped kitchens. Housekeeping service is available on request (extra charge), and some apartments have elevators, air-conditioning, clothes washers, dishwashers, and a DSL Internet line. A distinct advantage is that credit cards are accepted. Someone is always on-call twenty-four hours a day if there are any problems. One of the best reasons to deal with France for Rent is Jamie Sommer; not only is she delightful, but her enthusiasm for Paris is infectious.

GUEST APARTMENT SERVICES (52)
9, Quai de Bourbon, 75004 (Île St-Louis)
Métro: Pont-Marie

TELEPHONE
01-44-07-06-20,
06-80-63-19-95 (cell phone)

FAX
01-46-33-37-73

Guest Apartment Services specializes in short-term rentals of some of the most beautiful Parisian apartments I have seen. Each exclusive property is carefully chosen for its innate charm and authentic character, and it has been decorated in a comfortable Parisian style with beautiful period furnishings, nicely equipped kitchens, and modern bathrooms. I can assure you they are wonderful . . . nothing is faded, out-of-date, or displays even a hint of that shabby-chic decor one often finds in French rental properties. All are located either on the beguiling Île St-Louis or in the Marais around place des Vosges. Some have quiet garden views; others have sweeping, panoramic picture-postcard outlooks. From the smallest studio on a quiet courtyard with a lovely magnolia tree to an elegant town house near place des Vosges, complete with indoor swimming pool and garden—and the staff to maintain them—you can be assured that Christophe Chastel and Philippe Pée and their staff will provide you with a memorable Parisian stay. All apartments include weekly housekeeping and linen service (daily housekeeping service is available), cable television, stereo with CD, private telephone and fax, and all major appliances. The small studios, however, do not have washer-dryers. Arrangements can be made for airport transfers, a car and driver during your stay or for trips out of Paris, a personal chef, babysitting . . . whatever is needed to enhance your stay.

EMAIL
guestapart@wanadoo.fr
INTERNET
www.guestapartment.com
CREDIT CARDS
MC, V
RATES
Per day: from 125€ for small studio; 400€ for luxurious apartment on Île St-Louis; fabulous town house 1,500€; lower rates for longer stays and in low-season
ENGLISH SPOKEN
Yes

HISTORIC RENTALS
100 W. Kennedy Boulevard, No. 260
Tampa, FL 33602

George Harris owns three beautiful one-bedroom apartments in Paris that he has completely restored. Two are located in the fifth arrondissement near the Panthéon, and the other on rue des Rosiers in the Jewish Quarter in the Marais. When I saw them, I thought they didn't look like rentals; they looked and felt like lovely homes. All three are decorated with charming furnishings, quality fabrics, and great attention to detail. Kitchens and bathrooms are small but completely up-to-date. The bedrooms have a king-size bed, and there is another comfortable couch in the living room that converts to a single bed with a trundle bed. There are plenty of electrical outlets suitable for plugging in laptops and always a comfortable work space with good lighting. These two features may sound routine, but let me assure you they are not. I cannot tell you the number of nice apartments and hotels in Paris with little or no work space, and plugs so far away that several extension cords snaking across the room are required. Guests also have a "pay as you go"

TELEPHONE
Toll-free in the U.S. 800-537-5408; outside the U.S. 813-765-4701
INTERNET
www.historicrentals.com
CREDIT CARDS
MC, V
RATES
Starting at $900 per week for 1 week, less for multiple weeks or in low season; $100 weekly supplement for special holidays (July 4, July 14, Thanksgiving, Christmas, New Year's, Easter, Fashion Week, French Open)
ENGLISH SPOKEN
Yes

cellular phone and a concierge book filled with helpful hints. Television, hair dryer, and utilities are included along with weekly cleaning and linen changes. There is a six-day minimum stay.

If your travels are taking you to Annecy, ask about his latest apartment venture located in the historic center of this picturesque town on a lake in the French alps. For something closer to home, he has eight apartments in the heart of the French Quarter in New Orleans, all fully furnished with air-conditioning, telephone, television, and parking.

IRVING HUTTON LTD (18)
Bill and Natalie Cameron Ward
3, rue Troyon 75017

Bill and Natalie Cameron Ward offer a number of exceptional apartments in the first, third, fourth, and fifth arrondissements. A stay in any one of them puts the visitor in an interesting, lively area with excellent access to bus and métro transportation, good restaurants, and wonderful neighborhood shopping. The apartments, which they own or exclusively manage, range in size from a roomy studio to a two-bedroom, two-bathroom apartment sleeping six. Each has its own character derived from quality furnishings and coordinated color schemes. Kitchens are fully fitted with everything from a paring knife and an electric tea kettle to a microwave, attractive china, glassware, and cutlery. Most have a washer and dryer and a dishwasher. All have cable TV reception, several have a high-speed Internet connection and DVD or VCR. All prices include utilities (with the exception of the telephone) and housekeeping service after ten days. Bill and Natalie are a charming hands-on team who inspect each property regularly, know the owners, and spare no effort in making their guests feel welcome and at home. All you have to do is arrive with your luggage, settle in, and enjoy home-sweet-home in Paris.

TELEPHONE
06-22-58-45-85 (cell phone)
01-40-55-46-19
FAX
01-42-67-93-09
EMAIL
cameron@wanadoo.fr
CREDIT CARDS
None, payment by check in U.S. dollars
RATES
From $735 per week for a studio to $2,065 per week for a 2-bedroom, 2-bathroom apartment
ENGLISH SPOKEN
Yes

KUDETA HOME (9)
Stéphan Martin and Pierre Filliole
22, rue Rambuteau, 75003
Métro: Rambuteau

Stéphane Martin was once the marketing manager for Galeries Lafayette, and Pierre Filliole was involved in international banking and finance. A few years ago they decided to change careers and subsequently went into the short-term apartment-rental business. They now own and

TELEPHONE & FAX
01-44-78-06-76
06-72-72-10-42 (cell phone)
EMAIL
stephane.martin@noos.fr,
filliole@libertysurf.fr
INTERNET
www.kudeta-home.com

manage a group of very attractive studios and apartments geared to all types of budgets. For the seriously budget-minded, they have a group of modestly priced studios located in the Marais and around rue Montorgueil, the colorful shopping street near Les Halles. These are both very trendy areas, full of bars, restaurants, and a stylish blend of fashionistas. While these studios are definitely budget in size and require some stair climbing, they have a certain simple charm . . . think Ikea with a smattering of beams, an antique door, or lovely mirror as accents, nice curtains, hardwood floors, and little kitchenettes. These studios are available for stays of two nights, one week, one month, or more. If you need more space, consider a larger studio, with antiques and a wood-burning fireplace located at the corner of place des Vosges. Another such option is a one- or two-bedroom apartment that has all the bells and whistles, plus quality furnishings and a wonderful atmosphere that invites you to move right in and begin your life as a temporary Parisian. All properties have cable television, phones, hair dryers, and Stéphane and Pierre on call. The more expensive apartments additionally include stereos, fax line, answering machine, and housekeepers on request. Depending on location, there will be a washer and dryer and dishwasher, and the largest has an elevator.

CREDIT CARDS
None, euros only

RATES
Small studios from 90€ per night (2-night minimum), 450€ per week, 1,100€ per month; medium studio 550€ per week, 1,300€ per month; large studio 750€ per week, 2,100€ per month; 1- and 2-bedroom apartments from 1,050€ per week, 2,800€ per month; lower rates for longer stays

ENGLISH SPOKEN
Yes

PANACHE
141 South Main Street
Cohasset, MA 02025

Connie Afshar specializes in excellent short-term apartment rentals in Paris that are centrally located in the Marais, Île St-Louis, Île de la Cité, les Halles, and near the Louvre. They range from basic-budget to lovely and lavish, and are equipped accordingly. It all depends on your pocketbook and your needs. Properties are inspected regularly, and detailed descriptions and pictures are available on the Website. In addition to securing your perfect Parisian apartment, Connie and her resourceful staff can help with travel arrangements, engage a chef to prepare your meals, or book you into other properties they have throughout France or in Venice, London, and Scotland.

TELEPHONE
781-383-6006

FAX
781-383-6087

EMAIL
info@PanacheRental.com

INTERNET
www.PanacheRental.com, www.OneWorld-Travel.com

CREDIT CARDS
Depends on apartment; otherwise, cash or check

RATES
$140–750 per night; lower rates for stays over 1 week

ENGLISH SPOKEN
Yes

PARIS APPARTEMENTS SERVICES (14)
20, rue Bachaumont, 75002
Métro: Sentier, Étienne-Marcel

TELEPHONE
01-40-28-01-28
FAX
01-40-28-92-01
INTERNET
www.paris-apts.com
CREDIT CARDS
AE, MC, V
RATES
Per week: studio from 135€,
1-bedroom from 183–214€;
continental breakfast 13€; *taxe
de séjour* 0.91€ per person, per
day
ENGLISH SPOKEN
Yes

Paris Appartements Services owns all of the one hundred apartments they rent. This insures that their properties will be uniformly decorated and regularly maintained by an in-house staff. Best of all, they will usually have something at the last minute and in a variety of price ranges. One-bedroom apartments have a sofabed in addition to a separate bedroom with a double bed, a bathroom with a tub and shower, and clothes washers and dryers. The studios for one or two have a main room with a double bed or sofabed and bathroom, but no washer-dryer. No matter where you stay, you will have a TV (some with international reception), a well-equipped kitchen, and a telephone. Linens are changed weekly, housekeeping service is included for stays of more than a week, and a congenial office staff with twenty-four-hour phone access is ready to troubleshoot. When reserving, ask for Meilee Carrette, the international sales manager.

PARIS VACATION APARTMENTS (12)
86, boulevard de Clichy, 75018
In the U.S.:
37 Somerset Road
Lexington, MA 02420-3519

TELEPHONE
France 01-44-92-06-55,
06-12-44-64-78 (cell phone);
U.S. 781-862-3304
FAX
01-42-64-20-03
EMAIL
pva@wfi.fr
INTERNET
www.parisvacationapart
ments.com
CREDIT CARDS
MC, V; also accepts wire
transfer, bank draft, money
order, or personal checks in
U.S. dollars
RATES
Small studios from $650 per
week; Montmartre apartments
$900–2,000 per week; Palais
Royal duplex $3,200–4,200 per
week, $4,900 during Christmas
and New Year's; lower rates for
stays over three weeks and in
off-season
ENGLISH SPOKEN
Yes

If you saw the Woody Allen film *Everyone Says I Love You (Tout le Monde Dit I Love You),* you will remember the Montmartre *pied-à-terre* he rented to impress his would-be lover, played by Julia Roberts, and the spectacular view it had of the Sacré Coeur. For the film actors, it was just a temporary on-site set location. For you, an apartment with the same fabulous view can be your home in Paris.

American Erica Berman and her French business partner, Alex Mony, are young, energetic, artistic, and full of great ideas. They have taken several Montmartre apartments—two right on the Palais Royale gardens—and renovated them into smart, stylish, uncluttered, wonderful accommodations that all say, "This is Paris!" Being American, Erica knows the mindset of her compatriots and has designed the apartments to appeal to American visitors. She has used simple colors, sprinkled the rooms with antiques, and fitted the kitchens and baths to American standards and tastes. Erica and Alex live in Paris and are always accessible to their clients. Upon arrival, they meet you on-site and provide you with the necessary details, and are available 24/7 to make sure you feel at home during your stay.

Their Palais Royal three-bedroom, three-bathroom duplex apartment sleeps up to ten, and it is nothing short of sensational. This stunning location has doors opening from the living room onto a balcony overlooking the lovely Palais Royal gardens, plus another terrace off the master bedroom. In addition to all the amenities guests enjoy in the other apartments, this one includes air-conditioning, a private safe, fireplace, housekeeping service five days a week, fax, DVD, VCR, and a full security system. Their studios are on rue Lepic, the colorful Montmartre shopping street. These are very nice but small. They have no lift or laundry facilities, but they do have cable TV, a CD player, a kitchenette with a microwave, and showers in the bathroom. All the other apartments have weekly housekeeping service along with cable television, washer-dryer, dishwasher, DSL line, stereo systems, elevator, and utilities (except telephone and fax charges) as standard issue. No pets are accepted, but children certainly are, and they will be happy to provide baby beds, babysitters, and safety gates in apartments with stairs. If you need a private car and driver, they will arrange for it. Prices are fair, and my recommendation continues to be very high.

RENDEZ-VOUS À PARIS LTD

Katrine Grillard has a roster of twenty-five or more marvelous apartments that she exclusively manages. It is easy to see why these are always full. Leaving nothing to chance, Katrine has personally decorated each property in her own tasteful French style, and they are all lovely. I can additionally assure you without question that these are dynamite apartments in locations that every visitor clamors to be in: Île St-Louis, St-Germain-des-Prés, and near Alma in the eighth. The apartments range in size from one to four bedrooms, and always the bedrooms are on the back, away from Paris early morning or late night street noise. They have cable television (where possible), stereo music systems, telephones with answering machines, washers and dryers, dishwashers and housekeeping service for stays of over one month, or on request. The kitchens are fitted with matching china, nice glassware and cutlery, good cooking facilities, and proper stoves and ovens in addition to microwaves.

TELEPHONE
06-15-26-30-04

FAX
01-56-24-19-06

EMAIL
rendez-vous@wfi.fr

INTERNET
www.rendez-vousaparis.com

CREDIT CARDS
None, payment in euros

RATES
From 150–500€ per night, 3,000–4,000€ per month; lower rates for longer stays and in low season; 5-night minimum

ENGLISH SPOKEN
Yes

RENTVILLAS.COM
700 East Main Street
Ventura, CA 93001

TELEPHONE
805-641-1650, toll-free in U.S.
800-726-6702

FAX
805-641-1630

INTERNET
www.rentvillas.com

CREDIT CARDS
MC, V

RATES
From $1,000 per month,
1-week minimum; no Sun
arrivals

ENGLISH SPOKEN
Yes

Rentvillas.com has an enviable track record of being one of the most customer-focused rental companies in the industry. Founded by Suzanne Pidduck, it has grown from covering only Italian properties to being a thoroughly computerized operation with properties all over Europe, including Paris and the French countryside. Every time I have used Suzanne to help me organize a long-term stay, I have been very pleased, and I have been impressed with the backup provided in several emergency situations. Everyone on staff has extensive travel experience and many are multilingual. You will be matched with a travel advisor who has expertise in your area of interest. Their excellent Website is an easy way to find and reserve just the property you want.

ROTHRAY (19)
10, rue Nicolas-Flamel, 75004
Métro: Châtelet

TELEPHONE
01-48-87-13-37

FAX
01-42-78-17-72

EMAIL
rothray@online.fr

INTERNET
www.rothray.free.fr

CREDIT CARDS
None; cash or personal checks
in your currency. Prices are
converted to your currency at
the rate of exchange on the day
you are paying.

RATES
80–200€ per day; 1,650–
4,800€ per month. Prices vary
according to size and location as
well as length of stay (7-day
minimum; stays of 1 month or
more preferred)

ENGLISH SPOKEN
Yes

It is an undisputed fact that RothRay apartments are tops . . . and some of the best in Paris. Period. This opinion is shared not only by all of their loyal and contented clients but by the rest of the competition! I absolutely agree—after one stay, I vowed to always let competent Ray Lampard and his capable partner, Roth, arrange my living accommodations anytime I am in Paris. The problem is that their apartments are always full, usually a year in advance! Some short-term private apartment rentals in Paris can be potluck affairs: you find unwelcome surprises on arrival, and during your stay you must contend with strange decor, varying amenities and levels of cleanliness, and haphazard services by the agency in charge, which shows little interest in you after they have your money . . . up front. You will find none of these problems in any apartment rented through RothRay. Their apartments are located in interesting *quartiers,* where a stroll around a corner will put picturesque Paris at your feet. After a few days you will discover what fun it is to actually be a part of Paris, and you'll probably spend a good deal of your time trying to make more permanent arrangements or figuring out how to return again more often. It will be love at first sight when you walk into one of their nicely furnished and beautifully equipped studios and apartments. In addition to attractive furnishings, most have cable televisions, stereo systems, washers and dryers, dishwashers, and American-style kitchens beautifully equipped with nice china, crystal, and utensils. You can only fully appreciate the quality of their kitchens if you have ever tried to prepare a meal in a French closet-style kitchen with a mishmash of "rental" pots and pans and chipped, unmatched dishes for serving. Their own apartments are constantly being improved to meet the exacting standards of Roth, who will spend days locating just the right knobs for new kitchen cabinets or will move a wall a few centimeters to allow for a washer-dryer to be installed. Before guests arrive, he personally inspects the apartment to make sure everything is in order, and both he and Ray are available in Paris for problem-solving. This is an important point: you are not dealing with a local representative of the person or company you rented from. With RothRay you are dealing with the two people who are the owners and who are in charge of, and responsible for, everything. Weekly housekeeping service, linen changes, and a refrigerator stocked with fruit juices, wine, and beer are included. As one guest happily told me, "There is RothRay, and then everyone else, just trying to catch up." How very true that is. RothRay Apartments are in such demand that they are booked usually a year in advance, so please make your reservation the minute you know your dates in Paris. There is a seven day minimum, and they prefer one month rentals.

Exclusive for readers of the tenth-anniversary edition of *Great Sleeps Paris:* When reserving one of their apartments, *Great Sleeps Paris* readers who mention the book will get a complimentary taxi ride from the airport to their apartment, where upon they will be personally welcomed by Ray Lampard and reimbursed for the taxi trip. Just be sure to save your receipt.

Bed and Breakfast in a Private Home

ALCÔVE & AGAPES, LE BED & BREAKFAST À PARIS

TELEPHONE
01-44-85-06-05

FAX
01-44-85-06-14

INTERNET
www.bed-and-breakfast-in-paris.com

CREDIT CARDS
V only for B&B fee; euros only, must be paid to host upon arrival

RATES
1–2 people: room with shared bath 55–70€ per night; room with private bath 70–110€; 1st-class room 110–195€; discounts after 10 days; no registration fee, no minimum stay

ENGLISH SPOKEN
Yes

Françoise Foret has developed a roster of over eighty Parisian hosts who offer bed-and-breakfast accommodations in their homes ranging from Haussmann apartments, private mansions, artists' workshops, and lively family homes. As she puts it, "Alcôve & Agapes can offer guest rooms that cater to the businessperson, please the budget-conscious, and charm the first-class traveler." For those who want to personalize their stay and learn more about French culture in general and life in Paris in particular, a stay in a private home in Paris is a welcome opportunity. Françoise personally visits every home at least twice a year to ensure that her standards of cleanliness and comfort are being met. All are located in Paris and are within walking distance to a métro. The majority are nonsmoking. Her hosts range in age from twenty-five to sixty-five years and usually speak fluent English. Some homes have shared bathrooms and/or toilets, have adored family pets, are up a few flights of stairs, or have strictly residential locations. Others are deluxe in every way, are in the most desirable tourist areas, and have hosts who will prepare three-course dinners (for a fee, of course).

To avoid any unpleasant surprises, Françoise provides detailed descriptions and photos, which are available on the Website or can be sent to prospective guests. Taking the guesswork out of selecting the right B&B, these fact sheets provide details about the host, home, bedroom, neighborhood, distance from tourist sites, and directions on how to get there. Whatever your bottom line, Françoise says, "We take great care to ensure a pleasant stay in the City of Lights and trust that you will be among our many satisfied guests who arrive as clients and leave as friends."

Boat on the Seine

BATEAU SYMPATICO (11)
Port du Suffren, 75007
Métro: Bir Hakeim; RER Champ-de-Mars–Tour Eiffel

Bob Abrams's love of boats is evident the minute you step off the *quai* along the Seine and into his meticulously restored *peniche* (barge). He has spent upwards of twenty years on the project, and the results are remarkable. The main part consists of one great room (800 square feet!), trimmed in highly polished wood with gleaming brass fittings. It is furnished with a leather settee, comfortable chairs, a dining table and chairs, and many fascinating objects he has collected over many years of globetrotting. If you need to stay connected with the outside world, you will have a telephone, Internet connection, and television with a VCR. There is a king-size bed, plus a trundle bed suitable for a child. However, no children under ten are accepted, and neither are smokers or animals. Hardly a galley, the kitchen is big enough for you to cook your Christmas goose in the oven and prepare all the side dishes on the four-burner stove. Of course, the kitchen is equipped with all the pots, pans, and necessary implements to do it in great style. For simple heating and eating, there is a microwave. The large bathroom has a shower and a washer and dryer. If you are here in the warm months, you will be able to relax on the deck in a lounge chair and watch all the activities taking place along this interesting part of the Seine. And you'll be right under the shadow of the Eiffel Tower and only a three-minute walk from a métro stop. For a different, yet totally romantic and very memorable time in Paris, a stay on the romantic *Bateau Sympatico* will be impossible to top.

TELEPHONE & FAX
01-47-53-02-79

INTERNET
quai48parisvacation.com

CREDIT CARDS
None; cash, bank transfer, or traveler's check in dollars

RATES
2 people $1,820; 1-week minimum May–Aug; 30% supplement for Christmas through New Year's; reservations required as far in advance as possible; all utilities included except telephone

ENGLISH SPOKEN
Yes

Camping Out

LES CAMPINGS DU BOIS DE BOULOGNE
Allée du Bord de l'Eau, Bois de Boulogne, 75016
Métro: Porte-Maillot, then take camp shuttle bus or public bus No. 244

TELEPHONE
01-45-24-30-00
FAX
01-42-24-42-95
EMAIL
camping-boulogne@stereau.fr
INTERNET
www.abccamping.com (select campingdeparis), www.hotelparispleinair.com
CREDIT CARDS
AE, MC, V
RATES
All rates are per night: 1–2 persons, no car, tent site without electricity 15€, with electricity 19€; with car, tent site without electricity 24€; with electricity 28€; RV (camper van) site with electricity and water hookups 31€. Mobile home rental (including electricity & water) for 2–4 people 66€ per night. Lower rates Sept–June; *taxe de séjour* on all rates 0.20€ per person, per day
BREAKFAST
Not available
ENGLISH SPOKEN
Yes

Coleman stoves, tents, inflatable mattresses, and citronella candles may not be on everyone's packing list for a trip to Paris, but they might be on yours if you are a camper. Yes, it is possible to pitch a tent in Paris! Les Campings in the Bois de Boulogne is next to the Seine on the far edge of the park and provides the only true rustic opportunity for those who like to pitch a tent under the stars. Geared to students and hearty international travelers, or those with RVs, the campground is located four kilometers away from the nearest métro, making it almost essential that you have your own set of wheels. Otherwise, there is a camp bus, but its schedule may not match yours, and then you ll be forced to walk. At the campground, there's a convenience store, hot showers, a coin-operated washer and dryer, and a restaurant. The office is open from 7 A.M. until 10 P.M. and accepts no reservations for campsites, but it will accept them for RV bookings and large camping groups. Everything is always on a first-come, first-served basis.

NOTE: To reach the campground from the Porte-Maillot métro station, exit the station at *sortie* André Maurois and take a shuttle bus, which runs April to October every half hour during much of the day (but not between noon and 6 P.M.) and some of the night; it's free in July and August. Alternatively, take public bus No. 244 from the Porte-Maillot métro station, get off at route des Moulins, and walk down the path to the right. Do not follow misleading signs to the left on the main road.

FACILITIES AND SERVICES: Open year-round, convenience store, coin-operated washing machines and dryers, information office, free hot showers, shuttle bus service, and restaurant from April to October

NEAREST TOURIST ATTRACTIONS: None

Hostels

Hostels appeal to travelers with youth on their side and wanderlust in their hearts. Only one of the hostels listed here has an age limit, but otherwise, they all follow the same general guidelines: shared rooms, public facilities, lockouts in the afternoon, and sometimes a sheaf of other rules and restrictions regarding drinking, smoking, guests, curfews, and so on. However, they often make up in camaraderie what they lack in luxury, and you are almost certain to meet like-minded budget travelers who will be more than willing to share their tales of Parisian adventures.

If you are serious about hostelling, then you should consider becoming a member of Hostelling International/American Youth Hostel (HI/AYH), which runs forty five hundred hostels in seventy countries. There is no age limit (13 percent of members are senior citizens), and they offer other services as well. If you are not already a member when you arrive at an affiliated hostel, you will be charged a supplement per night for six nights, which will then qualify you as a member. Auberge Jules Ferry (see page 313) is the best located HI hostel in Paris. For general information on Hostelling International and a list of their other Paris hostels, see La Centrale de Réservations below or log onto their Website at www.hiayh.org.

HOSTELS

Aloha Hostel (15th)	**311**
Auberge International des Jeunes (11th)	**312**
Auberge Jules Ferry (11th)	**313**
La Centrale de Réservations (FUAJ; 18th)	**313**
La Maison (15th)	**314**
Le Village Hostel–Montmartre (18th)	**314**
3 Ducks Hostel (15th)	**315**
Woodstock Hostel (9th)	**315**
Young & Happy (Y & H) Hostel (5th)	**316**

ALOHA HOSTEL (18)
1, rue Borromée, 75015
Métro: Volontaires

60 beds, 8 rooms with showers, none with toilets

Two brothers own the Aloha Hostel and five other hostels in Paris: La Maison, Le Village Hostel–Montmartre, 3 Ducks Hostel, Woodstock Hostel, and Young & Happy Hostel. In addition, they operate three bottom-of-the-barrel budget hotels that I do not include because, in my opinion, the neighborhoods are not safe after dark, and in one, the management is creepy.

While each hostel has its own personality, all have many similarities in rates, services, and amenities. Unless

TELEPHONE
01-42-73-03-03

FAX
01-42-73-14-14

EMAIL
friends@aloha.fr

INTERNET
www.hiphophostels.com,
www.aloha.fr

CREDIT CARDS
None; euro cash or traveler's checks only

RATES
Double room 25€, dorm (4–8 people) 22€ per person; showers free; lower rates in off-season; *taxe de séjour* included

BREAKFAST
Included

ENGLISH SPOKEN
Yes

otherwise stated, the following information applies to all six hostels. They are open year-round, but during the summer high-season between April and October, all stays are generally limited to two weeks. There is no age limit for guests. Every day there is a cleaning lockout between 11 A.M. and 5 P.M. and a strict 2 A.M. curfew, though reception is open daily from 8 A.M. to 2 A.M. No booze is allowed and no credit cards are accepted—it is euro cash only or traveler's checks in euros. There are lower rates in winter from November through March. Don't ask for a refund—they don't exist. Breakfast, which consists of bread and coffee, tea, or hot chocolate, is included, and so are showers and the *taxe de séjour*. If you do not BYO sheets and towels, count on spending around 3€ plus 7€ deposit for sheets and 2€ plus 2€ deposit for a towel. You can surf the Internet or send and receive emails for a nominal charge. There are kitchen privileges, a TV in the lounge, and always a friendly atmosphere and helpful, English-speaking staff. Extensions must be made by 9:30 P.M. the day before.

At the Aloha Hostel in particular, guests can mingle in the backpack-laden reception area, comparing cheap travel tips gleaned from years of surviving on the edge. Rooms have benefited from a redecoration project; beams were added and so were new showers. There are no singles. The working-class neighborhood is full of supermarkets, bakeries, banks, and other survival-type shopping. Otherwise, it's at least twenty minutes to tourist destinations.

FACILITIES AND SERVICES: Bar in summer, communal kitchen, no elevator (3 floors), Internet in lounge, luggage room (unlocked), no lockers, French TV in lounge (videos in English), showers on every floor, safe in office (no charge), no smoking in rooms

NEAREST TOURIST ATTRACTIONS (LEFT BANK): None; must use public transportation

AUBERGE INTERNATIONAL DES JEUNES (18)
10, rue Trousseau, 75011
Métro: Ledru-Rollin
190 beds

TELEPHONE
01-47-00-62-00

FAX
01-47-00-33-16

INTERNET
www.aijparis.com

CREDIT CARDS
AE, MC, V

It is clean, you can book ahead, and you can pay by credit card. When you arrive, you will have a spartan clean room that is shared by two to four people. Rooms for four have private facilities. Sinks are in all the other rooms, toilets and free showers in the hall. There is no curfew, no age limit, and no ban on groups, but you will have to observe a cleaning lockout from 10 A.M. to 3 P.M.

FACILITIES AND SERVICES: No elevator (4 floors), Internet in lounge, locked luggage area, office safe (no charge), no smoking or booze allowed

NEAREST TOURIST ATTRACTIONS (RIGHT BANK): Nightlife around the Bastille

RATES
March–Oct 15€ per person; Nov–Feb 14€ per person; towel rental 1€; *taxe de séjour* included

BREAKFAST
Continental included

ENGLISH SPOKEN
Yes

AUBERGE JULES FERRY (1)
8, boulevard Jules Ferry, 75011
Métro: République
99 beds

No curfew, no age limit, no reservations, no groups, and no stays over one week in this sanctioned Hostelling International choice near place de la République. An International Youth Hostel Card is required. Rooms sleep from two to six, and the price includes breakfast, showers, and sheets. No towels are provided. Cleaning lockout is from noon to 2:00 P.M.; the office is open 24/7.

FACILITIES AND SERVICES: Elevator, Internet in lounge, lockers (BYO locks), microwave, communal refrigerator, coin-operated washer and dryer

NEAREST TOURIST ATTRACTIONS (RIGHT BANK): Nothing, must use public transportation

TELEPHONE
01-43-57-55-60

FAX
01-43-14-82-09

EMAIL
auberge@micronet.fr

INTERNET
www.fuaj.fr

CREDIT CARDS
MC, V

RATES
19€ per person; small lockers free, large lockers 1.55€ per day; *taxe de séjour* included

BREAKFAST
Included

ENGLISH SPOKEN
Yes

LA CENTRALE DE RÉSERVATIONS (FUAJ; 3)
27, rue Pajol, 75018
Métro: Marx-Dormoy

La Centrale de Réservations (FUAJ), run by Hostelling International, is a good place to go to get a cheap student bed in Paris, or anywhere else in Europe. Membership in Hostelling International is required; when purchased in the United States, it costs around $12 if you are twenty-six years old or younger, or around $18 if you are over twenty-six. If you buy your card in France, it will cost more. Cards are good for one year from date of purchase. A trip to one of their Paris offices will provide you with a same-day reservation in any of their affiliated hostels or budget hotels. Not only can you book a bed, but you can make on-going travel arrangements by bus, boat, or air; book tours to other parts of the world; or nail down an excursion in Paris. There will be a reservation fee, payable at the time of booking, but it is deducted from the cost of your bed. The office is open Monday to Friday from 9:30 A.M. to 5 P.M., Saturday 10 A.M. to 4 P.M.

TELEPHONE
01-44-89-87-27

FAX
01-44-89-87-10/49

INTERNET
www.fuaj.org

CREDIT CARDS
MC, V

RATES
Must be an HI member. rates are per person in dorm rooms 20.60€; showers free; rental towels 3€; paper sheets 1.60€; *taxe de séjour* 1€ per person, per day

BREAKFAST
Continental 4€ per person

ENGLISH SPOKEN
Yes

NOTE: If you can't get to the office in the eighteenth arrondissement, a more convenient office is near the Centre Georges Pompidou at 9 rue Brantôme, 75003; Métro: Rambuteau; Tel: 01-48-04-70-40; Fax: 01-42-77-03-29. Office hours are Monday to Friday 10 A.M. to 6 P.M., Saturday 10 A.M. to 5 P.M.

LA MAISON (24)
67 bis, rue Dutot and rue de la Procession, 75015
Métro: Vaugirard

27 rooms, all with shower and toilet

TELEPHONE
01-42-73-10-10
FAX
01-42-73-08-08
INTERNET
www.mamaison.fr
RATES
Twin or double bed 24€ per person; 3–4 beds 21€ per person

La Maison is a good hostel for families and senior citizens hell-bent on spending as little as possible to sleep cheap in Paris. Accommodations are in twin-bedded rooms or dorms for three or four people. All rooms have their own showers and toilets. It is located next to the Ministère de l'Éducation in a safe but dull area (at least for tourists), where you will find a supermarket, laundromat, post office, and plenty of bakeries. There is a maximum seven-day stay. Lockout is from 11 A.M. to 4 P.M., curfew is at 2 A.M., and you pay the day before for the next night. Towel rental is 1€ plus 0.50€ deposit; sheet rental is 2.50€ plus 10€ deposit. For a complete description of rules, regulations, and perks, see Aloha Hostel (page 311).

FACILITIES AND SERVICES: Elevator, Internet in lounge, kitchen privileges, no TV, office safe (no charge)

NEAREST TOURIST ATTRACTIONS (LEFT BANK): None; must use public transportation

LE VILLAGE HOSTEL–MONTMARTRE (14)
20, rue d'Orsel, 75018
Métro: Anvers

75 beds in rooms for 2–6 persons, all with shower and toilet

TELEPHONE
01-42-64-22-02
FAX
01-42-64-22-04
INTERNET
www.villagehostel.fr
RATES
Double 50€ for 2 people, dorm (4–6 people) 21.50€ per person, triple 23€ per person

At this hostel, all the rooms have private facilities, and six rooms (Nos. 201, 205, 302, 305, 401, and 406) have views of Sacré Coeur and the gardens surrounding it. If these rooms are not available, you can enjoy the view from the small hostel terrace. The hostel is on a street lined with fabric shops, and the famed bargain-bin department store Tati is at the corner. Montmartre can be fun if you don't mind the hikes around the *butte,* and if you revel in the laid-back party atmosphere that permeates the more tourist-saturated parts of this special area of Paris. Note that for you, anyway, partying can't go on forever because of the 2 A.M. curfew. For a complete description, see Aloha Hostel (page 311).

FACILITIES AND SERVICES: Elevator, Internet in lounge, kitchen privileges, TV with international reception in lounge, office safe (no charge)

NEAREST TOURIST ATTRACTIONS (RIGHT BANK): Montmartre

3 DUCKS HOSTEL (19)
6, place Étienne Pernet, 75015
Métro: Félix-Faure, Commerce

70 beds in shared rooms; 6 rooms also have showers only

This youthful hangout is not the sort of place moms and dads would check into—nor is it one you would want them to check out on your behalf. Its rugged appeal draws backpackers and other wanderers who value camaraderie along with wild and ribald fun over esthetics or a peaceful night's rest. The relaxed management requires shirts and shoes to be worn at all times and provides cooking facilities, hot showers, a TV in a casual bar with cheap beer, and rooms for two, three, or four persons. There are no lockers, only a storage room. The reception and bar are open all day, there is a lockout from 11 A.M. to 5 P.M., but there is a shower, bathroom, and kitchen open during this time. For a complete description, see Aloha Hostel (page 311).

NOTE: 3 Ducks Hostel is on the right side of Jean Baptiste de Grenelle Church, at the end of rue de Commerce.

FACILITIES AND SERVICES: Bar with beer and soft drinks, no elevator (3 floors), Internet in lounge, kitchen privileges, French TV in bar, office safe (no charge)

NEAREST TOURIST ATTRACTIONS (LEFT BANK): Far from everything, must use public transportation

TELEPHONE
01-48-42-04-05
FAX
01-48-42-99-99
INTERNET
www.3ducks.fr
RATES
Double 24€ per person, 4–10 people in dorm 21€ per person

WOODSTOCK HOSTEL (2)
48, rue Rodier, 75009
Métro: Anvers, Poissonnière

58 beds

Woodstock Hostel is about a ten-minute walk from the Gare du Nord and Gare de l'Est train stations and across the street from a pretty park where you can enjoy a picnic lunch or watch the children playing. Also close by are bakeries, a grocery, and a laundromat. Even though it is close to Pigalle and all the sleaze of that area, the hostel is in a safe pocket. But do be aware that the Anvers métro station is not considered safe at night. For a complete description, see Aloha Hostel (page 311).

FACILITIES AND SERVICES: No elevator (3 floors), Internet in lounge, kitchen privileges, office safe (no charge)

TELEPHONE
01-48-78-87-76
FAX
01-48-78-01-63
INTERNET
www.woodstock.fr
RATES
Double 23€ per person, 4–6 people in dorm 20€ per person

NEAREST TOURIST ATTRACTIONS (RIGHT BANK): Fifteen-minute walk to Sacré Coeur; otherwise, must use public transportation

YOUNG & HAPPY (Y & H) HOSTEL (37)
80, rue Mouffetard, 75005
Métro: Place Monge, Censier-Daubenton
65 beds

TELEPHONE
01-47-07-47-07

FAX
01-47-07-22-24

INTERNET
www.youngandhappy.fr

RATES
Double 25€ per person, 4–5 people in dorm 22€ per person

The Young & Happy Hostel is so named because it's friendly and everyone who stays here has such a good time. It is located on rue Mouffetard, a famous *marché* street with loads of cheap eats—everything from crêpes and croissants to pizza slices and dripping Greek sandwiches. It is also close to the Latin Quarter. You can reserve with a one-night advance deposit, or arrive when they open and hope for the best. For a complete description, see Aloha Hostel (page 311).

FACILITIES AND SERVICES: No elevator (4 floors), Internet in lounge, kitchen privileges, French TV in lounge, office safe (no charge)

NEAREST TOURIST ATTRACTIONS (LEFT BANK): Rue Mouffetard, Panthéon

Residence Hotels

Residence hotels are a popular concept because they combine many of the services and amenities you find in regular hotels with the advantages of having your own apartment. They generally come with a fully equipped kitchen, are usually roomier, and have more closet space than most deluxe hotel rooms, and often include some sort of housekeeping service. They are nice options for travelers staying for longer periods of time, and they bear absolutely no resemblance to the down-and-out accommodations that often go by the name "residence hotels" in the States.

Note that residence hotels in France can choose whether or not to apply for a star rating, and many do not. If a place listed below possesses no stars, that does not mean it is a "no star"; it could be luxurious and expensive—it just doesn't have the stars to prove it.

RESIDENCE HOTELS

Centre Parisien de Zen (12th)	**317**
Family Hôtel Résidence (15th)	**318**
Home Plazza Bastille (11th) ★★★	**319**
Home Plazza Saint-Antoine (11th) ★★★	**320**
Hôtel Résidence des Arts (6th, $)	**320**
Libertel Résidence–Villa Daubenton (5th)	**321**
Pierre & Vacances Résidence Montmartre (18th)	**321**
Résidence Hôtel des Trois Poussins (9th) ★★★	**322**

($) indicates a Big Splurge

CENTRE PARISIEN DE ZEN (23)
35, rue de Lyon, 75012
Métro: Gare de Lyon, Bastille

6 studios with kitchenettes

Peace and serenity are the by-words of this calming alternative to a stressful hotel stay. Grazyna and Jacob Perl, both Polish and both Zen masters, have opened six studio apartments and a meditation center in an old school building. When I first heard about it, I definitely had my doubts. Once I saw the amazingly low prices for the sparkling clean, whitewashed, wood-floor or carpeted studios surrounding a leafy, cobbled courtyard, I was ready to check in. Each bright, sunny, Ikea-furnished unit sleeps two on a good mattress with an orthopedic pillow (on request) and a duvet cover. In addition to a private bath and shower, there is a kitchen corner with two burners, refrigerator, sink, and all the utensils and dishes you will need. With one exception (No. 24), closet and drawer space is certainly adequate. Nice touches include Grazyna's framed paintings and a few paperback books.

TELEPHONE
01-44-87-08-13

FAX
01-44-87-09-07

EMAIL
maisonzen@pariszencenter.com.

INTERNET
www.maisonzen.com

CREDIT CARDS
None, cash only

RATES
rates are per week: Single 310–350€; double 425–450€; lower rates for longer stays; *taxe de séjour* included

BREAKFAST
Not served

ENGLISH SPOKEN
Yes, fluently, and Polish and Russian

The only television and telephone are in the common room, but if you are staying a month or more, you can get your own telephone line and private number. Once-a-week housekeeping service and linen change is included. The meditation room is open to everyone.

The neighborhood is a ten-minute walk from the Bastille, and the Marais and place des Vosges are a twenty-minute stroll. If you are a night owl, there is the fun and frivolity along rue de Lappe and rue de la Roquette. On Thursday and Sunday there is a huge open-air market at Bastille, and plenty of little food shops are nearby. A minimum stay of one week is required, and longer stays are welcomed. No smoking is allowed, and neither are shoes.

FACILITIES AND SERVICES: No elevator (3 floors), meditation room, communal French TV, office safe (no charge), no smoking allowed

NEAREST TOURIST ATTRACTIONS (RIGHT BANK): Bastille Opéra, Marais, place des Vosges

FAMILY HÔTEL RÉSIDENCE (8)
23, rue Fondary, 75015
Métro: Dupleix, Avenue Émile-Zola, La Motte Picquet–Grenelle
21 studios, all with kitchenette, shower, and toilet

These plain-as-a-pin studios in the middle of the working-class fifteenth arrondissement put the B on Basic. The twenty-one bargain sites are geared for economizers who are in for the long haul and want only a clean place to cook, eat, sleep, and take a shower, and nothing more. Fifteen have French TV; some have sofabeds, and others proper double or twin beds. The low-maintenance floors are white tile, bathrooms are reminiscent of train compartments, and the closets are designed for those who travel light and never shop. The colors match and so does the simple furniture. Kitchens are stocked with the barest essentials you will need to do simple cooking. There are two burners for cooking, but no microwave or oven. The units are kept clean, thanks to the housekeepers who swoop through three times a week. The operation is owned and run by Au Pacific Hôtel just down the street, where you pick up your keys and pay your bill (see page 248).

FACILITIES AND SERVICES: Direct-dial phone with separate line for each studio, elevator, kitchenettes, housekeeping service, French TV (in most rooms), office safe at Pacific Hôtel (no charge)

NEAREST TOURIST ATTRACTIONS (LEFT BANK): Eiffel Tower

TELEPHONE
01-43-92-42-42 (9 A.M.–7 P.M. daily)

FAX
01-45-77-70-73

EMAIL
pacifichotel@wanadoo.fr

INTERNET
www.familyresidence75.com

CREDIT CARDS
MC, V

RATES
Single 38€ (sofabed, no TV); 1–2 persons 44€ (double sofabed, no TV), 62–70€ (double or twin beds, TV); 74€ triple (double and single beds, TV); 20% discount after 7 nights, 30% discount after 15 nights; utilities, except the phone, included; *taxe de séjour* included

BREAKFAST
Not available

ENGLISH SPOKEN
Yes

HOME PLAZZA RÉSIDENCE HÔTELS: BASTILLE AND SAINT-ANTOINE

The two Home Plazza residences are in the eleventh arrondissement, a part of Paris that once was a tourist wilderness and now is close to the thick of things. The two residence hotels offer equipped studios and flats furnished in a modern, recently refurbished style that holds up well under hard use. While the Bastille résidence has the edge on location and amenities, the Saint-Antoine site is less impersonal and sterile. At both, impressive discounts can be negotiated during the low season and for longer stays, but during the fashion shows, the Paris Air Show, and any other internationally publicized events or conferences, there are outrageous supplements.

NOTE: The following information is the same for both Bastille and Saint-Antoine.

CENTRAL RESERVATIONS: 01-40-21-22-23/81; toll-free in U.S. 800-44-UTELL

FAX: 01-47-00-82-40

INTERNET: www.homeplazza.com

CREDIT CARDS: AE, DC, MC, V

RATES: From 1-person singles 230€ to 6-person rooms 725€; lower rates on request, in low season, and for long stays; *taxe de séjour* included

BREAKFAST: Buffet 18€ per person

ENGLISH SPOKEN: Yes

HOME PLAZZA BASTILLE ★★★ (11)
74, rue Amelot, 75011
Métro: St-Sebastien–Froissart, Chemin Vert
290 studios and apartments, fully furnished with equipped kitchens

FACILITIES AND SERVICES: Air-conditioning, bar, conference room, direct-dial phone, elevator, hair dryer, 7 rooms handicapped accessible, iron, laundry service, luggage storage, modem (150€ deposit!), complimentary newspapers, parking (23€ per day), restaurant, TV with international reception, room safe (no charge), 23 non-smoking rooms

NEAREST TOURIST ATTRACTIONS (RIGHT BANK): Marais, place des Vosges, Bastille, Musée National Picasso

TELEPHONE
01-40-21-20-00

FAX
01-47-00-82-40

EMAIL
resabastille@homeplazza.com

HOME PLAZZA SAINT-ANTOINE ★★★ (22)
289 bis, rue du Faubourg St-Antoine, 75011
Métro: Nation

TELEPHONE
01-40-09-40-94/00

FAX
01-40-09-11-55

EMAIL
resanation@home-plazza.com,
resabastille@homeplazza.com

INTERNET
www.1st-paris-
hotelsplazza.com

89 studios and apartments, fully furnished with equipped kitchens

From a security standpoint, I would avoid the rooms on the garden level.

FACILITIES AND SERVICES: Air-conditioning, conference room, direct-dial phone & fax, elevator, hair dryer, iron, laundry service, parking (23€ per day), TV with international reception, room safe (no charge), 1 floor non-smoking

NEAREST TOURIST ATTRACTIONS (RIGHT BANK): Nothing; must use public transportation

HÔTEL RÉSIDENCE DES ARTS ($, 23)
14, rue Gît-le-Coeur, 75006
Métro: Odéon, St-Michel; RER St-Michel–Notre-Dame

TELEPHONE
01-55-42-71-11

FAX
01-55-42-71-00

EMAIL
RDesarts@aol.com

INTERNET
www.arts-residence-paris.com

CREDIT CARDS
AE, MC, V

RATES
Studio 130–180€, suite 230–
280€, apartment 274–340€,
studio & suite combined 352–
430€; lower rates in off-season
and for longer stays; *taxe de
séjour* included

BREAKFAST
Continental 8€ per person

ENGLISH SPOKEN
Yes

5 studios, 5 suites, 1 large penthouse apartment

If you are looking for the ease of independent living combined with the full services of a hotel, the posh Résidence des Arts is for you. Pivotally located in the very core of St-Germain-des-Prés, the fifteenth-century private residence hotel offers five beautiful studios, five suites, and one stunning penthouse apartment, each combining luxurious touches with the convenience of a kitchen and individual service. Starting from the top, No. 6, the penthouse, is a large one-bedroom choice with mansard windows. The sitting room has a desk, large-screen television, and comfortable seating. The bedroom has a spacious bath with a separate bathtub and enclosed stall shower. The corner kitchen is well stocked for light cooking. As with all of the units, there is a private telephone line, modem connection, and air-conditioning. Next in size are the suites. I like No. 22, with a king-size bed and two windows looking toward the street. The studios are small, but they are certainly comfortable for one or two for a short stay. The bathroom comes with a stall shower, and all the other comforts are here. One benefit of the studios and suites is that they can be combined into large two-bedroom apartments, which is convenient for families.

FACILITIES AND SERVICES: Air-conditioning, direct-dial phone with private line, hair dryer, elevator, daily housekeeping service, daily towel and linen change, kitchen with microwave, laundry service, TV with international reception, room safe (no charge)

NEAREST TOURIST ATTRACTIONS (LEFT BANK): St-Germain-des-Prés, St-Michel, Seine, Île de la Cité, Île St-Louis

LIBERTEL RÉSIDENCE–VILLA DAUBENTON (42)
34, rue de l'Arbalète, 75005
Métro: Censier-Daubenton

16 studios and apartments

From a day-to-day living standpoint, the location is interesting because it is within easy walking distance to rue Mouffetard, one of the most famous market streets on the Left Bank, and the roving market at place Monge, where stalls are set up on Wednesday, Friday, and Sunday mornings. Walkers will enjoy strolling through the nearby Jardin des Plants or Jardin du Luxembourg. The accommodations are exceptional. There are only three per floor, so that alone is a plus. All of them, including the studios, have enough room, excellent bathrooms, and good closet space. Two one-bedroom units have a private terrace, and No. 601, an airy two-level duplex, has two terraces. The color of choice is blue, which can be a bit tiring, but you are not moving in forever . . . just a week or two. Daily housekeeping service is included.

FACILITIES AND SERVICES: Direct-dial phone, elevator, hair dryer, equipped kitchen, laundry services, parking TV with international reception, office safe (no charge)

NEAREST TOURIST ATTRACTIONS (LEFT BANK): Rue Mouffetard, Jardin des Plants

TELEPHONE
01-55-43-25-50

FAX
01-55-43-81-40

EMAIL
H2786@accor-hotels.com

INTERNET
www.accorhotels.com

CREDIT CARDS
AE, DC, MC, V

RATES
Studios for 1–2 people 163–195€; apartments for 1–6 people 163–269€; duplex for 4–6 people 227–259€; parking 13€ per day; *taxe de séjour* included

BREAKFAST
Buffet or Continental 13€ per person

ENGLISH SPOKEN
Yes

PIERRE & VACANCES–RÉSIDENCE MONTMARTRE (17)
10, place Charles Dullin, 75018
Métro: Abbesses, Anvers

76 studios and apartments

Pierre & Vacances is a large company that has many vacation-residence hotels throughout France. This is their only property in Paris, and it's located on a quiet cul-de-sac in Montmartre. Staying anywhere in Montmartre will require walking up and down hills, but the payoff is the villagelike community and all the picturesque little streets and alleyways you will discover in your travels. Thanks to a recent facelift that involved painting and recarpeting, this once worn-out establishment has improved. Unfortunately, this has not extended to the lobby and reception, which have had the same ugly black leather sofas for fifteen years. The impersonal yellow, blue, and white accommodations are spacious and simply furnished in wash-and-wipe white laminate. Most units have a microwave, all have a dishwasher and weekly housekeeping service. Frankly, it is not my first choice, but it is a good fall-back address to remember, especially if you like Montmarte.

TELEPHONE
01-42-57-14-55

FAX
01-42-54-48-87

INTERNET
www.pierre-vacances.fr

CREDIT CARDS
AE, DC, MC, V

RATES
Studio for 1–4 people 110–140€; apartments for 2–6 people 170–215€; 10% discount after 8 days, 20% discount after 28 days; *taxe de séjour* 0.86€ per person, per day

BREAKFAST
Continental 8.50€ per person

ENGLISH SPOKEN
Yes

FACILITIES AND SERVICES: Direct-dial phone, laundry services, elevator, equipped kitchens, TV with international reception, office safe (no charge)

NEAREST TOURIST ATTRACTIONS (RIGHT BANK): Montmartre, Sacré Coeur

RÉSIDENCE HÔTEL DES TROIS POUSSINS ★★★ (4)
15, rue Clauzel, 75009
Métro: St-Georges
40 rooms: 24 studios with kitchens, 16 hotel rooms, all with bath or shower and toilet

TELEPHONE
01-53-32-81-81

FAX
01-53-32-81-82

INTERNET
www.les3poussins.com

CREDIT CARDS
AE, MC, V

RATES
Hotel single 125–136€, double 140–197€, triple or quad 210–254€, studio with kitchenette 15€ supplement; extra bed 28€; seasonal & weekend discounts; *taxe de séjour* included

BREAKFAST
Buffet 10€ per person

ENGLISH SPOKEN
Yes

In its former life, the Résidence Hôtel des Trois Poussins was a fleabag bunker for young, hard-partying backpackers who were more interested in the earthly activities around Pigalle than in a decent place to stay. To say the place has been renovated is an injustice. It has been totally transformed and is now a very smart-looking address geared toward a discriminating clientele who are accustomed to the better things in life. The hotel is a combination of regular hotel rooms and studios with kitchenettes, allowing you to choose whichever style of accommodation suits your needs. Finally, its location in a small, nice neighborhood enclave is light-years away in spirit from the seamier neighborhood next to it.

Everything in the hotel has been well conceived, from the small, fitted kitchens, to the coordinated checks and prints that decorate the pretty rooms, to the garden where summer breakfasts are served. Many of the sixth-floor rooms have views that stretch from the Panthéon and Notre Dame to L'Église Notre Dame de Lorette. One of the most popular, especially for honeymooners, is No. 602, which has large windows encompassing this wide view and a lovely new bathroom. Those on the fourth floor are bathed in sunshine. The staff has a sense of what personal service is . . . and they deliver it. Nearby is an interesting market street, and you are within brisk walking distance to Montmartre. Special rates during the low season and for stays that include Friday, Saturday, and Sunday nights are available on request.

FACILITIES AND SERVICES: Air-conditioning, direct-dial phone and fax, elevator, hair dryer, 2 handicapped-accessible rooms, daily housekeeping service in studios, kitchens in studios, laundry service, TV with international reception, room safe (no charge)

NEAREST TOURIST ATTRACTIONS (RIGHT BANK): Nothing, must use public transportation

Student Accommodations

There are more than ten thousand student beds in Paris. The following list of both public and private sources offers help in finding low-cost student accommodations year-round. Most sites have a minimum stay in the summer, and curfews are not uncommon. All will give you the rules of the road before you get your bed, so there will be no excuses for improper conduct or pleading ignorance. It is critically important to remember that often only cash is accepted, and that most times you must either be an enrolled student or within a certain age bracket.

Any student can take advantage of the French government–run and –subsidized student lodgings as well as a wide range of other student discounts. To qualify for the *tarif étudiant,* you are required to show proof of full-time student status, in addition to your university or college ID, or if you are not a student, prove you are between the ages of twelve and twenty-five. The best way to show this additional proof is with the International Student Identity Card (ISIC) or with the Go-25 card (if you are between twelve and twenty-five years old and not a student). Both cards entitle you to savings on selected museum entry fees, film and theater tickets, transportation costs, meals at certain student dining halls, and of course, lodgings. Teachers can get some of the same discounts and all of the benefits by purchasing the International Teacher Identity Card (ITIC). In the United States the cards cost around $25, require a one-inch-size passport photo, and are available through STA (see below). The card can also be issued in Paris at the CROUS office at 39, avenue Georges-Bernanos, 5th, Métro: Port-Royal, Tel: 01-40-51-36-00, office open Monday to Friday 9 A.M. to 4:30 P.M. One of the best benefits of the student and teacher cards is the health insurance, which provides you with the following coverage at no additional cost: hospital coverage (sixty-day maximum stay), accident, accidental death, emergency medical evacuation and medical escort, and repatriation of remains. In addition, an ISIC card will save on airfares, transportation, attractions, and accommodations in more than ninety countries. It also provides users with a twenty-four-hour emergency help line and worldwide voice mail, fax messaging, and phone-card service through its ISIConnect feature. It is an unbelievable bargain. If you send for the card, allow three weeks; if you go to your local office, it will be issued on the spot. For more information, log onto the Websites www.isic.org. or www.statravel.com.

For information about work-study programs, contact the Council on International Education Exchange (CIEE) headquarters, 205 East 42nd Street, 16th Floor, New York, NY 10017, or call 1-800-407-8839. For worldwide reservations, contact STA at 6 Hamilton Place, 4th Floor, Boston, MA 02108, or call 1-800-226-8624. Hours are Monday to Friday 8 A.M. to 9 P.M. and Saturday 10 A.M. to 7 P.M. For information about their educational programs, call 1-800-407-8839; hours are Monday to Friday 9 A.M. to 5 P.M., Saturday 11 A.M. to 3 P.M. You can also visit their Website at www.ciee.org/isp for more information.

STUDENT ACCOMMODATIONS

Bureau des Voyages de la Jeunesse (BVJ; 1st, 5th) **324**
CROUS Académie de Paris (5th) **325**
Maison Internationale de la Jeunesse et des
    Étudiants (MIJE; 4th) **325**
Maison Internationale des Jeunes (MIJCP; 11th) **326**
OTU Voyage (4th) **326**

BUREAU DES VOYAGES DE LA JEUNESSE (BVJ)

Paris/Louvre location (47)
20, rue Jean-Jacques Rousseau, 75001
Métro: Louvre-Rivoli
200 beds, none with shower, bath, or toilet

Quartier Latin location (18)
44, rue des Bernardins, 75005
Métro: Maubert-Mutualité
113 beds, all rooms with shower, none with bath or toilet

TELEPHONE
Paris/Louvre: 01-53-00-90-90
Quartier Latin: 01-43-29-34-80
Group reservations (both locations): 01-53-00-90-95

FAX
Both locations: 01-53-00-90-91

EMAIL
Both locations: bvj@wanadoo.fr

INTERNET
Both locations: www.bvjhotel.com

CREDIT CARDS
MC, V (both at Paris/Louvre but only for groups)

RATES
All rates are per person. Louvre: twin double 27€, 4–8 bed dorm 24€. Quartier Latin: single 30€, 2–3 beds 27€, 5 beds 25€; *taxe de séjour* included

BREAKFAST
Continental included

ENGLISH SPOKEN
Yes

There are 313 beds for young people (ages eighteen to thirty-five) available in the heart of Paris, either on the Right Bank near the Louvre (called Paris/Louvre) or on the Left Bank in the Latin Quarter (at Quartier Latin). Most of the clientele travel light with only a backpack and don't mind sharing dorm rooms with up to eight other weary travelers. The good news: the prices are reasonable; there are some single and double accommodations in addition to the shared dorm rooms (for up to eight); and there is no daytime lockout or midnight curfew. The key is to land in a room with as few roommates as possible. The hall showers are free at Paris/Louvre, but at Quartier Latin, all rooms have a shower. No towels or soap are provided at either location, lockers cost 2€ per opening, and are worth it. Individual travelers usually need a two- or three-day advance reservation, but groups should reserve as far ahead as possible. The type of room cannot be guaranteed, but you don't have to pay for it until you see it upon arrival. There is a maximum one-week stay, with extensions only if space is available.

FACILITIES AND SERVICES: No elevators (6 floors), Internet in lobby and TV at Quartier Latin, no safe, no smoking allowed at either location

NEAREST TOURIST ATTRACTIONS: Paris/Louvre location (Right Bank): Louvre, Palais Royal, Centre Georges Pompidou (Beaubourg), Les Halles & Forum des Halles. Quartier Latin location (Left Bank): St-Michel, Latin Quarter, Seine, Île de la Cité, Île St-Louis

CROUS ACADÉMIE DE PARIS (40)
39, avenue Georges-Bernanos, 75005
Métro: RER Line B Port-Royal

CROUS plays a vital role in the life of a student in Paris. This organization is in charge of all University of Paris student residences, and offers beds during the French university vacation and a listing of short-term student foyers. It's the clearinghouse for foreign-student grants and operates student cafeterias providing students with inexpensive meals in its Restos-U (see *Great Eats Paris*). It is also a source of cheap trips and discount tickets for theater and cultural events, and the ISIC card is sold here. The address above is the main office where you should start your search, whether it be for meal tickets, a bed for your stay, or a trip outside of Paris. Hours are Monday to Friday from 9 A.M. to 4:30 P.M. English is spoken most of the time.

TELEPHONE
01-40-51-36-00
01-40-51-55-55
FAX
01-40-51-36-99
INTERNET
www.crous-paris.fr
ENGLISH SPOKEN
Generally

MAISON INTERNATIONALE DE LA JEUNESSE ET DES ÉTUDIANTS (MIJE, 44)
6, rue de Fourcy, 75004
Métro: St-Paul

MIJE offers some of the best student beds in Paris in two converted seventeenth-century historic mansions and a former convent. Each room holds from two to ten people; all rooms have a sink and shower. The address given above (Le Fourcy) is also the main office where all reservations are made. There is also a dining room here that is open to anyone staying in the three hostels. Sheets are provided, but no towels or soap. There is a 2.50€ one-year membership fee, the maximum stay is seven nights, and no one over thirty is accepted. No smoking or booze is allowed, and there is a room lockout from noon to 3 P.M., and a 1 A.M. curfew. Advanced reservations by telephone *only* are accepted a week before arrival. They do not accept reservations by email or fax.

NOTE: The other two locations are Fauconnier, 11, rue Fauconnier (4th), Métro: St-Paul; and Maubuisson, 12, rue des Barres (4th), Métro: Hôtel-de-Ville.

FACILITIES AND SERVICES: Elevator (Fourcy), Internet facilities at Fourcy and Fauconnier; restaurant at Fourcy, office safe (no charge for groups, individuals pay 1€ for the key)

NEAREST TOURIST ATTRACTIONS (RIGHT BANK): Marais, place des Vosges, Musée National Picasso, Seine, St-Michel, St-Germain-des-Prés, Bastille Opéra

TELEPHONE
01-42-74-23-45
FAX
01-40-27-81-64
INTERNET
www.mije.com
CREDIT CARDS
None, cash only
RATES
All rates are per person: single 40€, double 30€, triple 26€, quad 25€, dorm (5 to 10 persons) 24€; restaurant, lunch or dinner 11€, three courses; *taxe de séjour* included
BREAKFAST
Included
ENGLISH SPOKEN
Yes

MAISON INTERNATIONALE DES JEUNES (MIJCP, 19)
4, rue Titon, 75011
Métro: Faidherbe-Chaligny
170 beds, no private facilities

TELEPHONE
01-43-71-99-21

FAX
01-43-71-78-58

EMAIL
mij.cp@wanadoo.fr

CREDIT CARDS
None, cash only

RATES
20€ per person; free shower;
sheet rental 2.30€, towel rental
1€; *taxe de séjour* included

BREAKFAST
Included

ENGLISH SPOKEN
Yes

Open to people age eighteen to thirty (older if with a group), the MIJCP offers clean rooms with two to eight basic bunks and not much else. Even the neighborhood is boring. The maximum length of stay is between three and four nights. Breakfast and a free shower are included in the daily rate; everything else is extra. Facilities are nil: no safes, lockers, laundry, TV, or even bed lights, and you must bring your own sheets, soap, and towels or rent them here. There is a 2 A.M. curfew and a daily cleaning lockout from 10 A.M. until 5 P.M. The office is open from 8 A.M. to 1 A.M. This is one to keep in mind when all else fails.

FACILITIES AND SERVICES: None

NEAREST TOURIST ATTRACTIONS (RIGHT BANK): Nothing, must use public transportation

OTU VOYAGE (11)
119, rue St-Martin, Parvis de Beaubourg, 75004
Métro: Rambuteau

TELEPHONE
01-40-29-12-22

FAX
01-40-29-12-20

EMAIL
paris.beaubourg@.fr

INTERNET
www.otu.fr

CREDIT CARDS
MC, V

ENGLISH SPOKEN
Yes

Located across the square from the Centre Georges Pompidou (Beaubourg), OTU provides discount travel help and information on accommodations, travel, and many other related items of interest to anyone age eighteen to thirty. Office hours are Monday to Friday 9:30 A.M. to 6:30 P.M., Saturday 10 A.M. to 5 P.M. They also sell the ISIC card, which every student or teacher should have in their possession (see page 323).

Shopping: Great Chic

**Paris is wrenchingly beautiful, and so are many of its people.
If you use your eyes and take in everything, you can learn
more about true style in a weekend than in a lifetime's perusal
of fashion magazines.**
                                        —*Lucia Van der Post*

A museum is a museum, but a bargain is forever. . . .
                    —*Suzy K. Gershman,* Born to Shop Paris

Paris is a shopper's dream world. Even those who claim to dislike shopping are bound to be attracted by the unending selection of shops with beautiful window displays. The haute couture, open air *marchés* overflowing with beautiful foods, extravagant toy shops, and the dazzling displays of jewelry, antiques, and collectibles tempt everyone from the serious buyer to the casual browser. There has always been something very stylish about the French. Just the addition of the word French to everyday objects such as jeans, silk, perfume, bread, wine, cheese, and toast lifts them out of the ordinary. For many of us, going to Paris is a dream come true, but it isn't quite enough . . . we want to bring something of Paris home with us. However, a recent study showed Paris to be the most expensive city in Europe for buying clothes and shoes. What are we to do—those of us who cannot afford to pay the astronomically high prices that come with such glorious merchandise? Become a Parisian smart shopper.

After you have been in Paris for a day or so, you will realize that style counts: the French do not just get dressed—they get turned out, many in *couturière* battle dress, with the emphasis on quality not quantity. You will no doubt wonder how a modest shop clerk manages to look so elegant, considering his or her low wages and the high price tags for clothing. The answer is simple: savvy Parisian shoppers know where to go for the best quality and value, and they seldom pay full price.

Shopping the secondhand clothing stores was once reserved for a minority who seldom admitted it, but this has now become a mainstream activity in Paris. Paying less has been given a new cachet. Determined discount bounty hunters shop with a vengeance for vintage clothing, which has become so "in" that designers have based entire collections on specific retro looks. As a lifelong, dedicated discount shopper with a black belt in the art, I know that bargain shopping of any kind can be both frustrating and exhausting—until you find that fabulous designer suit in your size and favorite color for half price. Any type of discount shopping in Paris takes a good eye, limitless patience, endurance, and comfortable shoes. In Paris, of all places, it should be more than just a quest to track down the cheapest items available . . . it should be fun. Finding something *très à la mode* at below retail in Paris is not that difficult once you know how. The trick is in knowing when and where to shop to get the most for your money. That is what this chapter will help you to do: transform your T-shirt into a significant outfit, with just the right pair of pants, a sassy jacket, and perfect accessories for the moment—all for reduced prices and, more importantly, for less than you would pay at home.

With all discount shopping, especially in clothing stores, the selections will vary from day to day and season to season. Shops also come and go. What is here today and very "in" may be gone tomorrow. Not all shops take credit cards, so be prepared with euros. The comfort of the customer is seldom a top priority if you are on the designer discount beat. As a result, many of these places do not have proper dressing rooms, most are jammed with merchandise, there is limited individual attention, and in many cases, only fragmented English is spoken. And never mind the ice-maiden *vendeuse* who has an innate knack for sizing you up and pricing everything you are wearing in one glance. Believe me, it is all worth it because nothing is more satisfying than being clad in designer labels at knockdown prices.

In addition to leading you to fabulous discount clothing buys, this chapter guides you to a gamut of great shopping: from the best English-language bookstores, children's toys and clothes, cosmetics, kitchen supplies, and jewelry to flea and antique markets, produce markets, museum shops, historic *passages,* and department stores. Armed with "Great Chic," you are bound to find great gifts and clothes, save money, and come home with unique discoveries your friends will die over. *Bon chance!* And please, if you uncover something wonderful, let me know.

Tips for Great Shopping

> Nobody who has not lived in Paris can appreciate the unique savor of that word *femmes*.
>
> —*Arnold Bennett,* Paris Nights *(1913)*

1. Know the prices at home so you will be able to spot a bargain when you see it in Paris. Carry a calculator to be sure you are getting the bargain you think you are.

2. Form is very important for the French. When you enter a store, you will be greeted with *Bonjour, Madame* (or *Monsieur*), and when you leave, *Au revoir, Madame* (or *Monsieur*), *merci.* Please respond in kind, with *Bonjour, Mademoiselle,* and so on. It is considered extremely bad form not to acknowledge the salespeople when entering or leaving a store.

3. If you like something, can afford it, and can get it home, buy it when you see it. If you wait until later, it probably will not be there when you go back, or you will see it when you get home for twice the price.

4. Look for these signs in the windows—they mean lower prices:

Soldes	a sale in progress
Fin de Séries	end of collection
Dégriffés	labels cut out
Stock	overstock
Dépôt Vente	resale
Fripes	used clothing
Troc, brocante	secondhand

5. Seldom in small shops will you be able to return something, and if you manage to do so, the hassle will probably not be worth it. To avoid this time-consuming headache, be sure when you buy something from a small shopkeeper that it does not have flaws, that it fits, and that it's what you want. However, most major department stores, including Monoprix, will accept returns for full refund from thirty days of the date purchased with the receipt.

6. If you have a consumer complaint with a shop or store, write to Direction Départmentale de la Concurrence, de la Consommation, et la Repression des Fraudes, 8, rue Froissart, 75153 Paris, Tel: 01-40-27-16 00 (Mon–Fri 9 A.M.–noon, 2–5:30 P.M.). This office is in the Ministry of Finance. Be sure to include an explanation, copies of your receipt, and any correspondence you have had with the seller.

7. Never change money at a shop. The rate will not be in your favor. Go instead to a bank or ATM, or use a credit card.

8. If you are shopping at one of the flea markets, you can definitely bargain. The asking price is not the price you are expected to pay. You should be able to get the price down by 15 to 30 percent. Also, bring cash: plastic is not part of a bargaining discussion, and most sellers do not take credit cards of any type.

9. Pharmacies are marked with a green cross on a white background. They are the places to go if you need a prescription filled or advice on cold remedies. In addition many pharmacies also carry excellent hair and skin products that you never see at home. But everyday toiletries and basic cosmetics will be cheaper in supermarkets or at Monoprix.

10. Pack an empty, soft-folding suitcase in your luggage so you can transport your treasures without the extra bother and expense of mailing. An extra bag on an airline (over the limit of two, plus a carry-on) will cost around a hundred dollars, and that will be *less* than you will have to pay the store, Federal Express, or UPS to have it sent, never mind the time and hassle to pack and get your items there. That said, if you do have a major department store mail your packages, the *détaxe* is automatically deducted from the total price, so that could be an incentive (See "Getting It All Home," page 335).

11. Be sure to get the 10 percent discount card issued to all foreigners who shop at the major department stores (with the exception of

Bon Marché and Monoprix). If you add this savings to the *détaxe* (which is 13 percent), the savings can be considerable (see "Department Stores," page 333).

12. If you are eligible for a tax refund, take the time to fill out the *détaxe* form, and remember to turn it into the customs officials at the airport before you relinquish your luggage or go through customs or passport control (see "Tax Refund: *Détaxe,*" page 331).

13. When returning to the United States, remember these points when going through customs:

   • You and every member of your family, regardless of age, can bring back $800 worth of purchases duty-free. Family members can pool their duty-free purchases (see "Customs," page 332).

   • Don't cheat, don't smuggle, and above all, don't carry drugs.

   • Be nice.

Shopping Hours

Generally speaking, shopping hours are Monday through Saturday from 9:30 or 10 A.M. to 7 P.M. Large department stores are open later one night a week. Small shops sometimes close Monday morning, for lunch, and often for all or part of August. Food markets are usually open Sunday morning but closed on Monday. With the exception of the heavily touristed areas, all stores are closed on Sunday and major holidays.

Size Conversion Charts

Many French off-the-rack manufacturers have their own cuts, and sizes are not always uniform. Whenever possible, it is important to try on clothing before you buy. However, that is not always possible, so bring your measurements and carry a tape measure showing both inches and centimeters. Be careful with men's shirt sleeves, as the length is not always given; be prepared to measure. Table and bed linen sizes are also different from those in the States.

Women's dresses: To change French dress sizes to U.S. sizes, subtract 28 from the French dress size. To change U.S. dress sizes to French, add 28 to the U.S. dress size.

French	32	34	36	38	40	42	44
U.S.	4	6	8	10	12	14	16

Women's sweaters and blouses: To change French sizes to U.S., subtract 8 from the French blouse or sweater size. To change U.S. sizes to French, add 8 to the U.S. size.

French	38	40	42	44	46	48	50
U.S.	30	32	34	36	38	40	42

Men's suits: To change French suit sizes to U.S. sizes, subtract 10 from the French suit size. To change U.S. suit sizes to French, add 10 to the U.S. size.

French	46	48	50	52	54	56	58
U.S.	36	38	40	42	44	46	48

Men's shirts: To change French shirt sizes to U.S., subtract 8 from the French size and divide by 2. To change U.S. shirt sizes to French, multiply the U.S. size by 2 and add 8.

French	36	37	38	39	40	41	42	43
U.S.	14	14.5	15	15.5	16	16.5	17	17.5

Women's Shoes: To change French shoe sizes to U.S., subtract 32 from the French size. To change U.S. shoe sizes to French, add 32 to the U.S. shoe size.

French	36	37	38	39	40	41	42	43	44
U.S.	4	5	6	7	8	9	10	11½	12

Men's Shoes

French	39	40	41	42	43	44	45	46
U.S.	7	7½	8	8½	9½	10½	11	11½

Children's clothing: French children's clothes are sized according to the child's age. Look for the abbreviations "m" and "a," which stand for month and year (in French, "m" stands for *mois*, or "month," and "a" stands for *ans*, or "years"). Thus, 2m means two months, 16m means sixteen months, 2a means two years, 6a means six years, and so on.

Tax Refund: *Détaxe*

Every non–European Union resident spending six months or less in France is entitled to a 12 to 14 percent *détaxe* (tax rebate) for minimum purchases of 175 to 200€ (depending on the store), made on the same day in the same store. In smaller shops you usually must ask for the form, but in the big department stores, you can get it from the Tax Refund Desk. You must always present your passport for identification. If shopping with a friend, combine your purchases to reach the total and share the proceeds when they arrive. You and the store representative fill out the simple paperwork. At your point of exit from France, or another EU country, present your tax refund forms and have your purchases ready for inspection at the customs office in the last country you visit in the European Union. At the airport, look for the window that says *douane de détaxe* and allow an extra half hour to accomplish the mission. After having customs stamp the forms, you must send back the pink form(s) in the self addressed, stamped envelope given to you by the store at the time of purchase. There is usually a mailbox next to the customs office. You have three months following the month you made your purchases to do this. That's it.

On the *détaxe* form, you will be asked to state whether you want the refund mailed to you in a euro check or to have it credited to your credit card. Obtaining your refund by check is not recommended because it is hard to deal with in the United States and getting it can take forever. Ask for the rebate on your credit card—your credit card company will credit the refund to you in U.S. dollars. Expect a delay of two to three months. For items shipped directly from the store, the *détaxe* is automatically deducted without any paperwork. Yes, it all does take some extra time and effort, but the savings do add up, so persevere.

NOTE: The *détaxe* does not apply for services, food, drink, medicine, unset gems, antiques, works of art, automobiles or their parts, or commercial purchases.

Customs

Each U.S. citizen, even a week-old baby, is entitled to bring back $800 worth of duty-free goods acquired abroad. Families can pool their duty-free purchases, so you can use what your spouse and children do not. After the $800 point, there will be a duty charged. Have your receipts ready and make sure they coincide with what you filled out on the landing card. Don't cheat or lie, as you will invariably be caught. If that happens, you and your luggage will undergo exhaustive searches, and that will just be for openers. Any purchase worth less than $100 can be shipped back to the States as an unsolicited gift and is considered duty-free, and it does not count in your $800 limit. You can send as many of these unsolicited gifts as you wish, but only one unsolicited gift per person for each mailing, and don't mail anything to yourself. If your package worth exceeds $100, you will pay duty.

Antiques must be over one hundred years old to be duty-free.

A work of art is duty-free, and it does not matter when it was created or who the artist was.

If you have expensive cameras, piles of imported luggage, fancy watches, or valuable jewelry, carry the receipts for them, or you could be questioned about them and even end up paying duty on them.

Finally, it's simply a fact of customs: people who look like hippies get stopped and have their bags searched. The same goes for bejeweled and bedecked women wrapped in full-length furs and carrying expensive designer luggage.

For more information on U.S. Customs rules and regulations, send for the free brochure *Know Before You Go,* available from the Department of the Treasury, U.S. Customs Service, Washington, D.C., 20229; Tel: 202-927-1700 or 202-354-1000; Internet: www.cpb.gov.

Consignment Shops: *Dépôts-Ventes*

Consignment shops sell previously owned items at a fraction of original cost. Some people balk at the idea of wearing "used" clothing, but please, try to shed this reluctance. Keep in mind that many of the items are barely worn; they are being consigned so that their owner will have more money to spend in the designer boutiques . . . only to recycle them again after one wearing. In Paris, it is considered very fashionable to resurrect something from oblivion and incorporate it into your wardrobe, or to outsmart retail buyers by finding a fabulous Armani suit for a fraction of what they paid for it. Believe me, this is big business in Paris and you would be surprised at the number of very sophisticated and well-known fellow bargain-inspired shoppers you may recognize standing next to you searching the racks for just the perfect "previously owned" outfit.

For a complete list of all the consignment shops in this book, see page 399.

Department Stores

Bargain shoppers take note: Most of the department stores listed here will issue a 10 percent discount shopping card upon presentation of your passport. Just go to the Welcome Desk; someone who speaks English will be there to issue you the card. When paying, you may have to go to a special *caisse* (a cashier's desk) to pay, and then take your paid receipt back to the department where you initially found the item. It's a bit of a drag . . . but it is 10 percent, and that can add up. The exceptions are Tati, Monoprix, and Bon Marché.

On top of that, don't forget that you will qualify for the 12 to 14 percent *détaxe* if you spend (depending on department store) 175 to 200€ in the same store. Unfortunately, that amount is not cumulative over several shopping trips; it is per day. But if you plan accordingly and combine it with your 10 percent discount card, you can save 23 percent. Keep this in mind especially if you are shopping for items that may be sold elsewhere in Paris in specialty boutiques. For example, many Americans have a love affair with Mephisto and Arche shoes, and know that they are cheaper in Paris. Both Galeries Lafayette and Au Printemps carry these shoes . . . so, why buy them someplace else if you can buy them here and save an additional 10 percent plus the *détaxe?*

For a complete list of all the department stores in this book, see page 400.

Designer Discount Boutiques

Anyone can pay retail . . . . It takes talent, dedication, and hard work to get a good deal.
—Diana Withee, art historian and
veteran shopper

These boutiques sell designer label stock at well below the retail prices you will pay elsewhere in Paris for exactly the same items, but you will be looking at last season's collections. Sometimes the labels have been cut out.

For a complete list of all the designer discount boutiques in this book, see page 400.

DISCOUNT SHOPPING MALL: LA VALLÉE OUTLET SHOPPING VILLAGE

3 cours de la Garonne, 77700 Serris, Marne-la-Vallée
TELEPHONE: 01-60-42-35-00
INTERNET: www.lavalleevillage.com
CREDIT CARDS: Depends on shop, but usually MC, V
OPEN: Mon–Sat 10 A.M.–7 P.M., Sun 11 A.M.–7 P.M. (these hours can vary slightly)

For a total immersion in discount shopping, go to La Vallée Outlet Shopping Village, a very posh outlet shopping mall open seven days a week, and a forty-five-minute RER ride from Paris. For the nonshoppers in your party, Paris Disney is only a five-minute RER ride from the discount mall, and even closer is the Sealife Aquarium next door. An on-call shuttle service is available to and from Disney hotels and the Val d'Europe RER station. The shops are well laid out on a winding walkway that is designed to look like a provincial market town. The list of designers represented is impressive, and so are the discounts: at least 30 percent for openers, and in some cases, up to 60 percent. Okay, so the items are last season or end of stock, but there are plenty of classic staples from names we all love: Kenzo, Versace, Givenchy, Max Mara, Charles Jourdain, Reebok, Calvin Klein, Diesel, Jean-Charles de Castelbajac, Prada, Christian Lacroix, and many more. Don't forget to get the *détaxe* on purchases that total over 175€ made in the same store (see "Tax Refund: *Détaxe*," page 331). Go on a weekday and you will have the shops and the salespeople almost to yourself. There are no restaurants here, but there are nice bathrooms and a play area for children. In the regular-price mall next door, there are plenty of places to eat, the Sealife Aquarium as well as an immense Auchan hypermarket with thirty checkout stands.

How to get there: From Châtelet–Les Halles, take the RER A line that goes to Disney Paris. On the train platform, look for the light that is on next to Val d'Europe. This is the train you want, because that is your stop. Before leaving the station at Val d'Europe, check on the return train times for Paris.

Sales: *Soldes*

During most of the year, when you venture into one of the designer shops, they are quiet enough for you to hear the rustle of money being spent by wealthy customers. However, we less-affluent mortals also have a chance in these stores. It is hard to imagine the U.S. government dictating to stores the dates on which they can hold sales . . . but that is exactly what happens in France. As it now stands, during the first three weeks in January and six weeks beginning the last week of June through July, the French *ministre de shopping* has declared that *toute* Paris will be on sale. In addition, Galeries Lafayette, Au Printemps, and many other large department stores have special offers throughout the rest of the year. But the real bargains are found during the January and July sales, when the crowds of shoppers move with dizzying swiftness, all zeroing in on the considerable savings. If you can brave these shopping pros, this is the time to go to the designer boutiques and pick up a little number for about one-third the U.S. retail price. In October, Hèrmes has its annual sale. The line forms the night before, with shoppers eager to pay 50 percent less for the famous signature scarves (currently retailing for over $250), ties, leather goods, and conservative line of clothing. Again, if you do not mind standing in line and fighting crowds packed in ten-deep, then this sale is a must for Hèrmes fans.

Getting It All Home

I recommend taking an extra fold-up suitcase if you are a dedicated shop hound. This way, you can take your purchases with you on the plane, they arrive when you do, and at worst, you have to pay the extra bag charge of around $125. If you buy such a suitcase in Paris, you get to keep the bag for the next trip. Some stores, including the major department stores, will ship items. If you have spent over their limit for the *détaxe* (see page 331), they will deduct the *détaxe* from your total on the spot. Otherwise, you have three options, two of which will cost about the same as the extra bag on the airplane, maybe more, and all three will entail work on your part. These options are Federal Express, UPS, and the French post office. Think about carrying heavy boxes or the contents to pack on site, through several métro changes, or in a taxi, and believe me, the airline option looks great.

FEDERAL EXPRESS
63, boulevard Haussmann, 75009
Métro: Havre-Caumartin

The folks at Fedex speak English, have boxes, and will pick up your parcels (3€ extra). Their prices are very expensive and are based on weight, contents, and destination. For example: 10kg, 131€; 25kg, 196€.

TELEPHONE: 08-00-12-38-00

CREDIT CARDS: AE, MC, V

OPEN: Mon–Fri 9 A.M.–7 P.M. (by 5:45 P.M. for same day sending), Sat 9 A.M.–5 P.M. (by 4:45 P.M. for same day sending)

UPS
Corner rue Réaumur & rue Montmartre, 75002
Métro: Sentier

They also have shipping boxes, and prices based on weight, contents, and destination. However, their rates are even higher than Fedex.

OPEN: Mon–Fri 11 A.M.–8:30 P.M.

POST OFFICE (PTT)

Post offices *(bureaux de poste)* are in every *quartier*. The best one in Paris is the main post office at 52, rue du Louvre, 75001, Métro: Louvre-Rivoli, Tel. 01-40-28-76-00. It is open 24 hours a day, 365 days a year; it is the only post office in France with these hours. At all post offices, you can purchase boxes in various sizes. There are two types: one marked

Chronopost for mailing within France, and another marked Colissimo, which you will need if you are sending items to the U.S. The price of the box includes the postage, and there is no weight limit. Figure around 35€ for the largest box. The hours at all other post offices are Mon–Fri 8 A.M.–7 P.M., and Sat 8 A.M.–noon.

Shopping Areas

PLACE DES VICTOIRES, 75001 (27; see map page 62)
Métro: Étienne-Marcel, Palais-Royal–Musée du Louvre

This is a smart shopping section nestled behind Palais-Royal. After going around the place des Victoires, branch out down the side streets. This is an area of many fashion innovators and well worth serious time just to see what you will be wearing two years from now. The prices are not bargains unless you happen to hit a sale.

PLACE VENDÔME, 75001 (12; see map page 62)
Métro: Tuileries, Opéra

Cartier, Van Cleef & Arpels, Trussardi, Bulgari, and international banks cater to the needs of the guests at the Hôtel Ritz around place Vendôme.

MARAIS AND PLACE DES VOSGES, 75003 AND 75004 (15 and 42; see map page 84)
Métro: St-Paul

The Marais is the oldest *quartier* in Paris. The kosher food shops along rue des Rosiers, the trendy boutiques along rue Francs Bourgeois, the menswear shops lining the rue de Turenne, and the avant-garde designers make shopping in the Marais an excellent adventure. The place des Vosges, which Henri IV had constructed between 1605 and 1612, was the first planned square to be built in Paris. Today, the symmetrical, soft-pink stone square made up of thirty-six slate-roof town homes is lovely. Be sure to include a stroll through the shops and galleries in the stone arcades and sit in one of the cafés. Most of the shops along Francs Bourgeois and in the place des Vosges are open on Sunday (see *Great Eats Paris*).

VILLAGE ST-PAUL, RUE ST-PAUL, AND RUE DU PONT LOUIS PHILIPPE, 75004 (49; see map page 84)
Métro: St-Paul

The Village St-Paul is a collective name for the fifty or more antique and *brocante* dealers who line rue St-Paul and the courtyard squares surrounding it. It's a favorite Sunday destination for many Parisians because the shops are all open. One of my favorites is Baïkal at 24, rue St-Paul. This interesting shop, run by Michael Monlaü and his partner, Thierry de la Salmoniere, specializes in Asian artifacts and antiques. For almost seventy years, the shop was a local bar run by the same woman and by her parents before that. When Michael and Thierry took it over, they saved and restored the old bar and countertop, which had stood in the same place for a century. For all those years, the locals spent part of their lives here and left part of their souls, leaning against the bar and tossing down their daily quotas. Today it's still in the middle of the shop. The bar is not for sale, but everything else is. Tel.: 01-42-74-73-39; Internet: www.baikal.fr

On the rue du Pont Louis Philippe, you will find calligraphy and paper shops and stores selling perfumed candles.

ST-GERMAIN-DES-PRÉS, 75006 (13; see map page 140)
Métro: St-Germain-des-Prés

Sensational shopping can be found on the rue de Sèvres, rue Bonaparte, rue du Four, rue St-Sulpice, rue Jacob, rue de Saints-Pères, rue de Grenelle, rue du Bac, and the rue de Seine, to mention only a few of the streets that line this *quartier,* which is literally packed with fashion boutiques, antique shops, art galleries, bookshops, and the magnificent Le Bon Marché department store. In fact, if you have only a short time to devote to shopping and browsing, this is where you should go.

CHAMPS-ÉLYSÉES, 75008 (11; see map page 202)
Métro: Charles-de-Gaulle-Étoile

The Champs-Élysées is enjoying a renaissance for shopping and entertainment. There are still waves of tourists (300,000 per day) flowing up one side and down the other of the most famous avenue in the world. Now, in addition to the movie theaters, airline offices, banks, car dealers, fast-food outlets, mini-malls, and outdoor cafés—all charging top prices for everything—lining each side of the majestic avenue, fashion boutiques and multipurpose stores are making their presence known. The Virgin Megastore, Séphora cosmetics and perfume supermarket, and the Peugeot showroom redone by Sir Terence Conran into a design and dining space are only a few of the blockbuster addresses Parisians are flocking to. No one said anything about bargains, either in food, goods, or drink, but a stroll along the Champs-Élysées, a look into these amazing shopping venues, and sipping a drink at a café, all the while engaging in fascinating people-watching, is one of the must-dos of Paris and is now more enjoyable than ever. For further information consult www.champs-elysees.org. Please beware: Pickpockets continue to work both sides of the street and they are pros . . . watch out!

RUE ROYALE, 75008 (50; see map page 202)
Métro: Concorde, Madeleine

Rue Royale runs from the place de la Concorde to the Madeleine Church. It is a short stretch but packed with shopping treasures that are not only *très chic,* but *très cher.* In addition to admiring the window displays, be sure to stop at Ladurée, which opened on rue Royale in 1862. Ladurée is credited with inventing the macaroon, and theirs are without question the best. Obviously, Parisians agree—3,000 are sold daily. Be sure to wander into the pedestrian passages that flow off of rue Royale—the glass-roofed Galerie de la Madeleine, the Galerie Royale, and Le Village Royale—for more elegantly magical shopping. Along one side of the church is a colorful flower market, and lining the streets behind it are the finest gourmet shops in the city.

THE GOLDEN TRIANGLE, 75008 (see map page 202)
Métro: Alma-Marceau

When cost is not an object, come to the Golden Triangle, which is formed by Avenue George-V, avenue Marceau, avenue Montaigne, and rue François 1er. For window-shopping and dreaming of the highest order, these five premier shopping streets are to designer fashion and haute couture what the Louvre is to priceless art. The boutiques and shops are not to be missed, even if you only stroll by the elegant window displays.

RUE DE PASSY AND AVENUE VICTOR HUGO, 75016 (24 and 2; see map page 256)
Métro: Passy, Victor Hugo

Walking down either of these streets in the sixteenth arrondissement will give you an idea of what it is like to be upper-middle-class and living in Paris. You will see few tourists, no razor-shaved haircuts, and certainly no hawkers waving T-shirts or plastic replicas of the Eiffel Tower. This is the land of the BCBGs (French yuppies), old money, and tradition. There are several cafés if someone in your party would rather sit and have a beer while watching the world wander by.

Discount Shopping Streets

Just as Paris has its high-priced shopping streets, it also has its discount shopping streets. No dedicated discount shopper will want to miss a trip to one of these streets where, if you are lucky, you will bring home something marvelous that your friends would kill for . . . even at three times the price you paid.

Note that most shops will take Visa or MasterCard, not American Express or Diners Club. Hours vary with each shop; however, in general stores are open Monday 2 to 7 P.M., and Tuesday to Saturday 10 A.M. to 7 P.M.

RUE MESLAY, 75003 (2; see map page 84)
Métro: République

One entire street devoted to shoes—one store after the other—with everything from clodhoppers to four-inch red-satin sling pumps. Prices are good. The best advice is to browse first, then go back and do serious buying. Finding the perfect pair of shoes takes time and energy, not to say patience. Don't try to squeeze this one in . . . allow time and leave nonshopping pals at the hotel.

RUE ST-PLACIDE, 75006 (43; see map page 140)
Métro: Sèvres-Babylone

Bargain fever has hit Paris in a cluster of boutiques along rue St-Placide. Start at Bon Marché department store and work both sides of the street. This can be frustrating if the crowds are out in force, especially at lunchtime when the office workers surge through and on Saturday when housewives leave *les enfants* at home and make the pilgrimage. Best buys are in casual sportswear and teenage "must-haves" of the moment. There are no top-name designers, but everything is *au courant*. Windows are often more appealing than the stuffy, cramped interiors. Sharpen your elbows for this—and watch your handbag carefully.

RUE ST-DOMINIQUE, 75007 (5; see map page 176)
Métro: Latour-Maubourg

It isn't as good as it used to be, but along rue St-Dominique from avenue Bosquet to boulevard de Latour-Maubourg, shops sell clothing for men, women, and children from designer *dégriffés* (labels cut out) to bins of last season's T-shirts. Affordable.

RUE DE PARADIS, 75010
Métro: Château d'Eau, Gare de l'Est

This is the best area in Paris for china and crystal, in one crowded shop after another. Be sure to look at the magnificent Baccarat crystal store, and check their back table with the red dots on end-of-the-line designs, which sell for up to half regular price. Baccarat is at 32, rue de Paradis; it's open Monday to Friday 9 A.M. to 6 P.M., Saturday 10 A.M. to noon, 2 to 5 P.M. Other worthwhile stops are at La Maison de la Porcelaine at 21, rue de Paradis, with over 100,000 articles of Limoges porcelain in stock, and Limoges Unic, 34 & 58 rue de Paradis. Staff at all shops speak English; the *détaxe* is available, and they ship.

RUE D'ALÉSIA, 75014 (26; see map page 240)
Métro: Alésia

Both sides of rue d'Alésia are home to an assortment of outlet shops carrying last season's lines of designers, some of whom you have heard of and some you never will. The best line of attack is to go up one side and down the other to get an overview, and then come back to those that seem promising. The worst time to go is on Saturday. Some of the better shops are the following: SR (Sonya Rykiel), No. 110 & No. 64; Dorotennis Stock (Dorothée Bis), No. 74; Evolutif: Georges Rech, Kenzo, YSL, Givenchy, Armani, all for men, No. 90; Franck B., No. 96; Tout Compte Fait, No. 103; Petits Petons, No. 113; Cacharel, No. 114; Café Cotton, No. 115; Amazone, No. 118; Chevignon, No. 122; and two Monoprix stores with regular prices.

WARNING: The numbering system is crazy, but these are close.

Passages

Long before anyone heard of shopping malls, Paris had galleries and *passages*—skylighted, decorated, tiled, and beautiful. Built in the early nineteenth century for wealthy shoppers, they are a reflection of the prosperity and flamboyance of the Belle Epoque era. Tucked away off major commercial streets, mainly in the second and ninth arrondissements, they are easy to miss if you are not looking for them. Unfortunately, in a few, commercialism has taken over and there are some low-end shops. On the other hand, the occupants of the spaces come and go, and it is still fun to stroll through one or two if only to see a sampling of the old-fashioned shops selling handmade dolls, fancy pipes, old books, 78-RPM records, model trains, and toys.

In general, you can count on most shops being open Monday afternoon to Saturday 10 A.M. to 7 P.M.

GALERIE VÉRO-DODAT (44; see map page 62)
19, rue Jean-Jacques Rousseau & 2, rue du Bouloi, 75001
Métro: Palais-Royal–Musée du Louvre

This Empire-style *passage* opened in 1826 and has an ornate interior with facades of dark wood and a mosaic-tile floor. There are some interesting shops, including an old toy shop, but my favorite is Anne Galerie, which sells beautiful scarves and magnificent shawls that are truly works of art. Credit Cards: MC, V; Open: Tues–Sat 9 A.M.–6 P.M., Fri noon–6 P.M.; closed 15 days in Aug (dates vary).

GALERIE VIVIENNE (15; see map page 62)
4, rue des Petits-Champs; 5, rue de la Banque; and 6, rue Vivienne 75002
Métro: Bourse

The most beautiful *passage* of all opened in 1823. The shops reflect their elegant surroundings. While here, be sure to stop at Lucien Legrand, a famous wine shop that now serves light lunches.

PASSAGE DES PANORAMAS (3; see map page 62)
10, rue Saint-Marc & 11, boulevard Montmartre, 75002
Métro: Grands Boulevards

One of the oldest, dating from 1800, its name is taken from the panoramas of Rome, Jerusalem, London, Athens, and other world capitals. The most interesting things to see here are the stamp and coin dealers and the shop selling old postcards.

PASSAGE DU GRAND-CERF (33; see map page 62)
145, rue Saint-Denis, or 10, rue Dussouds, 75002
Métro: Étienne-Marcel

Paved in marble, the *passage* has a high glass roof, wrought-iron walkways, and wood-framed windows in shops devoted to contemporary design.

PASSAGE JOUFFROY (19; see map page 202)
10–12, boulevard Montmartre & 9, rue de la Grange-Batelière, 75009
Métro: Grands Boulevards

Built in 1846, this was the first *passage* to be heated. It also contains the Hôtel Chopin (see page 217) and the Musée Grevin, the hundred-year-old Paris wax museum inspired by Madame Tussaud's in London.

PASSAGE VERDEAU (16; see map page 202)
31 bis, rue du Faubourg-Montmartre & 6, rue de la Grange-Batelière, 75009
Métro: Richelieu-Drouot, Grands Boulevards

Shops have been here since 1847, and some of the merchandise in the collectibles shops looks it; check out books, old prints, old postcards, a shop selling vintage cameras, and another devoted to embroidery.

Shopping Malls

Indoor shopping complexes are popping up all over Paris. They are not my favorite shopping venues, but if you need several items and only have a short time to shop, they are useful.

CARROUSEL DU LOUVRE (46; see map page 62)
99, rue de Rivoli, 75001
Metro: Palais-Royal–Museé du Louvre

Combine your visit to the Louvre with a shopping stroll through the tempting boutiques here, which range from Limoges and Lalique to a Virgin Megastore, and from clothing boutiques to tourist kitsch and a post office . . . you name it, and they have it. One of the best all-purpose shopping destinations in Paris, and it is open on Sunday! See *Great Eats Paris* for details on the Carrousel du Louvre food court.

TELEPHONE: 01-43-16-47-15
CREDIT CARDS: Depends on shop, but always MC, V
OPEN: Daily 10 A.M.–8 P.M.

FORUM DES HALLES (48; see map page 62)
rue Pierre Lescott (main entry), 75001
Métro: Les Halles, Étienne-Marcel

This is the result of filling the hole left after the wholesale food market Les Halles was moved to Rungis. The Forum des Halles is the largest commercial project in France, and the largest métro station in the world lies under it. But please be careful: this is not considered a safe place to wander late at night. When it opened, the multilevel complex attracted forty million shoppers a year. On the weekend, it feels as though half of them are either milling around outside or roaming the mall inside. Even though the area has lost its original luster and allure, those youthful in mind, body, and spirit still gravitate to this covered shopping wonderland to check out the general scene, cruise the shops, eat in the fast-food joints, hang out in FNAC (see page 377), and try the hair salons offering sculpted cuts or dye jobs in glowing pink, green, or yellow. If you don't feel like doing any of the above, you can watch a film in the Cine Cité multiplex (which has over thirty theaters), swim in the public swimming pool, or just hang out and enjoy the fauna and flora as it walks by.

TELEPHONE: 01-40-39-38-74

CREDIT CARDS: Depends on shop, but usually MC, V

OPEN: Mon–Sat 10:30 A.M.–7:30 P.M. for the shops, 10 A.M.–1:30 A.M. for films

LE MARCHÉ SAINT GERMAIN (34; see map page 140)
Entrances on rue Lobineau, rue Fléiabien, rue Clément, rue Mabillon, 75006
Métro: Odéon

In addition to a section devoted to food stalls, this small, enclosed mall has all the usual mall shopping adventures and offers liquid sustenance in a popular Irish pub. On Saturday, outside and under the arches, sellers set up makeshift stalls. Be sure to see the one selling hand-smocked children's clothes at cut-rate prices. Look carefully before you buy: these are made in the Philippines, and the quality of workmanship varies.

CREDIT CARDS: Depends on shop

OPEN: Food stalls Tues–Sat 8 A.M.–1:30 P.M., 4–8 P.M., Sun 8 A.M.–1 P.M.; shops Mon–Sat 10 A.M.–6 P.M.

LES TROIS QUARTIERS (47; see map page 202)
23, boulevard de la Madeleine, 75008
Métro: Madeleine

At this shopping mall you'll find seventy-five boutiques and a sports store to behold. Prices are high, but stroll through anyway to get an idea of how much you will save by shopping at the other shops listed in this book. The quality is better than at Forum des Halles, but the spirit is really dead.

TELEPHONE: 01-42-97-80-12

CREDIT CARDS: Depends on boutique, but usually MC, V

OPEN: Mon–Sat 10 A.M.–7 P.M.

BERCY VILLAGE
9, Cour St-Emilion, 75012
Métro: Cour St-Emilion

Shopping, entertainment, bars, banks, and restaurants in an American-like mall that pulls in the crowds, especially on the weekends. What to expect? Everything from a huge pet store selling live animals and guppies, to a beautiful garden shop, houseware warehouse, computer store, three-level sport fishing store, movie multiplex, and much more. It is probably more of a unique experience for Parisians than for Americans, but it is interesting to see what Parisians think is so *au courant*.

NOTE: When you are here, you are two métro stops away from the François Mitterand Bibliothèque Nationale, quai François-Mauriac

(13th); Métro: Bibliothèque or Quai de la Gare; Open: Tues–Sat 10 A.M.–8 P.M., Sun noon–7 P.M. This was Mitterand's final project, but it was completed after his death. The library has over ten million books and enough space for three thousand people (to use the library you must be over 18 years old).

TELEPHONE: Not available
INTERNET: www.bercyvillage.com
CREDIT CARDS: Depends on store, generally MC, V
OPEN: Shops, daily 11 A.M.–9 P.M., restaurants close at 2 A.M.

MAINE-MONTPARNASSE (9; see map page 240)
Tour, Maine-Montparnasse, 75014
Métro: Montparnasse-Bienvenüe

Round up the usual chain stores, stick them in a mundane indoor mall at the Montparnasse-Bienvenüe métro station, and you have this shopping mall. It does have a small Galeries Lafayette, but it is certainly not worth a special trip. If you are here, fine; otherwise, never mind.

TELEPHONE: Not available
CREDIT CARDS: MC, V (depends on store)
OPEN: Mon–Sat 10 A.M.–7 P.M. (stores vary)

PASSY PLAZA (26; see map page 256)
Corner rue Jean Bologne and rue de Passy, 75016
Métro: Passy, La Muette

This shopping mall has middle-of-the-road boutiques with lots of clothes for the junior set or for something to knock around in and still feel fashionable. Also a very good supermarket, Inno.

CREDIT CARDS: Varies with each shop
OPEN: Shops Mon–Sat 10 A.M.–7:30 P.M.; supermarket Mon–Sat 9 A.M.–8 P.M.

Store Listings by Arrondissement

FIRST ARRONDISSEMENT (see map page 62)

Shops

Boutique Paris-Musées	344
Catherine Perfumes and Cosmetics	345
Colette	345
Dehillerin	346
Du Pareil au Même	346
Du Pareil au Même Bébé	346
Galignani	347
Herboristerie du Palais Royal	347
La Dame Blanche	347
La Droguerie	348
La Samaritaine	348
Le Cèdre Rouge	348
Le Louvre des Antiquaires	349
Le Prince Jardinier	349
L'Espace Créateurs	349
Madelios	350
Maréchal	350
Oliver B	350
Scooter	350
W. H. Smith	351

Shopping Areas

Place des Victoires	336
Place Vendôme	336

***Passages* and Shopping Malls**

Galerie Véro-Dodat	340
Carrousel du Louvre	341
Forum des Halles	341

BOUTIQUE PARIS-MUSÉES (48)
Forum des Halles
1, rue Pierre Lescott, 75001
Métro: Les Halles

There are three of these museum boutiques in Paris offering reproductions of items from the various permanent collections of the city's big museums. This boutique specializes in contemporary design reproductions, the other two in classic. Here you will find a wonderful selection of jewelry and household goods. Though the address is Forum des Halles, it is located on your left as you enter the Forum from rue Pierre Lescott.

The other two locations are in the third and fourth arrondissements (see pages 355 and 358).

TELEPHONE: 01-40-26-56-65
CREDIT CARDS: AE, V
OPEN: Mon 2–7 P.M., Tues–Sat 10:30 A.M.–7 P.M.

CATHERINE PERFUMES AND COSMETICS (16)
7, rue de Castiglione, 75001
Métro: Tuileries

Jacques Levy, his wife, and their two daughters run this boutique. They offer an excellent selection of perfumes, cosmetics, scarves, hair ornaments, jewelry, and ties. They speak English and don't employ "hard sell" tactics. To begin, you will receive a tax-free price of 20 to 25 percent off on anything in the shop. If you purchase over 175€ worth of merchandise, you get the original 20 to 25 percent off plus the 13 percent *détaxe,* which translates into a savings of up to 38 percent. If you are a collector of old perfumes, talk with Jacques, who has an excellent selection of hard-to-find scents. For mail orders, which you can do by fax, the same discounts are offered.

TELEPHONE: 01-42-61-02-89
FAX: 01-42-61-02-35
CREDIT CARDS: AE, DC, MC, V
OPEN: Mon 11 A.M.–7 P.M., Tues–Sat 9:30 A.M.–7 P.M.; closed Aug 15–31, 1 week after Jan 15th

COLETTE (22)
213, rue St-Honoré, 75001
Métro: Tuileries

Colette bills itself as a *styledesignartfood* concept store. It is one of the "hot" addresses in Paris, but frankly I think it is a shopping experience best characterized as "overpriced boutique chic meets designer kitsch at rip-off prices," which the customer is supposed to consider *la dernière cri* in cutting-edge fashion and minimalistic accessories. A band of ohhh, so cool *vendeuses,* dressed in skin-tight designer (of course!) jeans and spray-on sleeveless T-shirts, cruise the aisles trying to look busy. Models wander around dressed in over-the-top outfits no one would ever wear . . . even if they could afford them. Big, burly, muscle-flexing bouncers man the doors, scowling at anything they don't like, including this writer, who was literally thrown out of the store for looking and taking notes. The shop has three levels, and downstairs is a stylized food and designer water bar with prices as high as the noses of the diners and drinkers. Go to Colette, don't miss it in fact, because it is the city's only Museum of the Outrageous. Just remember: look, buy if you must, but don't take notes.

TELEPHONE: 01-55-35-33-90
INTERNET: www.colette.fr
CREDIT CARDS: AE, DC, MC, V
OPEN: Mon–Sat 10:30 A.M.–7:30 P.M.

DEHILLERIN (37)
18–20 rue Coquillière and 51, rue Jean-Jacques Rousseau, 75001
Métro: Louvre-Rivoli, Les Halles

Since 1820, the Dehillerin family has been supplying chefs and serious cooks with every utensil and cooking accessory needed to create the perfect dish. The selection is vast, and should you forget something, they have an English catalog and will ship. This is a must-go place for anyone who loves to spend time in the kitchen.

TELEPHONE: 01-42-36-53-13
FAX: 01-42-36-54-80
EMAIL: www.e.dehillerin@wanadoo.fr
INTERNET: www.e-dehillerin.fr
CREDIT CARDS: MC, V
OPEN: Mon 8 A.M.–12:30 P.M., 2–6 P.M.; Tues–Sat 8 A.M.–6 P.M.

DU PAREIL AU MÊME (48)
Forum des Halles, Niveau 2 (second level), 75001
Métro: Les Halles

Finally, adorable French children's clothing we all can afford. If you have shopped for children in Paris before, you know how prohibitive the prices are . . . a little play outfit could cost $100, and a tiny bikini, $50. Take heart, and take your credit card to this mecca for mommies: Du Pareil au Même. If you have anyone on your list between the ages of one and twelve years, you absolutely must include one of these shops on your Paris A-list of things to do. At last count, there were twenty shops well positioned throughout Paris. There are also shops in every major French city. If France is not on your travel map, don't worry; you can shop with Du Pareil au Même online and have your purchases sent. This is a major breakthrough in French merchandizing for children, and it has captured everyone's attention. Don't miss it. Consult their Website, or pick up a card, which lists all of their many locations throughout Paris and France.

TELEPHONE: 01-40-13-95-29
INTERNET: www.dpam.fr
CREDIT CARDS: AE, MC, V
OPEN: Generally Mon–Sat 10 A.M.–7 P.M.; hours vary slightly at each location

DU PAREIL AU MÊME BÉBÉ (58)
1, rue Saint-Denis, corner avenue Victoria, 75001
Métro: Châtelet

Du Pareil au Même has created a shop exclusively for babies, with numerous locations around Paris. The discount clothing for the tiny ones is just as adorable as what the other stores sell for the older children. This one is not far from the Du Pareil au Même in Forum des Halles.

TELEPHONE: 01-42-36-26-53
INTERNET: www.dpam.fr

CREDIT CARDS: AE, MC, V

OPEN: Generally Mon–Sat 10 A.M.–7 P.M.; hours vary slightly at each location

GALIGNANI (24)
224, rue de Rivoli, 75001
Métro: Tuileries

Galignani has the distinction of being the first English language bookstore established on the continent of Europe. It is everything book lovers want in a quality bookstore, including a knowledgeable staff willing to assist. Galignani is known for its fine selection of decorative art books and for filling worldwide special mail orders.

TELEPHONE: 01-42-60-76-07

FAX: 01-42-86-91-31

EMAIL: galignani@wanadoo.fr

CREDIT CARDS: MC, V

OPEN: Mon–Sat 10 A.M.–7 P.M.

HERBORISTERIE DU PALAIS ROYAL (11)
11, rue des Petits-Champs, 75001
Métro: Pyramides

This shop stocks between five and six hundred types of herbal teas and makes their own plant-based soaps and cosmetics (try the carrot face oil). They also sell nutritionally correct cereals, cookies, bottled juices, honey, essential oils, herbal remedies, and vitamins. But you had better know what you want, since you can't count on too much English.

TELEPHONE: 01-42-97-54-68

CREDIT CARDS: MC, V

OPEN: Mon–Fri 9:30 A.M.–7 P.M., Sat 10:30 A.M.–6:30 P.M.

LA DAME BLANCHE (41)
186, rue de Rivoli, 75001
Métro: Palais-Royal–Musée du Louvre

You will soon become dizzy and confused walking along the tourist trail that leads from place de la Concorde down rue de Rivoli. The area has one of the highest concentrations of tourist merchandise in the city. You know the type: plastic Eiffel Towers, T-shirts with the Mona Lisa and a smart remark, gaudy scarves, and wild ties your husband would blush wearing. However, dedicated shop hounds know that with a little digging, treasures are here. Where? At Michael and Suzanne's La Dame Blanche, which was started by their mother in 1969 as a small glove boutique. The windows of their side-by-side shops are jam-packed with Limoges boxes that collectors will go mad over, Le Faïence de Quimper, dolls from Provence, leather gloves, authentic French berets, small and large tapestries, and more. Do not let this confusing clutter deter you from exploring one of the best shops along this stretch. Not only is the selection the best, so are the prices. If you want a special Limoges box, ask

Michael and he can have it made for you. Both Michael and Suzanne speak English, offer excellent service, and are delightful besides. They ship worldwide. Don't forget to fill out the paperwork for the *détaxe* if you spend 185€ or more.

TELEPHONE: 01-42-96-31-56
FAX: 01-42-96-02-11
CREDIT CARDS: AE, DC, MC, V
OPEN: Mon–Sat 10 A.M.–6:30 P.M.

LA DROGUERIE (38)
9–11, rue du Jour, 75001
Métro: Les Halles (exit Turbigo-Rambuteau)

It doesn't look like much when you walk by it, but once inside, it is an Ali Baba's cave of glorious ribbons, yarn, trim, buttons, feathers, and glitter, plus the glue to put it all together. If you are into jewelry making, beading, knitting, making your own purses—or any other creative DIY hobby—you will love this treasure trove. Do yourself a favor and try to avoid coming on Saturday, when they are absolutely swamped with eager customers.

TELEPHONE: 01-43-08-93-27
CREDIT CARDS: MC, V
OPEN: Mon 2–6:45 P.M., Tues–Sat 10:30 A.M.–6:45 P.M.

LA SAMARITAINE (54)
19, rue de la Monnaie, 75001
Métro: Pont-Neuf

The view of Paris from the top floor of La Samaritaine on rue de la Monnaie is justly famous. At an altitude of 243 feet, you have a 360-degree panoramic view of Paris, with a table to help you pick the main sights . . . and it costs you nothing. The perfume and cosmetics department on the ground floor has a l'Occitane stand, often with special promotions. The store participates in the 10 percent discount to foreigners, and the *détaxe* after 200€. Great changes for this Parisian landmark are in the offing. The store was recently taken over by LVMH and is undergoing extensive redesigning.

TELEPHONE: Welcome Service 01-40-41-22-68, Store 01-40-41-20-20
CREDIT CARDS: AE, DC, MC, V
OPEN: Mon–Fri 9:30 A.M.–7 P.M. (Thur until 9 P.M., Sat until 8 P.M.)

LE CÈDRE ROUGE (56)
22, avenue Victoria, 75001
Métro: Châtelet

Le Cèdre Rouge has five Paris stores showcasing elegant home and garden decor and accessories. Most of of what you see, you will not be able to take home, but you can always take new ideas with you, or perhaps a pretty pillow or set of unusual table linens.

TELEPHONE: 01-42-33-71-05
INTERNET: www.lecedrerouge.com

CREDIT CARDS: AE, MC, V

OPEN: Mon 1–7 P.M., Tues–Sat 10:30 A.M.–7:30 P.M.

LE LOUVRE DES ANTIQUAIRES (42)
2, place du Palais-Royal, 75001
Métro: Palais-Royal–Musée du Louvre

Here you will find more than two hundred dealers selling antiques from all over the world, and at world-class prices. Each piece comes with a certificate of guarantee. You don't have to buy, but it is interesting to see such a concentration of magnificent, museum-quality antiques.

TELEPHONE: 01-42-97-27-00

INTERNET: www.louvre-antiquaires.com

CREDIT CARDS: Varies, but generally MC, V

OPEN: Tues–Sun 11 A.M.– 7 P.M., closed Sun–Mon, Aug, all holidays

LE PRINCE JARDINIER (21)
117–121 Jardins du Palais Royal, Arcade Valois, 75001
Métro: Palais-Royal–Musée du Louvre

The Palais Royal gardens are known and loved as some of the most beautiful in Paris. Now, in addition to admiring the palace built by Cardinal Richelieu in 1632, you have another enchanted garden to visit. Prince Louis-Albert de Broglie, a young Paris banker, has opened Le Prince Jardinier, a charming garden boutique along the arcades of the Palais Royal. Not only does he sell seeds and spades, he has handcrafted garden tools, brass buckets and stainless steel watering cans, and tools that fit into custom-made aprons and sacks. On the main floor are displays of garden attire for the stylish gardener—aprons, bags, hats, smocks, and coats—along with gardening tools, plants, herbal teas, and spices. Upstairs are botanical prints, books, and farm implements made into sculptures. One titled customer has found Prince Broglie's wares irresistible, and he uses them on his Highgrove estate. Who? Prince Charles.

TELEPHONE: 01-42-60-37-13

INTERNET: www.princejardinier.fr

CREDIT CARDS: MC, V

OPEN: Mon–Sat 10 A.M.–7 P.M., closed Mon & Tues from 1–2 P.M.

L'ESPACE CRÉATEURS (48)
Forum des Halles, Niveau 1, Porte Berger (Berger Gate)
Entrance on rue Pierre Lescot or rue Berger, 75001
Métro: Les Halles

Fifty young designers have joined forces to display their creations in the Forum des Halles. Aimed at a young, buff, fashion-conscious audience, this is the place to check out what new talent is around and to spot that which has an edge on the future.

TELEPHONE: 06-21-02-69-65

CREDIT CARDS: Depends on designer

OPEN: Mon–Sat 11 A.M.–7 P.M.

MADELIOS (7)
23, boulevard de la Madeleine, 75001
Métro: Madeleine

Madelios is a megastore for men featuring top brand names. The store offers a 10 percent discount on purchases, as well as an immediate 15 percent tax refund (in cash or on your credit card) after you spend 175€ in the store.

TELEPHONE: 01-53-45-00-00
INTERNET: www.madelios.com
CREDIT CARDS: AE, DC, MC, V
OPEN: Mon–Sat 10 A.M.–7 P.M.

MARÉCHAL (23)
232, rue de Rivoli, 75001
Métro: Tuileries

If you cannot find a Limoges box here to suit you, they will have one custom designed for you and shipped anywhere you like. In addition to their fabulous selection of well-displayed Limoges boxes, they have a good selection of quality Paris souvenirs. They also have a shipping and a mail-order service.

TELEPHONE: 01-42-60-71-83
FAX: 01-42-60-33-76
EMAIL: marechalparis@wanadoo.fr
INTERNET: www.marechal-paris.com
CREDIT CARDS: AE, MC, V
OPEN: Mon–Sat 10:30 A.M.–6:30 P.M., Sun 11 A.M.–6:30 P.M.

OLIVER B (40)
21, rue Pierre Lescot, 75001
Métro: Étienne-Marcel, Les Halles

At Oliver B you will find inexpensive separates that are easy to wear and cheap enough to toss out after a season or two. Lots of sizes and nothing too far out. The clothes are poorly displayed, but at least they are organized by color. Don't expect much help from the bored (and often smoking) sales babes. The store has good sales in January and July.

TELEPHONE: 01-40-26-26-26
CREDIT CARDS: AE, MC, V
OPEN: Mon–Sat 10:30 A.M.–7 P.M.

SCOOTER (39)
10, rue de Turbigo, 75001
Métro: Étienne-Marcel

Scooter specializes in jewelry, accessories, and clothing of the moment that are young, fun, and inexpensive. They have several locations, but this is the main boutique.

TELEPHONE: 01-45-08-50-54
CREDIT CARDS: MC, V
OPEN: Mon 2–7 P.M., Tues–Sat 11 A.M.–7 P.M.

W. H. SMITH (18)
248, rue de Rivoli, 75001
Métro: Concorde

If you forgot to bring along a book to read, long for an English-language magazine, or need a travel guide (especially one on Paris or France), W. H. Smith will come to your rescue. The British-based bookstore has two floors filled to the brim with English-language books, newspapers, magazines, and videos. It also has a wonderful travel book section that stocks the books in the Great Sleeps and Eats series.

TELEPHONE: 01-44-77-88-99
EMAIL: whsmith.france@wanadoo.fr
INTERNET: www.whsmith.fr
CREDIT CARDS: AE, MC, V
OPEN: Mon–Sat 9 A.M.–7:30 P.M., Sun 1–7:30 P.M.

SECOND ARRONDISSEMENT (see map page 62)

Shops

A. Simon	**351**
Anthony Peto	**352**
Brentano's	**352**
Debauve & Gallais	**352**
Et Vous Stock	**353**
Explora	**353**
Lollipops	**353**
Stock Kookaï	**353**
Tati Or	**354**
Village Jové Club–La Passion de Jouet	**354**

Passages and Shopping Malls

Galerie Vivienne	**340**
Passage des Panoramas	**340**
Passage du Grand-Cerf	**340**

Food Shopping

Rue Montorgueil	**394**

A. SIMON (28)
52 & 58, rue Montmartre, 75002
Métro: Étienne-Marcel

Calling all chefs, gourmets, and gourmands—whether past, present, or budding—as well as anyone with a love of cooking and good food. For one hundred years, A. Simon occupied the corner of 36, rue Étienne Marcel. When their lease ran out, they had to move to smaller quarters in two shops on rue Montmartre. At the two side-by-side A. Simon shops, you will still find all the French cooking and dining essentials you will ever need. With its broad inventory of cooking utensils of every known type and variety and its fascinating array of tableware, this is the Rolls Royce in its field. Prices are geared for the volume buyer, but anyone is welcome, and you will be graciously treated whether you outfit a restaurant or buy a tiny *pichet* for your *vin du table*.

TELEPHONE: 01-42-33-71-65
EMAIL: simon.sa@wanadoo.fr
INTERNET: www.simon-a.com
CREDIT CARDS: AE, MC, V
OPEN: Mon 1:30–6:30 P.M., Tues–Sat 9 A.M.–6:30 P.M.

ANTHONY PETO (30)
56, rue Tiquetonne, 75002
Métro: Étienne-Marcel

Hats off to these fabulous *chapeaux!* I love hats and wear them often, especially when traveling. Anthony Peto runs his hat shop in conjunction with Marie Mercié, who has her own location and her own hats in the sixth arrondissement (see page 370). Between the two stores, their hats run the gamut from frankly fanciful to downright sane and sensible. If you need a hat for any occasion, or, like me, just enjoy wearing—or admiring —them, please make a point of seeing some of the best hats in Paris. Anthony's shop is geared for men, though he carries some unisex hats. I like his summer Panama hats that you can roll up in your suitcase; they just pop back into shape when ready to wear.

TELEPHONE: 01-40-26-60-68
CREDIT CARDS: AE, MC, V
OPEN: Mon–Sat 11 A.M.–7 P.M.; closed middle of Aug

BRENTANO'S (9)
37, avenue de l'Opéra, 75002
Métro: Opéra

This shop has two levels of books as well as a wide selection of stationery and greeting cards, all in English.

TELEPHONE: 01-42-61-52-50
INTERNET: www.brentanos.fr
CREDIT CARDS: AE, MC, V
OPEN: Mon–Sat 10 A.M.–7:30 P.M.

DEBAUVE & GALLAIS (1)
33, rue Vivienne, 75002
Métro: Bourse

For details about this famous chocolate maker and supplier to the kings of France since 1800, please see page 374. All other information is the same.

TELEPHONE: 01-40-39-05-50
OPEN: Mon–Sat 9 A.M.–6:30 P.M.

ET VOUS STOCK (35)
17, rue de Turbigo, 75002
Métro: Étienne-Marcel

They offer up to 50 percent off on the simply styled Et Vous brand of men's and women's clothing, which almost anyone can wear.

TELEPHONE: 01-40-13-04-12

CREDIT CARDS: AE, MC, V

OPEN: Mon–Sat noon–7 P.M.

EXPLORA (32)
46, rue Tiquetonne, 75002
Métro: Étienne-Marcel

I was first drawn to the beautifully colored line of clothing and accessories—geared toward active, eclectic women—before I knew about the store. The Explora line is designed in Paris and uses only high-quality fabrics such as pima cotton, cashmere, and alpaca. You will see the Explora label in Vogue magazine, Le Bon Marché department store in Paris, and in Neiman Marcus in the United States, but for the best selection and prices, come to the source. The *détaxe* starts after 200€.

TELEPHONE: 01-40-41-00-33

EMAIL: expl46@aol.com

INTERNET: www.explora-paris.com

CREDIT CARDS: AE, MC, V

OPEN: Mon–Fri 10 A.M.–1:30 P.M., 3–6:30 P.M., Sat 1:30–7 P.M.; closed 2 weeks in Aug

LOLLIPOPS (31)
60, rue Tiquetonne, 75002
Métro: Étienne-Marcel

Fantasy accessories with the emphasis on glam, glitter, and great fun for the young at heart from nine to ninety. Several locations in Paris, including boutiques in the Les Halles behemoth, Galeries Lafayette, and Au Printemps.

TELEPHONE: 01-42-33-15-72

INTERNET: www.lollipops.fr

CREDIT CARDS: AE, MC, V

OPEN: Mon–Sat 11 A.M.–7:30 P.M.; closed 1 week in Aug

STOCK KOOKAÏ (13)
82, rue Réaumur at corner of rue St-Denis, 75002
Métro: Réaumur-Sebastapol

There are Kookaï boutiques worldwide, but this is the only showroom devoted to permanent sale items from the line. There are two sections, with the newer, regularly priced clothing toward the back. You can tell which section is which easily: the clothing in front is last season's collection, and it is where fellow savvy shoppers are plying the goods. Dressing rooms are miniscule, and there is only a communal mirror.

TELEPHONE: 01-45-08-93-69
INTERNET: www.kookai.fr
CREDIT CARDS: AE, DC, MC, V
OPEN: Mon 11:30 A.M.–7:30 P.M., Tues–Sat 10:30 A.M.–7:30 P.M.

TATI OR (6)
19, rue de la Paix, 75002
Métro: Opéra

What!? A Tati jewelry store four doors down from Cartier and only a block or two from place Vendôme, home of Van Cleef & Arpels and the Ritz Hotel!! *Quelle horreur.* As you are walking down rue de la Paix, you can't help but notice the Tati awning covering the sidewalk from the door to the street . . . just like Alain Figaret's does, the expensive men's store next door. If Cartier and the like are beyond your budget, now you have Tati Or, a ninety-square-meter boutique selling discount gold jewelry, with prices starting around 10€ for gold stud earrings, 3€ for a little gold heart, and 300€ for a one-carat diamond ring. Engraving is free.

The chairman of Bucheron jewelers was quoted as saying, "You have Lasserre and Taillevent restaurants, but there is also McDonald's." This is definitely the McDonald's of jewelry stores. Obviously, owner Fabien Ouaki knew what he was doing when he signed the original lease requiring a monthly rent in excess of $25,000 (which is a lot of gold hearts). Now there are Tati Or shops in almost every arrondissement in Paris and in at least a dozen cities throughout France.

TELEPHONE: Not available
CREDIT CARDS: MC, V
OPEN: Mon–Sat 10 A.M.–6 P.M.

VILLAGE JOVÉ CLUB–LA PASSION DE JOUET (4)
5, boulevard des Italiens, 75002
Métro: Richelieu-Drouot

If it is on the toy market, chances are you will find it in this two-level mall devoted exclusively to toys appealing to the child in all of us. In addition to all the toys, educational and creative learning games, dolls, stuffed animals, and art supplies, there is a children's *coiffeur,* a one-hour photo service, and pleasant red-vested sales personnel to guide you through this wonderland.

TELEPHONE: 01-53-45-41-41
CREDIT CARDS: MC, V
OPEN: Mon–Sat 10 A.M.–8 P.M.

THIRD ARRONDISSEMENT (see map page 84)

Shops

Boutique Majolique	355
Boutique Paris-Musées	355
DOT–Diffusion d'Objets de Table	355
Laurent Guillot	356
Patyka	356
Tati	356

Shopping Areas

Marais	336

Discount Shopping Streets

Rue Meslay	338

BOUTIQUE MAJOLIQUE (13)
79, rue Vieille-du-Temple 75003
Metro: Rambuteau

All the beautifully embroidered linens and cottons you see in this boutique will require some ironing. If you love beautiful table linens and accessories, it will be worth the effort. Everything is French-designed but made in Vietnam. There is another shop in the sixth (see page 366).

TELEPHONE: 01-42-78-38-81
INTERNET: www.majolique.fr
CREDIT CARDS: AE, MC, V
OPEN: Mon–Sat noon–7 P.M., Sun & holidays 2–7 P.M.

BOUTIQUE PARIS-MUSÉES (28)
Musée Carnavalet, 23, rue de Sévigné, 75003
Métro: St-Paul

Inside Musée Carnavalet, which explores the history of Paris, this shop specializes in books. For a full description of this museum shop, see page 344.

TELEPHONE: None
OPEN: Mon 2–7 P.M., Tues–Sat 11 A.M.–1 P.M., 2–7 P.M., Sun 11 A.M.–7 P.M.

DOT–DIFFUSION D'OBJETS DE TABLE (7)
47, rue de Saintonge, 75003
Métro: Filles-du-Calvaire

I love this store. You will too if you are a devotée of French bistro ware, unusual glass and crystal pieces, vintage children's books, enamel boxes, and wooden kitchen utensils, all gathered together under one roof. Garage sale and flea market addicts won't want to miss the basement, which is literally piled to the ceiling with things that have not sold upstairs. There is absolutely no order to the basement, but the good part is that everything in this dugout is half price. I suggest that you wear old clothes, bring a pair of rubber gloves, and have a great time digging.

Chances are great you will find something you *must* have. Email them if you want to be on their mailing list, and check out their Website where you can order on line, but above all, visit them the next time you are in Paris. The staff is as much fun as the store.

TELEPHONE: 01-40-29-90-34
EMAIL: dot.bon@wanadoo.fr
INTERNET: www.dot-france.com
CREDIT CARDS: AE, MC, V
OPEN: Mon–Fri 9 A.M.–6 P.M.

LAURENT GUILLOT (14)
48, rue de Turenne, 75003
Métro: Chemin Vert

Laurent Guillot's crystal and Plexiglas jewelry trimmed in gold and silver appears on the pages of *Elle, Vogue,* and almost every other fashion magazine on the stands. He also supplies many of the top-name designers with jewelry used during the Paris fashion shows. This is his display/boutique in Paris, and it is worth seeing if you like beautifully handcrafted, contemporary jewelry at surprisingly reasonable prices.

NOTE· Rue de Turenne is lined with men's clothing stores.
TELEPHONE: 01-48-87-87-69
EMAIL: l.guillot.pa@infonie.fr
CREDIT CARDS: MC, V
OPEN: Mon–Sat 11 A.M.–12:30 P.M., 1:30–7 P.M.

PATYKA (10)
14, rue Rambuteau, 75003
Métro: Rambuteau

Founded in Budapest in 1922, the Patyka line of beauty products is made from pure, natural ingredients and based on the traditions of living in harmony with nature. This is a small, independent company of European artisans and aromatherapists, headed by Phylyppe and his wife, Caroline, who believe in a world where simplicity and quality are one. I am a committed admirer of their creams and oils, their beautifully scented candles, and their relaxing bath products. Shipping is available.

TELEPHONE: 01-40-29-49-49
INTERNET: www.patyka.com
CREDIT CARDS: MC, V
OPEN: Daily noon–8 P.M.

TATI (4)
174, rue du Temple, 75003
Métro: Temple, République,

Attention, shoppers! If you love swap meets, garage sales, and basement fire sales, then Tati is for you. The crowds are impossible, especially on Saturday, but for truly amazing bargains hidden among some real junk, join the diverse crowd at Tati. Prices defy the competition on stock that ranges from bridal wear to linen slacks, cheap silk shirts, cheaper shoes, baby gear, and kitchen equipment, and now separate jewelers and opticians. Be sure to check each item carefully because quality control is not a priority when this much volume is concerned.

TELEPHONE: Not available
CREDIT CARDS: MC, V
OPEN: Mon–Fri 9:30 A.M.–7 P.M.

FOURTH ARRONDISSEMENT (see map page 84)

Shops

A la Bonne Renommee	357
BHV–Bazar de l'Hôtel de Ville	358
Biscuit	358
Boutique Paris-Musées	358
C & P	359
Faïenceries de Quimper	359
Krystyna Bukowska	359
L'Écritoire	359
L'Occitane	360
Matière Première	360
Monoprix	360
PWS–Prices Without Surprise	361
The Red Wheelbarrow Bookstore	361
Sidney Carron	361
Stock Griffes	362

Shopping Areas

Place des Vosges	336
Village St-Paul, Rue St-Paul, and Rue du Pont Louis Philippe	336

Food Shopping

Marché Place Baudoyer	396

A LA BONNE RENOMMÉE (26)
20, rue Vieille du Temple, 75004
Métro: St-Paul

A la Bonne Renommee became famous for its multifabric and multi-colored handbags. Now they have expanded into men's and women's clothing and accessories, both for wearing and using in the home. Some of the colors and fabric mixes leave me wondering, and so do most of the prices, but if you can find something you like on sale, it will be a good buy . . . and will probably last a long time.

TELEPHONE: 01-42-72-03-86
EMAIL: a.la.bonne.renommee@wanadoo.fr
INTERNET: www.labonnerenommee.com
CREDIT CARDS: AE, DC, MC, V
OPEN: Mon–Sat 11 A.M.–7 P.M., Sun 2–7 P.M.

BHV–BAZAR DE L'HÔTEL DE VILLE (29)
52–64, rue de Rivoli, 75004
Métro: Hôtel de Ville

This is a shopping experience no do-it-yourselfer should miss, except on Saturday when an estimated twenty-five thousand shoppers stream through the store. It is famous for its basement hardware department, which is a Parisian DIY experience in itself—with vast kitchen and automotive sections not to mention paints, electrical, and a series of classes held to teach you how to do-it-all-yourself. While in the basement, don't miss the Bricolo Café, which looks like a 1920 garage. The rest of the multilevel store is ho-hum in terms of anything very exciting. The store offers a 10 percent discount for non-EU citizens, but you first must physically go to get a discount voucher from the Quick Hamburger Restaurant, 66, rue de Rivoli, just across the side street from the department store, bring the voucher back along with your passport to the store's Welcome Desk (some welcome), where you are issued the store discount card. Sometimes the vouchers are available in hotels. Who thought this one up? Really, this takes the booby prize for customer service and convenience. The store also grants a 12 percent *detaxe* when purchases total 175€ or more, and you don't have to leave the store and go to a greasy spoon to complete the paperwork. You can do it in the store.

TELEPHONE: 01-42-74-90-00
INTERNET: www.bhv.fr
CREDIT CARDS: AE, MC, V
OPEN: Mon–Tues, Thur–Sat 9:30 A.M.–7 P.M., Wed 9:30 A.M.–8:30 P.M.

BISCUIT (48)
15, rue Beautreillis, 75004
Métro: St-Paul, Bastille

I found Michiko and her children's *depôt vent* and design boutique just a week after she opened. I must say I am very impressed with the quality and condition of the formerly owned clothes she stocks. I also think her own designs are adorable. Her clothes sizes are from newborn to ten years. Prices are tempting, and it will be hard to leave without buying something you and your children or grandchildren will love—I left with five dresses.

TELEPHONE: 01-42-71-43-73
OPEN: Tues–Sat 10:30 A.M.–6:30 P.M.

BOUTIQUE PARIS-MUSÉES (27)
29 bis, rue des Francs-Bourgeois, 75004
Métro: St-Paul

For a description of this museum store, see page 344.

TELEPHONE: 01-42-74-13-02
OPEN: Mon 2–7 P.M., Tues–Sat 11 A.M.–7 P.M., Sun 11 A.M.–6:30 P.M.

C & P (45)
16, rue du Pont Louis-Philippe, 75004
Métro: Pont-Marie, St-Paul

Patrick Poirier designs fluid, wearable clothing that never seems to go out of style. These are the clothes you always reach for in your closet when you are dressing for the day or packing for a trip. The colors are simple: black, blue, gray, beige, and white. Fabrics are excellent and the prices affordable when you think how long you are going to enjoy the outfit.

TELEPHONE: 01-42-74-22-34
CREDIT CARDS: MC, V
OPEN: Mon 2–7 P.M., Tues–Sat 11 A.M.–7 P.M.

FAÏENCERIES DE QUIMPER (16)
84, rue St-Martin, 75004
Métro: Hôtel de Ville, Rambuteau

Here you can find everything for the Quimper collector, including paper napkins, Christmas ornaments, linens, and numbers or name tiles for your home. The display is excellent, and so is the friendly sales staff. They will ship.

TELEPHONE: 01-42-71-93-03
CREDIT CARDS: MC, V
INTERNET: hb-henriot.com
OPEN: Mon–Sat 11 A.M.–7 P.M.

KRYSTYNA BUKOWSKA (46)
1, rue du Pont-Louis-Philippe, 75004
Métro: Hôtel de Ville

The word here is interesting as it applies to jewelry, scarves, and the clothes that will make a statement and not cost the moon.

TELEPHONE: 01-42-77-87-58
CREDIT CARDS: MC, V
OPEN: Mon 3–7 P.M., Tues–Sat 11:30 A.M.–7 P.M.

L'ÉCRITOIRE (17)
61, rue Saint Martin, 75004
Métro: Châtelet, Hôtel de Ville

Here's where you'll find inks, inkpots, journals and diaries, desk accessories, pretty papers, and greeting cards destined to please all of us who still remember the postman.

TELEPHONE: 01-42-78-01-18
CREDIT CARDS: MC, V
OPEN: Mon–Sat 11 A.M.–8 P.M., Sun (in Aug only) 1–8 P.M.

L'OCCITANE
17, rue des Francs-Bourgeois, 75004 (31)
18, place des Vosges, 75004 (38)
55, rue St-Louis-en-l'Île, 75004 (57)
Métro: St-Paul, Pont-Marie

For the best in natural, vegetable-based cosmetics, go to L'Occitane. All the products are from Provence and include cosmetics, essential oils, soaps, creams, perfumes, and bath accessories. It is worth a trip to the shop just to smell the aromas and admire the beautiful displays. Whatever you buy will be beautifully gift-wrapped. These three shops in the fourth arrondissement are my favorites, but there are branches all over Paris. At last count, the company had shops in Europe, the United States, Mexico, Asia, the Middle East, Oceania, and Africa. But you are lucky . . . the prices in France are up to one-third less than elsewhere. These three branches are open on Sunday as is the L'Occitane in the first arrondissement in the Carrousel du Louvre shopping mall (see page 341), and I've noted several other convenient L'Occitanes throughout the shopping section.

TELEPHONE: 01-42-77-96-67 (rue des Francs Bourgeois); 01-42-72-60-36 (place des Vosges); 01-40-46-81-71 (l'Île St-Louis)

INTERNET: www.loccitane.com

CREDIT CARDS: MC, V

OPEN: Mon–Sat 10:30 A.M.–7 P.M., Sun noon–7 P.M.

MATIÈRE PREMIÈRE (33)
12, rue de Sévigné, 75004
Métro: St-Paul

Baubles, bangles, and beads—either assemble your own or buy ready-made necklaces, earrings, and pins at decent prices. There is another shop in the sixth arrondissement (see page 371).

TELEPHONE: 01-42-78-40-87

EMAIL: matierepremiere@wanadoo.fr

INTERNET: www.matierepremiere.fr

CREDIT CARDS: MC, V

OPEN: Mon–Sat 10:30 A.M.–7:30 P.M., Sun 3–7 P.M.

MONOPRIX (22)
88, rue de Rivoli, at rue St-Martin, 75004
Métro: Châtelet

When Marks and Spencer moved out, Monoprix moved in with its usual stock of budget cosmetics, snappy seasonal outfits on the ground floor, children's wear and lingerie on the first, housewares on the second, and food in the basement.

TELEPHONE: Not available

CREDIT CARDS: AE, MC, V

OPEN: Mon–Sat 9 A.M.–9:30 P.M., Thurs until 10 P.M.

PWS–PRICES WITHOUT SURPRISE (32)
13, rue de Sévigné, 75004
Métro: St-Paul

Owner Claude Windisch got the idea for his discount store after visiting the United States and seeing all the cut-price stores. Although he has some women's apparel, he is better with men's. He stocks everything for the man in your life, from top-name (YSL, Louis Feraud, Pierre Cardin, and Cerruti) to no-name designer clothing. Prices are 20 percent off the marked prices on this season's clothing. He does not stock last year's collections. If you spend 185€, you will qualify for a 15 percent discount on the marked price, plus another 15 percent for the *détaxe*. Manager Miriam Benarroche speaks English and is very helpful.

NOTE: The shop is in a courtyard. Look for the PWS flag hanging next to the archway on the street that leads to the courtyard.

TELEPHONE: 01-44-54-09-09
INTERNET: www.parispws.com
CREDIT CARDS: MC, V
OPEN: Mon 2–7 P.M., Tues–Sat 10 A.M.–7 P.M.

THE RED WHEELBARROW BOOKSTORE (50)
13, rue Charles V, 75004
Métro: St-Paul, Bastille, Sully-Morland

Penelope Fletcher-Le Masson owns and runs this charming Anglophone bookstore. Her stock is excellent, especially in children's books and contemporary literature. She is young, enthusiastic, and a consummate bookseller who is passionate about her profession. Penelope also runs a second location at 22, rue St-Paul (Tel: 01-48-04-75-08).

TELEPHONE: 01-42-77-42-17
CREDIT CARDS: MC, V
OPEN: Mon–Sat 9:30 A.M.–7 P.M., Sun 2–6 P.M.

SIDNEY CARRON (12)
37, rue des Archives, 75004
Métro: Hôtel de Ville, Rambuteau

The window displays of unusual jewelry caught my eye . . . and then I looked at the prices charged by this talented designer in his workshop/boutique. For the beautifully crafted silver and gold jewelry, the prices are excellent. Carron also makes jewelry for the Salvador Dali Museum in Montmartre (11, rue Poulbot, 75018).

TELEPHONE: 01-48-87-27-70
EMAIL: sidneycarron@yahoo.fr
CREDIT CARDS: None, cash only
OPEN: Mon–Fri 9:30 A.M.–7:30 P.M., Sat 11 A.M.–7:30 P.M.

STOCK GRIFFES (25)
17, rue Vieille du Temple, 75004
Métro: St-Paul

It is not my first choice for low-cost duds, but if you are nearby and swing through, you might get lucky. There is another location in the eighteenth arrondissement (see page 391).

TELEPHONE: 01-48-04-82-34

CREDIT CARDS: MC, V

OPEN: Tues–Sat 10:30 A.M.–7:30 P.M.

FIFTH ARRONDISSEMENT (see map page 108)

Shops

The Abbey Bookshop	362
Au Vieux Campeur	363
Diptyque	363
La Tuile à Loup	363
Le Rouvray	364
Les Artisans du Rêve: Breiz Norway	364
L'Occitane	364

Food Shopping

Rue Mouffetard	394
Marché Carmes	396
Marché Monge	396

THE ABBEY BOOKSHOP (8)
29, rue de la Parcheminerie, 75005
Métro: St-Michel, Cluny–La Sorbonne

Canadian Brian Spence stocks new and used English books that he trades and sells. He also takes special orders, will ship, and holds literary events in his bookshop near the Cluny Museum. Once a month a book club (in English) meets, and on Sunday, he leads hiking trips to the countryside. Check his Website for the events schedule, or email him and ask to be put on the activities list.

TELEPHONE: 01-46-33-16-24

FAX: 01-46-33-03-33

EMAIL: abparis@compuserve.com

INTERNET: www.abbeybookshop.com

CREDIT CARDS: AE, MC, V

OPEN: Mon–Sat 10 A.M.–7 P.M., sometimes also on Sun; closed 1 week Aug (dates vary)

AU VIEUX CAMPEUR (16)
48, rue des Écoles, 75005
Métro: Maubert-Mutualité

Outdoor enthusiasts and sports-minded people must make a pilgrimage to one of the nineteen stores under the Au Vieux Campeur umbrella. If it has to do with the outdoors or sports, they stock it and probably in several brands and models. Drop into their main store at the above address and pick up a sheet (which includes a map) that gives the addresses of their other stores, all located within a few blocks of each other between rue des Écoles and boulevard St-Germain. Avoid Saturday, when the crowds are so lethal you cannot get down the aisles.

TELEPHONE: 01-53-10-48-48
INTERNET: www.au-vieux-campeur.com
CREDIT CARDS: MC, V
OPEN: Mon–Fri 11 A.M.–7:30 P.M., Sat 9:30 A.M.–7:30 P.M.

DIPTYQUE (15)
34, boulevard St-Germain, 75005
Métro: Maubert-Mutualité

Join Puff Daddy, Elton John, and scores of other celebrities who light scented candles from Diptyque. The seven-ounce glass containers hold every wonderful scent you have heard of . . . and plenty you haven't. Traditionalists can buy rose, lilac, cinnamon, or hyacinth, but why not experiment with something unusual: fig tree, newly mown hay, Mexican orange blossom, or myrrh? Room sprays that match the candle scents enhance the experience. Go one step further and wear a matching *eau de toilette* in the same fragrance. Don't leave without a bottle of *vinaigre de toilette*. Based on a nineteenth-century recipe using plants, woods, and spices, this elixir has many uses. In the bath it revives and refreshes; as an aftershave or face spray, it tones and refreshes; and a capful in a bowl of boiling water will remove cooking and tobacco smells from a room. Loyalists know to stock up on their favorite Diptyque products in Paris. For instance, a perfumed candle sells in Paris for 32€ (under $40). Buy it in London and you will spend £28 (about $48) or in New York for $45. One candle lasts fifty hours.

TELEPHONE: 01-43-26-45-27
INTERNET: www.diptyque.tm.fr
CREDIT CARDS: AE, MC, V
OPEN: Mon–Sat 10 A.M.–7 P.M.

LA TUILE À LOUP (38)
35, rue Daubenton, 75005
Métro: Censier-Daubenton

Marie-France and Michel Joblin-Dépalle stock regional tableware and housewares from all over France. True, the pieces are heavy and probably too bulky for a suitcase, but they will insure and ship your purchases.

TELEPHONE: 01-47-07-28-90
FAX: 01-43-36-40-95
EMAIL: tuilealoup@aol.com

INTERNET: www.latuilealoup.com
CREDIT CARDS: AE, MC, V
OPEN: Mon 1–7 P.M., Tues–Sat 10:30 A.M.–7 P.M.; closed in Aug (dates vary)

LE ROUVRAY (5)
3, rue de la Bucherie, 75005
Métro: Maubert-Mutualité, St-Michel

Le Rouvray's motto says it all: "We speak patchwork fluently." It is a wonderful shop if you sew and love homespun fabrics. The shop stocks two thousand fabrics featuring Provençal prints and *toiles de jouy,* offers classes, and fills mail orders. In addition, they will sell you all the supplies you need to create your own work of art.

TELEPHONE: 01-43-25-00-45
FAX: 01-43-25-51-61
EMAIL: lerouvray@easyconnect.fr
INTERNET: www.lerouvray.com
CREDIT CARDS: MC, V
OPEN: Tues–Sat 10 A.M.–6:30 P.M.

LES ARTISANS DU RÊVE: BREIZ NORWAY (35)
33, rue Gay-Lussac, 75005
Métro: Luxembourg

All things from Brittany . . . and the genuine articles: pea coats for adults and children, wool sweaters, authentic striped Breton T-shirts, BZH (a powerful Breton apéritif), and a few pieces of old Quimper. You can also order new, individual Quimper-like pottery bowls and have them personalized with your own name. They also carry Celtic jewelry and Scandinavian items. For Finnish and Austrian products, go to their shop at 25, rue Gay-Lussac.

TELEPHONE: 01-43-29-47-82
CREDIT CARDS: AE, DC, MC, V
OPEN: Mon 1–7 P.M., Tues–Sat 10 A.M.–7 P.M.; hours vary in Aug

L'OCCITANE (39)
130, Rue Mouffetard, 75005
Métro: Monge

Natural cosmetics and body products. For a description, see page 360.

TELEPHONE: 01-43-31-98-12
OPEN: Tues–Sat 9:30 A.M.–7:30 P.M., Sun 9:30 A.M.–1 P.M.

SIXTH ARRONDISSEMENT (see map page 140)

Shops

Arzat	**365**
Boutique Majolique	**366**
Cartes d'Art	**366**
Chercheminippes	**366**
Christian Lu	**366**
Dépôt–Vente de Buci	**367**
Du Pareil au Même	**367**
Du Pareil au Même Bébé	**367**
Flamant	**367**
Galerie Documents	**368**
Gilbert Joseph Papeterie	**368**
Graphigro	**368**
La Cie de Provence	**369**
La Dernière Goutte	**369**
Les Couturiers de la Nature	**369**
Les Olivades	**370**
Les Trois Marches de Catherine B	**370**
L'Occitane	**370**
Marie Mercié	**370**
Matière Première	**371**
Monoprix	**371**
Petit Faune	**371**
Pierre Frey	**372**
The San Francisco Book Company	**372**
Scooter	**372**
Souleiado	**372**
Tout Compte Fait . . .	**373**

Shopping Areas

St-Germain-des-Prés	**337**

Discount Shopping Streets

Rue St-Placide	**339**

***Passages* and Shopping Malls**

Le Marché Saint Germain	**342**

Food Shopping

Rue de Buci and Rue de Seine	**394**
Marché Raspail	**396**

ARZAT (44)
6, rue St-Placide, 75006
Métro: Sévres-Babylone, St-Placide

Silver collectors might find just the thing they have been searching for at this narrow shop sandwiched in among all the discount clothing stores that line both sides of rue St-Placide. None of it is new, and neither are the assorted pieces of china and crystal. If you have a piece that needs restoring, this is where to bring it.

TELEPHONE: 01-42-84-20-66
EMAIL: arzat@net-up.com
INTERNET: www.arzat.com
CREDIT CARDS: AE, DC, MC, V
OPEN: Mon 2–7 P.M., Tues–Sat 11 A.M.–7 P.M.; closed Aug 10–20

BOUTIQUE MAJOLIQUE (6)
42, rue Dauphine, 75006
Métro: St-Germain-des-Prés

For a description of this shop selling hand-embroidered linens, see page 355.
TELEPHONE: 01-55-42-93-55
CREDIT CARDS: AE, MC, V
OPEN: Mon–Sat 10 A.M.–7 P.M.

CARTES D'ART (17)
9, rue du Dragon, 75006
Métro: St-Germain-des-Prés

Most of the postcards are printed exclusively for Cartes d'Art. You will see their designs all over town, but here is the source for their whimsical takes on Paris life, her monuments, and places of interest. They also stock literally thousands of other postcards, all arranged by type. In addition, you will find greeting cards and other stationery products that make nice gifts or souvenirs for yourself. If you don't see what you want, just ask and they probably have it someplace.
TELEPHONE: 01-42-22-86-15
EMAIL: cartesdart@easynet.fr
CREDIT CARDS: AE, DC, MC, V
OPEN: Mon–Sat 11 A.M.–7 P.M.

CHERCHEMINIPPES (56)
109, rue du Cherche-Midi, 75006
Métro: Duroc

Between street Nos. 102 and 124, rue de Cherche-Midi, Cherche-minippes has five *dépôt vents* selling previously owned clothing for men, women, and children, toys, and decorative items. I think the most interesting shop is the decoration shop at 109, which has lots of little things for less than 10€.
TELEPHONE: 01-42-22-45-23
CREDIT CARDS: MC, V
OPEN: Mon–Sat 10:30 A.M.–7 P.M.; closed July 20–Sept 1

CHRISTIAN LU (55)
86, rue de Vaugirard, 75006
Métro: St-Placide, Rennes

Christian Lu designs all the silks you see in her colorful shop and often waits on you herself. Everything is made in China, but the quality and craftsmanship are very high. She has large, hand-rolled scarves; mix-and-match skirts, blouses, and trousers; and some dresses. The scarves make great gifts. Everything is hand washable.

TELEPHONE: 01-45-44-93-37
CREDIT CARDS: V
OPEN: Mon noon–7 P.M., Tues–Sat 10:30 A.M.–7 P.M.

DÉPÔT–VENTE DE BUCI (15)
4, rue de Bourbon-le-Château, off rue de Buci, 75006
Métro: Mabillon

These two side-by-side boutiques run by a mother and daughter team are well worth a few moments if you like being clad in Chanel, Hèrmes, YSL, Dior, Fendi, and Louis Vuitton, but don't want to pay the asking prices in their boutiques. One side is definitely more *haute* than the other, but all the previously owned clothes, accessories, and housewares are in good condition. This is a very popular shopping destination for many style mavens in the tony sixth.

TELEPHONE: 01-46-34-45-05, 01-46-34-28-28
CREDIT CARDS: AE, MC, V
OPEN: Tues–Sat 11 A.M.–7:30 P.M.; closed Aug 10–15

DU PAREIL AU MÊME (49)
7, 14 & 34, Rue St-Placide, 75006
Métro: St-Placide

For a description of these well-priced children's clothing stores, see page 346.

TELEPHONE: 01-45-44-04-40

DU PAREIL AU MÊME (19)
168, boulevard Saint-Germain, 75006
Métro: St-Germain-des-Prés

For a description of this children's clothing store, see page 346.

TELEPHONE: 01-46-33-87-85

DU PAREIL AU MÊME BÉBÉ (60)
17, Rue Vavin, 75006
Métro: Vavin

For a description of this baby clothing store, see page 346.

TELEPHONE: 01-43-54-12-34

FLAMANT (7)
8, rue Furstemberg & 8, rue de l'Abbaye, 75006
Métro: St-Germain-des-Pres

Flamant is a world-class theme park showcasing the latest in home accessories, gourmet treats, candies, and books on gardening and design targeted for the elegant shopper with impeccable tastes and prepared to give a real workout to a credit card. The trendy gathering rooms meander from one high-ticket display to another, offering a mother lode of stylish ideas. Should you need strength to carry on, lunch is served from noon to 3 P.M., and tea until 6:30 P.M.

TELEPHONE: Not available
CREDIT CARDS: MC, V
OPEN: Mon–Sat 10A.M.–6:30 P.M.

GALERIE DOCUMENTS (5)
53, rue de Seine, 75006
Métro: Mabillon

Mireille Romand, the great-great granddaughter of the founder, is keeping the tradition of selling original posters, all with historic interest and value. She also has a fascinating collection of framed advertisements, theater programs, illustrated menus, and sheet music. The prices start around 25€. They are easy and light to carry with you, or she will wrap and ship your purchases.

TELEPHONE: 01-43-54-50-68
FAX: 01-43-29-10-25
EMAIL: gal.documents@easynet.fr
CREDIT CARDS: MC, V
OPEN: Mon 2:30 7 P.M., Tues–Sat 10:30–7 P.M.; Aug closing (dates vary)

GILBERT JOSEPH PAPETERIE (32)
30, boulevard St-Michel, 75006
Métro: St-Michel

Gilbert Joseph is omnipresent in this part of Paris. What started out as a bookstore over a hundred years ago has grown into a conglomerate of stores selling books, videos and CDs, art supplies, and every type of stationery known to civilized humanity. The bookstores are not of as much interest to most visiting shoppers as this stationery store, where the merchandise is spread out over three floors.

TELEPHONE: 01-44-41-88-66
CREDIT CARDS: MC, V
OPEN: Mon–Sat 10 A.M.–7 P.M.

GRAPHIGRO (57)
133, rue de Rennes, 75006
Métro: St-Placide

No artist should miss this three-level emporium dedicated to the needs of artists of all types and levels of ability.

TELEPHONE: 01-53-63-60-00
INTERNET: www.graphigro.com
CREDIT CARDS: MC, V
OPEN: Mon–Sat 10 A.M.–7 P.M.

LA CIE DE PROVENCE (64)
5, rue Bréa, 75006
Métro: Vavin

Savon de Marseille is one of the most well-known French soaps. In their only Parisian boutique, you can indulge in a wide variety of their bath and body care products geared to pamper and promote a feeling of well-being.

TELEPHONE: 01-43-26-39-53
EMAIL: lcdp@free.fr
CREDIT CARDS: AE, MC, V
OPEN: Mon–Sat 10:30–7 P.M.

LA DERNIÈRE GOUTTE (14)
6, rue de Bourbon-le-Château near rue de Buci, 75006
Métro: St-Germain-des-Prés

Juan Sanchez is the multidimensional American owner of this wine shop near the St-Germain-des-Prés Church and the famous Les Deux Magots café. He features lesser-known estate-bottled regional French wines at prices that are 30 to 40 percent less than you would pay elsewhere. Tastings are usually held on Saturday, and often the winemaker is present to talk about his wines. If you are close by, stop in, have a taste, and you will probably leave with several bottles to sample in Paris or to take home. If you are buying in bulk, Juan has a delivery service within Paris.

TELEPHONE: 01-43-29-11-62
FAX: 01-46-34-63-41
EMAIL: goutte@club-internet.fr
CREDIT CARDS: AE, MC, V
OPEN: Mon 4–8:30 P.M., Tues–Sat 10 A.M.–8:30 P.M., Sun 11 A.M.–7 P.M

LES COUTURIERS DE LA NATURE (51)
16, rue de Vaugirard, 75006
Métro: Odéon

Brigitte Half makes the most beautiful dried floral arrangements I have ever seen. And I don't like dried or fake flowers . . . but I make an exception with hers because they are works of art. The topiary bouquets come in all sizes and are made with real roses, lilacs, other blooms, and greenery that have been specially treated to retain their true, natural color. I bought my first arrangement five years ago hoping it would keep its color through the summer. I am now wondering if it ever will fade or look tired—it is still just as pretty as the day I bought it. Don't worry about getting your flowers home. She ships all over the world or will wrap them in such a way that nothing will be damaged. Even if you don't buy a thing, her little shop is lovely to look at.

TELEPHONE & FAX: 01-43-26-18-25
EMAIL: lescouturiersdelanature@hotmail.com
INTERNET: www.lescouturiersdelanature.com

CREDIT CARDS: MC, V
OPEN: Mon–Sat 10 A.M.–7:30 P.M.

LES OLIVADES (35)
95, rue de Seine, 75006
Métro: Odéon

Les Olivades celebrates the textile traditions of Provence in a wide range of products designed to decorate you and your home to reflect the warm colors of the south of France. The quality is excellent and the prices below the competition across the street at Souleiado (see page 372).

TELEPHONE: 01-56-24-29-19
INTERNET: www.les-olivades.com
CREDIT CARDS: AE, DC, MC, V
OPEN: Mon 1–7 P.M., Tues, Wed, Fri 10 A.M.–2 P.M., 3–7 P.M., Thur 10 A.M.–7 P.M., Sat 10 A.M.–noon, 1–7 P.M.

LES TROIS MARCHES DE CATHERINE B (36)
1–3, rue Guisarde, 75006
Métro: Mabillon, Odéon

The shops specialize in vintage Chanel, Hermès, and Louis Vuitton clothing, jewelry, scarves, and other accessories. If you know the name of a particular Hèrmes scarf, they can find it for you.

TELEPHONE: 01-43-54-74-18
INTERNET: www.catherine-b.com
CREDIT CARDS: MC, V
OPEN: Mon 2:30–7:30 P.M., Tues–Sat 10:30 A.M.–7:30 P.M.

L'OCCITANE (61)
26, rue Vavin, 75006
Métro: Vavin

For a description of this store selling natural cosmetics and body products, see page 360.

TELEPHONE: 01-43-25-07-71
OPEN: Mon–Sat 10 A.M.–2 P.M., 3–7 P.M., Sun 10 A.M.–7 P.M.

MARIE MERCIÉ (39)
23, rue St-Sulpice, 75006
Métro: Odéon, St-Sulpice

Marie Mercié runs her hat shop in conjunction with Anthony Peto, who has his own store in the second arrondissement (see page 352). Marie makes theatrical hats exclusively for women, and her creations are almost museum quality—suitable for a day at Ascot, the wardrobe department of a film studio, or the most elaborate fashion event imaginable. She will also do custom orders.

TELEPHONE: 01-43-26-45-83
CREDIT CARDS: AE, DC, MC, V
OPEN: Mon–Sat 11 A.M.–7 P.M.; closed middle of Aug

MATIÈRE PREMIÈRE (30)
89, rue de Seine, 75006
Métro: Odéon

This shop specializes in antique beads. For a complete description of both Matière Première shops, see page 360.

TELEPHONE: 01-44-07-39-07
OPEN: Mon–Sat 10 A.M.–12:30 P.M., 1:30–7 P.M.

MONOPRIX (18)
50, rue de Rennes, 75006
Métro: St-Germain-des-Prés

A complete renovation has transformed this once grubby Monoprix into a contemporary shopping experience, befitting its neighbor, Emporio Armani, which occupies the corner location we all knew and loved as Le Drug Store. Upstairs is a small women's ready-to-wear department plus an Express Manicurist, free "flash" makeup services, and a free skin diagnostic. Downstairs has an enormous grocery, deli, health bar with soup and fruit juice, a bar and café, bakery, and sushi stand where you can eat in or take it out. You'll almost forget this is a Monoprix . . . until it's time to check out, and then you'll be snaked behind ten or fifteen other frustrated customers waiting for your turn to pay. Some things never change, and the lines at Monoprix are one of them.

Monoprix stores are all over Paris. Another central location is in the eighth arrondissement (see page 379).

TELEPHONE: 01-45-48-18-08
CREDIT CARDS: AE, MC, V
OPEN: Mon–Sat 9 A.M.–10 P.M.

PETIT FAUNE (3)
33, rue Jacob, 75006
Métro: St-Germain-des-Prés

For the most adorable classic French baby and children's clothing (birth to twelve years), look no further than this beguiling shop. They also do personalized dishes, which make perfect gifts to commemorate a birth or birthday. Prices are high, that is true. But I think the clothes are worth the money because of the quality and fine workmanship, and they wear like iron. Look at it this way: these are investment purchases for both the present and future generations of children in your family. In January and July, they have super sales. There is a second location at 13, rue Mézières, 75006, Tel: 01-42-22-63-69, Métro: St-Sulpice.

TELEPHONE: 01-42-60-80-72
INTERNET: www.petitfaune.com
CREDIT CARDS: AE, MC, V
OPEN: Mon–Sat 10 A.M.–7 P.M.; closed 2 weeks mid-August

PIERRE FREY (8)
1–2 , rue de Furstemberg, 75006
Métro: St-Germain-des-Prés

Pierre Frey was founded in 1935 in Paris. Since then, the company has become synonymous with the finest in French home furnishing fabrics and home accessories. There are shops worldwide, but it is always special to visit the source, which includes several shops next to each other.

TELEPHONE: 01-46-33-73-00
INTERNET: www.pierrefrey.com
CREDIT CARDS: AE, MC, V
OPEN: Mon–Sat 10 A.M.–6:30 P.M.

THE SAN FRANCISCO BOOK COMPANY (41)
17, rue Monsieur-le-Prince, 75006
Métro: Odéon

It is messy and cluttered, and the second-hand English-language books are stacked two deep, so finding something you are looking for literally resembles looking for a needle in a haystack. Then again, if you don't want to pay retail, it sometimes takes a little extra effort, and you will expend it here. Actually, it is a nice place to while away an hour or so just rummaging, and the good news is that you will usually run across something of interest.

TELEPHONE: 01-43-29-15-70
EMAIL: sfbooks@easynet.fr
CREDIT CARDS: MC, V
OPEN: Mon–Sat 11 A.M.–9 P.M. (Thur until 8 P.M.), Sun 2–7 P.M.

SCOOTER (26)
19, rue du Dragon, 75006
Métro: St-Germain-des-Prés

This is a smaller branch, selling jewelry, a few handbags, and some clothing. For a complete description, see page 350.

TELEPHONE: 01-45-49-48-28

SOULEIADO (37)
78, rue de Siene, 75006
Metro: Odéon, Mabillon

For beautiful prints and products from Provence, Souleiado is the name everyone knows. No one said anything about it being cheap, but the quality is superb and the selection runs all the way from a lavender sachet to outfitting your entire home and wardrobe á la Souleiado.

TELEPHONE: 01-43-54-62-25
INTERNET: www.souleiado.com
CREDIT CARDS: AE, DC, MC, V
OPEN: Mon 10:30 A.M.–1 P.M., 2–7 P.M., Tues–Fri 10:30 A.M.–7 P.M., Sat 11 A.M.–7 P.M.

TOUT COMPTE FAIT . . . (52)
31, rue St-Placide, 75006
Métro: St-Placide

For trendy French children's clothes that don't cost an arm and a leg, Tout Compte Fait . . . runs a close second to Du Pareil au Même (see page 346). Their stores are all over Paris (see pages 384 and 390).

TELEPHONE: 01-42-22-45-64
INTERNET: www.toutcomptefait.com
CREDIT CARDS: MC, V
OPEN: Mon–Sat 10 A.M.–7 P.M.

SEVENTH ARRONDISSEMENT (see map page 176)

Shops

Au Nom de la Rose	373
À Votre Idée Broderie	374
Bonpoint	374
Bonton	374
Debauve & Gallais	374
Le Bon Marché and La Grande Épicerie de Paris	375
L'Occitane	375

Discount Shopping Streets

Rue St-Dominique	339

Food Shopping

Rue Cler	394
Marché Saxe-Breteuil	396

AU NOM DE LA ROSE (29)
46, rue du Bac, 75007
Métro: Rue du Bac

Everything is coming up roses at this colorful boutique devoted to the rose. I like the rose petal bubble bath, the perfumed candles, and the rose syrup to drink with champagne. These are only a few of the multitude of rose-inspired temptations: scarves, sachets, jam, hats and handbags decorated with roses, perfume, Limoges china. Oh, yes, they do sell beautiful fresh roses. This is the only shop with a boutique. The original shop is at 4, rue de Tournon (75006), and there are branches throughout Paris that are easily recognizable by the rose petals strewn on the sidewalk in front of the shops.

TELEPHONE: 01-42-22-22-12
INTERNET: www.aunomdelarose.fr
CREDIT CARDS: AE, MC, V
OPEN: Flower shop Mon–Sat 9 A.M.–9 P.M., boutique Mon–Sat 10 A.M.–7 P.M.; closed 2 weeks mid-Aug (dates vary)

À VOTRE IDÉE BRODERIE (7)
11, rue Amèlie, 75007
Métro: Latour-Maubourg, École-Militaire

Everything in this tiny shop can be personalized. I think the children's camp chairs, embroidered in the color and name of your choice, and weighing only five pounds, are one of the more unusual buys *grand-mères* will not be able to resist.

TELEPHONE & FAX: 01-45-55-55-48
EMAIL: www.avotreidee@aol.com
CREDIT CARDS: None, cash only
OPEN: Mon 2–7 P.M., Tues–Sat 9 A.M.–1 P.M., 3–7 P.M.

BONPOINT (17)
42, rue de l'Université, 75007
Métro: Rue du Bac

If you can afford to shop at Bonpoint for your children's clothes, then you don't need this book, since this is probably the most expensive store for outfitting babies and children in Paris. However, this Bonpoint discounts last season's collections and anything else the other stores can't sell. While it still doesn't quality as cheap, the quality is superb, and the clothes last for generations. They offer even better prices during the sales in January and at the end of June.

TELEPHONE: 01-40-20-10-55
INTERNET: www.bonpoint.com
CREDIT CARDS: AE, MC, V
OPEN: Mon–Sat 10:30 A.M.–6:30 P.M.; closed 3 weeks in Aug (dates vary)

BONTON (30)
82, rue de Grenelle, 75007
Métro: Rue du Bac

Bonton stocks the latest trends in children's clothing from birth to ten years. The displays are great, and so are the clothes, which are hardly bargains, but your child will stand out with panache in a Bonton outfit. There is also a *coiffeur* ready to style the locks of the entire family.

TELEPHONE: 01-44-39-09-20
CREDIT CARDS: AE, MC, V
OPEN: Mon–Sat 10 A.M.–7 P.M.

DEBAUVE & GALLAIS (21)
30, rue des Saints Pères, 75007
Métro: St-Germain-des-Prés

Debauve & Gallais, founded in 1800, are the oldest makers of chocolate in Paris. And are they popular! In its two shops, Parisians spend over 2.5 millions euros annually on thirty tons of chocolate. Only the highest quality, pure ingredients are used, along with the best cocoa beans from three continents. Discerning gourmet chocolate lovers owe themselves a visit to this beautiful shop, which is listed as a national public monument. The chocolates are magnificently displayed on a half-moon carved-wood counter that has been in place since 1819. If you can't wait until your next trip to Paris for one of their divine chocolates, you can shop online and have yours delivered via Federal Express to your door. The other shop is in the second arrondissement (see page 352).

TELEPHONE: 01-45-48-54-67

INTERNET: www.debauve-et-gallais.com

CREDIT CARDS: AE, MC, V

OPEN: Mon–Sat 9 A.M.–7 P.M.

LE BON MARCHÉ AND LA GRANDE ÉPICERIE DE PARIS (35)
38, rue de Sèvres, at rue du Bac, 75007
Métro: Sèvres-Babylone

The first department store in Paris, and still my favorite, this showplace store has balustrades and balconies designed by Gustave Eiffel. It is Paris's premier department store, combining the elegant and the practical, and it is easy to manage. To make several purchases anywhere in the store and not have to carry them, ask at any information desk for a purchase booklet. Your selections are noted in the book and taken to the third floor, where you can make just one payment, and do the *détaxe*. The only drawback at Le Bon Marché is that they do not offer a 10 percent discount to foreigners, but they do have a 12 percent *détaxe* after 175€.

La Grande Épicerie de Paris is a gourmet *supermarché* to behold, with over 30,000 items in stock, not counting the 5,000 bottles of wine. Even if you never cook, it is a fabulous feast for the eyes (see *Great Eats Paris*).

TELEPHONE: 01-44-39-80-00, customer service 01-44-39-82-80

CREDIT CARDS: AE, DC, MC, V

INTERNET: www.lebonmarche.fr

OPEN: Department store Mon–Tues, Wed, Fri 9:30 A.M.–7 P.M.; Thur 10 A.M.–9 P.M., Sat 9:30 A.M.–8 P.M. Food store Mon–Sat 8:30 A.M.–9 P.M.

L'OCCITANE (34)
90, rue du Bac, 75007
Métro: Rue du Bac

For a description of this shop selling natural cosmetics and body products, see page 360.

TELEPHONE: Not available

EIGHTH ARRONDISSEMENT (see map page 202)

Shops

Allix	**376**
Anna Lowe	**376**
Fauchon	**377**
FNAC	**377**
Franchi Chausseurs	**377**
Hediard	**377**
Kiosque Théâtre	**378**
L'Occitane	**378**
Maille	**378**
Maxim's	**379**
Miss "Griffes"	**379**
Monoprix	**379**
Sephora	**380**
Virgin Megastore	**380**

Shopping Areas

Champs-Élysées	**337**
Rue Royale	**337**
The Golden Triangle	**338**

***Passages* and Shopping Malls**

Les Trois Quartiers	**342**

ALLIX (40)
6, rue de Surène, 75008
Métro: Madeleine

Aline Rodriguez makes simple, unusual handbags that are sold throughout the world at three or four times the prices you will pay here. They also stock selected items of jewelry. The merchandise is very well displayed, and English is spoken.

TELEPHONE: 01-42-65-10-79

CREDIT CARDS: MC, V

OPEN: Mon–Fri 11 A.M.–2:30 P.M., 3:30–6:30 P.M.; closed Aug (call to check)

ANNA LOWE (22)
104, rue du Faubourg du St-Honorè, 75008
Métro: Miromesnil, St-Philippe-du-Roule

Anna Lowe is one of the best designer discount stores in Paris. The location is great, next door to the famous Hôtel Bristol and in the midst of many top fashion houses and designers. You will find all the top-name French and Italian designers, including Chanel, and a fabulous selection of evening wear at reduced prices. All labels are left in. There are sensational July and mid-December sales and fast alterations.

TELEPHONE: 01-42-66-11-32, 01-40-06-02-42

EMAIL: annaloweparis@aol.com

INTERNET: www.annaloweparis.com

CREDIT CARDS: AE, DC, MC, V

OPEN: Mon–Sat 10 A.M.–7 P.M.

FAUCHON (42)
30, place de la Madeleine, 75008
Métro: Madeleine

Fauchon is to grocery shopping what the Ritz is to hotels . . . *le ne plus ultra.* A trip to the famed shop and amazing *charcuterie* epitomizes gourmet grocery shopping. A jar of *herbes de provence,* fancy honey, or tin of cookies with the Fauchon label is a very much appreciated gift.

TELEPHONE: 01-47-42-60-11

CREDIT CARDS: AE, DC, MC, V

OPEN: Mon–Sat 9:30 A.M.–8 P.M.

FNAC (26)
74, avenue des Champs Elysées (in Galerie du Claridge), 75008
Métro: George V

FNAC is the place to go for a wide range of music and tickets to whatever is playing. You can either stand in line for hours to book concert seats or log onto their Website. FNAC also sells books (in French, naturally), computers, stereos, mobile telephones, photography equipment, and videos. There are branches in Forum des Halles (75001); at 136, rue de Rennes, 75006; and (music only) at 4, place de la Bastille, 75004.

TELEPHONE: 01-53-53-64-64

INTERNET: www.fnac.com

CREDIT CARDS: AE, MC, V

OPEN: Mon–Sat 10 A.M.–midnight, Sun noon–midnight

FRANCHI CHAUSSEURS (8)
15, rue de la Pépinière, 75008
Métro: St-Augustin

They might have Charles Jourdan shoes at half price, but the styles are dated. They also have end-of-series shoes and Italian designs at good prices, but there's no place to really sit to try them on unless you count the one stool by the door. Remember, this is a discount store, and comfortable shopping is not included in the price.

There is another location in the eighth: 10, rue de Rome, 75008; Tel: 01-43-87-42-59; Métro: Saint-Lazare; same hours, but closed in July, open August.

TELEPHONE: 01-42-94-28-88

CREDIT CARDS: AE, MC, V

OPEN: Mon–Sat 10:30 A.M.–7 P.M.; closed Aug

HEDIARD (41)
21, place de la Madeleine, 75008
Métro: Madeleine

Hediard has several other luscious gourmet food locations, but this is its first, anchoring an entire corner of the gourmet food strip surrounding the Madeleine Church. It offers a true feast for the eyes, and it stocks everything a foodie could dream of finding under one roof, whether it be smoked salmon from Norway; a tin of beluga caviar (100g, 424€!); their own brand of spices, herbs, jams and jellies, foie gras *d'oie* (228€ per kilo); unblemished fresh fruits and vegetables from around the world; wine, coffee, tea, and much more. If you don't feel in the mood to cook yourself, they have complete meals at the ready, and the perfect wines to accompany them. Upstairs is a restaurant serving coffee from Monday to Friday, lunch and tea Monday to Saturday, and dinner Monday to Friday. For a meal, do make a reservation. There is another branch in the eighth on avenue Georges V, and one in the seventh behind Le Bon Marché department store on rue du Bac.

TELEPHONE: 01-43-12-88-88, restaurant reservations 01-43-12-88-99
INTERNET: www.hediard.fr
CREDIT CARDS: AE, DC, MC, V
OPEN: Mon–Sat 9 A.M.–9 P.M., Sun in Dec 10 A.M.–8 P.M.

KIOSQUE THÉÂTRE (45)
15, place de la Madeleine
Métro: Madeleine

This is where you can buy same-day tickets for participating theatrical, dance, and circus performances, and some special events for 50 percent off, plus a 3 percent commission per ticket.

TELEPHONE: Not available
CREDIT CARDS: None, cash only
OPEN: Tues–Sat 12:30–8 P.M., Sun 12:30–4 P.M.

L'OCCITANE (24)
Galerie des Champs Élysées, 84, avenue Champs-Élysées, 75008
Métro: Franklin-D-Roosevelt

For a description, see page 360.

TELEPHONE: Not available

MAILLE (46)
6, place de la Madeleine, 75008
Métro: Madeleine

The Maille boutique is devoted to products from the best and most famous name in mustards. There are over twenty varieties, many of which are attractively gift packaged with recipes included (in French, but if you speak any French, simple enough to follow). In addition, the boutique stocks vinegars, oils, herbs, mustard pots, pickles, and olives. Prices start as low as 3.81€, and the more unusual mustard varieties make great gifts. They also pump two types of fresh mustard (white wine and a fruity chablis) into a pot that you buy, and top it off with a cork. When the mustard is gone, bring the pot and the cork back, and you only pay for the fresh mustard. They do mail orders.

TELEPHONE: 01-40-15-06-00
FAX: 01-40-15-06-11

EMAIL: am-parisboutique@unilever.com
CREDIT CARDS: MC, V
OPEN: Mon–Sat 10 A.M.–7 P.M.

MAXIM'S (52)
5, rue Royale, 75008
Métro: Concorde, Madeleine

Maxim's is synonymous with over-the-top-glamour, moneyed moguls, and the best that excess can offer. Located a few steps from the famed restaurant is this boutique selling everything with the Maxim's stamp of approval proudly displayed. I have to give master merchandiser Pierre Cardin (who is at the helm of the Maxim's enterprises) credit for having something for all budgets. Prices start at 50 euro cents for a book of matches and continue on to 5 to 10€ for their signature pasta, more for a jar of colorful cooked veggies. Not interested in matches or food? Okay, there are pens, watches, a menu from the restaurant (7€), jams, jellies, teas, coffees, and a 37€ apron to wear while you heat up that pasta. You can also buy crockery from the restaurant, reproduction Art Nouveau lamps, candles, and champagne buckets. You name it, and Maxim's has it covered.

TELEPHONE: 01-47-42-01-72
INTERNET: www.maxims-de-paris.co
CREDIT CARDS: AE, DC, MC, V
OPEN: Mon–Sat 10 A.M.–6:45 P.M.

MISS "GRIFFES" (21)
19, rue de Penthièvre, 75008
Metro: Miromesnil

The shop has been in business for more than a half century, and it is now run by its third owner, Mme. Vincent, who has been here for more than twenty years. I think it is one of the best in the discount hunt for women's clothing, shoes, handbags, and accessories from all the top names, including Chanel, Armani, Ungaro, and Valentino. Prices are high at first glance, but not when you consider what you would pay retail in the boutiques. Also available are prototype collections of last season's models, a few of Mme. Vincent's own designs, and wonderful custom-made blazers. Free alterations are ready in two days.

TELEPHONE: 01-42-65-10-00
CREDIT CARDS: AE, DC, MC, V
OPEN: Mon–Fri 11 A.M.–7 P.M., Sat noon–7 P.M.; closed middle 2 weeks in Aug

MONOPRIX (27)
52, avenue des Champs-Élysées, at rue La Boétie, 75008
Métro: Franklin-D-Roosevelt

If you are a Kmart or Target shopper, you will be a Monoprix shopper in Paris. Stores dot the landscape and vary in size and atmosphere, but this is the one that has the longest hours and is the one most tourists will see. All

Monoprix stores are good to keep in mind for quick-fix cosmetic buys (including Bourjois, which all smart discount shoppers know is the prototype for Chanel and is sold at a fraction of cost of the designer brand), cotton underwear, fashion accessories of the moment, toothbrushes, and housewares. Here there is a tourist souvenir corner, basement grocery, and thousands of other daily shoppers in addition to you. Because of the inadequate ratio of cash registers to shoppers, you may feel as if you are in the checkout line behind them all.

Other locations are in the first and sixth arrondissements (see pages 360 and 371).

TELEPHONE: 01-42-25-27-60
CREDIT CARDS: MC, V
OPEN: Mon–Sat 9 A.M.–midnight

SEPHORA (25)
70, avenue des Champs-Élysées, 75008
Métro: Georges-V

Bouncers guard the front doors of the Champs-Élysées Sephora, probably to try to stem the virtual sea of people who stream through here to revel in the absolutely mind-boggling collection of cosmetics, perfumes, and miscellaneous beauty accessories. All the big name lines are here, including Bourjois (the prototype for Chanel). There is a special room for customers to test makeup under lighting conditions from day to night. Perfumes are arranged in alphabetical order, and as you walk in, there is a circular booth where you can sample many of the scents. No *détaxe,* but competitive prices make them worth a look. Sephora is now opening in the States, so it may not be the experience it once was, but if you are near this flagship store, take a look.

There are also two locations in the first arrondissement in the Forum des Halles (see page 341) and on rue de Rivoli near La Samaritaine department store (see page 348), and one in the sixteenth on rue de Passy (see page 390).

TELEPHONE: 01-53-93-22-50
INTERNET: www.sephora.com
CREDIT CARDS: AE, MC, V
OPEN: Mon–Sat 10 A.M.–midnight, Sun noon–9 P.M.

VIRGIN MEGASTORE (28)
52–60, avenue des Champs-Élysées, 75008
Métro: Franklin-D-Roosevelt

Go to the top-floor café for the dazzling view, and then work your way down through an equally dazzling stock of CDs and videos. There is a branch at the Carrousel du Louvre (see page 341).

TELEPHONE: 01-49-53-50-00
CREDIT CARDS: AE, MC, V
OPEN: Café daily 10 A.M.–7:30 P.M., store Mon–Sat 10 A.M.–midnight, Sun noon–midnight

NINTH ARRONDISSEMENT (see map page 202)

Shops

Annexe des Créateurs	**381**
Au Printemps	**381**
Freddy	**382**
Galeries Lafayette	**382**
Haut de Gamme Stock	**382**
Louis Pion	**383**
Musée de la Parfumerie Fragonard	**383**
Pharmacie T. LeClerc	**383**
Sulmaco	**384**
Tout Compte Fait . . .	**384**

***Passages* and Shopping Malls**

Passage Jouffroy	**341**
Passage Verdeau	**341**

ANNEXE DES CRÉATEURS (38)
19, rue Godot-de-Mauroy, 75009
Métro: Madeleine

No Chanel or Yves St-Laurent, but they have last season's fashions for women from French, Italian, and Japanese manufacturers. Labels are left in, and quality varies. There are two shops next to each other, one for dressy attire, the other for sportswear and separates. They also have hats, jewelry, coats, bags, and wedding gowns. Prices are from 40 to 60 percent off retail. Sales are in January and July.

TELEPHONE: 01-42-65-46-40
CREDIT CARDS: AE, MC, V
OPEN: Mon–Sat 10:30 A.M.–7 P.M.

AU PRINTEMPS (14)
64, boulevard Haussmann, 75009
Métro: Havre-Caumartin

This is known as "The Most Parisian Department Store." Famous designer boutiques, a separate men's store, and an excellent leather and cosmetic department are on the ground floor. Also, there's a fabulous umbrella section, which sells thirty thousand *parapluies* per year! The shoe department is excellent, with over forty-one different brands on display. Ask about the shopping booklet, which lets you shop the store and pay only once. Personal shoppers are available, as is a beauty institute, theater and concert reservations, a travel agency, and branches of Mariage Frères, Ladurée, and Brasserie Flo. Don't miss the beautiful views of Paris from a window perch in the cafeteria or outdoor terrace on the top floor; have a coffee if you must while you're here, but don't waste time or money on the dismal food.

TELEPHONE: 01-42-82-50-00
INTERNET: www.printemps.com

CREDIT CARDS: AE, DC, MC, V
OPEN: Mon–Sat 9:30 A.M.–7 P.M., Thur 9:30 A.M.–10 P.M.

FREDDY (44)
3, rue Scribe, 75009
Métro: Opéra

Freddy specializes in perfumes but also stocks scarves, ties, cosmetics, and costume jewelry. Forty percent is taken off if you spend 185€; if you spend less, you will get a 30 percent discount. Prices are marked with the discount already taken off. If you show a copy of *Great Sleeps Paris,* you will receive a small gift.

TELEPHONE: 01-47-42-63-41
CREDIT CARDS: AE, DC, MC, V
OPEN: Mon–Sat 9 A.M.–7 P.M.

GALERIES LAFAYETTE (15)
40, boulevard Haussmann, 75009
Métro: Chaussée d'Antin–La Fayette

Galeries Lafayette carries the top names in fashion, featuring 75,000 brand names, including their own label, all laid out in 110 departments. It also boasts a record number of daily shoppers. More than a hundred thousand people per day stream through their Haussmann store, and of course, they want you to be one of them during your Parisian stay. In addition to a huge perfume and cosmetic section, the top names in French fashion, including the avant guard, they have one floor devoted to lingerie, another to home decorating, and everything else you can imagine—including a one-hour photo service, *bureau de change,* car park, restaurants (including McDonald's in the toy department, naturally), travel and theater agencies, and a watch and shoe repair department. Gourmets and gourmands will want to visit their grocery department (Lafayette Gourmet), which borders on the inspirational: its dazzling array of delicacies features everything a gastronome could possibly want, including food stations where you can stop for a plate of just-made pasta, a sampling of sushi, a quick cappuccino, or a pastry (see *Great Eats Paris*), or contemplate which of the sixty types of cigars to buy. Even dedicated noncooks will want to see this beautiful section of Galeries Lafayette.

TELEPHONE: 01-42-82-34-56, fashion-show reservation 01-42-82-30-85
FAX: 01-42-82-80-18
INTERNET: www.galerieslafayette.com
CREDIT CARDS: AE, MC, V
OPEN: Mon–Sat 9:30 A.M.–7:30 P.M., Thur 9:30 A.M.–9 P.M.

HAUT DE GAMME STOCK (39)
9, rue Scribe, 75009
Métro: Opéra

The shop is located in a courtyard and features two sections of designer clothing for men and women at discounted prices. Not always the top names, but usually a few Armani or Versace pieces mixed in.

TELEPHONE: 01-40-07-10-20
CREDIT CARDS: AE, DC, MC, V
OPEN: Mon–Sat 10 A.M.–7 P.M.

LOUIS PION (36)
9, rue Auber, 75009
Metro: Opéra

Fashion and fun watches for everyone on your list at prices starting at 10€ for an alarm clock and 15€ for a watch. There are several locations throughout Paris.

TELEPHONE: 01-42-65-40-33
CREDIT CARDS: AE, DC, MC, V
OPEN: Mon–Sat 9:30 A.M.–7 P.M.

MUSÉE DE LA PARFUMERIE FRAGONARD (31)
9, rue Scribe, 75009
Métro: Opéra

In the museum you will see displays showing the perfume-making process according to Fragonard and a collection of their perfume bottles. This part is free; then you exit through the boutique, where a patient multilingual sales force is available to help you decide on just the right fragrance. I think the best buy is the box of five perfumes, which you can divide into five separate gifts. It isn't all perfume. The boutique stocks beautifully packaged soaps, cosmetics, and candles. If you are having trouble making up your mind, remember the words of Coco Chanel, who quoted Paul Éluard, a poet friend of Picasso: "A woman who doesn't perfume herself has no future!"

Note that the museum closes half an hour before the boutique does.

TELEPHONE: 01-47-42-04-56
INTERNET: www.fragonard.com
CREDIT CARDS: AE, DC, MC, V
OPEN: boutique: Mon–Sat 9 A.M.–6 P.M., Sun 9 A.M.–6 P.M. from mid-March–Oct; Mon–Sat 9:30 A.M.–4 P.M. from Oct–mid-March

PHARMACIE T. LECLERC (43)
10, rue Vignon, at rue de Sèze, 75009
Métro: Madeleine

T. LeClerc is a 120-year-old pharmacy stocking their own line of cosmetic products. You will see some of their products in other pharmacies and in all the department stores, but here they have the full line and a very helpful staff to help you to get exactly the right products for your skin type. I like their face powders, which are packaged in twenty different tints including banana, apricot, and orchid, their nail polish, and waterproof mascara. They do mail orders.

TELEPHONE: 01-47-42-04-59
FAX: 01-47-42-75-13
INTERNET: www.t-leclerc.com

CREDIT CARDS: AE, MC, V
OPEN: Mon–Sat 8:30 A.M.–7:30 P.M.

SULMACO (17)
13, rue de Trévise, 75009
Métro: Grands Boulevards

English-speaking owner Philippe Madar offers an excellent selection of designer men's fashions and accessories at below retail. In addition to off-the-rack clothing, it is possible to order custom-made clothes. The detail in the double-lined tailor-made suits is superb. Ready-made suits start around 450€, and tailor-made, with your initials inside, begin around 1000€. These are good prices when you consider you can deduct the 13 percent *détaxe* after spending only 175€. Two master tailors are employed to do alterations, which are included in the price of the garment except during sales. Tailor-made suits are guaranteed ready in four weeks for a first fitting, and delivery in the next three days. If a French tailor-made suit appeals to you, make Sulmaco your first shopping stop in Paris. Sales are held at the end of December and January and during the first part of July (dates vary).

TELEPHONE: 01 48-24-89-00
EMAIL: sulmaco@noos.fr
CREDIT CARDS: AE, DC, MC, V
OPEN: Mon–Sat 10:30 A.M.–7 P.M.; in Aug, Mon–Sat noon–6:30 P.M.; closed middle 10 days of Aug

TOUT COMPTE FAIT . . . (6)
62, rue de la Chaussée d'Antin, 75009
Métro: Chaussée d'Antin–La Fayette

For a description of this children's store, see page 373.
TELEPHONE: 01-48-74-16-54

ELEVENTH ARRONDISSEMENT (see map page 222)

Shops

Allicante	385
Anne Willi	385
Porcelaine de Paris	385

Food Shopping

Marché Richard-Lenoir	396

ALLICANTE (14)
26, boulevard Beaumarchais, 75011
Métro: Bastille, Chemin Vert

Allicante specializes in oils from France, but it also carries oils from Italy, Greece, Spain, Portugal, Israel, and Tunesia, all bottled on site by the grower. The selection is daunting, but you can sample to your heart's content before deciding which to buy. Not all the oils are olive—you can sample and purchase sesame, raisin, or pistachio oil, aromatic oils, essential oils, and therapeutic oils. It is quite an interesting learning and tasting experience.

TELEPHONE: 01-43-55-13-02
INTERNET: www.allicante.com
CREDIT CARDS: MC, V
OPEN: Daily 10 A.M.–7:30 P.M.,

ANNE WILLI (16)
13, rue Keller, 75011
Métro: Ledru-Rollin, Bastille

Anne Willi is a talented young designer who makes and sells her line of clothes and jewelry for active young women in this workshop and boutique. Her clothing is not expensive. Many of the separates are reversible, which makes mixing and matching an easy way to maximize an outfit. After the birth of her child, she added a limited amount of baby clothes.

TELEPHONE: 01-48-06-74-06
EMAIL: anne.willi@wanadoo.fr
CREDIT CARDS: MC, V
OPEN: Mon 2–8 P.M., Tues–Sat 11.30 A.M. 8 P.M ; closed 2 weeks in Aug

PORCELAINE DE PARIS (2)
13, rue de la Pierre-Levée, 75011
Métro: Parmentier

Porcelaine de Paris is the second-oldest porcelain manufacturer in France (after Sèvres) and the last porcelain manufacturer still actively working in Paris. It is interesting to note that only women work here, with the exception of the production manager. I don't have to tell you about the high quality of this magnificent china, which includes everything from a small pin dish to complete kitchens, bathrooms, and countless table settings. You will see Porcelaine de Paris proudly displayed in every fine department or home furnishing store. However, you do not have to pay these retail prices. End of series and seconds are available, and special promotions are held. Shipping is available. Before you buy a complete dinner set, be sure to inquire about the lead count, as some of the patterns will not meet the strict U.S. guidelines.

TELEPHONE & FAX: 01-40-21-37-90
INTERNET: www.porcelaine-paris.com
CREDIT CARDS: MC, V
OPEN: Tues–Fri 10 A.M.–2 P.M., 3–7 P.M., Sat noon–7 P.M.; closed Aug

TWELFTH ARRONDISSEMENT (see map page 222)

Shops
Betty	386
Viaduc des Arts	386

***Passages* and Shopping Malls**
Bercy Village	342

Flea Markets
Marché d'Aligre	392

Food Shopping
Rue d'Aligre	395

BETTY (21)
10, place d'Aligre, 75012
Métro: Ledru-Rollin

Betty is not worth a separate journey, but it is worth a quick look. Probably the best time to check Betty is early Sunday morning; combine it with a trip to the flea market at place d'Aligre. Upstairs they say they have last season's designer labels, but not many on most top-ten lists. The prices are low, and if you want something French and don't care about famous designer labels, you might find this interesting.

TELEPHONE: 01-43-07-40-64

CREDIT CARDS: MC, V

OPEN: Tues, Wed, Fri, Sun 9 A.M.–12:30 P.M., Thur & Sat 9 A.M.–12:30 P.M., 2:30–7 P.M.

VIADUC DES ARTS (24)
9–129, avenue Daumesnil, 75012
Métro: Ledru-Rollin, Gare de Lyon

The railway tracks on top of the stone viaduct carried the suburban railway from Bastille. Now the vaulted archways are enclosed and house a variety of artists' workshops, galleries, boutiques, and a café. The rail tracks have been replaced by a walkway with trees and gardens that goes all the way to the Bois de Vincennes.

TELEPHONE: Not available

CREDIT CARDS: Depends on shop

INTERNET: www.viaduc-des-arts.com

OPEN: Tues–Sat noon–7 P.M., Sun 11 A.M.–7 P.M. (some stores may differ)

FOURTEENTH ARRONDISSEMENT (see map page 240)

Shops
Divine	**387**
Galeries Lafayette	**387**
La Boutique de l'Artisanat Monastique	**387**

Discount Shopping Streets
Rue d'Alésia	**339**

***Passages* and Shopping Malls**
Maine-Montparnasse	**343**

Flea Markets
Marché de Vanves	**392**

Food Shopping
Rue Daguerre	**395**

DIVINE (21)
39, rue Daguerre, 75014
Métro: Denfert-Rochereau

Hats, berets, bonnets, scarves, and gloves for men and women are piled high in this shop. When I asked, "How many hats do you have?" the answer was, "Too many to count!" When you go, you will believe it.

TELEPHONE: 01-43-22-28-10
CREDIT CARDS: MC, V
OPEN: Tues–Sat 10:30 A.M.–1 P.M., 3–7:30 P.M.

GALERIES LAFAYETTE (9)
Centre Commercial Montparnasse, Tour Montparnasse Complex, 212, rue du Départ, 75014
Métro: Montparnasse-Bienvenüe

This location is rather boring and limited compared to the flagship main store. For a complete description, see page 382.

TELEPHONE: 01-45-38-52-87
OPEN: Mon–Sat 9:45 A.M.–7:30 P.M.

LA BOUTIQUE DE L'ARTISANAT MONASTIQUE (17)
68 bis, avenue Denfert-Rochereau, 75014
Métro: Denfert-Rochereau

Doting *grand-mères*, beware! What a find for adorable children's clothing (including christening outfits that are destined to become family heirlooms), layettes, handicrafts, new and antique embroidered linens and laces, cosmetics, food products, and beautiful robes and nightgowns . . . all made by French monks and nuns in 360 convents and monasteries throughout France. The quality is beautiful, and whatever you buy will show the name of the convent or monastery where it was made, and it will be hand-signed by the sister or monk who made it. A volunteer staff of 121 sweet, gray-haired lady volunteers graciously assist you, wrap your purchase, and take your money. Even if you only buy a candle or a bar of soap, it is worth a visit. There are other boutique locations throughout France.

TELEPHONE: 01-43-35-15-76

EMAIL: monastic.secretariat@wanadoo.fr

CREDIT CARDS: MC, V

OPEN: Mon–Fri noon–6:30 P.M., Sat 2–7 P.M.; closed holidays, last week of July, and Aug

---

FIFTEENTH ARRONDISSEMENT (see map page 240)
Food Shopping

Rue du Commerce	395
Marché Dupleix	397

SIXTEENTH ARRONDISSEMENT (see map page 256)
Shops

Dépôt–Vente de Passy	388
Du Pareil au Même	389
Franck et Fils	389
L'Affair d'Un Soir	389
L'Occitane	389
Réciproque	390
Sephora	390
Tout Compte Fait . . .	390

Shopping Areas

Rue de Passy and Avenue Victor Hugo	338

***Passages* and Shopping Malls**

Passy Plaza	343

Food Shopping

Marché Cours de la Reine	397

DÉPÔT–VENTE DE PASSY (16)
14–16, rue de la Tour, 75116
Métro: Passy

This is one of the best consignment shops, offering a super selection of clothing in mint condition featuring all the biggies for women, from Chanel and Hermès accessories to Dior, Gucci, and Prada. It has a nice staff, fair prices of about 40 to 50 percent off regular retail (only 20 percent for Chanel), and good dressing rooms. This is one of the favorites of smart French discount denizens.

TELEPHONE: 01-45-20-95-21

CREDIT CARDS: AE, MC, V

OPEN: Mon 2–7 P.M., Tues–Sat 10 A.M.–7 P.M.; closed Aug

DU PAREIL AU MÊME (9)
97, avenue Victor Hugo, 75116
Métro: Victor-Hugo

For a description of this children's clothing store, see page 346.

TELEPHONE: 01-47-37-06-31

FRANCK ET FILS (19)
80, rue de Passy, 75116
Métro: La Muette, Passy

This small, elegant department store sells traditional clothing to the women of Passy, one of Paris's most expensive neighborhoods. You will get a 10 percent discount on anything you buy, plus the *détaxe*, if you spend 185€. The store has all the high-quality designers, including Chanel, and an excellent lingerie department. And it is easily manageable.

TELEPHONE: 01-44-14-38-00
CREDIT CARDS: AE, DC, MC, V
OPEN: Mon–Sat 10 A.M.–7 P.M.

L'AFFAIR D'UN SOIR (11)
147, rue de la Pompe, 75116
Métro: Victor-Hugo

The shop is located in one of the poshest neighborhoods of Paris, so this tells you another secret of the well-dressed French woman— maybe she leases! If you have been invited to the Élysée Palace and "haven't a thing to wear," don't worry, call L'Affair d'un Soir for your dress-rental appointment. For women soirée-goers, silk dresses, ball gowns, hats, and elegant accessories are available. They will also rent just one necklace, or a hat, if that is all you need to complete an ensemble. For the men, tuxedos and everything to go with them are also here. Sophie de Mestier designs two original collections each year that she rents to her elegant clientele. Many customers rent an outfit and cannot bear to part with it, so they end up buying it. Prices for rentals are between 80€ and 385€, plus a deposit of 500€ (and up) depending on the garment. Cleaning and alterations are included. They also have an exotic tearoom where you can sit on pillows and pretend you are sipping mint tea in a real casbah.

TELEPHONE: 01-47-27-37-50
INTERNET: www.laffairedunsoir.com
CREDIT CARDS: MC, V
OPEN: Mon 2–7 P.M., Tues–Sat 10:30 A.M.–7 P.M.

L'OCCITANE (8)
109, Avenue Victor Hugo, 75116
Métro: Victor-Hugo

For a description, see page 360.

TELEPHONE: Not available
OPEN: Mon–Sat 10:30 A.M.–2 P.M., 3–7 P.M.

RÉCIPROQUE (14)
88, 89, 92, 93, 95, 97, 101, 123, rue de la Pompe, 75116
Métro: Rue de la Pompe

The grande dame of formerly worn designer fashions for a fraction of their original retail price displayed in a series of shops makes Réciproque the largest consignment shop in Paris. It has everything from gifts and antiques to estate jewelry, shoes, bags, clothes, furs, evening wear, and men's clothing. The sheer volume is staggering, so allow plenty of time if this type of *haute* thrift shopping is your forte. Sales are held in January, July, and August. Look for the orange signs indicating their shops along rue de la Pompe. The staff can be helpful.

TELEPHONE: 01-47-04-30-28 (main office), 01-47-04-82-24
CREDIT CARDS: AE, MC, V
OPEN: Tues–Fri 11 A.M.–7:30 P.M., Sat 10:30 A.M.–7:30 P.M.

SEPHORA (25)
50, rue de Passy, 75116
Métro: Passy

For a complete description of this cosmetics and perfume wonderland, see page 380.

TELEPHONE: Not available

TOUT COMPTE FAIT . . . (10)
115, avenue Victor Hugo, 75116
Métro: Victor-Hugo

For a description of this children's clothing store, see page 373.

TELEPHONE: 01-47-55-63-36

SEVENTEENTH ARRONDISSEMENT (see map page 272)
Shops

Accessories à Soie	**390**
Gianni d'Arno Pur Réve de Soie	**391**

Food Shopping

Rue de Lévis	**395**
Rue Poncelet	**395**
Marché des Batignolles	**397**

ACCESSORIES À SOIE (13)
21, rue des Acacias, 75017
Métro: Argentine, Charles-de-Gaulle-Étoile

Scarves by Nini Ricci, YSL, pretty silk sweaters, belts, ties, and shirts for the man in your life—all at discount prices. The scarves are beautifully wrapped in the designer box they came in.

TELEPHONE: 01-42-27-78-77
CREDIT CARDS: AE, DC, MC, V
OPEN: Mon–Sat 10:30 A.M.–2 P.M., 3–7:30 P.M.

GIANNI D'ARNO PUR RÉVE DE SOIE (2)
55, rue Tocqueville, 75017
Métro: Malsherbes, Villiers

Come here for the best-priced washable silk blouses in Paris in a rainbow of colors, patterns, and styles. No Chinese imitation imports . . . all are French or Italian silk. Custom-made orders are the same price and take fifteen days for delivery in Paris, or they will send.

TELEPHONE AND FAX: 01-42-36-98-73
CREDIT CARDS: MC, V
OPEN: Tues–Sat 11 A.M.–7 P.M.; sales in Jan and July

EIGHTEENTH ARRONDISSEMENT (see map page 288)

Shops
Marché Saint Pierre	**391**
Stock Griffes	**391**
Tati	**392**

Flea Markets
Marché de Clignancourt	**393**

Food Shopping
Rue Lepic	**395**

MARCHÉ SAINT PIERRE (11)
2–5 rue Charles-Nodier and 1, place St-Pierre, 75018
Métro: Anvers

Every Parisian interior designer knows this is the only place to come for wonderful fabrics and trimmings in all types, sizes, and price ranges All the shops are centered around rue Charles-Nodier and place St-Pierre. At Dreyfus, 2, rue Charles-Nodier, you will find discounted bolts of fabric; at Tissues Reine, 5, place St-Pierre, silks and luxury fabrics are sold; and at Moline, 1, place St-Pierre, you have upholstery.

TELEPHONE: Dreyfus 01-46-06-92-25; Tissues Reine 01-46-06-02-31; Moline 01-46-06-14 66
CREDIT CARDS: MC, V
OPEN: Depends on store, but generally Mon 2–6 P.M., Tues–Sat 10 A.M.–6 P.M.

STOCK GRIFFES (15)
1, rue des Trois Frères, 75018
Métro: Pigalle, Abbesses

For a description of this discount clothing store, see page 362.

TELEPHONE: 01-42-55-42-49
OPEN: Mon–Sat 10:30 A.M.–7 P.M.

TATI (16)
4–30, boulevard de Rochechouart, 75018
Métro: Barbès-Rochechouart, Anvers
For a complete description of this department store, see page 356. At this location, watch out for pickpockets, especially children.
TELEPHONE: 01-55-29-50-00

Flea Markets: Les Marchés aux Puces

What to do on a Saturday or Sunday morning? Go early to the flea market. Wear old clothes and comfortable shoes, beware of pickpockets, and bring cash. You will have a good time even if you don't buy a thing. The days of finding a fabulous antique for a few euros are gone, but you will probably find a keepsake or two. If you have nothing special on your list, just people-watch; the wildlife at the *puces* beats that at the zoo.

FLEA MARKETS: *LES MARCHÉS AUX PUCES*

Marché d'Aligre (12th)	392
Marché de Vanves (14th)	392
Marché de Clignancourt (18th)	393
Marché de Montreuil (20th)	393

MARCHÉ D'ALIGRE (25; see map page 222)
Place d'Aligre, 75012
Métro: Ledru-Rollin
Marché d'Aligre is an Arab-influenced market with bottom-of-the-barrel prices. That's also where most of the quality is, especially for the produce. Wear a concealed money belt and go on a Sunday morning when it is really jumping. Prowl through the little shops, which have the lowest prices on baskets, tea glasses, *couscousières,* teapots, and Middle Eastern kitsch. You can bargain a little and probably save 30 or 40 percent over what you would pay in an uptown shop. In the center of it all is a small flea market selling little objects, antique buttons, bric-a-brac, and tacky clothes. Fashion mavens might want to swing through Betty, a designer discount shop that at times has something interesting (see page 386).
OPEN: Tues–Sun 7:30 A.M. –1 P.M.

MARCHÉ DE VANVES (27; see map page 240)
Avenue Georges-Lafenestre, 75014
Métro: Porte de Vanves
This is a good place for small antiques and collectibles that tuck easily into a suitcase. Start by walking along avenue Marc-Sangier, and in a morning, you will be able to browse and bargain your way through it and come away with a treasure or two. The locals know to come way before noon, when most of the serious sellers fold up their stalls. Every Sunday morning from March to October, the Square Georges-Lafenestre is an open-air art gallery where you can buy directly from the artists.

MARCHÉ DE CLIGNANCOURT (1; see map page 288)
Avenue Michelet at rue des Rosiers, 75018
Métro: Porte de Clignancourt

Clignancourt is the largest flea and antique market in the world—too
big to conquer in only a day. More than 11 million bargain hunters come
every year, making this the number four tourist site in France. There are
over 2500 dealers here set up in permanent shops. Once you get past the
piles of jeans and the Indians selling cheap beads, head for the Marché
Biron on the corner of 85, rue des Rosiers. It has the most expensive
sellers, but it's the most serious for furniture and art. The Paul Bert
Marché, at 110, rue des Rosiers, and 18, rue Paul Bert, has an unusual
collection of Art Deco pieces and antiques from the late 1890s. The
Marché Jules-Valles at 7, rue Jules Valles, has the least expensive items,
and lots of 1920s and 1930s lace and postcards. For vintage clothing, the
Marché Malik at 53, rue Jules-Valles, is the place. Bring cash, expect to
bargain, and wear a money belt. Pickpockets are pros here.

NOTE: When you exit the métro station, simply head north, following
the crowds and the signs, to find the flea market. Cross boulevard Ney
onto avenue de la Porte de Clignancourt, and you can't miss it.

INTERNET: www.antikita.com
OPEN: Sat 8 or 9 A.M.–6 P.M., Sun–Mon 10 or 11 A.M.–6 P.M.

MARCHÉ DE MONTREUIL
Place de la Porte de Montreuil, 75020
Métro: Porte de Montreuil

The huge market begins once you get through the long line of vendors
hawking cheap trash on the bridge, but even then, you will wonder why
you came. It's all basically cheap junk of little value or interest for most of
us unless you are looking for tools, domestic appliances, or beat-up
furniture.

OPEN: Sat–Mon 9 A.M.–5 P.M.

Food Shopping Streets and Outdoor Roving Markets

**Paris in the early morning has a cheerful, bustling aspect—
a promise of things to come.**
> —*Nancy Mitford,* The Pursuit of Love

There are two types of markets in Paris (in addition to the growing
number of *supermarchés*): *rue commerçantes*—stationary indoor/outdoor markets along certain streets that are open six days a week, including Sunday
morning, but not on Monday—and the *marchés volants*—outdoor roving
markets of independent merchants who move from one neighborhood to
another on Tuesday to Sunday mornings only, never in the afternoon. A

visit to one of these markets provides a real look at an old, unchanging way of daily Paris life. When you go, take your camera, don't touch the merchandise, and watch your wallet. I guarantee you that a trip or two to a Paris market will spoil you for your hometown supermarket. In Paris markets, fruits and vegetables of every variety are arranged with the skill and precision usually reserved for fine jewelry store windows. Equal care and attention is given to the displays of meats, fish, cheese, and fresh flowers. Everyone has a favorite vendor for each item on their shopping list, and vendors respond with very personal service. It is not unusual for a fruit seller to ask you not only what day you want to eat your melon or peaches, but at what time, and to select the fruit accordingly. A few favorites are listed here.

Food Shopping Streets: *Rues Commerçantes*

Generally, these are open Tuesday to Sunday 8:30 A.M. to 1 P.M. and 4:30 to 7 P.M.; closed Monday all day and Sunday afternoon. You can usually use credit cards for larger purchases.

RUE MONTORGUEIL, 75002 (29; see map page 62)
Métro: Étienne-Marcel, Sentier

Rue Montorgueil is crowded with dogs, children, motor scooters, and people of all ages and persuasions, who create a great, lively Parisian ambience on one of the best shopping streets in Paris. The street is lined with three supermarkets, six *boulangeries/pâtisseries,* four produce stands, meat (including horse) markets, fishmongers, cheese and wine shops, three florists, pharmacies, cleaners, phone and photo shops, a hardware store, bars and cafés galore, and a four-star hotel.

OPEN: With the exception of the bakeries, most of the food shops are closed Mon, but open Tues–Sat 8:30 A.M.–7 P.M., Sun 8:30 A.M.–1 P.M.

RUE MOUFFETARD, 75005 (41; see map page 108)
Métro: Censier-Daubenton, Place Monge

One of the most photographed and colorful street markets in Paris, but the quality is sometimes suspect and the prices tend to be high. The best times to experience the market street is on Saturday and Sunday mornings.

RUE DE BUCI AND RUE DE SEINE, 75006 (16; see map page 140)
Métro: Odéon

Loud, colorful, and tourist-infested—and it has high prices for daily shopping needs. It's sociologically interesting to sit at one of the outdoor cafés and watch the crowd.

RUE CLER, 75007 (24; see map page 176)
Métro: École-Militaire

This is the gathering place for aristocratic shoppers in the tony seventh arrondissement, but frankly, the quality has slipped, and the prices have gone up.

RUE D'ALIGRE, 75012 (25; see map page 222)
Métro: Ledru-Rollin

The street stalls are open only in the morning, selling an amazing array of North African and Caribbean produce and fruit in addition to seasonal French produce. Prices are low and quality varies. For an even more ethnic shopping experience, browse through the shops that line both sides of rue d'Aligre. The covered market on place d'Aligre is open in the afternoon. On Sunday morning there is a flea market on place d'Aligre with stalls selling mostly *junque*. There may be a hidden treasure, but I have never thought it was worth the digging. If you like wonderful, whole grain, organic breads, join the queue at Moisan, 5, place d'Aligre. Moisan is open Tues–Sat 7 A.M.–1:30 P.M., 3–8 P.M., Sun 7 A.M.–2 P.M.; Tel: 01-43-45-46-60; no credit cards.

RUE DAGUERRE, 75014 (23; see map page 240)
Métro: Denfert-Rochereau

Here you'll find lots of cafés filled with people-watchers, a Monoprix on the corner, and the markets with good-quality products at fair prices.

RUE DU COMMERCE, 75015 (2; see map page 240)
Métro: Commerce, La Motte-Picquet–Grenelle

This provides an interesting look at blue-collar Paris.

RUE DE LÉVIS, 75017 (7; see map page 272)
Métro: Villiers

There is plenty here to tempt you—from bakeries and wine shops to a Monoprix.

RUE PONCELET, 75017 (12; see map page 272)
Métro: Ternes

This is a popular shopping destination with good cheese shops and colorful food hawkers.

RUE LEPIC, 75018 (13; see map page 288)
Métro: Abbesses, Blanche

This runs up the hill from boulevard de Clichy and merges into the heart of this side of the Butte Montmartre.

Outdoor Roving Food Markets: *Marchés Volants*

These are open on the days listed, unless otherwise noted, from 8 A.M. to 1:30 P.M. only. At the markets, look for the sign *producteur,* which usually hangs along the back of the stall. It means the merchant is selling foods or products he or she grew or produced, and the quality is usually better.

MARCHÉ PLACE BAUDOYER (36; see map page 84)
Place Baudoyer, off rue de Rivoli, 75004
Métro: Hôtel de Ville

This is the only afternoon market held in Paris. The location is central, but the stands are few. However, prices are competitive, and there are several above-average stalls including one selling plants and flowers, another stirring a huge dish of paella, and another hawking hot and cold *charcuterie*.

OPEN: Wed 3–8 P.M., Sat 7–2:30 P.M.

MARCHÉ CARMES (11; see map page 108)
Place Maubert, 75005
Métro: Maubert-Mutualité

This market is small with the usual food stalls, but also those selling foie gras, spices, a variety of olive oils and balsamic vinegar, clothing, rugs, quilts, Provençal prints, as well as a Senegalese merchant selling African art. Thursday is the best day for non-food items.

OPEN: Tues, Thur, Sat 8 A.M.–1 P.M.

MARCHÉ MONGE (34; see map page 108)
Place Monge, 75005
Métro: Place Monge

This market is smaller than most, so it's easy to look it all over before deciding what looks the best. Friday is the best day for non-food items.

OPEN: Wed, Fri, Sun 8 A.M.–1 P.M.

MARCHÉ RASPAIL (45; see map page 140)
Boulevard Raspail, between rue du Cherche-Midi and rue de Rennes, 75006
Métro: Rennes, Sèvres-Babylone

On Sunday the bio-products are from local growers and producers offering excellent organic fruits and veggies, even sulfate-free wines. If you are a health foodie, you will love it.

OPEN: Tues & Fri (not organic), Sun (organic), 9 A.M.–1 P.M.

MARCHÉ SAXE-BRETEUIL (36; see map page 176)
Avenue de Saxe, from place de Breteuil to place de Fontenoy, 75007
Métro: Sèvres-Lecourbe, Duroc

The Eiffel Tower serves as a beacon between the lines of food sellers. What a great photo op!

OPEN: Thur, Sat

MARCHÉ RICHARD-LENOIR (17; see map page 222)
Boulevard Richard-Lenoir, at rue Amelot, 75011
Métro: Bastille, Richard-Lenoir

Not far from the Bastille, enormous, and very local.

OPEN: Thur, Sun

MARCHÉ DUPLEIX (1; see map page 240)
Boulevard du Grenelle, between rue de Lourmel and rue de Commerce, 75015
Métro: Dupleix, La Motte-Piquet–Grenelle

This is considered one of the best roving markets in Paris because it's so big and has everything, and it's well worth an hour or so on a Sunday morning. In addition to food, you can buy suitcases, smocked dresses, violins, and much more. Despite its proximity to the Eiffel Tower, it's not touristy; in fact, Parisians love to live in the fifteenth arrondissement simply because of this market.

OPEN: Wed, Sun

MARCHÉ COURS DE LA REINE (15; see map page 256)
Avenue du Président Wilson, 75016
Métro: Alma Marceau, Iéna

Big, beautiful with lots of luxurious foodstuffs befitting the exclusive neighborhood.

OPEN: Wed, Sat

MARCHÉ DES BATIGNOLLES (5; see map page 272)
Boulevard des Batignolles between rue de Rome and place de Clichy, 75017
Métro: Place Clichy, Rome

On Saturday, stalls sell organic products directly from the growers. Look for the sweet woman selling crêpes made to order.

OPEN: Sat

A Shopper's Glossary

These are a few words and phrases to help you during your shopping adventures. For a larger glossary, see page 403.

How much does this cost?	*Ça coute combien?*
Do you have a smaller/larger size?	*Auriez-vous la taille au dessous/endussus?*
I am a size 36.	*Je fait un 36.*
I will take it.	*Je le prends.*
Do you accept credit cards?	*Acceptez-vous les cartes de crédit?*
Do you ship to the U.S.?	*Est-ce que vous envoyez au Etats-Unis?*
alteration(s)	*retouche(s)*
apron	*tablier*
belt	*ceinture*
blue cotton worker's uniform	*bleus de travail*
cash	*espèces*
bottle (perfume)	*flacon*
boxer shorts	*caleçons*
chef's hat	*toque*

closed	*fermé*
coat	*manteau*
department store	*magasin*
do-it-yourselfers	*bricoleurs*
down comforter	*duvet*
dress	*robe*
dressing gown, robe	*peignoir*
end of the collection	*fin de series*
expensive custom-made designer clothing	*haute couture*
first floor above ground (second floor in U.S.)	*premier étage*
flea market	*marché aux puces*
French cuff(s)	*manchette(s)*
glove	*gant*
good deal	*bonne affair*
ground floor (first floor in U.S.)	*rez-de-chausée*
hand-painted pottery	*faïence*
in style	*à la mode*
labels cut out	*dégriffés*
large department store	*grand magasin*
market	*marché*
MasterCard charge card	*Eurocard*
open	*ouvert*
overstock	*stock*
pants	*pantalons*
perfume store	*parfumerie*
poster	*affiche*
purse	*sac*
ready-to-wear	*prêt-a-porter*
resale consignment shop	*dépôt vente*
sales	*soldes*
scarf	*écharpe*
second-hand clothes (à la thrift shops)	*fripes*
second-hand dealer	*brocanteur*
shoes	*chaussures*
size	*taille*
skirt	*jupe*
stockings	*bas*
sweater	*pull*
tax refund	*détaxe*
tie	*cravate*
Visa charge card	*Carte Bleu*
workshop	*atelier*

Shops by Type

Antiques
Le Louvre des Antiquaires   **349**

Art Supplies/Stationery
Gilbert Joseph Papeterie   **368**
Graphigro   **368**
L'Écritoire   **359**

Bookstores
Abbey Bookshop, The   **362**
Boutique Paris-Musées   **344, 355, 358**
Brentano's   **352**
Galignani   **347**
Red Wheelbarrow Bookstore, The   **361**
San Francisco Book Company, The   **372**
W. H. Smith   **351**

Children's Clothing
Bonpoint   **374**
Bonton   **374**
Du Pareil au Même   **346, 367, 389**
Du Pareil au Même Bébé   **346, 367**
Petit Faune   **371**
Tout Compte Fait . . .   **373, 384, 390**

China and Crystal
Faïenceries de Quimper   **359**
Porcelaine de Paris   **385**

Clothing and Accessories
A la Bonne Renommée   **357**
Allix   **376**
Anne Willi   **385**
C & P   **359**
Colette   **345**
Divine   **387**
Explora   **353**
Krystyna Bukowska   **359**
L'Espace Créateurs   **349**
Lollipops   **353**
Oliver B   **350**

Consignment
Biscuit   **358**
Chercheminippes   **366**
Dépôt–Vente de Buci   **367**
Dépôt–Vente de Passy   **388**
Réciproque   **390**

Cosmetics and Perfume

Catherine Perfumes and Cosmetics — **345**
Freddy — **382**
La Cie de Provence — **369**
L'Occitane — **360, 364, 370, 375, 378, 389**
Musée de la Parfumerie Fragonard — **383**
Patyka — **356**
Pharmacie T. LeClerc — **383**
Sephora — **380, 390**

Department Stores

Au Printemps — **381**
BHV — **358**
FNAC — **377**
Franck et Fils — **389**
Galeries Lafayette — **382, 387**
La Samaritaine — **348**
Le Bon Marché — **375**
Madelios — **350**
Monoprix — **360, 371, 379**
Tati — **356, 392**
Virgin Megastore — **380**

Discount Shopping Mall

La Vallée Outlet Shopping Village — **334**
Discount Shopping Streets — **338**

Discount Shops

Anna Lowe — **376**
Annexe des Créateurs — **381**
Betty — **386**
Et Vous Stock — **353**
Franchi Chausseurs — **377**
Haut de Gamme Stock — **382**
Les Trois Marchés de Catherine B — **370**
Miss "Griffes" — **379**
Oliver B — **350**
PWS–Prices Without Surprise — **361**
Stock Griffes — **362, 391**
Stock Kookaï — **353**
Sulmaco — **384**

Discount Theater Tickets

Kiosque Théâtre — **378**

Fabrics

Le Rouvray — **364**
Marché Saint Pierre — **391**
Flea Markets — **392**

Food Shopping Streets and Outdoor Roving Markets — **393**

Gifts

Arzat	**365**
Au Nom de la Rose	**373**
À Votre Idée Broderie	**374**
Boutique Majolique	**355, 366**
Boutique Paris-Musées	**344, 355, 358**
Cartes d'Art	**366**
Colette	**345**
Diptyque	**363**
DOT–Diffusion d'Objets de Table	**355**
Faïenceries de Quimper	**359**
Galerie Documents	**368**
La Boutique de l'Artisanat Monastique	**387**
La Dame Blanche	**347**
La Tuile à Loup	**363**
L'Écritoire	**359**
Le Prince Jardinier	**349**
Les Artisans du Rêve: Breiz Norway	**364**
Les Couturiers de la Nature	**369**
Les Olivades	**370**
Louis Pion	**383**
Maréchal	**350**
Souleiado	**372**
Viaduc des Arts	**386**

Gourmet Foods

Allicante	**385**
Debauve & Gallais	**352, 374**
Fauchon	**377**
Galeries Lafayette	**382, 387**
Hediard	**377**
La Grande Épicerie de Paris	**375**
Maille	**378**
Maxim's	**379**

Hairdresser

Franck Fann Coiffeur	**33**

Handcrafts/DIY

La Droguerie	**348**
Le Rouvray	**364**
Matière Première	**360, 371**

Hats

Anthony Peto	**352**
Divine	**387**
Marie Mercié	**370**

Herbalist

Herboristerie du Palais Royal	**347**

House and Garden
Flamant 367
Le Cèdre Rouge 348
Le Prince Jardinier 349
Les Olivades 370
Pierre Frey 372
Souleiado 372
Jewelry
Laurent Guillot 356
Matière Première 360, 371
Scooter 350, 372
Sidney Carron 361
Tati Or 354
Kitchen/Cooking Utensils
A. Simon 351
Dehillerin 346
Menswear
Accessories à Soie 390
Anthony Peto 352
Madelios 350
PWS–Prices Without Surprise 361
Sulmaco 384
Passages 340
Renting Dress Clothes
L'Affair d'Un Soir 389
Shoes
Franchi Chausseurs 377
Rue Meslay 338
Shopping Malls 341
Silk
Accessories à Soie 390
Christian Lu 366
Gianni d'Arno Pur Réve du Soie 391
Sporting Goods
Au Vieux Campeur 363
Toys
Village Jové Club–La Passion de Jouet 354
Wine
La Dernière Goutte 369

Glossary of French Words and Phrases

The French are surprisingly tolerant of foreigners who make an attempt to speak a few words. If you combine that with a smile and some sign language, and liberal use of *Madame* and *Monsieur, s'il vous plaît,* and *merci beaucoup,* you will be surprised how far you will get. Before your trip, buy some French language tapes or check them out from the library, and listen to them whenever you can. You will be amazed at how much you will absorb. For a list of shopping terms, see page 397.

At the Hotel

a room for one/two persons	*une chambre pour une/deux personnes*
a double bed	*un lit double, un grand lit*
twin beds	*deux lits*
a room with an extra bed	*une chambre avec un lit supplémentaire*
a room with running water and bidet	*une chambre avec cabinet de toilette*
a room with shower and toilet	*une chambre avec douche et WC*
a room with bath and toilet	*une chambre avec salle de bain et WC*
for one/two/three nights	*pour une/deux/troix nuits*
suite	*appartment*
two-level suite	*duplex*
a room on the courtyard	*une chambre sur la cour*
a room over the street	*une chambre sur la rue*
ground floor	*rez-de-chaussée*
first floor	*premier étage*
second floor	*deuxième étage*
sixth floor	*seizième étage*
with a view	*avec vue*
quiet	*calme*
noisy	*bruyant*
breakfast included	*le petit déjeuner compris*
I would like breakfast.	*Je voudrais prendre le petit déjeuner.*
I do not want breakfast.	*Je ne veux pas de petit déjeuner.*
air-conditioning	*climatisé*
blankets	*couvertures*
elevator, lift	*ascenseur*
heat	*chauffage*
to iron	*repasser*
key	*clef*
to do laundry	*faire la lessive*
pillow	*oreiller*
sheets	*draps*

Emergencies

police	*police*
Stop!	*Arrêtez!*
help/help me!	*Au secours!/Aidez-moi!*
Leave me alone.	*Laissez-moi tranquille.*
I am sick.	*Je suis malade.*
Call a doctor.	*Appelez un médecin.*
in case of emergency	*en cas d'urgence*
hospital	*l'hôpital*
drugstore	*pharmacie*
prescription	*ordonnance*
medicine	*médicament*
aspirin	*aspirine*

General Phrases

yes/no	*oui/non*
okay	*d'accord*
please	*s'il vous plaît*
thank you (very much)	*merci (beaucoup)*
You are welcome.	*De rien.*
excuse me	*excusez-moi, pardon*
I am very sorry.	*Désolé(e).*
Sir, Mr.	*Monsieur*
Madame, Mrs.	*Madame*
Miss	*Mademoiselle*
good morning, good afternoon, hello	*bonjour*
good evening, goodbye	*bonsoir, au revoir*
Hi (familiar)	*salut*
How are you?	*Comment allez-vous? Vous allez bien?*
How is it going?	*Comment ça va? Ca va? (familiar)*
Fine, thank you, and you?	*Très bien, merci, et vous?*
What is your name?	*Comment vous appellez-vous?*
My name is . . .	*Je m'appelle . . .*
at what time	*à quelle heure*
Who is calling?	*C'est de la part de qui?*
hold the line (telephone)	*ne quittez pas*
good/well/bad/badly	*bon (bonne)/bien/mauvais(e)/mal*
small/big	*petit(e)/grand(e)*
beautiful	*beau/belle*
expensive/cheap	*cher/pas cher*
free (without charge)	*gratuit*
free (unoccupied)	*libre*
and/or	*et/ou*
with/without	*avec/sans*
because	*parce que*

a little/a lot	*un peu/beaucoup*
hot/cold	*chaud/froid*

Getting Around

Do you speak English?	*Parlez-vous anglais?*
I don't speak French.	*Je ne parle pas français.*
I don't understand.	*Je ne comprends pas.*
Speak more slowly, please.	*Parlez plus lentement, s'il vous plaît.*
I am American/British.	*Je suis Américain(e)/Anglais(e).*
Where is the nearest métro?	*Où est le métro le plus proche?*
When is the next train for . . . ?	*C'est quand le prochain train pour . . . ?*
I want to get off at . . .	*Je voudrais descendre à . . .*
Ticket	*billet*
far/near	*loin/pas loin*
street	*la rue*
street map	*le plan*
road map	*la carte*
Where are the toilets?	*Où sont les toilettes?*
What is it?	*Qu'est-ce que c'est?*
who	*qui*
what	*quoi*
where	*où*
when	*quand*
why	*pourquoi*
which	*quel*
how	*comment*
here/there	*ici/là*
right/left	*à droit/à gauche*
straight ahead	*tout droit*
red/green stoplight	*feu rouge/vert*
far/near	*loin/pas loin*
to cross	*traverser*
How much/ how many?	*Combien?*
How much does it cost?	*C'est combien?/Ça coûte combien?*
Do you take credit cards?	*Est-ce que vous acceptez les cartes de crédit?*
I would like . . .	*Je voudrais . . .*
I am going . . .	*Je vais . . .*
It is/It is not	*C'est/Ce n'est pas*

Places

airport	*l'aéroport*
bank	*banque*
basement	*sous-sol*
bookstore	*librairie*
bridge	*pont*

bus stop	*l'arrêt de bus*
church	*église*
city hall	*hôtel de ville*
department store	*grand magasin*
district, neighborhood	*quartier*
garden	*jardin*
laundromat	*laverie*
market	*marché*
museum	*musée*
post office (stamp)	*la poste (timbre)*
private home	*hôtel particuliere*
street	*rue*
subway	*métro*
ticket office	*vente de billets*
tobacconist	*tabac*
train station/railway/platform	*gare/chemin de fer/quai*

Signs

caisse	cashier
complet	full (restaurant or hotel)
défense de fumer, nonfumer	no smoking
entrée/sortie	entrance/exit
fermeture annuelle	annual closing
hors service/en panne	out of order
interdit/sens interdit	forbidden/no entry
ouvert/fermé	open/closed
stationnement interdit	no parking
tous les jours	daily
zone piétonne	pedestrian zone

Time

What time is it?	*Quelle heure est-il?*
At what time?	*A quelle heure?*
What time does the train leave?	*Le train part à quelle heure?*
today/yesterday/tomorrow	*aujourd'hui/hier/demain*
this morning	*ce matin*
this afternoon	*cet après-midi*
tonight	*ce soir*
daily	*tous les jours*

Days

Sunday	*dimanche*
Monday	*lundi*
Tuesday	*mardi*
Wednesday	*mercredi*
Thursday	*jeudi*

Friday	*vendredi*
Saturday	*samedi*

Months

January	*janvier*
February	*fevrier*
March	*mars*
April	*avril*
May	*mai*
June	*juin*
July	*juillet*
August	*août*
September	*septembre*
October	*octobre*
November	*novembre*
December	*decembre*

Seasons

spring	*printemps*
summer	*été*
autumn	*automne*
winter	*hiver*

Numbers

0	*zéro*
1	*un, une*
2	*deux*
3	*trois*
4	*quatre*
5	*cinq*
6	*six*
7	*sept*
8	*huit*
9	*neuf*
10	*dix*
11	*onze*
12	*douze*
13	*treize*
14	*quatorze*
15	*quinze*
16	*seize*
17	*dix-sept*
18	*dix-huit*
19	*dix-neuf*
20	*vingt*
21	*vingt-et-un*

22	*vingt-deux*
30	*trente*
40	*quarante*
50	*cinquante*
60	*soixante*
70	*soixante-dix*
80	*quatre-vingts*
90	*quatre-vingt-dix*
100	*cent*
1,000	*mille*
1,000,000	*million*
first	*premier*
second	*deuxième*
third	*troisième*
fourth	*quatrième*
fifth	*cinquième*
sixth	*sixième*
seventh	*septième*
eighth	*huitième*
ninth	*neuvième*
tenth	*dixième*
twentieth	*vingtième*
one-hundredth	*centième*

Colors

black	*noir*
blue	*bleu*
brown	*marron/brun*
green	*vert*
orange	*orange*
pink	*rose*
purple	*violet*
red	*rouge*
white	*blanc*
yellow	*jaune*

Index of Accommodations

Alcôve & Agapes, Le Bed & Breakfast à Paris **308**

Aloha Hostel **311**

Artus Hotel ★★★ ($) **142**

Atlantis Saint-Germain-des-Prés ★★★ **143**

Auberge International des Jeunes **312**

Auberge Jules Ferry **313**

Au Manoir Saint-Germain-des-Prés ★★★★ ($) **144**

Au Pacific Hotel ★★ **248**

Au Palais de Chaillot Hôtel ★★ **258**

Austin's Arts et Métiers Hôtel ★★★ **86**

Bateau Sympatico **309**

Bureau des Voyages de la Jeunesse (BVJ) **324**

Centre Parisien de Zen **317**

Centre Ville Étoile ★★★ **274**

Chambellan Morgane ★★★ **259**

Chez Vous **299**

CROUS Académie de Paris **325**

Daval Hôtel ★★ **224**

De Circourt Associates **299**

Dhely's Hôtel ★ **145**

Lrmitage Hôtel ★★ **287**

Familia Hôtel ★★ **111**

Family Hôtel Résidence **318**

France for Rent **300**

Galileo Hôtel ★★★ **204**

Garden Hôtel ★★ **224**

Golden Opéra de Noailles ★★★★ ($) **79**

Grand Hôtel de Champagne ★★★ **64**

Grand Hôtel de l'Univers ★★★ ($) **145**

Grand Hôtel des Balcons ★★ **146**

Grand Hôtel du Palais Royal ★★ **65**

Grand Hôtel Jeanne d'Arc ★★ **92**

Grand Hôtel Lévêque ★★ **178**

Grand Hôtel Malher ★★ **92**

Grand Hôtel St-Michel ★★★ **112**

Guest Apartment Services **300**

Historic Rentals **301**

Home Plazza Bastille ★★★ **319**

Home Plazza Saint-Antoine ★★★ **320**

Hospitel–Hôtel Dieu Paris ★★★ **93**

Hôtel Abbatial Saint-Germain ★★★ **113**

Hôtel Agora ★★ **66**

Hôtel Agora St-Germain ★★★ **113**

Hôtel Antin Trinité ★★ **216**

Hôtel Astrid ★★★ **274**

Hôtel Aviatic ★★★ ($) **147**

Hôtel Axial Beaubourg ★★★ **94**

Hôtel Balmoral ★★★ **275**

Hôtel Bastille de Launay ★★ **225**

Hôtel Baudelaire Opéra ★★★ **80**

Hôtel Beaugrenelle St-Charles ★★ **249**

Hôtel Beaumarchais ★★★ **225**

Hôtel Bedford ★★★★ ($) **205**

Hôtel Bélidor ★ (¢) **276**

Hôtel Bersoly's Saint-Germain ★★★ **178**

Hôtel Bonséjour (NO STARS, ¢) **290**

Hôtel Bourgogne & Montana ★★★★ ($) **179**

Hôtel Bourg Tibourg ★★★ ($) **95**

Hôtel Brighton ★★★ ($) **67**

Hôtel Britannique ★★★ **68**

Hôtel Caron de Beaumarchais ★★★ **96**

Hôtel Chopin ★★ **217**

Hôtel Claude Bernard ★★★ **114**

Hôtel Concortel ★★★ **206**

Hôtel Daguerre ★★★ **239**

Hôtel d'Albe ★★★ **115**

Hôtel Danemark ★★★ **148**

Hôtel Danube ★★★ **149**

Hôtel d'Argenson ★★ **206**

Hôtel Dauphine Saint-Germain-des-Prés ★★★ ($) **150**

Hôtel de Banville ★★★ ($) **277**

Hôtel de Blois ★ (¢) **242**

Hôtel de Chevreuse ★ **151**

Hôtel de Fleurie ★★★ **151**

Hôtel de l'Abbaye ★★★ ($) **152**

Hôtel de la Bretonnerie ★★★ **97**

Hôtel Delambre ★★★ **243**

Hôtel de la Paix ★★ **180**

Hôtel de la Place des Vosges ★★ **98**

Hôtel de la Place du Louvre ★★★ **69**

Hôtel de l'Arcade ★★★ **207**

Hôtel de l'Avre ★★ **250**
Hôtel de la Sorbonne ★★ **116**
Hôtel de la Tulipe ★★★ **181**
Hôtel de l'Espérance (5th) ★★ **116**
Hôtel de l'Espérance (14th, NO STARS, ¢) **243**
Hôtel de l'Odéon ★★★ **154**
Hôtel de Londres Eiffel ★★★ **181**
Hôtel de l'Université ★★★ **182**
Hôtel de Lutèce ★★★ **99**
Hôtel de Nevers ★ (¢) **226**
Hôtel de Nice ★★ **99**
Hôtel de Notre Dame ★★★ **117**
Hôtel des Académies ★ (¢) **154**
Hôtel des Allies ★ (¢) **118**
Hôtel des Arts ★★ **290**
Hôtel des Bains ★ **244**
Hôtel des Champs-Élysées ★★ **208**
Hôtel des Chevaliers ★★★ **86**
Hôtel des Deux Acacias ★★ **279**
Hôtel des Deux-Îles ★★★ **100**
Hôtel des Ducs de Bourgogne ★★★ **70**
Hôtel de Sévigné ★★★ **259**
Hôtel des Grandes Écoles ★★★ **119**
Hôtel des Grands Hommes ★★★ ($) **119**
Hôtel des Jardins du Luxembourg ★★★ **120**
Hôtel des 3 Collèges ★★ **121**
Hôtel de Varenne ★★★ **183**
Hôtel d'Orsay ★★★ **184**
Hôtel du Bois ★★★ **261**
Hôtel Duc de Saint-Simon ★★★ ($) **185**
Hôtel du Champ de Mars ★★ **186**
Hôtel du Collège de France ★★ **122**
Hôtel du Continent ★★★ **71**
Hôtel du Cygne ★★ **71**
Hôtel du Dragon (NO STARS) **155**
Hôtel du Jeu de Paume ★★★★ ($) **101**
Hôtel du Lys ★★ **156**
Hôtel du Palais Bourbon ★★ **187**
Hôtel du Panthéon ★★★ ($) **122**
Hôtel du Rond-Point de Longchamp ★★★ **261**
Hôtel du Séjour (NO STARS, ¢) **87**
Hôtel du 7e Art ★★ **102**
Hôtel Eber Mars ★★ **188**
Hôtel Eber Monceau ★★★ **280**
Hôtel Élysées-Mermoz ★★★ **209**
Hôtel Esmeralda ★ **123**

Hôtel Étoile Péreire ★★★ **281**
Hôtel Excelsior ★ **124**
Hôtel Ferrandi ★★★ **157**
Hôtel Flaubert ★★ **282**
Hôtel Folkestone Opéra ★★★ **209**
Hôtel Gavarni ★★★ ($) **262**
Hôtel Henri IV (1st, NO STARS, ¢) **72**
Hôtel Henri IV (5th) ★★★ **125**
Hôtel Istria ★★ **245**
Hôtel Jardin de Villiers ★★★ **283**
Hôtel Jardin Le Bréa ★★★ **158**
Hôtel Kensington ★★ **189**
Hôtel Keppler ★★ **264**
Hôtel l'Aiglon ★★★ **246**
Hôtel La Manufacture ★★★ **236**
Hôtel Langlois ★★ **218**
Hôtel La Régence Étoile ★★★ **283**
Hôtel Latour-Maubourg ★★★ **190**
Hôtel le Bouquet de Montmartre ★★ **291**
Hôtel Left Bank Saint-Germain ★★★ ($) **158**
Hôtel Le Lavoisier ★★★★ ($) **210**
Hôtel le Loiret ★★★ **73**
Hôtel le Notre Dame ★★★ ($) **126**
Hôtel Lenox Montparnasse ★★★ **247**
Hôtel Lenox Saint-Germain ★★★ **191**
Hôtel le Pavillon Bastille ★★★ **233**
Hôtel le Régent ★★★ ($) **159**
Hôtel Le Relais Médicis ★★★ ($) **161**
Hôtel le Sainte-Beuve ★★★ **162**
Hôtel le Saint-Grégoire ★★★★ ($) **163**
Hôtel les Jardins d'Eiffel ★★★ **192**
Hôtel le Tourville ★★★★ ($) **193**
Hôtel Louvre Sainte-Anne ★★★ **74**
Hôtel Lyon-Mulhouse ★★ **227**
Hôtel Mansart ★★★ ($) **74**
Hôtel Marignan ★ **127**
Hôtel Marigny ★★ **211**
Hôtel Minerve ★★★ **128**
Hôtel Molière ★★★ **76**
Hôtel Muguet ★★ **194**
Hôtel Newton Opéra ★★★ ($) **212**
Hôtel Nicolo ★★ **265**
Hôtel Notre-Dame ★★ **227**
Hôtel Novanox ★★★ **164**
Hôtel Parc Saint-Séverin ★★★ **129**
Hôtel Passy Eiffel ★★★ **266**
Hôtel Plessis ★★ **228**

Hôtel Prima-Lepic ★★ **292**
Hôtel Queen Mary ★★★ **213**
Hôtel Regent's Garden ★★★ ($) **284**
Hôtel Regina de Passy ★★★ **266**
Hôtel Relais Bosquet ★★★ **195**
Hôtel Relais Saint-Jacques ★★★★ ($) **130**
Hôtel Relais Saint-Sulpice ★★★ ($) **165**
Hôtel Résidence Alhambra ★★ **229**
Hôtel Résidence des Arts ($) **320**
Hôtel Résidence Foch ★★★ **267**
Hôtel Résidence Henri IV ★★★ **131**
Hôtel Résidence Lord Byron ★★★ **214**
Hôtel Résidence Monge ★★ **132**
Hôtel Rhetia ★ (¢) **230**
Hôtel Roma Sacré-Coeur ★★ **292**
Hôtel Rotary (NO STARS, ¢) **219**
Hôtel Saint-André-des-Arts ★ **165**
Hôtel Saint-Dominique ★★ **196**
Hôtel Saint-Germain-des-Prés ★★★ ($) **166**
Hôtel Saint-Jacques ★★ **132**
Hôtel Saint-Louis ★★★ **103**
Hôtel Saint-Merry ★★★ ($) **104**
Hôtel Saint-Paul ★★★ **167**
Hotel Saint-Thomas-d'Aquin ★★ **197**
Hôtel Sansonnet ★★ **105**
Hôtel Thérèse ★★★ **77**
Hôtel Trocadéro La Tour ★★★ **268**
Hôtel Valadon ★★ **198**
Hôtel Verneuil ★★★ **199**
Hôtel Victor Hugo ★★★ **268**
Hôtel Villa des Ternes ★★★ **285**
Hôtel Vivienne ★★ **81**
Hôtel West End ★★★ ($) **215**
Innova Hôtel ★★ **250**
Irving Hutton Ltd **302**
Kudeta Home **302**
La Centrale de Réservations (FUAJ) **313**
La Maison **314**
Le Hameau de Passy ★★ **269**
Le Madison Hôtel ★★★ ($) **168**
Le Relais du Louvre ★★★ **77**
Le Relais Hôtel du Vieux Paris ★★★★ ($) **170**
Les Campings du Bois de Boulogne **310**
Les Degrés de Notre-Dame Hôtel (NO STARS) **133**
Le Vert Gallant ★★★ **237**
Le Village Hostel–Montmartre **314**

L'Hôtel du Bailli de Suffren-Tour Eiffel ★★★
    251
Libertel Croix de Malte ★★ **230**
Libertel Grand Turenne ★★★ **106**
Libertel Résidence–Villa Daubenton **321**
Maison Internationale de la Jeunesse et des
    Étudiants (MIJE) **325**
Maison Internationale des Jeunes (MIJCP) **326**
Mercure Paris Saint Charles ★★ **252**
Millésime Hôtel ★★★ ($) **171**
OTU Voyage **326**
Panache **303**
Paris Appartements Services **304**
Paris-France Hôtel ★★ **88**
Paris Vacation Apartments **304**
Pension les Marronniers (NO STARS, ¢) **172**
Perfect Hôtel ★ (¢) **220**
Pierre & Vacances—Résidence Montmartre
    321
Port-Royal Hôtel ★ **134**
Practic Hôtel (NO STARS) **253**
Rendez-Vous á Paris Ltd **305**
Rentvillas.com **306**
Résidence Hôtel des Trois Poussins ★★★ **322**
RothRay **306**
Select Hôtel ★★★ **136**
Splendid Hôtel ★★★ **200**
Terrass Hôtel ★★★★ ($) **293**
3 Ducks Hostel **315**
Timhôtel Montmartre ★★ **294**
Tiquetonne Hôtel ★ (¢) **82**
Tulip Inn Little Place ★★★ **88**
Welcome Hôtel ★★ **173**
Woodstock Hostel **315**
Young & Happy Hostel **316**

Big Splurges

Artus Hôtel ★★★ (6th) **142**
Au Manoir Saint-Germain-des-Prés ★★★★
    (6th) **144**
Golden Opéra de Noailles ★★★★ (2nd) **79**
Grand Hôtel de l'Univers ★★★ (6th) **145**
Hôtel Aviatic ★★★ (6th) **147**
Hôtel Bedford ★★★★ (8th) **205**
Hôtel Bourgogne & Montana ★★★★ (7th)
    179

Hôtel Bourg Tibourg ★★★ (4th) **95**
Hôtel Brighton ★★★ (1st) **67**
Hôtel Dauphine Saint-Germain-des-Prés ★★★
 (6th) **150**
Hôtel de Banville ★★★ (17th) **277**
Hôtel de l'Abbaye ★★★ (6th) **152**
Hôtel des Grands Hommes ★★★ (5th) **119**
Hôtel Duc de Saint-Simon ★★★ (7th) **185**
Hôtel du Jeu de Paume ★★★★ (4th) **101**
Hôtel du Panthéon ★★★ (5th) **122**
Hôtel Gavarni ★★★ (16th) **262**
Hôtel Left Bank Saint-Germain ★★★ (6th) **158**
Hôtel Le Lavoisier ★★★★ (8th) **210**
Hôtel le Notre Dame ★★★ (5th) **126**
Hôtel le Régent ★★★ (6th) **159**
Hôtel Le Relais Médicis ★★★ (6th) **161**
Hôtel le Saint-Grégoire ★★★★ (6th) **163**
Hôtel le Tourville ★★★★ (7th) **193**
Hôtel Mansart ★★★ (1st) **74**
Hôtel Newton-Opéra ★★★ (8th) **212**
Hôtel Regent's Garden ★★★ (17th) **284**
Hôtel Relais Saint-Jacques ★★★★ (5th) **130**
Hôtel Relais Saint-Sulpice ★★★ (6th) **165**
Hôtel Résidence des Arts (6th) **320**
Hôtel Saint-Germain-des-Prés ★★★ (6th) **166**
Hôtel Saint-Merry ★★★ (4th) **104**
Hôtel West End ★★★ (8th) **215**
Le Madison Hôtel ★★★ (6th) **168**
Le Relais Hôtel du Vieux Paris ★★★★ (6th) **170**
Millésime Hôtel ★★★ (6th) **171**
Terrass Hôtel ★★★★ (18th) **293**

Cheap Sleeps

Hôtel Bélidor ★ (17th) **276**
Hôtel Bonséjour (NO STARS, 18th) **290**
Hôtel de Blois ★ (14th) **242**
Hôtel de l'Espérance (NO STARS, 14th) **243**
Hôtel de Nevers ★ (11th) **226**
Hôtel des Académies ★ (6th) **154**
Hôtel des Allies ★ (5th) **118**
Hôtel du Séjour (NO STARS, 3rd) **87**
Hôtel Henri IV (NO STARS, 1st) **72**
Hôtel Rhetia ★ (11th) **230**
Hôtel Rotary (NO STARS, 9th) **219**
Pension les Marronniers (NO STARS, 6th) **172**

Perfect Hôtel ★ (9th) **220**
Tiquetonne Hôtel ★ (2nd) **82**

Nonsmoking Rooms

Alcôve & Agapes **308**
Auberge International des Jeunes **312**
Bateau Sympatico **309**
Centre Parisien de Zen **317**
Centre Ville Étoile ★★★ (17th) **274**
Chambellan Morgane ★★★ (16th) **259**
France for Rent **300**
Golden Opéra de Noailles ★★★★ (2nd) **79**
Grand Hôtel de Champagne ★★★ (1st) **64**
Grand Hôtel de l'Univers ★★★ (6th) **145**
Home Plazza Bastille **319**
Home Plazza Saint-Antoine **320**
Hospitel-Hôtel Dieu Paris ★★★ (4th) **93**
Hôtel Balmoral ★★★ (17th) **275**
Hôtel d'Albe ★★★ (5th) **115**
Hôtel Dauphine Saint-Germain des-Prés ★★★
 (6th) **150**
Hôtel de l'Arcade ★★★ (8th) **207**
Hôtel des Ducs de Bourgogne ★★★ (1st) **70**
Hôtel Étoile Péreire ★★★ (17th) **281**
Hôtel Folkstone Opéra ★★★ (8th) **209**
Hôtel Latour-Maubourg ★★★ (7th) **190**
Hôtel Left Bank St-Germain ★★★ (6th) **158**
Hôtel les Jardins d'Eiffel ★★★ (7th) **192**
Hôtel Muguet ★★ (7th) **194**
Hôtel Regent's Garden ★★★ (17th) **284**
Hôtel Relais Bosquet ★★★ (7th) **195**
Hôtel Relais Saint-Jacques ★★★★ (5th) **130**
Hôtel Trocadéro La Tour ★★★ (16th) **268**
Hôtel Valadon ★★ (7th) **198**
Hôtel Victor Hugo ★★★ (16th) **268**
Le Relais Hôtel de Vieux Paris ★★★★ (6th) **170**
L'Hôtel du Bailli de Suffren-Tour Eiffel ★★★
 (15th) **251**
Libertel Croix de Malte ★★ (11th) **230**
Libertel Grand Turenne ★★★ (4th) **106**
Millésime Hôtel ★★★ (6th) **171**
Terrass Hôtel ★★★★ (18th) **293**
Timhôtel Montmartre ★★ (18th) **294**

Index of Shops

Abbey Bookshop, The **362**
Accessories à Soie **390**
A la Bonne Renommee **357**
Allicante **385**
Allix **376**
Anna Lowe **376**
Anne Willi **385**
Annexe des Créateurs **381**
Anthony Peto **352**
Arzat **365**
A. Simon **351**
Au Nom de la Rose **373**
Au Printemps **381**
Au Vieux Campeur **363**
Avenue Victor Hugo **338**
À Votre Idée Broderie **374**
Bercy Village **342**
Betty **386**
BHV **358**
Biscuit **358**
Bonpoint **371**
Bonton **374**
Boutique Majolique **355, 366**
Boutique Paris-Musées **344, 355, 358**
Brentano's **352**
C & P **359**
Carrousel du Louvre **341**
Cartes d'Art **366**
Catherine Perfumes and Cosmetics **345**
Champs-Élysées **337**
Chercheminippes **366**
Christian Lu **366**
Colette **345**
Debauve & Gallais **352, 374**
Dehillerin **346**
Dépol–Vente de Buci **367**
Dépôt–Vente de Passy **388**
Diptyque **363**
Divine **387**
DOT–Diffusion d'Objets de Table **355**
Du Pareil au Même **346, 367, 389**
Du Pareil au Même Bébé **346, 367**

easyEverything **48**
Et Vous Stock **353**
Explora **353**
Faïenceries de Quimper **359**
Fauchon **377**
Flamant **367**
FNAC **377**
Forum des Halles **341**
Franchi Chausseurs **377**
Franck et Fils **389**
Freddy **382**
Galerie Documents **368**
Galerie Véro-Dodat **340**
Galerie Vivienne **340**
Galeries Lafayette **382, 387**
Galignani **347**
Gianni d'Arno Pur Réve de Soie **391**
Gilbert Joseph Papeterie **368**
Golden Triangle, The **338**
Graphigro **368**
Haut de Gamme Stock **382**
Hediard **377**
Herboristerie du Palais Royal **347**
Kiosque Théâtre **378**
Krystyna Bukowska **359**
La Boutique de l'Artisanat Monastique **387**
La Cie de Provence **369**
La Dame Blanche **347**
La Dernière Goutte **369**
La Droguerie **348**
L'Affair d'Un Soir **389**
La Samaritaine **348**
La Tuile à Loup **363**
Laurent Guillot **356**
La Vallée Outlet Shopping Village **334**
Le Bon Marché and La Grande Épicerie de Paris **375**
Le Cèdre Rouge **348**
L'Écritoire **359**
Le Louvre des Antiquaires **349**
Le Marché Saint Germain **342**
Le Prince Jardinier **349**

Le Rouvray **364**
Les Artisans du Rêve: Breiz Norway **364**
Les Couturiers de la Nature **369**
Les Olivades **370**
L'Espace Créateurs **349**
Les Trois Marchés de Catherine B **370**
Les Trois Quartiers **342**
L'Occitane **360, 364, 370, 375, 378, 389**
Lollipops **353**
Louis Pion **383**
Madelios **350**
Maille **378**
Maine-Montparnasse **343**
Marais **336**
Marché Carmes **396**
Marché Cours de la Reine **397**
Marché d'Aligre **392**
Marché de Clignancourt **393**
Marché de Montreuil **393**
Marché des Batignolles **397**
Marché de Vanves **392**
Marché Dupleix **397**
Marché Monge **396**
Marché Place Baudoyer **396**
Marché Raspail **396**
Marché Richard-Lenoir **396**
Marché Saint Pierre **391**
Marché Saxe-Breteuil **396**
Maréchal **350**
Marie Mercié **370**
Matière Première **360, 371**
Maxim's **379**
Miss "Griffes" **379**
Monoprix **360, 371, 379**
Musée de la Parfumerie Fragonard **383**
Oliver B **350**
Passage des Panoramas **340**
Passage du Grand-Cerf **340**
Passage Jouffroy **341**
Passage Verdeau **341**
Passy Plaza **343**
Patyka **356**
Petit Faune **371**
Pharmacie T. LeClerc **383**

Pierre Frey **372**
Place des Victoires **336**
Place des Vosges **336**
Place Vendôme **336**
Porcelaine de Paris **385**
PWS–Prices Without Surprise **361**
Réciproque **390**
Red Wheelbarrow Bookstore, The **361**
Rue Cler **394**
Rue d'Alésia **339**
Rue d'Aligre **395**
Rue Daguerre **395**
Rue de Buci and Rue de Seine **394**
Rue de Lévis **395**
Rue de Paradis **339**
Rue de Passy and Avenue Victor Hugo **338**
Rue du Commerce **395**
Rue Lepic **395**
Rue Meslay **338**
Rue Montorgueil **394**
Rue Mouffetard **394**
Rue Poncelet **395**
Rue Royale **337**
Rue St-Placide **339**
Rue St-Dominique **339**
San Francisco Book Company, The **372**
Scooter **350, 372**
Sephora **380, 390**
Sidney Carron **361**
Souleiado **372**
St-Germain-des-Prés **337**
Stock Griffes **362, 391**
Stock Kookaï **353**
Sulmaco **384**
Tati **356, 392**
Tati Or **354**
Tout Compte Fait . . . **373, 384, 390**
Viaduc des Arts **386**
Village St-Paul **336**
Village Jové Club–La Passion de Jouet **354**
Virgin Megastore **380**
Web Bar **48**
W. H. Smith **351**
Zeidnet **48**

Readers' Comments

While every effort has been taken to provide accurate information in this guide, the publisher and author cannot be held responsible for changes in any of the listings due to rate increases, inflation, the rise and fall of the dollar, the passage of time, management changes or attitudes, or any other problems—financial or otherwise—that occur between a reader and any person or establishment listed here.

Great Sleeps Paris is updated and revised on a regular basis. If you find a change before I do, make an important discovery you want to pass along to me, or just want to tell me about your trip to Paris, please send me a note stating the name and address of the hotel or shop, the date of your visit, and a description of your findings. Or if you prefer, visit my Website (www.greateatsandsleeps.com) and leave your comment on my message board. As the many readers who have written to me know, your comments are very important to me, and I respond to as many as possible. Thank you, in advance, for taking the time to write. For current information on any of the guides in the series, readers can also visit www.chroniclebooks.com.

Please send your letters to Sandra A. Gustafson, *Great Sleeps Paris,* c/o Chronicle Books, 85 Second Street, Sixth Floor, San Francisco, CA 94105.